GW00708299

Legal Practice
Companion

בס"ד

**'A woman of valour - who can find [one]?
Her value is far beyond pearls'**

Book of Proverbs (Mishlei), Ch.31, v.10

I thank God every day that He has given me the merit to find one. This book is for my amazing wife, Daniella, who makes life's journey through the 'corridor' to the 'palace' full of joy.

It is also for Eliezer, Rafi and Shimon. For a little while each year, you allow me to use a little of our precious time together to produce this book - thank you.

**'There are three partners in [a] man -
The Lord (Blessed be He), his [the man's] father and his mother.'**

Babylonian Talmud, Tractate Niddah 31a

I continue to thank them all. Without the continuing investment of those three partners, nothing would be possible.

M.W.

For Charlotte, for her own 'special box', like Zac has for his.

G.F.H.M and F.H.M.

Legal Practice Companion

Gerald Montagu

BA (Hons), MA, Solicitor

Mark Weston

LLB (Hons), Solicitor

Seventeenth edition (2011-2012)

Foreword to the
Legal Practice Companion and the *Companion* series

The Right Honourable Lord Woolf
former Lord Chief Justice

Foreword to the
Legal Practice Companion

Sir Gavin Lightman
former judge of the High Court of Justice

Bloomsbury Professional

Seventeenth edition first published in Great Britain in 2011 by
Bloomsbury Professional Limited
Maxwelton House
41-43 Boltro Road
Haywards Heath
West Sussex
RH16 1BJ

Bloomsbury Professional Limited is an imprint of Bloomsbury Publishing Plc

© GFH Montagu, F H Montagu, M Weston, and D Weston 2011

This publication is sold with the understanding that neither the publisher, nor the authors, are engaged in rendering legal, accounting or other professional services.   If legal advice is required, the services of a competent professional person should be sought.

Sixteenth edition (2010) and fifteenth edition (2009) published by Bloomsbury Professional Limited.
Thirteenth edition (2007) and fourteenth edition (2008) published by Tottel Publishing Limited
Eleventh edition (2005 and reprinted 2006), and twelfth edition (2006) published by Law Matters Limited
Ninth (2003), tenth (2004 and reprinted 2005) editions published by Cavendish Publishing Limited
Eighth edition (2002) published by Oxford University Press
Fourth (1998), fifth (1999), sixth (2000) and seventh (2001) editions published by Blackstone Press Limited
First (1995), second (1996) and third (1997) editions published by CLT Professional Publishing

Gerald Montagu Fiona Montagu, Mark Weston and Daniella Weston have asserted their moral rights under the Copyright, Designs and Patents Act 1988

The authors and publisher acknowledge Crown copyright in all statutory materials in this work

All rights reserved. No part of this publication may be reproduced, stored in a retrieval system, or transmitted, in any form or by any means, electronic, mechanical, photocopying, recording, scanning or otherwise, without the prior permission in writing of the copyright holders (or as expressly permitted by law), or under the terms agreed with the appropriate reprographics rights organisation. Enquiries concerning reproduction outside the scope of the above should be sent to the publisher at the address above.

You must not circulate this book in any other binding or cover and you must impose the same condition on any acquirer.

British Library Cataloguing in Publication Data
Montagu, Gerald
Montagu, Fiona
Weston, Mark
Weston, Daniella
Legal Practice Companion 2011/2012
1 Law - England 2 Law - Wales
3 Procedure (Law) - England 4 Procedure (Law) - Wales
I Title II Weston, Mark
349.4'2

Library of Congress Cataloguing in Publication Data
Data available

ISBN 978 1 84766 745 8

Typeset (other than the index and tables) by Fiona Montagu and Daniella Weston
Index and tables typeset by Phoenix Photosetting, Chatham, Kent
Printed and bound in Great Britain by CPI Group (UK) Ltd, Croydon, CR0 4YY

Foreword to the *Legal Practice Companion*

The *Legal Practice Companion* is intended as a companion, friend and guide to the student and newly qualified practitioner. Its purpose is achieved with distinction. This work sets out the principles of substantive law in the areas where the reader will need to tread; and civil procedure can no longer be a mystery to those who have this book at hand. The quality of the contents and the clarity of thought and presentation combine to enable the authors, in one volume, to provide a map and a guided tour of legal practice today. Seasoned practitioners will find it valuable to have at their elbows such an up-to-date and reliable summary, and most certainly the *Legal Practice Companion* will occupy a place on my bookshelf.

Sir Gavin Lightman

former *Judge of the High Court of Justice*

Foreword to the *Companions*

I am wholly in favour of the Companions. Legal text books are not often to the fore when it comes to presenting legal information in an attractive, readily understandable and digestible form. However, this is exactly what the Companion series achieves. The law is becoming ever more complex and there is undoubtedly a need to find new methods of communicating it to those who need to know, whether they be members of the public, law students, practitioners or for that matter judges. They will all find that it is a great advantage to have access to a Companion.

This is why the original volume in the series, The Legal Practice Companion (LPC) has proved to be a success. It is now in its seventeenth edition, having been first published in 1995. The Intellectual Property and Media Law Companion and the Banking and Capital Markets Companion are worthy successors to the core volume, LPC.

Some of the subjects which are now dealt with by the Companions are not ones with which I am particularly familiar and so I was able to find out for myself in practice whether they work. I can assure the potential reader that they do work as far as I am concerned and that they are very user friendly. The very clear method of presentation both provided an overview of the subject and a step by step guide. I feel confident that they will translate well to multimedia formats since their present style will be very familiar to regular users of information technology.

My enthusiasm for the *Companion* series is in part because they complement the reforms I recommended for civil procedure and which I hoped would make our Civil Justice System an appropriate one for this 21st century. I am very conscious that a weakness of the reforms is that in general they were confined to procedural law and left substantive law intact and in a state which means that in the majority of areas it is impenetrable to those to whom it is unfamiliar. This creates a real impediment to access to justice. The virtue of the *Companion* series is that it provides a clear path through what is so often a jungle. While the *Companion* series will usually provide all that the reader requires, when this is not the case they will be a solid base from which to embark on a more detailed investigation of the tangled undergrowth of the law.

That I find the *Companion* series refreshing is no doubt due to the fact that the authors are (by judicial standards) younger and obviously very bright. Having been schooled in the law and practice in more recent times, they know the needs of others in their position and how the existing texts do not always meet those needs. They have decided that something can and should be done to provide a solution. LPC was the start and the other *Companions* followed. They deserved to achieve the success that they have done and I believe that they will continue to succeed in meeting that need. I congratulate the team on their initiative and on what they are achieving and I look forward to the continued growth of the *Companion* series.

The Right Honourable Lord Woolf

former *Lord Chief Justice*

Introduction

Welcome to the *Legal Practice Companion*!

To the Practitioner

This book aims to help provide a guide to law and practice beyond your areas of specialisation. It sets out the context, general 'feel' and basic concepts of an area of English law. Its purpose is to serve as a prelude to detailed research. The numerous references aid 'mapping out' research, before clients are given more considered advice based on that research.

The book is intended to provide an *overview* for the practitioner. It is *not* comprehensive; there are numerous specialist works on particular topics that are intended for that purpose. For example, the demands of converting highly complex statutes into digestible points have forced us to focus on those points that seem most relevant. When giving advice, original sources should *always* be checked. For example, we set out in the criminal sections the law applying to adults only and without taking into account the special provisions for sexual offences or terrorism offences.

Meeting the needs of practitioners has required an original approach. After discussions with solicitors and trainees, we have evolved a novel format that represents something of a departure for legal publishing. This is reflected in both the choice of material and its presentation.

In this book:

1. Procedures are often broken down into steps or flowcharts, so that they can easily be followed.

2. The law is set out schematically and areas are linked together as appropriate. For example, the *Business* section gives an integrated overview of the legal framework within which businesses operate, dealing with corporate governance, employment, and commercial agreements.

3. All this is packaged in one convenient volume. Therefore, for example, the conveyancer will find an outline of the possible tax treatment of the transaction a few pages away - the importance of which has been highlighted by Lightman J.'s judgment in *Hurlingham Estates Ltd v Wilde & Partners* [1997] STC 627).

4. This book also flags statutes which have received Royal Assent (or will shortly receive it), which are not yet in force but are awaiting orders to bring them into force. This should help maintain an awareness of how the law *will* work (as well as how it *does* work).

We believe that this book will become a valued tool. It is a trusty companion for the practitioner whom will, we hope, keep a copy within reach of his or her desk.

Introduction

Welcome to the *Legal Practice Companion*!

To the Student

The **Legal Practice Course** (LPC), the BVC and QLTT all move the worlds of study and practice closer together than ever before. This volume is intended to help in both.

Information required for the compulsory topics and the pervasive topics on the LPC, as well as topics throughout the BVC and QLTT, is presented here in one volume. After completing any of these courses, the references throughout to source materials (such as sections in statutes or cases) lay the basis for your research in practice and are included in a format which will quickly become familiar.

Other books and materials usually contain unwieldy blocks of text, which are often split over numerous pages and volumes. This often hinders grasping masses of information which appears unconnected and unclear. The Legal Practice Companion breaks new ground by presenting the relevant law and practice in a step by step format - it is all in one volume, and frequently one topic is presented per page. Charts, flow charts and summaries provide an accessible, clear and straightforward overview of modern legal practice. Please note that the book does assume some prior knowledge and comprehension of basic concepts - it is aimed at students undertaking the courses above or equivalent professional examinations - but can also be used at a wholly different level (using the referenced sources) when you get to practice. The Legal Practice Companion, for example, will not define a 'shelf' company or an 'either way' offence, but it will summarise what to do with respect to them and the procedures that apply to them.

This book is intended:

1. To explain complex parts of the course that you have already covered.
2. To provide a breakdown (aiding comprehension) for parts of the course that you are about to tackle.
3. To present an area of law coherently in one place (for example, taxation and conduct are grouped in their own sections).
4. To split topics up so that they appear where they fit best.

For you, the student, this book is intended to cover the core material that you need for your courses, and to help you beyond into the world of work. No doubt your annotations will soon cover the pages. This is entirely suitable and to be encouraged, not least because the precise focus of what is taught and examinations varies from course to course. For those who can take books into examinations (or who chop the pages out, hole-punch them and then pop them into their files), this presentation of the course, together with your annotations, should be invaluable in helping you pass your exams well.

Acknowledgements

Access to ... the law ... and to justice

In 1995, the *Legal Practice Companion* was launched into what was then a stormy debate over legal education. Since then, over 40,000 copies have been sold, and the book now finds itself in its seventeenth edition.

Over the last 17 years we have witnessed the legislature 'rewrite' virtually every aspect of the law covered by this book. In fact, not one page of this book remains the same as in the first edition 17 years ago. With a new coalition government in place and no money left for the country to spend implementing expensive legislative schemes, we hope that the pace of legislative change may abate a little.

Autumn 2009 witnessed certain reforms to the Legal Practice Course, including shortening the course, which we advocated back in 1995 and which we hoped to advance though the publication of this book. Although there were some within the Law Society who reacted with fury to this agenda when the book was first published, we are glad that these reforms have been implemented and hope that in some small way, the approach taken by this book helped to show the way.

Tackling all these changes has been possible so far due to the many who deserve our thanks. We start by thanking our readers and the former Lord Chief Justice and Sir Gavin Lightman for their whole-hearted support and encouragement.

Continuing growth...

A fifth edition of the *Banking and Capital Markets Companion* was published in March 2011 and a fourth edition of the *Intellectual Property and Media Law Companion* was published in 2010. The *Companions* continue to meet what, judging from the response, is a very real need both in the legal profession and further afield. We continue to look to expand the series - if you are interested in helping us do this (either as an author or as someone with ideas) - then please write to us!

Our thanks to...

Our thanks go to all at Bloomsbury Professional and, in particular, to Martin Casimir, Jenny Burdett, Jubriel Hanid and Stephen Hughes. We are delighted still to be sharing publishers with the likes of J.K. Rowling - may we merit her sales figures! However, don't expect to see a

'Legal-Practice-Companion-World' any time soon. On the other hand, we pride ourselves on being entrepreneurial...

Behind the scenes ...

We would like to thank (as always) Mark's wife, Daniella, for her typesetting, proof reading, RSI-busting typing and her continual support and madness at putting up with it all - while juggling work, home, kids and life in general. Gerald's wife, Fiona, has put her hand to the tiller and kindly cast a sharp eye over some of the drier aspects of the text and taking on some of the typesetting.

Mark is also particularly grateful to his mother, Diana Weston for the huge amount she does and the huge support she provides.

And of course - no *Legal Practice Companion* would be complete without mentioning Gill Zeiner who developed the original typeset for our approach nearly two decades ago, and Moira Greenhalgh who (at something approaching warp speed, and drawing on considerable reserves of patience) has produced the tables and index ever since the fourth edition.

We hope that readers will continue to write to us at our firms with suggestions on how the *Legal Practice Companion* can become even more helpful.

Without which ...

And of course, many thanks to our families and friends who put up with us during the writing process and to anyone inadvertently missing ...

The law ...

As usual, we cover English law only. The law is generally as stated at **22 July, 2011**, except where indicated otherwise. Please note that all references to the *Criminal Procedure Rules 2011* are to the rules as they will be, as of 3 October 2011. Also, references to the *Legal Services Act 2007* are to that Act as the various elements of it will be in force as of 31 December 2011. We continue to try and be the most up to date book on the market!

Gerald Montagu and Mark Weston,

Shenfield and London, 6 August, 2011.

'Many rough and cragged by-ways have been ... trodden towards the intricate problems of the Law's mysteries, but no foot-path ... [has been] plainley beaten, so that anyone could ... find the way without being subject to any Aberrations [and which] should safely conduct the Zealous Pilgrim through the sullen deserts, and over the craggy precipicies of this Herculean voyage.'

Compleat Solicitor (London, 1668)

Contents

Conduct

Accounts

Taxation

Wills, probate and administration

Boxes and citations - conventions

I   Boxes

> **Legal points** and principles
>
> ➤ Square boxes contain information relating to a specific area of law or legal principle.

> **Practice points** and principles
>
> ➤ Round boxes contain information relating to information that is useful in practice.

II   Legislative citations

➤ At the time of going to press, certain legislation awaits an order from a Minister before it comes into force (this is dependent on the drafting and approval of secondary legislation and/or regulatory codes).

> **Where legislation is not yet in force, this is indicated by '[not yet in force]' and the presentation of text and bullets in italics.**
>
> **The repeal of legislation with effect from a future date is indicated by a ✄ symbol.**

➤ We have generally addressed the law as it is, or will be during the life of this edition.

III   Bullet conventions

➤ Often, a point will be made using one level of bullet (eg: this arrow bullet).

  ◆ A sub-point may be made about something related to that main point (eg: this diamond bullet is a sub-point to the arrow bullet above).

  ◆ When reading at a 'high' level, the sub-points can be ignored without impairing the conceptual integrity of the text at the higher level (ie: in this example, you can read just the arrow bullets, ignoring all diamond bullets).

➤ It is therefore possible to read the next main point (ie: this arrow bullet), having missed out the sub-points in between (eg: the diamond bullets above).

Table of abbreviations

Statutes

LD(A)A 1888	Law of Distress (Amendment) Act 1888.
LLCA 1975	Local Land Charges Act 1975.
LLPA 2000	Limited Liability Partnerships Act 2000.
LPA	Law of Property Act 1925.
LPCD(I)A 1998	Late Payment of Commercial Debts (Interest) Act 1998.
LP(JT)A 1964	Law of Property (Joint Tenants) Act 1964.
LP(MP)A 1989	Law of Property (Miscellaneous Provisions) Act 1989.
LP(MP)A 1994	Law of Property (Miscellaneous Provisions) Act 1994.
LP(R)A 1938	Leasehold Property (Repairs) Act 1938.
LRA 1967	Leasehold Reform Act 1967.
LRA 2002	Land Registration Act 2002.
LR(CN)A 1945	Law Reform (Contributory Negligence) Act 1945.
LRHUDA 1993	Leasehold Reform Housing and Urban Development Act 1993.
LR(MP)A 1934	Law Reform (Miscellaneous Provisions) Act 1934.
LR(PI)A 1948	Law Reform (Personal Injuries) Act 1948.
LR(S)A 1995	Law Reform (Succession) Act 1995.
LTA 1927	Landlord and Tenant Act 1927.
LTA 1954	Landlord and Tenant Act 1954.
LTA 1985	Landlord and Tenant Act 1985.
LTA 1987	Landlord and Tenant Act 1987.
LTA 1988	Landlord and Tenant Act 1988.
LT(C)A 1995	Landlord and Tenants (Covenants) Act 1995.

M

MA 1967	Misrepresentation Act 1967.
MCA 1980	Magistrates' Courts Act 1980.
MCA 1987	Minors' Contracts Act 1987.
MCA 2005	Mental Capacity Act 2005.
MHA 1983	Matrimonial Homes Act 1983.

N

NAA 1948	National Assistance Act 1948.

O

OA 1978	Oaths Act 1978.
OAPA 1861	Offences Against the Person Act 1861.
OLA 1984	Occupiers' Liability Act 1984.

P

PA 1890	Partnership Act 1890.
PA 1911	Perjury Act 1911.
PAA 1971	Powers of Attorney Act 1971.
PACE	Police and Criminal Evidence Act 1984.
PCA 1994	Proceeds of Crime Act 1994.
PCA 2002	Proceeds of Crime Act 2002.
PCC(S)A 2000	Powers of Criminal Courts (Sentencing) Act 2000.
P(DB)A 2011	Police (Detention and Bail) Act 2011.
PEA 1977	Protection from Eviction Act 1977.
PHA 1997	Protection from Harassment Act 1997.
PIL(MP)A 1995	Private International Law (Miscellaneous Provisions) Act 1995.
PJA 2006	Police and Justice Act 2006.
P(LBCA)A 1990	Planning (Listed Buildings and Conservation Areas) Act 1990.
POA 1985	Prosecution of Offences Act 1985.
POA 1986	Public Order Act 1986.

R

ROA 1974	Rehabilitation of Offenders Act 1974.
RRA 1976	Race Relations Act 1976.
RSA 2006	Road Safety Act 2006.
RTA 1988	Road Traffic Act 1988.
RTA 1991	Road Traffic Act 1991.
RT(NC)A 1999	Road Traffic (NHS Charges) Act 1999.
RTOA 1988	Road Traffic Offenders Act 1988.

S

SA 1891	Stamp Act 1891.
SA 1974	Solicitors' Act 1974.
SCA 1981	Senior Courts Act 1981.
SDA 1975	Sex Discrimination Act 1975.
SDA 1986	Sex Discrimination Act 1986.
SGA 1979	Sales of Goods Act 1979.
SG(A)A 1995	Sale of Goods (Amendment) Act 1995.
SGSA 1982	Supply of Goods and Services Act 1982.
SG(IT)A 1973	Supply of Goods (Implied Terms) Act 1973.
SG(A)A 1995	Sale of Goods (Amendment) Act 1995.
SLA 1925	Settled Land Act 1925.
SOCPA 2005	Serious Organised Crime and Police Act 2005.
SSGA 1994	Sale and Supply of Goods Act 1994.
SS(RB)A 1997	Social Security (Recovery of Benefits) Act 1997.

T

TA 1925	Trustee Act 1925.
TA 1968	Theft Act 1968.

TA 2000	Trustee Act 2000.
TCE 2007	Tribunals, Courts and Enforcement Act 2007.
TCGA 1992	Taxation of Chargeable Gains Act 1992.
TCPA 1990	Town and Country Planning Act 1990.
TDA 1999	Trustee Delegation Act 1999.
TIA 1961	Trustee Investments Act 1961.
T(IOP)A 2010	Taxation (International and Other Provisions) Act 2010.
TLATA 1996	Trusts of Land and Appointment of Trustees Act 1996.
TMA 1970	Taxes Management Act 1970.
TULR(C)A 1992	Trade Union and Labour Relations (Consolidation) Act 1992.

U

UCTA 1977	Unfair Contract Terms Act 1977.

V

VATA and VATA 1994	
	Value Added Tax Act 1994.
VCRA 2006	Violent Crime Reduction Act 2006.

W

WA 1837	Wills Act 1837.
WA 1968	Wills Act 1968.
WIA 1991	Water Industry Act 1991.
WRPA 1999	Welfare Reform and Pensions Act 1999.

Y

YJCEA 1999	Youth Justice and Criminal Evidence Act 1999.

Table of abbreviations

Statutory Instruments / SRA codes / FSA rules

A

AIEDPO 1986 — Administration of Insolvent Estates of Deceased Persons Order 1986.

AJA(DA)O 2000 — Access to Justice Act 1999 (Destination of Appeals) Order 2000.

ATAO(F)R 1988 — Assured Tenancies and Agricultural Occupational (Forms) Regulations 1988.

AT(A)(E)0 2010 — Assured Tenancies (Amendment) (England) Order 2010.

B

BPMMR 2008 — Business Protection from Misleading Marketing Regulations 2008.

C

CA(CA(CD)R 1993 — Commercial Agents (Council Directive) Regulations 1993.

CA(DTP)O 2000 — Competition Act (Determination of Turnover for Penalties) Order 2000.

CA(EBPM)O 2003 — Capital Allowances (Environmentally Beneficial Plant and Machinery) Order 2003.

CA(EBPM)(A)O 2009 — Capital Allowances (Environmentally Beneficial Plant and Machinery) (Amendment) Order 2009.

CA(ESPM)O 2001 — Capital Allowances (Energy-saving Plant and Machinery) Order 2001.

CA(ESPM)(A)O 2009 — Capital Allowances (Energy-saving Plant and Machinery) (Amendment) Order 2009.

CA 1998 (LAER)O 2004 — Competition Act 1998 (Land Agreements Exclusion and Revocation) Order 2004.

CA 1998(LAER)O 2010 — Competition Act 1998 (Land Agreements Exclusion and Revocation) Order 2010.

CA(A,R,A)R 2009 — Companies Act 2006 (Accounts, Report and Audit) Regulations 2009.

CA(ARSA)R 2008 — Companies Act 2006 (Annual Return and Service Addresses) Regulations 2008.

CALLP(TPS)(A)R 2009 — The Companies Act 2006 and Limited Liability Partnerships (Transitional Provisions and Savings) (Amendment) Regulations 2009.

C(AM)R 2009 — Companies (Authorised Minimum) Regulations 2009.

CA(SACMS)R 2000 — Competition Act (Small Agreements and Conduct of Minor Significance) Regulations 2000.

CBN(MP)R 2009 — Company and Business Names (Miscellaneous Provisions) Regulations 2009.

C(CBM)R 2007 — Companies (Cross-Border Mergers) Regulations 2007.

CCFAR 2000 — Collective Conditional Fee Agreements Regulations 2000.

CCR — County Court Rules (CPR Sch 2).

C(DA)R 2009 — Companies (Disclosure of Address) Regulations 2009.

CDA(SOPE)R 2005 — Crime and Disorder Act (Scope of Prosecution Evidence) Regulations 2005.

CDS(CO)R 2009 — The Criminal Defence Service (Contribution Orders) Regulations 2009.

CDS(FE) R 2006 — Criminal Defence Service (Financial Eligibility) Regulations 2006.

CDS(G2)R 2001 — Criminal Defence Service (General)(No.2) Regulations 2001.

CDS(IJ)R 2009 — The Criminal Defence Service (Interests of Justice) Regulations 2009.

CDS(RDCO)R 2001 — Criminal Defence Service (Recovery of Defence Costs Orders) Regulations 2001.

CDS(ROA)R 2006 — Criminal Defence Service (Representation Orders: Appeals etc.) Regulations 2006.

CDS(RO(A))R 2009 — The Criminal Defence Service (Representation Orders) (Amendment) Regulations 2009.

CDS(ROA)AR 2010 — The Criminal Defence Service (Representation Orders: Appeals etc.) (Amendment) Regulations 2010.

CDS(ROCA)R 2006 — Criminal Defence Service (Representation Orders and Consequential Amendments) Regulations 2006.

CFAO 2000 — Conditional Fee Agreements Order 2000.

CITEPPOR 2005 — Charge to Income Tax By Reference to Enjoyment of Property Previously Owned Regulations 2005.

Table of authorities
Cases

Case	Page

Table of authorities

Statutes/UK, European and International legislation

H

Table of authorities

Statutory instruments and other rules/Codes/European secondary legislation

T

U

V

Statutory Codes

Non-statutory Codes/Rules/Regulations

CONDUCT

This chapter examines:

Note: This book assumes all provisions of the SRA Code are in force (although some are, in fact, subject to transitional provisions on Chapter 15 of the SRA Code.)

Note: Some provisions of the SRA Code are not applicable to in-house practices. This book does not cover the requirements for in-house practices.

The *SRA Code of Conduct*

➤ The Solicitors Regulation Authority ('SRA') regulates solicitors' compliance with the *SRA Code of Conduct*.

➤ The *SRA Code of Conduct* is on the SRA's website: **www.sra.org.uk**

➤ The *SRA Code of Conduct* sets outs outcomes-focused regulation (known as 'OFR').

 ◆ It sets out positive outcomes which, when achieved, will benefit and protect clients and the public.

 ◆ Solicitors must uphold the letter - and the intention - of the *SRA Code of Conduct*.

➤ The *SRA Code of Conduct* is underpinned by SRA supervision and enforcement.

Graphical overview of scope of all SRA rules

10 Principles permeate everything

- ◆ SRA Code of Conduct → Outcome-focused provisions about matters of conduct

- ◆ SRA Accounts Rules → Provisions about protecting client money

- ◆ SRA Authorisation and Practising Requirements consist of:
  - SRA Practice Framework Rules
  - SRA Authorisation Rules for Legal Services Bodies and Licensable Bodies
  - SRA Practising Regulations
  - SRA Recognised Bodies Regulations
  - SRA Training Regulations
  - SRA Admission Regulations
  - SRA Qualified Lawyers Transfer Scheme Regulations
  - SRA Higher Rights of Audience Regulations
  - SRA Suitability Test
  - Solicitors Keeping of the Roll Regulations.

  → The SRA approach to authorisation, appointing compliance officers (COLP and COFA), notification requirements, admission requirements, education requirements

- ◆ SRA Introduction to Client Protection consists of:
  - SRA Indemnity Insurance Rules
  - SRA Indemnity (Enactment) Rules
  - SRA Compensation Fund Rules
  - SRA Intervention Powers (Statutory Trust) Rules.

  → The SRA rules for disciplining firms

- ◆ SRA Introduction to discipline and costs recovery consists of:
  - SRA Disciplinary Procedure Rules
  - SRA Cost of Investigation Rules

  → The SRA rules for indemnity insurance and the Compensation Fund

- ◆ The SRA Introduction to Specialist Services consists of:
  - SRA European Cross-border Practice Rules (applicable to European cross-border practice)
  - SRA Property Selling Rules (applicable to providing property selling services through your law firm)
  - SRA Financial Services (Scope) Rules and the SRA Financial Services (Conduct of Business) Rules (applicable when you are not authorised by the Financial Services Authority and carry on exempt regulated activities for your clients)

A   The *SRA Code of Conduct* and its 10 Principles

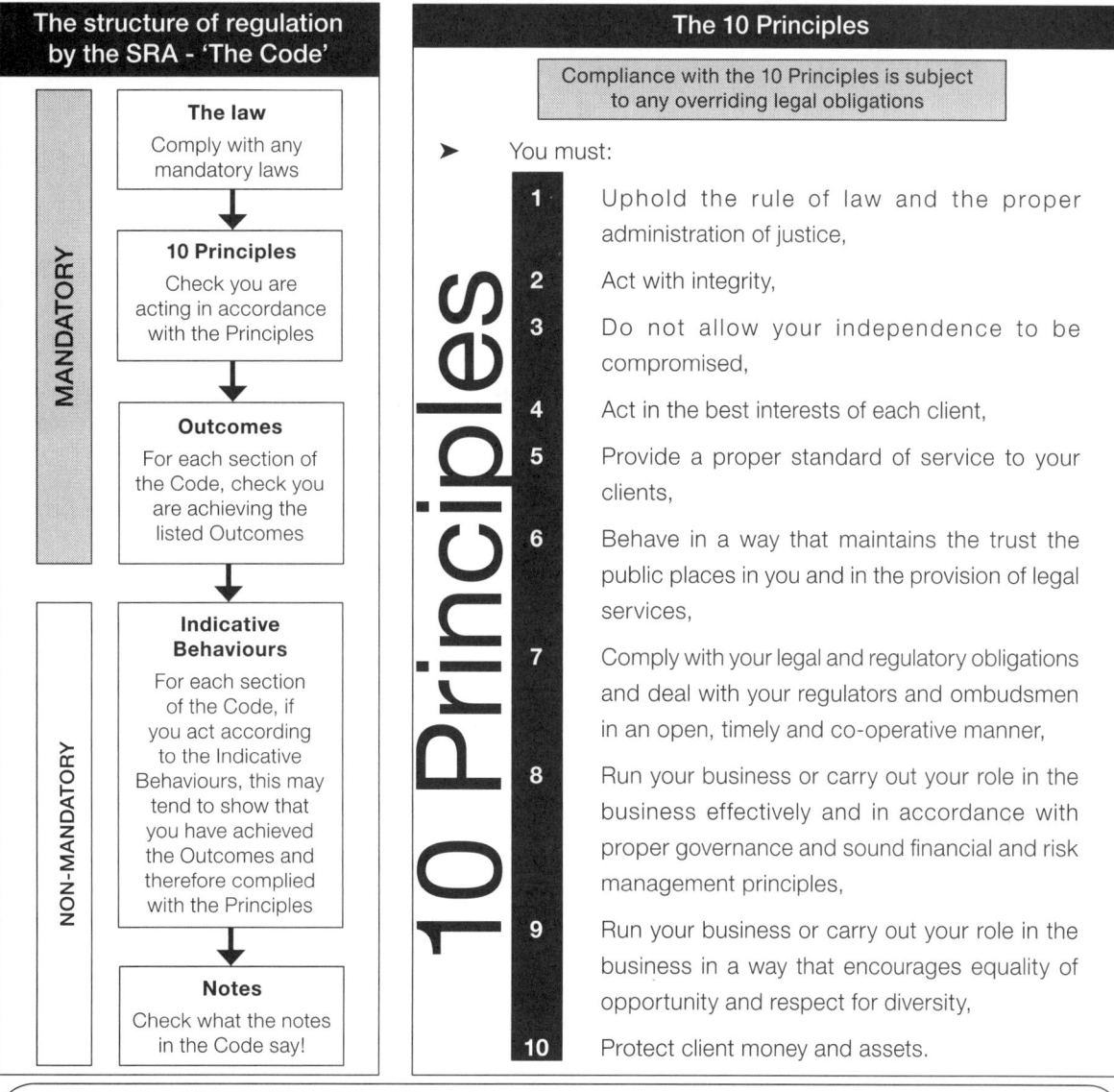

The structure of regulation by the SRA - 'The Code'

MANDATORY

The law
Comply with any mandatory laws

↓

10 Principles
Check you are acting in accordance with the Principles

↓

Outcomes
For each section of the Code, check you are achieving the listed Outcomes

↓

NON-MANDATORY

Indicative Behaviours
For each section of the Code, if you act according to the Indicative Behaviours, this may tend to show that you have achieved the Outcomes and therefore complied with the Principles

↓

Notes
Check what the notes in the Code say!

The 10 Principles

Compliance with the 10 Principles is subject to any overriding legal obligations

➤ You must:

10 Principles

1. Uphold the rule of law and the proper administration of justice,

2. Act with integrity,

3. Do not allow your independence to be compromised,

4. Act in the best interests of each client,

5. Provide a proper standard of service to your clients,

6. Behave in a way that maintains the trust the public places in you and in the provision of legal services,

7. Comply with your legal and regulatory obligations and deal with your regulators and ombudsmen in an open, timely and co-operative manner,

8. Run your business or carry out your role in the business effectively and in accordance with proper governance and sound financial and risk management principles,

9. Run your business or carry out your role in the business in a way that encourages equality of opportunity and respect for diversity,

10. Protect client money and assets.

What are the 10 Principles?

➤ The 10 mandatory Principles are all-pervasive for solicitors.

  ♦ They are the starting point for considering any action or inaction.

  ♦ They are the definition of all fundamental ethical and professional standards expected of all firms and individuals (including owners who may not be lawyers) when providing legal services.

Conflict among the Principles

➤ If Principles conflict with each other, the one which best serves the public interest in the particular circumstances (especially the public interest in the proper administration of justice) takes precedence.

Status of Indicative Behaviours

➤ Indicative Behaviours are not the only way to show compliance.

➤ Firms must demonstrate that they are meeting the outcomes and complying with the Principles.

B You and your client

I   Client care
II Equality and diversity
III Conflicts of interests
IV Confidentiality and disclosure
V   Your client and the court
VI Your client and introductions to third parties

I   Client care

Outcomes which MUST be achieved: Client care

➤ You treat your clients fairly (*O(1.1)*).

➤ You provide services to your clients in a manner which protects their interests in their matter (subject to the proper administration of justice) (*O(1.2)*).

➤ When deciding whether to act, or terminate your instructions, you comply with the law and the Code (*O(1.3)*).

➤ You have the resources, skills and procedures to carry out your clients' instructions (*O(1.4)*).

➤ The service you provide to clients is competent, delivered in a timely manner and takes account of your clients' needs and circumstances (*O(1.5)*).

➤ You only enter into fee agreements with your clients that are legal, and which you consider are suitable for the client's needs and take account of the client's best interests (*O(1.6)*).

➤ You inform clients whether and how the services you provide are regulated and how this affects the protections available to the client (*O(1.7)*).

➤ Clients have the benefit of your compulsory professional indemnity insurance and you do not exclude or attempt to exclude liability below the minimum level of cover required by the *SRA Indemnity Insurance Rules* (*O(1.8)*).

➤ Clients are informed in writing at the outset of their matter of their right to complain and how complaints can be made (*O(1.9)*).

➤ Clients are informed in writing, both at the time of engagement and at the conclusion of your complaints procedure, of their right to complain to the Legal Ombudsman, the time frame for doing so and full details of how to contact the Legal Ombudsman (*O(1.10)*). (See also p 41.)

➤ Clients' complaints are dealt with promptly, fairly, openly and effectively (*O(1.11)*).

➤ Clients are in a position to make informed decisions about the services they need, how their matter will be handled and the options available to them (*O(1.12)*).

➤ Clients receive the best possible information, both at the time of engagement and when appropriate as their matter progresses, about the likely overall cost of their matter (*O(1.13)*).

➤ Clients are informed of their right to challenge or complain about your bill and the circumstances in which they may be liable to pay interest on an unpaid bill (*O(1.14)*).

➤ You properly account to clients for any financial benefit you receive as a result of your instructions (*O(1.15)*).

➤ You inform clients if you discover any act/omission which could give rise to a claim by them against you (*O(1.16)*).

  ◆ Such an act/omission will cause an own interest conflict (see p 10) and you will need to cease acting.

Indicative Behaviours: Dealing with the client's matter

➤ Agreeing an appropriate level of service with your client, eg: type and frequency of communications (*IB(1.1)*).

➤ Explaining your responsibilities and those of the client (*IB(1.2)*).

➤ Ensuring that the client is told, in writing, the name and status of the person(s) dealing with the matter and the name and status of the person responsible for its overall supervision (*IB(1.3)*).

➤ Explaining any arrangements, such as fee sharing or referral arrangements, which are relevant to the client's instructions (*IB(1.4)*).

➤ Explaining any limitations or conditions on what you can do for the client, eg: because of the way the client's matter is funded (*IB(1.5)*).

➤ In taking instructions and during the course of the retainer, having proper regard to your client's mental capacity or other vulnerability, such as incapacity or duress (*IB(1.6)*).

IB(1.6): Does the client have capacity?

➤ A person is assumed to have capacity, unless it is established that he lacks capacity (*MCA 2005 s 1(2)*).

  ◆ A person is not treated as being unable to make a decision unless all practical steps have been taken, without success, to help him to make that decision (*MCA 2005 s 1(3)*).

  ◆ A person lacks capacity for a matter if, at the material time, he is unable to make a decision for himself because of an impairment, or disturbance in the functioning of, mind or brain (*MCA 2005 s 1(3)*).

➤ Provided a solicitor is not negligent, he is protected from criminal and civil liability in relation to each of his acts in connection with the care of a person if (broadly) (*MCA 2005 s 5*):

  a) the solicitor takes reasonable steps, before each act, to establish whether a person lacks capacity in relation to the matter in question, *and*

  b) when the solicitor acts, he reasonably believes that:

    i) the person lacks capacity in relation to the matter, *and*

    ii) it will be in the person's best interest for the act to be done.

➤ A solicitor is under a duty to have regard to the *MCA 2005 Code of Practice* issued by the Lord Chancellor on 23 April 2007 in relation to matters covered by the *MCA 2005* (*MCA 2005 s 42*).

  ◆ *MCA 2005* does not displace the common law test for capacity to make a will (*Scammell and another v Farmer* [2008] EWHC 1100 (Ch)).

➤ Considering whether you should decline to act or cease to act because you cannot act in the client's best interests (*IB(1.7)*).

➤ If you seek to limit your liability to your client to a level above the minimum required by the *SRA Indemnity Insurance Rules*, ensuring that this limitation is in writing and is brought to the client's attention (*IB(1.8)*).

  ◆ The sum insured for any one claim (exclusive of defence costs) must be, where the insured firm is a relevant recognised body, at least £3 million, and in all other cases, at least £2 million (*SRA IIR 2.1*).

➤ Refusing to act where your client proposes to make a gift of significant value to you or a member of your family, or a member of your firm or their family, unless the client takes independent legal advice (*IB(1.9)*).

➤ If you have to cease acting for a client, explaining to the client their possible options for pursuing their matter (*IB(1.10)*).

➤ You inform clients if they are not entitled to the protections of the SRA Compensation Fund (*IB(1.11)*).

➤ Considering whether a conflict of interests has arisen or whether the client should be advised to obtain independent advice where the client notifies you of their intention to make a claim or if you discover an act or omission which might give rise to a claim (*IB(1.12)*).

Indicative Behaviours: Fee arrangements with your client

➤ Discussing whether the potential outcomes of the client's matter are likely to justify the expense or risk involved, including any risk of having to pay someone else's legal fees (*IB(1.13)*).

➤ Clearly explaining your fees and if and when they are likely to change (*IB(1.14)*).

➤ Warning about any other payments for which the client may be responsible (*IB(1.15)*).

➤ Discussing how the client will pay, including whether public funding may be available, whether the client has insurance that might cover the fees, and whether the fees may be paid by someone else such as a trade union (*IB(1.16)*).

➤ Where you are acting for a client under a fee arrangement governed by statute, such as a conditional fee agreement, giving the client all relevant information relating to that arrangement (*IB(1.17)*).

➤ Where you are acting for a publicly funded client, explaining how their publicly funded status affects the costs (*IB(1.18)*).

➤ Providing the information in a clear and accessible form which is appropriate to the needs and circumstances of the client (*IB(1.19)*).

➤ Where you receive a financial benefit as a result of acting for a client, either (*IB(1.20)*):

   ◆ paying it to the client, *or*

   ◆ offsetting it against your fees, *or*

   ◆ keeping it only where you can justify keeping it, you have told the client the amount of the benefit (or an approximation if you do not know the exact amount) and the client has agreed that you can keep it.

➤ Ensuring that disbursements included in your bill reflect the actual amount spent or to be spent on behalf of the client (*IB(1.21)*).

Fees, quotations and estimates

➤ If a solicitor gives a quotation instead of an estimate, he must do the job for that price.

➤ An estimate of fees should make clear how costs will be calculated; the solicitor must inform the client if it appears likely that costs will exceed the estimate.

➤ If VAT is not mentioned, the client is entitled to assume the price is inclusive of VAT (*VATA 1994 s 89*).

➤ For conditional fee agreements, see pp 31 et seq.

Types of costs a client will have to bear: 2 classes

1 **Solicitor-own-client costs:** these are all expenses which the solicitor incurs on the client's behalf, eg: solicitor's own fees, fees for counsel/experts, applications for police accident reports, etc. The solicitor usually asks for payment on account for expenses he expects to incur.

2 **Inter partes costs:** in a civil claim, these are expenses which other parties to a claim incur and are usually the responsibility of whichever party loses litigation (subject to the court's ruling on costs, see pp 461 et seq).

For further information on civil costs see pp 461 et seq

Some practical considerations: acting for a client

In (civil) contentious matters, it is sensible for you to explain to a client:

For private clients:	For CLS funded clients:
◆ the client's potential liability for his own costs and those of any other party	◆ the circumstances in which the client may be liable for the solicitor's costs
◆ the fact that the client will be responsible for paying the firm's bill in full regardless of any order for costs made against the opponent	◆ the effect of the statutory charge
◆ the probability that the client will have to pay both its opponent's costs and the client's own costs if the case is lost	◆ the client's duty to pay any fixed or periodic contribution assessed and the consequences of failing to do so
◆ the fact that even if the client wins, the opponent may not be ordered to pay or be capable of paying the full amount of the client's costs	◆ the fact that even if the client is successful, the opponent may not be ordered to pay or may not be in a position to pay them
◆ the fact that if the opponent is LSC funded, the client may not recover costs even if successful	

If advising on a dispute, you should discuss if ADR may be more appropriate than litigation, arbitration or other formal processes. Otherwise there may be costs sanctions if a party refuses ADR (*Halsey v Milton Keynes NHS Trust* [2004] EWCA (Civ) 576).

Scope of solicitor authority

➤ **Non-contentious work** (pre-litigation): a solicitor has 'ostensible authority' to act on the client's behalf.

➤ **Contentious work**: a solicitor has 'actual authority' to act on a client's behalf and to bind a client.

◆ You should always obtain a client's express authority, preferably in writing, before making any commitment on the client's behalf, unless the matter is urgent.

◆ Acting without client consent may make you liable to a third party for breach of warranty of authority.

Ceasing to act

➤ The retainer is a contractual relationship and subject to legal considerations.

◆ A client can end the retainer with the solicitor at any time and for any reason.

◆ The retainer may be ended automatically by law eg: on the client's bankruptcy.

➤ If the solicitor ceases to act, he needs to consider what should be done with the paperwork.

◆ The solicitor must hand over the client's files promptly on request subject to the solicitor's right to exercise a lien in respect of outstanding costs. If possible, an undertaking to secure costs from the new solicitor should be secured as an alternative to a lien.

◆ The solicitor should try to ensure the client's position is not prejudiced.

◆ The solicitor should also bear in mind the client's rights under the *Data Protection Act 1998*.

Indicative Behaviours that Principles have NOT been complied with: Accepting and refusing instructions

➤ Acting for a client when instructions are given by someone else, or by only one client when you act jointly for others unless you are satisfied that the person providing the instructions has the authority to do so on behalf of all of the clients (*IB(1.25)*).

➤ Ceasing to act for a client without good reason and without providing reasonable notice (*IB(1.26)*).

➤ Entering into unlawful fee arrangements such as an unlawful contingency fee (*IB(1.27)*).

➤ Acting for a client when there are reasonable grounds for believing that the instructions are affected by duress or undue influence without satisfying yourself that they represent the client's wishes (*IB(1.28)*).

Indicative Behaviours: Complaints handling

➤ Having a written complaints procedure which (*IB(1.22)*):

- ◆ is brought to clients' attention at the outset of the matter, *and*

- ◆ is easy for clients to use and understand, allowing for complaints to be made by any reasonable means, *and*

- ◆ is responsive to the needs of individual clients, especially those who are vulnerable, *and*

- ◆ enables complaints to be dealt with promptly and fairly, with decisions based on a sufficient investigation of the circumstances, *and*

- ◆ provides for appropriate remedies, *and*

- ◆ does not involve any charges to clients for handling their complaints.

➤ Providing the client with a copy of the firm's complaints procedure on request (*IB(1.23)*).

➤ In the event that a client makes a complaint, providing them with all necessary information concerning the handling of the complaint (*IB(1.24)*).

Some practical considerations: complaints

Acknowledging a complaint

➤ A well-written acknowledgement of a complaint should:

- ◆ include details of the Legal Ombudsman (LO), with its contact details, *and*

- ◆ state that the client(s) can ask the LO to become involved at the end of the firm's own complaints procedure if they are unhappy with the outcome, *and*

- ◆ state the time limit for submitting a complaint to the LO.

➤ See p 41 for further details.

Assessment of a bill

➤ A client is entitled to apply to the High Court for a detailed assessment of a bill (see p 466) (*SA 1974 ss 70, 71, 72*).

- ◆ In a detailed assessment, if the client is not funded by legal aid, costs are assessed on an indemnity basis (see p 461) but are presumed (*CPR r 48.8*):

  - • to have been reasonably incurred if incurred with the client's express or implied approval, *and*

  - • to be reasonable in amount if their amount was expressly or impliedly approved by the client, *and*

  - • to have been unreasonably incurred if:

    - ▪ they are of an unusual nature or amount, *and*

    - ▪ the solicitor did not tell his client that some costs might not be recovered from the other party.

➤ **If a conditional fee arrangement is in place,** where the court is considering a percentage increase, the court will have regard to all the relevant factors as they reasonably appeared to the solicitor or counsel when the conditional fee agreement was entered into or varied (*CPR r 48.8(3)*).

II Equality and diversity

The law
➤ Ensure you comply with the *Equality Act 2010*.

Have you checked the Principles first?

Outcomes which MUST be achieved: Equality and diversity

➤ You do not discriminate unlawfully, or victimise or harass anyone, in the course of your professional dealings (*O(2.1)*).

➤ You provide services to clients in a way that respects diversity (*O(2.2)*).

➤ You make reasonable adjustments to ensure that disabled clients, employees or managers are not placed at a substantial disadvantage compared to those who are not disabled, and you do not pass on the costs of these adjustments to these disabled clients, employees or managers (*O(2.3)*).

➤ Your approach to recruitment and employment encourages equality of opportunity and respect for diversity (*O(2.4)*).

➤ Complaints of discrimination are dealt with promptly, fairly, openly, and effectively (*O(2.5)*).

Systems and controls

➤ There is an obligation to put systems and controls in place to comply with these rules (see p 35).

Indicative Behaviours: Equality and diversity

➤ Having a written equality and diversity policy which is appropriate to the size and nature of the firm and includes the following features (*IB(2.1)*):

♦ a commitment to the principles of equality and diversity and legislative requirements,

♦ a requirement that all employees and managers comply with the outcomes,

♦ provisions to encompass your recruitment and interview processes,

♦ details of how the firm will implement, monitor, evaluate and update the policy,

♦ details of how the firm will ensure equality in relation to the treatment of employees, managers, clients and third parties instructed in connection with client matters,

♦ details of how complaints and disciplinary issues are to be dealt with.

♦ details of arrangements for workforce diversity and monitoring.

♦ details of how the firm will communicate policy to employees, managers and clients.

➤ Providing employees and managers with training and information about complying with equality and diversity requirements (*IB(2.2)*).

➤ Monitoring and responding to issues identified by your policy and reviewing and updating your policy (*IB(2.3)*).

 ### Indicative Behaviours that Principles have NOT been complied with: Equality and diversity

➤ Being subject to any decision of a court or tribunal of the UK , that you have committed, or are to be treated as having committed, an unlawful act of discrimination (*IB(2.4)*).

➤ Discriminating unlawfully when accepting or refusing instructions to act for a client (*IB(2.5)*).

III   Conflicts of interests

Outcomes which MUST be achieved (Prohibition on acting in a conflict)

➤ You do not act if there is an own interest conflict or a significant risk of an own interest conflict (*O(3.4)*.)

➤ You do not act if there is a client conflict, or a significant risk of a client conflict, unless the circumstances set out in Outcomes 3.6 or 3.7 apply (*O(3.5)*).

An 'own interest conflict' is a conflict between you and one or more current clients

A 'client conflict' is a conflict between two or more current clients

Outcomes which MUST be achieved (Client conflict exceptions when you may act)

➤ Where there is a client conflict and the clients have a substantially common interest in relation to a matter or a particular aspect of it, you only act if (*O(3.6)*):

   a) you have explained the relevant issues and risks to the clients and you have a reasonable belief that they understand those issues and risks, *and*

   b) all the clients have given informed consent in writing to you acting, *and*

   c) you are satisfied that it is reasonable for you to act for all the clients and that it is in their best interests, *and*

   d) you are satisfied that the benefits to the clients of you doing so outweigh the risks.

➤ Where there is a client conflict and the clients are competing for the same objective, you only act if (*O(3.7)*):

   a) you have explained the relevant issues and risks to the clients and you have a reasonable belief that they understand those issues and risks, *and*

   b) the clients have confirmed in writing that they want you to act, in the knowledge that you act, or may act, for one or more other clients who are competing for the same objective, *and*

   c) there is no other client conflict in relation to that matter, *and*

   d) unless the clients specifically agree, no individual acts for, or is responsible for the supervision of work done for, more than one of the clients in that matter, *and*

   e) you are satisfied that it is reasonable for you to act for all the clients and that the benefits to the clients of you doing so outweigh the risks.

Outcomes which MUST be achieved (Systems in place)

➤ You have effective systems and controls in place to enable you to identify and assess potential conflicts of interests (*O(3.1)*).

➤ Your systems and controls for identifying own interest conflicts are appropriate to the size and complexity of the firm and the nature of the work undertaken, and enable you to assess all the relevant circumstances, including whether your ability as an individual, or that of anyone within your firm, to act in the best interests of the client(s), is impaired by (*O(3.2)*):

   ◆ any financial interest, *or*   ◆ a personal relationship, *or*

   ◆ the appointment of you, or a member of your firm or family, to public office, *or*

   ◆ commercial relationships, *or*   ◆ your employment.

➤ Your systems and controls for identifying client conflicts are appropriate to the size and complexity of the firm and the nature of the work undertaken, and enable you to assess all relevant circumstances, including whether (*O(3.3)*):

   ◆ the clients' interests are different, *or*

   ◆ your ability to give independent advice to the clients may be fettered, *or*

   ◆ there is a need to negotiate between the clients, *or*

   ◆ there is an imbalance in bargaining power between the clients, *or*

   ◆ any client is vulnerable.

Have you checked the Principles first?

Indicative Behaviours: Conflicts of interests

➤ Training employees and managers to identify and assess potential conflicts of interests (*(IB(3.1)*).

➤ Declining to act for clients whose interests are in direct conflict, for example claimant and defendant in litigation (*(IB(3.2)*).

➤ Declining to act for clients where you may need to negotiate on matters of substance on their behalf, for example negotiating on price between a buyer and seller of a property (*(IB(3.3)*).

➤ Declining to act where there is unequal bargaining power between the clients, for example acting for a seller and buyer where a builder is selling to a non-commercial client (*(IB(3.4)*).

➤ Declining to act for clients under Outcomes 3.6 or 3.7 (competing for the same objective) where the clients cannot be represented even-handedly, or will be prejudiced by lack of separate representation (*(IB(3.5)*).

➤ Acting for clients under Outcome 3.7 (competing for the same objective) only where the clients are sophisticated users of legal services (*(IB(3.6)*).

➤ Acting for clients who are the lender and borrower on the grant of a mortgage of land only where (*(IB(3.7)*):

   a) the mortgage is a standard mortgage (ie: one provided in the normal course of the lender's activities, where a significant part of the lender's activities consists of lending and the mortgage is on standard terms) of property to be used as the borrower's private residence, *and*

   b) you are satisfied that it is reasonable and in the clients' best interests for you to act, *and*

   c) the certificate of title required by the lender is in the form approved by the Society and the Council of Mortgage Lenders.

Indicative Behaviours that Principles have NOT been complied with: Conflicts of interests

➤ In a personal capacity, selling to or buying from, lending to or borrowing from a client, unless the client has obtained independent legal advice (*IB(3.8)*).

➤ Advising a client to invest in a business, in which you have an interest which affects your ability to provide impartial advice (*IB(3.9)*).

➤ Where you hold a power of attorney for a client, using that power to gain a benefit for yourself which in your professional capacity you would not have been prepared to allow to a third party (*IB(3.10)*).

➤ Acting for two or more clients in a conflict of interests under Outcome 3.6 (substantially common interest) where the clients' interests in the end result are not the same, for example one partner buying out the interest of the other partner in their joint business or a seller transferring a property to a buyer (*IB(3.11)*).

➤ Acting for two or more clients in a conflict of interests under Outcome 3.6 where it is unreasonable to act because there is unequal bargaining power (*IB(3.12)*).

➤ Acting for two buyers where there is a conflict of interests under Outcome 3.7, for example where two buyers are competing for a residential property (*IB(3.13)*).

➤ Acting for a buyer (including a lessee) and seller (including a lessor) in a transaction relating to the transfer of land for value, the grant or assignment of a lease or some other interest in land for value (*IB(3.14)*).

IV   Confidentiality and disclosure

Outcomes which MUST be achieved: Confidentiality and disclosure

➤ You keep the affairs of clients confidential unless disclosure is required or permitted by law or the client consents (*O(4.1)*).

➤ Any individual who is advising a client makes that client aware of all information material to that retainer of which the individual has personal knowledge (*O(4.2)*).

➤ You ensure that where your duty of confidentiality to one client comes into conflict with your duty of disclosure to another client, your duty of confidentiality takes precedence (*O(4.3)*).

➤ You do not act for A in a matter where A has an interest adverse to B, and B is a client for whom you hold confidential information which is material to A in that matter, unless the confidential information can be protected by the use of safeguards, and (*O(4.4)*):

  a) you reasonably believe that A is aware of, and understands, the relevant issues and gives informed consent, *and*
  b) *either* (i) B gives informed consent and you agree with B the safeguards to protect B's information, *or* (ii) where this is not possible, you put in place effective safeguards including information barriers which comply with the common law, *and*
  c) it is reasonable in all the circumstances to act for A with such safeguards in place.

➤ You have effective systems and controls in place to enable you to identify risks to client confidentiality and to mitigate those risks (*O(4.5)*).

Indicative Behaviours: Confidentiality and disclosure

➤ Your systems and controls for identifying risks to client confidentiality are appropriate to the size and complexity of the firm or in-house practice and the nature of the work undertaken, and enable you to assess all the relevant circumstances (*IB(4.1)*).

➤ You comply with the law in respect of your fiduciary duties in relation to confidentiality and disclosure (*IB(4.2)*).

➤ You only outsource services when you are satisfied that the provider has taken all appropriate steps to ensure that your clients' confidential information will be protected (*IB(4.3)*).

➤ Where you are an individual who has responsibility for acting for a client or supervising a client's matter, you disclose to the client all information material to the client's matter of which you are personally aware, except when (*IB(4.4)*):

  ◆ the client gives specific informed consent to non-disclosure or a different standard of disclosure arises, *or*
  ◆ there is evidence that serious physical or mental injury will be caused to a person(s) if the information is disclosed to the client, *or*
  ◆ legal restrictions effectively prohibit you from passing the information to the client, such as the provisions in the money-laundering and anti-terrorism legislation, *or*
  ◆ it is obvious that privileged documents have been mistakenly disclosed to you, *or*
  ◆ you come into possession of information relating to state security or intelligence matters to which the *Official Secrets Act 1989* applies.

➤ Not acting for A where B is a client for whom you hold confidential information which is material to A unless the confidential information can be protected (*IB(4.5)*).

Indicative Behaviours that Principles have NOT been complied with: Confidentiality and disclosure

➤ Disclosing the content of a will on the death of a client unless consent has been provided by the personal representatives for the content to be released (*IB(4.6)*).

➤ Disclosing details of bills sent to clients to third parties, such as debt factoring companies in relation to the collection of book debts, unless the client has consented. (*IB(4.7)*).

V   Your client and the court

Outcomes which MUST be achieved: Your client and the court

➤ You do not attempt to deceive or knowingly or recklessly mislead the court (*O(5.1)*).

➤ You are not complicit in another person deceiving or misleading the court (*O(5.2)*).

➤ You comply with court orders which place obligations on you (*O(5.3)*).

➤ You do not place yourself in contempt of court (*O(5.4)*).

➤ Where relevant, clients are informed of the circumstances in which your duties to the court outweigh your obligations to your client (*O(5.5)*).

➤ You comply with your duties to the court (*O(5.6)*).

➤ You ensure that evidence relating to sensitive issues is not misused (*O(5.7)*).

➤ You do not make or offer to make payments to witnesses dependent upon their evidence or the outcome of the case (*O(5.8)*).

Have you checked the Principles first?

Indicative Behaviours: Your client and the court

➤ Advising your clients to comply with court orders made against them, and advising them of the consequences of failing to comply (*IB(5.1)*).

➤ Drawing the court's attention to relevant cases and statutory provisions, and any material procedural irregularity (*IB(5.2)*).

➤ Ensuring child witness evidence is kept securely and not released to clients or third parties (*IB(5.3)*).

➤ Immediately informing the court, with your client's consent, if during the course of proceedings you become aware that you have inadvertently misled the court, or ceasing to act if the client does not consent to you informing the court (*IB(5.4)*).

➤ Refusing to continue acting for a client if you become aware they have committed perjury or misled the court, or attempted to mislead the court, in any material matter unless the client agrees to disclose the truth to the court (*IB(5.5)*).

➤ Not appearing as an advocate, or acting in litigation, if it is clear that you, or anyone within your firm, will be called as a witness in the matter unless you are satisfied that this will not prejudice your independence as an advocate, or litigator, or the interests of your clients or the interests of justice (*IB(5.6)*).

Indicative Behaviours that Principles have NOT been complied with: Your client and the court

➤ Constructing facts supporting your client's case or drafting any documents relating to any proceedings containing (*IB(5.7)*):

  ◆ any contention which you do not consider to be properly arguable, *or*

  ◆ any allegation of fraud, unless you are instructed to do so and you have material which you reasonably believe shows, on the face of it, a case of fraud.

➤ Suggesting that any person is guilty of a crime, fraud or misconduct unless such allegations (*IB(5.8)*):

  ◆ go to a matter in issue which is material to your own client's case, *and*

  ◆ appear to you to be supported by reasonable grounds.

➤ Calling a witness whose evidence you know is untrue (*IB(5.9)*).

➤ Attempting to influence a witness, when taking a statement from that witness, with regard to the contents of their statement (*IB(5.10)*).

Indicative Behaviours that Principles have NOT been complied with: Your client and the court

➤ Tampering with evidence or seeking to persuade a witness to change their evidence (*IB(5.11)*).

➤ When acting as an advocate, naming in open court any third party whose character would thereby be called into question, unless it is necessary for the proper conduct of the case (*IB(5.12)*).

➤ When acting as an advocate, calling into question the character of a witness you have crossexamined unless the witness has had the opportunity to answer the allegations during crossexamination (*IB(5.13)*).

Some practical considerations

Civil litigation

➤ **The overriding duty:** the solicitor has an overriding duty to the court when appearing before it or when conducting litigation, to act with independence in the interests of justice (*LSA 2007 s 188* and cf. p 378).

➤ **Disclosure:** the solicitor should make a client aware that it is important to preserve carefully all documents for disclosure whether they help or harm the client's case.

Criminal litigation

➤ In a criminal case, a solicitor can put the prosecution to proof even if the client admits guilt to the solicitor. However, assisting a client to give perjured evidence would breach the solicitor's duty to the court, and the solicitor should refuse to act if a client attempts this.

➤ A solicitor is not obliged to inform the court if it is mistaken about a defendant's criminal record, provided the court does not request any positive representation. If a court requests information, the solicitor must advise the client to tell the truth, and must refuse to act if the client declines.

➤ **When the client admits guilt to the solicitor,** the solicitor is unable to act by positively misleading the court. However, on a plea of 'not guilty', a solicitor can still put the prosecution to proof.

♦ However, it is important to remember that cases can be adjourned and reopened in the interests of justice (*Khatibi v DPP* [2004] 168 JP 361).

➤ **When the client pleads 'guilty', but has a defence,** the solicitor can act. He can put the client's defence, but must advise that in mitigation it may not be possible to rely on the facts constituting the defence.

➤ **When the client gives inconsistent instructions,** the solicitor can act (if there is no false evidence).

➤ **The solicitor has a positive duty to assist the court on points of law.**

➤ **The solicitor has a negative duty - not to mislead the court on points of fact.**

➤ **If the client wishes to give a false name or address to the court,** the solicitor must try to persuade the client to be truthful. If he does not succeed, the solicitor cannot act.

➤ **If the court has an incorrect list of the client's previous convictions,** the solicitor may not correct the list without the consent of the client. If there is no such consent, the solicitor must refuse to act.

➤ **If for *any* reason, the solicitor is unable to act, he may not be able to say why without breaching a client confidence.** He should just say that it is impossible for him to act, without saying why.

➤ **If the prosecution does not realise that its detention limits are about to run out,** the defence owes a duty to the client not to remind the prosecution of this (see p 550).

VI   Your client and introductions to third parties

Have you checked the Principles first?

Outcomes which MUST be achieved : Your client and introductions to third parties

➤ Whenever you recommend that a client uses a particular person or business, your recommendation is in the best interests of the client and does not compromise your independence (*O(6.1)*).

➤ Clients are fully informed of any financial or other interest which you have in referring the client to another person or business (*O(6.2)*).

➤ If a client is likely to need advice on investments, such as life insurance with an investment element or pension policies, you refer them only to an independent intermediary (*O(6.3)*).

Indicative Behaviours: Your client and introductions to third parties

➤ Any arrangement you enter into in respect of regulated mortgage contracts, general insurance contracts (including after the event insurance) or pure protection contracts, provides that referrals will only be made where this is in the best interests of the particular client and the contract is suitable for the needs of that client (*IB(6.1)*).

➤ Any referral in respect of regulated mortgage contracts, general insurance contracts and pure protection contracts to a third party that can only offer products from one source, is made only after the client has been informed of this limitation (*IB(6.2)*).

Indicative Behaviours that Principles have NOT been complied with: Your client and introductions to third parties

➤ Entering into any arrangement which restricts your freedom to recommend any particular business, except in respect of regulated mortgage contracts, general insurance contracts or pure protection contracts (*IB(6.3)*).

➤ Being an appointed representative (*IB(6.4)*) (in terms of *FSMA 2000*).

C   Money laundering

➤   The *PCA 2002* defines 5 offences on money laundering, all carrying strict criminal penalties.

1. Concealing (*s 327*)

➤   **The offence:** concealing, disguising, converting or transferring criminal property or removing criminal property from England and Wales.

♦   'Concealing or disguising' includes concealing or disguising its nature, source, location, disposition, movement or ownership or any rights with respect to it.

DEFENCES:
See box at bottom of page.

2. Arranging (*s 328*)

➤   **The offence:** entering into or becoming concerned in 'an arrangement' which he knows or suspects facilitates (by whatever means) the acquisition, retention, use or control of criminal property by or on behalf of another person. (See also p 18.)

DEFENCES:
See box at bottom of page.

3. Acquiring, using and possessing (*s 329*)

➤   **The offence:** acquiring, using or possessing criminal property.

EXTRA DEFENCE: A person does not commit such an offence if he acquired or used or had possession of the property for adequate consideration.

DEFENCES:
See box at bottom of page plus

Defences to offences 1, 2 and 3 above (*ss 327, 328, 329, 338*)

➤   **Defences:** A person does not commit an offence under *ss 327, 328 or 329* if:

♦   he makes an authorised disclosure to the police or a Money Laundering Officer (MLO) before the prohibited act and he has the appropriate consent to do the act, *or*

♦   he makes an authorised disclosure to the police or an MLO while the alleged offender is doing the prohibited act, and the offender began the act when the act was not a prohibited act (because he did not then know or suspect that the property constituted or represented a person's benefit from criminal conduct), and the disclosure is made on his own initiative and as soon as is practicable after he first knows or suspects that the property constitutes or represents a person's benefit from criminal conduct, *or*

♦   he makes an authorised disclosure to the police or an MLO after the prohibited act and he has a reasonable excuse for his failure to make the disclosure before the act and the disclosure is made on his own initiative and as soon as practicable, *or*

♦   he intended to make such a disclosure but had a reasonable excuse for not doing so, *or*

♦   the act is done in carrying out a function he has relating to the enforcement of any provision of *PCA 2002* or of any other enactment relating to criminal conduct or benefit from it, *or*

♦   he knows, or believes on reasonable grounds, that the relevant criminal conduct occurred in a particular country/territory outside the UK *and* the relevant criminal conduct was not, at the time it occurred, unlawful under the criminal law then applying in that country/territory, and is not of a description prescribed by an order made by the Secretary of State, *or*

♦   for deposit taking institutions only: an account is maintained with such an institution and the criminal property involved is under £250 (although this amount may be varied in certain circumstances).

These sections only apply to business in the regulated sector (PCA 2002 Schedule 9). Much of the business of a law firm is in the regulated sector but some is not. Law firms typically treat all business as being in the regulated sector for the purpose of complying with these sections - better safe than sorry!

4. Failing to disclose (ss 330-332) (as amended by SOCPA 2005 ss 102, 104)

➤ **The offence:** A person commits an offence if:

A he knows or suspects or has reasonable grounds for knowing or suspecting, that another person is engaged in money laundering, *and*

B the information or other matter on which his knowledge or suspicion is based, or which gives reasonable grounds for such knowledge or suspicion, came to him in the course of his business in a regulated sector (which includes legal services providers eg: lawyers), *and*

C he:
- can identify the other person mentioned in A or the whereabouts of any of the laundered property, *or*
- believes, or it is reasonable to expect him to believe, that the information or other matter mentioned in B will or may assist in identifying that other person or the whereabouts of any of the laundered property, *and*

D he does not make the 'required disclosure', as soon as is practicable after the information or other matter in B comes to him, to a nominated officer (ie: the MLO of the firm) or to a person authorised by the Serious Organised Crime Agency (SOCA).

➤ **Defences:** A person does not commit an offence if:

◆ he has a reasonable excuse for not making the 'required disclosure', *or*

◆ he is a professional legal adviser (or relevant specified professional adviser, eg: accountant, auditor, tax adviser etc), *and*:
- if he knows either of i) or ii) below (see 'required disclosure'), that he knows that thing because of information or other matter that came to him in privileged circumstances, *or*
- the information or other matter mentioned in offence element B above came to him in privileged circumstances, *or*

◆ he does not know or suspect that another person is engaged in money laundering *and* he has not been provided by his employer with certain specified mandated training, *or*

◆ he knows, or believes on reasonable grounds, that the money laundering is occurring in a particular country/territory outside the UK, *and* the money laundering is not unlawful under the criminal law applying in that country/ territory and is not prescribed by an order made by the Secretary of State, *or*

◆ he is employed by (or is in partnership with) a professional legal adviser (or a relevant professional adviser) to provide the adviser with assistance or support, *and* the information or other matter mentioned in offence element B above comes to the person in connection with the provision of such assistance or support, *and* the information or other matter came to the adviser in privileged circumstances.

➤ **The 'required disclosure' is:** a disclosure of:

i) the identity of the other person mentioned in offence element A above, if he knows it, *and*

ii) the whereabouts of the laundered property, so far as he knows it, *and*

iii) the information or other matter mentioned in offence element B above.

➤ Legal privilege applies if information (or other matter) comes to a solicitor when it is *not* given with the intention of furthering a criminal purpose and is communicated or given to him:

◆ by (or by a representative of) a client of his in connection with the giving by the solicitor of legal advice to the client, *or*

◆ by (or by a representative of) a person seeking legal advice from the solicitor, or

◆ by a person in connection with legal proceedings or contemplated legal proceedings.

Reinterpretation by *Bowman v Fels [2005] EWCA Civ 226* (Court of Appeal)

➤ **Litigation is not an 'arrangement' for the purposes of *PCA 2002 s 328* (see p 16).**

➤ Lord Justice Brooke delivered the judgment of the court and said:

◆ *s 328* cannot have been intended to affect the ordinary conduct of litigation by legal professionals.

● This includes any step taken by legal professionals in litigation from the issue of proceedings and the securing of injunctive relief or a freezing order up to its final disposal by judgment.

◆ The European/UK legislator could not have envisaged that any of these ordinary activities could fall within the concept of 'concerned in an arrangement ...'.

◆ Legal proceedings are a state-provided mechanism for the resolution of issues according to law. Everyone has the right to a fair and public trial in the determination of his civil rights and duties which is secured by *ECHR Art 6*.

◆ Parliament could not have intended that proceedings or steps taken by lawyers in order to determine or secure legal rights and remedies for their clients should involve them in 'becoming concerned in an arrangement ...', *even if they suspected that the outcome of such proceedings might have such an effect*.

◆ If the court was wrong in its interpretation of *s 328* and Parliament *had* intended to override legal professional privilege, then the legislation had to be clearer and should be amended to state this intention expressly.

5. Tipping off offences (*s 333A*)

➤ **Offence 1:** A person commits an offence if (*s 333A(1)-(2)*):

◆ he discloses that X has made a Primary Disclosure to an MLO or the police (or certain other officers), *and*

● A Primary Disclosure is a disclosure of information that came to X in the course of a business in the regulated sector.

◆ the disclosure is likely to prejudice any investigation that might be conducted following that Primary Disclosure, *and*

◆ the information on which the disclosure is based came to the person in the course of a business in the regulated sector.

➤ **Offence 2:** A person commits an offence if (*s 333A(3)*):

◆ that person discloses that an investigation into allegations that an offence under *PCA 2002 ss 327-340* has been committed is being contemplated or is being carried out, *and*

◆ the disclosure is likely to prejudice that investigation, *and*

◆ the information on which the disclosure is based came to the person in the course of a business in the regulated sector.

This section only applies to business in the regulated sector (PCA 2002 Schedule 9). Much of the business of a law firm is in the regulated sector but some is not. Law firms typically treat all business as being in the regulated sector for the purpose of complying with this section – better safe than sorry!

5. Tipping off defences (ss 333B-333E)

➤ **Defences:**

◆ An employee, officer or partner of an undertaking does not commit an offence if the disclosure is to an employee, officer or partner of the same undertaking (s 333B(1)).

◆ A legal adviser does not commit an offence if (s 333B(4)):

  ● the disclosure is to a professional legal adviser, *and*

  ● both the person making the disclosure and the person to whom it is made carry on business in an EEA State or in a country or territory imposing equivalent money laundering requirements, *and*

  ● those persons perform their professional activities within different undertakings that share common ownership, management or control.

◆ A professional legal adviser does not commit an offence when disclosing to another professional legal adviser if (s 333C):

  ● the disclosure relates to:

    ▪ a client or former client of the institution or adviser making the disclosure and the institution or adviser to whom it is made, *or*

    ▪ a transaction involving them both, *or*

    ▪ the provision of a service involving them both, *and*

  ● the disclosure is for the purpose only of preventing an offence under *PCA 2002 ss 327-340*, *and*

  ● the institution or adviser to whom the disclosure is made is situated in an EEA State or in a country or territory imposing equivalent money laundering requirements, *and*

  ● the institution or adviser making the disclosure and the institution or adviser to whom it is made are subject to equivalent duties of professional confidentiality and the protection of personal data.

◆ A person does not commit an offence if the disclosure is (s 333D(1)):

  ● to the Law Society (*MLR 2007 Schedule 3*), *or*

  ● for the purpose of the detection, investigation or prosecution of a criminal offence (whether in the UK or elsewhere), *or*

  ● for the purpose of an investigation under *PCA 2002*, *or*

  ● for the purpose of the enforcement of any order of a court under *PCA 2002*.

◆ A professional legal adviser does not commit an offence if the disclosure is (s 333D(2)):

  ● to the adviser's client, *and*

  ● is made for the purpose of dissuading the client from engaging in conduct amounting to an offence.

◆ A person does not commit an offence under *s 333A(1)-(2)*, if the person does not know or suspect that the disclosure is likely to prejudice any investigation that might be conducted following that Primary Disclosure (s 333D(3)).

◆ A person does not commit an offence under *s 333A(3)* if the person does not know or suspect that the disclosure is likely prejudice that investigation (s 333D(4)).

Money Laundering Regulations 2007

➤ To prevent activities related to money laundering and terrorist financing, a solicitor must have policies and procedures in place relating to (*MLR 2007 r 20(1)*):

a) customer due diligence and ongoing monitoring, *and*

- Certain simplified customer due diligence measures apply for certain products, customers and transactions (eg: dealing with companies on a regulated market, dealing with UK public authorities, dealing with credit or financial institutions who are subject to the money laundering directive) (*MLR 2007 r 13*).

b) reporting, *and*

c) record-keeping, *and*

d) internal control, *and*

e) risk assessment and management, *and*

f) monitoring and management of compliance with, and internal communication of, such policies and procedures.

◆ These include policies and procedures (*MLR 2007 r 20(2)*):

- which provide for the identification and scrutiny of:

  ▪ complex or unusually large transactions, *and*

  ▪ unusual patterns of transactions which have no apparent economic or visible lawful purpose, *and*

  ▪ any other activity which the relevant person regards as particularly likely by its nature to be related to money laundering or terrorist financing,

- which specify the taking of additional measures, where appropriate, to prevent the use for money laundering or terrorist financing of products and transactions which might favour anonymity,

- to determine whether a customer is a **Politically Exposed Person**,

  ▪ This is an individual who is or has, at any time in the preceding year, been entrusted with a prominent public function by a state other than the UK, an EU institution or an international body - or certain family members or close associates of that individual.

- under which a Money Laundering Officer is appointed and procedures exist for reporting of knowledge or suspicions appropriately up the relevant chain.

➤ A solicitor must take appropriate measures so that all relevant employees are (*r 21*):

◆ made aware of the law relating to money laundering and terrorist financing, *and*

◆ regularly given training in how to recognise and deal with transactions and other activities which may be related to money laundering or terrorist financing.

Failure to comply with the rules (*MLR 2007 r 45*)

➤ A person who breaches the rules may be liable to:

◆ on summary conviction, a fine, *or*

◆ on indictment, imprisonment for up to 2 years and/or a fine.

Money Laundering Regulations 2007

What is customer due diligence? (*MLR 2007 rr 5-6*)

➤ 'Customer due diligence' means:

   ◆ identifying the client and verifying the client's identity on the basis of documents, data or information obtained from a reliable and independent source ('Requirement 1'), *and*

   ◆ if there is a beneficial owner who is not the client, identifying that beneficial owner and taking adequate measures, on a risk-sensitive basis, to verify his identity so that the solicitor is satisfied that he knows who the beneficial owner is ('Requirement 2'), *and*

      ● For a non-human, this includes understanding the ownership and control structure.

      ● For a company or partnership, 'beneficial owner' means whoever controls more than 25% of the shares/votes or whoever otherwise exercises control over management.

   ◆ obtaining information on the purpose and intended nature of the business relationship ('Requirement 3').

Extent of customer due diligence (*MLR 2007 r 7(3)*)

➤ A solicitor must determine the extent of customer due diligence measures on a risk-sensitive basis depending on the type of customer, business relationship, product or transaction.

➤ A solicitor must be able to demonstrate that the extent of the measures is appropriate in view of the risks of money laundering and terrorist financing.

Customer due diligence measures (*MLR 2007 rr 7, 8, 9*)

➤ A solicitor must apply customer due diligence measures when he (*r 7(1)*):

a) establishes a business relationship, *or*

   ● Requirement 1 and Requirement 2 of customer due diligence must be done before the relationship is established (*r 9(2)*).

      ▪ However, the verification may be completed during the establishment of the business relationship if this is necessary not to interrupt the normal conduct of business and there is little risk of money laundering or terrorist financing occurring. This is only allowed though if the verification is completed as soon as practicable after contact is first established (*r 9(3)*).

b) carries out an occasional transaction, *or*

c) suspects money laundering or terrorist financing, *or*

d) doubts the veracity or adequacy of documents, data or information previously obtained for the purposes of identification or verification.

➤ **Existing customers:** A solicitor must apply customer due diligence measures at other appropriate times to existing customers on a risk-sensitive basis (*r 7(2)*).

➤ **Ongoing monitoring** of a business relationship must be conducted (*r 8*). This means:

   ◆ scrutiny of transactions undertaken throughout the course of the relationship (including, where necessary, the source of funds) to ensure that the transactions are consistent with the relevant person's knowledge of the customer, his business and risk profile, *and*

   ◆ keeping the documents, data or information obtained for the purpose of applying customer due diligence measures up-to-date.

Money Laundering Regulations 2007

Enhanced customer due diligence and ongoing monitoring (*MLR 2007 r 14*)

➤ A solicitor must apply on a risk-sensitive basis enhanced customer due diligence measures and enhanced ongoing monitoring ...

- ... where the client has not been physically present for identification purposes, the solicitor must take specific and adequate measures to compensate for the higher risk, eg:

  - ensuring that the client's identity is established by additional documents, data or information, *and/or*

  - using supplementary measures to verify or certify the documents supplied, or requiring confirmatory certification by a credit or financial institution which is subject to the money laundering directive, *and/or*

  - ensuring that the first payment is carried out through an account opened in the client's name with a credit institution.

- ... where a solicitor who proposes to have a business relationship or carry out an occasional transaction with a **Politically Exposed Person** in which case the solicitor must:

  - have approval from senior management to establish the business relationship, *and*

  - take adequate measures to establish the source of wealth and source of funds which are involved in the proposed business relationship or occasional transaction, *and*

  - where the business relationship is entered into, conduct enhanced ongoing monitoring of the relationship.

- ... in any other situation which by its nature can present a higher risk of money laundering or terrorist financing.

Failure to apply customer due diligence measures (*MLR 2007 r 11*)

➤ Where a solicitor is unable to apply customer due diligence measures, the solicitor must:

- not carry out a transaction with or for the client through a bank account, *and*

- not establish a business relationship or carry out an occasional transaction, *and*

- terminate any existing business relationship with the client, *and*

- consider whether he is required to make a disclosure under *PCA 2002*.

➤ Exception: This does not apply where a solicitor is in the course of ascertaining the legal position for the client (or defending or representing that client in, or concerning, legal proceedings).

Record keeping (*MLR 2007 r 19*)

➤ A solicitor must keep the following records:

- a copy of (or references to) the evidence of the client's identity, *and*

  - These must be kept for a minimum of 5 years beginning on the date when the occasional transaction completes or the business relationship ends.

- supporting records (ie: original documents or copies) for a business relationship or occasional transaction which is the subject of customer due diligence or ongoing monitoring.

  - These must be kept for a minimum of 5 years beginning with: i) the date on which the transaction is completed (where the records relate to a particular transaction), *or* ii) the date on which the business relationship ends (for all other records).

D Help in funding a case

I LSC funding generally
II Civil: CLS help (general treatment)
III Criminal: CDS help (general treatment)
IV 'contingency' v 'conditional' fees
V Conditional fee agreements
VI After The Event (ATE) insurance

I LSC funding generally

➤ The Legal Services Commission (LSC) provides legal funding help.

♦ The LSC pays set rates to solicitors who do legal work for people who need government help to fund legal cases/advice.

➤ The LSC is responsible for running 2 schemes (*AJA 1999*):

♦ for civil matters: **the Community Legal Service (CLS)**, *and*

♦ for criminal matters: **the Criminal Defence Service (CDS)**.

> ### *Legal Aid, Sentencing And Punishment Of Offenders Bill: published on 21 June 2011*
>
> ➤ *Part 1 of LASPOB 2011 (currently before Parliament) provides for the abolition of the LSC and the transfer of the day-to-day administration of legal aid to the Lord Chancellor.*
>
> ♦ *In practice, this administration will be done by civil servants in an executive agency of the Ministry of Justice. However, decisions on legal aid in individual cases will be taken by a statutory office holder: a civil servant designated by the Lord Chancellor as the Director of Legal Aid Casework. The Lord Chancellor will have no power to direct or issue guidance to the Director in relation to individual cases.*
>
> ♦ *The Lord Chancellor will have power to set quality standards for those providing legal aid services and to make arrangements for accreditation and monitoring of such providers.*
>
> ➤ *LASPOB is the framework to implement the government's wish to cut massively the legal aid budget and to restrict the scope of legal aid generally.*
>
> ➤ *LASPOB will do away with - and completely replace - the AJA 1999 framework for legal aid.*

II Civil: CLS help (general treatment)

➤ Solicitors can provide advice or representation funded by the LSC (via the CLS) only if they have a special contract with the LSC.

♦ For family cases and specialist areas like immigration and clinical negligence, only specialist firms are funded to do the work.

♦ Claims for personal injury (except clinical negligence) are not funded by the LSC. Such cases can instead be pursued under conditional fee agreements between solicitors and clients (see pp 31 et seq).

♦ Firms are audited against their LSC contract to check they continue to meet quality standards.

➤ The CLS cannot be used to fund services (beyond the provision of general information about the law and the legal system and the availability of legal services) in relation to (*AJA 1999 Sch 2, CJA 2009 s 150*):

   ◆ allegations of personal injury or death, other than allegations relating to clinical negligence, *or*

   ◆ allegations of negligently caused damage to property, *or*

   ◆ conveyancing, *or*

   ◆ boundary disputes, *or*

   ◆ the making of wills, *or*

   ◆ matters of trust law, *or*

   ◆ defamation or malicious falsehood, *or*

   ◆ matters of company or partnership law, *or*

   ◆ certain areas under *MCA 2005*, *or*

   ◆ services consisting of the provision of help to an individual in relation to matters arising out of or in connection with:

      ● a proposal by that individual to establish a business, *or*

      ● the carrying on of a business by that individual (whether or not the business is being carried on at the time the services are provided), *or*

      ● the termination or transfer of a business that was being carried on by that individual.

➤ The primary practical document to consult on the funding rules is the Funding Code.

   ◆ This can be found at: http://www.legalservices.gov.uk/civil/guidance/funding_code.asp#.

➤ The LSC funds a range of legal services. There are 5 main forms of civil legal aid:

Types of civil legal aid (*CLS(F)R 2000*)	
Covered in this book	**Not covered in this book**
1 **Legal Help**	4 **Family Help**
2 **Help At Court**	◆ **Purpose:** a level of service, the grant of which authorises help in relation to a family dispute (including assistance in resolving that dispute through negotiation or otherwise). Does not include provision of mediation services but does cover help and advice in support of Family Mediation. Does include all services within the scope of either Legal Help or Legal Representation other than preparation for or representation at a contested final hearing or appeal.
3 **Legal Representation:**	
Type 1:	
◆ Investigative Help	
Type 2:	
◆ Full Representation	
	5 **Family Mediation**
	◆ **Purpose:** covers mediation for a family dispute.

> **Note**
> Special criteria apply to:
> very expensive cases, judicial review, claims against public authorities, clinical negligence, housing, mental health, immigration and quasi-criminal proceedings
> (none of these are dealt with in this book)

1   **Legal Help**

➤ **Purpose:** advice/assistance with any legal problem. It covers general advice, writing letters, negotiating, getting a barrister's opinion, preparing a written case if going before a court or tribunal.

➤ **Criteria:**

◆ **Sufficient Benefit Test** (*Funding Code r 5.2.1*): Help may only be provided where there is sufficient benefit to the client, having regard to the circumstances of the matter, including the personal circumstances of the client, to justify work or further work being carried out.

◆ **Funding as part of CLS** (*Funding Code r 5.2.2*): Help may only be provided if it is reasonable for the matter to be funded out of the Community Legal Service Fund, having regard to any other potential sources of funding.

➤ **Financial restrictions:**

◆ Capital and income must be within certain prescribed financial limits.

◆ No contribution is payable by the applicant.

◆ Initially, the level of work which can be undertaken is set by reference to a standard rate. Authority for any further work must be sought from the LSC regional office.

◆ The statutory charge will apply to any money or property recovered or preserved for cases going beyond Legal Help.

2   **Help At Court**

➤ **Purpose:** allows for a solicitor or adviser to speak at court hearings, without acting for the client in the whole proceedings.

➤ **Criteria:**

◆ **Sufficient Benefit Test** (*Funding Code r 5.2.1, r 5.3.1*): Help may only be provided where there is sufficient benefit to the client, having regard to the circumstances of the matter, including the personal circumstances of the client, to justify work or further work being carried out.

◆ **Funding as part of CLS** (*Funding Code r 5.2.2, r 5.3.1*): Help may only be provided if it is reasonable for the matter to be funded out of the Community Legal Service Fund, having regard to any other potential sources of funding.

◆ **The Need for Representation** (*Funding Code r 5.3.2*): Help at Court may only be provided if the nature of the proceedings and the circumstances of the hearing and the client are such that advocacy is appropriate and will be of real benefit to the client.

◆ **Legal Representation** (*Funding Code r 5.3.3*): Help at Court may not be provided if the contested nature of the proceedings or the nature of the hearing is such that, if any help is to be provided, it is more appropriate that it should be given through Legal Representation.

➤ **Financial restrictions:**

◆ Capital and income must be within certain prescribed financial limits.

◆ No contribution is payable by the applicant.

◆ Initially, the level of work which can be undertaken is set by reference to a standard rate. Authority for any further work must be sought from the LSC regional office.

◆ The statutory charge will apply to any money or property recovered or preserved for cases going beyond Help At Court.

3   **Legal Representation (2 types):**

Type 1:   Investigative Help

➤ **Purpose:** investigation of the strength of a proposed claim where the prospects of success are not clear and the investigation is likely to be expensive. It covers the issue and conduct of proceedings only so far as these are necessary to obtain disclosure of relevant information or to protect a position in relation to an urgent hearing or a time limit for the issue of proceedings.

➤ **Criteria:**

♦ **Potential for a Conditional Fee Agreement** (*Funding Code r 5.6.1*): Investigative Help may be refused if the nature of the case and circumstances of the client are such that investigative work should be carried out privately with a view to a conditional fee agreement.

♦ **The Need for Investigation** (*Funding Code r 5.6.2*): Investigative Help may only be granted where the prospects of success of the claim are uncertain and substantial investigative work is required before those prospects can be determined. Guidance may indicate what constitutes substantial investigative work for this purpose.

♦ **Damages** (*Funding Code r 5.6.3*): If the client's claim is primarily for damages and has no significant wider public interest, Investigative Help will be refused unless damages are likely to exceed £5,000.

♦ **Prospects after Investigation** (*Funding Code r 5.6.4*): Investigative Help may only be granted if there are reasonable grounds for believing that when the investigative work has been carried out the claim will be strong enough, in terms of prospects of success and cost benefit, to satisfy the relevant criteria for Full Representation.

Type 2:   Full Representation

➤ **Purpose:** for representation in legal proceedings to trial and beyond.

➤ **Criteria:**

♦ Conditional Fee Agreements (*Funding Code r 5.7.1*): If the nature of the case is suitable for a CFA, and the client is likely to be able to avail himself of a CFA, Full Representation will be refused.

♦ Prospects of Success (*Funding Code r 5.7.2*): Full Representation will be refused if:

● Prospects of success are unclear, *or*

● Prospects of success are borderline and the case does not appear to have a significant wider public interest or to be of overwhelming importance to the client, *or*

● Prospects of success are poor.

♦ Cost Benefit (Quantifiable Claims) (*Funding Code r 5.7.3*): If the claim is primarily a claim for damages by the client and does not have a significant wider public interest, Full Representation will be refused unless the following cost benefit criteria are satisfied:

● If success prospects are very good (80% or more), likely damages must exceed likely costs.

● If success prospects are good (60%-80%), likely damages must exceed likely costs by 2:1.

● If success prospects are moderate (50%-60%), likely damages must exceed likely costs by 4:1.

♦ Cost Benefit (Unquantifiable Claims) (*Funding Code r 5.7.4*): If the claim is not primarily a claim for damages (including any application by a defendant or a case which has overwhelming importance to the client), but does not have a significant wider public interest, Full Representation will be refused unless the likely benefits to be gained from the proceedings justify the likely costs, such that a reasonable private paying client would be prepared to litigate, having regard to the prospects of success and all other circumstances.

♦ Cost Benefit (Public Interest Cases) (*Funding Code r 5.7.5*): If the claim has a significant wider public interest, Full Representation may be refused unless the likely benefits of the proceedings justify the likely costs, having regard to the prospects of success and all other circumstances.

EMERGENCIES (*Funding Code r 5.5*):: It is also possible for either type of Legal Representation to be granted on an emergency basis where the matter is urgent and meets the criteria.

For Type 1 or Type 2:

➤ **Criteria:**

◆ **Alternative Funding** (*Funding Code r 5.4.2*): An application may be refused if alternative funding is available to the client (through insurance or otherwise) or if there are other persons or bodies, including those who might benefit from the proceedings, who can reasonably be expected to bring or fund the case.

• For the purpose of this criterion only, alternative funding does not include funding by means of a conditional fee agreement.

◆ **Alternatives to Litigation** (*Funding Code r 5.4.3*): An application may be refused if there are complaint systems, ombudsman schemes or forms of alternative dispute resolution which should be tried before litigation is pursued.

◆ **Other Levels of Service** (*Funding Code r 5.4.4*): An application may be refused if it appears premature or if it appears more appropriate for the client to be assisted by some other level of service under the Funding Code, such as Legal Help or Help at Court.

◆ **The Need for Representation** (*Funding Code r 5.4.5*): An application may be refused if it appears unreasonable to fund representation, for example in the light of the nature and complexity of the issues, the existence of other proceedings or the interests of other parties in the proceedings to which the application relates.

◆ **Small Claims** (*Funding Code r 5.4.6*): An application will be refused if the case has been or is likely to be allocated to the small claims track.

➤ **Procedure:** an organisation with an LSC contract applies on behalf of the applicant to the LSC regional office, which decides (usually within 2 weeks) whether it meets the funding criteria. The regional office can either grant or refuse the application.

◆ If the application is refused, there is a right of review by an LSC director and ultimately by an LSC adjudicator (*Funding Code, Part 2, C19, C22*).

◆ If the application is granted and no contribution is payable, the LSC regional office sends a certificate detailing the scope of the funding (*Funding Code, Part 2, C14*).

◆ If the application is granted and a contribution is payable, the LSC regional office sends an offer to the applicant (detailing the scope of the contribution), which, if accepted by the applicant, results in a certificate being sent to the applicant detailing the scope of the funding (*Funding Code, Part 2, C15*).

➤ **The certificate:**

◆ Copies are sent to the applicant and the solicitor and notice of issue is served on any other parties (*Funding Code, Part 2, C16*).
NB: No notice of any limitation or restrictions on the legal aid must be given to other parties.

◆ If the certificate needs to be amended, an amended certificate is issued and notice must be served on all parties to the dispute.

➤ **Financial restrictions:**

◆ The calculation is based on the applicant's disposable capital and disposable income (together with that of a spouse/civil partner/unmarried partner, provided that there is no conflict of interest between them).

◆ Capital and income must be within certain prescribed financial limits.

• Reassessments of income/capital may happen any time while the certificate is in force (*Funding Code, Part 2, C51*).

◆ A contribution may be payable by the applicant.

◆ The statutory charge will apply to any money or property recovered or preserved.

III Criminal: CDS help (general treatment)

➤ Solicitors can carry out criminal defence work funded by the LSC (via the CDS) only if they have a special contract with the LSC.

◆ Firms are audited against that contract to ensure they continue to meet quality assurance standards.

➤ The LSC also directly employs some criminal defence lawyers (known as public defenders) who can provide any CDS criminal services. Public Defenders are subject to a strict code of conduct.

➤ There are 2 main forms of CDS-provided help:

1 **Advice and Assistance (this covers advice and assistance on criminal matters)**

2 **Full representation for criminal offences (under a 'representation' order)**

1 Advice and Assistance

Scope (CDS(G2)R 2001 reg 4)
➤ **Scope:** The LSC funds such advice and assistance as it considers appropriate for any individual who: ◆ is the subject of an investigation which may lead to criminal proceedings, *or* ◆ is the subject of criminal proceedings, *or* ◆ requires advice and assistance regarding an appeal or potential appeal against the outcome of any criminal proceedings or an application to vary a sentence, *or* ◆ requires advice and assistance regarding a sentence, *or* ◆ requires advice and assistance regarding an application or potential application to the Criminal Cases Review Commission, *or* ◆ requires advice and assistance regarding his treatment or discipline in prison (other than in respect of actual or contemplated proceedings regarding personal injury, death or damage to property), *or* ◆ is the subject of proceedings before the Parole Board, *or* ◆ requires advice and assistance regarding representations to the Home Office in relation to a mandatory life sentence or other parole review, *or* ◆ is a witness in criminal proceedings and requires advice regarding self-incrimination, *or* ◆ is a volunteer, *or* ◆ is detained under *Terrorism Act 2000 Sch 7.*

➤ **Purpose:** It enables people of moderate means to get a solicitor's help including giving general advice, writing letters, negotiating, getting a barrister's opinion and preparing a written case. It does not cover court representation. (It is not available during criminal proceedings after charge or summons.)

➤ **Procedure:** The solicitor decides, based on the tests below, if LSC funded help can be given. He can refuse advice without a reason but may have to explain reasons for refusal to the LSC regional office.

➤ **Age:** Children are eligible for Advice and Assistance, but usually where a child is under 17, a parent/guardian should apply on his behalf. Sometimes a solicitor can advise a child directly.

➤ **Means test:** Unless the advice and assistance falls into one of the main 3 subcategories (dealt with below), an applicant's disposable capital and disposable income must be below set financial limits (*CDS(G2)R 2001 reg 5* and *Schedule 1*).

◆ If the applicant is in receipt of certain state benefits, his disposable income is ignored.

◆ If the applicant has a spouse/civil partner then joint capital and income are considered unless the parties live apart or there is a conflict of interest between them.

➤ **Merit test:** whether it is reasonable that approval should be granted in the particular circumstances of the case or the case involves one of the *AJA 1999 Sch 3* criteria (listed on p 30).

Subcategory 1: Advocacy Assistance before a Magistrates' Court or the Crown Court

➤ **Purpose:** This covers the cost of a solicitor preparing a case and *initial* representation in certain proceedings in both the Magistrates' Court and the Crown Court.

◆ It also covers representation for prisoners facing disciplinary charges before the prison governor/controller, and for discretionary and automatic lifers and those detained at Her Majesty's Pleasure whose cases are referred to the Parole Board. It also covers representation for those who have failed to pay a civil fine or obey a civil court order of the Magistrates' Court and are at risk of imprisonment and applications for ASBOs and some closure orders.

➤ **Procedure:** The solicitor decides whether this will be available based on the restrictions below (it is a devolved power from the LSC). The LSC pays the solicitor's bill if the merits restrictions test is met.

➤ **Means test:** There is no financial test (unless the advice and assistance is to be provided in the prison law class of work) (*CDS(G2)R 2001 reg 5(1)(b)*).

➤ **Merit test:** Advocacy assistance may not be granted if it appears unreasonable that approval should be granted in the particular circumstances of the case or if the case does not involve one of the *AJA 1999 Sch 3* criteria (listed on p 30).

Subcategory 2: Advice & assistance if arrested and held in custody at a police station/other premises

➤ **Purpose:** If the police question an alleged offender about an offence (whether or not he has been arrested and whether at a police station or elsewhere) there is a right to free legal advice from a contracted solicitor. The police must contact a duty solicitor or the alleged offender's own solicitor or a solicitor on a police-kept list of local solicitors.

➤ **Tests:** None (*CDS(G2)R 2001 reg 5(1)(a)*).

Subcategory 3: The court duty solicitor scheme

➤ **Purpose:** If an alleged offender has to go to a Magistrates' Court and does not have his own solicitor there will usually be a duty solicitor available either at the court or on call to give free advice and representation on his first appearance.

➤ **Tests:** None (*CDS(G2)R 2001 reg 5(1)(c)*).

2 Representation for criminal offences

➤ **Purpose:** Anyone charged with a criminal offence can apply. It covers the cost of a solicitor preparing a defence before going to court and representation there. It may also be available to apply for bail.

◆ A representation order granted while proceedings are in a Magistrates' Court includes representation in the Crown Court, if the proceedings continue there (except where they do so by way of appeal) (*CDS(ROCA)R 2006 reg 4, CDS(RO(A))R 2009*).

◆ A representation order must be granted to an individual for proceedings in the Crown Court if proceedings continue to the Crown Court where he has applied for a representation order for proceedings in a Magistrates' Court (and in the Crown Court, should they continue there) and either the individual is not financially eligible for such an order for the proceedings in the Magistrates' Court or the representation authority considers that the interests of justice do not require the individual to be represented in such proceedings (*CDS(ROCA)R 2006 reg 4A, CDS(RO(A))R 2009*).

➤ **Procedure:** An application for a representation order for proceedings in a Magistrates' Court or the Crown Court must be made in writing to the representation authority at the relevant Magistrates' Court (usually where the case will be heard). Court staff, acting on behalf of the LSC, decide whether to grant representation if the applicant passes both a means test and a merits test (*CDS(G2)R 2001 reg 9(1)*).

◆ If an application is refused for representation for proceedings in a Magistrates' Court, the appropriate officer must write giving reasons for refusal and details of the appeal process (*CDS(G2)R 2001 reg 9(2)*).

➤ **Age:** Where the person who requires representation is less than 18, the application for the grant of a representation order may be made by his parent or guardian on his behalf (*CDS(G2)R 2001 reg 6(5)*).

Representation: MEANS TEST

The test looks at the applicant's gross annual income and gross disposable income
(adjusted to take children into account) and the test applies to (*CDS(FE)R 2006 reg 9*):
- ◆ most criminal proceedings in a Magistrates' Court, *and*
- ◆ criminal proceedings where the individual has been committed to the Crown Court for sentence and did not apply for, or was not granted, a representation order in a Magistrates' Court.

➤ **Automatically eligible** (*CDS(FE)R 2006 reg 5*): i) individuals receiving certain benefits (eg: income support), *or* ii) those under 18.

➤ **Calculation:** If the individual has a spouse/civil partner, the other person's resources are treated as those of the individual, unless the other person has a contrary interest in the proceedings (*CDS(FE)R 2006 reg 7*).

➤ **Evidence:** The applicant may have to provide evidence to support the application. If he fails to do so, any representation order is normally withdrawn (*CDS(FE)R 2006 regs 6 and 15*).

➤ Applicants with <u>income below</u> the lower threshold automatically qualify (*CDS(FE)R 2006 reg 9*).

➤ Applicants with <u>income above</u> the upper threshold are ineligible and are expected to meet the full costs of representation before the Magistrates' Court (*CDS(FE)R 2006 reg 9*).

➤ Applicants with <u>income between the higher/lower amounts</u> have a more detailed assessment. The applicant's gross annual income is calculated (making deductions for income tax, national insurance, council tax, housing expenses, child-care costs, maintenance and living expenses). An applicant is eligible if the annual disposable income remaining does not exceed a fixed sum (*CDS(FE)R 2006 reg 10*).

➤ **Failure:** Those who fail the means test may be able to take advantage of special hardship criteria.

➤ **No appeal:** There is no right of appeal to court in relation to the application of the means test (unless there is a change in his financial circumstances which might affect his eligibility for a representation order). Any complaints about miscalculation are dealt with administratively by the representation authority or the LSC (although judicial review is still an option) (*CDS(ROA)R 2006) reg 5, CDS(FE)R 2006 regs 11, 13 and 14*).

➤ **Contributions:** Contribution orders may be made for the cost of publicly funded representation in criminal trials in, and appeals to, the Crown Court (*CDS(CO)R 2009*). Defendants who are applying for publicly funded representation must provide details of their income and capital (except for certain special defendants).

- ◆ If acquitted, no contribution towards defence costs is payable and the defendant must be repaid amounts he has already paid under a contribution order.

- ◆ If convicted, the costs of the defendant's representation are determined after he has been convicted and liability under a contribution order is calculated based on the defendant's capital.

- ◆ Also, if convicted, in a Magistrates' Court usually no contribution towards defence costs is payable but in other courts, the judge must usually make a 'Recovery of Defence Costs Order' (RDCO) for the accused to pay some/all of the representation cost (but not if the accused is in receipt of certain benefits or has low assets or it would not otherwise be reasonable and not if it would mean double-paying for anything already paid under a contribution order) (*CDS(G2)R 2001, CDS(RDCO)R 2001*).

Representation: MERIT TEST

The test is known as the 'interests of justice' test

➤ Representation will be granted/provisionally granted **if it is in the 'interests of justice'** that the applicant should be represented at the LSC's expense. The decision is based on information given in the application form. Some circumstances appropriate to give LSC funding are when (*AJA 1999 Sch 3*):

- ◆ there is a likelihood of a custodial sentence, loss of livelihood, or serious damage to reputation, *or*
- ◆ there is a substantial question of law involved (eg: evidential difficulties), *or*
- ◆ a disability/linguistic barrier prevents the defendant from understanding the proceedings, *or*
- ◆ tracing or interviewing or expert cross-examination of witnesses is necessary, *or*
- ◆ the case involves expert cross-examination of a prosecution witness, *or*
- ◆ it is in the interests of someone other than the accused that the accused is represented.

AJA 1999 Sch 3 criteria

➤ *Appeal:* In the case of proceedings in Magistrates' Courts, the individual may make a renewed application to the authority responsible for granting representation orders in Magistrates' Courts, after which the individual may appeal to the court (*CDS(ROA)R 2006 reg 4, CDS(ROA)AR 2010*). In the case of proceedings in the Crown Court, an individual may make a renewed application to the person who refused the application (and that person may refer it to a Crown Court judge) (*CDS(ROA)R 2006 reg 6*). Where a representation order is withdrawn, the individual may apply for the withdrawal to be set aside (*CDS(ROA)R 2006 reg 9*).

➤ **Deemed interests of justice:** It is deemed to be in the interests of justice for an individual who is the subject of a trial on indictment in, or committal for sentence to, the Crown Court to be granted a publicly funded right to representation (*CDS(IJ)R 2009*).

IV   'contingency' v 'conditional' fees

Contingency fee agreements

➤   'Contingency fee' agreements include but are wider than 'conditional fee' agreements.

➤   The term 'contingency fee' covers **all** agreements where the fee is payable only in the event of success.

◆   The fee may be fixed, or calculated as a percentage of the proceeds recovered, or otherwise.

● Historically, 'contingency fee' agreements have been where a fee is calculated as a percentage of the proceeds recovered. Such an agreement is only permissible in non-contentious matters and if a conditional fee agreement is entered into (as specified below).

Conditional fee agreements

➤   A conditional fee agreement is a special type of agreement created by statute where certain fees are payable only in specified circumstances.

◆   The fee charged depends whether the case is won or lost (ie: 'no win, no fee' agreements).

● The fee may consist of (*CFAO 2000*): i) basic or reduced costs, *or* ii) basic costs plus a 'success fee' of anything up to 100% of the basic costs.

V   Conditional fee agreements

Conditional fee agreements (*CLSA 1990 s 58, CFAO 2000*)

➤   *CLSA 1990 s 58* allows the use of conditional fee agreements in such types of case as is specified by order (and subject to any requirements made in regulations).

◆   *CLSA 1990 s 58A(1)* excludes from conditional fees most criminal and family proceedings.

➤   The maximum uplift that can be charged if a lawyer is successful is 100% of the normal fees.

◆   In *Morris v John Dennis (Barnsley) Ltd* [2008] EWHC 90112 (Costs) an administration charge (of £150) was permitted in addition to a 100% success fee.

➤   The arrangements must be in writing (*CLSA 1990 s 58(3)(a)*).

➤   Insurance policies are available to cover the costs of the other party and the client's own costs (including, if not a conditional fee case, the client's solicitor's fees) if the case is lost. The *AJA 1999* makes a success fee under a conditional fee agreement recoverable and also makes any premium paid for protective insurance recoverable too (*AJA 1999 s 29*).

➤   *Callery v Gray* [2002] UKHL 28 and *Halloran v Delaney* [2002] EWCA Civ 1258 give key principles.

◆   A claimant may enter a conditional fee agreement (CFA) and take out after-the-event (ATE) insurance on first consulting a solicitor, *before* the writing of a letter of claim and response.

◆   Reasonable ATE premiums are in principle recoverable as part of a claimant's costs, even though a claim may be resolved without proceedings.

➤   CFAs may also apply in a case resolved by arbitration, provided all the requirements specified by regulations as to the form and content of the agreement are complied with (*Bevan Ashford v Geoff Yeandle (Contractors) Ltd* [1999] Ch 239).

Abrogation of the 'indemnity principle'

➤ Although the client is liable to pay his solicitor's fees and expenses, a CFA is enforceable only if and to the extent that the client recovers damages or costs from the other party to the proceedings.

➤ For these special type CFAs, the old 'indemnity principle' is abolished, ie: the principle that the amount which can be awarded to a party in respect of costs to be paid by him to his solicitor is limited to what would have been payable by him to his solicitor if he had not been awarded costs.

➤ A solicitor can now lawfully agree with a client not to seek to recover by way of costs anything in excess of what the court awards, or what it is agreed will be paid.

A note on a CFA in road traffic cases

➤ For simple road traffic personal injury cases where a CFA is agreed at the outset, 12.5% is the *maximum* uplift that is allowed if the claim concludes before a trial has commenced, or the dispute is settled before a claim is issued (and 100% if the claim concludes at trial) (*CPR 45.16*).

Results of a challenge to a CFA by the paying party

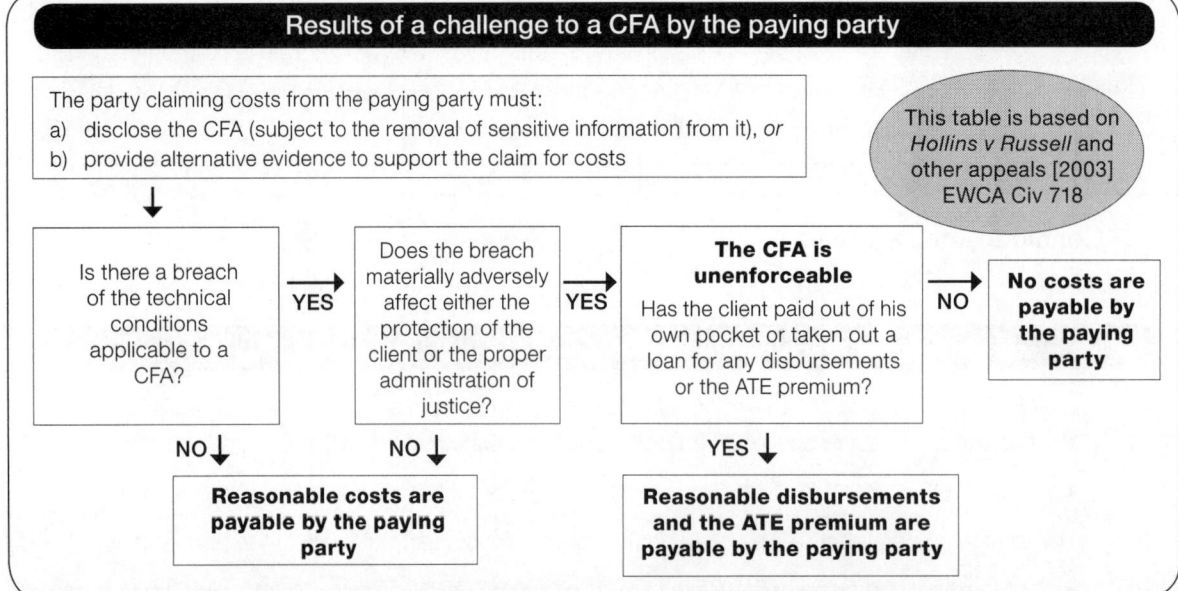

The party claiming costs from the paying party must:
a) disclose the CFA (subject to the removal of sensitive information from it), *or*
b) provide alternative evidence to support the claim for costs

This table is based on *Hollins v Russell* and other appeals [2003] EWCA Civ 718

Legal Aid, Sentencing And Punishment Of Offenders Bill: published on 21 June 2011

➤ *Under LASPOB 2011 (currently going through Parliament) it is proposed that:*

♦ *personal injury success fees will be capped at 25%, raising general damages by 10%, and*

♦ *lawyers will no longer be able to recover success fees from losing defendants.*

VI   After The Event (ATE) insurance

➤ After the Event Insurance (ATE Insurance) can be taken out once legal proceedings are contemplated.

➤ ATE Insurance indemnifies the insured's own disbursements and the opponent's costs and disbursements if the legal action is ultimately discontinued or lost at trial.

➤ The ATE market came into being in April 2000 under the *AJA 1999*, which provided that the successful party to litigation could recover the cost of his ATE policy from the opponent.

E   Bills

I   Contentious work: what can be billed?
II   Non-contentious work: what can be billed?
III   The client fails to pay: what next?

I   Contentious work: what can be billed?

➤   See 'Costs' p 461 et seq.

II   Non-contentious work: what can be billed?

Non-contentious business: what can be billed?

➤   A solicitor's costs must be fair and reasonable having regard to all the circumstances of the case and in particular to (*S(NCB)RO 2009 r 3*):

   ◆   the complexity of the matter or the difficulty or novelty of the questions raised, *and*

   ◆   the skill, labour, specialised knowledge and responsibility involved, *and*

   ◆   the time spent on the business, *and*

   ◆   the number and importance of the documents prepared or considered, ignoring length, *and*

   ◆   the place where, and circumstances in which, the business or any part of it is transacted, *and*

   ◆   the amount or value of any money or property involved, *and*

   ◆   whether any land involved is registered land, *and*

   ◆   the importance of the matter to the client, *and*

   ◆   the approval (express or implied) of the client to:

      ●   the solicitor undertaking all or any part of the work giving rise to the costs, *or*

      ●   the amount of the costs.

Mandatory rules about bills

➤   A bill must state separately:

   ◆   if VAT is included (and if the bill does not mention VAT, then VAT is taken to be included), *and*

   ◆   bill disbursements (eg: experts' fees) (*SA 1974 s 67*).

Security for costs

➤   A solicitor may take from his client security for the payment of any costs, including the amount of any interest to which the solicitor may become entitled (*S(NCB)RO 2009 r 4*).

> ## Interest

> ➤ A solicitor may charge interest on the unpaid amount of costs plus any paid disbursements and VAT (*S(NCB)RO 2009 r 5*).

>> ◆ Where an entitlement to interest arises (above) the period for which interest may be charged runs from 1 month after the date of delivery of a bill.

>>> • The solicitor and client can agree differently as between themselves.

>> ◆ The rate of interest must not exceed the rate payable on judgment debts (see p 470).

>>> • The solicitor and client can agree differently as between themselves.

>>> • Interest must be calculated, where applicable, by reference to :

>>>> ▪ the amount specified in a determination of costs by the Law Society under *SA 1974 Sch 1A*, *and/or*

>>>> ▪ the amount ascertained on assessment of the bill (if the client has applied for an assessment).

III   The client fails to pay: what next?

> ➤ Usually, a solicitor can only sue on a bill (or threaten to do so), if:

>> ◆ 1 month has passed since the bill was delivered to the client (unless the court grants leave to sue earlier than this) (*SA 1974 s 69(1)*), *and*

>> ◆ the bill has (*SA 1974 s 69(2A)*):

>>> • been signed by the solicitor (or on his behalf by an employee of the solicitor authorised by the solicitor to sign, *or*

>>>> ▪ Note: the signature may be an electronic signature (*SA 1974 s 69(2B)*).

>>> • the bill has been enclosed in, or accompanied by, a letter which is signed as mentioned in the circle bullet above, *and*

>> ◆ the bill has been delivered to the party to be charged with the bill (*SA 1974 s 69(2C)*):

>>> • personally, *or*

>>> • by being sent to him by post to, or left for him at, his place of business, dwelling-house or last known place of abode, *or*

>>> • by an electronic communications network (where the party being charged with the bill has indicated to the deliverer of the bill willingness to accept delivery of a bill sent in the form and manner used), *or*

>>> • by other means but in a form that nevertheless requires the use of apparatus by the recipient to render it intelligible (where the party being charged with the bill has indicated to the deliverer of the bill willingness to accept delivery of a bill sent in the form and manner used).

F   You and your business

I   Management of your business
II   Publicity
III   Fee sharing and referrals

I   Management of your business

Have you checked the Principles first?

Outcomes which MUST be achieved: Management of your business

➤ You have a clear and effective governance structure and reporting lines (*O(7.1)*).

➤ You have effective systems and controls in place to achieve and comply with all the Principles, rules and outcomes and other requirements of the Handbook, where applicable (*O(7.2)*).

➤ You identify, monitor and manage risks to compliance with all the Principles, rules and outcomes and other requirements of the Handbook, if applicable to you, and take steps to address issues identified (*O(7.3)*).

➤ You maintain systems and controls for monitoring the financial stability of your firm and risks to money and assets entrusted to you by clients and others, and you take steps to address issues identified (*O(7.4)*).

➤ You comply with legislation applicable to your business, including anti-money laundering and data protection legislation (*O(7.5)*).

➤ You train individuals working in the firm to maintain a level of competence appropriate to their work

➤ and level of responsibility (*O(7.6)*).

➤ You comply with the statutory requirements for the direction and supervision of reserved legal activities and immigration work (*O(7.7)*).

➤ You have a system for supervising clients' matters, to include the regular checking of the quality of work by suitably competent and experienced people (*O(7.8)*).

➤ You do not outsource reserved legal activities to a person who is not authorised to conduct such activities (*O(7.9)*).

➤ Subject to Outcome 7.9, where you outsource legal activities or any operational functions that are critical to the delivery of any legal activities, you ensure such outsourcing (*O(7.10)*):

a) does not adversely affect your ability to comply with, or the SRA's ability to monitor your compliance with, your obligations in the Code, *and*
b) is subject to contractual arrangements that enable the SRA or its agent to obtain information from, inspect the records (including electronic records) of, or enter the premises of, the third party, in relation to the outsourced activities or functions, *and*
c) does not alter your obligations towards your clients, *and*
d) does not cause you to breach the conditions with which you must comply in order to be authorised and to remain so.

Indicative Behaviours: Management of your business

➤ Safekeeping of documents and assets entrusted to the firm (*IB(7.1)*).

➤ Controlling budgets, expenditure and cash flow (*IB(7.2)*).

➤ Identifying and monitoring financial, operational and business continuity risks including complaints, credit risks and exposure, claims under legislation relating to matters such as data protection, IT failures and abuses, and damage to offices (*IB(7.3)*).

➤ Making arrangements for the continuation of your firm in the event of absences and emergencies, for example holiday or sick leave, with the minimum interruption to clients' business (*IB(7.4)*).

The *SRA Authorisation Rules*

➤ The *SRA Authorisation Rules* contain requirements that mean that all firms which are authorised by the SRA (but not in-house legal teams) will need to appoint compliance officers for:

◆ legal practice (called a Compliance Officer for Legal Practice or COLP), *and*

◆ for finance and administration (called a Compliance Officer for Finance and Administration or COFA).

COLP

➤ The COLP must:

◆ take all reasonable steps:

• to ensure that the authorised body complies with all terms and conditions of its authorisation (except any obligations imposed under the *SRA Accounts Rules*), *and*

• to ensure that the authorised body complies with relevant statutory obligations, *and*

• to record any failure to comply with authorisation or statutory obligations and make such records available to the SRA, *and*

◆ report any material failure (either taken on its own or as part of a pattern of failures) to the SRA as soon as reasonably practical.

➤ The COLP is responsible for ensuring that the firm has systems and controls in place to enable the firm, its managers and employees and anyone who has any interest in the firm to comply with the SRA codes and regulations and requirements on them.

COFA

➤ The COFA must:

◆ take all reasonable steps to ensure that the authorised body, its employees and managers, comply with any obligations imposed under the *SRA Accounts Rules*.

◆ keep a record of any failure to comply and make this record available to the SRA.

◆ report any material failure (either taken on its own or as part of a pattern of failures) to the SRA as soon as reasonably practical.

➤ The COFA is responsible for ensuring that the firm has systems and controls in place to enable the firm, its managers and employees and anyone who has any interest in the firm to comply with the *SRA Accounts Rules*.

Dates

➤ An existing recognised body i.e. any firm (including a sole practitioner from the later to occur of 31 March 2012 or the date on which a relevant order is made under *LSA 2007 s 69*) which is not planning to convert to be an ABS, must nominate its COLP and COFA for approval by 31 March 2012 and they will be authorised from 31 October 2012.

➤ New recognised bodies must apply from 28 February 2012 under the new *SRA Authorisation Rules* and will need to nominate a COLP and COFA for approval as part of the authorisation process. The COLP and COFA will be authorised as from 31 October 2012.

➤ All LDPs with non-lawyer managers are ABSs and have a grace period but will need to become licensed as such by 31 October 2012 at the latest.

◆ This will be dealt with by the **SRA as a passporting exercise.**

◆ Firms will be able to be passported from 6 October 2011.

• They will need to apply for approval of their designated COLP and **COFA which can be done from 10 August 2011.**

◆ Firms wanting to use the **grace period must designate COLPs and COFAs by 31 March 2012.**

➤ New ABSs will have to nominate a COLP and COFA for approval as part of the authorisation process and they will take up their responsibilities at the point when the firm is authorised.

II Publicity

Have you checked the Principles first?

Outcomes which MUST be achieved: Publicity

➤ Your publicity in relation to your firm or in-house practice or for any other business is accurate and not misleading, and is not likely to diminish the trust the public places in you and in the provision of legal services (O(8.1)).

➤ Your publicity relating to charges is clearly expressed and identifies whether VAT and disbursements are included (O(8.2)).

➤ You do not make unsolicited approaches in person or by telephone to members of the public in order to publicise your firm or in-house practice or another business (O(8.3)).

➤ Clients and the public have appropriate information about you, your firm and how you are regulated (O(8.4)).

➤ Your letterhead, website and e-mails show the words "authorised and regulated by the Solicitors Regulation Authority" and either the firm's registered name and number if it is an LLP or company or, if the firm is a partnership or sole practitioner, the name under which it is licensed/authorised by the SRA and the number allocated to it by the SRA (O(8.5)).

Indicative Behaviours: Publicity

➤ Where you conduct other regulated activities your publicity discloses the manner in which you are regulated in relation to those activities (IB(8.1)).

➤ Where your firm is a multi-disciplinary practice, any publicity in relation to that practice makes clear which services are regulated legal services and which are not (IB(8.2)).

➤ Any publicity intended for a jurisdiction outside England and Wales complies with the Principles, voluntary codes and the rules in force in that jurisdiction concerning publicity (IB(8.3)).

➤ Where you and another business jointly market services, the nature of the services provided by each business is clear (IB(8.4)).

Indicative Behaviours that Principles have NOT been complied with: Publicity

➤ Approaching people in the street, at ports of entry, in hospital or at the scene of an accident; including approaching people to conduct a survey which involves collecting contact details of potential clients, or otherwise promotes your firm or in-house practice (IB(8.5)).

➤ Allowing any other person to conduct publicity for your firm or in-house practice in a way that would breach the Principles (IB(8.6))

➤ Advertising an estimated fee which is pitched at an unrealistically low level (IB(8.7)).

➤ Describing overheads of your firm (such a normal postage, telephone calls and charges arising in respect of client due diligence under the Money Laundering Regulations 2007) as disbursements in your advertisements (IB(8.8)).

➤ Advertising an estimated or fixed fee without making it clear that additional charges may be payable, if that is the case (IB(8.9))

➤ Using a name or description of your firm or in-house practice that includes the word "solicitor(s)" if none of the managers are solicitors (IB(8.10)).

➤ Advertising your firm or in-house practice in a way that suggests that services provided by another business are provided by your firm or in-house practice (IB(8.11)).

➤ Producing misleading information (IB(8.12)).

III   Fee sharing and referrals

Have you checked the Principles first?

Outcomes which MUST be achieved: Fee sharing and referrals

➤ Your independence and your professional judgement are not prejudiced by virtue of any arrangement with another person (*O(9.1)*).

➤ Your clients' interests are protected regardless of the interests of an introducer or fee sharer or your interest in receiving referrals (*O(9.2)*).

➤ Clients are in a position to make informed decisions about how to pursue their matter (*O(9.3)*).

➤ Clients are informed of any financial or other interest which an introducer has in referring the client to you (*O(9.4)*).

➤ Clients are informed of any fee sharing arrangement that is relevant to their matter (*O(9.5)*).

➤ You do not make payments to an introducer in respect of clients who are the subject of criminal proceedings or who have the benefit of public funding (*O(9.6)*).

➤ Where you enter into a financial arrangement with an introducer you ensure that the agreement is in writing (*O(9.7)*).

Indicative Behaviours: Fee sharing and referrals

➤ Only entering into arrangements with reputable third parties and monitoring the outcome of those arrangements to ensure that clients are treated fairly (*IB(9.1)*).

➤ In any case where a client has entered into, or is proposing to enter into, an arrangement with an introducer in connection with their matter, which is not in their best interests, advising the client that this is the case (*IB(9.2)*).

➤ Terminating any arrangement with an introducer or fee sharer which is causing you to breach the Principles or any requirements of the Code (*IB(9.3)*).

➤ Being satisfied that any client referred by an introducer has not been acquired as a result of marketing or other activities which, if done by a person regulated by the SRA, would be contrary to the Principles or any requirements of the Code (*IB(9.4)*).

➤ Drawing the client's attention to any payments you make, or other consideration you provide, in connection with any referral (*IB(9.5)*).

➤ Where information needs to be given to a client, ensuring the information is clear and in writing or in a form appropriate to the client's needs (*IB(9.6)*).

Indicative Behaviours that Principles have NOT been complied with: Fee sharing and referrals

➤ Entering into any type of business relationship with a third party, such as an unauthorised partnership, which places you in breach of the SRA Authorisation Rules or any other regulatory requirements in the Handbook (*IB(9.7)*).

➤ Allowing an introducer or fee sharer to influence the advice you give to clients (*IB(9.8)*).

➤ Accepting referrals where you have reason to believe that clients have been pressurised or misled into instructing you (*IB(9.9)*).

G You and others

I Relations with third parties
II Separate businesses

I Relations with third parties

Have you checked the
Principles first?

Outcomes which MUST be achieved: Relations with third parties

➤ You do not take unfair advantage of third parties in either your professional or personal capacity (O(11.1)).

➤ You perform all undertakings given by you within an agreed timescale or within a reasonable amount of time (O(11.2)).

➤ Where you act for a seller of land, you inform all buyers immediately of the seller's intention to deal with more than one buyer (O(11.3)).

➤ You properly administer oaths, affirmations or declarations where you are authorised to do so (O(11.1)).

Indicative Behaviours: Relations with third parties

➤ Providing sufficient time and information to enable the costs in any matter to be agreed (IB(11.1)).

➤ Returning documents or money sent subject to an express condition if you are unable to comply with that condition (IB(11.2)).

➤ Returning documents or money on demand if they are sent on condition that they are held to the sender's order (IB(11.3)).

➤ Ensuring that you do not communicate with another party when you are aware that the other party has retained a lawyer in a matter, except (IB(11.4)):

   ◆ to request the name and address of the other party's lawyer, or

   ◆ the other party's lawyer consents to you communicating with the client, or

   ◆ where there are exceptional circumstances.

➤ Maintaining an effective system which records when undertakings have been given and when they have been discharged (IB(11.5)).

➤ Where an undertaking is given which is dependent upon the happening of a future event and it becomes apparent the future event will not occur, notifying the recipient of this (IB(11.6)).

Indicative Behaviours that Principles have NOT been complied with: Relations with third parties

➤ Taking unfair advantage of an opposing party's lack of legal knowledge where they have not instructed a lawyer (IB(11.7)).

➤ Demanding anything for yourself or on behalf of your client, that is not legally recoverable, such as when you are instructed to collect a simple debt, demanding from the debtor the cost of the letter of claim since it cannot be said at that stage that such a cost is legally recoverable (IB(11.8)).

➤ Using your professional status or qualification to take unfair advantage of another person in order to advance your personal interests (IB(11.9)).

➤ Taking unfair advantage of a public office held by you, or a member of your family, or a member of your firm or their family (IB(11.10)).

Undertakings

➤ To avoid incurring liability, a solicitor should follow these 5 steps before giving an undertaking.

Steps	
1	Ensure that it will be possible to fulfil the undertaking.
2	Obtain a client's authority before giving the undertaking.
3	Put the undertaking in writing.
4	Mark the client's file *on the outside* to warn everyone dealing with it of the undertaking.
5	Ask the recipient for a written discharge, and keep it on the client's file.

➤ It might be a good idea to observe a 'house rule' that only (lawyer) partners can give undertakings.

➤ **Note:** a solicitor is not released if default is due to circumstances beyond his control.

➤ The Law Society has drafted 'model' undertakings for use in certain situations (eg: conveyancing).

II   Separate businesses

Have you checked the Principles first?

Outcomes which MUST be achieved: Separate businesses

➤ You do not (*O(12.1)*):

   a) own, *or*

   b) have a significant interest in, *or*

   c) actively participate in,

   a separate business which conducts prohibited separate business activities.

> Definitions of "permitted separate business" and "prohibited separate business activities" appear in the Glossary in Chapter 14 of the Code.

➤ If you are a firm, you are not owned by, or connected with, a separate business which conducts prohibited separate business activities (*O(12.2)*).

➤ Where you (*O(12.3)*):

   a) have a significant interest in, *or*

   b) actively participate in, *or*

   c) own, *or*

   d) are a firm and owned by or connected with,

   a permitted separate business, you have safeguards in place to ensure that clients are not misled about the extent to which the services that you and the separate business offer are regulated.

➤ You do not represent any permitted separate business as being regulated by the SRA or any of its activities as being provided by an individual who is regulated by the SRA (*O(12.4)*).

➤ You are only connected with reputable separate businesses (*O(12.5)*)

➤ You are only connected with a permitted separate business which is an appointed representative if it is an appointed representative of an independent financial adviser (*O(12.6)*).

Indicative Behaviours: Separate businesses

➤ Ensuring that client information and records are not disclosed to the permitted separate business, without the express consent of the client (*IB(12.1)*).

➤ Complying with the *SRA Accounts Rules* and not allowing the client account to be used to hold money for the permitted separate business (*IB(12.2)*).

➤ Where you are referring a client to a permitted separate business, informing the client of your interest in the separate business (*IB(12.3)*).

➤ Terminating any connection with a permitted separate business where you have reason to doubt the integrity or competence of that separate business (*IB(12.4)*).

H Complaints, Legal Ombudsman, SRA discipline

Disciplinary procedures

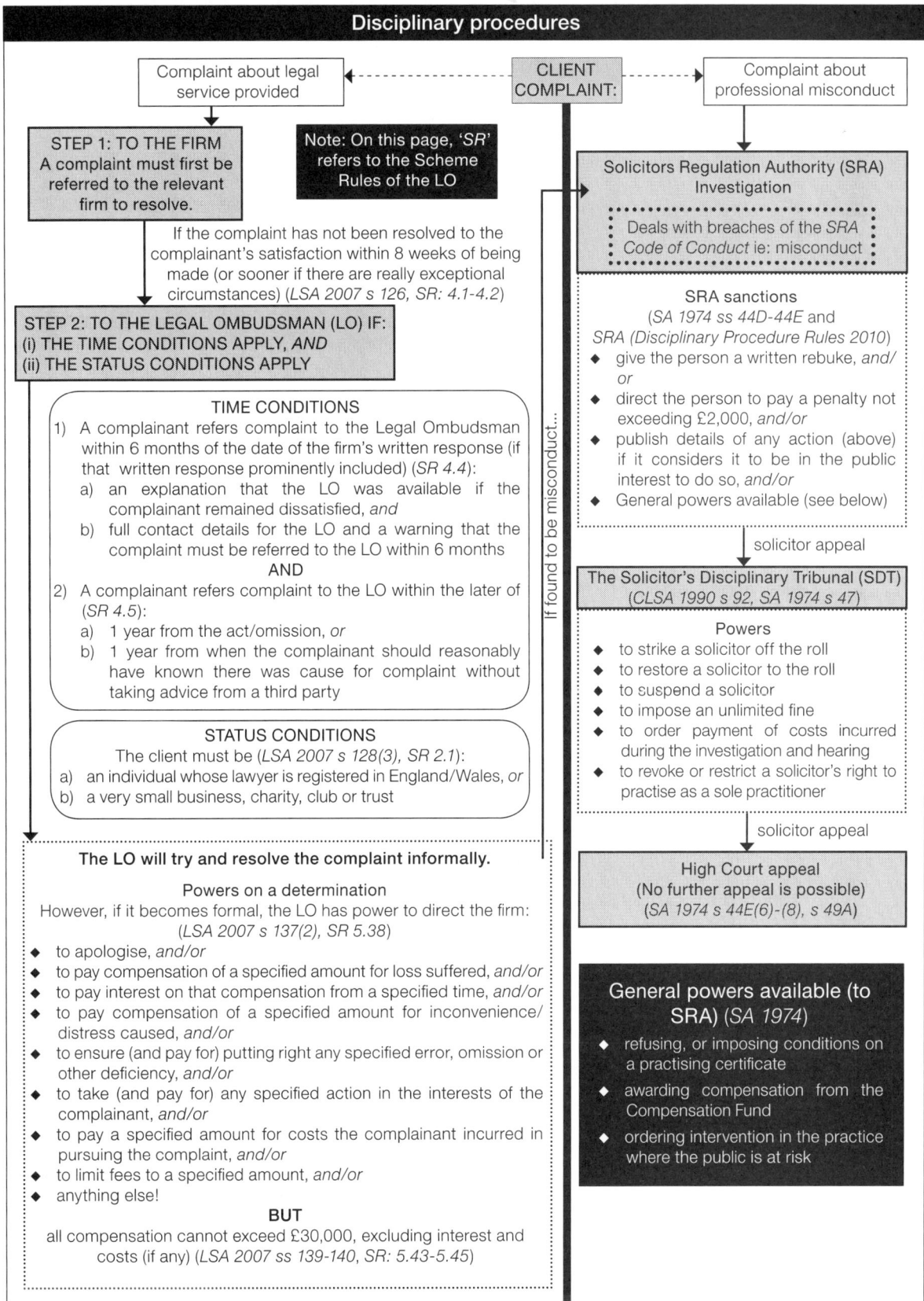

Complaint about legal service provided ←- - - - - - - - CLIENT COMPLAINT: - - - - - - - → Complaint about professional misconduct

STEP 1: TO THE FIRM
A complaint must first be referred to the relevant firm to resolve.

Note: On this page, '*SR*' refers to the Scheme Rules of the LO

If the complaint has not been resolved to the complainant's satisfaction within 8 weeks of being made (or sooner if there are really exceptional circumstances) (*LSA 2007 s 126, SR: 4.1-4.2*)

STEP 2: TO THE LEGAL OMBUDSMAN (LO) IF:
(i) THE TIME CONDITIONS APPLY, *AND*
(ii) THE STATUS CONDITIONS APPLY

TIME CONDITIONS
1) A complainant refers complaint to the Legal Ombudsman within 6 months of the date of the firm's written response (if that written response prominently included) (*SR 4.4*):
    a) an explanation that the LO was available if the complainant remained dissatisfied, *and*
    b) full contact details for the LO and a warning that the complaint must be referred to the LO within 6 months
    AND
2) A complainant refers complaint to the LO within the later of (*SR 4.5*):
    a) 1 year from the act/omission, *or*
    b) 1 year from when the complainant should reasonably have known there was cause for complaint without taking advice from a third party

STATUS CONDITIONS
The client must be (*LSA 2007 s 128(3), SR 2.1*):
a) an individual whose lawyer is registered in England/Wales, *or*
b) a very small business, charity, club or trust

The LO will try and resolve the complaint informally.

Powers on a determination
However, if it becomes formal, the LO has power to direct the firm: (*LSA 2007 s 137(2), SR 5.38*)
◆ to apologise, *and/or*
◆ to pay compensation of a specified amount for loss suffered, *and/or*
◆ to pay interest on that compensation from a specified time, *and/or*
◆ to pay compensation of a specified amount for inconvenience/distress caused, *and/or*
◆ to ensure (and pay for) putting right any specified error, omission or other deficiency, *and/or*
◆ to take (and pay for) any specified action in the interests of the complainant, *and/or*
◆ to pay a specified amount for costs the complainant incurred in pursuing the complaint, *and/or*
◆ to limit fees to a specified amount, *and/or*
◆ anything else!
BUT
all compensation cannot exceed £30,000, excluding interest and costs (if any) (*LSA 2007 ss 139-140, SR: 5.43-5.45*)

If found to be misconduct...

Solicitors Regulation Authority (SRA) Investigation

Deals with breaches of the *SRA Code of Conduct* ie: misconduct

SRA sanctions
(*SA 1974 ss 44D-44E* and *SRA (Disciplinary Procedure Rules 2010*)
◆ give the person a written rebuke, *and/or*
◆ direct the person to pay a penalty not exceeding £2,000, *and/or*
◆ publish details of any action (above) if it considers it to be in the public interest to do so, *and/or*
◆ General powers available (see below)

solicitor appeal

The Solicitor's Disciplinary Tribunal (SDT)
(*CLSA 1990 s 92, SA 1974 s 47*)

Powers
◆ to strike a solicitor off the roll
◆ to restore a solicitor to the roll
◆ to suspend a solicitor
◆ to impose an unlimited fine
◆ to order payment of costs incurred during the investigation and hearing
◆ to revoke or restrict a solicitor's right to practise as a sole practitioner

solicitor appeal

High Court appeal
(No further appeal is possible)
(*SA 1974 s 44E(6)-(8), s 49A*)

General powers available (to SRA) (*SA 1974*)
◆ refusing, or imposing conditions on a practising certificate
◆ awarding compensation from the Compensation Fund
◆ ordering intervention in the practice where the public is at risk

Fees charges by the Legal Ombudsman (*SR: 6*)

➤ A complaint to the Legal Ombudsman is potentially chargeable unless it is out of jurisdiction or it is dismissed or discontinued by the LO.

➤ No case fee is payable for the first 2 potentially chargeable complaints closed during the LO's financial year relating to:

◆ a business/partnership that is responsible for any act/omission of any employee/partner, *or*

◆ any individual authorised person for whom no business/partnership is responsible.

➤ A case fee is payable by the firm for every additional potentially chargeable complaint closed during the LO's financial year unless:

◆ the complaint was:

● abandoned or withdrawn, *or*

● settled, resolved or determined in favour of the firm, *and*

◆ the LO is satisfied that the firm took all reasonable steps, under its complaints procedures, to try to resolve the complaint.

➤ The case fee is £400 for all chargeable complaints.

➤ There is no charge to a complainant.

Actions on discovering grounds for a claim

➤ A solicitor should take the following actions on discovering that there are grounds for a claim.

Steps	
1	Inform the firm's insurers, and ask for their advice.
2	Advise the party concerned to seek independent legal advice and complaints routes.
3	Ensure all communications concerning this matter are confirmed in writing.
4	The solicitor must not admit liability without the insurer's consent.

Structures for handling complaints under *LSA 2007 ss 112-161* (assuming all is in force)

➤ The Office for Legal Complaints (OLC) has a chairman (who must be a lay person) and 6 to 8 members (the majority of whom must be lay persons) (*LSA 2007 Schedule 15*). The OLC:

◆ sets policy and rules in relation to complaints handling to ensure that best practice is promoted, *and*

◆ administers the Legal Ombudsman (LO) scheme by reference to rules devised by the OLC (and approved by the Legal Services Board (LSB)), called 'Scheme Rules'.

● The LO Scheme Rules can be found here: *www.legalombudsman.org.uk/downloads/documents/publications/OLC_Scheme%20rules_v1_201104-1_FINAL.pdf*

➤ The LO is:

◆ empowered to deal with all complaints about lawyers, *and*

◆ empowered, where appropriate, to provide redress to complainants of up to £30,000.

◆ expressly prohibited from taking any disciplinary action against a lawyer, the power to do so remains solely with the approved regulators (ie: the SRA for solicitors).

◆ The OLC is accountable to the LSB in respect of its targets and funding.

Financial Services

➤ The following summary is a bare outline of *FSMA 2000* (the 'framework' legislation for the financial services industry) and is intended to show the broad scope of activities which may be subject to FSA regulation.

➤ The industry is under a single regulator - the Financial Services Authority ('FSA') constituted by *FSMA 2000*.

➤ A specialised work should always be consulted before deciding whether an activity can be carried out without FSA authorisation and to ensure that if FSA authorisation is required, FSA rules are complied with.

The FSA and the *FSMA 2000*

➤ The FSA regulates financial services by pursuing the following regulatory objectives (*FSMA 2000 s 2(2)*):

a) a **market confidence objective** (*FSMA 2000 s 3*), *and*

  ● Maintaining confidence in the UK financial system (eg: financial markets, exchanges, regulated activities).

b) a **financial stability objective** (*FSMA 2000 s 3A*), *and*

  ● Contributing to the protection and enhancement of the stability of the UK financial system.

c) a **protection of consumers objective** (*FSMA 2000 s 5*), *and*

d) a **reduction of financial crime objective** (*FSMA 2000 s 6*).

➤ In discharging its general functions the FSA must have regard to (*FSMA 2000 s 2(3)*):

  ◆ the need to use its resources in the most efficient and economic way, *and*
  ◆ the responsibilities of those who manage the affairs of authorised persons, *and*
  ◆ the principle that a burden or restriction which is imposed on a person, or on the carrying on of an activity, should be proportionate to the benefits, considered in general terms, which are expected to result from the imposition of that burden or restriction, *and*
  ◆ the desirability of facilitating innovation in connection with regulated activities, *and*
  ◆ the international character of financial services and markets and the desirability of maintaining the competitive position of the UK, *and*
  ◆ the need to minimise the adverse effects on competition that may arise from anything done in the discharge of those functions, *and*
  ◆ the desirability of facilitating competition between those who are subject to any form of regulation by the FSA, *and*
  ◆ the desirability of enhancing the understanding and knowledge of members of the public of financial matters (including the UK financial system).
    ● The FSA also looks at representations from a Practitioner Panel and Consumer Panel (*FSMA 2000 s 11*).

➤ Under *FSMA 2000 Part XX* (*ss 325-333*), the FSA oversees the performance by members of the professions (eg: solicitors) of activities which are exempt from the general prohibition (*FSMA 2000 s 327*) (see p 44).

The 'financial promotion restriction'

➤ A person must not, in the course of business, communicate an invitation or inducement to engage in investment activity (unless that person is an authorised person, or the content of the communication is approved by an authorised person) (*FSMA 2000 s 21, FSMA(FP)O 2001*).

  ◆ The *FSMA(FP)O 2001 Sch 1* uses concepts of a 'controlled activity' and a 'controlled investment' which broadly mirror (but are not identical to) 'regulated activity' and 'investment' under *FSMA(RA)O 2001*.

    ● Activities not subject to the financial promotion restriction include certain communications: to persons outside the UK (*Art 12*), to an investment professional (*Art 19*), by a journalist (*Art 20*), to members or creditors of a body corporate (*Art 43*), to a certified high net worth individual (*Art 48*), to a high net worth company (*Art 49*), or to a sophisticated investor (*Art 50*), or by a PR or trustee (*Art 53-54*).

➤ Contravention of either the general prohibition in *s 19* or of *s 21* is a criminal offence punishable by a fine and up to 2 years' imprisonment (*FSMA 2000 ss 23/25*).

➤ An agreement made by/through a person in the course of carrying out a regulated activity in contravention of the general prohibition is unenforceable, unless a court permits otherwise (*FSMA 2000 ss 26-28*).

The 'general prohibition'

➤ No person may carry on a regulated activity with respect to an investment in the UK *unless* that person is an authorised person, or an exempt person (*FSMA 2000 s 19*).

◆ Certain exempt persons are identified by the *FSMA(E)O 2001*.

◆ The FSA may grant authorisation under *FSMA 2000 Part IV* (*ss 40-55*).

'Investments' (*FSMA 2000 Sch 2 Part II*)

◆ Securities (shares, stock, gilts, etc)

◆ Instruments creating/acknowledging indebtedness

◆ Units in collective investment schemes

◆ Options, futures, contracts for differences

◆ Contracts of insurance

◆ Participation in Lloyds syndicates

◆ Deposits

◆ Loans secured on land and other financial arrangements involving land

Regulated activities (*FSMA(RA)O 2001* amended by *FSMA(RA)(A)O 2009*) (see also *FSMA(CRAWB)O 2001*)

There are many more exclusions from these regulated activities - we present a selection of exclusions only.

◆ Accepting deposits (*Art 5*).

● Excluding sums received by a practising solicitor acting in the course of his profession. (*Art 7*)).

● Excluding sums paid by the Bank of England, the central bank of an EEA State other than the UK or the European Central Bank (*Art 6(1)(a)(i)*).

● Excluding sums paid by an authorised person who has permission to accept deposits, or to effect or carry out contracts of insurance; (*Art 6(1)(a)(ii)*).

● Excluding sums paid by the National Savings Bank (*Art 6(1)(a)(iv)*).

● Excluding sums paid by paid by a person in the course of carrying on a business consisting wholly or to a significant extent of lending money (*Art 6(1)(b)*).

● Excluding sums paid by one company to another at a time when both are members of the same group or when the same individual is a majority shareholder controller of both of them (*Art 6(1)(c)*).

● Excluding sums paid by a person who, at the time when it is paid, is a close relative of the person receiving it or who is, or is a close relative of, a director or manager of that person or who is, or is a close relative of, a controller of that person (*Art 6(1)(d)*).

◆ Issuing electronic money (*Art 9B*).

◆ Effecting and carrying out contracts of insurance (*Art 10*).

● Excluding breakdown insurance (*Art 12*).

◆ Dealing in investments as principal (*Art 14*) or as agent (*Art 21*).

● Excluded from *Art 14* are the sale of 50% or more of the voting shares in a body corporate (*Art 70*).

● Excluded from *Art 14* is the issue by a company of its own shares or share warrants and the issue by any person of his own debentures or debenture warrants (*Art 18*).

◆ Arranging deals in investments (*Art 25*).

● Excluded from *Art 25* are the sale of 50% or more of the voting shares in a body corporate (*Art 70*).

● Arrangements which do not cause a deal are excluded (*Art 26*).

◆ Arranging or advising on regulated mortgage contracts (*Art 25A, Art 53A*).

● Arrangements which do not cause a deal are excluded (*Art 26*) and advice in newspapers is excluded (*Art 54*).

◆ Managing investments (*Art 37*).

◆ Arranging or advising on regulated home reversion plans (*Art 25B, Art 53B*).

● Arrangements which do not cause a deal are excluded (*Art 26*) and advice in newspapers is excluded (*Art 54*).

◆ Arranging or advising on regulated home purchase plans (*Art 25C, Art 53C*).

● Arrangements which do not cause a deal are excluded (*Art 26*) and advice in newspapers is excluded (*Art 54*).

◆ Operating a multilateral trading facility (*Art 25D*).

◆ Arranging or advising on regulated sale and rent back agreements (*Art 25E, Art 53D*).

● Arrangements which do not cause a deal are excluded (*Art 26*) and advice in newspapers is excluded (*Art 54*).

◆ Assisting in the administration and performance of a contract of insurance (*Art 39A*).

◆ Safeguarding and administering investments (*Art 40*).

◆ Sending dematerialised instructions (*Art 45*).

◆ Establishing, operating or winding up a collective investment scheme (*Art 51*).

◆ Establishing, operating or winding up a stakeholder or personal pension scheme (*Art 52*).

◆ Providing basic advice to a retail consumer on a stakeholder product (*Art 52B*).

◆ Advising on investments (*Art 53*).

● Excluded from *Art 53* are the sale of 50% or more of the voting shares in a body corporate (*Art 70*).

● Advice in newspapers is excluded (*Art 54*).

◆ Lloyds activities (*Art 56*).

◆ Funeral plan contracts (*Art 59*).

◆ Regulated mortgage contracts (*Art 61*) (eg: mortgages over residential dwellings taken out by individuals).

◆ Entering into and administering regulated home reversion plans (*Art 63B*), regulated home purchase plans (*Art 63F*), regulated sale and rent back agreements (*Art 63J*),

◆ Agreeing to carry on specified activities (*Art 64*).

The Law Society and Solicitors

➤ The Law Society is a designated professional body ('DPB') for the purposes of *FSMA 2000 Part XX.*

- ◆ A DPB is required to have rules 'designed to secure that in providing a particular service to a particular client, the member carries on only regulated activities which arise out of, or are complementary to, the provision by him of that service to that client' (*FSMA 2000 s 332(4)).*

- ◆ The Law Society has agreed with the FSA the *Solicitors' Financial Services (Scope) Rules 2001* that define 'mainstream investment advice' which solicitors may give within the DPB regime.

- ◆ Following the policy of the *FSMA 2000* that the FSA is to be the sole regulator of financial services, the FSA is empowered to disapply the exemption under the DPB regime with respect to particular firms, activities or an entire profession (*FSMA 2000 ss 328-329).*

➤ The *SFS(S)R 2001* provide that a firm must not carry out 'prohibited activities' (without FSA regulation), eg: (*SFS(S)R 2001 r 3*):

a) market-make in investments, *or*

b) buy, sell, subscribe for or underwrite investments as principal where a firm holds itself out as engaging in the business of buying such investments with a view to sale, *or*

c) buy or sell investments to stabilise or maintain the market price, *or*

d) act as stakeholder pension scheme manager, establish, operate, or wind up such a scheme, *or*

e) enter into a broker fund arrangement, *or*

f) effect or carry out a contract of insurance as a principal, *or*

g) establish, operate, or wind-up a collective investment scheme, *or*

h) manage the underwriting capacity of a Lloyds syndicate as a managing agent, or advise a person to become a member of a particular Lloyds syndicate, *or*

i) enter as a provider into a funeral plan contract, *or*

j) enter into a regulated mortgage contract as a lender, or administer a regulated mortgage contract.

➤ A firm which carries on an activity within *FSMA(RA)O 2001* must ensure that (*SFS(S)R 2001 rr 4-5*):

a) that activity arises out of, or is complementary to, the provision of a particular professional service to a particular client, *and*

b) the provision of any service in the course of carrying out any regulated activity is incidental to the provision by the firm of professional services, *and*

c) the firm accounts to the client for any pecuniary reward, or other advantage, the firm receives from a third party, *and*

d) neither the activity, nor the investment are within an order under *FSMA 2000 s 327(6)* and the FSA has not made a direction or order under *FSMA 2000 ss 328-329, and*

e) the activity is not otherwise prohibited by the *SFS(S)R 2001* (eg: recommending a packaged product or a securities and contractually based investment (other than in certain restricted circumstances), discretionary management (unless in a capacity such as a trustee and advised by an authorised person or an exempt person), or certain corporate finance activities (eg: sponsor for securities to be admitted to trading on the London Stock Exchange)).

➤ Breach of the *SFS(S)R 2001* is a criminal offence under *FSMA 2000 s 23.*

J   Human rights

➤ Every solicitor should be aware of the impact of human rights law on all other areas of law.

➤ The European Convention for the Protection of Human Rights and Fundamental Freedoms (known as the European Convention on Human Rights or ECHR) was signed in Rome on 4 November 1950.

 ◆ The ECHR establishes a European Court of Human Rights (in Strasbourg).

➤ The ECHR established international protection for human rights and entitled individuals to apply to the European Court of Human Rights for enforcement. This still applies even after the *HRA 1998*.

➤ The ECHR is part of English law by virtue of *HRA 1998*.

European Convention for the Protection of Human Rights and Fundamental Freedoms				
Article	**Content**	**Article**	**Content**	
2	right to life	8	right to respect for family and private life	
3	prohibition of torture	9	freedom of thought, conscience and religion	
4	prohibition of slavery and forced labour	10	freedom of expression	
5	right to liberty and security	11	freedom of assembly and association	
	◆ includes right to be brought before a judge promptly if arrested or detained	12	right to marry	
		14	prohibition of discrimination	
	◆ includes compensation right if a victim of arrest / detention in held in contravention of this article	**1st Protocol**		
6	right to a fair trial	**1-3**	rights to protection of property, education and free elections	
	(includes the presumption of innocence until proven guilty)	**13th Protocol**	abolition of the death penalty	
7	no punishment without law (ie: victim must contravene a law in force at the time)			

Human Rights Act 1998

➤ The *HRA 1998* incorporates the Articles in the above table into English law.

 ◆ The *HRA 1998* tries to balance protection of human rights with Parliamentary sovereignty.

➤ **New legislation:** all new legislation must comply with the convention rights above.

 ◆ There must be a 'Declaration of Compatibility' before a second reading of a proposed Bill (*s 19*).

➤ **Existing legislation**

 a) All legislation must (as far as possible) be interpreted by the courts to be compatible with the ECHR (*s 3*).

 b) Courts and tribunals have jurisdiction to hear human rights arguments.

 c) The higher courts (eg: High Court, the Court of Appeal and the Supreme Court and some others) may make a 'Declaration of Incompatibility' that a law does not accord with ECHR rights (*s 4*).

 ◆ This does not affect the validity of the law.

 ◆ The Crown is put on notice by the court. The Crown may make a counter-argument (*s 5*).

 ◆ A Minister may draft a remedial order amending such legislation which must be approved by Parliament within 60 days in order to be effective (*s 10 and Sch 2*).

 • In cases of particular urgency, an order may be effective immediately but lapses if not approved by Parliament within 120 days.

➤ It is unlawful for a public authority to act in a way incompatible with the ECHR (*s 6*).

 ◆ Proceedings must be brought within 1 year or such other period as a Court finds equitable (*s 7(5)*).

➤ It is unclear if ECHR rights have horizontal effect between private parties, but Sedley LJ in *Douglas & others v Hello! Ltd (No.1)* [2001] QB 967 says that for *Art 10* rights at least, there is horizontal effect.

 ◆ See also *X v Y* [2004] EWCA Civ 662 regarding horizontal effect.

K *Legal Services Act 2007*

➤ *LSA 2007* sets out a new framework for the regulation of legal services.

Part	What *LSA 2007* provides
A guide to the *Legal Services Act 2007*	
Part 1 *s 1*	➤ **Regulatory objectives:** ◆ Sets out a new regulatory framework to replace the existing framework which comprises a number of oversight regulators with overlapping responsibilities. ◆ Sets out 8 regulatory objectives, which guides a new Legal Services Board (LSB), the approved regulators (including the Law Society) and a new Office for Legal Complaints (OLC).
Part 2 *ss 2-11*	➤ **Legal Services Board:** ◆ Establishes the LSB: a single oversight body, independent both from Government and from the "front-line" approved regulators such as the Law Society and Bar Council. ◆ Sets out the structure and functions of the LSB, including its duty to act compatibly with the regulatory objectives, to assist in the maintenance and development of standards in regulation, education and training and to establish a Consumer Panel. ◆ Also sets out the requirements for both appointment to, and membership of, the LSB and the powers that the Lord Chancellor has in relation to these processes.
Part 3 *ss* *12-26*	➤ **Reserved Legal Activities:** Lists and defines the reserved legal activities. ◆ Explains who is entitled to carry out these activities. ◆ Sets out the penalties for those who carry out, or pretend to be entitled to carry out, these activities where they are not entitled. ◆ Explains the process for altering the scope of the reserved legal activities. ➤ **Approved Regulators:** Approved regulators are the bodies that authorise and regulate persons to carry on reserved legal activities. ◆ Explains what an approved regulator is, lists those bodies designated by the Act as approved regulators, and explains how other bodies can become approved regulators in the future.
Part 4 *ss* *27-70*	➤ **Regulation of Approved Regulators:** Prescribes the general duties of approved regulators and the powers that the LSB has to ensure that these are being properly carried out.
Part 5 *ss* *71-111* **see** **p 49**	➤ **Alternative Business Structures (ABS):** Makes provision for the licensing of new business structures in legal services allowing lawyers and non-lawyers to work together to deliver legal and other services. ◆ Sets out the arrangements for authorisation, by the LSB, of licensing authorities and how, in the absence of an appropriate licensing authority, the LSB can license ABS firms directly. ◆ Makes provision for the regulation of ABS.
Part 6 *ss* *112-161*	➤ **Legal Complaints:** Establishes an independent OLC, which will be responsible for administering an ombudsman scheme, under which all complaints will be dealt with by a Chief Ombudsman, assistant ombudsmen, and staff appointed by the OLC. ◆ The OLC draws up scheme rules setting out the detail of the ombudsman scheme. ◆ Makes provision for the appointment process and terms of office for members of the OLC Board and the Chief Ombudsman and the assistant ombudsmen. ◆ Makes provision for the accountability of the OLC to the LSB, the framework of rules by which the OLC will establish its operating procedures, and changes to the regulatory arrangements of approved regulators.
Part 7 *ss* *162-175*	➤ **Further Provisions Relating to LSB/OLC:** Makes provision as to the guidance that the LSB may give. ◆ Requires the LSB to make rules for the payment by approved regulators of a levy, to recoup the expenditure of the LSB and OLC.
Part 8 *ss* *176-196*	➤ **Miscellaneous Provisions about Lawyers:** makes provision about several matters including: ◆ the requirement for alteration of the rules of the Solicitors Disciplinary Tribunal to be approved by the LSB, and empowering the LSB to give a limited range of directions to the Tribunal, *and* ◆ the making of costs orders in relation to pro bono legal representation.
Part 9 *ss197-214*	➤ **General provisions.**

The 8 regulatory objectives (*LSA 2007 s 1*)

➤ protecting and promoting the public interest, *and*

➤ supporting the constitutional principle of the rule of law, *and*

➤ improving access to justice, *and*

➤ protecting and promoting the interests of consumers, *and*

➤ promoting competition in the provision of legal services, *and*

➤ encouraging an independent, strong, diverse and effective legal profession, *and*

➤ increasing public understanding of the citizen's legal rights and duties, *and*

➤ promoting and maintaining adherence to the professional principles.

◆ The professional principles are:

● that authorised persons should act with independence and integrity, *and*

● that authorised persons should maintain proper standards of work, *and*

● that authorised persons should act in the best interests of their clients, *and*

● that persons who exercise before any court a right of audience, or conduct litigation in relation to proceedings in any court, by virtue of being authorised persons should comply with their duty to the court to act with independence in the interests of justice, *and*

● that the affairs of clients should be kept confidential.

Some selected interesting aspects of *LSA 2007*

➤ The LSB must set up and maintain a Consumer Panel (*LSA 2007 s 8*).

◆ This is a panel of persons whose task will be to represent the interests of consumers (as defined in *LSA 2007 s 207*).

◆ Appointments to the Panel will be made by the LSB with the approval of the Lord Chancellor and one of the Panel members will be appointed as chairman of the Panel by the LSB.

➤ Existing regulators which *LSA 2007* recognises as approved regulators includes the Law Society.

➤ A person (including a body corporate or an unincorporated body) is entitled to carry on a 'Reserved Legal Activity' (see p 49) only if the person is (*LSA 2007 s 13*):

◆ an authorised person (*defined in LSA 2007 s 18*), *or*

● A person is an "authorised person" in relation to a particular reserved legal activity if the person is authorised to carry on that activity by a relevant approved regulator *(other than by virtue of a licence under LSA 2007 Part 5 (ss 71-111)) or the person is a licensable body and holds a licence under LSA 2007 Part 5 (ss 71-111) which authorises the carrying on of the activity [words in italics not yet in force]*.

◆ an exempt person (*defined in LSA 2007 s 19* and *Schedule 3*).

● Eg: an individual who carries on probate activities other than for fee, gain or reward is exempt.

Reserved legal activities (*LSA 2007 s 12*)

➤ The right of audience in the courts.

➤ The right to conduct litigation.

➤ Reserved instrument activities.

➤ Probate activities.

➤ Notarial activities.

➤ The administration of oaths.

A guide to the *Legal Services Act 2007 Part 5* - LDPs and ABSs

➤ **LDPs:**

   ◆ From 31 March 2009, legal disciplinary practices (LDPs) can be set up (*Legal Services Act 2007 (Commencement No. 4, Transitory and Transitional Provisions and Appointed Day) Order 2009* and *The Solicitors Recognised Bodies (Amendment) Order 2009*).

   • LDPs can be owned and managed by different types of lawyer and up to 25% non-lawyers.

   • There can be no external ownership of an LDP.

   ◆ The SRA can regulate LDPs.

   • Some LDPs may have a choice of regulator depending on the services they want to provide.

   ▪ Approved regulators will only be able to regulate firms providing a particular range of legal services, depending on the scope of the particular regulator's authority.

➤ **ABSs:**

   ◆ From 6 October 2011, the first alternative business structures (ABS) will be able to open for business in the legal services marketplace in England and Wales.

   • This will mean that for the first time non-lawyers will be able to fully own and invest in law firms.

   ◆ This will allow lawyers to form multidisciplinary practices offering legal services in conjunction with non-legal services.

   • The SRA has been designated by the Legal Services Board (LSB) as a licensing authority for ABSs.

   ◆ **Benefits of ABSs:**

   • ABSs will increase access to finance.

   ▪ Before ABSs, providers could face constraints on the amount of equity (usually debt equity) that could be raised.

   • ABSs allow for increased flexibility as non-legal firms (eg: insurance companies, estate agents and banks) will be able to 'partner' legal firms.

   • ABSs allow easier hiring and retention of high-quality non-legal staff and will be able to reward non-legal staff in the same way as they reward lawyers.

   • ABSs should lead to innovation and price reductions which should result in more people being able to access legal services.

   ◆ **Safeguards:** A non-lawyer owning more than 10% of the ABS is subject to a 'fitness-to-own' test.

ACCOUNTS

This chapter examines:

Conventions in the presentation of accounts

➤ If a figure is underlined, this means it is being added or subtracted along with those *above* it.

➤ The answer may be placed in the column to the right of the underlined figure if there is one, or if there is no such column, directly below.

➤ The purpose of this is to help in the addition or subtraction of totals and subtotals.

➤ Final answers are usually double-underlined.

A   Basic bookkeeping

Step 1	Produce 'T' accounts

➤   In a double entry accounting system, every transaction is recorded twice in order to produce an ongoing error check in the figures.

◆   'T' accounts are used, named after the shape of the lines drawn.

●   These are 'fictional' devices which set out what is happening to particular items in a business.

■   Items can be assets, liabilities, receipts in or payments out eg: cash, a vehicle, debtors, etc.

NB: 'T' accounts are *not* real accounts in the sense of a bank account.

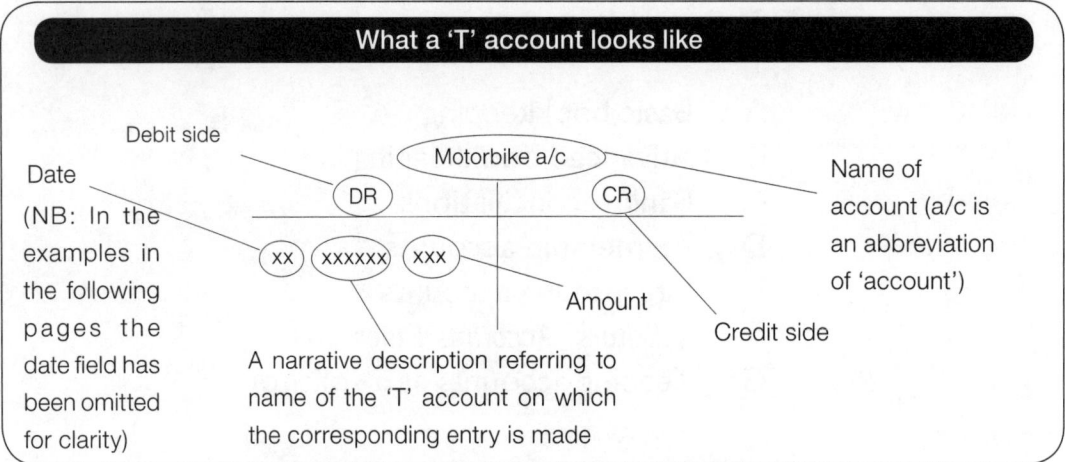

➤   A debit on 1 side of a 'T' account = a credit on 1 side of another 'T' account.

◆   Total debits *must* equal total credits.

➤   As many 'T' accounts as necessary are used. It is easiest to start with the cash account entry.

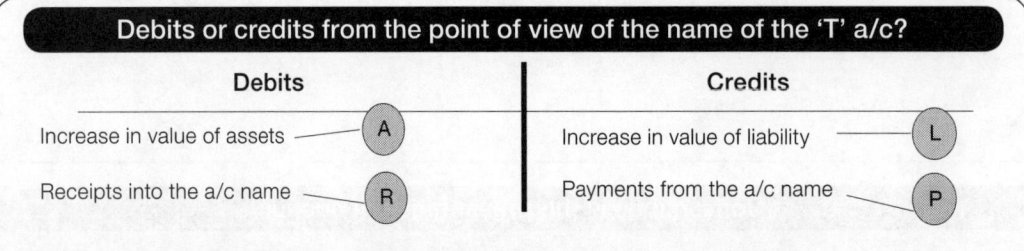

➤   The collection of 'T' accounts taken together' is known as:

◆   the general ledger, *or*

◆   the nominal ledger.

Step 1	Example

Facts: Alpha and Beta start together as solicitors on 1 January 2018. Each puts £15,000 into the new partnership. In the first year the following events occur:

	DR	CR
Staff salaries	27,000	
Rent	10,000	
Company motorbike	4,000	
Office equipment bought on credit	6,500	
Misc. and general expenses	1,500	
Bills delivered		90,000

They have only collected £62,000 of bills delivered and you will see that they still owe £6,500 for the office equipment.

Hint: Start with the cash account and work through the other accounts.

The 'T' accounts

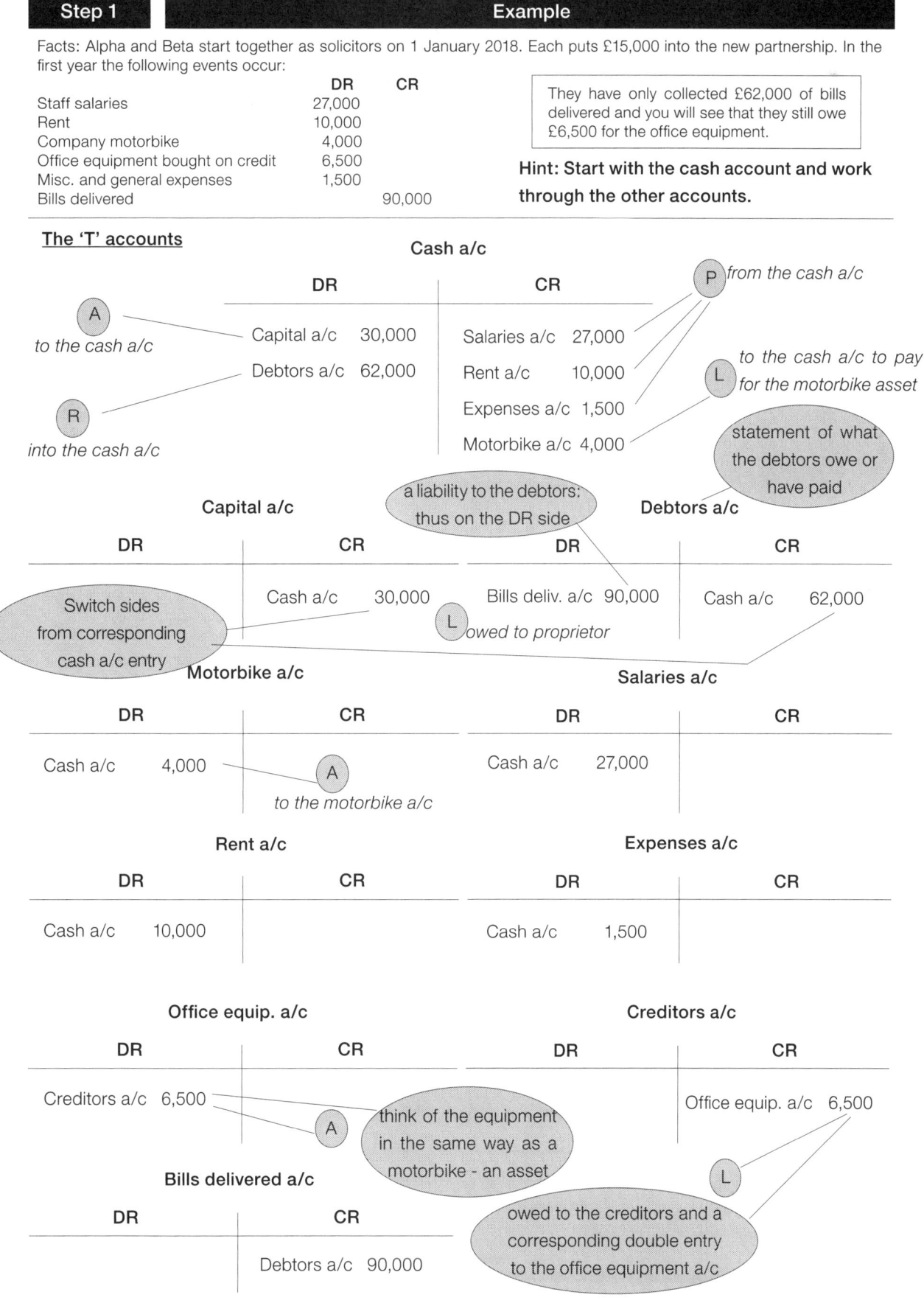

53

| Step 2 | Balance the 'T' accounts and produce a trial balance |

A   Balancing the 'T' accounts

➤   The aim of balancing accounts is to draw the line under everything that has occurred so far in each 'T' account and carry on into the next period with just one figure - so starting the process for each 'T' account all over again.

➤   Balancing off the 'T' accounts is the process of adding all the entries on each side of a 'T' account and working out what the difference is and on which side that difference falls.

➤   The balance is carried forward to the next period.

➤   There are 5 steps in this procedure which are set out (❶ to ❺) in the example opposite.

B   Producing the trial balance

➤   The purpose of producing a trial balance is to check the arithmetic in all of the 'T' accounts.

➤   A trial balance is produced as follows:

   ◆   take each of the DR 'balance brought forward' entries (from the 'T' accounts with a balance brought forward on the DR side) and add them together to reach a total, *and*

   ◆   take each of the CR 'balance brought forward' entries (from the 'T' accounts with a balance forward on the CR side) and add them together to reach a total, *and*

   ◆   if the arithmetic is correct, the totals should be the same because of the double entry system whereby every time a CR is made, a corresponding DR is made, so total CR = total DR.

➤   The method of setting this out is illustrated in the example opposite.

Step 2	Example

Facts: Continued from step 1.

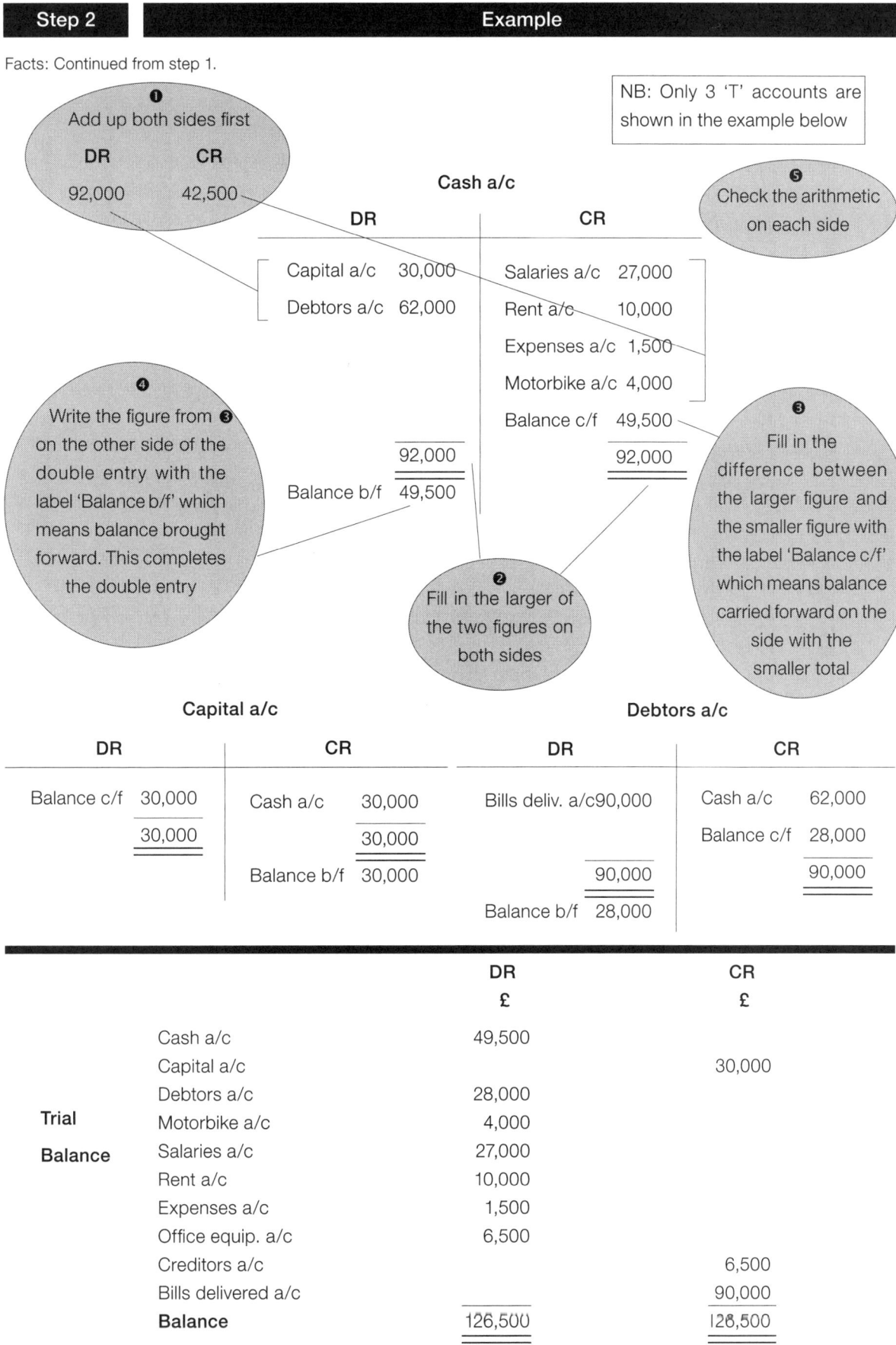

❶ Add up both sides first

DR	CR
92,000	42,500

NB: Only 3 'T' accounts are shown in the example below

❺ Check the arithmetic on each side

Cash a/c

DR		CR	
Capital a/c	30,000	Salaries a/c	27,000
Debtors a/c	62,000	Rent a/c	10,000
		Expenses a/c	1,500
		Motorbike a/c	4,000
		Balance c/f	49,500
	92,000		92,000
Balance b/f	49,500		

❹ Write the figure from **❸** on the other side of the double entry with the label 'Balance b/f' which means balance brought forward. This completes the double entry

❸ Fill in the difference between the larger figure and the smaller figure with the label 'Balance c/f' which means balance carried forward on the side with the smaller total

❷ Fill in the larger of the two figures on both sides

Capital a/c

DR		CR	
Balance c/f	30,000	Cash a/c	30,000
	30,000		30,000
		Balance b/f	30,000

Debtors a/c

DR		CR	
Bills deliv. a/c	90,000	Cash a/c	62,000
		Balance c/f	28,000
	90,000		90,000
Balance b/f	28,000		

		DR £	CR £
	Cash a/c	49,500	
	Capital a/c		30,000
	Debtors a/c	28,000	
Trial	Motorbike a/c	4,000	
Balance	Salaries a/c	27,000	
	Rent a/c	10,000	
	Expenses a/c	1,500	
	Office equip. a/c	6,500	
	Creditors a/c		6,500
	Bills delivered a/c		90,000
	Balance	126,500	126,500

Step 3	Produce final accounts (Profit & loss account and balance sheet)

Stage 1: Mark up the trial balance

➤ In order to produce the 2 final accounts, it is necessary to mark every item on the trial balance as being destined for the profit & loss account or the balance sheet.

◆ Receipts and payments will go on the profit and loss account.

● Receipts and payments have the nature of being ephemeral - coming and going.

◆ Assets and liabilities will go on the balance sheet.

● Assets and liabilities have a more permanent nature.

➤ An example of this marking is shown in the example opposite.

Stage 2: Make any necessary adjustments as per pp 60-63

➤ The example on the right has no necessary adjustments to make.

Stage 3: Produce the profit & loss account

➤ The profit & loss account shows the profits or losses that the business has made during a particular period.

➤ The profit & loss account is part of the double entry system.

◆ This means that to put entries into the profit & loss account, it is necessary to close off the relevant 'T' account.

NB: Relevant 'T' accounts are those which are relevant to the profit & loss account from the marking up of the trial balance.

● This means writing an entry labelled 'P&L a/c' on the opposite side to the 'balance b/f' entry with the same figure.

● Then complete the double entry in the profit & loss 'T' a/c.

◆ The relevant 'T' accounts for which this has been done are at zero and are said to be closed for the period in question. The new period will start from a zero balance again.

➤ There are 2 'styles' of presenting a profit and loss account.

◆ Style 'A' is technical and is a presentation of the profit & loss 'T' account itself.

◆ Style 'B' is more user-friendly and is a re-writing of the profit & loss 'T' account.

Step 3	Example

Facts: Continued from step 2.

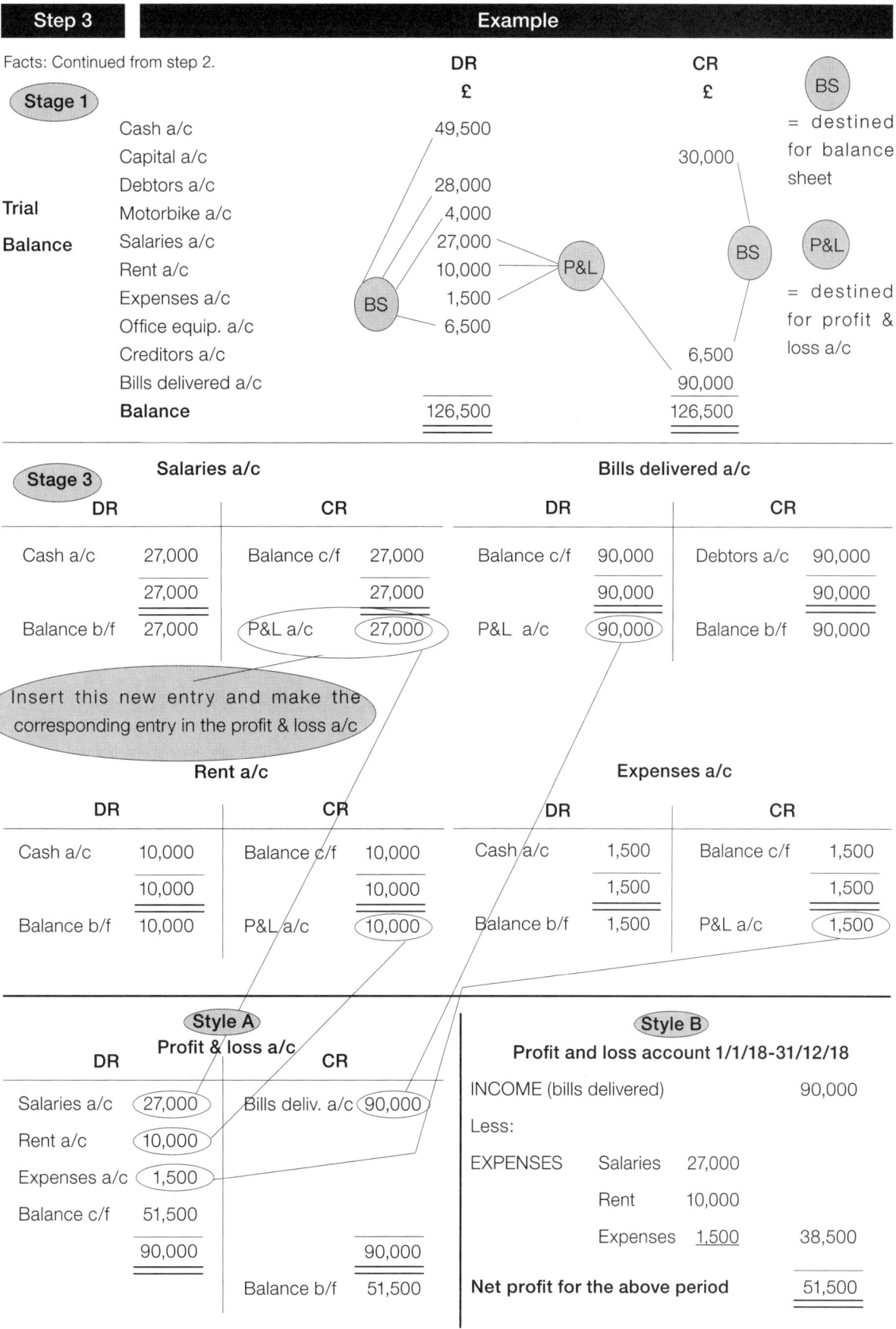

Stage 1

Trial Balance

	DR £	CR £	
Cash a/c	49,500		
Capital a/c		30,000	
Debtors a/c	28,000		
Motorbike a/c	4,000		
Salaries a/c	27,000		
Rent a/c	10,000		
Expenses a/c	1,500		
Office equip. a/c	6,500		
Creditors a/c		6,500	
Bills delivered a/c		90,000	
Balance	126,500	126,500	

BS = destined for balance sheet

P&L = destined for profit & loss a/c

Stage 3

Salaries a/c

DR		CR	
Cash a/c	27,000	Balance c/f	27,000
	27,000		27,000
Balance b/f	27,000	P&L a/c	27,000

Insert this new entry and make the corresponding entry in the profit & loss a/c

Bills delivered a/c

DR		CR	
Balance c/f	90,000	Debtors a/c	90,000
	90,000		90,000
P&L a/c	90,000	Balance b/f	90,000

Rent a/c

DR		CR	
Cash a/c	10,000	Balance c/f	10,000
	10,000		10,000
Balance b/f	10,000	P&L a/c	10,000

Expenses a/c

DR		CR	
Cash a/c	1,500	Balance c/f	1,500
	1,500		1,500
Balance b/f	1,500	P&L a/c	1,500

Style A

Profit & loss a/c

DR		CR	
Salaries a/c	27,000	Bills deliv. a/c	90,000
Rent a/c	10,000		
Expenses a/c	1,500		
Balance c/f	51,500		
	90,000		90,000
		Balance b/f	51,500

Style B

Profit and loss account 1/1/18-31/12/18

INCOME (bills delivered)			90,000
Less:			
EXPENSES	Salaries	27,000	
	Rent	10,000	
	Expenses	1,500	38,500
Net profit for the above period			51,500

Step 3...	Produce final accounts (Profit & loss account and balance sheet)

Stage 4: Produce the balance sheet

➤ The balance sheet performs 2 functions:

   a) it is a snapshot of the business's assets and liabilities at a particular date, *and*

   b) it is a check that 'Assets of the business = Liabilities of the business (ie: capital employed)'.

      ◆ The form of the balance sheet is derived from the equation as follows:

      Assets = Liabilities

      Assets = Inside liabilities (owed to the proprietor ie: capital and profit) + Outside Liabilities

      Assets = (Opening capital and profit) + Outside liabilities

      Assets - Outside liabilities = Opening capital and profit

➤ The balance sheet is *not* part of the double entry system.

      ◆ This means there is no adjustment to the 'T' accounts.

➤ The balance sheet is made up by taking the items from the marked up trial balance *and* taking the final figure from the profit and loss account and putting them into the balance sheet form. There is a pro forma balance sheet set out on p 66.

➤ The net assets [ie: (fixed + current assets) less (fixed + current liabilities)] should match the opening capital and profit. This is because it shows how the company capital is employed and tied up in assets and liabilities.

Step 3...	Example (cont.)

Stage 4

A 'snapshot' as of this date

Balance sheet as at 31st December, 2018

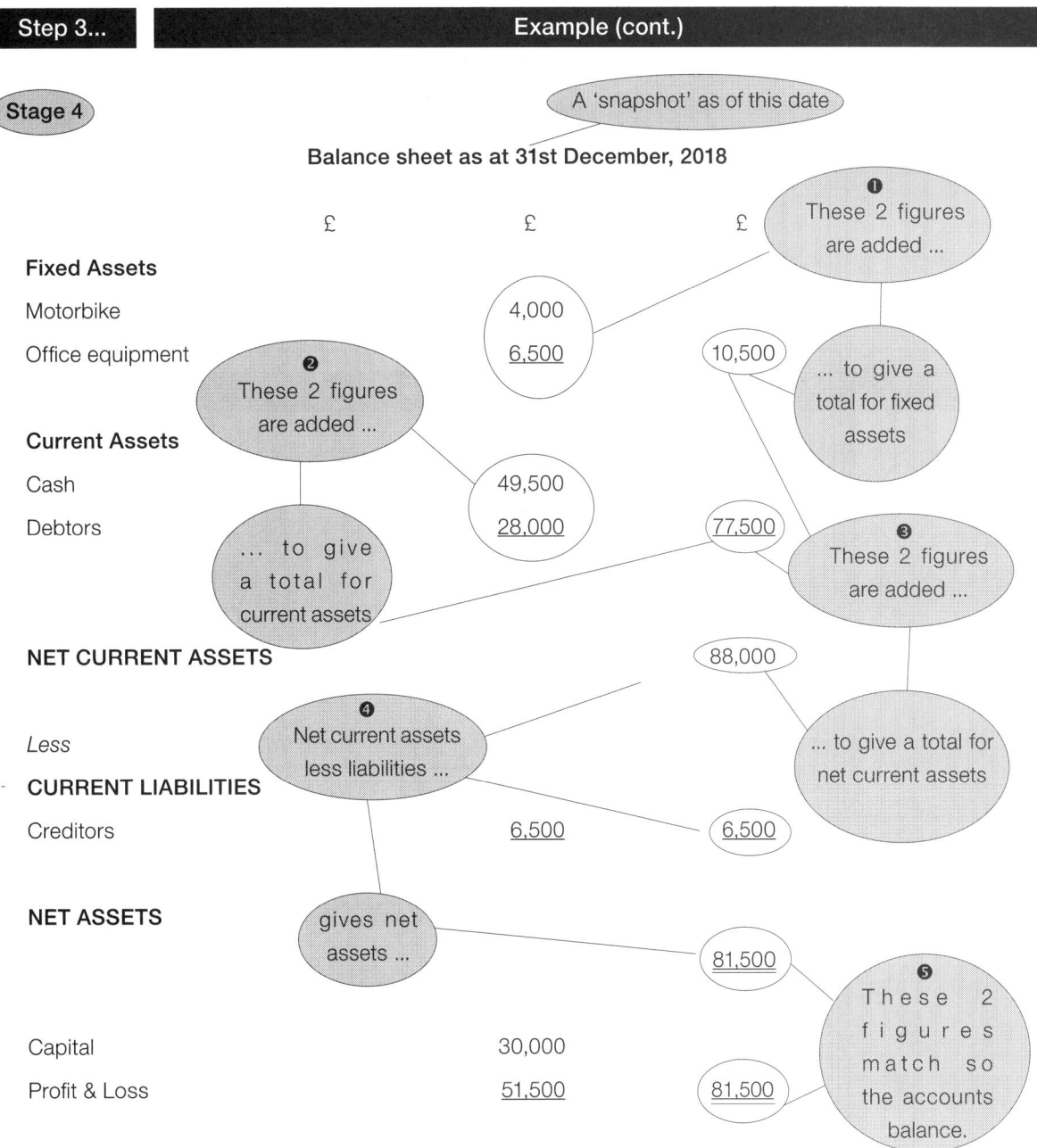

❶ These 2 figures are added ...

... to give a total for fixed assets

Fixed Assets

Motorbike — 4,000

Office equipment — 6,500

10,500

❷ These 2 figures are added ...

... to give a total for current assets

Current Assets

Cash — 49,500

Debtors — 28,000

77,500

❸ These 2 figures are added ...

... to give a total for net current assets

88,000

NET CURRENT ASSETS

Less

❹ Net current assets less liabilities ...

CURRENT LIABILITIES

Creditors — 6,500 — 6,500

NET ASSETS

gives net assets ... — 81,500

❺ These 2 figures match so the accounts balance.

Capital — 30,000

Profit & Loss — 51,500 — 81,500

All figures used on this balance sheet are from the marked up trial balance

59

B Advanced bookkeeping

All advanced bookkeeping in this section (A-G) necessitates changes to the profit & loss account (and other relevant 'T' accounts) and to the balance sheet. There is a fully worked example on pp 64-65.

A Work in progress

➤ Work in progress is work that is being undertaken by the firm but which has not yet been billed.

➤ It has value and this value must be shown in the same period as the expenses spent to produce it.

End of period 1 - taking period 1 work in progress into account

Profit & loss account	Balance sheet
◆ The work in progress 'T' a/c should be debited with the period 1 work in progress figure (see p 52 because it is an asset).	◆ Add work in progress under CURRENT ASSETS as per the pro forma on p 66.
◆ The profit & loss a/c should be credited with the period 1 work in progress figure (completing the double entry).	
◆ If presenting the account in style B (see p 56), add the work in progress for period 1 to bills delivered.	

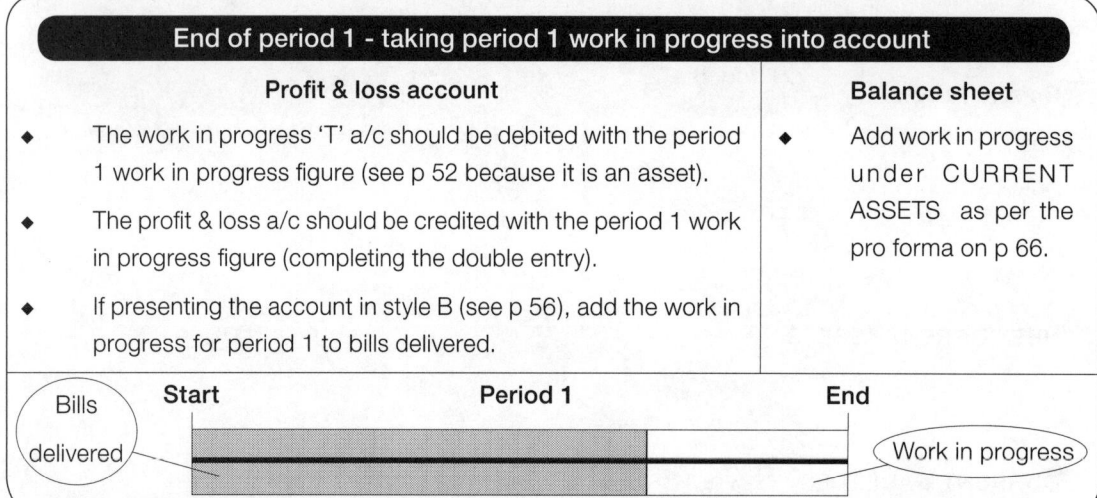

End of period 2 - taking period 2 work in progress into account and taking out period 1 work in progress from account

Profit & loss account	Balance sheet
◆ The work in progress 'T' a/c should be debited with the period 2 work in progress figure (see p 52 because it is an asset).	◆ Add work in progress under CURRENT ASSETS as per the pro forma on p 66.
◆ The profit & loss a/c should be credited with the period 2 work in progress figure (completing the double entry).	

- The 'T' a/cs will now be accurate as the period 1 work in progress was billed and gradually paid, the necessary entries will have been made in the work in progress a/c to bring the period 1 work in progress a/c to zero.

◆ If presenting the account in style B (see p 56), add the work in progress from period 2 to bills delivered and subtract the work in progress from period 1 from bills delivered.

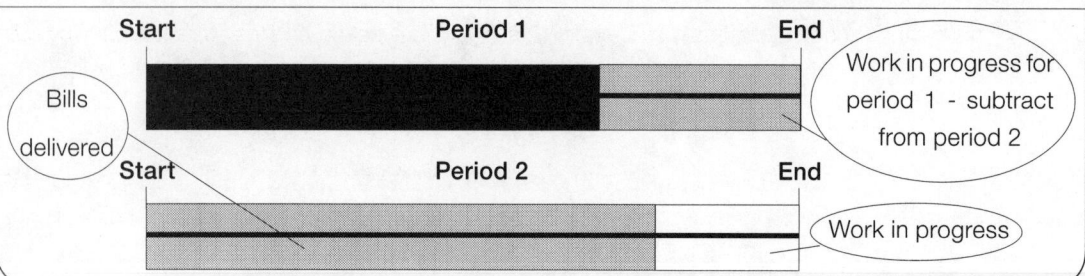

B   Bad debts

➤ Sometimes it is obvious that specific debts will not be paid by specific debtors and it is necessary to write off those debts.

➤ Adjustments:

◆ the balance sheet, by amending the profit & loss figure (see below) and the current assets, *and*

◆ the profit & loss account and other 'T' accounts:

● The debtors a/c is credited with an entry labelled 'bad debts a/c' and the amount.

● The bad debts a/c is debited with an entry labelled 'debtors a/c' and the amount. This is then closed off to the profit & loss account.

▪ In Style 'B' presentations, bad debts is an expense of the business.

Eg: (showing the amendments to 'T' accounts only):

The facts are as on pp 53, 55 and 57 but it becomes obvious that £1,500 will never be paid:

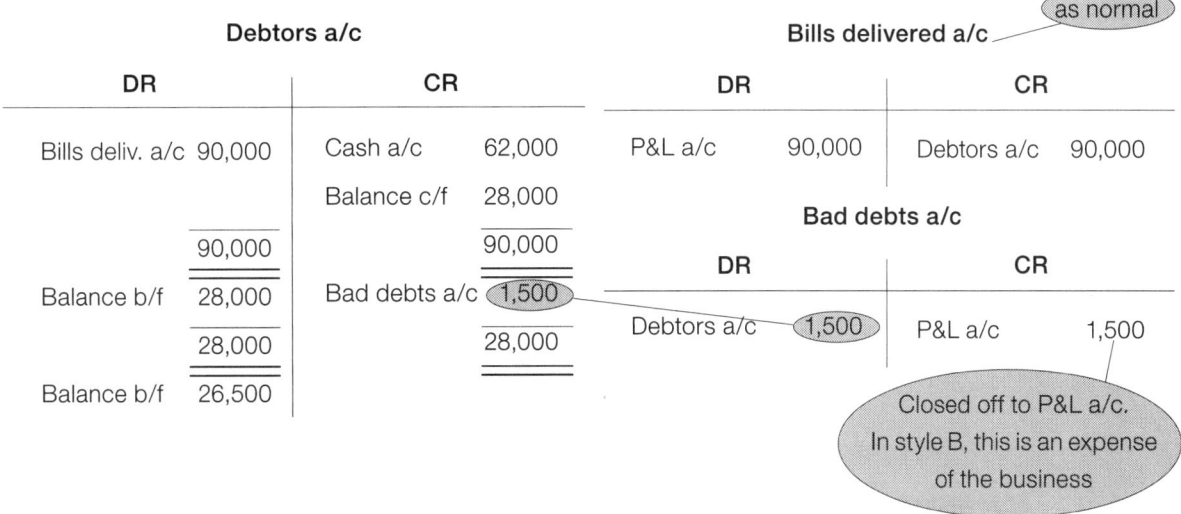

C   Doubtful debts

➤ It is careful accounting to make a provision for doubtful debts (unlike bad debts which is knowledge that a *specific* debtor will not pay).

◆ The figure chosen is based on experience of debts that as a fact have not been paid in the past and is usually a percentage of total debtors.

➤ Adjustments:

◆ the balance sheet, by amending the profit & loss figure (see below) and the current assets (by subtracting the figure from debtors), *and*

◆ the profit & loss account and other 'T' accounts:

● The doubtful debts a/c is credited with an entry labelled 'profit & loss a/c' and the amount.

● The profit & loss a/c is debited with an entry labelled 'doubtful debts a/c' and the amount.

▪ In Style 'B' presentations, the doubtful debts are an expense of the business.

D Payments in advance (prepayments)

➤ These are payments made in the current accounting period for goods/services in the following period.

➤ Adjustments:

◆ the balance sheet, by adding the prepayment as a current asset and amending the profit & loss figure (see below), *and*

◆ the profit & loss account and other 'T' accounts:

● if the account with the prepayment is for example, rent, close off from the rent a/c to the profit & loss account the amount actually paid out for the period less the prepayment. The prepayment goes in in the CR column (of the rent a/c) (under the profit and loss a/c entry) as the 'balance c/f' figure with the corresponding double entry figure being in the DR column as the balance b/f. This is the amount brought forward into the next accounting period.

NB: the cash a/c should always reflect the sums actually paid during the account period.

■ In Style B presentations, subtract the prepayment from the rent figure.

E Payments in arrears (accruals)

➤ These are payments that will be made in the next accounting period for goods/services used in the current accounting period.

➤ Adjustments:

◆ the balance sheet, by subtracting the accrual by putting it in as a current liability and amending the profit & loss figure (see below), *and*

◆ the profit & loss account and other 'T' accounts:

● if the account with the accrual is for example, water, only close off from the water account to the profit & loss a/c an amount equal to the cash paid out less the prepayment. Carry forward the prepayment into the next account period.

■ In Style B presentations, add the accrual to the water figure for the period.

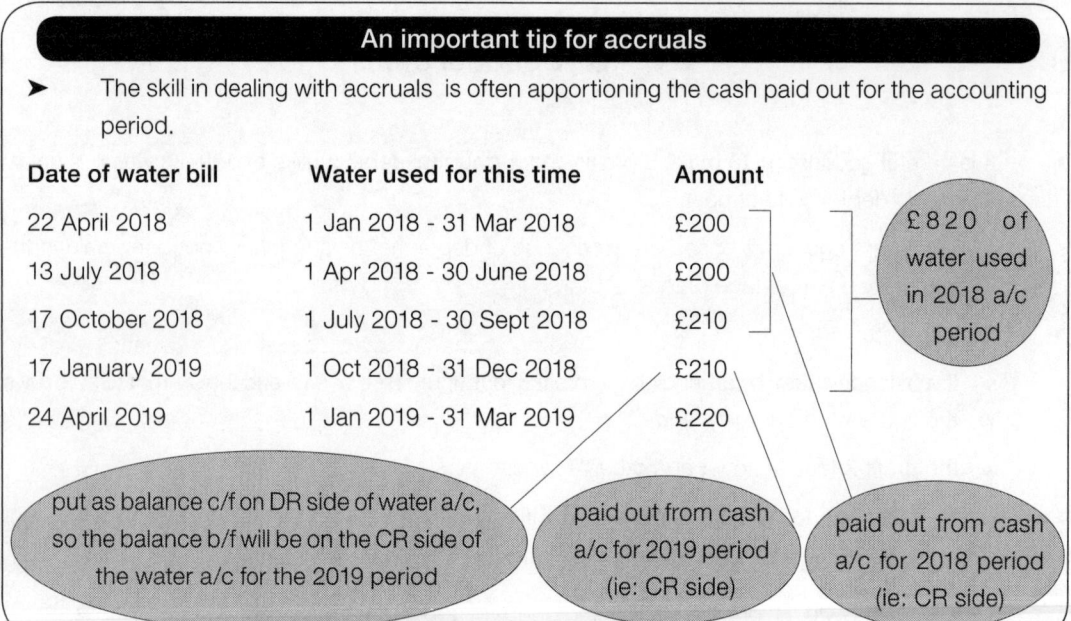

An important tip for accruals

➤ The skill in dealing with accruals is often apportioning the cash paid out for the accounting period.

Date of water bill	Water used for this time	Amount
22 April 2018	1 Jan 2018 - 31 Mar 2018	£200
13 July 2018	1 Apr 2018 - 30 June 2018	£200
17 October 2018	1 July 2018 - 30 Sept 2018	£210
17 January 2019	1 Oct 2018 - 31 Dec 2018	£210
24 April 2019	1 Jan 2019 - 31 Mar 2019	£220

£820 of water used in 2018 a/c period

put as balance c/f on DR side of water a/c, so the balance b/f will be on the CR side of the water a/c for the 2019 period

paid out from cash a/c for 2019 period (ie: CR side)

paid out from cash a/c for 2018 period (ie: CR side)

F Depreciation

➤ Depreciation is a charge made to the business each year to reflect the loss in value of an asset, eg: if a £5,000 motorbike is expected to last the business for 5 years, we will charge a cost of £1,000 per year to the business.

◆ The actual figure charged per year, although a 'guesstimate', is usually based on the experience of accountants.

➤ Adjustments:

◆ using the motorbike example above, each year on the balance sheet under the fixed asset 'motorbike' there should be an entry labelled 'accumulated depreciation'. This will be listed as £1,000 in the first year, £2,000 in the next year until it reads £5,000 in the fifth year giving an asset value of nil.

◆ 'T' accounts:

● the motorbike a/c will have already have £5,000 listed on the DR side (as it is an asset, see p 52).

● the accumulated depreciation a/c will already have the accumulated depreciation (for previous accounting years) listed on the CR side. Add to the CR side the depreciation for this year's accounting period and perform the 'balance c/f' and 'balance b/f' procedure to give a total figure for accumulated depreciation (for previous accounting periods and this accounting period) on the CR side.

● the depreciation a/c should have this year's (and only this year's) motorbike depreciation put on the DR side and the account should be closed off to the profit & loss account.

■ In Style B presentations, this year's depreciation is an expense of the business.

G Disposal of fixed assets

➤ When a business sells assets, it will make a profit or loss on the sale.

➤ This profit is reported at the end of the profit & loss account as a separate figure from the main profit figure of the business. (Since the mainstream income of the business is not derived from the buying and selling of assets, the figure from this is listed as separate, otherwise this would confuse the true profit and loss figures.)

➤ When asset A is sold:

◆ put in the CR column of the asset A a/c, the label 'transfer to disposal a/c' and the cost price - this clears the asset A 'T' account, *and*

◆ put in the DR column of the accumulation depreciation a/c the accumulated depreciation for asset A and update the accumulation a/c by doing the balance c/f - balance b/f procedure, *and*

◆ put in the DR column of the fixed asset disposal a/c the label 'Asset A a/c' and the cost figure (thus completing the double entry for (a) above), *and*

◆ put in the CR column of the fixed asset a/c the label 'accumulated depreciation a/c' and the final accumulated depreciation figure for asset A (thus completing the double entry for (b) above), *and*

So far this has cleared off asset A from the main accounts into a special asset disposal account.

◆ put in the DR column of the cash account the sale price, *and*

◆ put in the CR column of the fixed asset disposal a/c, the sale price. Balance off the fixed asset disposal a/c and take the profit to the profit & loss a/c.

● Style B presentations and adjustments to the balance sheet are self-explanatory.

Fully worked example

Sue, Grabbit & Run, a firm of successful solicitors in Erehwon, set up business on 1 January 2018. The accountants draw up a trial balance as at 31 December 2018 for the 2018 year of business. Produce a balance sheet and profit & loss account based on the following trial balance and extra facts:

Trial balance:	£	£
Opening capital in the business		50,000
Bank loan		80,000
Loan interest	9,000	
Balance in office account - cash	110,000	
Office equipment and computers - cost	20,000	
Office equipment and computers - accumulated depreciation		10,000
Messengers motorbikes - cost	14,000	
Messengers motorbikes - accumulated depreciation		4,000
Bills delivered		170,000
Work in progress as at 31 December 2017	80,000	
Debtors	13,500	
Creditors		8,500
Salaries	60,000	
Office rent	13,500	
Electricity	2,000	
Water	500	
	322,500	322,500

❶

Mark all items on the trial balance as destined for the BS or the P&L a/c

☐ BS

▨ P&L

Unmarked BS and P&L

- The office owes party contractors (ie: creditors) £1,000 (not yet in the account) for the 2018 office Xmas party.
- The office rent paid in advance at 31 Dec. 2018 is £2,000.
- The electricity accrued as at 31 Dec. 2018 is £400.
- The water accrued as at 31 Dec. 2018 is £100.
- It has been decided that a provision for doubtful debts of £8,500 should be made.
- Depreciation for the year is 20% of cost on office computers and equipment.
- Depreciation for the year is 15% of cost on messengers motorbikes.
- Work in progress at 31 December 2018 is £40,000.

❷
BS and P&L

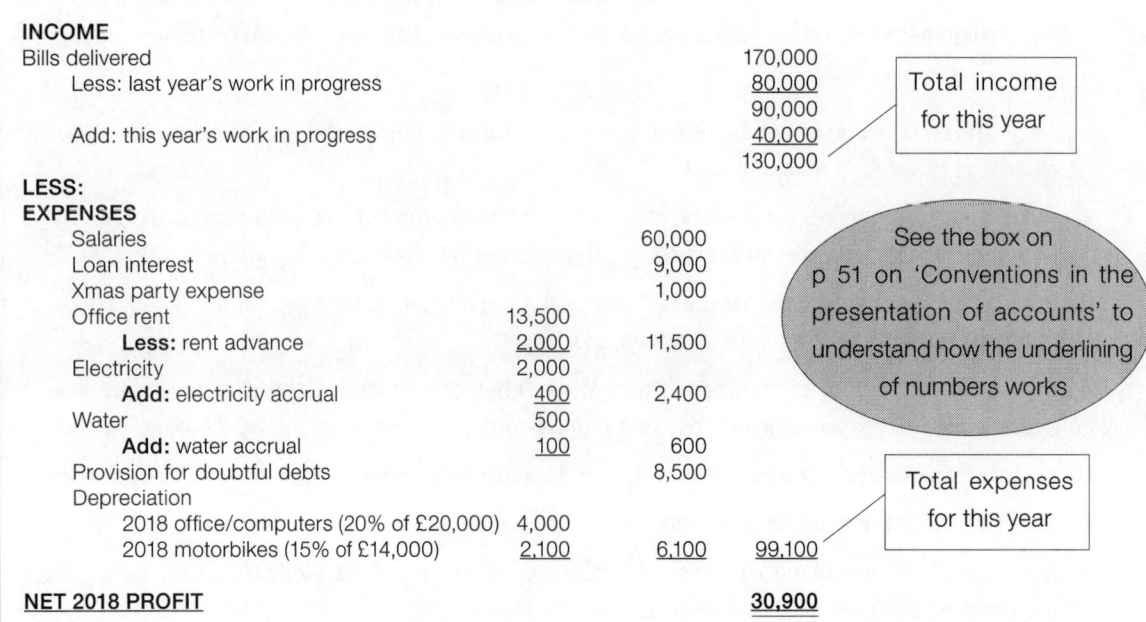

Profit & Loss account for Sue Grabbit & Run for 2018 a/c period

INCOME

Bills delivered		170,000
Less: last year's work in progress		80,000
		90,000
Add: this year's work in progress		40,000
		130,000

Total income for this year

LESS:
EXPENSES

Salaries		60,000	
Loan interest		9,000	
Xmas party expense		1,000	
Office rent	13,500		
Less: rent advance	2,000	11,500	
Electricity	2,000		
Add: electricity accrual	400	2,400	
Water	500		
Add: water accrual	100	600	
Provision for doubtful debts		8,500	
Depreciation			
2018 office/computers (20% of £20,000)	4,000		
2018 motorbikes (15% of £14,000)	2,100	6,100	99,100
NET 2018 PROFIT			**30,900**

See the box on p 51 on 'Conventions in the presentation of accounts' to understand how the underlining of numbers works

Total expenses for this year

Fully worked example (continued)

Balance sheet of Sue, Grabbit & Run as of 31st December, 2018

FIXED ASSETS

			pre 2018 office equipment depreciation	2018 office equipment depreciation		

Office equipment and computers - cost			20,000			
Less accumulated depreciation (10,000+4,000)			14,000	6,000		
Messengers motorbikes - cost			14,000			
Less accumulated depreciation (4,000+2,100)			6,100	7,900	13,900	

pre 2018 motorbike depreciation   2018 motorbike depreciation

ADD: CURRENT ASSETS

Work in progress 2018		40,000		
Debtors	13,500			
Less provision for doubtful debts	8,500	5,000		
Prepayments		2,000		
Cash		110,000	157,000	

LESS: CURRENT LIABILITIES

Creditors	8,500		
Add creditors not yet in accounts	1,000	9,500	
Accruals			
Electricity	400		
Water	100	500	10,000

NET CURRENT ASSETS	**160,900**

LESS: LONG TERM LIABILITIES

Bank loan	80,000
NET ASSETS	**80,900**

Capital and profit

Capital	50,000	
Net 2018 profit	30,900	**80,900**

Pro-forma balance sheet

Balance sheet of [   ] as of [   ]

> V-W should equal AA+BB

FIXED ASSETS

Asset 1 - cost	A		
Less accumulated depreciation for asset 1	B	C (A+B)	
Asset 2 - cost	D		
Less accumulated depreciation for asset 2	E	F (D+E)	G (C+F)

ADD: CURRENT ASSETS

Work in progress current period		H	
Debtors	I		
Less provision for doubtful debts	J		
Less provision for bad debts	K	L(I+J+K)	
Prepayments (X+X+X+X+X+X+X etc.)		M	
Cash at bank		N	
Petty cash		O	P(H+L+M+N+P)

LESS: CURRENT LIABILITIES

Creditors	Q		
Add creditors not yet in accounts	R	S(Q+R)	
Accruals (X+X+X+X+X+X+X+X etc.)		T	U(S+T)

CLIENT BALANCES

Client bank account	Y		
Less client ledgers (owed to clients)	Y	NIL(Y-Y)	NIL

NET CURRENT ASSETS   **V(G+P-U)**

LESS: LONG TERM LIABILITIES

Bank loan   W

NET ASSETS   **V-W**

Capital employed

Capital	if partnership accounts, this is the partners'	AA	
Net [year] profit	capital and current accounts (see p 68)	BB	**AA+BB**

C   Bank reconciliations

➤ It is often necessary to 'reconcile' the bank statements of the business with the cash ledger (ie: the cash 'T' account) as a cheque on the double entry accounting. They may not match up because of:

♦ bank charges/bank interest on the statement but not in the cash book, *and/or*

♦ cheques received by the business but not yet paid into/credited to the bank account, *and/or*

♦ cheques paid out by the business but not yet cashed by those to whom they have been given, *and/or*

♦ error on the bank statement (quite common!) or in the cash book.

❶ Make sure the starting balances on the cash ledger and the bank statement are the same by bringing the previous month's transactions up to date. Then, cross off all similar items that appear in both the bank statement and the cash ledger and circle those that are different.

❷ Write into the cash ledger all outstanding items (see grey boxes below).

❸ Draw up a reconciliation statement to match the bank statement to the cash ledger - the end figures should be the same!

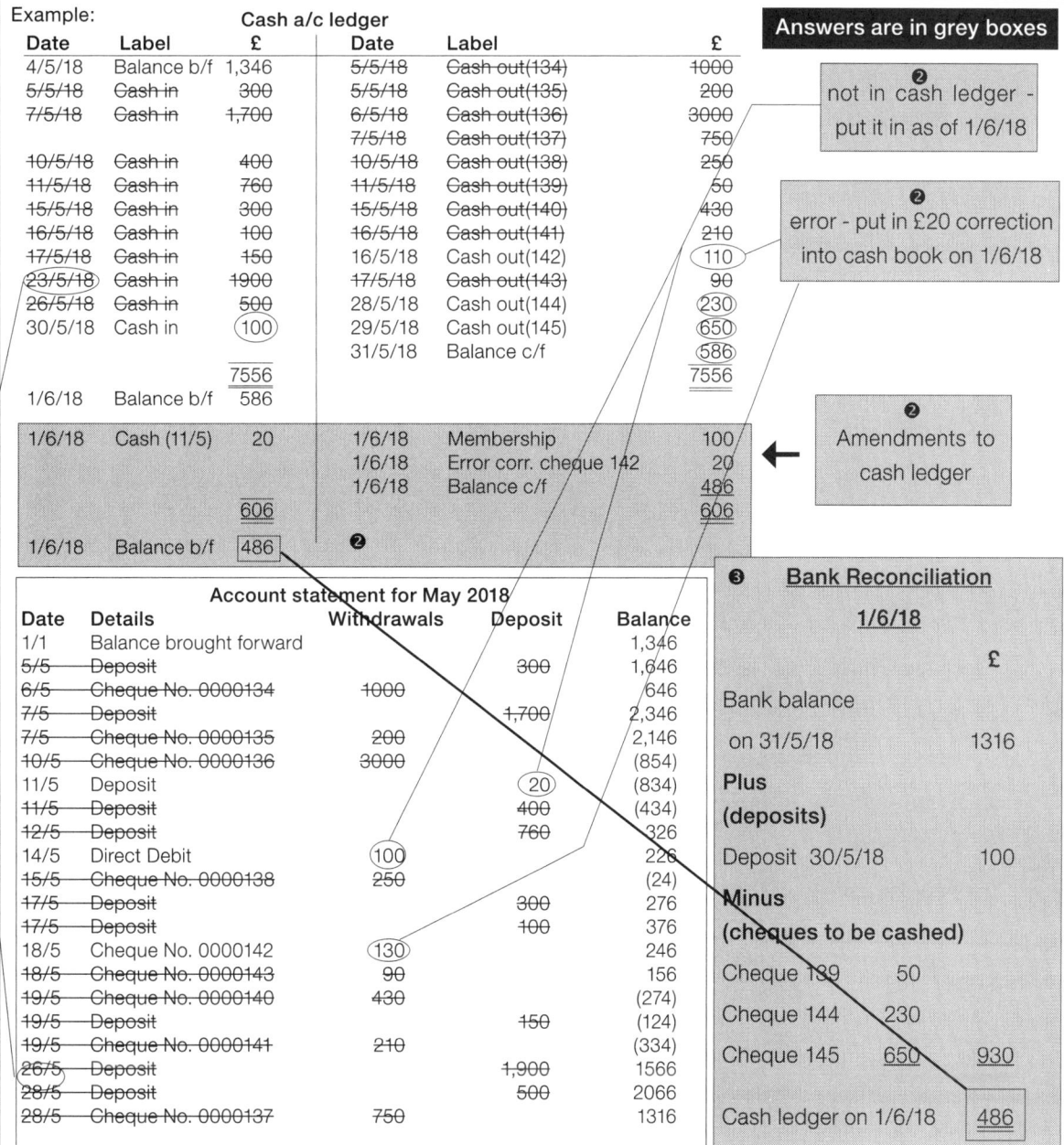

Example:

Cash a/c ledger

Date	Label	£	Date	Label	£
4/5/18	Balance b/f	1,346	5/5/18	Cash out(134)	1000
5/5/18	Cash in	300	5/5/18	Cash out(135)	200
7/5/18	Cash in	1,700	6/5/18	Cash out(136)	3000
			7/5/18	Cash out(137)	750
10/5/18	Cash in	400	10/5/18	Cash out(138)	250
11/5/18	Cash in	760	11/5/18	Cash out(139)	50
15/5/18	Cash in	300	15/5/18	Cash out(140)	430
16/5/18	Cash in	100	16/5/18	Cash out(141)	210
17/5/18	Cash in	150	16/5/18	Cash out(142)	(110)
23/5/18	Cash in	1900	17/5/18	Cash out(143)	90
26/5/18	Cash in	500	28/5/18	Cash out(144)	(230)
30/5/18	Cash in	(100)	29/5/18	Cash out(145)	(650)
			31/5/18	Balance c/f	(586)
		7556			7556
1/6/18	Balance b/f	586			
1/6/18	Cash (11/5)	20	1/6/18	Membership	100
			1/6/18	Error corr. cheque 142	20
			1/6/18	Balance c/f	486
		606			606
1/6/18	Balance b/f	486			

Answers are in grey boxes

❷ not in cash ledger - put it in as of 1/6/18

❷ error - put in £20 correction into cash book on 1/6/18

❷ Amendments to cash ledger

❶ eg: of a match to cross out

Account statement for May 2018

Date	Details	Withdrawals	Deposit	Balance
1/1	Balance brought forward			1,346
5/5	Deposit		300	1,646
6/5	Cheque No. 0000134	1000		646
7/5	Deposit		1,700	2,346
7/5	Cheque No. 0000135	200		2,146
10/5	Cheque No. 0000136	3000		(854)
11/5	Deposit		(20)	(834)
11/5	Deposit		400	(434)
12/5	Deposit		760	326
14/5	Direct Debit	(100)		226
15/5	Cheque No. 0000138	250		(24)
17/5	Deposit		300	276
17/5	Deposit		100	376
18/5	Cheque No. 0000142	(130)		246
18/5	Cheque No. 0000143	90		156
19/5	Cheque No. 0000140	430		(274)
19/5	Deposit		150	(124)
19/5	Cheque No. 0000141	210		(334)
26/5	Deposit		1,900	1566
28/5	Deposit		500	2066
28/5	Cheque No. 0000137	750		1316

❸ **Bank Reconciliation**

1/6/18

£

Bank balance

on 31/5/18   1316

Plus

(deposits)

Deposit 30/5/18   100

Minus

(cheques to be cashed)

Cheque 139	50	
Cheque 144	230	
Cheque 145	650	930

Cash ledger on 1/6/18   486

67

D   Partnership accounts

➤ With partnership accounts, certain changes are made to the different areas of the accounts.

➤ The differences when dealing with partnerships are 4:

a) partners may take interest on their capital contributions to the partnership, *and/or*

b) partners may draw a salary for themselves, *and/or*

c) partners will share profits according to a set formula (usually based on an agreed %age), *and/or*

d) partners may take drawings from the business for themselves.

A   The trial balance

➤ Remember - a trial balance is a listing of all the balances of the 'T' accounts. Although the changes below are listed from the trial balance stage, they in fact occur much earlier when the individual 'T' accounts are worked on.

➤ In addition to the usual trial balance (p 54), the following changes should be made:

◆ any net profit listed on the trial balance is usually, by convention, a figure taken before any of (a)-(d) above have been taken out.

◆ the capital account entry is split into an entry per partner:

eg: trial balance excerpt:

Non-partnership accounts	DR	CR		Partnership accounts	DR	CR
capital		X	➡	Partner's 1 capital		A
				Partner's 2 capital		B
				Partner's 3 capital		C

B   The appropriation accounts

➤ An appropriation account is a breakdown of how profit is distributed to each partner. It is not a 'T' account.

➤ The appropriation account lists the profit for the relevant period broken down into 3 elements:

a) interest on capital, *and*

b) salary, *and*

c) profit division.

➤ The appropriation account is usually broken down into as many time segments as is necessary for the accounting period. Each segment represents a fixed group of partners *and* fixed levels of the list of (a)-(c) at the top of this page. If any of these change (eg: new partners are taken on, partners retire, profit share ratio changes etc.) it is necessary to start a new appropriation account for the new segment of time.

➤ The worked example opposite sets out how to set out the appropriation account.

Fully worked example

Alpha runs his garage business but due to pressure of work he decides to take on a new partner. On 1 August 2018 he takes on Beta who in exchange for a 35% partnership and a yearly salary of £2,000, agrees to put £10,000 in to the partnership. Alpha decides to take £1,000 p.a. salary from the time Beta joins. Both partners agree to take 5% p.a. interest on capital from the time Beta joins. Below is a trial balance for the 2018 period. Draw up the appropriation account and the partners' current accounts (for current a/cs, see p 70, Section C   The current accounts).

Trial Balance for period ending 31 December 2018

	DR £	CR £
Cash a/c	49,500	
Recovery van a/c	4,000	
Mechanical equip. a/c	6,500	
Staff salaries a/c	17,000	
Expenses a/c	12,500	
Rent a/c	10,000	
Debtors a/c	28,000	
Creditors a/c		7,500
Bills paid		139,500
Partners' capital accounts:		
Alpha		20,000
Beta		10,000
Partners' drawings:		
Alpha	45,500	
Beta	4,000	
Balance	177,000	177,000

NB: Profit for the period is bills paid (£139,500) less staff salaries (£17,000), expenses (£12,500) and rent (£10,000) = £100,000

Alpha & Beta
Appropriation account
1 January 2018 - 31 July 2018

	£	£	£
Net profit (7 out of 12 months = 7/12 of total profit) ie 100,000 x (7/12)			58,333.33
Alpha (the owner)			58,333.33

Alpha & Beta
Appropriation account
1 August 2018 - 31 December 2018

	£	£	£
Net profit (5 out of 12 months = 5/12 of total profit) ie 100,000 x (5/12)			41,666.67 ❶

Interest on capital
Alpha (5/12 x £20,000 x 5%)   416.67
Beta (5/12 x £10,000 x 5%)   208.33   625.00 ❷

Partners' salaries
Alpha (5/12 x £1,000)   416.67
Beta (5/12 x £2,000)   833.33   1,250.00 ❸

Profit division
Alpha (65%)   25,864.59 ❺
Beta (35%)   13,927.08   39,791.67 ❹

41,666.67 ❶

First: write these
Second: calculate interest on capital and total
Third: calculate partners' salaries and total
Fourth: write in profit division [❶-(❷+❸)]
Fifth: split ❹ into individual partners

69

C The current accounts

➤ Each partner will have a current account, showing how much the business owes him (or how much he owes the business!).

➤ Each current account will be in a 'T' a/c format.

◆ The example below is based on the facts on the previous page:

Current a/c - Alpha			
DR		CR	
		31.12.18	
		profit div no.1	58,333.33
		31.12.18	
		int. on capital	416.67
31.7.18		**31.12.18**	
Drawings	45,500.00	partner salary	416.67
31.7.18		**31.12.18**	
balance c/f	39,531.26	profit div no.2	25,864.59
	85,031.26		85,031.26
		31.7.18	
		balance b/f	39,531.26

Current a/c - Beta			
DR		CR	
		31.12.18	
		int. on capital	208.33
31.7.18		**31.12.18**	
Drawings	4,000.00	partner salary	833.33
31.7.18		**31.12.18**	
balance c/f	10,968.74	profit div	13,927.08
	14,968.74		14,968.74
		31.7.18	
		balance b/f	10,968.74

➤ The current accounts are also presented in a certain format as notes to the balance sheet (see D below).

D The balance sheet

➤ The 'capital employed' section of the pro forma balance sheet (p 66) is made up of:

◆ the partners' capital accounts, *and*

◆ the partners' current accounts.

➤ A note to the balance sheet lists the make-up of the current accounts.

➤ ALWAYS do the capital account first, followed by the balance sheet, even though they are displayed the other way round.

➤ An example based on the facts from the previous example is on the facing page.

E Revaluations of assets

➤ A revaluation of each asset is usually carried out on a change in the partnership or a change in the profit-sharing ratio between them.

➤ A revaluation 'T' a/c is opened and the following adjustments are made:

	Revaluation a/c	Asset a/c	Partner capital a/c
Increase in asset value	CREDIT	DEBIT	
Decrease in asset value	DEBIT	CREDIT	
Profit on revaluation (close revaluation a/c)	DEBIT		CREDIT
Loss on revaluation (close revaluation a/c)	CREDIT		DEBIT

any credits/debits are in the agreed partner ratio of sharing profits and losses

Fully worked example (continued)

Balance sheet of Alpha and Beta as of 31st December 2018

	£	£	£
FIXED ASSETS			
Recovery van - cost		4,000	
Mechanical equipment - cost		6,500	10,500
ADD: CURRENT ASSETS			
Debtors		28,000	
Cash at bank		49,500	77,500
LESS: CURRENT LIABILITIES			
Creditors		7,500	7,500
NET CURRENT ASSETS			80,500
NET ASSETS			80,500
Capital employed			
Capital accounts			
Alpha	20,000		
Beta	10,000	30,000	
Current accounts (see note 1)			
Alpha	39,531.26		
Beta	10,968.74	50,500	80,500

Do the balance sheet after the current accounts

Do this first

Put these figures into the balance sheet

Notes to the balance sheet
Note (1)

Current accounts	Alpha	Beta
Interest on capital	416.67	208.33
Partners' salaries	416.67	803.33
Profit division no. 1	58,333.33	0.00
Profit division no. 2	25,864.59	13,927.08
	85,031.26	14,938.74
Less drawings	45,500.00	4,000.00
Balance	39,531.26	10,938.74

E   Interpreting accounts

I   Generally

II   Ratios

I   Generally

➤   When compiling accounts, accountants use guidance which the accountancy profession produces under the auspices, in the UK, of the Accounting Standards Board. ASB guidance sets out UK generally accepted accounting practice ('UK GAAP').

➤   For accounting periods beginning on or after 1 January 2005:

a)   an EU company with listed equity securities is required to draw up group accounts in accordance with International Financial Reporting Standards ('IFRS') (overseen by the International Accounting Standards Board) as endorsed by the EU Commission, *and*

b)   other companies and LLPs incorporated under English law may elect to adopt IFRS.

●   For more on this, see the *Banking & Capital Markets Companion*.

➤   Where a feature of the accounts is unusual, or requires explanation, it should be explained in the 'Notes' found at the back of the accounts.   These 'Notes' are an important aid to understanding accounts.

➤   In addition to information to be found in the 'Notes' the use of ratios provides a rough and ready way to:

◆   identify trends in a business (by comparing ratios in successive sets of accounts), *and/or*

◆   compare a business with other businesses in the same sector, or of a similar size.

➤   Some frequently used ratios, which are examined below, are designed to measure:

a)   profitability, *or*

b)   financial risk, *or*

c)   cashflow.

●   Ratios should be used with caution - like all statistics they are misleading if looked at in isolation. Ratios are best used as a stimulus to ask questions about an enterprise (eg: why is 'dividend cover' so low?) rather than as a source of objective information.

II   Ratios

A Profitability

➤   The ratios which are used to assess a business's profitability, including the following:

1   Return on capital employed ('ROCE')

➤   This ratio relates 'profit before interest and tax' ('PBIT') to the working capital invested in a business.

➤   ROCE can be expressed as:

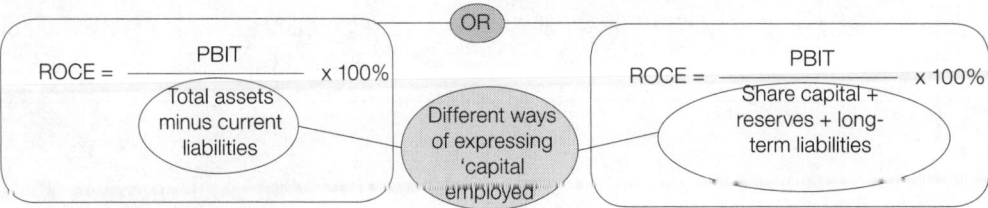

$$ROCE = \frac{PBIT}{\text{Total assets minus current liabilities}} \times 100\%$$

OR   Different ways of expressing 'capital employed'

$$ROCE = \frac{PBIT}{\text{Share capital + reserves + long-term liabilities}} \times 100\%$$

2 Asset turnover

➤ This ratio indicates the volume of sales the enterprise is generating using its assets/capital.

➤ The formula is:

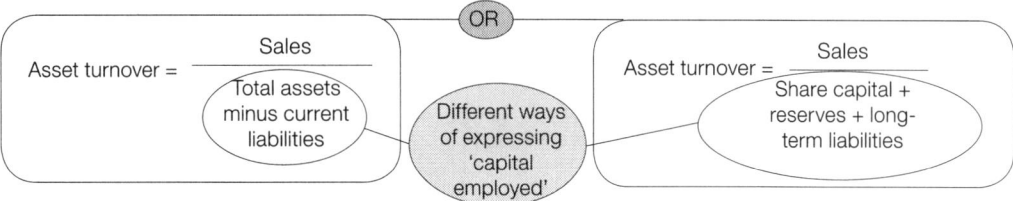

3 Profit margin

➤ This ratio can be used to measure an enterprise's gross profit margin (before general expenses are deducted) or net profit margin (after general expenses are deducted).

$$\text{Gross margin} = \frac{\text{Gross profit (sales less cost of sales)}}{\text{Sales turnover}} \times 100\%$$

$$\text{Net margin} = \frac{\text{Net profit (sales less all costs)}}{\text{Sales turnover}} \times 100\%$$

4 Ratios for companies with share capital

➤ Earnings per share ('EPS'): this shows how much profit is earned on each share.

$$\text{Earnings per share} = \frac{\text{Profit}}{\text{Number of issued shares}}$$

◆ EPS has in the past frequently been used (indeed over used) as an indicator of whether shares are under or over priced.

● EPS is open to abuse, as the calculation of 'profit' or the use of complex capital structures mean that it can be manipulated.

● Note also the importance of cultural/economic influences when interpreting EPS as, for instance, the EPS is traditionally lower in the UK and the USA (eg: 10x-15x) than on the Japanese market (eg: 20x-25x) while an internet ('.com') stock may have a large market capitalisation running into billions of dollars but generate no profit (or even incur a loss).

➤ Dividend cover: this relates the dividends a company pays to the profits the company earns.

$$\text{Dividend cover} = \frac{\text{Earnings per share}}{\text{Dividend per share}}$$

◆ Note that a dividend cover of less than 1 means that the company is paying dividends out of retained profits earned in previous years, a cover of 1 or more indicates dividends are being paid out of current earnings.

● Public companies often maintain a dividend cover of 1.5 to 3 (eg: in the latter case £1 paid out for every £3 of profits).

B Financial risk

➤ The following ratios are used to assess whether a company is likely to be unable to meet its obligations to its creditors.

1 Gearing

➤ Gearing relates debt finance to equity finance.

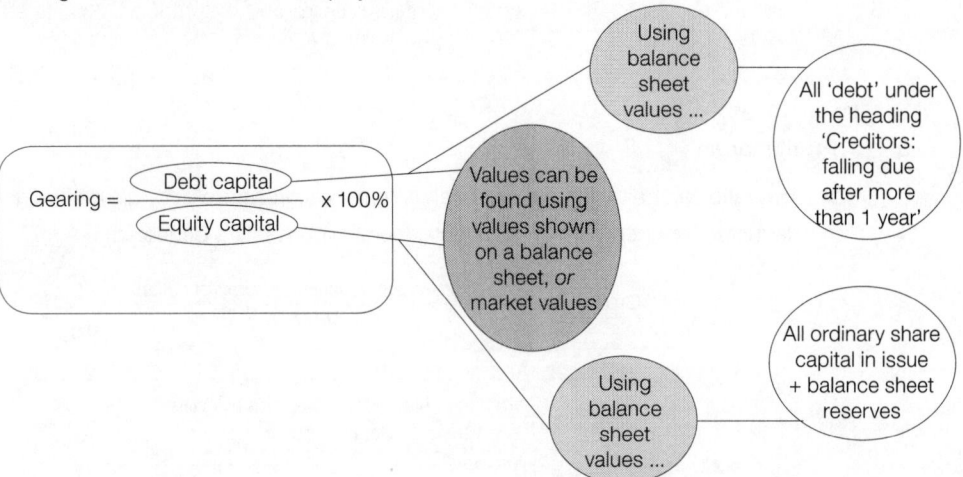

- ◆ Gearing can be measured in a number of different ways. For example, 'Total capital' can be used instead of equity capital.

➤ Whether 'gearing' (also known as 'leverage') is too high, or too low, depends on market conditions and the business sector in which the enterprise is operating. The higher the gearing, the more the equity capital may be perceived to be at risk.

2 Interest cover

➤ This ratio is a measure of credit risk - it shows how comfortably an enterprise can meet its interest obligations to creditors.

$$\text{Interest cover} = \frac{\text{PBIT (profit before interest and tax)}}{\text{Interest charges}}$$

3 Working capital

➤ This ratio reflects the amount of capital which is used to finance the enterprise from day-to-day.

$$\text{Working capital} = \text{'Current Assets' - 'Current Liabilities'}$$

- ◆ Put another way, 'working capital' equals 'net current assets'.

C   Cashflow

➤   Cashflow is essential to any enterprise.   Without sufficient liquidity to pay its liabilities as they fall due even an enterprise which on paper is extremely profitable will go bust.

➤   The following ratios offer a measure of how liquid an enterprise is:

1   Stock turnover ratio

➤   This ratio shows the average number of days it takes an enterprise to turn its stock over.

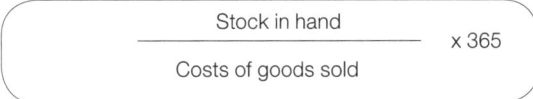

$$\frac{\text{Stock in hand}}{\text{Costs of goods sold}} \times 365$$

2   Debtor days

➤   This ratio reveals the average number of days' credit which the enterprise's customers are allowed.

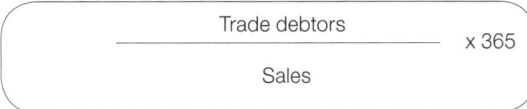

$$\frac{\text{Trade debtors}}{\text{Sales}} \times 365$$

3   'Acid test' ratio

➤   This ratio can be useful if an enterprise necessarily has a slow stock turnover and it should normally exceed 1:1.

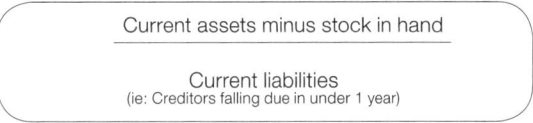

$$\frac{\text{Current assets minus stock in hand}}{\text{Current liabilities} \text{ (ie: Creditors falling due in under 1 year)}}$$

4   Current ratio

➤   This ratio demonstrates whether an enterprise can meet its current liabilities.

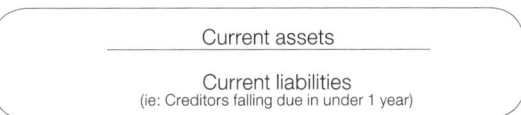

$$\frac{\text{Current assets}}{\text{Current liabilities} \text{ (ie: Creditors falling due in under 1 year)}}$$

F   *Solicitors' Accounts Rules 2011*

I   Generally

II   Interest

I   Generally

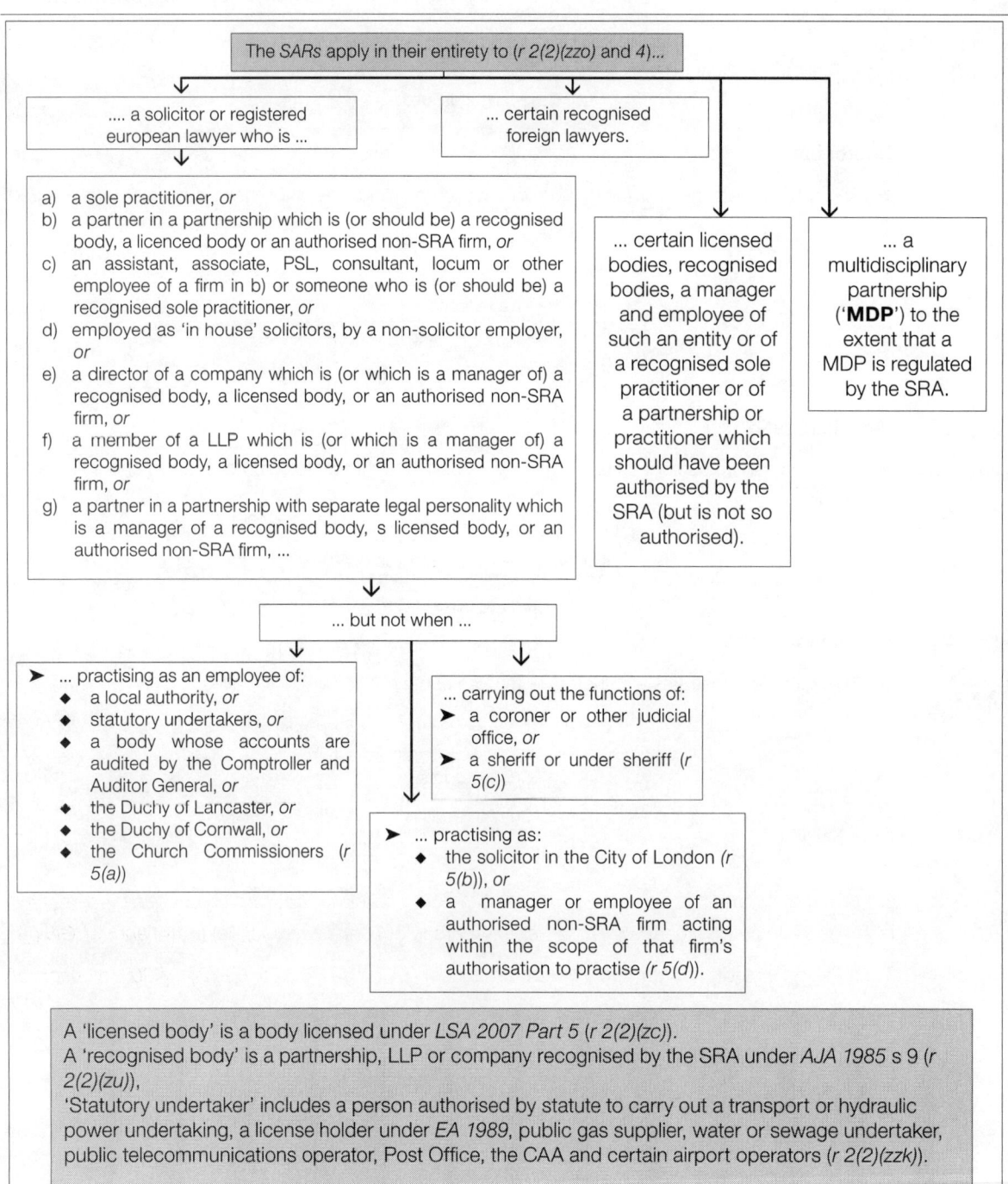

The *SARs* apply in their entirety to (*r 2(2)(zzo)* and *4*)...

.... a solicitor or registered european lawyer who is ...

a) a sole practitioner, *or*
b) a partner in a partnership which is (or should be) a recognised body, a licenced body or an authorised non-SRA firm, *or*
c) an assistant, associate, PSL, consultant, locum or other employee of a firm in b) or someone who is (or should be) a recognised sole practitioner, *or*
d) employed as 'in house' solicitors, by a non-solicitor employer, *or*
e) a director of a company which is (or which is a manager of) a recognised body, a licensed body, or an authorised non-SRA firm, *or*
f) a member of a LLP which is (or which is a manager of) a recognised body, a licensed body, or an authorised non-SRA firm, *or*
g) a partner in a partnership with separate legal personality which is a manager of a recognised body, s licensed body, or an authorised non-SRA firm, ...

... certain recognised foreign lawyers.

... certain licensed bodies, recognised bodies, a manager and employee of such an entity or of a recognised sole practitioner or of a partnership or practitioner which should have been authorised by the SRA (but is not so authorised).

... a multidisciplinary partnership ('**MDP**') to the extent that a MDP is regulated by the SRA.

... but not when ...

➤ ... practising as an employee of:
   ◆ a local authority, *or*
   ◆ statutory undertakers, *or*
   ◆ a body whose accounts are audited by the Comptroller and Auditor General, *or*
   ◆ the Duchy of Lancaster, *or*
   ◆ the Duchy of Cornwall, *or*
   ◆ the Church Commissioners (*r 5(a)*)

... carrying out the functions of:
➤ a coroner or other judicial office, *or*
➤ a sheriff or under sheriff (*r 5(c)*)

➤ ... practising as:
   ◆ the solicitor in the City of London (*r 5(b)*), *or*
   ◆ a manager or employee of an authorised non-SRA firm acting within the scope of that firm's authorisation to practise (*r 5(d)*).

A 'licensed body' is a body licensed under *LSA 2007 Part 5* (*r 2(2)(zc)*).
A 'recognised body' is a partnership, LLP or company recognised by the SRA under *AJA 1985 s 9* (*r 2(2)(zu)*),
'Statutory undertaker' includes a person authorised by statute to carry out a transport or hydraulic power undertaking, a license holder under *EA 1989*, public gas supplier, water or sewage undertaker, public telecommunications operator, Post Office, the CAA and certain airport operators (*r 2(2)(zzk)*).

'Solicitor', for the remainder of this section, refers to anyone subject to the SARs in their entirety

Overarching objective and underlying principles (*r 1*)

➤ The over arching objective of these rules is for client money to be kept safe.

➤ A solicitor must comply with the Principles set out in the SRA Handbook and the *SRA SCC r 1.* In particular, a solicitor must:

a) keep other people's money separate from money belonging to the solicitor *or* the solicitor's firm, *and*

b) keep other people's money safely in a 'bank' *or* 'building society' account identifiable as a client account except where the rules specifically provide otherwise, *and*

- A 'bank' is an institution authorised under the Banking Act 1987, the Post Office, or the Bank of England (*r 2(2)(g)*).

- A 'building society' is a society within the meaning of the Building Societies Act 1986 (*r 2(2)(h)*).

d) use each client's money for each client's matters only, *and*

e) use money held as trustee of a trust for the purposes of that trust only, *and*

f) establish and maintain proper accounting systems, and proper internal controls over those systems, to ensure compliance with the *SARs*, *and*

g) keep proper accounting records to show accurately the position with regard to the money held for each client and each trust, *and*

h) account for interest on other people's money in accordance with the rules, *and*

i) co-operate with the SRA in checking compliance with these rules, *and*

j) deliver annual accountant's reports as required by the rules.

1 Responsibility for compliance (*r 6*)

➤ A principal (and a director of a recognised body and a COFA) must ensure compliance by him or herself and everyone employed in a practice (and, in the case of a director, by a recognised body).

- A 'COFA' is a compliance officer for finance and administration appointed in accordance with *SRA Authorisation Rules for Legal Services Bodies and Licenced Bodies 2011, r 8(5)*.

- Guidance notes (cited in this Section as 'GN') set out in the *SARs* do not form part of the rules (*r 2(1)*).

➤ A person who acts as a trustee in a purely personal capacity outside any legal practice is not subject to the *SARs* in respect of that trusteeship; a trustee who charges for acting as a trustee does not act in a personal capacity

- The use of professional notepaper indicates that a trusteeship is not undertaken in a purely personal capacity (*r 4:GN (iii)*).

➤ A person may continue to be bound by some of the *SARs* if that person has held or received client money, and ceases to do so (irrespective of whether that person continues to practice) (*r 4(4) and r 4:GN (i)*).

- These rules include *r 7* (*duty to remedy breaches*), *r 17(2), 17(8), 29(15)-(24), r 30* (*retention of records*), *r 31* (*production of records*), *Part F* (*accountants' reports*) (*r 4:GN (ii)*).

2 Duty to remedy breaches (*r 7*)

➤ Any breach must be remedied promptly upon discovery.

- This includes replacing money improperly withheld or withdrawn from client account - if necessary by the principals in the practice using their own resources (irrespective of whether a claim is subsequently made under the firm's insurance or the Compensation Fund).

Money a solicitor holds or receives in the course of practise is either (*r 12*):

Client money
Money held and received from a client or as trustee and all other money which is not office money

↓

Includes money held or received:

a) as trustee, *or*
b) as agent, bailee, stakeholder, donee of power of attorney, liquidator, trustee in bankruptcy, Court of Protection deputy, or trustee of an occupational pension scheme, *or*
c) for payment of unpaid professional disbursements, *or*
d) for payment of stamp duty, Land Registry/court fees etc, where the solicitor has not already incurred an obligation to the pay the sum, *or*
e) as a payment on account of costs generally, *or*
f) as a financial benefit (unless the client has given prior authority to retain it under *SRA SCC Ch 1 Outcome 1.15 and Indicative Behaviour 1.20*), *or*
g) jointly with another person outside the firm, *or*
h) to the sender's order
  - NB: a cheque or draft held to a sender's order must not be presented for payment without the sender's consent .
➤ An advance to a client is client money.
➤ A cheque in respect of damages or costs, payable to the client but paid into client account under *r 14(2)(b)* is client money.

Office money
Money which belongs to the solicitor or the firm

↓

Includes:

a) money held or received in connection with running a firm (PAYE, VAT, firm's fees), and
b) interest on general client accounts, *and*
c) payments received in respect of:
d) fees due against a bill or written notification of costs (see *r 17(2)*).
e) disbursements already paid.
f) disbursements incurred (but not paid) (excluding unpaid professional disbursements).
g) money paid for or towards an agreed fee, *and*
h) money held in client account and earmarked for costs under *r 17(3)*, and
i) money held or received from the Legal Services Commission as a regular payment.

Money held for a principal of the firm will be office money (as a solicitor cannot act as his own client) unless the circumstances dictate otherwise, e.g:

- money is held jointly for a principal and a spouse who is not a principal.
- the firm also acts for a lender and money is held for that lender.
- the firm acts for one of its employees, consultants, etc.

➤ Money which is held by a MDP, in relation to activities with respect to which the MDP is not regulated by the SRA, is 'out of scope money' and is not generally subject to these rules (*rr 2(2)(zn)* and *11*).

- Where a MDP receives funds which include out of scope money which is mixed with other types of money *rr 17-18* apply

➤ The *SARs* do not affect a solicitor's rights by way of lien, set off, counterclaim or otherwise against money standing to the credit of client account (*r 11*).

Categories of money *paid into* client account

May be paid into client account (*r 14(2)*)	a) the firm's own money to open or maintain the account, *or* b) an advance from the firm to fund payment on behalf of a client or trust (being in excess of money held for that client or trust), *or* c) money paid in to replace money that has been withdrawn in breach of the *r 20*, *or* d) interest which is paid into client account to enable payment from client account of all money owed to the client *or* e) a cheque in respect of damages and costs, payable by the client, which is paid into client account pursuant to the Law Society's Conditional Fee Agreement.
Must be paid into client account	➤ Client money (*r 14(1)*). ◆ This must be done 'without delay', ie: in normal circumstances, the day of receipt or, if that is not possible, the next working day (*r 2(2)(zzn)*). ➤ However, client money need **not** be paid into client account if the client instructs otherwise, the money is held outside client account for the client's convenience, and those instructions are given in writing or are confirmed in writing (it is improper to seek to take such instructions in the form of terms and conditions or a blanket agreement); *r 15*)
May be withheld from client account (*r 16*)	➤ Client money which is: a) cash received and without delay paid in cash in the ordinary course of business to the client, or on the client's behalf to a third party, or paid in cash in the execution of a trust to a beneficiary or a third party, *or* b) a cheque or banker's draft received and endorsed over in the ordinary course of business to the client, or on the client's behalf to a third party, or without delay endorsed over in the execution of a trust to a beneficiary or a third party, *or* c) money which the client instructs the solicitor not to pay into client account, for the client's own convenience, and instructions are given in writing or are given by other means and confirmed by the solicitor to the client in writing (*SAR r 15*), *or* d) money which, in accordance with a trustee's powers, is paid into or retained in an account of the trustee which is not a client account (eg: an account outside England and Wales), or properly retained in cash in the performance of the trustee's duties, *or* e) unpaid professional disbursements included in a payment of costs under *r 17(1)(b)* or *r 19*, *or* f) withheld on the written authorisation of the SRA.

Categories of money *withdrawn* from client account (*r 20*)

Client money	Office money
↓	

a) properly required for a payment to or on behalf of a client (or another person on whose behalf the money is being held), *or*

b) properly required for a payment in the execution of a trust, including the purchase of an investment (other than money) in accordance with the trustee's powers, *or*

c) properly required for the payment of a disbursement on behalf of the client or trust, *or*

d) properly required in full or partial reimbursement of money spent by the solicitor on behalf of the client or trust, *or*

e) transferred to another client account, *or*

f) withdrawn on the client's instructions, provided the instructions are for the client's convenience and are given in writing or by other means and confirmed by the solicitor to the client in writing, *or*

g) transferred to an account other than a client account (eg: an account outside England and Wales), or retained in cash, by a trustee in the proper performance of his duties, *or*

h) a refund to the solicitor of an advance no longer required to fund a payment on behalf of a client or trust, *or*

i) money paid in breach of the rules, *or*

j) money not covered by a) to i) above, where the solicitor pays a sum not exceeding £50 to charity (having first fulfilled various procedural requirements), *or*

k) money not covered by a) to i) above, withdrawn on the written SRA authorisation, *or*

l) out of scope money (in accordance with *rr 17-18*).

a) paid in to open the account or maintain it under *r 14(2)(a)*, *or*

b) properly required for payment of the solicitor's costs under (*r 17(2)-(3)*), *or*

c) the whole or part of a payment into client account under *r 17(1)*), *or*

d) part of a mixed payment placed in client account under *r 18(2)(b)*.

A Types of client account

➤ A solicitor who holds or receives client money must generally keep a client account at a 'bank' or a 'building society'; the naming of the account must comply with certain formal requirements (*r 13(1)-(3)*).

◆ A bank account or building society account must be at a branch or a head office in England and Wales (*r 13(4)*).

● A 'bank' means an institution with permission to accept deposits under *FSMA 2000 Part IV* (including a UK branch of an EEA firm permitted in another EC member state to accept deposits), the Post Office, or the Bank of England (*r 2(2)(g)*).

● A 'building society' means a building society for the purposes of the *BSA 1986* (*r 2(2)(h)*).

➤ A client account may be either (*r 13(5)*):

a) a separate designated client account - a deposit or share account relating to a single client, other person or trust, *or*

b) a general client account.

B Mixed payments into client account

➤ A mixed payment includes both client money and office money.

➤ A mixed payment must either be *(r 18(2))*:

a) split as appropriate, *or*

b) placed without delay in client account (in which case all office money and out-of-scope money must be transferred out of client account within 14 days of receipt (*r 18(3)*).

C Withdrawing money from client account

➤ Money paid into client account in breach of the rules must be withdrawn promptly on discovery (*r 20(5)*).

◆ Out-of-scope money must be withdrawn in accordance with rules *17(1)(a)*, *17(1)(c)* and *18* (*r 20(4)*).

➤ Money withdrawn from a general client account must not exceed the money held on behalf of the particular client or trust in all the solicitor's general client accounts unless:

a) sufficient money is held for that client or trust in a separate designated client account, *and*

b) the appropriate transfer from the separate designated client account to a general client account is made immediately (*r 20(6)-(7)*).

➤ Money held for a particular client or trust must not be used for payments for another client or trust (*r 20(8)*).

➤ A client account must not be overdrawn except in the following circumstances (*r 20(9)*):

a) a separate designated client account of solicitor trustees, if the trustee(s) makes payments on behalf of the trust (eg: for IHT) before realising sufficient assets to cover the payments, *or*

b) a sole practitioner dies and his or client accounts are frozen, in which case the solicitor-manager can operate client accounts which are overdrawn to the extent of money held in the frozen accounts.

D   Receipt and transfer of costs

➤ A solicitor who properly requires payment of fees from money held for a client or trust in client account must first give or send a bill of costs, or other notification of costs, to the client or paying party (*r 17(2)*).

◆ When this has been done, money earmarked for costs becomes office money and must be transferred out of client account within 14 days (*r 17(3)*).

➤ Where a fee is fixed (this does not include a fee that can be varied upwards or that is dependent on a transaction being completed) it must be paid into office account (and the fee must be evidenced in writing) (*r 17(5)*).

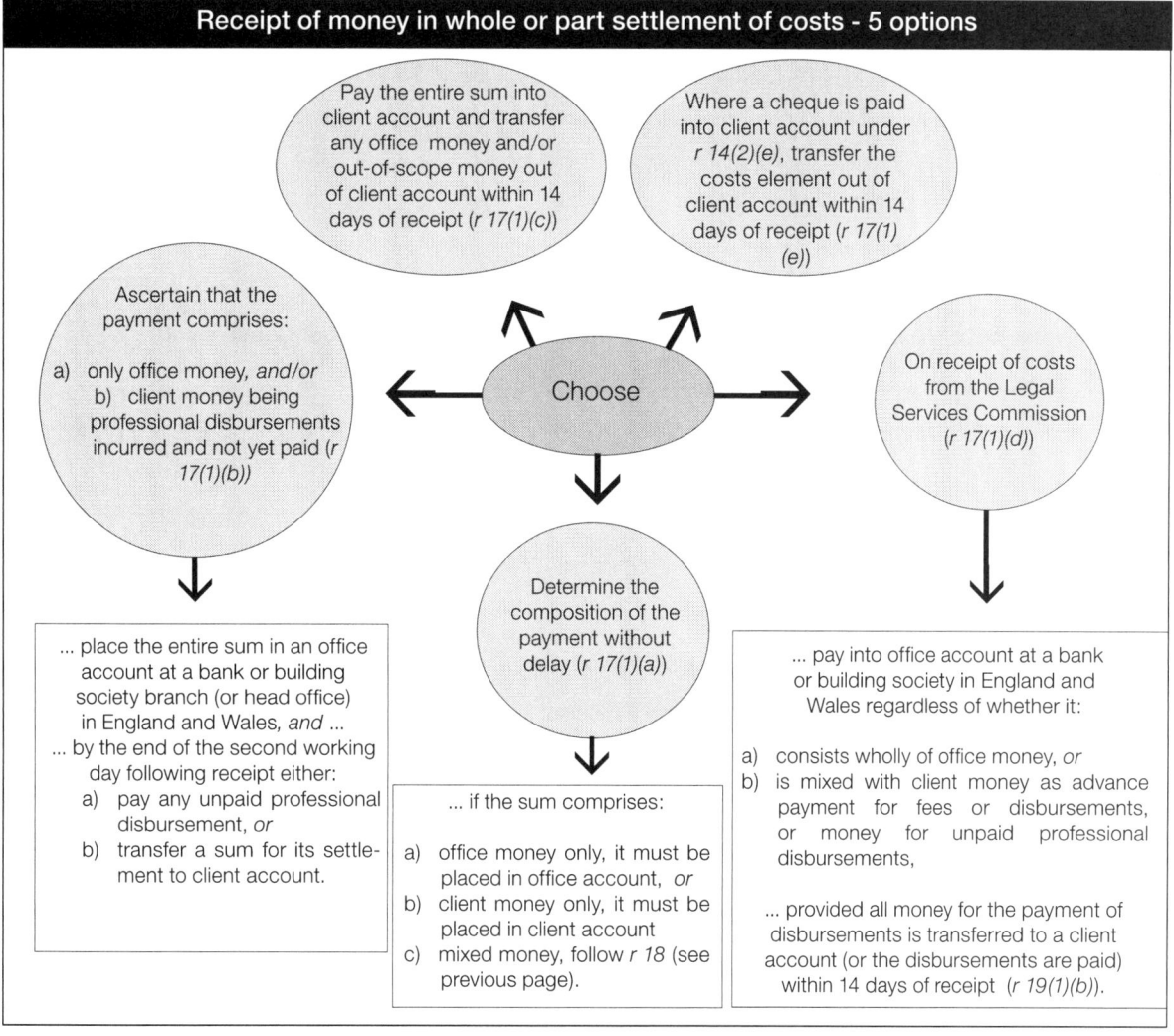

➤ Client money must be returned to a client promptly, as soon as there is no longer any proper reason to retain it (*r 14(3)*).

◆ A solicitor must promptly notify a client in writing of the amount of any client money which the solicitor retains at the end (or substantial conclusion of) a matter and the reason for retaining that money (*r 14(4)*).

● This notification must be updated at least once every 12 months (*r 14(4)*).

➤ Where an amount does no exceed £50 in relation to an individual matter, a solicitor may pay funds to a charity provided the solicitor:

a)   establishes the identity of the owner (or makes reasonable attempts to do so, unless the cost of doing so would be excessive), *and*

b)   records the steps taken under a) and the payment (including a receipt from the charity), *and*

c)   keeps a central register of such payments in accordance with *r 29(22)* (*r 22(2)*).

E Payments to Legal Aid practitioners

1   **Payments from the Legal Services Commission (the 'Commission')**

➤ An advance which may include client money may be placed in office account (*r 19(1)(a)*).

◆ This may be done only if the Commission instructs in writing that this may be done.

➤ A payment for costs may be paid into office account (*r 19(1)(b)*) (see previous page).

➤ A payment for regular work (eg: regular payments under civil or legal aid contracting arrangements) must be paid into office account at a bank or building society in England and Wales (*r 19(2)(b)*).

➤ Within 28 days of submitting a report to the Commission notifying it of completion of a matter (or, if permitted by the Commission to notify it at other stages, within 28 days of submitting such a report), a solicitor must either:

a) pay any unpaid professional disbursements, *or*

b) transfer to client account an amount equivalent to any unpaid professional disbursements relating to that matter (*r 19(2)(c)-(d)*).

2   **Payments from a third party where payment previously received from the Commission**

➤ When the Commission has made payments of (*r 19(3)*):

a) costs to a solicitor or to a previously nominated solicitor (advice and assistance costs, legal help costs, advance payments or interim costs), *or*

b) professional disbursements direct, *and ....*

... costs are subsequently settled by a third party:

▪ the entire third party payment must be paid into client account, *and*

▪ a sum representing payments made by the Commission must be retained in client account, *and*

▪ any balance belonging to the solicitor must be transferred to an office account within 14 days of the solicitor sending a report to the Commission containing details of the third party payment, *and*

▪ the sum retained in client account (as representing payments made by the Commission) must be either:

i) recorded in the individual client's ledger account and identified as the Commission's money, *or*

ii) recorded in a ledger account in the Commission's name and identified by reference to the client or matter, *and*

... kept in the client account until notification from the Commission that it has recouped an equivalent sum from subsequent legal help payments due to the solicitor (the retained sum must be transferred to office account within 14 days of notification).

➤ Any part of a third party payment which relates to unpaid professional disbursements or outstanding costs of a client's previous firm is client money, and must be kept in client account until those disbursements or costs are paid (*r 19(4)*).

Some definitions in the *SARs*

'without delay'   in normal circumstances, either the day of receipt or the next day (*r 2(2)(zzn)*)
'costs'   fees and disbursements (*r 2(2)(o)*)
'disbursement'   any sum spent or to be spent by a solicitor on behalf of a client or trust (incl. VAT) (*r 2(2)(r)*)
'professional disbursement' the fees of counsel, lawyer, or of a professional or agent instructed by a solicitor (*r 2(2)(zt)*)
'fees'   a solicitor's own charges or profit costs (incl. VAT) (*r 2(2)(v)*)

Record keeping

➤ A solicitor must keep a properly written up record of all dealings with client money (ie: client money received, held or paid by the solicitor) *(r 29(1))*.

 ◆ The record (ie: a client ledger) must also distinguish a particular client's money from other money held in client account.

 ◆ Each client ledger must show a current balance (but there is no requirement to keep a historic record of previous balances) *(r 29(9))*.

 ◆ Transfers between client ledgers must be recorded through the cash account, or a separate record (often known as a transfer journal, or 'TJ') *(r 29(2))*.

 ◆ A solicitor must keep a record of all bills of costs (distinguishing between profit costs and disbursements), and must record all bills and intimations of costs delivered to clients *(r 29(15))*.

➤ There is no obligation to keep a separate client ledger for a borrower and lender in a conveyancing transaction provided that *(r 29(10))*:

 a) the funds belonging to each client are 'clearly identifiable' (eg: the fact that an amount represents a mortgage advance from a particular lender must be clearly stated in the borrower's ledger), *and*

 b) the lender is an institutional lender providing mortgages in the normal course of its activities. (Consequently, this relaxation of the general rule does not apply if the lender is a private individual.)

➤ At least once every 5 weeks (at least once every 14 weeks in the case of money held by solicitor trustees in a pass-book operated designated client account) a solicitor must *(r 29(12))*:

 a) compare the balances in client ledgers with the cash account balance, *and*

 b) prepare a reconciliation showing the cause of any difference between the two balances and reconcile the cash account with balances shown on client account pass books or statements and money held elsewhere.

➤ A withdrawal from client account must not be made unless there is specific authority signed by an appropriate person (or persons) in accordance with a firm's procedures for signing on client account *(r 21(1))*.

 ◆ An authority may be signed electronically (subject to appropriate safeguards and controls).

  • A firm must put in place systems and controls governing withdrawals from client account. A non-manager owner or a non-employee of an owner of a licensed body may not be permitted to give such authorisation *(r 21(4))*.

 ◆ This rule does not apply to transfers from one general client account to another general client account at the same bank or building society *(r 21(3))*.

 ◆ A solicitor must keep all cheques and copies of authorities (other than cheques) signed under *SAR r 21(1)* for at least 2 years, or must seek written confirmation from a bank or building society that it will retain them for at least 2 years *(r 29(18))*.

➤ A solicitor must keep all accounts, books, ledgers, records, and bank statements as printed and issued by a bank or building society, for at least 6 years from the date of last entry in each document *(r 32(17))*.

II   Interest

1   General obligation to account for interest

➤ A solicitor must account for interest on a client account when it is fair and reasonable to do so to (*r 22(1)*):

◆ a client or trust, if a solicitor holds money in such an account for a client or trust, *or*

◆ a person funding all or part of the solicitor's fees (ie: if a solicitor holds money for such a person).

● A firm must have a written policy which seeks to provide a fair outcome (for the client/trust and the firm) with respect to the payment of interest (*r 22(3)*).

■ A fair outcome is 'unlikely':

a) to provide for a client or trust to receive a sum of interest which is as high as the client could obtain by placing the relevant funds on deposit (*r 22: GN (i)*), *or*

b) to involve only looking at the lowest rate of interest obtainable (*r 23: GN (ii)*), *or*

c) to reflect any arbitrage which arises by reference to the firm's overall banking arrangements (e.g. a lower rate of interest on a client account to reflect more favourable terms on a firm's office account) (*r 23: GN (iii)*).

■ The rate of interest will 'usually' be based on client money being placed in an instant access account to facilitate a transaction (*r 22: GN (ii)*). A firm's policy with respect to interest should take into account (*r 23: GN (ii)*):

a) the amount held, *and*

b) the length of time for which cleared funds are held, *and*

c) the need for instant access to those funds, *and*

d) the rate of interest paid on instant access accounts at the institution where the account is kept, *and*

e) how frequently interest is compounded by that institution.

■ It is good practice to explain a firm's interest rate arrangements to a client (*r 22: GN (iii)*).

■ If a firm wishes to retain part of the interest which accrues money should be held in a general client account (rather than a separate designated account), and interest on that account should be paid into office account (in accordance with *r 12(7)*) (*r 22: GN (iv)*).

■ A firm may decide not to pay interest below a *de minimis* amount (e.g. £20), provided that this amount is reviewed regularly in light to prevailing interest rates (*r 22: GN (v)*).

■ Where a substantial sum is held for a lengthy period of time it is 'likely' to be appropriate for a firm to account for all the interest which accrues in relation to that sum (*r 22: GN (vi)*).

■ Money held in respect of different matters for the same client may 'normally' be treated separately, unless the relevant matters are closely connected (*r 22: GN (vii)*).

➤ This obligation also applies to money which (*r 22(1)*):

◆ should have been held on client account (but was not), *or*

◆ withheld (or which should have been withheld) from client account on a client's instructions (see *r 15*), *or*

◆ is paid into or retained in an account of a trustee (which is not a client account), or properly retained in cash in performance of a trustee's duties (see *r 16(d)*).

➤ The obligation to account for interest does **not** apply (*r 22(2)*):

a) to money held for the payment of a professional disbursement, once counsel has requested a delay in settlement, *or*

b) money held for the Legal Services Commission, *or*

c) on an advance from the solicitor's firm under *r 14(2)(b)* to fund a payment on behalf of a client or trust in excess of the funds held for that client or trust, *or*

d) if there is an agreement in accordance with *r 25* to contract out of the obligation to account for interest, *or*

e) where money is held outside client account on a client's instructions in such a manner that no interest accrues on that money (*r 22: GN (viii)*), or where that money is held in an account in the client's name (ie. as the interest on such an account belongs to the client) (*r 22: GN (ix)*).

2 Special situations

➤ When a firm acts liquidator, trustee in bankruptcy, court of protection deputy, or trustee of an occupational pension scheme, statutory rules may prevent money being held in client account; where such client money is held outside client account the obligation to account for interest does not apply (*r 8 and r 22: GN (xii)*).

➤ The obligation to account for interest does not apply where money is held in a joint account (*r 9 and r 22: GN (xiii)*).

➤ A firm may enter into a written agreement to contract out of the obligation to account for interest which is imposed by *r 22* (*r 25*).

◆ A firm must act fairly towards its client if it and the client agree to contract out; this includes providing the client with sufficient information at the outset to enable the client to give informed consent (*r 25(2)*).

➤ When a firm acts as stakeholder, a firm must account for interest, in accordance with *r 22*, to the person to whom the stake is paid (unless the firm has contracted out of *r 22* with the agreement of its client and other person for whom the stake is held) (*r 24 and r 25(3)*).

G   Keeping accounts as a solicitor

I	Generally
II	Particular entries

I   Generally

➤ In order to comply with *SAR r 1*, a solicitor must use separate bank accounts for client money and office money. Separate cash account ledgers must be kept for each bank (or building society) account (these show amounts paid into / withdrawn from each account).

➤ A solicitor must keep a separate ledger for each client (*SAR r 29*) (these show amounts received from/paid out for each client).

◆ Since there are two separate cash accounts (one for office money and the other for client money), each client effectively has two ledgers - one dealing with that client's 'client money' and the other with that client's 'office money'.

➤ The diagram below shows how the 2 sets of ledgers relate to each other.

◆ The Cash Account shows two separate accounts kept with a bank or building society (client account and office account). The Client Ledger shows the money which the firm is liable to the client for (client money) and which the client owes to the firm (office money).

◆ Note that double entries are never made between the 'office' and 'client' ledgers, but between the those ledgers and the related ledgers in the Cash Account (for instance, when money is paid out of one account and into the other, eg: when a bill of costs is settled).

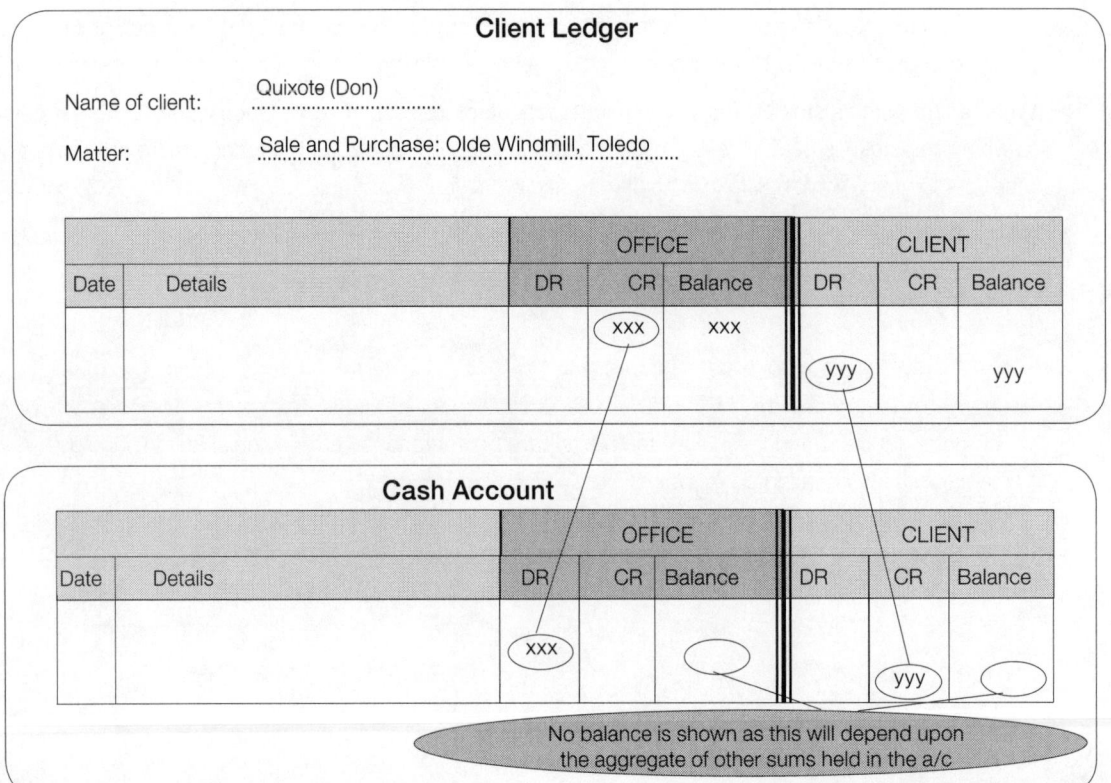

➤ Various formats can be used for ledgers, but the example below illustrates some important features of a Client Ledger comprising two separate sets of 'T' accounts (known as 'ledgers'), one showing office money and the other client money:

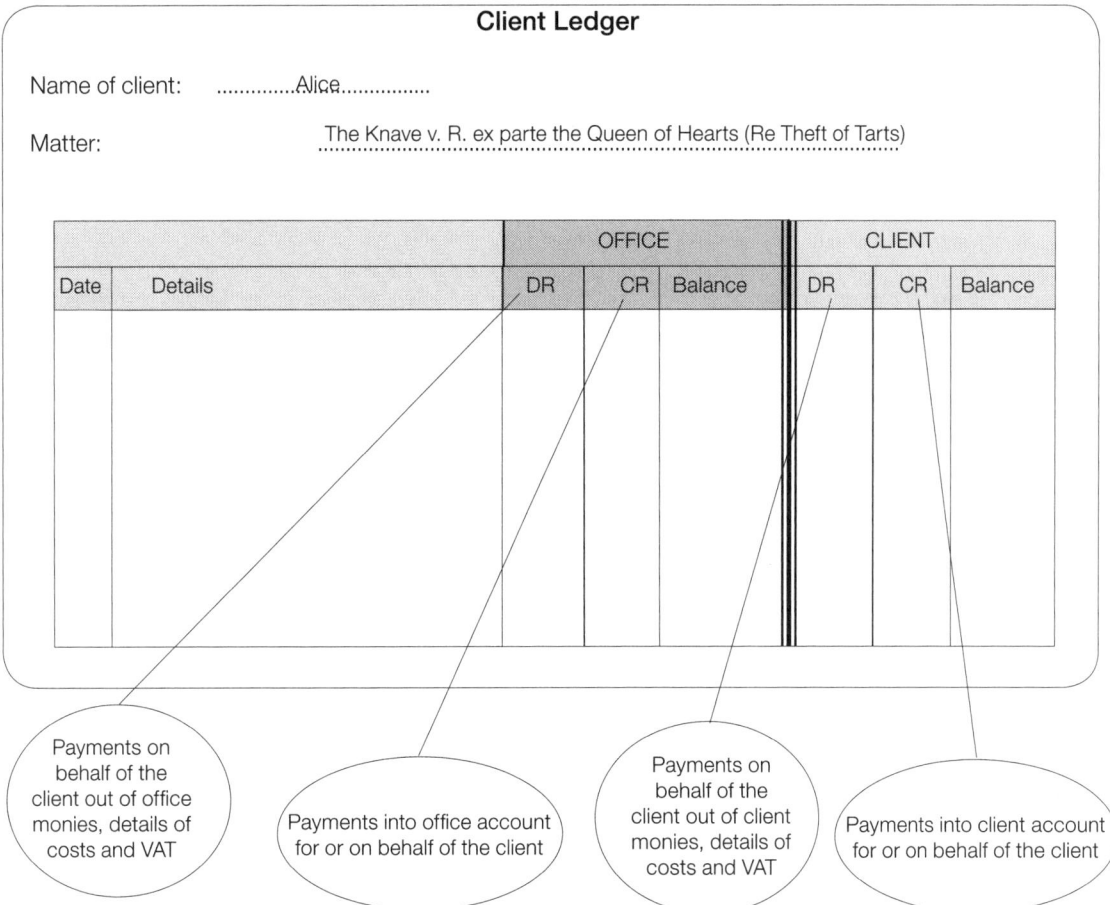

Client Ledger

Name of client: ....Alice...............

Matter: The Knave v. R. ex parte the Queen of Hearts (Re Theft of Tarts)

Date	Details	OFFICE			CLIENT		
		DR	CR	Balance	DR	CR	Balance

- Payments on behalf of the client out of office monies, details of costs and VAT
- Payments into office account for or on behalf of the client
- Payments on behalf of the client out of client monies, details of costs and VAT
- Payments into client account for or on behalf of the client

➤ **The balance in the office ledger should be a debit balance** - it indicates how much the client owes the firm for costs, disbursements etc.

◆ A credit balance (shown by putting 'CR' after the balance) indicates that more has been paid into the office account than is owed by the client to the solicitor - this usually (but not always, see below for the treatment of 'agreed fees') shows that the *SARs* have been breached.

➤ **The balance in the client ledger should be a credit balance** - it indicates how much money the solicitor holds on the client's behalf.

◆ A debit balance (shown by putting 'DR' after the balance) indicates that money has been withdrawn which does not belong to the client - the *SARs* have been breached and remedial action should be taken immediately (ie: by making good the deficiency with office money).

➤ **Description** - always 'describe' the corresponding account entry (so that you can match the entries to each other) then add any further information (see next page for an example).

A note on terminology

In the following pages the word 'Ledger' (with an upper case 'L') is used
to refer to the Client Ledger recording office and client money associated
with a particular client. It is also used to refer to Cash Account and other
ledgers recording client or office monies (eg: Profit Costs a/c).
A 'ledger' ('l' in lower case) dealing with 'client money' or 'office money'
is called a 'column'. This is purely to avoid the confusion sometimes
occasioned by accounting terminology which uses the term 'ledger' in more
than one context. Thus, the 'columns' are themselves 'ledgers' (ie: separate
'T' accounts) relating respectively to 'office money' and 'client money'
which are written up, for the sake of convenience, in the same 'Ledger'.

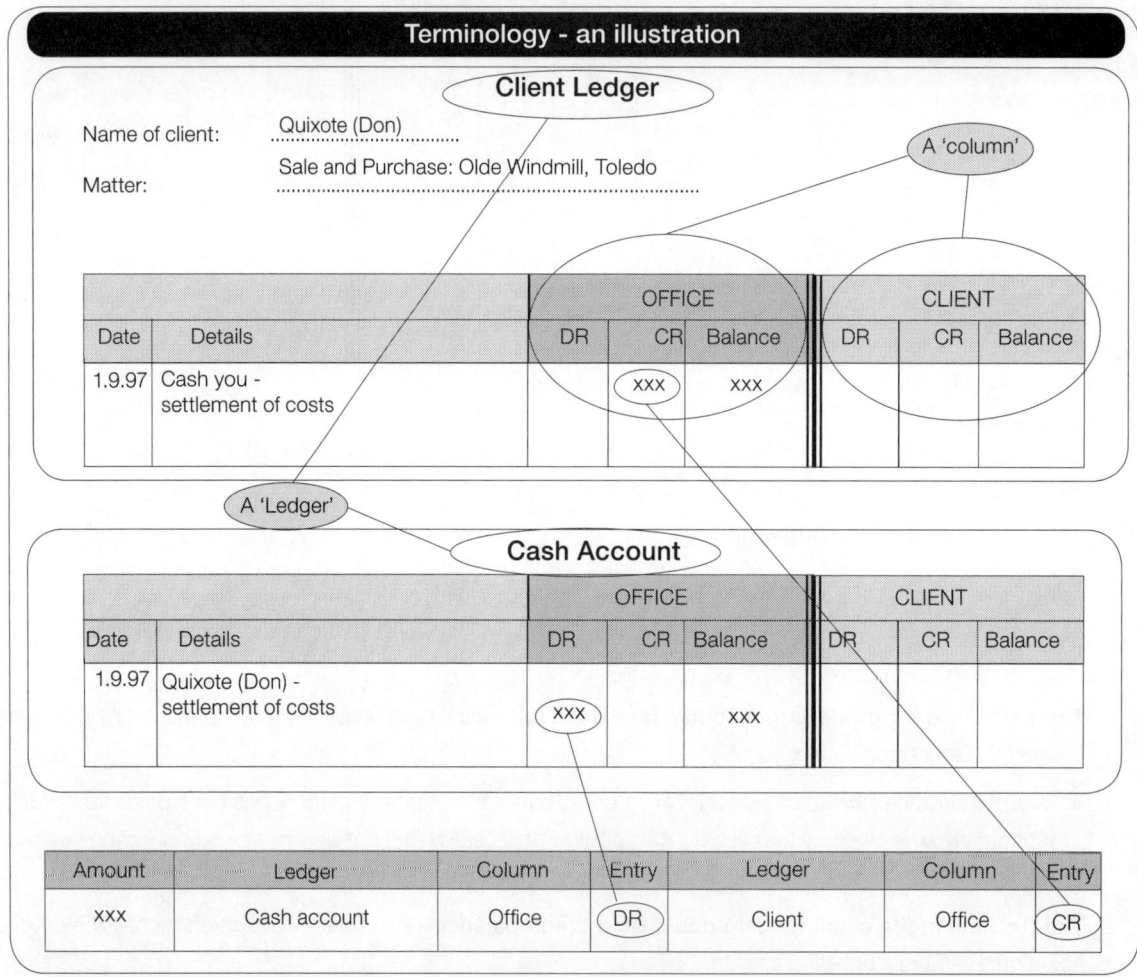

Terminology - an illustration

Client Ledger

Name of client: Quixote (Don)

Matter: Sale and Purchase: Olde Windmill, Toledo

A 'column'

Date	Details	OFFICE			CLIENT		
		DR	CR	Balance	DR	CR	Balance
1.9.97	Cash you - settlement of costs		xxx	xxx			

A 'Ledger'

Cash Account

Date	Details	OFFICE			CLIENT		
		DR	CR	Balance	DR	CR	Balance
1.9.97	Quixote (Don) - settlement of costs	xxx		xxx			

Amount	Ledger	Column	Entry	Ledger	Column	Entry
xxx	Cash account	Office	DR	Client	Office	CR

Problem solving hints

➤ Get into the habit of thinking of entries in a particular order with its own logic, eg: (following the cash)

a) is it client money or office money? (This dictates which 'column' is correct)

b) is it a receipt into Cash Account (always DR) or a payment out of Cash Account (always a CR)?

c) which Ledger should the corresponding CR entry (or DR entry) go in?

... does the column 'balance' as it should, or would the proposed entries breach the *SARs*?

I   Particular entries

1   Costs and disbursements

➤ When a bill of costs is delivered to a client the following entries are made:

Amount	Ledger	Column	Entry	Ledger	Column	Entry
Costs	Client	Office	DR	Profit costs account	Office	CR

➤ When the bill is paid either:

a) the payment should be paid into office account as office money (*SAR rr 17(1)(a)-(b)*), or

Amount	Ledger	Column	Entry	Ledger	Column	Entry
Costs	Cash account	Office	DR	Office	Office	CR

- By the end of the 2nd working day following receipt, either (*SAR r 19(1)(b)*):

  - unpaid professional disbursements must be paid, *or*

Amount	Ledger	Column	Entry	Ledger	Column	Entry
Unpaid disbursement	Cash account	Office	CR	Office	Office	DR

  - a sum must have been transferred for the settlement of those disbursements to client account.

Out of office a/c

Amount	Ledger	Column	Entry	Ledger	Column	Entry
Unpaid disbursement	Cash account	Office	CR	Office	Office	DR

In to client a/c

Amount	Ledger	Column	Entry	Ledger	Column	Entry
Unpaid disbursement	Cash account	Client	DR	Client	Client	CR

b) pay the entire sum into client account and transfer any office money out of client account within 14 days (*SAR r 17(1)(c)*).

Into client a/c

Amount	Ledger	Column	Entry	Ledger	Column	Entry
Payment	Cash account	Client	DR	Client	Client	CR

Out of client a/c

Amount	Ledger	Column	Entry	Ledger	Column	Entry
Costs	Cash account	Client	CR	Client	Client	DR

Into office a/c

Amount	Ledger	Column	Entry	Ledger	Column	Entry
Costs	Cash account	Office	DR	Client	Office	CR

c) if the payment is mixed with other monies which are client money, and the solicitor does not split the cheque, the cheque should be paid into client account and the relevant amount subsequently transferred to office account (*SAR rr 17(1)(a), 18*). (The entries are as in b) above)

- Note that it is very unusual to 'split' a cheque as cheques are nowadays often crossed 'a/c payee' and so cannot be split. If a cheque is 'split', both portions are accounted for as separate payments into office and client account.

➤ Disbursements and sums paid on the client's behalf may be paid from client account if there is a sufficient balance and the solicitor has express or implied authority to make the payment. If there is not enough money in client account, then office money must be used.

2   **Sums received on account of costs**

➤ These are client money and should be entered on the client account.

Amount	Ledger	Column	Entry	Ledger	Column	Entry
Costs	Cash account	Client	DR	Client	Client	CR

3   **VAT**

➤ These are client money and should be entered on the client account.

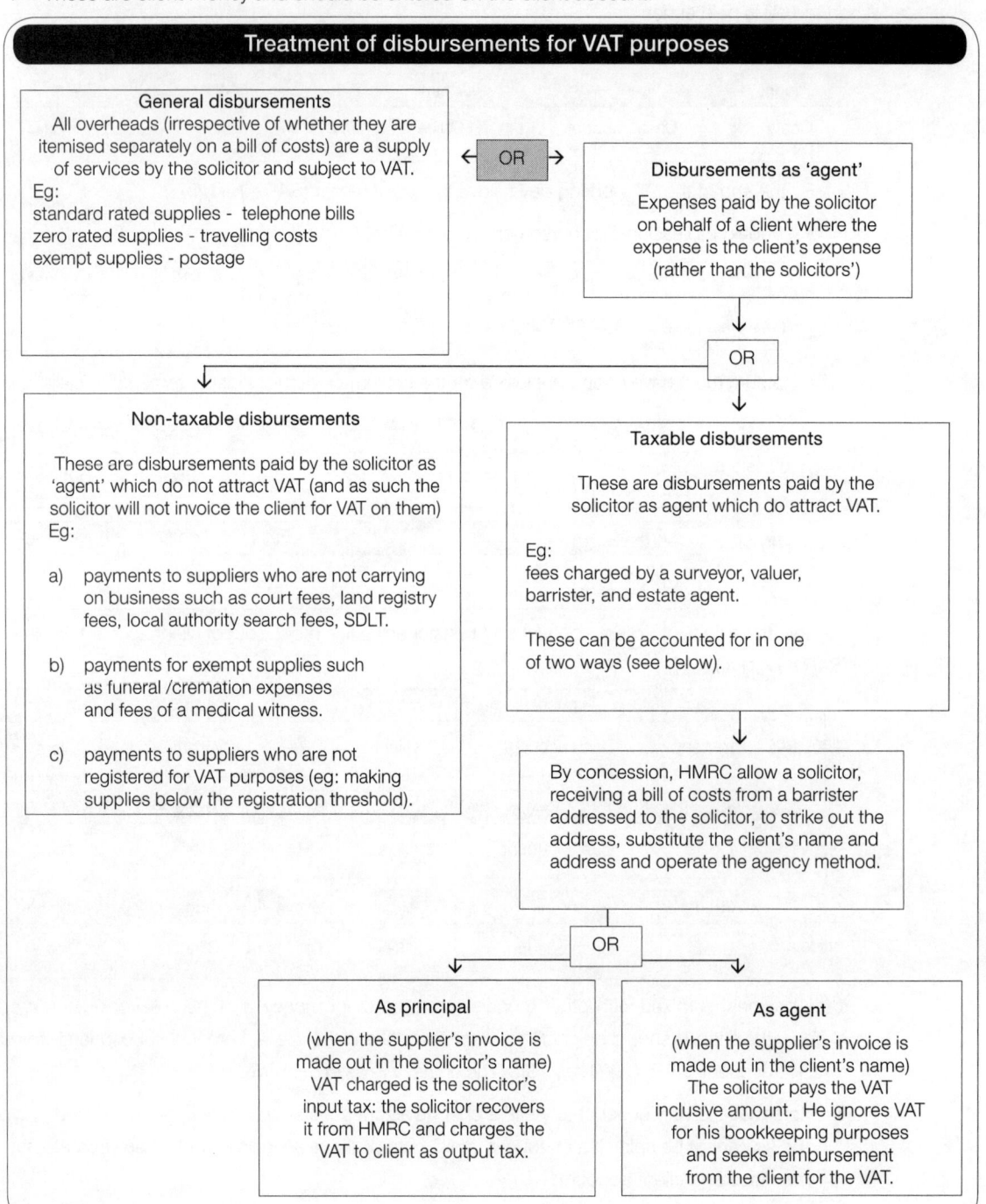

Treatment of disbursements for VAT purposes

General disbursements
All overheads (irrespective of whether they are itemised separately on a bill of costs) are a supply of services by the solicitor and subject to VAT.
Eg:
standard rated supplies - telephone bills
zero rated supplies - travelling costs
exempt supplies - postage

← OR →

Disbursements as 'agent'
Expenses paid by the solicitor on behalf of a client where the expense is the client's expense (rather than the solicitors')

OR

Non-taxable disbursements

These are disbursements paid by the solicitor as 'agent' which do not attract VAT (and as such the solicitor will not invoice the client for VAT on them)
Eg:

a) payments to suppliers who are not carrying on business such as court fees, land registry fees, local authority search fees, SDLT.

b) payments for exempt supplies such as funeral /cremation expenses and fees of a medical witness.

c) payments to suppliers who are not registered for VAT purposes (eg: making supplies below the registration threshold).

Taxable disbursements

These are disbursements paid by the solicitor as agent which do attract VAT.

Eg:
fees charged by a surveyor, valuer, barrister, and estate agent.

These can be accounted for in one of two ways (see below).

By concession, HMRC allow a solicitor, receiving a bill of costs from a barrister addressed to the solicitor, to strike out the address, substitute the client's name and address and operate the agency method.

OR

As principal

(when the supplier's invoice is made out in the solicitor's name)
VAT charged is the solicitor's input tax: the solicitor recovers it from HMRC and charges the VAT to client as output tax.

As agent

(when the supplier's invoice is made out in the client's name)
The solicitor pays the VAT inclusive amount. He ignores VAT for his bookkeeping purposes and seeks reimbursement from the client for the VAT.

➤ A solicitor, like any taxable person, is obliged to charge VAT ('output tax') on supplies of services and may recover VAT ('input tax') on supplies attributable to taxable supplies which he or she makes.

➤ A taxable person's liability to HMRC is recorded in an HMRC account.

➤ When a bill of costs is delivered to a client the following double entries must be made:

Amount	Ledger	Column	Entry	Ledger	Column	Entry
Costs (ex VAT)	Client	Office	DR	Profit costs account	Office	CR

Amount	Ledger	Column	Entry	Ledger	Column	Entry
VAT	Client	Office	DR	HMRC a/c	Office	CR

➤ When an expense is paid (including VAT) the following double entries must be made:

Ledger	Column	Entry	Amount	Ledger	Column	Entry
Cash account	Office	CR	← Expense including VAT →	Nominal expenses	Office	DR
			→	HMRC		

• In order to ease a subsequent bank reconciliation the apportionment between the expense and the VAT is recorded as in the following example:

Cash Account

			OFFICE			CLIENT		
Date	Details		DR	CR	Balance	DR	CR	Balance
1.1.1998	Mousetraps 240 VAT 42 282						282	

➤ When net VAT is paid to HMRC (ie: output tax exceeds input tax for the accounting period) the following double entries must be made:

Amount	Ledger	Column	Entry	Ledger	Column	Entry
Net VAT	Cash account	Office	CR	HMRC a/c	Office	DR

➤ For guidance, approved by HMRC, on the VAT treatment of legal aid payments, see the Law Society's 'VAT on legal aid work practice note', dated 4 July 2008.

4 Agreed fees

➤ A payment from a client in respect of agreed fees is office money and should not be paid into client account (*SAR r 12*). (This may create a credit ('CR') balance in the office account - but this will be cancelled by a corresponding debit ('DR') in the office account when the solicitor issues his bill.)

5   **Deposits (Conveyancing transactions)**

➤   A deposit can be held as agent for the seller, or as stakeholder.   In both cases a deposit is 'client money' (*SAR r 12*).

➤   The accounting treatment differs depending on how deposit monies are held.

◆   **As agent:** the solicitor may account immediately to the client for the deposit.

Amount	Ledger	Column	Entry	Ledger	Column	Entry
Deposit	Cash account	Client	DR	Client	Client	CR

◆   **As stakeholder:**

a)   The solicitor should not account immediately to the client for the deposit - the deposit is recorded in a separate ledger, the 'stakeholder account'.

Amount	Ledger	Column	Entry	Ledger	Column	Entry
Deposit	Cash account	Client	DR	Stakeholder a/c	Client	CR

b)   On completion, a transfer is made from the 'stakeholder account' to the client's ledger account. This transfer between the 'stakeholder account' and the client's ledger is a transfer between client ledgers and although there is therefore no need to record the transfer in the cash account (as no money is being withdrawn from client account), the transfer must be noted in both client accounts (*SAR r 32*), stating in both cases 'transfer of deposit TJ' (for 'transfer journal')

Amount	Ledger	Column	Entry	Ledger	Column	Entry
Deposit	Stakeholder a/c	Client	DR	Client	Client	CR

●   One 'stakeholder account' ledger will suffice for all stakeholder monies held by a solicitor (as it is all 'client money'); there is no need to have a separate ledger for each client in relation to whom the solicitor is a stakeholder.

6   **Mortgages**

➤   A solicitor may either treat an institutional lender as a separate client, or may take advantage of *SAR r 29(10)* and simply record a mortgage advance in the buyer's ledger noting the lender's interest.

7   **Insurance premiums**

➤   When a solicitor receives an insurance premium from a client, prior to accounting to an insurance company for the net premium (ie: the gross premium less any commission for the solicitor), the insurance company is treated as the solicitor's client for the purposes of the *SARs*.

➤   If the solicitor receives commission **without accounting to policyholder** for it the double entries are:

a)   On payment by the policyholder:

Amount	Ledger	Column	Entry	Ledger	Column	Entry
Commission	Client (Insurance Co)	Office	DR	Commission account	Office	CR

Amount	Ledger	Column	Entry	Ledger	Column	Entry
Gross premium	Cash account	Client	DR	Client (Insurance Co)	Client	CR

•   Note that there is no entry in the ledger account of the policyholder (assuming the policyholder is a client of the solicitor) as the payment is received as 'client money' held on behalf of the insurance company.

b)   On payment by the solicitor to the insurance company.

	Amount	Ledger	Column	Entry	Ledger	Column	Entry
Out of client a/c	Net premium	Cash account	Client	CR	Client (Insurance Co)	Client	DR

	Amount	Ledger	Column	Entry	Ledger	Column	Entry
Out of client a/c	Commission	Cash account	Client	CR	Client (Insurance Co)	Client	DR

	Amount	Ledger	Column	Entry	Ledger	Column	Entry
Into office a/c	Commission	Cash a/c	Office	DR	Client (Insurance Co)	Office	CR

•   The commission account is an office ledger - at the end of the year the balance will be closed off to the solicitor's profit and loss account as income.

➤   If the solicitor receives commission **for which he is obliged to account to policyholder**.

Amount	Ledger	Column	Entry	Ledger	Column	Entry
Gross premium	Cash account	Client	DR	Client (Insurance Co)	Client	CR

Amount	Ledger	Column	Entry	Ledger	Column	Entry
Commission	Client ledger (Insurance Co)	Client	DR	Client (Policyholder)	Client	CR

•   There is an entry in the ledger account of the policyholder as the payment is received as 'client money' for which the solicitor must account to the policyholder.

▪   Mark the entry as being 'a transfer of commission TJ' as a transfer between client ledgers (*SAR r 29*).

- No entries are made in the Commission account as the commission is accounted for to the policyholder as 'client money'. An internal transfer between client ledgers is made (which does not therefore go through the cash account as no money is drawn out of client account.

Amount	Ledger	Column	Entry	Ledger	Column	Entry
Net premium	Cash account	Client	CR	Client (Insurance Co)	Client	DR

8 Returned cheques

➤ A solicitor must record a cheque received from a client in that client's ledger without delay (*SAR r 14(1)*). Consequently, a client ledger may show uncleared funds as well as cleared funds.

Amount	Ledger	Column	Entry	Ledger	Column	Entry
Cheque	Cash account	Client	DR	Client	Client	CR

➤ If a client's cheque bounces the solicitor must make entries in the client's ledger and cash account showing that the cheque has been returned (ie: these reverse the entries made when the money was received).

Amount	Ledger	Column	Entry	Ledger	Column	Entry
Returned cheque	Cash account	Client	CR	Client	Office	DR

➤ If the solicitor has drawn on uncleared funds there will have been a breach of the *SAR*s as the money drawn from client account will effectively belong to other clients of the solicitor. The solicitor must immediately make good this breach by making a compensating transfer from office account into client account.

- Note that drawing on uncleared funds is not itself a breach of the *SAR*s.

9 Deposit interest

➤ The accounting treatment depends upon whether interest is held on a separate designated deposit account (ie: an account in the client's name, solely for holding money belonging to the named client), or the solicitor accounts to the client for interest.

➤ If a designated deposit account is used:

a) the solicitor must record the transfer of money to the designated deposit cash account.

Amount	Ledger	Column	Entry	Ledger	Column	Entry
Payment in	Cash account	Client	DR	Design. deposit a/c	Client	CR

b) on an interest payment by the bank:

Amount	Ledger	Column	Entry	Ledger	Column	Entry
Interest	Desig. deposit a/c	Client	DR	Client	Client	CR

c) in order to draw money from the designated deposit account the solicitor will have to transfer monies from the designated deposit account to general client account (ie: an account containing mixed client monies) as there will not generally be a cheque book facility on a designated deposit account. This involves reversing the entries in a) above

Amount	Ledger	Column	Entry	Ledger	Column	Entry
Payment out	Cash account	Client	CR	Design. deposit a/c	Client	DR

- If money is transferred to a designated deposit account no entry need be actually made in the client ledger (as the credit balance indicating the funds owed to the client does not change), but it is good practice to record on the ledger that money has been placed in a designated deposit account

➤ If a solicitor pays money in lieu of interest:

a) the solicitor must make a payment out of his own funds in lieu of interest. This can be done either:

- by a transfer from office account to client account, *or*

Amount	Ledger	Column	Entry	Ledger	Column	Entry
Interest	Cash account	Office	CR	Interest paid a/c	Office	DR

Amount	Ledger	Column	Entry	Ledger	Column	Entry
Interest	Cash account	Client	DR	Client	Client	CR

- by an office account cheque paid to the client.

Amount	Ledger	Column	Entry	Ledger	Column	Entry
Interest	Cash account	Office	CR	Interest paid a/c	Office	DR

10   Abatements and bad debts

➤ When a solicitor reduces a bill (known as 'abatement'), the client ledger must record the abatement and corresponding entries must be made in respect of VAT relating to the amount written off. The double entries are as follows:

Amount	Ledger	Column	Entry	Ledger	Column	Entry
Write off	Client	Office	CR	Costs abatement a/c	Office	DR

Amount	Ledger	Column	Entry	Ledger	Column	Entry
VAT on write off	Client	Office	CR	HMRC a/c	Office	DR

➤ If client debt which has been outstanding for more than 6 months is written off, a solicitor may generally claim VAT relief in respect of the 'output tax' that the solicitor will have paid to HMRC one month after the end of the accounting period during which the supply to which the debt relates was made (*VATA 1994 ss 26A, 36*, see also *VATR 1995 rr 165-172*). A successful claim will be recorded by the following double entries:

Amount	Ledger	Column	Entry	Ledger	Column	Entry
VAT relief	Client	Office	CR	HMRC a/c	Office	DR

➤ Any bad debt is treated on the same principles as an abatement.

TAXATION

This chapter examines:

Income or capital?

Income is usually a receipt or expense which recurs, eg: rent or buying paperclips.

Capital is usually a one-off payment for an asset, eg: paying for office furniture.

Individuals are presumed to be domiciled, resident and ordinarily resident in the UK.

Companies are presumed to be resident solely in the UK and trading in the UK

A Income tax (IT)

References in this section are to the IT(TOI)A 2005, unless otherwise stated.

I Calculation

A Individuals as private persons

Steps	See *ITA s 23*
1	Calculate 'total income'
2	Calculate 'net income' ('total income' minus *s 24* reliefs)
3	Deduct allowances from 'net income'
4	Calculate tax due at the applicable rate for the remaining components of net income
5	Add together the tax calculated at Step 4
6	Deduct tax reductions
7	Add any 'additional tax' to give the income tax liability for a tax year

Step 1	Calculate 'total income'

➤ Different rules govern assessment in respect of each component of income. A loss in respect of a component gives a nil assessment for that component.

Components of income
Profits of a trade, vocation, or profession (*s 3, Part 2*)
Profits from a property business (*s 263, Part 3*)
Savings, and investment income (*s 365 , Part 4*)
Employment, pension and social security income (*IT(EP)A 2003 s 1*)
Miscellaneous income (*s 574, Part 5*)
NB: Special rules, beyond the scope of this book, apply to relevant foreign income (*Part 8*)

Some exemptions from income tax (not exhaustive)

- Interest on National Savings certificates (*s 692*)
- Income from the sale of electricity generated by a domestic microgeneration system, or receipt by an individual of a renewables certificate (*ss 782A-782B*)
- Payments to adopters (*s 744*), and foster carers with respect to certain foster care receipts (*s 803*)
- Interest on personal injury damages or death damages (*s 751*)
- Certain social security benefits (eg: child benefit) (*IT(EP)A 2003 s 677*)
- Certain annual payments under an immediate needs annuity (*s 725*)
- Scholarship income (*s 776*), provided it is not chargeable under *IT(EP)A 2003 ss 211-214*
- Gross income up to £4,250 from letting a furnished room in a 'main residence' (*s 785*)
- Maintenance from a former spouse/civil partner under a court order or written agreement (*s 727*)

➤ Where tax is deducted at source, 'gross up' the income to its value *before* tax was deducted to arrive at the 'statutory income' (eg: multiply by 100/80 if income tax has been deducted at the lower rate of 20%).

Profits from a trade, etc

➤ The profits of a trade are calculated in accordance with generally accepted accounting practice, subject to any adjustment required or authorised by law (*s 25*).

◆ Whether an amount is income is a question of fact, determined in accordance with case law (rather than accounting practice).

● An amount which is capital, rather than income, is not brought into account (*s 96*).

◆ A deduction is not allowed, eg:

● for items of a capital nature (*s 33*), *or*

● for expenses not incurred wholly and exclusively for the purposes of a trade (*s 34, Mallalieu v. Drummond* [1983] 2 AC 861), *or*

● for a debt, unless the debt is bad, estimated to be bad, or released as part of an insolvency arrangement (*s 35*), *or*

● for providing entertainment or gifts in connection with a trade (*s 45*) (subject to limited exceptions in *ss 46-47*), *or*

● for social security contributions (other than an employer's Class 1 contribution, a Class 1A contribution, or a Class 1B contribution) (*s 53*), *or*

● for any penalty or interest incurred in relation to certain provisions relating to income tax, capital gains tax, corporation tax, VAT, excise duties, insurance premium tax, climate change/aggregates levy, landfill tax, or SDLT (*s 54*), *or*

● crime-related payments (*s 55*).

◆ A deduction is allowed in respect of certain expenses, eg:

● pre-trading expenditure (as if expenses were incurred on the first day of the trade) (*s 57*), *and*

● subsistence expenses (*s 57A* as inserted by *EE-SCO 2009 r 3*), *and,*

● certain incidental costs of obtaining loan finance (*ss 58-59*), *and*

● a payment for a restrictive employment undertaking (*s 69*), *and*

● counselling, or retraining (*ss 73-75*), *and*

● redundancy/approved contractual payments (*s 76*), *and*

● personal security (*s 81*), *and*

● a contribution to an enterprise organisation, or an urban regeneration company (*s 82*), *and*

● scientific research and development (*s 87*).

◆ A charge arising under *CAA 2001* is treated as a receipt of a trade, and an allowance arising under that Act is treated as an expense of a trade (*s 28*).

➤ Profits from a profession or vocation, are generally calculated in the same way as profits from a trade (*ss 24, 32*).

◆ Special rules apply for ministers of religion (*s 159*), barristers of not more than 7 years call (*s 160*), creative artists, and farmers whose profits fluctuate (*ss 221-225*).

Profits from a property business

➤ Income generated from land by exploiting an estate, interest or right in or over land as a source of rents or other receipts (*s 266*), and distributions in respect of a REIT's tax-exempt business (*CA 2010 s 548*).

➤ The amount of income is generally calculated in the same way as the profits of a trade (*s 272*).

   ◆ Part of a premium on the grant of a lease with a term not exceeding 50 years, or on the surrender or variation / waiver of a lease (even if the original term exceeded 50 years), may be treated as an income receipt and as a part disposal for CGT (see also *TCGA 1992 Sch 8* for CGT treatment) (*ss 276-307*).

Savings and investment income

➤ Sources of income arising on or after 6 April 1994 are assessed on the current year basis (ie: the tax year in which income accrues), although for a partnership with savings income its basis period serves as the period of assessment if this differs from its accounting period (*ss 852-853*).

   ◆ An individual receives interest from a UK bank or UK building society (*ITA s 851*), and annual interest from other UK companies (*ITA s 874*), net of tax at the basic rate (currently, 20%) (ie: for £100 of interest, the individual receives £80 and the payer accounts to HMRC for £20).

Non-taxpayer	20% taxpayer	40%/50% taxpayer
↓	↓	↓
Full rebate (20%)	No more tax to pay	25%/37.5% more tax to pay under *Step 4*

   • Bank/Building Society interest: a non-taxpayer can receive the gross amount, without a deduction at source, if he or she sends the correct form to the bank/building society.

   • National Savings certificates and accounts: tax is not deducted at source; interest is paid gross.

   • A payment representing interest from the Financial Services Compensation Scheme is treated as interest (*s 380A* and *ITA s 979A*).

   ◆ Annual payments are subject to a deduction at source at the basic rate (20%) (*ITA s 900*).

   ◆ Deduction at source (also known as a 'withholding tax') makes tax collection easier/more reliable and gives the Government a cashflow advantage as institutions account for tax quarterly (*viz*: before payment of tax falls due under self assessment).

➤ Although no deductible expenditure is permitted in calculating savings and investment income, if a debenture holder borrows to lend money to a company then the interest may give rise to a relief under *Step 2*.

➤ Distributions (*ss 383, 397*): for a fuller explanation see p 129:

Non-taxpayer	20% taxpayer	40%/50% taxpayer
↓	↓	↓
No more tax to pay - no rebate	No more tax to pay	32.5%/42.5% more tax to pay under *Step 4*

➤ A close company writes off a loan to a participator: the amount written off is 'grossed up' so that the income is treated as having been subject to tax at the dividend ordinary rate (10%), and the participator is assessed on the gross income (*CA 2010 Part 10 Chapter 3*).

   ◆ Since the company has already, with the payment to HMRC, satisfied the shareholder's liability for basic rate tax, the shareholder has effectively postponed liability for higher rate tax.

Non-taxpayer, 20% taxpayer	40%/50% taxpayer
↓	↓
No more tax to pay	32.5%/42.5% more tax to pay under *Step 4*

➤ A company repurchases its own shares: the difference between the original issue price of the shares and their value on sale may be taxed as if it were a dividend. Alternatively, the gain may be subject to CGT if conditions set out on p 314 are fulfilled.

Employment income, pensions income and social security income

References are to IT(EP)A 2003, unless stated otherwise

➤ Tax is imposed on 'employment income' (*Parts 2-7*), pensions income (*Part 9*) and social security income (*Part 10*) and deducted from pay under 'pay as you earn' (known as 'PAYE') (*Part 11*).

➤ 'Employment income' is divided into 'general earnings' and 'specific employment income' (*s 6*).

   ◆ 'General earnings' includes any salary, wages, or fee, any benefit if it is money or money's worth, and any other emolument of employment (*s 62*).

   ◆ 'Specific employment income' includes income in *Part 6* (*Income which is not earnings or share related*) and is not exempt under *Part 4* (*Exemptions*) or subject to *Part 7* (*Share related income*) (*ss 7(4)-(6)*).

      • *Part 6* imposes tax on payments to and benefits from unapproved pension schemes (*ss 386-400*) and payments and benefits on the termination of employment in excess of £30,000 (*ss 401-416*).

      • *Part 7* provides that tax is chargeable on a gain on the occurrence of a chargeable event in relation to employment related securities, or the exercise of a share option (*ss 471-484*).

         ■ There is an exemption for: any gain on the exercise of an option granted under an approved share incentive plan (*ss 488-515*), an approved SAYE scheme (*ss 516-519*), an approved CSOP scheme (*ss 521-526*), or an enterprise management incentive ('EMI') (*ss 527-541*).

➤ An individual is chargeable to tax in respect of employment income on the amount of his/her 'net taxable earnings' and 'net taxable specific income' (*ss 9-10*).

   ◆ 'Net taxable earnings' and ''net taxable specific income' are calculated by deducting from 'taxable earnings'/'taxable specific income' deductions which are allowed (*ss 11-12*) (see 'Deductions' below).

   ◆ 'Taxable earnings': where an individual is resident, ordinarily resident and domiciled in the UK this are calculated in accordance *ss 14-19*, otherwise *ss 20-41* apply (the rules relating to individuals not resident, ordinarily resident and domiciled in the UK are beyond the scope of this book).

Deductions

➤ Deductions:
   a) are not allowed from earnings from other employments, *and*
   b) may not exceed earnings, must not be in duplicate for the same costs or expenses (*ss 327-330*), *and*
   c) are allowed in the order resulting in the greatest reduction in the liability to tax (subject to special rules for chargeable overseas expenses and seafarers) (*s 331*).

➤ A deduction for an employee's expenses, broadly, is allowed *either*:
 	
   A: a) when an employee is obliged to incur and pay an amount as holder of the employment, *and*
 	
      b) the amount is incurred wholly, exclusively and necessarily in the performance of the duties of employment (*s 336*), *or*
 	
   B: for travel expenses are incurred in certain specific circumstances, eg:
 	
      a) where an employee is obliged to incur and pay an amount, eg: incurred in travelling in performance of employment duties, for necessary attendance at a place in performance of employment duties, *or* between employments by companies which are members of the same group of companies (*ss 337-340*), *and*
 	
      b) at the start or finish of an overseas employment, and travel between employments when duties are performed abroad (*ss 341-342*), *and*
 	
      c) where a company vehicle is not used, no mileage allowance payment is made and no mileage allowance relief is available (*s 359*).

Deductions (cont.)

C: for travel costs and expenses incurred where duties are performed abroad (*ss 370-372*).

D: for certain fees and annual subscriptions (eg: professional fees) (*ss 342-344*).

E: when liability is incurred to discharge an employment related liability, proceedings are conducted in respect of such a liability, or a premium is paid for insurance in respect of such a liability (*ss 346-350*).

F: when business entertainment and gift expenses are incurred which are *either*:

    a) not deductible for an employer, *or*

    b) are:

        i) also provided for others, *and*

        ii) their provision for employees is incidental to their provision for others (*ss 356-358*).

➤ A fixed sum is allowable as a deduction in relation to certain annual expenses incurred in respect of the repair and maintenance of work equipment (*s 367*).

➤ A deduction is allowed in respect of personal security assets and services where a special threat to personal physical security arises wholly or mainly because of employment (*s 377*).

➤ Benefits in non-cash form are taxed under the 'benefits code'.

◆ Certain benefits (marked in the 'Benefits code' box below with a '†' are not taxable in the hands of an employee who earns less than £8,500 a year, *and* is *either*:

a) not a director, *or*

b) a director who does not own a material interest (5%) in the company, *and either*

    i) that director is a full time working director, *or*

    ii) the company is non-profit making or established for charitable purposes (*ss 216-220*).

◆ An amount equal to the cost to an employer of providing a benefit is usually taxable, although special rules, some of which are outlined in the 'Benefits code' box below, apply to certain types of benefit.

Benefits code

➤ The following are taxable benefits under the benefits code:

a) sums in respect of expenses (*ss 70-72*)[†].

b) cash vouchers (*ss 73-81*) and non-cash vouchers/credit tokens (*ss 82-96*).

  ● There is an exception for: vouchers/tokens made available to the public generally (*ss 78, 85, 93*), cash vouchers issued under an approved scheme (*s 79*), and cash vouchers where payment of a sum would have been exempt from tax (*s 80*).

c) living accommodation (*ss 97-113*).

  ● There is an exception for: certain accommodation provided by a local authority, accommodation provided for the better performance of duties where it is customary to provide such accommodation, accommodation provided as a result of a security threat (*ss 98-100*), and homes outside the UK owned through a company (*ss 100A-B*).

  ● Special rules govern the tax assessable with respect to cost of providing accommodation where that cost exceeds £75,000 (*ss 103-107*).

Benefits code (cont.)

d) cars, vans and related benefits (ss 114-171)[†].

- The cash equivalent of a car is calculated by reference to CO_2 emissions (ss 133-142).

- There is an exemption in respect of:

  - mileage allowance payments (ss 229-236), and passenger payments (ss 233-236).

  - the provision of workplace parking (s 237).

  - modest private use of a heavy goods vehicle (s 238).

  - support for public bus services (s 243).

  - cycles and cyclist's safety equipment (s 244),

  - travelling and subsistence during public transport strikes (s 245).

  - disabled employee's work/home transport (ss 245-246), and provision of cars (s 247).

  - late night transport home (s 248).

e) taxable cheap loans (s 175).[†]

- The cash equivalent is calculated by reference to interest saved by comparison with an official rate which is set periodically.

- There is an exception for: a loan on ordinary commercial terms (s 176), a loan qualifying for tax relief (s 177), an advance for necessary expenses (s 179), and loan under £5,000 (s 180).

f) notional loans for the acquisition of shares (ss 192-197) and a disposal of shares for more than market value (ss 198-200).[†]

g) other benefits (ss 201-215).

- There is an exception for:

  - an expense 'made good' by the employee (s 203(2)).

  - incidental overnight expenses (£5 for each night wholly in the UK, else £10) (ss 240-241).

  - work related training (ss 250-254), contributions to individual learning accounting training (ss 255-260).

  - subsidised meals (s 317), eye tests and corrective appliances (s 320A).

  - recreational benefits (ss 261-263), annual party to £150 a head (s 264), third party entertainment (s 265).

  - childcare (ss 318-318D).

  - a (single) mobile telephone for an employee (s 319 as substituted by FA 2006).

  - removal expenses not exceeding £8,000 (ss 271-289).

  - certain repairs to living accommodation (s 313), and accommodation, supplies and services used in performing duties of employment (s 316).

  - overseas medical treatment (s 325).

  - pension provision (ss 306-307).

  - up to £1,000 if service not less than 20 years (s 323), small gifts from third parties not exceeding £250 (s 324), encouragement award to £25 and financial suggestion award to £5,000 (ss 321-322).

  - redundancy payments (s 309).

  - counselling on termination of employment and outplacement (s 310), retraining courses (s 311).

➤ PAYE generally obliges an employer to pay tax directly to HMRC within 14 days of the fifth of the month following the month in which either the payment takes place, or the benefit is conferred.

'Personal service companies' and 'managed service companies'

- ➤ An individual is treated as receiving a deemed employment payment from a personal service provider if (*IT(EP)A 2003 ss 49-50*):

  a) an individual (the 'worker') personally performs, or is under an obligation personally to perform, services for another person (the 'client'), *and*

  b) the services are provided not under a contract directly between the client and the worker but under arrangements involving an intermediary (the 'intermediary'), *and*

  c) the services were provided under a contract directly between the client and the worker, the worker would be regarded for tax purposes as the client's employee, *and if the intermediary is*:

    i) a company in which the worker has a 'material interest', *or*

      - A 'material interest' is an entitlement to more than 5% of the company's ordinary share capital, a right to more than 5% of the company's distributions, *or* a right to more than 5% of the company's assets on a winding-up (*IT(EP)A 2003 s 51*).

    ii) a partnership, *or*

      - The worker (and his relatives) are *either:*

        - entitled to 60% or more of partnership profits, *or*

        - most of the partnership profits derive from the client and its associates, *or*

        - the profit share of any of the partners is based on the income generated by that partner through the provision of services under engagements to which these rules *IT(EP)A 2003 Ch 8* apply (*IT(EP)A 2003 s 52*), *or*

    iii) an individual.

      - The payment/benefit is received or receivable:

        - by the worker directly from the intermediary, *and*

        - can reasonably be taken to represent remuneration for services provided by the worker to the client (*IT(EP)A 2003 s 53*).

- ➤ These provisions were introduced to counter perceived avoidance of PAYE and NICs.

  - ◆ The deemed payment is calculated by *IT(EP)A 2003 ss 54-55* and PAYE applies *IT(EP)A 2003 s 56*.

- ➤ Equivalent provisions apply to 'managed service companies' (*IT(EP)A 2003 ss 61A-61J, 688A* and *IT(TOI)A 2005 164A*). A company is a 'managed service company' if:

  a) its business consists wholly or mainly of providing (directly or indirectly) the services of an individual to other persons, *and*

  b) payments are made (directly or indirectly) to the individual (or associates of the individual) of an amount equal to the greater part or all of the consideration for the provision of the services, *and*

  c) the way in which those payments are made would result in the individual (or associates) receiving payments of an amount (net of tax and NI) exceeding that which would be received (net of tax and national insurance) if every payment in respect of the services were employment income of the individual, *and*

  d) a person who carries on a business of promoting or facilitating the use of companies to provide the services of individuals is involved with the company (*IT(EP)A 2003 s 61B(1)*).

Miscellaneous income

- ➤ This covers income listed in *s 574*, including the 'full amount' of any income not caught elsewhere (*s 687*).

| Step 2 | Calculate 'net income' ('total income' minus 's 24 reliefs') |

➤ *ITA s 24* provides that the following reliefs may be deducted in calculating an individual's 'net income'.

  a) Relief for interest on a qualifying loan which a taxpayer takes out (*ITA s 383*):

- to invest in a partnership (*ITA ss 398, 401*): buy a share in, lend or contribute capital to a partnership/LLP.

  ■ In the case of a LLP, the LLP must not be not an 'investment LLP' whose purpose consists wholly or mainly in making investments (*ITA s 399*).

- to invest in a close company (but not a close investment holding company) (*ITA ss 392-395*)).

- to invest in an 'employee controlled company' (*ITA s 396*).

  ■ An 'employee controlled company' is a company in which: 50%+ of the voting rights and ordinary shares are held by employees, and none of whose shares is listed on the LSE's Official List (*ITA s 397*).

  ■ The taxpayer works full time for the company (or a 51% subsidiary) and *either*:
    i) lends money to a trading company or the holding company of a trading group, *or*
    ii) acquires ordinary shares in such a company or pays off a loan financing such an acquisition.

- as a PR to pay inheritance tax (*ITA s 403*).

> Relief is not available under *ITA s 383* in respect of interest payable on a loan if there are arrangements which are very likely to produce a post-tax advantage, and those arrangements seem designed to reduce a liability to income tax or capital gains tax (*ITA s 384A* introduced by *FA 2009 Sch 30*).

  b) Relief for a gift of shares, securities and real property to a charity (*ITA s 431-446*).

- Relief is denied if a donation is 'tainted' (*ITA ss 809ZH-809ZR* inserted by *FA 2011 Sch 3*).

  c) Share loss relief on the sale of shares in a qualifying unquoted trading company (eg: for shares issued on or after 6 April 1998, EIS shares) for which the individual was the original subscriber (*ITA ss 131-133*).

  d) Relief for a payment to a trade union or a police organisation (*ITA s 457-458*).

  e) Excess relief under a net pay arrangement for a pension scheme (*FA 2004 s 193(4)*).

  f) Loss reliefs arising in connection with a trade or business (see Section C below).

| Step 3 | Deduct allowances from 'net income' |

➤ These allowances depend on an individual's personal circumstances.

Personal allowances (*ITA ss 35-37*): dependent on age		
Under 65 (*ITA s 35*) †	£7,475	
Over 65, but under 75 (*ITA s 36*)*	£9,940	
Over 75 (*ITA s 37*)*	£10,090	
Other *additional* allowance		
Blind person (*ITA ss 38-41*)	£1,980	If the taxpayer is registered blind A husband and a wife, or civil partners, can both claim this relief

*   Relief is *only* available on income up to £24,000, and is reduced by half the excess over £24,000 but not so that the overall relief is below the personal allowance given by under *ITA s 35* (*ITA ss 36-37*).
†   For 2011-2012 and subsequent years, for each £2 of income over £100,000 the allowance is reduced by £1 (*FA 2009 s 3*).

Step 4 | **Calculate tax at the applicable rate from the remaining components of net income**

➤ Savings income £0 - £2,560: savings income is taxed at the 'starting rate for savings', of 10% to the extent that an individual does not have taxable non-savings income above £2,560 (*ITA ss 7, 12*) (where tax has been paid at the basic rate, instead of at the starting rate for savings, a repayment may be claimed (*ITA s 17*)), otherwise ...

➤ Taxable income £0 - £35,000: taxed at the 'basic rate' of 20% (*ITA s 6*).

◆ Note that the basic rate limit (£35,000) can be increased in certain circumstances (*ITA s 10(6)*):

a) where an individual makes a qualifying donation to a charity, and the donor makes a gift aid declaration, the basic rate limit is increased by an amount equal to the grossed-up amount of the gift (*ITA s 414*).

▪ A gift is grossed-up because is treated as having been made after deduction of income tax at the basic rate (ie: if the gift is £80, a charity can reclaim £20 from HMRC, receiving £100 in total).

b) to give effect to relief for certain pension contributions (*FA 2004 s 192(4)*).

➤ Taxable income £35,000-£150,000: taxed at the 'higher rate' of 40% (*ITA s 6(1)(c), 10, 20(3)*).

➤ Taxable income over £150,000: taxed at the 'additional rate' of 50%.

◆ Savings and dividend income are treated as the highest part of total income (*ITA s 16*).

Trustees

➤ UK resident trustees to whom accumulated or discretionary income arises generally pay income tax at the trusts rate, currently 40% (*ITA s 479*).

◆ Distributions are taxable at the dividend trust rate of 42.5% (*ITA s 479(3)*).

● Income that does not exceed £1,000 is not chargeable at the rate applicable to trusts, or the dividend trust rate. Instead, it is chargeable at the rate of 20% (*ITA s 491*).

● If a beneficiary is a 'vulnerable beneficiary', and a valid election is made, trustees may claim relief so that the tax payable is reduced to the amount that would have been payable if the income had arisen directly to the beneficiary (*FA 2005 ss 23-45*).

▪ A 'vulnerable beneficiary' is a person who is disabled, or a person under 18 at least one of whose parent's has died (*FA 2005 ss 38-39*).

➤ Trustees of fixed interest trusts have tax at 20% deducted at source on savings income, and are subject to basic rate tax at 20% on other income.

➤ Trustees have no personal allowances, but may claim capital allowances and loss relief in respect of any trade they carry on as trustees.

Step 5 | **Add together amounts of tax calculated at *Step 4***

| Step 6 | Deduct tax reductions |

➤ 'Tax reductions' include:

◆ reductions for married couples and civil partners.

Married couples/civil partners if born before 6 April 1935 (*ITA ss 42-55*)		
Either spouse or civil partner over 75 at some time during the tax year*†	£7,295	The couple/civil partners live together for part of the year
		By default this relief goes to a husband, unless the couple elect before the beginning of the tax year to share it differently
		The spouse or civil partner can claim any allowance unused by the other spouse/partner at the end of the year
		The allowance can be reduced below the basic personal allowance where the income is above £100,000
* Relief is *only* available on income up to £24,000, and is reduced by half the excess over £24,000 less any reduction in personal allowances under *ITA ss 35-37* (*ITA ss 45-46*).		
† Relief is restricted to 10% (*ITA ss 45-46*)		

◆ EIS relief (*ITA Ch 1 of Part 5*).

◆ VCT relief (*ITA Ch 2 of Part 6*).

◆ community investment tax relief (*ITA Ch 1 of Part 7*).

◆ qualifying maintenance payments (*ITA s 453*).

◆ relief for foreign tax (*TA ss 788, 790*).

| Step 7 | Add any 'additional tax' to give the income tax liability for a tax year |

➤ If the taxpayer is an individual, 'additional tax' includes (*ITA s 30(1)*):

◆ tax is imposed in respect of gift aid (*ITA s 414*) if:

... the total amount of tax treated as deducted from qualifying donations made by that individual in a tax year, exceeds ...

... the sum of the amount of income tax and capital gains tax to which the individual is charged for that tax year (*ITA s 424*).

◆ tax in respect of pension schemes, eg:

a) the short service refund lump sum charge (*FA 2004 s 205*), *and*

b) the special lump sum death benefits charge (*FA 2004 s 206*), *and*

c) the unauthorised payments charge (*FA 2004 s 208(2)(a)*), *and*

d) the unauthorised payments surcharge (*FA 2004 s 209(3)(a)*), *and*

e) the lifetime allowance charge (*FA 2004 s 214*) (see p 166), *and*

f) annual allowance charge (*FA 2004 s 227*), *and*

◆ tax in respect of a social security lump sum (*F(No2)A 2005 s 7*).

B Individuals as sole traders/partners

Follow the 4 steps in *'A Individuals as private persons'*,

BUT use these additional rules.

Step 1	Set the 'accounting date'

➤ The profits chargeable in respect of a tax year, are the profits of the 'basis period' for that year (*s 7*).

   ◆ A 'basis period' is the period of 12 months ending with the 'accounting date' falling in a tax year (*s 198*), unless special circumstances set out in *s 198(2)* arise, eg:

   a) the first years in which a person carries on a trade.

   ● Special rules set the basis period during the first 3 years of a trade. During the first year, the basis period runs from commencement to the following 5 April (*s 199*). Thereafter, the rules align the basis period with the accounting period as quickly as possible.

   ▪ Alignment happens in year 2 if *either*:

   i) there are 12 months or more between commencement and the accounting date (*s 200(3)*), *or*

   ii) there is a change of accounting date between years 1 and 2 (*s 214*), ...

   ... in which case the basis period is the 12 months to the new accounting date.

   ▪ Alignment happens in year 3 if *either*:

   i) there are 12 months or less between commencement and the accounting date (*s 200(2)*), *or*

   ii) the accounting date is changed in years 1 or 2 so that the new date is less than 12 months after the business began (*s 215*), *or*

   iii) the basis period for year 2 actually ends in year 3 (*s 200(4)*), ...

   ... in the case of i) and ii) the basis period in year 2 is the first 12 months, but for iii) the basis period is the tax year itself.

   b) the final tax year in which a person carries on a business (*s 202*).

   c) the accounting date is changed and conditions set out in *ss 217-18* are satisfied (including that the change is made for commercial reasons).

➤ The 'accounting date' is the date in a tax year to which accounts are drawn up (or, if there are 2 dates, the later of them) (*s 197*).

   ◆ Special rules apply if:

   ● an accounting date falls on one of 7 (or in February, 8) consecutive days; these rules allow the taxpayer to elect that the fourth of those dates is to be treated as the accounting date (*ss 211-13*), *or*

   ● an accounting date falls on 31 March-4 April, or there is no accounting date in a tax year (*ss 208-210*).

Step 2	Claim any 'overlap relief'

➤ When basis periods overlap, 'overlap relief' is available. The profit from the preceding year attributable to the overlapping days is apportioned, and used as a deduction to prevent a double liability (*s 220*).

➤ A loss cannot be used more than once, so overlap relief cannot be used to recycle any other form of loss relief such as relief under *ITA s 64 (IT(TOI)A s 206)*.

Step 3	Deduct any loss relief from 'total income' in calculating 'net income'

➤ *References in this Step are to the ITA, unless otherwise stated.*

	Period	Loss claimed on ...	Use on ...
Early trade relief *s 72*	First 4 tax years	... over the 3 tax years before the year in which the loss incurred	... any income
Terminal trade loss relief *s 89*	Final year	... the final tax year and the 3 years preceding it	... trading income
Property relief *s 118*	Any accounting year	... the next tax year of taxable income, any excess in future years	... property business income
Trade loss relief *s 64*[†]			
Carry forward trade loss relief *s 83*		... the tax year in which the accounting year of the loss ends, and the preceding year	... any income
		... the next tax year with taxable profit; any excess in future years	... trading income

➤ Using *s 64* wastes personal reliefs as this relief must be used on the whole of income
➤ Using *s 83* allows personal reliefs to be set off against other income
➤ *s 83* can be claimed whether *s 64* is used or not
➤ If *s 83* is used with a *s 64* loss, then *s 83* can only be claimed to the extent that a loss remains unused after *s 64* has been claimed

[†] Trading losses made in 2008-2009 and 2009-2010 can be carried back for up to 3 years, although there is a cap of £50,000 on the trading losses which may be carried back beyond 1 year (*FA 2009 Sch 6*).

Relief on incorporation of a business *s 86*

If a trading loss is unrelieved when a business is transferred to a company 'wholly or mainly in return for the issue of shares' (ie: shares form at least 80% of the consideration), this loss can be carried forward and provide relief against dividends *or* salary which the former trader or partner gains from the company in future years

➤ Relief which an individual who is a partner (*s 104*), or an individual who is a member of a LLP (*ss 107-114*), can claim for interest and trading losses against other income is restricted to that partner's/member's capital contribution to the partnership/LLP and his or her entitlement to undistributed profit.

  ◆ A charge to income tax is imposed where an individual has made a claim for relief under *ss 104, 107, 110* and receives non-taxable consideration (*ITA s 792*).

➤ The amount of loss relief which an individual (other than a partner) who is not active in a trade, or a non-active partner/member of a LLP, can claim for any tax year in respect of losses is limited to £25,000 (*ITA s 74A-D, 103C*).

➤ For R & D tax credits, see p 128.

The detailed rules relating to tax efficient investments such as venture capital trusts (*ITA s 258-332, TCGA 1992 s 100*), the Enterprise Investment Scheme (*ITA ss 156-257, TCGA 1992 ss 150-150D, Sch 5B-BA*) and ISAs, are beyond the scope of this book, however, for an outline see pp 161-162

C Partnerships

Steps

1 Send in the partnership return

2 Split the profit or loss amongst the individual partners

Step 1   Send in the partnership return

➤ The partnership must send in a return giving details of the firm's business for an accounting period (eg: partnership income, profit allocation and any capital allowances claimed) (*TMA 1970 s 9*).

➤ Claims for expenditure and capital allowances etc which affect profits and losses of the partnership are made when the partnership return is completed (*TMA 1970 s 42*).

   ◆ Expenditure incurred by a partner must be included on the partnership return; a claim as an individual will be disallowed.

   ◆ Claims for allowances for plant and machinery owned by a partner, and used by the partnership, must generally be made on the partnership return (*CAA 2001 s 264*).

Step 2   Split the profit or loss amongst the individual partners

➤ Profit and loss are calculated for the partnership as a whole (*s 848*).

➤ Partners complete individual self assessments, each being liable for their own share of the profits under the profit sharing ratio during the period of assessment concerned (net of any deductions successfully claimed by the partnership) (*s 850*).

   ◆ Partners are generally not jointly and severally liable for taxation arising on the profit earned by each other (*ss 246(3)-(4), 353(2)-(3), 854(1)*).

Continuance of partnerships
➤ Under the old rules, before the introduction of self assessment on 6 April 1994, a partnership was deemed to discontinue if its membership changed, unless the partners elected for it to continue.
➤ If the membership of a partnership changes on or after 6 April 1994, then it is deemed to continue unless none of the partners continues in the business (*ss 246(3)-(4), 353(2)-(3)*).

D Limited liability partnership incorporated under the *LPA 2000*

➤ A trade, profession or business carried on by a LLP with a view to profit is generally treated as a partnership carried on by its members (and not by the LLP itself) (*s 983* (for IT), *CA 2009 s 1273* (for CT)).

   ◆ The property and income of a LLP are treated as the property or income of the members of the LLP.

   ◆ If a liquidator is appointed, or the court makes an order for the winding-up of the LLP, the LLP is treated as a body corporate subject to corporation tax.

B Capital allowances

I What allowances are and how they may be used?
II Who can claim allowances for expenditure on plant and machinery?
III What allowances can be claimed?

I What allowances are and how they may be used

A What allowances are

➤ Capital allowances allow the depreciation of capital assets to be brought into account for taxation purposes and offset against income profit (earned by sole traders, partners and companies).

B How allowances may be used

➤ Capital allowances can be claimed and set against 'income profits' and used to create a loss for the purposes of income tax, or corporation tax in respect of income.

 ◆ If there is more than one item of plant /machinery, an allowance is granted on a 'pool'.

  • Expenditure on 'long life' assets, thermal insulation and integral features is allocated to a special rate pool (*CAA 2001 ss 104A-E*).

➤ Some allowances are granted on a 'reducing balance' basis which allows expenditure to be depreciated over a number of years:

20% reducing balance			
Period	Reducing balance	Depreciation	and so on ... until allowances reach £100. The majority of the value of a 20% allowance is extracted over 8 years, thereafter the allowance becomes less significant
1	£100	£20 (20% of £100)	
2	£64	£16 (20% of £80)	
3	£51.2	£12.8 (20% of £64)	

➤ When a 'disposal event' occurs in respect of a capital asset, the sum written down against the capital allowance is compared with the disposal value to determine whether a balancing charge or balancing allowance arises (*CAA 2001 ss 55-56*).

 ◆ If the sale proceeds (or original cost if less) exceed the sum written down (in respect of the asset, or the pool if there is a pool), a balancing charge arises on the excess taxed as a chargeable receipt of the trade/property business, etc.

 ◆ If the proceeds are less than the sum written down, the shortfall is deductible as a balancing allowance from the chargeable receipts of the trade/property business, etc.

  • A 'disposal event' includes where a person ceases to own plant or machinery, a qualifying activity is permanently discontinued, or equipment is destroyed (*CAA 2001 s 61*).

II   Who can claim allowances for expenditure on plant and machinery?

➤ For plant and machinery, the general rule is that a person may claim capital allowances if that person carries on a 'qualifying activity' and incurs 'qualifying expenditure' (*CAA 2001 s 11(1)*).

   ◆ A 'qualifying activity' includes a UK property business, an overseas property business, a trade, profession or vocation, or the special leasing of plant or machinery (*CAA 2001 s 15(1)*).

   ◆ 'Qualifying expenditure' exists where there is:

   a) i) capital expenditure on the provision of plant or machinery wholly or partly for the purposes of a qualifying activity carried on by the person incurring the expenditure, *and*

   ii) the person owns the plant or machinery as a result of incurring the expenditure (*CAA 2001 s 11(4)*), *and*

   b) expenditure which is not excluded, see eg: *CAA 2001 ss 21-23* (expenditure on buildings, etc is excluded).

➤ Special rules govern how allowances may be claimed in respect of expenditure incurred on plant or machinery which becomes a fixture to land (*CAA 2001 ss 172-204*).

➤ Anti-avoidance rules can restrict, or deny allowances.

   ◆ Eg: *FA 2006* introduced special rules in respect of 'long funding leases' (*CAA 2001 ss 70A-YJ, TA ss 502A-L* (for CT purposes), *IT(TOI)A 2005 ss 148A-J* (for IT purposes)).

   • Under the *FA 2006* rules, allowances go to the lessee (rather than the lessor).

III   What capital allowances can be claimed?

➤ A capital allowance can be claimed at the rate of:

a) 100% in respect of an 'annual investment allowance' of up to £100,000 (£25,000 from April 2012) (*CAA 2001 ss 38A-38B* and *51A-51N*).

   ◆ Certain types of expenditure, such as expenditure on a car or expenditure in which a qualifying activity is permanently discontinued, are excluded.

   ◆ An annual investment allowance is available to:

   i) an individual, *and*

   ii) a partnership consisting only of individuals, *and*

   iii) a company.

      • Where businesses are related as a result of being controlled by a person (or persons) and either use shared premises or engage in similar activities, a single annual investment allowance must be shared by the relevant businesses.

b) 100% for expenditure incurred before 1 April 2013 on:

   i) natural gas, biogas, or hydrogen refuelling equipment (*CAA 2001 s 45D*), *or*

   ii) cars with low CO_2 emissions (*CAA 2001 s 45E*).

c) 100% on expenditure in energy efficient or water efficient technology (*CAA 2001 ss 45A, 45H*).

- A company which incurs a loss carrying on an activity for the purposes of which it incurs such expenditure may claim a 19% tax credit (*CAA 2001 Sch A1*).

  - This credit is capped at the greater of i) £250,000, and ii) the total of that company's PAYE and NIC liabilities for payment periods ending in the relevant chargeable period.

- Qualifying energy efficient technology is identified on a list issued by the Secretary of State for Climate Change on 8 November 2010 (*CA(ESPM)O 2001* as amended by *CA(ESPM)(A)O 2010*).

- Qualifying water efficient technology is identified on a list issued by the Environment, Food and Rural Affairs on 8 November 2010 (*CA(EBPM)O 2003* as amended by *CA(EBPM)(A)O 2010*).

  - On 23 March 2011 it was announced that the Treasury would make further amendment orders but none have been made as at the time of going to press; the lists of qualifying machinery are reviewed annually.

d) 20% (18% from April 2012) on a reducing balance basis for expenditure on plant and machinery (*CAA 2001 s 56*).

e) 10% (8% from April 2012) on a reducing balance basis for expenditure on 'integral features' of a building used for a qualifying activity (*CAA 2001 s 33A-B*).

- Eg. electrical/lighting system, cold water system, water heating system, air cooling/purification, lift, escalator, external solar shading.

f) 10% (8% from April 2012) on a reducing balance basis on thermal insulation of buildings (*CAA 2001 s 28*).

g) 10% (8% from April 2012) on a reducing balance basis for certain plant and machinery which constitute 'long life assets' that can reasonably be expected to have a useful economic life of at least 25 years (*CAA 2001 ss 91, 102*). This treatment does not apply to:

i) a person (other than a lessor) who incurs expenditure during a chargeable period of 12 months not exceeding £100,000 (*CAA 2001 ss 98-100*).

ii) expenditure on any of the following:

- machinery or plant which is a fixture in, or provided for use in, any building which is wholly or mainly for use as a dwelling house, retail shop, showroom, hotel or office (*CAA 2001 s 93*).

- a car (*CAA 2001 s 96*).

- prior to 1 January 2011 certain types of ship (basically seagoing vessels) (*CAA 2001 s 94*).

- prior to 1 January 2011 the provision of a railway asset wholly and exclusively for the purposes of a railway business (*CAA 2001 s 95*).

➤ In certain other cases allowances are accelerated and/or offered on special terms, eg: renovating business premises in deprived areas (*CAA 2001 Part 3A*), agriculture and forestry (*CAA 2001 Part 4*), conversion or renovation of flats for rental over shops or commercial premises (*CAA 2001 Part 4A*), mineral extraction (*CAA 2001 Parts 5-5A*), research and development (*CAA 2001 Part 6*), know-how (*CAA 2001 Part 7*), patents (*CAA 2001 Part 8*), dredging (*CAA 2001 Part 9*) and assured tenancies (*CAA 2001 Part 10*).

C   Capital gains tax (CGT)

References in this section are to the Taxation of Chargeable Gains Act 1992, unless stated otherwise.

I   Calculation

Steps	
1	Identify the disposal
2	Calculate the 'chargeable gain' or 'allowable loss' on a disposal
3	Calculate the 'taxable gain' for the tax year on all disposals of chargeable assets, taking due account of exemptions and reliefs
4	Calculate the tax due

Step 1 — Identify the disposal (*ss 22-28*)

➤ A sale *or* gift of a 'chargeable asset' (*s 15(2)*).

♦ Note that a disposal to a co-habiting spouse (*s 58*), co-habiting civil partner (*FA 2005 s 103*), or charity (*s 257*), does not give rise to a 'chargeable gain' or an 'allowable loss' for CGT purposes.

Step 2 — Calculate the 'chargeable gain' or 'allowable loss' on *a* disposal

Steps

1   **Take either:**

a) the consideration on disposal, *or*

b) if the disposal is either:

   i) not a bargain at arm's length, *or*

   ii) the persons who dispose of and acquire the asset are 'connected',

   ... the market value of the asset *(ss 17-18)*.

2   **Subtract the 'allowable expenditure'.**

'Allowable expenditure'
➤ Allowable expenditure is calculated by adding up the following: ♦ the initial cost of the asset.   • If the asset was acquired before 31 March 1982, then use its market value on that date (*s 35 as amended by FA 2008 Sch 2 para 58*). ♦ any expense 'wholly and exclusively' incurred in enhancing the asset's value (not routine maintenance) (*s 38*). ♦ the cost of establishing title to the asset, and any costs incurred in disposing of it (*s 38*).

Step 3   **Calculate the 'taxable gain' for the tax year**

➤ Add up the total 'chargeable gains' for the tax year and deduct:

- ◆ any 'allowable losses' from that tax year (*s 2(2)(a)*), *and*

- ◆ any 'allowable losses' from previous tax years not previously brought into account for CGT (*s 2(2)(b)*).

➤ Ensure that relevant exemptions and reliefs are left out of account:

Exemptions
➤ Annual exemption of £10,600 for the tax year 2011/2012 for individuals, disabled trusts, and PRs for the year of death and 2 years thereafter (*s 3(2)*). £5,300 for other trusts.
➤ 'Wasting assets' which have a life of under 50 years (*ss 44-45*).
➤ Tangible moveables if the consideration is less than £6,000 (*s 262*).
➤ A private dwelling house which is used as a 'main residence' (or which has been used as such during the period of ownership) and land up to half a hectare (*s 222*).

- ◆ The following periods of absence are permitted:

  - • the first year of ownership (*Extra Statutory Concession D49*).

  - • up to 3 years' absence for any reason, split over relevant periods (*s 223(3)(a)*).

  - • for as long as the owner is employed outside the UK (not self-employed) or lived with a spouse or civil partner who worked in such an employment (*s 223(3)(b)*).

  - • up to 4 years of absence within the UK at the reasonable behest of an employer (*s 223(3)(c)*).

  - • any period(s) of absence not exceeding 4 years throughout which the individual lived with a spouse or civil partner in respect of whom *s 223(3)(c)* applied in respect of such period(s).

  - • the last 3 years of ownership (*s 223(1)*).

- ◆ Married couples/civil partners can only use this exemption for one house - if they own more than one, they should choose which qualifies for the exemption (*s 222(5)*).

- ◆ The exemption is reduced in proportion to any use for business purposes (*s 223(2)*).

- ◆ Trustees of a settlement can claim exemption from CGT so long as the occupier was entitled to occupy the house *either*:

  a) as tenant for life, *or*

  b) under the terms of the trust (*s 225*).

- ◆ PRs can claim exemption if certain conditions are satisfied (*s 225A*).

- ◆ Land over half a hectare will not come within the exemption unless the owner can show it is for the 'reasonable enjoyment' of the house (*s 222(2)-(3)*).

- ◆ If land of up to half a hectare is sold off, but the house is retained, the exemption will apply to the land sold (*s 222(4)*).

- ◆ The exemption also applies:

  - • if a couple cease to live together and a disposal is subsequently made as part of a divorce settlement (*s 225B*), *or*

  - • in respect of a share of any profit made when a home is sold because of employment needs and, pursuant to a home purchase agreement entered into with an employer, within 3 years of that disposal a home is sold on (*s 225C*).

Reliefs

Roll-over relief on the replacement of 'qualifying assets' (*ss 152-157*)

Qualifying assets: a) goodwill *and* b) land *and* c) fixed plant and machinery.

➤ A replacement is acquired *either* within 1 year prior to the disposal *or* within 3 years after the disposal.

➤ The replacement asset does not have to be of the same kind as the asset disposed of.

NB: For a shareholder the assets must be used by a personal trading company.

NB: Relief is restricted if the asset is not used in the seller's trade throughout the period of ownership *or* if the whole proceeds are not reinvested in a new qualifying asset.

Roll-over relief on EIS investments (*ss150-150D, Sch 5B-BA*)

➤ Any gain on the disposal of assets sold to subscribe for shares issued by an EIS company.

➤ A company may be a 'qualifying company' for the EIS if:

a) it has gross assets of less than £7 million (£15 million from 5 April 2012) before an investment, *and*
b) does not raise over £2 million (£10 million from 5 April 2012) in a 12 month period from EIS/VCT investors, *and*
c) it has fewer than 50 employees (250 from 5 April 2012), *and*
d) it is not an excluded company. It should not be excluded if it carries on a 'qualifying trade' or is the parent company of a trading group.
Note that activities such as property backed activities are excluded, eg: farming, operating or managing nursing or residential care homes, property development and forestry.

◆ The replacement shares are acquired within 1 year prior to the disposal *or* within 3 years after the disposal.

Roll-over relief on the incorporation of a business (*s 162*)

➤ The business is transferred to a corporate body as a going concern.

◆ The business is transferred with all its assets (ignore cash).

◆ The relief only applies to the proportion of the gain for which the consideration is in shares.

➤ It is possible to elect for this relief not to apply (*s 162A*).

Hold-over relief on gifts of business assets (*ss 165-165A, Sch 7*)

Qualifying assets: a) used by the business, *or* b) shares in a personal trading company, *or* c) unquoted shares.

➤ The disposal is a gift, *or* at below market value - and the transferee is not a settlor interested settlement.

➤ If a qualifying asset is shares or securities, relief is not available if the transferee is a company.

➤ There must be a joint election for relief by the donor and the donee.

NB: any IHT due is deductible from CGT as an 'expense' (*s 260(7), s 165(11)*).

Relief is denied, or may be clawed back, if a gift is made to the trustees of a settlement in which the donor has an interest or arrangements exist, or arrangements subsist under which such an interest may be acquired by the donor (*ss 169A-169G*).

Entrepreneurs' relief (*ss 169H-169S* introduced by *FA 2008 Sch 3*)

An individual makes a 'material disposal' of 'business assets' if he or she disposes of:

a) all or part of a trade carried on alone or in partnership + business owned throughout 1 year prior to disposal, *or*

b) the assets of a trade after the trade ceases + business owned throughout 1 year prior to cessation + disposal of assets within 3 years of cessation, *or*

c) shares or securities:

i) in a 'personal' trading company and the individual is an officer or employee during 1 year before the disposal, *or*

ii) the conditions in i) are met within met throughout the 1 year ending when a company ceases to be a trading company or a member of trading group, and the disposal is made within 3 years of that cessation.

▪ A company is a 'personal' company if an individual owns at least 5% of the ordinary share capital and at least 5% of the voting rights in the company are exercisable by the individual by virtue of that holding.

➤ The rate of tax is 10%.

➤ There is a lifetime limit of gains of £10 million (disposals before 6 April 2008 are ignored).

➤ Relief is also available in other special circumstances (eg: if trustees make a disposal).

Step 4	Calculate the tax due

➤ **Individuals:** 18%, *or*

28% if an individual is subject to income tax at the higher rate or dividend upper rate, *or*

28% if the amount chargeable to capital gains tax exceeds the amount at which that individual is subject to income tax at the basic rate, *or*

10% to the extent that Entrepreneurs' Relief applies to a chargeable gain.

(*s 4* as substituted by *F(No.2)A 2010 Sch 1* for disposals on or after 23 June 2010).

➤ **Trustees / PRs:** 28% for trustees of settled property and PRs (*s 4* post *F(No.2)A 2010 Sch 1*).

◆ If a beneficiary is a 'vulnerable beneficiary', and a valid election is made, trustees can claim relief so that the tax charge is reduced to that which it would have been if the chargeable gain had arisen directly to the vulnerable beneficiary (*FA 2005 ss 30-32*).

➤ **Partnerships:** calculate the 'chargeable gain' by subtracting a partner's share of an asset's acquisition cost from that partner's share of the asset's disposal value.

◆ It is the individual responsibility of each partner to ensure that his CGT is paid (*s 59*).

➤ **LLPs:** where a LLP carries on a trade or business with a view to profit, assets held by a LLP are treated for CGT purposes as being held by its partners and tax on a disposal of such assets is assessed and charged on the partners separately (and not on the LLP) (*s 59A(1)*).

➤ If a LLP ceases to carry on a trade or business with a view to profit (eg: a liquidator is appointed, or a court makes an order for the LLP to be wound-up) tax is assessed and charged on (*s 59A(5)*):

◆ the LLP in respect of any chargeable gains accruing on the disposal of its assets, *and*

◆ the LLP's members in respect of chargeable gains accruing on the disposal of their capital interests in the LLP (see also *s 169A*).

Instalment option

➤ The instalment option enables tax to be paid in 10 annual instalments, where:

a) the disposal was a gift (*s 281(1)(a)*), *and*

b) hold-over relief is not available, as opposed to not claimed (*s 281(1)(b)*), *and*

• Normally, the 'instalment option' is not available for sole traders/partners/members of a LLP incorporated under the *LPA 2000* as 'hold over' relief is available.

c) the property disposed of was (*s 281(3)*):

• land, *or*

• a controlling shareholding in a quoted or unquoted company, *or*

• a minority holding in an unquoted company.

D   Inheritance tax (IHT)

➤ *References in this section are to the Inheritance Tax Act 1984, unless otherwise stated.*

I   Liability
II   Calculation

I   Liability

Property	Liability for IHT		Burden (if a will is silent)
Vesting in the PRs	PRs: are liable to the extent that resources fall into their hands or would do so but for their default (*ss 200, 204*)		Residuary beneficiary
Jointly and nominated			Beneficiary
LCTs, PETs	Donor and donee (*s 199*)	PRs for IHT which is unpaid after 1 year after the end of the month of death (*s 204(8)*)	Donee
GBRs			
Life interest in possession	Donee and trustees (*s 199*)		Donee and trust fund

II   Calculation

During life (L)

Steps

L1 Identify a 'transfer of value' which reduces the estate's value

L2 Value the transfer

L3 Deduct any exemptions or reliefs

L4 Cumulate transfers over 7 years and calculate the tax due

On death (D)

Steps

D1 Identify property deemed to pass on death: 'the free estate'

D2 Value the 'free estate'

D3 Deduct any exemptions, reliefs or deductible property

D4 Calculate IHT on death, on pre-death chargeable transfers (LCTs, PETs, GBRs)

'PET' - Potentially Exempt Transfer
'LCT' - Lifetime Chargeable Transfer
'GBR' - Gift in respect of a which a donor Reserves a Benefit under *FA 1986 ss 102-102C*

Step L1/L4	**Identify the lifetime transfer and calculate the tax due**

Lifetime transfers which are potentially chargeable

Transfer	Definition	Tax on transfer	Cumulation on death	Tax on death
Lifetime chargeable (s 2)	a) To a trust (other than for a disabled person) b) To a company	Up to £325,000 at 0% Over £325,000 at 20% Cumulate LCTs over 7 years prior to the LCT	LCTs and chargeable PETs over 7 years prior to death	Tapering relief: year 6-7: 8% year 5-6: 16% year 4-5: 24% year 3-4: 32% Otherwise death rate at 40% Credit is given for tax already paid
Potentially exempt (s 3A)	To an individual	Nil, unless the donor dies within 7 years, then cumulate LCTs over 7 years prior to the PET	If a PET becomes chargeable, add it to the cumulative total	Tapering relief applies (as above)

Step L2/D2	**Value the transfer and/or the 'free estate'**

➤ The value of a lifetime transfer is the value of the asset transferred at the time of the transfer (s 160).

➤ The probate value of the free estate is the value of the death estate minus any lifetime transfers of value.

Valuation

Bank, building society a/c	The balance of the account and interest which has accrued to the date of death
Debts	Sums owed to the deceased. Overpaid income tax is reclaimed and accounted for on *IHT 30* (s 174)
Life interest in trust	The capital value of the beneficial interest which the deceased enjoyed *and* income accrued but unpaid at death (s 49)
Insurance	If a policy matures on the deceased's death and the estate is beneficially entitled, the sum it produces on maturity. If it matures on another event, the value of premiums paid less any sum paid to surrender rights under the policy before death (s 167)
Quoted shares	In accordance with the Stock Exchange's *Daily Official List* on the day of death. The value is the 'sell' price plus one quarter of the difference between the 'sell' and the 'buy' price. Prices are usually quoted 'cum div.' (ie: with the right to the next dividend). If the dividend has been declared but not paid, the price is quoted 'ex div.' as only those registered on the company's Register of Members when the dividend is declared are entitled to receive the dividend. If the testator dies before payment of the dividend, his estate is entitled to any declared dividend. The dividend is treated as a separate asset in the estate, and the estate's gross value is calculated by adding the dividend to the 'ex div.' price of the shares
Unquoted shares	The open market value. The firm's accountants and the firm itself will advise on a valuation. The latest annual accounts should be consulted as a guide (s 168)
Land	The open market value. Estate agents will advise on this. The figure must be agreed with the local district valuer before the estate is wound up (s 160)

Loss relief on death

➤ For some assets, the sale price may replace the probate value *if* the sale price is less than the probate value.

➤ Sale within 1 year of shares and securities quoted on a recognised stock exchange at death, or of units in an authorised unit trust (ss 178-189).

    Note: if qualifying investments are cancelled (and not replaced by the institution which issued them), they are treated as having been sold.

➤ Sale within 4 years of land (ss 190-198).

Step L3/D3	Deduct any exemptions, reliefs and (on death) deductible property

Exemptions *available on lifetime transfers only per tax year*

- ➤ £3,000 per annum, which can be carried forward for 1 year so that £6,000 becomes available in a given year.
- ➤ Normal expenditure (*s 21*).
  - ◆ Regular payments + the transfer is from income + the transferor retains sufficient income to maintain his standard of living.
- ➤ PETs which are not yet chargeable *or* have become extinct as they occurred more than 7 years before death.
- ➤ £250 small gift exemption for gifts up to this sum to any particular individual (*s 20*).
- ➤ Marriage: a) up to £5,000 from a parent, b) up to £2,500 from a remoter relation, c) up to £1,000 from a non-relation (*s 22*).

Exemptions and reliefs *on lifetime transfers and on death*

Exemptions	➤ Gift to spouse (*s 18*) or civil partner (*FA 2005 s 103*) ◆ The transfer of a lifetime interest in possession is treated as capital within this exemption ◆ On death, a gift qualifies for exemption if it is immediate *or* conditional on survivorship for up to 1 year ➤ Gift to charity (*ss 23-26*) ➤ Gift for the public benefit (*ss 30-35*). Providing that: a) the Treasury classes the asset as being as of national, artistic, historic or scientific interest, *and* b) an undertaking is given that the asset will i) remain in the UK, *and* ii) be preserved, *and* iii) be open to public access

Business property relief (*s 105*)	Relief is at 100%	➤ A business *or* an interest in a business property ➤ Any shares in an unquoted company
	Relief is at 50%	➤ Quoted shares if the transferror had control of the company immediately before the transfer ➤ The transferor is a partner or controls a company *and* transfers land, buildings, machinery or plant which were wholly or mainly used for the business
	Property must be owned for 2 or more years before the transfer takes place (*s 106*)	
Agricultural property relief (*ss 115-24*)	Relief is at 100%	➤ The transferor used the property in the EEA (Channel Islands or Isle of Man) ('relevant land') for agriculture for 2 years prior to the transfer, *or* ➤ The transferor owned relevant land used for agricultural purposes during the last 7 years and is entitled to occupy it within 1 year (or the land is let under an agricultural tenancy granted on or after 1 September 1995)
	Relief is at 50%	➤ The transferor owned relevant land used for agricultural purposes during the last 7 years and the land is subject to a tenancy granted before 1 September 1995

Exemptions, reliefs and deductible items *available on death only*

Unused nil rate band (*ss 8A-8C*)	If the deceased has a spouse or civil partner immediately before death, the deceased's unused nil rate band may be transferred to the survivor.	➤ The percentage of the nil rate band which is unused at the deceased's death is applied to the nil rate band limit on the survivor's death. ➤ A transfer may be claimed if the survivor died on or after 9 October 2007.
Quick succession (*s 141*)	Relief is a fraction of the tax already paid on a previous transfer: 1-2 years before death: 80% 2-3 years before death: 60% 3-4 years before death: 40% 4-5 years before death: 20%	➤ Tax paid on a chargeable transfer to the deceased within the last 5 years ➤ Tax is payable on the deceased's estate
Woodlands (*ss 125-130*)	Timber is exempt	➤ Timbered land in the EEA not qualifying for agricultural property relief ➤ Timber itself (not the land) is exempt provided the land was bought at least 5 years before death
Funerals (*s 162*)	Fully deductible	➤ Reasonable burial expenses are deductible
Debts (*s 505*)		➤ Debts incurred for money or money's worth are deductible

Liabilities are deductible (*s 5(3)*) unless the deduction is excluded (*s 162*) (More complex liabilities are not dealt with here)

Step L3/D3	Deduct any exemptions, reliefs and (on death) deductible property

Identifying the 'free estate' on death (*IHTA 1984 ss 5, 200*)

➤ Assets to which the testator is beneficially entitled and which pass under the will or on intestacy

➤ Assets passing outside the will or intestacy:

◆ to which the deceased is beneficially entitled under property law: joint tenancies, nominated property, *and*

◆ friendly society/Industrial and provident society accounts, *and*

◆ assets to which the deceased is deemed to be beneficially entitled for IHT purposes:

a) a GBR, *and*

b) a life interest in possession which (broadly speaking) is **not**:

   i) an 'immediate post-death' interest (*s 49A*), *or*

      ■ An 'immediate post-death interest' is an interest in settled property:

         A) where the individual became beneficially entitled on the death of a testate or intestate person, *and*

         B) the settled property neither is (nor was at any time since the individual became beneficially entitled) property settled on a bereaved minor (within *s 71A*), nor a disabled person's interest.

   ii) a disabled person's interest (*s 89B*), *or*

   iii) a 'transitional serial interest' (*ss 49A-E*).

      ■ A 'transitional serial interest' is an interest in settled property, where the settlement commenced before 22 March 2006, and either:

         A) the individual became beneficially entitled aa) during the period between 22 March 2006 and 5 October 2008, *or* bb) on the death of a spouse/CP on or after 5 October 2008, *or*

         B) the settlement consisted of, or included, rights under an insurance policy entered into before 22 March 2006.

Step D4	Calculate IHT on death and on pre-death chargeable transfers

Calculation of IHT on the death estate

LCTs and PETs	Any of these occurring within 7 years prior to the death represent additional liability	(See *Step L1*, p 119)
Tax rate on 'free estate' (after taking account of exemptions/reliefs)	Not exceeding £325,000 at 0% Exceeding £325,000 at 40%	

Note
In calculating these bands, cumulate LCTs and PETs which occurred in the 7 years prior to death

Apportionment of IHT over the estate

Subject to instructions to the contrary in the will, the IHT burden is 'apportioned' over the whole estate by the formula:

$$\text{Estate rate} = \frac{\text{Tax payable}}{\text{Taxable estate}}$$

The tax due on each asset is calculated by multiplying the value of the asset by the 'estate rate'

E   Corporation tax (CT)

References in this section are to the CA 2009, unless otherwise stated.

I	Calculation
II	Loss relief/R&D tax relief

I   Calculation

Steps	*(CA 2010 s 4)*
1	Calculate the amount chargeable to CT as income
2	Calculate the amount chargeable to CT as chargeable gains
3	Calculate the 'total profits'
4	Deduct amounts relievable against total profits
5	Calculate the corporation tax due on profits

Step 1 — Calculate the amount chargeable to CT as income

Income taxed as trade profits (*Part 3*)

➤ Profit is calculated in accordance with generally accepted accounting practice, unless any adjustment is required or authorised by law (*s 46*).

➤ A deduction is not allowed if expenditure is: of a capital nature (*s 53*) , not 'wholly and exclusively' incurred for the purposes of a trade (*s 54*), for (subject to limited exceptions) for entertainment (*ss 1298-1299*).

➤ Subtract any capital allowances, or add any balancing charges see p 111.

➤ Note that if a company does not carry on a trade, and carries on Investment business instead, certain expenses (eg expenses of management) may be deductible (*Part 16*).

Income taxed as profits of a UK or overseas property business (*Part 4*)

➤ Profit is calculated in the same way as profits of a trade (*s 210(1)*).

   ◆ This includes distributions in respect of a REIT's tax-exempt business (*CA 2010 s 548*).

➤ Part of a premium received on the grant of a lease with a term not exceeding 50 years, or on the surrender or variation / waiver of a lease (even if the original term exceeded 50 years), may be treated as an income receipt and as a part disposal for CGT purposes - for the apportionment see *s 217* (see also *TCGA 1992 Sch 8* for CGT treatment).

   ◆ Remediation relief (at the rate of 150% of the actual expenditure incurred) may be claimed for expenditure incurred in cleaning up contaminated or derelict land (*Part 14*).

➤ Subtract any capital allowances, or add any balancing charges see p 111.

Profits on 'loan relationships' (*Part 5*), and 'derivative contracts' (*Part 7*)

➤ A company has a 'loan relationship' when:

a) it stands in the position of a creditor or a debtor as respects a money debt, *and*

b) the debt arises from a transaction for the lending of money (*s 302(1)*) (eg: not a trade debt).

- A 'money debt' is a debt which is, or has been, a debt in any currency which falls (or may at the option of the debtor or creditor fall), to be settled by the payment of money, *or* the transfer of a right to settlement of a debt which is a money debt (*s 303*).

NB: *Part 6* provides for other matters to be treated as loan relationships in certain circumstances (eg: certain non-lending relationships, some interests in collective investment schemes, alternative finance arrangements, shares accounted for as liabilities, or arrangements giving rise to disguised interest).

➤ Profits and losses are calculated in accordance with generally accepted accounting practice (*ss 307-312*; 'generally accepted accounting practice' is defined by *CA 2010 s 1127(1)* and *(3)*).

- An amortised cost basis of accounting (rather than fair value accounting) must be used in certain circumstances (eg: *ss 348-349*) (*parties to a loan relationship are connected*).

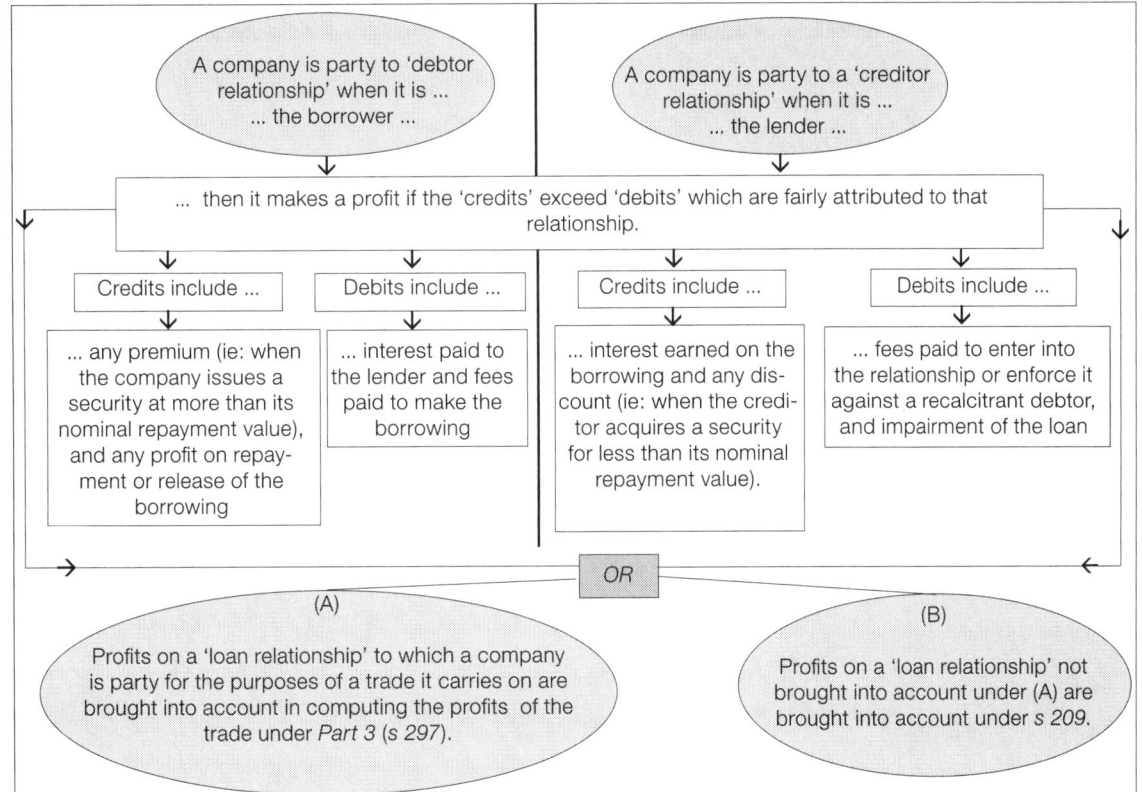

➤ Various anti-avoidance provisions may prevent a company gaining deductions in respect of interest or other 'debits'. Details are beyond the scope of this book.

- Provisions of general application include *CA 2010 Part 23*, and *ss 441-442* (*loan relationship for unallowable purpose*).

- There are also rules which apply in particular circumstances, eg: *s 354* which restricts the availability of 'debits' when an impairment loss (eg: a bad debt) arises for a creditor when a debt is between connected parties.

- *T(IOP)A 2010 Part 7* can disallow a deduction in respect of financing expenses if the UK net debt of a group of companies exceeds 75% of the worldwide group's gross debt.

➤ The general intention is that 'capital' gains and losses (as well as 'income' profits and losses, and including forex gains and losses) on a money debt should be taxed and relieved as income.

➤ Gains and losses on derivative contracts (eg: options, swaps and derivatives) are brought into account under legislation which aims (as with loan relationships) to follow generally accepted accounting practice (*Part 7*).

➤ Profits on a 'loan relationship' or a derivative contract to which a company is party for the purposes of a trade are brought into account in computing the profits and gains of the trade under *Part 3* (*ss 297, 573*).

   ◆ Otherwise, profits are brought into account under *ss 299-301, 574*.

Profits from intangible fixed assets (including goodwill and intellectual property) (*Part 8*)

➤ 'Capital' gains and losses (as well as 'income' profits and losses) may be taxed and relieved as income following generally accepted accounting practice.

   ◆ Note *Part 8* does not apply to intangible fixed assets treated as being created before 1 April 2002.

➤ Profits on intangible fixed assets held for the purposes of a trade or property business are brought into account in computing the profits and gains of that trade under *Part 3* (*s 747*) or of that property business (*s 748*).

   ◆ Otherwise, profits are brought into account under *ss 751-753*.

Miscellaneous income (*Part 10*)

Step 2	Calculate amount chargeable to CT as chargeable gains

Steps

I Identify the disposal

II Calculate the 'taxable gain' or loss on *a* disposal

III Calculate the 'taxable gain' on all disposals for the accounting period, taking account of exemptions and reliefs

Step I	Identify the disposal (*TCGA 1992 ss 22-28*)

➤ A sale *or* gift of a 'chargeable asset' (*TCGA 1992 s 15(2)*).

Step II	Calculate the 'taxable gain' or 'allowable loss' on disposal

➤ Take *either* the market value of the asset on its 'disposal' (*TCGA 1992 s 17*) *or* the consideration on its sale, and subtract the 'allowable expenditure'.

   ◆ The allowable expenditure is calculated by adding up the following:

   • the initial cost of the asset. If the asset was acquired before 31 March 1982, use *either*:

   a) its value on that date, *or*

   b) the cost of acquisition, whichever produces a smaller loss or gain (*TCGA 1992 s 35*).

   • any expense 'wholly and exclusively' incurred in enhancing the asset's value (not routine maintenance) (*TCGA 1992 s 38*).

   • the cost of establishing title to the asset, and costs of disposal (*TCGA 1992 s 38*).

➤ Then subtract the 'indexation allowance', which accounts for the impact of inflation on the gain.

   ◆ Where an asset was owned on 31 March 1982, the allowance can be taken *either*

   a) from the asset's value on 31 March 1982, *or*

   b) rom the 'actual expenditure' on the asset (ie: acquisition, maintenance, etc), whichever carries a higher indexation (*TCGA 1992 s 54*).

NB: since 30 November 1993, this allowance only serves to reduce or extinguish a gain, it cannot be used to increase the size of a loss, nor to convert a gain into a loss.

Step III	Calculate the 'taxable gain' for the accounting period

➤ Add up the total 'chargeable gains' for the accounting period.

➤ Then deduct:

◆ any 'allowable losses' from that accounting period (*TCGA 1992 s 2(2)(a)*), *and*

◆ any 'allowable losses' from previous accounting periods not brought into account to corporation tax (*TCGA 1992 s 2(2)(b)*).

➤ Ensure relevant exemptions and reliefs are left out of account:

Exemptions
'Wasting assets' which have a life of under 50 years (*TCGA 1992 ss 44-45*)
Tangible moveables if the consideration is less than £6,000 (*TCGA 1992 s 262*)
Substantial shareholdings (*TCGA 1992 Sch 7AC*)
➤ A trading company disposes of a substantial (10% or more) shareholding in a trading company or a holding company of a trading group, *and* ➤ The investing company has held 10% or more of the ordinary shares in the company invested in for at least 12 months in the 2 years before the disposal

Reliefs
Roll-over relief on the replacement of 'qualifying assets' (*TCGA 1992 ss 152-157*)
Qualifying assets: a) goodwill *and* b) land *and* c) fixed plant and machinery (*ss 155-156*) ➤ A replacement is acquired *either* within 1 year prior to the disposal *or* within 3 years after the disposal ➤ The replacement asset does not have to be of the same kind as the asset disposed of NB: Relief is restricted if the asset is not used in the seller's trade throughout the period of ownership *or* if the whole proceeds are not reinvested in a new qualifying asset
Roll-over relief on paper for paper transactions (*TCGA 1992 ss 127-137A*)

Step 3	'Total profits' = 'income' + 'chargeable gains'

Step 4	Deduct amounts relievable against total profits

➤ Relief is available in respect (*CA 2010 Part 6*):

a) qualifying charitable donations, *and*

b) amounts allowed in respect of gifts of shares, etc to charities.

• Relief is denied if a donation is tainted *(CA 2010 ss 939A-939I* inserted by *FA 2011 Sch 3*).

Step 5	Calculate the corporation tax due on profits (*TA s 13*)

➤ The rates are fixed for a financial year (1 April to 31 March): if the rate changes during the accounting period, the taxable profit is apportioned across the applicable tax rates.

Full rate of 'mainstream corporation tax':   26[†]% on profits over £1,500,000.

Tax on profits between £300,000 and £1,500,000:   27.5% ⎯ relief is effectively given at this marginal rate

Tax on profits not exceeding £300,000:   20% ⎯ the 'small profits rate' of corporation tax

[†]   *The Government plans to reduce the mainstream rate by 1% a year until it reaches 23% on 1 April 2014.*

➤ Franked investment income is ignored when paying tax, but it is included when calculating the rate of tax applicable.

II   Loss relief / R&D tax relief

➤   Companies may use their losses in a number of ways.

	Loss can be claimed ...	Use on ...

Carry-across and carry-back relief CA 2010 s 37	a) ... for the accounting period, and
	b) ... any unrelieved loss may be carried back against any profits from an accounting period in the previous 1 year, *provided*:
	  i) the company is carrying on the same trade as it had been in the earlier year, *and*
	  ii) the loss is set against later year(s) first
		... total profits

Trading losses other than terminal CA 2010 s 45	... following accounting periods, against losses of the trade, for as long as the company carries on the trade	... trading income
UK property business CA 2010 s 62	a) ... for the accounting period, and b) ... any unrelieved loss may be carried forward if the company continues to carry on a UK property business in that succeeding period	... total profits

NB: special rules apply for losses of a trade carried on wholly outside the UK and losses under miscellaneous charges (*CA 2010 s 91*). Further rules, which are beyond the scope of this book, apply to restrict relief to the capital contributed by the company to the partnership (*CA 2010 s 56*).

NB: a company which is a member of a group of companies can claim group relief.

Loan relationships and derivative contracts

➤   'Debits' on 'loan relationships' to which a company is a party for the purposes of a trade carried on by it are deductible in computing the profits of that trade (*CA 2009 s 297(2)*) and losses may be relieved under the normal rules for the set-off of losses on income.

➤   All the 'debits' and 'credits' on 'loan relationships' to which a company is party otherwise than for the purposes of trade carried on by it are aggregated together.   If the 'non-trading debits' exceed the 'non-trading credits', a company has a 'non-trading deficit' on its 'loan relationships'. A 'non-trading deficit' may be dealt with in one of 4 ways (*CA 2009 s 456-463*):

  a) set-off against profits from the same accounting period (in the priority required by *CA 2009 s 461*).

  b) surrendered and relieved through group relief.

  c) carried back against profits of accounting periods during the previous 1 year (*CA 2009 s 463*).

  d) carried forward against profits for the next accounting period (provided the profits are not classed as trading income within *CA 2010 s 37*) - this option is used to the extent that the others are not claimed (*CA 2009 ss 457-458*).

➤   Similar rules also apply to derivative contract (*CTA 2009 Part 7*) losses.

R&D tax relief
'Small and medium sized enterprises' (*CA 2009 Part 13 Chapters 2-4*)

➤ R&D is an activity that is treated as research and development under guidelines published by the DTI in March 2004 (*ITA s 1006*).

➤ An R&D tax credit should be available if a company (*CA 2009 ss 1043-1050*):

a) is a 'small or medium sized enterprise' in an accounting period, *and*

- A 'small or medium sized enterprise' under Commission Recommendation 2003/361/EC except that the ceilings are 500 employees (rather than 250), EURO 100m (rather than EURO 50m), and EURO 86m (rather than EURO 43m) (*CA 2009 ss 1119-1120*).

b) incurs qualifying expenditure on R&D in an accounting period which is not less than the R&D threshold of £10,000 and would be allowable as a deduction in computing the profits of a trade carried on by a company (or would have been so allowable if the company had been carrying on a trade at the time).

- 'Qualifying expenditure' is (*CA 2009 s 1052*), eg:
  i) incurred on staff costs, software, consumable items, externally provided workers, or payments to subjects of a clinical trial, *and*
  ii) attributable to R&D carried on by the company or on its behalf, *and*
  iii) not incurred on activities contracted out to the company by another person, *and*
  iv) such that any intellectual property is or will be vested (at least in part) in the company, *and*
  v) not subsidised by any other person.
- For 'qualifying subcontracted R&D expenditure' see *CA 2009 s 1053*.

➤ Relief can also be claimed for R&D subcontracted to a SME (*CA 2009 ss 1063-1067*), and subsidised and capped expenditure by a SME on R&D (*CA 2009 ss 1068-1072*).

➤ If a company is (*CA 2009 ss 1054-1062 as amended by FA 2011 s 43*):

a) trading and has qualifying R&D expenditure which is allowable as a deduction it may deduct an amount equal to 200% (225% from April 2012) of the qualifying R&D expenditure in computing trade profit, *or*

b) not trading, but has qualifying R&D expenditure which would have been allowable if at that time it had been carrying on a trade consisting of the activities in respect of which the expenditure was incurred, it may elect to be treated as if it had incurred a trading loss in that period equal to 150% of the amount of its qualifying R&D expenditure.

- Where a company under a) has an unrelieved loss, or a company is treated as having an unrelieved loss under b), it may claim a credit equal to 12.5% of that loss (*CA 2009 s 1058*).

➤ The total R&D aid for a project is capped at EURO 7.5 million (*CA 2009 ss 1113-1118*).

Large companies (*CA 2009 Part 13 Chapter 5*)

➤ A company which: ...

- qualifies as a large company (ie: not small or medium sized) throughout a period, *and*
- incurs 'qualifying R&D expenditure' of not less than £10,000 in a 12 month accounting period ...

  ... is entitled to an additional deduction (ie: in addition to a deduction available under general principles) equal to 30% of such qualifying expenditure (*CA 2009 s 1074(7)*).

  - For this purpose qualifying expenditure comprises expenditure on direct R&D, subcontracted R&D expenditure' and contributions to independent R&D (NB: the tests are not the same as under the rules for' small and medium sized enterprises').

F   Distributions

I	Shareholder who is an individual
II	Corporation tax paying shareholder

I   Shareholder who is an individual

➤ A distribution by a UK resident company carries a tax credit of one nineth.

The tax credit
Distribution (of £100) on or after 6 April 1999
1/9^{th†} (£8.89) of the net distribution (£80) received by the shareholder
$\dagger$ This is equivalent to 10% of the gross distribution (£88.89) which the shareholder receives

➤ A distribution by a non-UK resident company carries a tax credit of one nineth where:

a) a person's shareholding is less than 10% in the ordinary share capital of that company (*IT(TOI)A ss 397A-C*), or

b) the distribution is made on or after 22 April 2009, an individual holds 10% or more of the ordinary share capital in that resident company and (*IT(TOI)A ss 397AA, 397BA*):

   i)   the source of the distribution is a territory with which the UK has a double taxation agreement, *and*

   ii) that double taxation agreement has a non-discrimination article.

➤ An individual who is a non-taxpayer (and a person benefiting from a tax exemption, eg: a charity or a pension fund) is not entitled to a repayment of the tax credit.

➤ An individual who is liable under the starting rate for savings (10%) or basic rate (20%) has no additional liability in relation to the distribution (*IT(TOI)A 2005 s 397*).   Liability is at the 'dividend ordinary rate' - 10% of the gross distribution (*ITA ss 8(1), 13*), and the tax credit satisfies this.

➤ An individual who is a higher-rate (40%) taxpayer owes an extra 32.5% more tax at the 'dividend upper rate' (*ITA ss 8(2), 13*).   This equates to 25% of the amount actually received by the shareholder.

Higher rate taxpayer's liability		
	Distributions on or after 6 April 1999	£
Distribution		80.00
Tax credit	(10% of 88.89, or 1/9th of 80)	8.89
Gross income		88.89
Higher rate tax	(32.5% of 88.89)	28.89
After tax income		60.00

➤ An individual who has income above the higher rate limit' (£150,000) is subject to tax at the 'dividend additional rate' (42.5%) (*FA 2009 s 6*) which equates to 36.11% of the amount actually received by the shareholder.

➤ Note that HMRC may restrict or deny a tax credit in certain circumstances, for instance if a distribution is abnormally large and not commercially justified (*ITA ss 682-713*).

◆ An anti-avoidance provision, *TA s 231B*, has been introduced to counteract arrangements designed to pass on the value of a tax credit to a person who would not (without such arrangements) be entitled to it.

II Corporation tax paying shareholder

➤ A distribution paid by a company prior to 1 July 2009 is exempt from corporation tax (*CA 2009 s 1285*).

➤ A distribution paid by a company on or after 1 July 2009 (*FA 2009 Sch 14 para 31*) is chargeable to corporation tax (*CA 2009 s 931A as amended by F(No.3)A 2010*).

◆ It is anticipated that most dividends will be exempt (see further below).

➤ A distribution, and the associated tax credit, may be taken into account in working out the rate of corporation tax applicable to a company for an accounting period (*CA 2010 s 32*).

➤ There are 6 categories of exempt distribution.

◆ In order for a distribution to be exempt (*CA 2009 ss 931B(b)-(c), 931D(b)-(c)*):

a) that distribution must not be treated as a distribution by virtute of anti-avoidance rules which apply (broadly) when a return is paid on a debt security the terms of which are designed to mirror equity (eg: interest exceeds a reasonable commercial return, or interest increases as profits increase), *and*

b) no deduction must be allowed to a resident of a territory outside the UK in respect of that distribution.

◆ The first category of exempt distribution applies only to small companies, and a dividend paid by a company which is a small company cannot take advantage of any of the other categories of exemption.

◆ There are 5 additional anti-avoidance rules, each of which can apply so as to prevent a distribution from being exempt.

◆ A company may elect, within 2 years of the end of the accounting period in which a distribution is received, for that distribution not to be exempt (*CA 2009 s 931R*).

➤ The 6 categories of exempt distribution are as follows:

1   The recipient of the distribution is a 'small company'

➤ A distribution is exempt if (*CA 2009 s 931B*):

a) the company making the distribution is resident in the UK or in a 'qualifying territory', *and*

■ A 'qualifying territory' is a territory with which the UK has a double taxation treaty which includes a non-discrimination provision (*CA 2009 s 931C*).

■ If a company is excluded from any benefit under a double taxation treaty, that company is an 'excluded company' and a distribution is not exempt under *CA 2009 s 931C (D(EC) R 2009 r 2)*.

b) the distribution is not part of a tax advantage scheme.

➤ A company is 'small' if in the relevant accounting period it is a micro or small enterprise as defined in the Annex to Commission recommendation 2003/361/EC of 6 May 2003, provided that it is not an open-ended investment company, an authorised unit trust scheme, an insurance company or a friendly society (*CA 2009 s 931S*).

2   The distribution is from a 'controlled' company

➤ Either (*CA 2009 s 931E(1)-(3)*):

a) the recipient company 'controls' the company making the distribution, or

b) the recipient company is 1 of 2 companies which 'controls' the company making the distribution and:

   i)   the recipient has interests, rights and powers which represent at least 40%, *and*

   ii) the other company has interests, rights and powers which represent at least 40% but not more than 55%,

       ... of the interests rights and powers by virtue of which both companies control the company making the payment.

• 'Control' means (*CA 2009 s 931E(4)*):

   ■ the power to secure by means of holding shares or the possession of voting power, or through the articles of association or any other document regulating the affairs of a company, that the affairs of the relevant company are conducted in accordance with a person's wishes (*TA s 755D(1)*), or

   ■ an entitlement to receive the greater part of the distributable income of a company, the proceeds on a disposal of its share capital, or of its assets on a winding-up (*TA s 755D(1A)*).

➤ The distribution is not (*CA 2009 s 931J*):

a) paid as part of a scheme a main purpose of which is to ensure that the distribution falls within this category, *and*

b) paid out of profits that arose prior to the requisite control existing.

3   The distribution is in respect of non-redeemable ordinary shares

➤ The distribution is made in respect of a share that is an ordinary share and is not redeemable (*CA 2009 s 931F*).

   ◆ 'Ordinary' means a share that does not carry any present or future right preferential rights to dividends or assets on a winding-up (*CA 2009 s 931U(1)*).

➤ The (*CA 2009 s 931K*):

a) distribution is not paid as part of a scheme a main purpose of which is to ensure that the distribution falls within this category, *and*

b) share would not be ordinary or redeemable if the rights under that scheme of the company receiving the distribution (or any person connected with it) were attached to the share.

4   The distribution is in respect of a 'portfolio holding'

➤ The recipient company (*CA 2009 s 931G*):

a) holds less than 10% of the issued share capital of the company making the distribution, *and*

b) is entitled to less than 10% of the profits of the company making the distribution available for distribution to holders of its issued share capital, *and*

c) would be entitled on a winding-up to less than 10% of the assets of the company making the distribution available for distribution to holders of its issued share capital.

➤ The distribution (*CA 2009 s 931L*):

a) is not paid as part of a scheme a main purpose of which is to ensure that the distribution falls within this category, *and*

b) would not be 'exempt' in this category if in applying the 10% tests, the rights of all persons connected with the recipient company were taken into account.

5   The distribution is derived from transactions not designed to avoid tax

➤ The distribution is not paid out of profits which reflect the results of a transaction or series of transactions which achieve a reduction in UK tax, and a main purpose of that transaction (or transactions) was to achieve that reduction (*CA 2009 s 931H*).

6   The distribution is in respect of a share which is accounted for as a liability

➤ The share in respect of which the distribution is made would be accounted for as a liability, and other conditions set out in *CA 2009 s 521C* are satisfied (*CA 2009 s 931I*).

Anti-avoidance (1) - Schemes in the nature of loan relationships

➤ A distribution is not exempt if (*CA 2009 s 931M*):

a) it would, were it not for this rule, be exempt under categories 1 or 3-6, *and*

b) it is made as part of a tax advantage scheme, *and*

c) various conditions are met, including in particular that the distribution constitutes part of a return produced by the scheme which is economically equivalent to interest, and the recipient and the payer would be connected for the purposes of *CA 2009 s 466*.

Anti-avoidance (2) - Schemes involving distributions for which deductions are given

➤ A distribution is not exempt if (*CA 2009 s 931N*):

a) it is made as part of a tax advantage scheme, *and*

b) a deduction is allowed to a resident of any territory outside the UK under the law of that territory in respect of an amount determined by reference to the distribution.

Anti-avoidance (3) - Schemes involving payments for distributions

➤ A distribution is not exempt if (*CA 2009 s 931O)*):

a) it is made as part of a tax advantage scheme, *and*

b) various conditions are met, including that the scheme includes the making of a payment, or the giving up of a right to income, under a liability incurred for consideration in money or money's worth consisting of (or of the right to receive) the distribution.

Anti-avoidance (4) - Schemes involving non-arm's length payments

➤ A distribution is not exempt if (*CA 2009 s 931P*):

a) it is made as part of a tax advantage scheme, *and*

b) various conditions are met, including that the scheme includes a payment or receipt, or giving up a right to income in respect of goods or services.

Anti-avoidance (5) - Schemes involving diversion of trading income

➤ A distribution is not exempt if (*CA 2009 s 931Q*):

a) the distribution is made as part of a scheme entered into by the recipient of the distribution and a person ('P') connected with that recipient, *and*

b) if P had received the distribution, the distribution would have been treated in P's hands as trading income under *CA 2009 Part 3, and*

c) a main purpose of the scheme is to ensure that the distribution is dealt with under these rules rather than under *CA 2009 Part 3*.

G Close companies

    I   Generally

    II   Taxation of a 'close company' and its 'participators'

I Generally

➤ For corporation tax purposes, a 'close company' is a company that is *either*:

a) 'controlled' by 5 or fewer 'participators', *or*

b) 'controlled' by 'participators' who are its directors, *or*

c) has amongst its shareholders 5 or fewer 'participators', or directors who are 'participators' *and* on a winding-up of the company these 'participators' would be entitled to receive the greater part of the company's assets.

    • 'Control' means control as defined in *CA 2010 s 450*.

        ■ For the definition of 'control' in *CA 2010 s 450*, and also for the (different) definition of 'control' in *CA 2010 s 1124/ITA s 995*, see p 136. (Both definitions are used in the *Taxes Act* and it is important to make sure that the correct definition is used in the right context.)

    • A 'participator' is a person who has a share or interest in the capital or the income of a company and specifically someone entitled to acquire capital or voting rights, or to ensure income or assets will be deployed for his benefit, or entitled to distributions or the proceeds of a premium or redemption paid by the company, or certain loan creditors (*CA 2010 s 454*).

    • The definition of 'director' is a wide one, and focuses on substance rather than the title (*CA 2010 s 452*).

➤ Companies which may not be close companies for corporation tax purposes include:

    ◆ companies not resident in the UK (*CA 2010 s 442*).

    ◆ quoted companies, if shares bearing not less than 35% of the votes at a general meeting have been unconditionally allotted or acquired so that members of the public enjoy them beneficially (*CA 2010 s 446*).

    ◆ companies controlled by one or more non-close companies and which could only be treated as a close company by including a non-close company as one of the 5 participators, or by including non-close loan creditors on a liquidation (*CA 2010 s 444*).

➤ The definition of a 'close company' is different in respect of the taxation of individuals who hold shares in such companies.

    ◆ For IHT purposes, the definition of a 'close company' is the same as for corporation tax purposes except that:

    a) it includes non-resident companies, *and*

    b) the test for a 'participator' disregards the interests of loan creditors (*IHTA 1984 s 94*).

    ◆ For capital gains tax purposes, the definition includes non-resident companies (*TCGA 1992 s 13*).

II   Taxation of a 'close company' and its participators

➤   The taxation treatment of a 'close company' depends on whether it is also a 'close investment holding company'.

➤   The rules in **A 'Close companies'** apply to all 'close companies', the additional rules in **B 'Close investment holding companies'** apply only to 'close investment holding companies'.

Definition of a 'close investment holding company'

➤   A close company is a 'close investment holding company' unless it exists during an accounting period 'wholly or mainly' for one of 6 purposes.

◆   These purposes include carrying on a trade on a commercial basis, and investing in land provided the land is not intended to be let to connected persons (*CA 2010 s 34)*).

A   'Close companies'

1   Loans to 'participators' (*CA 2010 Part 10, IT(TOI)A 2005 ss 415-421*)

➤   A company pays tax (at the rate of 25%) to HMRC in respect of a loan to a participator (eg: if the company wishes to lend £100 gross it pays £25 tax to the HMRC and the participator receives £75).

➤   This does not apply if *either*:

a)   the loan is in the usual course of business for a company whose business is money lending, *or*

b)   the following conditions are fulfilled (*CA 2010 s 456*):

i)   the company's total loans to the 'participator' stand at less than £15,000, *and*

ii)   the 'participator' owns 5% or less of the shares in the company, *and*

iii)   the 'participator' works full time for the company.

➤   If a claim for repayment of the tax is made within 6 years of the end of the accounting period in which the repayment of the loan is made, HMRC refund the tax to the company.

2   Expenses of 'participators', and their 'associates', taxed as distributions (*CA 2010 s 1064*)

➤   An expense to benefit a 'participator' or their 'associate' (eg: a spouse, or civil partner), is a 'qualifying distribution' on which the participator is taxed under *IT(TOI)A 2005 s 383*.

➤   A charge to tax under this section is excluded if the 'participator' is taxed on the benefit under *IT(EP) A 2003 Part 3* (*CA 2010 s 1065*).

3   Attribution of capital gains to a 'participator' (*TCGA 1992 s 13*)

➤   Capital gains made by a non-resident company (which would be close if UK resident) are apportioned to 'participators' in that company in proportion to their beneficial interest in the company.

4   Liability to IHT on a transfer of value by a 'close company' (*IHTA 1984 s 94(1)*)

➤   A transfer at an undervalue by a close company is treated as a transfer out of a 'participator's' estate and is chargeable to IHT.   Liability rests primarily on the company, although limited recovery is possible from each 'participator' or the transferee (*IHTA 1984 s 202(1)*).

◆   Altering the rights of unquoted share or loan capital is treated as a transfer (*IHTA 1984 s 98(1)*).

5   **Relief on interest on loan to, or to buy ordinary shares in, a close company (*ITA ss 392-395*)**

➤ The individual:

a) has a 'material interest'

- The individual is the beneficial owner of or is able to control more than 5% of the company's ordinary shares, or has or is entitled to acquire rights to more than 5% of the assets of the company distributable amongst its 'participators' on a winding-up or otherwise, *and*

a) the taxpayer spends the majority of time working for the company when the interest is paid, *and*

- lends money to a close company, *or*

- borrows money for the close company to use in the course of its business, *or*

- borrows to purchase ordinary shares in a close company.

B 'Close investment holding companies'

1   **Rate of corporation tax**

➤ Tax is paid at the full corporation tax rate of 26% (eg: not the smaller companies' rate of 21%).

2   **Abuse of tax credit**

➤ Anti-avoidance rules deny the benefit of a tax credit where arrangements are entered into under which a person obtains a payment representing a tax credit and those arrangements are entered into for an unallowable purpose (*TA s 231B*).

Principal definitions of 'control' in the *Taxes Act*

s 450 'control'

➤ The test is complex, but involves establishing that a person exercises, is able to exercise or entitled to acquire, direct or indirect control over a company's affairs.

- Examples of such control include the possession of, or entitlement to acquire:

a) the greater part of a company's issued share capital or of the voting power in a company.

b) enough of the company's issued share capital to entitle that person to receive the greater part of the income of the company if that income were to be distributed amongst the 'participators' in the company.

c) on a winding-up of the company, to receive the greater part of the assets of the company which would be available for distribution amongst the 'participators' in the company (*s 450(3)*).

CA 2010 s 1124, ITA s 995

➤ A person 'controls' a company (the 'relevant company') if that person has power to secure ...

a) by means of the holding of shares or the possession of voting power in or in relation to the relevant company or any other company, *or*

b) by virtue of any powers conferred by the articles of association or other document regulating the relevant company or any other company, ...

... that the affairs of the relevant company are conducted in accordance with the wishes of that person.

H Assessment and payment of tax (IT, CGT, IHT, CT)

I   Self assessment of income tax and capital gains tax

II   Payment of income tax and capital gains tax

III   Assessment of IHT on death

IV   Payment of IHT

V   Self assessment of corporation tax

VI   Payment of corporation tax

I   Self assessment of income tax and capital gains tax

References in this section are to TMA 1970, unless otherwise stated.

1   Notification of chargeability

➤ An individual is under a duty to notify HMRC of any chargeable income or capital gain within 6 months of the taxable event in respect of which tax falls due, unless the individual is exempt as:

   ◆ no chargeable income and gains arise in the year of assessment (above the exempt amount), *and*

   ◆ his net income tax liability is nil *or* tax deducted at source covers any liability (*s 7(3)-(7)*).

2   Filing a tax return

➤ An individual must submit a tax return stating his liability to income tax and capital gains tax (*s 8(1)(a)*).

➤ The filing date depends on whether the individual completes a self assessment.

   ◆ If he only wishes to supply information, without completing a self assessment, he must submit the return:

     a) on or before 30 September following the end of the tax year, or

     b) if a notice is issued after 31 July following the end of the tax year, within 2 months of the notice being issued (*s 9(2)*).

   ◆ If he assesses his own tax, he must submit:

     ● an electronic return on or before 31 January following the end of the tax year, *or*

     ● a paper return on or before 31 October following the end of the tax year,

       ... unless the return is issued late (after 31 July) in which case special rules apply (*ss 8(1)(a), 8(1D)-(1H)*).

   ◆ If a return is submitted, but the self assessment is not completed, HMRC is under a duty to complete it (*s 9(3)*).

➤ Penalties for failing to file a return on time are hefty.

◆ £100 automatically if a return is not submitted on time, *and*

◆ a further £100 if it is still outstanding 6 months later, *and*

◆ then up to £60 a day (*ss 93(2)-93(4)*).

➤ If no return is submitted, HMRC may, within 5 years of the end of the year of assessment, estimate the tax and make a determination stating the tax due (*s 28C*).

3 Records

➤ Records relevant to calculating tax liability must be kept: there is a fine of up to £3,000 for non-compliance (*s 12B(1)-(6)*).

	Individual	Sole trader/partner
Time the return is issued ...	... within 1 year of the filing date	... within 5 years of the filing date
Obligation to keep records expires	1 year after the filing date	5 years after the filing date, or when a formal HMRC enquiry is finished or becomes impossible

◆ Powers introduced by *FA 2008 Sch 37* enable HMRC to make regulations shortening the period during which records must be kept.

II Payment of income tax and capital gains tax

➤ Tax assessed under self assessment is payable 'on account' on 31 January during the year of assessment, and on 31 July following the end of the year. Any corrective 'balancing' payment is due on the next 31 January (*TMA 1970 s 59A(2)*).

◆ No payment need be made on account if the income tax due is *either:*

a) less than £1,000 (*IT(PA)(A)R 2008 r 2*), *or*

b) less than 20% of the taxpayer's total income tax liability for the year (ie: including income from which tax has been deducted at source) (*TMA 1970 s 59A(1)(c)-(d), IT(PA)R 1996*), ...

... in which case tax is payable on 31 January following the year of assessment.

◆ The taxpayer may opt for tax to be deducted under PAYE if the tax due is less than £2,500.

➤ Interest runs on tax due 'on account', or as a balancing payment (*TMA 1970 ss 59A-59B*) from the date the payment is due (*TMA 1970 s 86*). Interest on overpaid tax is paid to the taxpayer (*s 824, TCGA s 283*).

➤ A surcharge of 5% is levied on tax outstanding 28 days after it falls due, and there is a further 5% surcharge if the tax is still unpaid 6 months after it is due (*TMA 1970 s 59C*).

> ➤ If tax is paid by credit card:
>
> ◆ over the telephone, a fee equal to 0.91% of the payment must also be paid (*T(FPT)R 2008 r 2*), *or*
>
> ◆ over the internet, a fee equal to 1.4% of the payment must also be paid (*T(FPI) R 2011 r 2*).

III   Assessment of IHT on death

➤   A PR is not required to deliver an account in respect of an 'excepted estate' (*IT(DA)(EE)R 2004 r 3*).

   ◆   If an estate is an 'excepted estate' *form IHT 205* must be completed and delivered with an application for probate (*IT(DA)(EE)R 2004 r 6*).   The Probate Office send *form IHT 205* to HMRC.

   ◆   Where an estate is an excepted estate, a claim under *IHTA 1984 s 8A* in respect of a transferable nil rate band must be made on *form IHT 217*.

➤   An estate is an 'excepted estate' if (*IT(DA)(EE)R 2004 r 4* as amended by *IT(DA)(EE)(A)R 2011*):

   a)   the deceased was domiciled in the United Kingdom immediately before death, *and*

   b)   the value of the estate is attributable wholly to property passing under a will/intestacy, *or* nomination taking effect on death, *or* under a single settlement in which the deceased was entitled to interest in possession, *or* by survivorship in a beneficial joint tenancy, *and* of such property:

      i)   not more than £150,000 represented value attributable to settled property, *and*

      ii)   not more than £100,000 represented value attributable to assets outside the United Kingdom, *and*

   c)   any chargeable lifetime transfers ('specified transfers') within 7 years of death were only cash, shares, quoted securities, chattels, *or* land (not subject to a GBR) with a total value not exceeding £150,000 (including transfers within *IHTA 1984 s 21* totalling more than £3,000 and made within 7 years of the person's death),

   d)   the deceased died prior to 6 April 2011 and was not a person by reason of whose death an alternatively secured pension provision applied, *and*

   f)   *either:*

      i)   the value of the 'gross estate' (including any specified transfers (eg: (i) to a spouse/civil partner or charity) and 'specified exempt transfers' did not exceed the 'IHT threshold', *or*

      ii)   the value of the gross estate (as in i) above) did not exceed £1 million, and no tax is payable because the net chargeable value of the estate, after deduction of liabilities and the spouse/civil partner or charity exemption only, does not exceed the IHT threshold.

      ●   The 'gross estate' includes the deceased's share in any jointly owned assets and is calculated before debts, administrative expenses or IHT reliefs or exemptions are deducted.

      ●   The 'IHT threshold' is either (*IT(DA)(EE)R 2004 r 5A* as inserted by *IT(DA)(EE)(A)R 2011*):

         ▪   £325,000, *or*

         ▪   £650,000 where a claim is made under *IHTA 1984 s 8A* to benefit from a transferable nil rate band from a sole predeceased spouse (who died on or after 13 November 1974) or civil partner (who died on or after 5 December 2005).

         That predeceased person must have been domiciled in the UK at death, the value of his or her estate must have passed by will intestacy or survivorship and contained not more than £100,000 of non-UK situate property and the predeceased must not have made any chargeable transfers (or transfers within *IHTA 1984 s 21* totalling more than £3,000 and made within 7 years of the person's death) within 7 years of his or her death.

         The predeceased's death must not have caused the alternatively secured pension provisions to apply, nor must the value of a chargeable transfer on their death have been reduced by business property relief or agricultural property relief.

➤ If an estate is not an excepted estate, complete *form IHT 400,* then *form IHT 400* and *IHT 421* must be sent to HMRC Capital Taxes (the Court Service will not issue a grant until *form IHT 421* has been authorised by HMRC).

◆ Around 3 weeks before submitting *IHT 400* it is necessary to apply using *form IHT 422* for an IHT reference number and payslip (eg: a payslip is used where payment is to be made by cheque).

Filling in a reduced *form IHT 400*

➤ *IHT 400 Notes* (p 5) sets out when and how a reduced *form IHT 400* may be submitted, eg: when:

a) the deceased was UK domiciled, *and*

b) assets passing by will or intestacy mostly go to exempt beneficiaries (spouse or charity), *and*

c) the gross value of:

   i) the estate passing to non-exempt beneficiaries, *and*

   ii) assets not passing by will or on intestacy but which are chargeable on death (eg: property passing on survivorship), *and*

   iii) the chargeable value of transfers made within 7 years of death ...

... does not exceed the IHT threshold.

IV   Payment of IHT

References in this section are to IHTA 1984, unless otherwise stated.

➤   IHT is payable:

   a)   6 months from the end of the month of a chargeable transfer, *or*

   b)   for lifetime transfers made between 5 April and 1 October, 30 April in the next following year (*s 226*).

➤   IHT on 'installment property' is payable in 10 equal annual instalments, with the first due 6 months from the end of the month of death, rather than on delivery of HMRC account (*s 227*). It is available for:

   a)   land, *and*

   b)   an interest in a business, *and*

   c)   shares (quoted and unquoted) which entailed control of a company immediately prior to death, *and*

   d)   unquoted shares if *either*:

   •   they form a large holding (10% of the nominal capital of a company worth £20,000 or more), *or*

   •   HMRC accept 'undue hardship' would follow if payment was due immediately, *or*

   •   IHT on the installment option exceeds 20% of the total IHT due on the estate as a whole.

   ◆   If instalment property is sold, tax and interest are both payable immediately (*s 227(4)*).

➤   HMRC no longer automatically issues a receipt, and recommends that payment is made electronically if a receipt is required (*HMRC IHT Customer Newsletter*, 15 April 2009).

➤   Interest runs ...

   ...   6 months after a chargeable transfer: on non-instalment property vesting in PRs, land that is 'instalment property', GBRs, LCTs, PETs (on death) and life interests in possession (*s 233*).

   ...   from the instalment date: sums unpaid on the date they are due under the instalment option (*s 234*).

Paying IHT on non-instalment option property

➤   Tax which falls due immediately can be funded:

   a)   by assets for which a grant of representation is not needed, *and/or*

   b)   by a building society/ bank holding a deceased's current account and willing to release funds, *and/or*

   c)   by loans from ...

   ...   beneficiaries: they may be in position to help, particularly if they are the assignees or nominees of an insurance policy maturing on the deceased's death.

   ...   banks: they demand a commercial rate of interest.

➤   Interest on a loan for personalty vesting in PRs may be offset against the estate's income tax.

➤   A bank may require an undertaking from PRs to repay a loan as soon as the property is available.

   ◆   A voluntary 'direct payment' scheme, endorsed the British Bankers' Association and the Building Societies' Association enables funds held at the time of death to be used to pay IHT (*Inland Revenue Press Release, 27 March 2003* and HMRC Manual, IHTM 30184).

   •   PRs enquire if an institution is willing to assist, and if it is then, when PRs are ready to apply for probate, PRs send a form IHT 423 and the estate's IHT reference number (see p 140) to the institution which makes a payment direct to the CTO.

➤   For guidance with respect to using National Savings or British Government stock (gilts) held on the Bank of England Register to pay IHT, see HMRC's leaflet *IHT 11*.

V   Self assessment of corporation tax

References in this section are to FA 1998 Sch 18, unless otherwise stated.

Self assessment for corporation tax applies to accounting periods ending on or after 1 July 1999 (the law relating to accounting periods ending before 1 July 1999 is not dealt with here).

1   Notification of chargeability

➤ A person within the charge to corporation tax must notify HMRC if it is chargeable to corporation tax for an accounting period and it has not received a notice requiring a company tax return (*para 2*).

  ◆ A company must notify HMRC within 12 months of the end of the accounting period (or face a penalty not exceeding the tax payable in respect of that accounting period).

2   The company tax return

➤ HMRC may require a person to submit a 'company tax return' (*para 3(1)*).

  ◆ The term 'company tax return' (*Form CT 600*) includes such relevant information, accounts, reports, statements as may be reasonably required (*para 3(2)*).

  • Where *CA 2006* requires a company to produce accounts for a period, the power to require the delivery of accounts is limited to those accounts (*para 11*).

  ◆ A company tax return must include a self assessment of the amount of corporation tax payable by the company for an accounting period (*para 7*).

  • The corporation tax payable is calculated according to four steps (*para 8*):

Steps	
1	Calculate the tax due on the company's profits (*CA 2010 s 4(1)-(2)*) and apply the rate(s) of CT applicable to the company
2	Give effect any reliefs or set off available against corporation tax chargeable on profits, eg: any double taxation relief under *T(IOP)A 2010 ss 2, 6 or 18* (tax credits in respect of foreign tax).

3	Add amounts assessable or chargeable as though they were corporation tax:
	
	 a) any amount due in respect of a loan to a participator under *CA 2010 s 455, and*
	
	 b) any sum chargeable as the profits of a 'controlled foreign company' ('CFC') under *TA s 747(4)(a)*.
	
	    ▪ A CFC is a company which during an accounting period is controlled by a company within the charge to corporation tax and is subject to a lower level of taxation (less than 75% of tax payable in the UK) in the territory in which it is resident.
	
	    ▪ Unless an exemption applies the company submitting the self assessment must pay tax on the CFC's income profit, in proportion to its interest in the CFC.

4	Deduct any amounts to be set off against a company's overall tax liability for a period, eg: under *CA 2010 ss 967-968* (income tax borne by deduction)

3   **Filing a company tax return**

➤ The filing date for a company tax return is whichever of the following periods is last to end (*para 14*):

a) 12 months from the end of the period for which the return is made, *or*

b) if the relevant period of account is not longer than 18 months, 12 months from the end of that period, *or*

c) if a company's period of account is longer than 18 months, 30 months from the beginning of that period, *or*

d) 3 months from the date on which the notice requiring the return is served.

➤ If a company is required to deliver a company tax return and does not do so by the filing date, it is liable to a flat rate penalty of (*para 17*):

a) £100 if the return is delivered within 3 months of the filing date, *and*

b) £200 in any other case, *unless* ...

... it has an excuse for late filing (because it is required to deliver accounts under *CA 2006* for that period and the return is delivered no later than the last date allowed by *CA 2006* for delivering accounts to Companies House) (*para 19*).

• On the third successive failure, the figures in a) and b) are increased to £500 and £1,000 respectively.

➤ If a company is required to deliver a company tax return and fails to do so *either*:

a) within 18 months of the end of the accounting period for which the return is required, *or*

b) the filing date, if the filing date is later than the period in a) ...

... it is liable to a tax-related penalty (*para 18*).

• A tax-related penalty is:

▪ 10% of the unpaid tax if the company tax return is submitted within 2 years of the end of the period in respect of which the return is required, *or*

▪ 20% of the unpaid tax, in any other case.

➤ If company does not deliver a company tax return, HMRC can determine (to the best of its information and belief) the tax due (*paras 36-49*).

4   **Information and records**

➤ A company must preserve such records (*para 21*), or information (*para 22*), as are needed to enable it to complete a correct and complete return for an accounting period.

➤ The duty to preserve records or information exists (*para 21*):

a) for 6 years from the end of a period in respect of which a company may be required to submit a company tax return, *or*

b) if a company is required to submit a company tax return before the end of the 6 year period in a) until *either*:

i)   any HMRC enquiry into that return is completed, *or*

ii) if there is no enquiry, HMRC no longer has power to enquire into the return (broadly, if a return is submitted on or before the filing date (and is not subsequently amended), within 12 months of the filing date (*para 24*)).

• Powers introduced by *FA 2008 Sch 37* enable HMRC to make regulations shortening the period during which records must be kept.

◆ A company which fails to keep records required under *para 21* is liable to a penalty not exceeding £3,000 (*para 23*).

VI   Payment of corporation tax

References in this section are to CT(IP)R 1998, unless otherwise stated.

➤ Corporation tax falls due 9 months after the end of each accounting period (*TMA 1970 s 59(D)*), unless a company is a 'large company'.

◆ A company is a 'large company' if (*r 3*):

a) its profits in an accounting period exceed £1.5 million, *and*

b) its total corporation tax liability for that accounting period exceeds £10,000 (or a proportion of £10,000 if the accounting period is less than 12 months), *and*

c) it was a large company in the 12 months preceding that accounting period or its profits for that accounting period exceed £10 million.

➤ If a company is a 'large company' during an accounting period then the corporation tax for that period, broadly speaking, is due and payable:

a) where the length of the accounting period so allows, in instalments (not exceeding 4) at intervals of 3 months beginning on the date which is 6 months and 13 days from the start of the accounting period and ending on the date which is 3 months and 14 days from the end of the accounting period (*r 5(3)*), *or*

b) in other cases on a date 3 months and 14 days from the end of the accounting period (*r 5(2)*).

Eg: for an accounting period ending 31 December 2011, the payment dates are: 14 July 2011, 14 October 2011, 14 January 2012 and 14 April 2012.

➤ Where tax is payable in instalments, the amount due on each instalment is (*rr 4,6*):

$$\frac{3}{\text{The number of whole calendar months falling within the accounting period PLUS the number of days falling outside the accounting period divided by 30}} \quad \times \quad \text{Total corporation tax liability (as defined in r 2(3))}$$

First accounting period - duty to notify

➤ A company must give written notice to HMRC of the beginning of its first accounting period (*FA 2004 s 55*).

Duty of senior accounting officer of a qualifying company

➤ A senior accounting officer of a large company must take reasonable steps to ensure that the company and each of its subsidiaries maintain appropriate tax accounting arrangements (*FA 2009 Sch 46*).

◆ A company is 'qualifying company' if its turnover in the previous financial year exceeded £200 million and/or its balance sheet exceeded £2 billion (*FA 2009 Sch 46 para 15*).

◆ The officer is liable for a £5,000 penalty for breach of this obligation.

I   Value added tax (VAT)

I   Generally
II   VAT and land - the election to tax
III Capital goods scheme
IV   Penalties (outline)

I   Generally

➤ A registered person accounts periodically to HMRC for VAT on 'output' (sales) of goods and services in the course of business, and any VAT on 'inputs' (*VATA s 1*).

➤ VAT is designed, in theory, to pass a tax charge on the value added by manufacturers and suppliers to the final customer (a non-taxable person, or one who makes exempt supplies).

➤ A taxable person who can attribute all his inputs to taxable supplies (ie: all supplies other than exempt supplies) pays no tax insofar as he reclaims 'input' tax he has paid to his suppliers against 'output' tax which he receives from his customers.   The attribution of 'inputs' to 'outputs' is governed by *VATR 1995 rr 99-116*.

➤ A taxable person pays HMRC the amount by which a business's 'output' exceeds its 'input', unless 'input' exceeds 'output' in which case he claims a rebate of the excess 'input' tax.

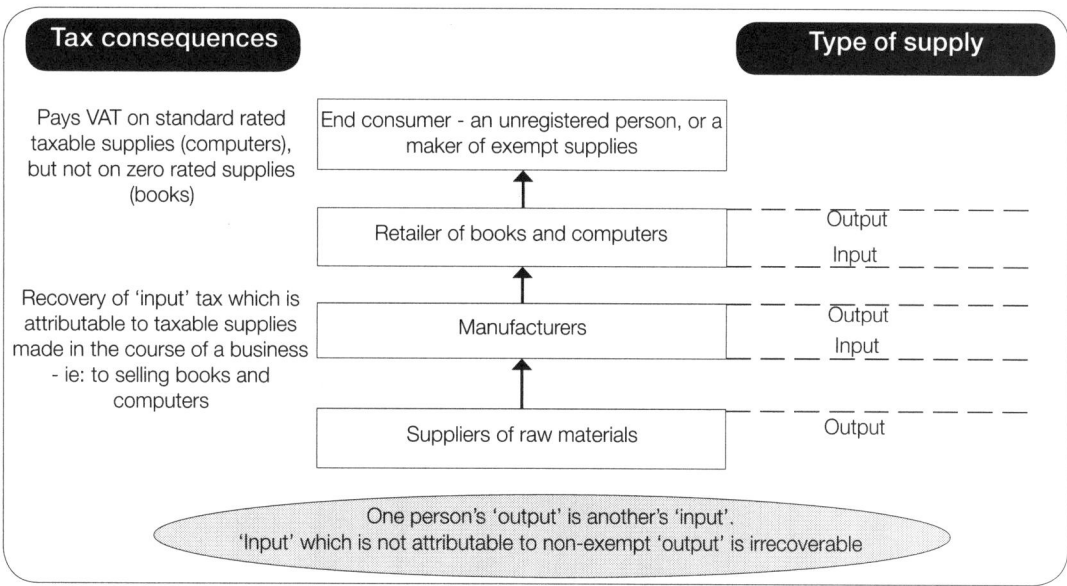

➤ A small business (annual taxable turnover not exceeding £150,000 and total turnover not exceeding £187,500) may opt to account for VAT under the 'flat rate scheme' (*VATA s 26B, VATR 1995 r 55L*).

   ◆ Under this scheme, a taxable person is liable to account to HMRC for a VAT on a percentage of the business's turnover.   By removing the need to attribute inputs to outputs, the intention is to ease the administration and lighten the compliance burden on small businesses.

➤ A sole trader, partnership, or company which makes 'taxable supplies' of goods or services in the course of a business exceeding £73,000 a year must register for VAT with HMRC as a 'taxable person' (*VATA 1994 s 2*).   Partners and trustees must register jointly.   For lower turnovers registration is optional; it is only advisable if reclaimable 'input' tax outweighs the extra cost to customers of the VAT which must be charged to them, and the administrative burden is not judged too inconvenient.

➤ Supplies of goods and services are standard rated at 20% unless they fall within the categories set out in the boxes below.

Exempt supplies (*VATA 1994 s 31(1), Sch 9*)

➤ Some grants (including assignments and surrenders) of interests in or over land (*Group 1*).
  ◆ Supplies which do not fall within this exemption are listed in *Items 1(a)-(n)* in *Group 1*. They include supplies which are zero rated and some which are standard rated.
  ◆ If the option to tax is exercised, the exemption does not apply.
➤ Insurance and reinsurance services (*Group 2*).
➤ Postal services (*Group 3*).
➤ Betting, gaming and lotteries (*Group 4*).
➤ Finance (*Group 5*).
  ◆ Supplies within this group include transactions in money, transactions in securities, underwriting security transactions, running current, deposit or savings accounts, and managing unit trust schemes.
➤ Education (*Group 6*).
  ◆ This exemption embraces education services by 'eligible bodies', examination services, certain private tuition, services provided by youth clubs, research and vocational training.
➤ Health and welfare services (*Group 7*).
➤ Burial services (*Group 8*).
➤ Trade union subscriptions (*Group 9*).
➤ Sporting services (*Group 10*).
➤ Works of art (*Group 11*).
➤ Fund-raising events (*Group 12*).

Zero rated (*VATA 1994 s 30(2), Sch 8*)

➤ Food (*Group 1*).
  ◆ Certain foods are, however, standard rated, eg: supplied in the course of a catering business, hot takeaways, or food sold for consumption on the premises where the supply is made, pet food, luxury and 'frivolous' foods.
➤ Sewage and water services (*Group 2*).
➤ Books and newspapers (*Group 3*).
➤ Talking books and wireless sets (*Group 4*).
➤ Certain buildings and civil engineering works (*Group 5*).
  ◆ This includes the first grant of a 'major interest' in land (ie: of a freehold or a lease with a term exceeding 21 years) by a person who:
    i) constructs a building designed as a dwelling, or converts a building or part of a building into one or more dwellings.
    ii) constructs a building, or converts a non-residential building or part of a building, for a 'relevant residential purpose'.
    iii) constructs a building for a 'relevant charitable purpose'.
➤ Supplies of and in relation to certain protected buildings that are listed buildings or scheduled monuments (*Group 6*).
➤ Certain international services (*Group 7*).
  ◆ Services on goods obtained in, or imported into, EEC States and for export from the EEC:
    a) i) by or on behalf of the supplier, or ii) where the recipient of the services belongs in a place outside the EEC.
  ◆ Making arrangements for i) the export of goods from the EEC, ii) a supply of services of the description in item a), or iii) any supply of services which is made outside the EEC.
➤ Transport (*Group 8*).
  ◆ This includes supplies of ships and aircraft, passenger transport services and some freight transport.
➤ Caravans and houseboats (*Group 9*).
➤ Gold (*Group 10*).
➤ Bank notes (*Group 11*).
➤ Drugs medicine and aids for the disabled (*Group 12*).
➤ Certain imports/exports (*Group 13*).
➤ Supplies to or by charities (*Group 15*).   (*Group 14* has been repealed)
➤ Clothing and footwear including pedal cycle helmets (*Group 16*).
➤ Commodities traded on terminal markets such as futures transactions (*VAT(TM)O 1973*).
➤ Goods exported to third countries (*VATA 1994 s 30(6)*).

Supplies rated at 5% (*VATA 1994 s 29A, Sch 7A*)

➤ Fuel and power (for domestic use, or use by a charity other than in the course of a business).
➤ Installation of energy saving materials
➤ Grant funded installation of heating equipment, security goods or connection of gas supply.
➤ Women's sanitary products, contraceptive products, over-the-counter supplies of smoking cessation products.
➤ Children's car seats.
➤ Supplies in the course of a residential conversion or renovation.
➤ Welfare advice and information.

➤ The transfer of a business as a going concern ('TOGC') is neither a supply of goods nor a supply of services (*VATA s 49, VAT(SP)O 1995 art 5*).

II VAT and land - the option to tax

➤ A taxable person may waive the exemption from VAT in respect of a supply of land which he would otherwise make as an exempt supply under *VATA 1994 Sch 9, Group 1*.

➤ This is known as the 'option to tax' and is governed by *VATA 1994 Sch 10* (as rewritten by the *VAT(LB)O 2008*). It is subject to some restrictions in that it:

◆ does not have effect in circumstances identified in *Sch 10 paras 5-12* (eg: a building is intended as a dwelling or for a relevant residential purpose, for a charitable purpose but not as an office), *and*

◆ if made in respect of part of a building, it covers the whole building (*VATA Sch 10 para 18*), *and*

◆ does not apply if at the time of the grant there is an intention or expectation that the land will become 'exempt land' and it is bought by a developer, financier or a connected person (broadly, land other than land used by a taxable person wholly or mainly for making supplies which are not exempt) (*VATA Sch 10 paras 12-16*).

➤ An election must fulfil the following conditions (with effect from 1 March 1995):

◆ it may be in any form, *but*

◆ it must be notified in writing to HMRC within 30 days of its being made (there is discretion to extend this period) (*VATA Sch 10 para 20*).

➤ From 1 June 2008, an election can be revoked if this is done *either*:

◆ within 6 months of the election becoming effective provided that no input tax has been recovered and the land has not been sold as part of a TOGC (*VATA Sch 10 para 23*), *or*

◆ 20 years or more after the election took effect (*VATA Sch 10 para 25*).

Some advantages and disadvantages of opting to tax	
✓ VAT on developing or purchasing the land or building will be recoverable	✗ Compliance costs associated with issuing VAT invoices etc
✓ Input tax will be recoverable on the landlord's overheads attributable to the taxable supply	✗ A future disposal of the building may be adversely affected as:
✓ A landlord will be able to recover VAT on continuing maintenance costs such as expenditure on service charges	a) the disposal may be standard rated, so SDLT will be paid on a greater amount, *and*
	b) even if the disposal is part of a TOGC (so that VAT will not fall due) the buyer will also have to opt to tax
✓ If a tenant is fully taxable, it will be able to recover VAT on service charges (this is impossible if the service charge is an exempt supply)	✗ Some tenants, whose business activities are not fully taxable, will have to bear the cost of VAT which they will be unable to recover (eg: insurers or underwriters who carry out exempt business)
	✗ The capital value of the property may be affected if local market conditions discriminate for or against buildings which are taxable

III   Capital goods scheme

➤ Under this scheme the 'input tax' recoverable in respect of a capital item is adjusted over a period of 5 (if under a) below) or 10 (if under b) below) years. (Further adjustments are made if, during the period over which the adjustment is made, the item is sold, lost or stolen, the taxable person de-registers, or a lease in respect of the item expires.) (*VATR 1995 rr 114-115*).

➤ A capital item qualifies for the scheme if it is:

a) of a value not less than £50,000 and is computer equipment (*VATR 1995 r 113(a)*), or

b) of a value not less than £250,000 and is:

   i)   an interest in land, a building (or part of a building), a civil engineering work (or part of civil engineering work) acquired as a standard rate supply (*VATR 1995 r 113(b)*), or

   ii) an interest when the taxable person changes the use of a building (or part of a building) which was previously used for a residential or charitable purpose (*VATR 1995 r 113(c)*), or

   iii) an interest in a building (or part of a building) when the taxable person either makes an exempt supply or ceases to be completely taxable (*VATR 1995 r 113(d)*), or

   iv) a building (or part of a building) which the owner constructed and used for the first time on or after 1 April 1990 (*VATR 1995 r 113(e)*), or

   v)   a building which has had its floor area increased by not less than 10% (*VATR 1995 r 113(f)*).

c) a building refurbished or fitted out by the owner if the expenditure on taxable supplies (other than zero rated supplies) of services and of goods fixed to the building is not less than £250,000 (*VATR 1995 r 113(h)*).

IV   Penalties (outline)

Penalties for evading VAT			
Offence	Statute	Penalty	Punishment
Default surcharge	VATA s 59	Civil	Failure to send in the 3 monthly return within 1 month of the end of each quarter: the surcharge rises to as much as 20% of the tax due over this period
Error in taxpayer's document	FA 2007 Sch 24 para 1	Civil	Penalty up to 100% of the tax evaded by understating a liability to tax, or a false or inflated claim to repayment of tax
Under assessment by HMRC	FA 2007 Sch 24 para 2	Civil	Penalty equal to up to 30% of the tax evaded where a return understates a liability to tax and the taxpayer does not take reasonable steps within 30 days of the assessment to notify HMRC of the under assessment
Failure to register	FA 2008 Sch 41	Civil	100% of potential lost revenue if deliberate and concealed, 70% of potential lost revenue if deliberate but not concealed, otherwise 30% of potential lost revenue
Breach of regulations	VATA s 69	Civil	Failure to keep certain records is punishable by a fine of up to £500 Other infringements carry a daily penalty
Fraudulent evasion	VATA s 72	Criminal	It is an indictable offence knowingly or deceitfully to avoid VAT. The penalty may be an unlimited fine and imprisonment for up to 7 years

J Stamp duty

    I   Calculation
    II   Collection and penalties

I   Calculation

Steps

1. Is there a dutiable instrument?
2. What is the head of charge and what is the rate of charge?
3. Is there an exemption or relief?

(This section focuses on stamp duty on selected heads of charge, as they apply on or after 1 December 2003)

Step 1 — Is there a dutiable instrument?

A Is there an 'instrument'?

➤ Stamp duty is a charge upon 'instruments'.

◆ Note that because stamp duty is chargeable on 'instruments', stamp duty can be avoided altogether if an agreement is oral and transfer is by delivery.

    ● However, in such cases care must be taken that the terms of the agreement are not subsequently recorded in a memorandum of agreement, as such a memorandum will be stampable (this is known as the 'memorandum rule').

    ● If the agreement relates to shares or securities consider whether there is an SDRT charge.

➤ An instrument must be properly stamped if it relates to any property situated or any matter or thing done or to be done in the UK, otherwise it will be inadmissible in evidence before a civil court in the UK (*SA 1891 s 14(4)*) and may not be registered (*SA 1891 s 17*).

B Does the 'instrument' relate to stampable property?

➤ A stamp duty charge only arises when an instrument relates to 'property' for which 'stampable consideration' is given.

◆ From 1 December 2003, stamp duty is only chargeable with respect to (*FA 2003 s 125*) stock or marketable securities (*FA 1999 Sch 13*) and bearer instruments (*FA 1999 Sch 15*).

◆ For the transfer of an interest in land to/from a partnership, or the transfer of a partnership interest, see special rules in *FA 2003 Sch 15 Part 3*.

C Is there 'stampable consideration'?

➤ Stampable consideration comprises money, stock/marketable securities (*SA 1891 s 55*) and debts (*SA 1891 s 57*).

| Step 2 | What is the head of charge and what is the rate of charge? |

A Generally

➤ Duty is calculated by reference to the value of the stampable consideration passing under the instrument (known as '*ad valorem*' duty).

B Heads of charge

➤ An instrument liable to stamp duty under 2 heads of charge may be charged to the higher (*Speyer Brothers v IRC* [1908] AC 92). But an instrument chargeable under a specific head of charge is not usually charged with greater duty under a more general head (*North of Scotland Bank* v. *IRC* 1 SC 149).

◆ Fixed duty of £5 has been abolished in respect of instruments executed on or after 13 March 2008 and not stamped before 19 March 2008 (*FA 2008 s 99*).

Heads of charge	
Head of charge	Rate of charge, etc
Transfer on sale (*FA 1999 Sch 13 Part I para 1*)	0.5% (*FA 1999 Sch 13 Part I para 3*)
Contracts or agreements for sale (*FA 1999 Sch 13 Part I para 7*)	➤ An agreement relating to an equitable interest is chargeable at the same rate as a transfer on sale. ◆ If such an agreement is stamped, and an instrument of transfer is subsequently executed in accordance with the agreement, there is no double charge to duty (but any excess consideration is chargeable to duty).
Repurchase of own shares by a company	➤ Duty is payable at the rate of 0.5% per £100 (*FA 1986 s 66*). ◆ When a company files a return at Companies House within 28 days of receiving the shares (*CA 2006 s 707(1)*), the return is treated as an 'instrument'.
Release or renunciation on sale	0.5% (*FA 1999 Sch 13 Part III para 7*).
Bearer instrument (On issue or first transfer) (*FA 1999 Sch 15*)	The details are beyond the range of this book; the rate of duty is 1.5%

> When any property is transfered:
> a) in consideration of a debt due to that person, *or*
> b) subject to the payment of money (whether secured or unsecured) (eg: a mortgage) ...
> ... the debt is treated as the consideration for the conveyance and is chargeable with *ad valorem* duty at the rate of 0.5% (*SA 1891 s 57*).

Step 3	Is there an exemption or relief?

1   Exemption from *ad valorem* duty for low value transactions

➤ No duty is chargeable if the stampable consideration is under £1,000, and the instrument is certified at £1,000 (*FA 1999 Sch 13 para 1(3A)* as introduced by *FA 2008 s 98*).

◆ The certificate states:

'I/we certify that the transaction effected by this instrument does not form part of a larger transaction or series of transactions in respect of which the amount or value, or aggregate amount or value, of the consideration exceeds £1,000.'

2   Loan capital (*FA 1986 s 79, FA 1999 Sch 13 Part IV para 3*)

➤ 'Loan capital' includes any debenture stock, corporation stock or funded debt, by whatever name known, issued by a body corporate or other body of persons, and any arrangements which fall within *s 48A FA 2005* relating to alternative finance investment bonds (ie: 'Islamic finance') (*FA 1986 s 78*).

➤ *FA 1986 s 79* provides an exemption for an instrument on transfer of 'loan capital' from all stamp duties (*FA 1986 s 79(4)*) unless:

a) at the time the instrument is executed, the instrument carries a right (exercisable then or later) of conversion into shares or other securities, or to the acquisition of shares or other securities, including loan capital of the same description (*FA 1986 s 79(5)*), or

b) at the time the instrument is executed or any earlier time, it carries or has carried a right (*FA 1986 s 79(5)*):

• to interest the amount of which exceeds a reasonable commercial return on the nominal amount of the capital, or

 ▪ This requirement does not apply to loan capital raised through alternative finance investment bonds (*s 79(8A)* introduced by *FA 2008 s 154*).

• to interest the amount of which falls or has fallen to be determined to any extent by reference to the results of, or of any part of, a business or to the value of any property, or

 ▪ An instrument is not treated as failing this condition for relief by virtue of:

 i) the amount of interest being determined by reference to a 'ratcheting margin' where the interest payable varies inversely to the performance of the borrower's business (eg: if the results of the business improve the interest rate goes down, and the results deteriorate the interest rate increases) (*s 79(7A)*), or

 ii) the instrument being a capital market investment, and the right to interest ceasing or reducing because the issuer has insufficient funds to pay all or part of the interest which would otherwise be due (*s 79(7B)* introduced by *FA 2008 s 101*).

• on repayment to an amount which exceeds the nominal amount of the capital and is not reasonably comparable with what is generally repayable under the terms of issue of loan capital listed in the FSA's Official List.

 ▪ In respect of an alternative finance bond, this condition applies so that it is satisfied if there is no right on repayment to an amount which exceeds the aggregate of:

 i) the amount paid for the issue of the bond, *and*

 ii) the amount of payments which would represent a reasonable commercial return on the bond over its term less the amount of payments actually made (*s 79(8A)* introduced by *FA 2008 s 148*).

3   **Mortgage granted after 1 August 1971**

➤ Mortgages granted after 1 August 1971 are exempt (*FA 1971 s 64, FA 1999 Sch 13 Part IV para 2*).

4   **Corporate reorganisations - under the head 'transfer on sale' (*FA 1986 ss 75-77*)**

5   **Transfer to a LLP incorporated under the *LPA 2000* (*LPA 2000 s 12*)**

➤ A transfer to a LPP in connection with its incorporation within 1 year of incorporation (if, broadly, there is no change in the partner's beneficial ownership in the assets) is exempt.

6   **Associated companies (*FA 1930 s 42*)**

7   **Examples of general exemptions (*FA 1999 Sch 13 Part IV*)**

➤ Transfers of shares in, or of, government stocks or funds or strips.

➤ Testaments, testamentary dispositions and dispositions *mortis causa* in Scotland.

➤ Renounceable letters of allotment (if rights renounceable not later than 6 months after issue).

II   Collection and penalties

➤   Duty may be paid without a penalty becoming payable within 30 days of the instrument being executed.

◆   If an instrument is executed outside the UK and does not relate to land in the UK, the 30 day period runs from when the instrument is first received into the UK.

◆   If an instrument relates to land in the UK, the 30 day period runs from the date of execution (irrespective of where the instrument is executed) (*SA 1891 s 15B(1)*).

➤   Late (or insufficient) stamping invites the following sanctions (in addition to the stamp duty due):

◆   if an instrument is not stamped within 30 days of execution, interest: (at a rate set by the Treasury) from the end of that 30 period to the day on which the instrument is stamped (but interest is not payable if an amount less than £25 is due) (*SA 1891 s 15A* as introduced by *FA 1999 s 109*), *and*

◆   a penalty; if there is no 'reasonable excuse' for late stamping.   The maximum penalty is:

●   the lesser of £300 and the unpaid duty - if the instrument is stamped within 1 year after the 30 day period ends, *or*

●   the greater of £300 and the unpaid duty - if the instrument is stamped 1 year after the end of the 30 day period (*SA 1891 s 15B(2)-(3)*).

➤   The *Stamp Acts* do not provide any general statements of who is liable to pay duty. However, an unstamped document may not generally be produced in evidence before a court (*SA 1891 s 14(4), Parinv (Hatfield) Limited v. IRC* [1998] STC 305), or enrolled on a register (*SA 1891 s 17*) (eg: a share register) so the onus is usually on whoever wishes to prove title (usually the transferee/buyer) to pay duty.

◆   Any arrangement or undertaking for assuming liability on account of the absence or insufficiency of stamp, or any indemnity against such liability, absence or insufficiently is void (*SA 1891 s 117*).

●   Attempts are sometimes made to circumvent this prohibition by covenanting to pay duty if and when an instrument executed outside the UK is received into the UK.   Opinion is divided as to whether such a covenant is enforceable.

➤   Different heads of charge used to have various fines and penalties. *Sch 17* to the *FA 1999* replaced fines with penalties which are recoverable by the Commissioners.

> For instruments executed on or after 1 October 1999:
> a)   amounts of stamp duty on a 'conveyance or transfer on sale' are rounded up to the nearest £5 (*FA 1999 s 112*), *and*
> b)   interest is are rounded down to the nearest £5 (*s 15A(4)*).

K Stamp duty reserve tax ('SDRT')

I   Generally
II   The principal charge

Generally

➤ Stamp duty reserve tax ('**SDRT**') is *not* a stamp duty.   It is a separate tax.

➤ SDRT is a tax on agreements relating to 'chargeable securities'.

 ◆ A 'chargeable security' includes:

 • stocks, shares or loan capital, *and*

 • interests in, or dividends, arising from stocks, shares, or loan capital, *and*

 • rights to allotments of, or to subscribe for, or options to acquire, stocks shares or loan capital, *and*

 • units under a unit trust scheme (*FA 1986 s 93(3)-6)(a)*), ...

 ... *unless* the securities are issued by a body corporate not incorporated in the UK *and* the securities are:

 ▪ not registered in a register kept in the United Kingdom by or on behalf of the body corporate by which the securities are issued, *or*

 ▪ in the case of shares they are not paired with shares issued by a body corporate incorporated in the United Kingdom (*FA 1986 s 93(4)*).

 ◆ Loan capital which is exempt from all stamp duties under the loan capital exemption in *FA 1986 s 79(4)* (see p 151) is not a 'chargeable security' (*FA 1986 s 99(5)*).

➤ SDRT arises on an agreement, not the instrument of transfer. Where there is an SDRT charge and within 6 years of the SDRT charge arising:

a) a transfer is executed in relation to the securities to which the agreement related, *and*

b) stamp duty paid on the transfer ...

 ... the SDRT charge is cancelled (*FA 1986 s 92*).

➤ On an agreement to transfer 'chargeable securities' an SDRT charge arises irrespective of whether:

a) the agreement, transfer, issue or appropriation in question is made or effected in the UK or elsewhere, *and*

b) any party to the agreement is resident or situate in any part of the UK (*FA 1986 s 86(4)*).

 • Note that an oral agreement is within the charge to SDRT.

II   The principal charge

➤   The 'principal charge' to SDRT is imposed when one person (A) agrees with another (B) to transfer (whether or not to B) 'chargeable securities' for money or money's worth (*s 87(1)*).

    ◆   There is an SDRT charge:

        a)   if the agreement is conditional, on the day on which the condition is satisfied, *and*

        b)   if the agreement is unconditional on the day on which the agreement is made (*s 87(3)*).

    ◆   Tax is charged at 0.5% (*s 87(6)*).   Liability to the SDRT charge falls upon (B) (*s 91(1)*).

➤   The precise requirements for the various exemptions are beyond the scope of this book, but note that the following 2 exemptions in particular exist:

    1   Intermediaries (*FA 1986 ss 88A-88B as amended by FA 2007 Sch 21*)

        ➤   The principal charge does not apply where (NB: this is not exhaustive):

            ◆   'B' is a member of a regulated market on which securities of the relevant kind are regularly traded, and 'B' is recognised as an intermediary by the market in accordance with arrangements arpproved by HMRC, *or*

            ◆   'B' is an intermediary approved by HMRC, and securities of the relevant kind are regularly traded on a regulated market, *or*

            ◆   'B' is a member of a multilateral trading facility or a recognised foreign exchange, on which securities of the relevant kind are regularly traded, 'B' is recognised as an intermediary by the facility/exchange in accordance with arrangements approved by HMRC, and the agreement is effected on the facility/exchange, *or*

            ◆   'B' is an intermediary approved by HMRC, securities of the relevant kind are regularly traded on a multilateral trading facility or recognised foreign exchange, and the agreement is effected on the facility/exchange, *or*

            ◆   'B' is a member of a regulated market, multilateral trading facility or recognised foreign options exchange, options to buy/sell securities of the relevant kind are regularly traded/listed/quoted on that market/facility/exchange, 'B' is an options intermediary recognised by that market/facility/exchange in accordance with approved by HMRC, and securities of the relevant kind are regularly traded on a regulated market.

    2   Public issues of securities (*FA 1986 s 89A*)

        ➤   This exemption applies to various categories of issuing houses and intermediaries who enter into agreements, conditional on the admission of the securities concerned to the Stock Exchange's Official List, for the transfer of chargeable securities in order to facilitate the offer of the securities to the public.

➤   There are other SDRT charges, in addition to the 'principal charge', but these are beyond the scope of the book, as are the precise requirements for the other exemptions to the 'principal charge' (see the *Banking & Capital Markets Companion*).

L   Stamp duty land tax ('SDLT')

References in this section are to the FA 2003, unless otherwise stated.

I   Calculation

II   Collection and penalties

I   Calculation

Steps	
1	Identify a 'land transaction'
2	Is there a 'chargeable transaction'?
3	Calculate the amount of tax due

(SDLT applies, subject to transitional rules which are not dealt with here, to transactions entered into on or after 1 December 2003; the special rules in Sch 15 relating to partnership transactions are beyond the scope of this book)

Step 1	Identify a 'land transaction'

➤   A 'land transaction' is the acquisition of a 'chargeable interest' (*s 43*).

     ◆   A 'chargeable interest' is:

       a)   an estate, interest, right or power in or over land in the United Kingdom, *or*

       b)   the benefit of an obligation, restriction or condition affecting the value of any such estate, interest, right or power ...

         ... other than an exempt interest (ie: a security interest, a licence to use or occupy land, or a tenancy at will, an advowson, franchise or manor) (*s 48*).

➤   If a contract for a land transaction is entered into, and that transaction is to be completed by conveyance, then:

     a)   if the transaction is completed without previously having been 'substantially performed', the contract and the transaction are treated as parts of a single land transaction (*s 44(3)*).

       •   The 'effective date' of the transaction is when completion takes place (*s 44(3)*).

     b)   if the transaction is 'substantially performed' without having being completed, the contract is treated as if it were the land transaction (*s 44(4)*).

       •   The 'effective date' of the transaction is when the contract is substantially performed (*s 44(4)*).

➤   A contract is 'substantially performed' when *either*:

     a)   the purchaser, or a person connected with the purchaser, takes 'possession' of the whole, or substantially the whole, of the subject matter of the contract (*s 44(5)(a)*), *or*

       •   'Possession' includes receipt of rents and profits or the right to receive them (it is immaterial whether it is under the contract or license/lease of temporary character) (*s 44(6)*).

     a)   a 'substantial amount' of the consideration is paid or provided (*s 44(5)(b)*):

       •   A 'substantial amount' means (*s 44(7)*):

         ❶   where there is no rent: all or substantially all the consideration is paid or provided, *and*

         ❷   where all the consideration is rent: when the first payment of rent is made, *and*

         ❸   when there is rent and other consideration: when ❶ or ❸ takes place.

➤ The acquisition of an option binding on the grantor, or a right of pre-emption preventing the grantor from entering into, or restricting the right of the grantor to enter into, a land transaction is a separate land transaction (ie: distinct from any land transaction resulting from the exercise of the option or right) (*s 46*).

➤ Where a land transaction is entered into by a purchaser in consideration of another land transaction as vendor, then each transaction is treated as a separate the distinct land transaction (*s 47*).

➤ Special rules apply where a contract provides for a conveyance to a third party (*s 44A*), or if rights under such a contract are subject to an assignment (*s 45A*).

Step 2	Is there a 'chargeable transaction'?

➤ A 'chargeable transaction' is any land transaction, other than a transaction which is exempt (*s 49*).

> ◆ The following transactions are exempt:
>
> a) a land transaction for which there is no 'chargeable consideration' (eg: a gift) (*Sch 3, para 1*).
>
> | **'Chargeable consideration'** |
> | --- |
> |
> > ➤ The general rule is that 'chargeable consideration' is any consideration in money or money's worth given for the subject matter of a chargeable transaction by the purchaser or a person 'connected' (for the purposes of *TA s 839*) with the purchaser (*Sch 4 para 1*).
> >
> > > ◆ 'Chargeable consideration' includes VAT (except for VAT chargeable by virtue of an option to tax exercised after the effective date of the transaction) (*Sch 4 para 2*).
> >
> > ➤ Debt as consideration: if the chargeable consideration includes the satisfaction or release of a debt due to the purchaser or owed by the vendor, or the assumption of an existing debt by the purchaser, the amount satisfied, released or assumed is treated as chargeable consideration (*Sch 4 para 8*).
> >
> > ➤ Non-monetary consideration (other than money or debt) is the market value of that consideration at the effective date of the transaction (*Sch 4 para 7*).
> >
> > ➤ Special rules apply in particular circumstances, eg:
> >
> > a) the carrying out of works (*Sch 4 para 10*, see also *para 17*).
> >
> > > • This is chargeable consideration except to the extent that:
> > >
> > > i) the works are carried out after the effective date of the transaction, *and*
> > >
> > > ii) the works are carried out on land acquired under the transaction or other land held by the purchaser (or a person connected with the purchaser), *and*
> > >
> > > iii) it is not a condition of the transaction that the works are carried out by the vendor or a person connected with the vendor.
> >
> > b) the provision of services (*Sch 4 para 11*).
> >
> > c) an indemnity given by the purchaser (not chargeable consideration) (*Sch 4 paras 13-15*).
>
> b) the grant of certain leases of registered social landlords (*Sch 3, para 2*).
>
> c) a transaction in connection with divorce/dissolution of a civil partnership (*Sch 3, para 3*).
>
> d) the variation of a testamentary disposition, if carried out within 2 years of death and for no consideration in money or money's worth (*Sch 3, para 4*).
>
> e) an initial transfer of assets to the trustees of a unit trust scheme (*s 64A*).
>
> f) an acquisition under an assent/appropriation by a PR (*s 3A*).

Step 3	Calculate the tax due

➤ The amount of tax is a percentage of the chargeable consideration for the transaction; the percentage depends on the type of land (*s 55*).

Consideration	Residential	Consideration	Non-residential or mixed
Not more than £125,000	0%	Not more than £150,000	0%
More than £125,000 and not more than £250,000	1%	More than £150,000 and not more than £250,000	1%
More than £250,000 and not more than £500,000		More than £250,000 and not more than £500,000	3%
More than £500,000	4%	More than £500,000	4%
More than £1,000,000	5%		

➤ Tax is also chargeable in respect of so much of the chargeable consideration as includes rent (*Sch 5 para 2*, see also *Sch 17A*).

◆ That tax is a percentage of the net present value of the rent payable over the term of the lease.

Relevant rental value	Residential	Relevant rental value	Non-residential or mixed
Not more than £125,000	0%	Not more than £150,000	0%
More than £125,000	1% over £125,000	More than £150,000	1% over £150,000

➤ The following reliefs from SDLT are available:

a) a land transaction with respect to residential land in a disadvantaged area: residential land may be exempt if the relevant consideration does not exceed £150,000 (*s 57, Sch 6*),

b) where a vendor and purchaser are members of the same group of companies (*Sch 7 paras 1-6*), *and*

c) reconstruction relief, where a company acquires the undertaking of another company (*Sch 7 paras 7-13*), *and*

d) charities relief, where the purchaser is a charity (*Sch 8*), *and*

e) for a right to buy transaction (*Sch 9*), *and*

f) certain acquisitions of residential property (for employment, by a property trader, etc) (*Sch 6A*), *and*

g) sale and leaseback transactions (*s 57A*), *and*

h) for a 'first time buyer' if the consideration is not more than £250,000 (*s 57AA*), *and*

i) acquisition of residential property: by a house building company or a property trader from an individual acquiring a new dwelling, by a property trader from PRs, by an employer or property trader on employment relocation (*s 58A, Sch 6A*)

j) first acquisition, prior to 1 October 2012, of a zero carbon flat; capped at consideration of £500,000 (*ss 58B-58C*), *and*

k) where a transfer involves multiple dwellings (*s 58D, Sch 6B inserted by FA 2011 Sch 22*), *and*

l) compulsory purchase facilitating development (*s 60*), *and*

m) compliance with planning obligations (*s 61*), *and*

n) on demutualisation of an insurance company or a building society (*ss 63-64*), *and*

o) on incorporation of a LLP (*s 65*), *and*

p) a transaction involving a public body (*s 66*), *and*

q) a land transaction in consequence of reorganisation of parliamentary constituency (*s 67*), *and*

r) on an acquisition by a body established for national purposes (*s 69*), *and*

s) certain acquisitions by a registered social landlord (*s 71*), *and*

t) alternative finance: land sold to financial institution and leased/resold to individual (*ss 71A, 72-73AB* and *FA 2009 Sch 61*), *and*

u) a land transaction on the collective enfranchisement of leaseholders (*s 74*), *and*

v) a land transaction with respect to a crofting community's right to buy (*s 75*).

II Collection and penalties

➤ The purchaser is liable for tax (*s 85*).

➤ The purchaser must, in the case of a 'notifiable transaction', deliver a land transaction return to HMRC before the end of the period of 30 days after the effective date of the transaction (*s 76(1)*).

> ◆ A 'notifiable transaction' is (for transactions on or after 12 March 2008):
>
> a) an acquisition of a major interest in land (*s 77*), other than (*s 77A*):
>
>   i) an acquisition which is exempt under *Sch 3, or*
>
>   ii) an acquisition (other than in respect of a lease) where the chargeable consideration is less than £40,000, *or*
>
>   iii) the grant of a lease for 7 years or more where the relevant rent is less than £1,000 and the chargeable consideration other than rent is less than £40,000, *or*
>
>   iv) the assignment or surrender of a lease where the original term was for 7 years or more and the chargeable consideration for the assignment or surrender is less than £40,000, *or*
>
>   v) the grant of a lease for less than 7 years (or the surrender or assignment of such a lease) and the chargeable consideration for the grant (or, as the case may be the surrender or assignment) does not exceed the 'zero rate threshold'.
>
>   ■ The 'zero rate threshold' is not exceeded if tax is not chargeable at a rate exceeding 1% or would not be so chargeable but for a relief.
>
> b) an acquisition of a chargeable interest (other than a major interest) where there is chargeable consideration in respect of which tax is chargeable at a rate of 1% or more, or would be so chargeable but for a relief, *or*
>
> c) a person is treated by *s 43A(3)* as entering into a land transaction by virtue of a contract providing for a conveyance to a third party, *or*
>
> d) a 'notional land transaction' within anti-avoidance rules in *s 75A*.
>
>   ● In England, a 'major interest' is a fee simple absolute or a term of years absolute (*s 117*).

◆ The return must be in the prescribed form (the main land transaction return is *Form SDLT 1*, and additional forms are available for use in particular circumstances) and include a declaration by the purchaser that the return is, to the best of the purchaser's knowledge, correct and complete.

◆ If the consideration is contingent or uncertain and falls (or may fall) to be paid on one or more occasions at least one of which is more than 6 months after the effective date of the transaction (and does not relate to rent), the purchaser can apply to defer payment of SDLT (*s 90*).

◆ A land transaction return includes a self-assessment of the tax that, on the basis of the information in the return, is chargeable (*s 76(3)*).

   ● The return and assessment, if submitted as hardcopy (rather than online), are sent to HMRC's central processing centre at Netherton, or via DX to HMRC's Rapid Data Capture Centre, DX725593, Bootle 9.

◆ A further return must be delivered where a relief (relief on an acquisition of residential property, group relief, reconstruction or acquisition relief, or charities relief) is withdrawn as a result of a disqualifying event (*s 81*), or as a result of a further linked transaction (*s 81A*).

➤ HM Land Registry will not register a land transaction (*s 79(1)-(2)*) unless *either*:

a) an application for registration is accompanied by a certificate of compliance with *FA 2003 Part 4*, *or*

> • A certificate of compliance must be a certificate by HMRC that a land transaction return has been delivered (*s 79(3)* as amended by *FA 2008 Sch 30 para 2*).

b) the entry is required to be made without any application, *or* the entry relates to an interest or right other than the chargeable interest acquired by the purchaser under the land transaction that gives rise to the application, *or*

c) a transaction treated as taking place under *s 44(4)* or *s 44A(3)* (or as applied respectively by *s 45* or *s 45A*).

➤ Tax must be paid not later than the filing date for relevant return (*s 86*) (as amended by *FA 2007*).

M Some planning ideas

➤ Often a transaction incurs liability for more than one tax - the transfer of an asset may incur CGT and IHT, and have income tax implications. Set out below are some approaches to tax-planning for individuals.

I During a client's lifetime

➤ Submit self assessment returns and make payments on account on time to avoid penalties/interest.

➤ UK tax may not chargeable if an individual is not UK resident (see *HMRC 6* and note *TCGA 1992 s 10A, IT(EP)A 2003 s 421(B)(7), ITA 2007 s 829* bringing gains/income of certain non-residents into charge), or relief is provided by a double taxation treaty.

➤ If an individual may be able to establish a non-UK domicile (eg: birth outside the UK, or regards another country as real home to which he intends to return), consider whether the £30,000 charge should be paid to take advantage of the 'remittance basis' of taxation (*ITA ss 809A-Z, TCGA ss 12, 16ZA-ZD*).

➤ Make full use of income tax loss reliefs.

➤ Make full use of a married couple's/civil partner's personal allowances and their individual basic rate bands. If the marriage/partnership is stable, consider transferring assets from one party to the other so that income is received more tax efficiently. (There is no CGT to pay, as transfers between cohabiting spouses or civil partners do not give rise to a 'chargeable gain' or an 'allowable loss'.)

➤ Consider investing in Enterprise Investment Scheme ('EIS') shares, a Venture Capital Trust ('VCT'), or an Individual Savings Account ('ISA') for various advantages with regard to both income tax and CGT.

The EIS (outline) (*ITA 2007 ss 156-257, TCGA 1992 ss 150-150D, Schs 5B-BA*)

➤ If a company raises money for a qualifying activity, and both the individual and the issuing company meet certain conditions for the relevant periods, then:

    a) a chargeable gain can be rolled over into a subscription for eligible shares, *and*

    b) any capital gain realised on a disposal of the eligible shares after 3 years is tax free, *and*

    c) income tax relief (at 30%) is granted at the time of the subscription for the shares, *and*

    d) if there is a loss on the disposal of EIS shares further income tax relief is available.

➤ An individual cannot invest more than £500,000 (£1 million from 5 April 2012) in a tax year under the EIS.

The VCT (outline) (*ITA 2007 ss 258-332, TCGA 1992 s 100*)

➤ Investment in a VCT may entitle the investor to:

    a) income tax relief (at the rate of 30%) on subscription for *new* shares in a VCT (for subscriptions up to £200,000 in a tax year) if the shares are retained for at least 5 years, *and*

    b) CGT exemption on the disposal of such shares (a loss on such a disposal will not be an allowable loss), *and*

    c) exemption from income tax on dividends in respect of ordinary shares (either purchased or subscribed for, at up to £200,000 in a tax year).

➤ A VCT does not pay tax on chargeable gains which it makes.

Individual savings accounts 'ISAs' (outline)

➤ An individual can invest up to a limit of £10,680 a year in an ISA.

➤ Investments in an ISA are described 'tax free'. In practice, this means that:

   a) interest and dividends are not subject to tax, *and*

   b) any gains are not subject to CGT (but any loss is not an 'allowable loss').

➤ Withdrawal can be instant and will not lead to the forfeiture of tax benefits (although if the maximum subscription for a tax year has been made more cannot be subscribed in that year).

➤ An investor may choose, for a tax year, either s 'stocks and shares' ISA and/or a 'cash' ISA:

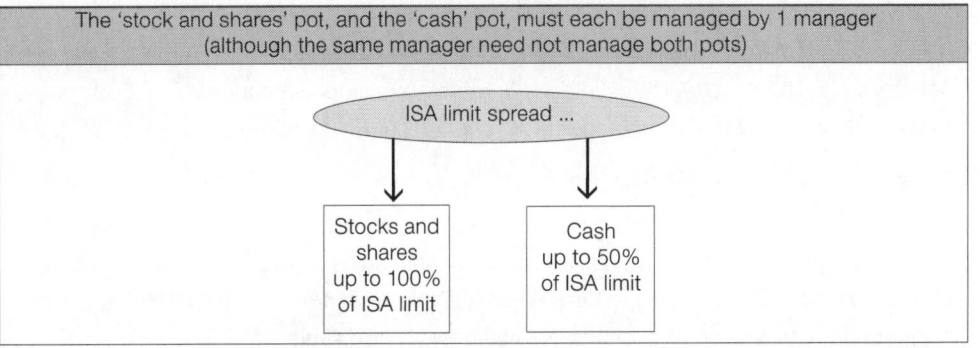

The 'stock and shares' pot, and the 'cash' pot, must each be managed by 1 manager (although the same manager need not manage both pots)

ISA limit spread ...

Stocks and shares up to 100% of ISA limit

Cash up to 50% of ISA limit

➤ Make full use of CGT 'allowable losses' and use exemptions or reliefs (roll-over or hold-over).

➤ Where 'related property' (property which is jointly owned) is valued for IHT, ensure it is discounted to reflect the unsaleability of the share concerned by itself - discounts of, eg: 10%-30% can be allowed.

➤ When making lifetime gifts, make full use of exemptions and reliefs.

   ◆ Time gifts to gain the benefit of tapering relief for IHT (eg: plan gifts while still in good health, and do not wait until approaching 100).

   ◆ On death, the value of the transfer is frozen at the value at the time of the *inter vivos* transfer.

      ● PETs: if the donor survives 7 years they are exempt.

      ● If a donor has plenty of disposable income, make regular gifts using the exemption under *IHTA 1984 s 21* - unlike a PET these gifts are completely exempt irrespective of whether the donor survives for 7 years.

➤ An *inter vivos* gift to a trust will, unless the transfer is to a disabled person's trust, be subject to an IHT charge at the rate of 20%.

   ◆ A further IHT charge arises:

   a) on each 10th anniversary of the original transfer to a trust (this charge is currently effectively capped at 6%), *and*

   b) when property ceases to be subject to the trust (known as an 'exit charge') (eg: on being distributed to a beneficiary).

      ● The tax chargeable on 'exit' is a fraction of the (6%) 10 yearly charge; the applicable rate is determined by reference to the number of complete quarters which have elapsed since the original transfer, or the date of the last 10 year anniversary of the transfer.

➤ Unlike an *inter vivos* gift to a trust, an 'immediate post-death interest' arising under a will or on intestacy and giving rise to an immediate interest in possession, is not subject to the 10 year/exit charge (*IHTA s 49A*) (although a charge to tax will arise on the surrender of an immediate post-death interest or the death of the beneficiary entitled to the interest in possession) (*IHTA s 51*).

➤ A transfer to a trust for a bereaved minor which is established on the death of a parent (step parent, or person with parental responsibility for a child) is not a LCT, and no exit charge/10 year charge arises if various conditions are satisfied, including that the child becomes absolutely entitled at 18 (*IHTA s 71A*).

   ◆ If a child does not become absolutely entitled at 18, but will become absolutely entitled no later than 25, a charge to IHT will arise not arise until 18 (and the IHT charge is effectively capped at 4.2% at current tax rates) (*IHTA 1984 ss 71D-71F*).

➤ Use the IHT nil rate band fully.

   ◆ Make full use of the ability to claim the benefit of any nil rate band which has not been utilised on the death of a spouse or civil partner.

➤ Avoid making gifts and reserving the benefit (GBRs).

   ◆ Note that where an individual (a 'chargeable person'):

   a) owned an interest in land, a chattel, or certain intangible property, on or after 17 March 1986, *and*

   b) disposed of that interest otherwise than through an excluded transaction (eg: arm's length sale, or where the transferee is a spouse/civil partner), *and*

   c) (in the case of land) land is occupied by the chargeable person, or (in the case of a chattel) the chargeable person has use or possession of that chattel,

   ... that chargeable person is chargeable to income tax by reference to the value of the land (ie: by reference to a notional market rent), chattel or intangible property, *unless either:*

   i) the chargeable person elected to take advantage of transitional rules under which the property is treated as having been subject to a GBR, *or*

   ii) the aggregate of certain amounts (eg: the notional value of the income to which the property is treated as giving rise) does not exceed £5,000 (*FA 2004 Sch 15*, see also *CITEPPOR 2005*).

➤ Do not resort to 'associated operations' (ie: a series of operations concerning a particular asset or a series of operations carried out by reference to each other which are designed to escape IHT). They will be ineffective as IHT is due under the anti-avoidance provisions (*IHTA 1984 s 268*).

Some additional factors when advising elderly donors ...

➤ Retain property necessary to maintain the donor's standard of living and security.

◆ If advising a client who is elderly, see the Law Society's practice note 'Making gifts of assets' (16 July 2009).

➤ Advise elderly clients considering disposing of their home of the consequences if they subsequently need residential care.

◆ The local authority determines the level of fees which the resident must contribute by reference to means testing under *NA(AR)R 1992 (as amended)*.

  • Means testing does not cover a minimum charge which is payable by the resident, and leaves the resident a personal allowance. The test relates to income and capital. Broadly, a resident is only entitled to have fees subsidised if their capital does not exceed £23,250, and he/she qualifies for a tapering subsidy below that figure. A home is taken into account unless:

    a) the property is occupied by a spouse, partner or relative who is *either*:

      i) incapacitated, *or*

      ii) aged 60 or over, *or*

      iii) a child under 16 whom the resident is obliged to maintain, *or*

    b) someone else occupies the property *and* the local authority uses its discretion, *or*

    c) the person's stay in care is only a temporary one.

◆ If the gift prevents the donor from funding care, the local authority may only fund a basic level of care. This may leave the donor dependent on others to supplement fees for better care.

◆ Where a resident is liable to pay for accommodation under *NAA 1948 Part 3* a local authority may enter into a deferred payment agreement with a resident which may provide for a resident to make deferred payment for care (and may include granting a charge over the resident's property) (*HSCA 2001 s 55*).

◆ The anti-avoidance provisions are formidable:

  • if a 'significant' motivation for a gift is to prevent a local authority imposing a charge on the client's home to pay for care, the authority can:

    a) place a charge on property transferred to a third party while the donor is in care, or within 6 months of the donor going into care (*HSSAA 1983 s 21*), *or*

    b) place a charge on property owned by a resident in a care home (interest runs from the date of death) (*HSSAA 1983 ss 22, 24*), *or*

    c) recover fees as a civil debt in the Magistrates' Court (*NAA 1948 s 56*).

  • When outstanding fees reach £750, a local authority can take insolvency proceedings and have the transaction set aside as a transaction at an undervalue, or as a transaction intended to defraud creditors (*IA 1986 ss 339-341, 423-425*).

Pensions

➤ New pensions rules, introduced by *FA 2004 Part 4,* came into force on 6 April 2006.

➤ The new rules introduced a universal system which operates by reference to:

a) a lifetime allowance on the amount of pensions savings that can benefit from tax relief of £1.8 million (to be reduced to £1.5 million on 6 April 2012), *and*

- Benefits under a defined benefit scheme which is not yet paying a pension are valued by being multiplied by 20 for the purposes of the lifetime allowance.

- If the lifetime allowance is exceeded a tax charge arises equal to 25% of the excess funds over the lifetime allowance (if such excess is taken as a lump sum, rather than as income, the rate of the tax charge is 55%) *(FA 2004 ss 214-215).*

b) an annual allowance of up to 100% of earnings subject to a cap. In 2011/2012 the cap is £50,000 *(FA 2004 s 228* as substituted by *FA 2011 Sch 17).*

- The contribution of a non-taxpayer is limited to £2,808 (with tax relief, the gross contribution which such a person may make in a tax year is, therefore, £3,600).

- An unused annual allowance from any of the 3 previous tax years can be carried forward and used in the current tax year *(FA 2004 s 228A* as inserted by *FA 2011 Sch 17).*

- Additional benefit which accrues in a tax year under a defined benefit arrangement is multiplied by 16 for the purposes of assessing whether the annual allowance has been exceeded *(FA 2004 s 234* as amended by *FA 2011 Sch 17).*

- There is an exemption from the annual allowance charge if an individual (who, in practice, is under 75) satisfies a 'serious ill-health condition' *(FA 2004 s 236* as amended by *FA 2011 Sch 17).*

- Any excess over the annual allowance is subject to tax at the individual's highest marginal rate of tax to the extent that income would be subject to tax at that rate *(FA 2004 s 227).*

➤ An individual is entitled to tax relief on a contribution it makes as follows:

a) **a non-tax payer/basic rate** taxpayer is entitled to tax relief at the rate of 20% (which the scheme provider claims from HMRC), *and*

b) a **higher rate** taxpayer or additional rate taxpayer is entitled to tax relief at the rate of 40% or 50%.

- The pension scheme provider claims 20% from HMRC, and the individual claims 20%/30% from HMRC when submitting his/her tax return by means of raising the threshold at which higher or additional rate tax is paid.

➤ The Labour Government intended, from 6 April 2011, to restrict relief claimed by an individual earning £130,000 or more to 20% by means of a 'high income excess relief charge' *(FA 2010 Sch 2).*

- ◆ 'An 'anti-forestalling measure' was introduced to prevent 'excessive' contributions being made to a pension during the 2009/2010 and 2010/2011 tax years. These rules operated by *(FA 2009 Sch 35 para 1* as amended by *FA 2010 s 48):*

a) bestowing a 'special allowance' on an individual who had relevant income of £130,000 or more in a relevant tax year (or either of the 2 tax years preceding that tax year), *and*

b) imposing a 'special allowance charge' on an individual who made contributions, or accrued benefit under a defined benefit scheme, of more than £20,000 (where an individual had made 'infrequent money purchase contributions' in 2006-2007, 2007-2008 and 2008-2009 the

Pensions (continued)

£20,000 restriction was substituted by an amount equal to the average of those contributions if that average was less than £30,000, or £30,000 if that average was £30,000 or more).

- The purpose of the 'special allowance charge' was to recover an amount equal to the higher rate tax relief, and therefore to restrict relief to the basic rate (20%).

- Where a person had been making regular contributions during the 3 years prior to 22 April 2009, an amount equal to the average of the contributions over those years was protected from the special allowance charge.

- In 2010/2011, where an individual was subject to income tax at the additional rate of 50% the special allowance charge was 30% to the extent that relief is claimed against income which was subject to tax at the 50% rate.

  ◆ *FA 2011* has softened the impact of the special allowance charge by allowing unused annual allowances to be carried forward from the previous 3 tax years.

➤ If an employer makes a contribution to a pension scheme, that contribution:

a) should be deductible by the employer for tax purposes (*FA 2004 ss 196-200*), *and*

b) is not treated as taxable income for the employee (*IT(EP)A 2003 s 308*).

➤ Neither capital gains tax, nor income tax, are payable in respect of assets held as an investment within a pension fund (*FA 2004 s 186, TCGA 1992 s 271(1A)*).

➤ The general retirement age, and hence the age at which a pension can be drawn, rose from 50 to 55 in 2010 (save in cases of ill health).

➤ A pension scheme can provide income for an individual by means of a drawdown pension (*FA 2004 Sch 28* as amended by *FA 2011 Sch 16*).

  ◆ Under a drawdown pension:

   • there is no requirement to draw down a minimum amount of income.

   • the amount of income which can be drawn may be capped at 100% of the single life annuity that an individual of the same sex and age could purchase based on rates published by the Government Actuary's Department.   The cap is generally reviewed every three years until age 75 and annually thereafter.

   • the cap will not apply to the extent that an individual satisfies the 'minimum income requirement' by having secure income for a tax year of not less than £20,000 which does not arise from a drawdown pension or a dependent's drawdown pension.

   • a tax-free lump sum may be paid after age 75 if an individual designates funds for income draw down (even if income is not drawn down).

➤ A pension scheme may pay out a tax free lump sum to a pensioner equal to the lower of:

a) 25% of the value of an individual's pension rights, *and*

b) 25% of the individual's lifetime allowance (*FA 2004 Sch 31*).

  ◆ If a lump sum payment is made on death (other than to charity), a scheme administrator is liable to a tax charge equal to 55% of that lump sum (*FA 2004 s 206* as amended by *FA 2011 Sch 16*).

II   On a client's death

➤   Alter gifts in a will by a disclaimer or a variation.

Disclaimers

➤   A disclaimer is a refusal of a gift (*Townson v. Tickell* (1819) B & Ald 31).   It:

   ◆   may relate to part of a gift provided the disclaimed part is severable and is not onerous (but it need not affect a separate gift under the same will).

   ◆   may not take effect if a beneficiary has benefited from property, but can be revocable.

   ◆   does not allow a disclaimor to determine property's destination unless a will permits this.

➤   The disclaimed property falls into residue (if residue is disclaimed, the property passes according to the intestacy rules) provided that there is no contrary intention in the will.

   ◆   Where an interest under the intestacy rules is disclaimed, the property is apportioned amongst the rest of the class who are entitled (or if there are none, to those next entitled).

Variations

➤   A variation enables a beneficiary to determine the destination of property.

➤   Written notice must be given to HMRC (whereas a disclaimer can be by conduct).

Some tax implications of disclaimers and variations

➤   The disclaimer or variation will not amount to a PET (*IHTA 1984 s 142*), nor will it be a chargeable transfer for CGT purposes (*TCGA 1992 s 62(6)*) if:

a)   it is made within 2 years of the death, *and*

b)   it is not for money or money's worth (except consideration for varying other dispositions), *and*

c)   if a variation, an election is in writing *and* that election is made within 6 months of the variation.

➤   The IHT and CGT elections are entirely independent of each other. If an election is made, the property is treated as if the alteration had been made by the testator, or written into the statutory trusts governing an intestacy.   If election(s) are not made, the transfer is treated as an ordinary *inter vivos* gift by the beneficiary, which qualifies as a PET/LCT and/or is subject to CGT on the gain realised by the donor on the disposal.

IHT elections

➤   A beneficiary making a variation must notify HMRC within 6 months of electing to vary the gift if the estate incurs additional IHT and the PRs should join that election (*IHTA s 218A*).

➤   In the case of a disclaimer, no election need be made (*IHTA 1984 s 142*).

CGT elections

➤   The PRs do not have to join in the election in the case of a variation, and HMRC need not be told of the election, although the instrument must contain a statement that it is intended to take effect for CGT purposes (*TCGA 1992 s 62(7)*).

➤   Make efficient use of IHT and CGT loss reliefs.

➤   Dispose of property so as to make full use of the 3 CGT annual exemptions which are available.

Anti-avoidance

➤ There is a fundamental distinction between:

a) tax evasion (which is illegal and is not dealt with here), *and*

b) tax avoidance (which is legal) (see, for example *IRC v Willoughby* [1997] STC 995, HL, *Ingram v IRC* [1999] STC 9).

◆ *Part 7* of *FA 2004* requires either the promoter of, or a party to, certain tax avoidance arrangements (specified in *TAS(PDA)R 2006*) to notify HMRC of those arrangements (giving information specified in *TAS(I)R 2004*).

- There is a disclosure obligation with respect to SDLT, where (broadly) arrangements relate to residential property with a value of at least £1 million, or non-residential property with a value of at least £5 miliion, and are not excluded (*SDLTAS(PDA)R 2005*).

- On 6 April 2011 arrangements which result in property becoming 'relevant property' (as defined by *IHTA 1984 s 58*) for IHT purposes as a result of a lifetime disposition must be disclosed (*ITAS(PDA)R 2011*).

- There are provisions, equivalent to those in *FA 2004 Part 7*, with respect to VAT in *VATA 1994 Sch 11A* requiring notification to HMRC of certain VAT arrangements.

➤ Counter-measures to restrict avoidance generally take 2 forms:

a) specific statutory provisions designed to block perceived 'loopholes', *and*

b) the development, by the judiciary, of principles of statutory construction under which certain transactions without a business purpose are disregarded for tax purposes.

- For the House of Lords/Supreme Court rulings which have shaped this judicial approach to a purposive interpretation of tax statutes, see *Barclays Mercantile Business Finance Ltd v Mawson (Inspector of Taxes)* ([2005] STC 1), *HMRC v Tower MCashback LLP1 & Anor* ([2011] UK SC 19) and *IRC v Scottish Provident Institution* [2005] STC 15.

Tax and the *Human Rights Act 1998*

➤ The following provisions of the European Convention on Human Rights may be particularly relevant to tax.

◆ Every ... person is entitled to the peaceful enjoyment of his possessions. No one shall be deprived of his possessions except in the public interest and subject ... to law. (*First Protocol, art 1(1)*) (On the construction of this article see, *National Provincial Building Society and others v UK [1997] STC 1466.*)

- This is subject to the proviso that this principle does not:

'in any way impair the right of the State to enforce such law as it deems necessary to control the use of property in accordance with the general interest or to secure the payment of taxes or other contributions or penalties' (*First Protocol, art 1(2)*).

(On the breadth of a State's prerogative in relation to tax, see *Gasus Dosier und Fördertechnik GmbH v Netherlands (1995) 20 EHRR 403.*)

◆ In tax appeals, consider *art. 6*: 'In the determination of his civil rights and obligations or of any criminal charge against him, everyone is entitled to a fair and public hearing within a reasonable time by an independent and impartial tribunal established by law'.

WILLS, PROBATE AND ADMINISTRATION

This chapter examines:

A   Valid wills

A   Generally

➤ There are 3 requirements for a valid will.

1 The testator has testamentary 'Capacity' (if not, the Court has power under *MCA 2005 s 18(1)(i)* and *Sch 2 paras 2-4* to authorise another person to execute a will on the testator's behalf).

2 The testator has general *and* specific 'Intention' to make the will.

3 The testator's signature and the form of the will must comply with the required 'Formalities'.

	Requirements	Presumed to be satisfied ...	Safeguards
1 **Capacity** (must have both a) and b))	a) 'Soundness of mind, memory, and understanding' (*Marquess of Winchester's Case* (1598) 6 Co Rep 32a)	... if the testator comprehends: the nature of the act, *and* the general extent of his property, *and* the moral claims on the estate. ... the will appears to be rational *and* the testator generally has capacity. ◆ A mental state is presumed to persist, so if the testator generally lacks capacity, it must be shown that he possessed it when making the will	➤ Obtain a written medical opinion on the testator's capacity, and ask the person giving this opinion to witness the will ➤ Make a detailed file note of the circumstances
	b) over 18 years of age*		
2 **Intention**	a) General: intention to make *a* will *and* b) Specific: intention to make *this particular* will The testator must intend a will to be valid unconditionally on execution (*Corbett v. Newey* [1996] 2 All ER 914, CA)	... if the testator has capacity when he executes the will. However, this presumption does not arise if: a) the testator is blind or illiterate, *or* b) 'suspicious circumstances' exist: the testator did not give free approval due to force, fear, undue influence, or because he mistook the will's contents	➤ Explain the meaning of all the clauses ➤ Ensure the client reads the will, and that it is as he wishes. If necessary, read it aloud in the presence of the witnesses, and alter the attestation clause to record this act ➤ If a gift to the solicitor is 'significant' (over £2,000 *or* 10% of the estate), recommend the client takes independent legal advice
	Intention and Capacity must be present *either*: a) when the will is executed (*Banks v. Goodfellow* (1870) LR 5 QB 549), *or* b) when the solicitor is instructed to prepare a will if a) these instructions are followed in the will, *and* b) when the testator executes the will, he comprehends that he previously gave instructions to draw it up (*Parker v. Felgate* (1883) 8 PD 171)		
3 **Formalities***	➤ A will may be handwritten, typed or printed ➤ The will is properly executed if: ◆ a testator, or another at his direction, signs anywhere on the will, *and* ◆ the signature is intended to validate the will, *and* ◆ 2 people witness the signature by signing the will *or* acknowledge the testator's mark in his presence *(WA 1837 s 9)* Note: a) a witness must be physically and mentally present at execution, and able to give evidence of this, eg: a child must understand the significance of acting as a witness b) a witness does not have to see the testator sign, or know the document is a will c) both witnesses must be present at the same time d) the testator need not see the witnesses sign		➤ An attestation clause is evidence that these requirements are met ➤ A witness who is blind, drunk, or mentally unsound is not suitable ➤ A witness must be *neither* a beneficiary, *nor* married to/a civil partner of, a beneficiary at the time, as a gift to such a person lapses. A partner must not witness a will with a charging clause for his firm (*WA 1837 s 15, CPA 2004 Sch 4 para 3*). But if 2 capable witnesses sign, a signature by a beneficiary or their spouse/civil partner will not cause a gift to lapse (*WA 1837 s 1*)
	Burden of proof: with the person relying on the will - the 'propounder' of the will (*Griffin & Amos v. Ferard* (1835) 1 Curt 97)		

* Not applicable to 'privileged' wills made by members of the armed forces on active service, or sailors at sea.

B Alterations

Wills Act 1837 s 21	Presumptions

➤ Before execution alterations are valid
➤ After execution alterations are void unless *either:*
  a) the testator and the witnesses initial the alteration in the margin, *or*
  b) a subsequent codicil republishes the will and confirms the alteration
	➤ Completed blanks predate execution (eg: date)
	➤ Other alterations postdate execution

Problems

If the alteration is void and the original wording is:
a) legible: the alteration is disregarded and the original is admitted to probate
b) illegible: probate is granted as if there is a blank, unless *either*:
  i) there is evidence that the testator intended to revoke the wording if the substitution was valid ('conditional revocation'), *or*
  ii) the testator had no intention to revoke the original wording, in which case the original wording is effective if extrinsic evidence reveals it, or if the original script can be successfully revealed

C Revocation

➤ There are 6 ways to revoke the whole *or* part of a will.

1 Express revocation (*WA 1837 s 20*)

➤ The insertion of suitable words in a subsequent will or a codicil executed as a will.

2 Implied revocation

➤ When a disposition is inconsistent with an earlier will, the original disposition is revoked and superseded in so far as it is incompatible with the subsequent disposition.

3 Dependant relative revocation (*Re Irvine* [1929] 2 IR 485)

➤ When the replacement of a disposition is conditional on a specified event: if the event does not occur, the earlier disposition remains valid, otherwise the conditional disposition is substituted for it.

4 Marriage (*WA 1837 ss 18, 18B*)

➤ Marriage, or the formation of a civil partnership, revokes a will, unless the will shows contrary intention.

➤ A will made on or after 1 January 1983 in anticipation of marriage, or after the *CPA 2004* came into force in anticipation of the formation of a civil partnership, with a clause displaying the testator's intent that the will (or part of it) should remain valid after marriage/formation, is valid, *provided that*:

  a) the will names a particular person as the intended spouse/civil partner, and this person is married/a civil partnership is formed with that person, *and*

  b) the testator's intention 'appears from the will . . . at the time it was made'; extrinsic evidence is inadmissible.

➤ Marriage does not revoke a mutual will as a trust arises on the death of the first to die, and this trust is not revoked by a subsequent marriage (*Re Goodchild (deceased)* [1996] 1 All ER 670, Ch D).

5 Divorce (*WA 1837 ss 18A, 18C*)

➤ If a marriage/civil partnership ends in divorce, dissolution, or annulment, the appointment of an ex-spouse/civil partner as executor *or* trustee, or a gift to the spouse/civil partner, take effect as if the former spouse/civil partner died on the day of the dissolution or annulment.

6 Destruction (*WA 1837 s 20*)

  a) Burning, tearing *or* otherwise destroying the will, *and*

  b) destruction by the testator *or* by some person in his presence and by his direction, *and*

  c) destruction with the intention of revoking the will.

    ◆ Destruction must be physical - crossing a will out, or writing 'revoked' across it is insufficient.

    ◆ Symbolic destruction is not sufficient. Destruction of part may revoke only the part destroyed; this depends on the condition of any remains and quite which part of the will is destroyed.

      • Destruction of a signature revokes the whole will (*Hobbs v. Knight* (1838) 1 Curt 768).

      • If parts are cut out, only those parts are revoked (*Re Everest* [1975] Fam 44).

    ◆ The presumption is that a missing will is intentionally destroyed.

B Contents of a will

I Common clauses
II Hints on drafting and interpretation

I Common clauses

---

1 Commencement

➤ States the testator's name and address.

➤ The words 'last will and testament' are evidence of an intention to make a will.

2 Revocation of previous wills

➤ Quite what is revoked depends on the wording of the clause.

◆ Wills' refers to wills and codicils.

◆ Testamentary dispositions' covers wills, codicils and privileged wills.

3 Disposal of remains

➤ This is a request, it does not bind the executors.

➤ If organ donation or medical research are envisaged, the testator should carry a donor card and inform his family. Details should be kept with the will of how to contact HM Inspector of Anatomy (organ donation) and/or the Department of Health (research).

4 Appointment of executors

➤ Individuals

◆ These should be suitable, willing and capable of taking a grant of representation (not a minor, a convicted criminal, or a bankrupt). Private individuals will not charge, but they may need to engage professionals who will bill the estate. It is advisable to appoint a minimum of 2 people.

➤ Trustees

◆ A maximum of 4 may apply for a grant of probate, so avoid appointing more than this.

➤ Banks and trust corporations

◆ For large complex estates, where the extra expense involved is justified, and the slightly more impersonal approach which may be taken is not a concern.

➤ Solicitors

◆ An individual partner may retire or cease to practice, so appoint the firm in the alternative.

i) Ensure the will appoints partners acting at death, rather than those at the time of the will, *and*

ii) provide for the firm's amalgamation, change of name, or future incorporation.

➤ Public trustee

◆ This is expensive and inconvenient, but available if there is no alternative.

5   Appointment of guardians (*ChA 1989*)

➤ A parent with 'parental responsibility' may appoint a guardian for a minor under the age of 18.

◆ An unmarried father does not have 'parental responsibility' unless he is granted it by a court order.

◆ If both parents have 'parental responsibility', then an appointment is effective on the death of both parents; where both appoint different guardians, the responsibilities are shared between them.

➤ An appointment must be written, dated and signed; it can be revoked in the same fashion *even* if the original appointment was by will *s 5(3)*. No codicil is needed to revoke an appointment, but divorce and annulment of a marriage, and dissolution or annulment of a civil partnership, revoke the appointment unless the appointment shows a contrary intention (*ChA 1989 s 6(3A)-(3B)*).

◆ Ensure both parents appoint the same guardian and that the person consents.

◆ Financial provision for the care of the children should be made by appointing the guardian trustee of a fund, with power to spend income and capital for a child's benefit.

6   Legacies

➤ These are classified as 'General', 'Demonstrative', 'Specific', 'Pecuniary' or 'Residuary' (see p 174).

7   Administrative powers

➤ PRs and trustees have powers under the general law to administer trust funds.

➤ The will may extend powers granted under the general law (see pp 175-176).

8   Attestation clause

➤ This is not compulsory, but it is evidence that the will has been properly executed.

Note: a space for the date is left either in the 'Commencement', or in the 'Attestation' clause.

II   Hints on drafting and interpretation

Class closing rules

Unless the will excludes the class closing rules, these will determine how a class gift is construed.

Vested gifts

a)   'To the children of X' - if there are members of the class alive at the time of the testator's death, the class closes then, otherwise it remains open until X dies.

b)   'To S for life, remainder to the children of X' - as in a), but the class *may* close from S's death.

Contingent gifts

c)   'To the children of X who attain the age of 21' - if the contingency has been fulfilled, the class closes at X's death, and it includes any children alive at the testator's death who have reached, or who may in the future reach 21. Otherwise the class closes as soon as one of X's children fulfils the contingency.

d)   'To S for life, remainder to the children of X who attain the age of 21' - as in c), but the class *may* close from S's death.

Gifts to individuals within a class: 'to *each* of the children of X' - the class closes on the testator's death.

Early closing: the class in b) and d) may close immediately the prior interest fails, then the gift operates like a) or c) respectively.

Legacies

General legacy	Demonstrative legacy	Specific legacy
Property in the estate	From a specific fund. If it does not exist on death, this is treated as a general legacy	A particular item, or items, in the estate

Identify the object to be given

Is it correctly described? A will speaks from death (*WA 1837 s 24*), *but* a reference to 'my' refers to property possessed when the will was made.

Can a beneficiary select an object? Provide for arbitration and a longstop date by which the choice must be made.

What is the interest? Is it vested or contingent? Is it in income or capital? Is the gift of a life interest, or absolute?

If the beneficiary may become insolvent, consider a protective trust (*TA 1925 s 33*) which provides an income stream, but protects capital from creditors.

Ancillary matters

Is the property mortgaged? Property carries any mortgage unless there is contrary intention shown (*AEA 1925 s 35*).

Who pays for insurance, packaging and transport - the estate *or* beneficiary?

Taxation

Is a gift 'free of tax' *or* 'subject to tax'? If 'free of tax', then tax is paid by the estate - a gift is presumed to be free of tax if no contrary intention is shown.

Pecuniary legacy

A gift of specific money

Identify the beneficiary

Is their identity clear? State a beneficiary's name and address, or class (eg: relationship to the testator).

Are specific beneficiaries named, or is there discretion? A list incorporated by reference binds the PRs, but is inflexible as it requires a codicil or a new will to alter it. A document may be incorporated into the will if 3 conditions are met:

a) the document is identified in the will, *and*
b) the document exists when the will is executed, *and*
c) the will refers to the document as existing at execution.

Alternatively, a gift to a named beneficiary, with a request that property should be disposed of in accordance with a memorandum found with the deceased's papers, can be altered merely by changing the memorandum. This is flexible, but is not legally enforceable.

Is a class properly described? 'Children' includes any *en ventre sa mere*, adopted, or illegitimate, unless a contrary intention is expressed.

Check a charity or unincorporated association exists and is named correctly (*Re Recher* [1972] Ch 526). A gift to a charity 'for its general charitable purposes' can save the gift for a related institution if the charity closes or amalgamates.

Ensure a beneficiary can give a good receipt. As minors (under 16 in England, under 14 in Scotland), and unincorporated associations may not do so, authorise PRs to take receipt from a parent or guardian of a minor, or from the treasurer of an unincorporated association.

Minors, or beneficiaries with an interest which is less than an absolute interest, take subject to a trust. Give trustees appropriate administrative powers and consider whether a power to re-appoint the trust (perhaps following a letter of wishes) would best enable the trust to adapt after death.

Consider a substitutional gift (see p 197).

Extra factors for gifts of residue

Provide for debts. The *AEA 1925* statutory order can be varied: 'subject to payment of debts, funeral and testamentary expenses'.

Survivorship: ensure property passes under this will rather than the *comorrientes* rule (*LPA 1925 s 184*). A 28 day period is convenient: IHT considerations dictate a maximum of 6 months.

Consider leaving a life interest to a spouse/ CP with power to advance capital, giving the trustees power to appoint funds to children, and a gift of the remainder to children.
As naming children excludes any born after the date of the will, rigid wording risks partial intestacy, so: 'such of my children as are living at the time of my death, and if more than one in equal shares ...'.

Residuary legacy

Whatever is left in an estate after the payment of debts, testamentary expenses and other legacies

Administration

Insurance (*TA 2000 s 34 substituting TA 1925 s 19*)

➤ **Power to insure** trust property against loss or damage and pay premiums from income or capital

Investment

➤ A general **power of investment**: power to make any kind of investment as if the trustee were absolutely entitled to the trust assets (*TA 2000 s 3(1)-(2)*).

   ◆ This power does not permit a trustee to make an investment in land, other than in loans secured on land (*TA 2000 s 3(3)-(6)*).

   ◆ A trustee must have regard to the standard investment criteria, which are (*TA 2000 s 4*):

   i) the suitability to the trust of investments of the same kind as any particular investment proposed to be made or retained and of that particular investment as an investment of that kind, *and*

   ii) the need for diversification of investments, in so far as is appropriate to the trust's circumstances.

   ◆ Unless a trustee reasonably concludes that it is unnecessary or inappropriate, he must obtain and consider proper advice before exercising the power of investment and when reviewing investments (*TA 2000 s 5*).

➤ A **power to acquire freehold or leasehold land in the UK**: as an investment, for occupation by a beneficiary, or for any other reason (*TA 2000 s 8*).

Land, etc

Powers under the general law	Drafting considerations
➤ Prior to 1 January 1997, land was held on a strict settlement under *SLA 1925* unless it is given to a trustee on an 'immediate binding trust for sale'. *TLATA 1996* prevents new strict settlements arising and creates a system of 'trusts of land'.	Consider how to achieve the testator's wishes under *TLATA 1996,* see further pp 92-105. *TLATA* only gives trustees of land a power to sell, so consider a power to sell personalty

Operate a business

Powers under the general law	Drafting considerations
➤ PRs can only run a business to preserve its sale value. They are restricted to using assets the business relied on at the testator's death (*Re Hodson, ex parte Richardson* (1818) 3 Madd 138)	PRs can be permitted to use assets from the general estate to run the business, or the business and assets used to carry on the business may be left as a specific legacy

Delegation, agency, etc

➤ **Power to authorise any person to exercise delegable functions as their agent** (*TA 2000 s 11*).

   ◆ A beneficiary may not act as an agent (*TA 2000 s 12(3)*) (for 'delegable functions', see p 186).

   ◆ An agent's authorisation in relation to asset management functions must be evidenced in writing and be accompanied by guidance (known as a 'policy statement') (*TA 2000 s 15*).

➤ **Power to appoint a nominee** (*TA 2000 s 16*) or **custodian** (*TA 2000 s 17*) (*TA 2000 Part IV*).

   ◆ The appointment must be evidenced in writing.

➤ Professionally drafted wills may continue to include express powers and duties. The statutory framework provided by *TLATA 1996/TA 2000* offers a 'safety net' in cases where specific provision is not made.

Administration (cont.)

Remuneration / Reimbursement

➤ An **entitlement to receive payment in respect of services** (*TA 2000 s 28*).

- ◆ This applies to a trust corporation or a trustee acting in a professional capacity if the trust instrument confers an entitlement to payment out of trust funds in respect of services provided by the trustee; it applies even if the services are capable of being provided by a lay trustee.

➤ An **entitlement to receive reasonable remuneration for services to the trust** (*TA 2000 s 29*).

- ◆ This applies to a trust corporation, or a trustee acting in a professional capacity (but not the trustee of a charitable trust) where no provision for remuneration has been made in the trust instrument.

- ◆ If a trustee acts in a professional capacity, each of the other trustees must agree in writing.

➤ An **entitlement to reimbursement of/payment for a trustee's expenses** (*TA 2000 s 31*).

➤ A **power to remunerate an agent/nominee/custodian** (*TA 2000 s 32*).

Distribution

Appropriation

Powers under the general law	Drafting considerations
➤ PRs can appropriate property to pay a pecuniary legacy provided that (*AEA 1925 s 41*): a) a beneficiary does not suffer, *and* b) that beneficiary consents	Relieve PRs of the duty to obtain a beneficiary's formal consent

Apportionment

Powers under the general law	Drafting considerations
➤ *Howe v. Dartmouth* (1802) 7 Ves 137: 'wasting, hazardous and unauthorised' assets, and those which produce no income are sold, so that a life tenant benefits from capital ➤ *Allhusen v. Whittell* (1867) LR 4 Eq 295: debts, administration and tax are apportioned between capital and income ➤ *AA 1870 s 2*: rent/dividends are income arising daily: they are treated as capital before death, and income thereafter	These complex bureaucratic rules can be expressly excluded to assist the administration of the trust If the will creates a trust of land under *TLATA 1996*, then the rule in *Howe v. Dartmouth* may be automatically excluded (*Re Pitcairn* [1896] 2 Ch 199). However, this will only occur if a will trust contains land so exclude the rules expressly

Receipt

Powers under the general law	Drafting considerations
➤ A married minor can only give receipt for income (*LPA s 21*) ➤ PRs can accept receipt on behalf of minors with an absolute interest from trustees who may be appointed for this purpose (*AEA 1925 s 42*).	Authorise PRs to accept receipt from a parent/guardian of a minor under 16, to avoid appointing trustees Cater for receipt if a minor's interest is contingent, *or* if a married minor receives capital

Income / Capital

Powers under the general law	Drafting considerations
Income for 'maintenance, education or benefit', acting 'reasonably' and with regard to other resources (*TA 1925 s 31*)	Give the trustees discretion to make payments as they think fit
➤ At 18 a beneficiary of an absolute or contingent interest is entitled to income ➤ Accumulated income is released if a beneficiary has a life interest in capital, otherwise accumulations and capital are retained until the gift vests absolutely	Postpone a beneficiary's right to receive income, and/or capital, until after the statutory age of 18
Capital for 'advancement or benefit' whether an interest is absolute or contingent (*TA 1925 s 32*)	
➤ Payments are subtracted when capital vests absolutely	Increase the capital which trustees can advance
➤ A holder of a prior life interest must consent in writing ➤ Only half a presumptive/ vested interest may be advanced	Give the trustees discretion to distribute capital without making deductions in respect of prior advancements

C Intestacy

Steps	
1	Discover the extent of the estate passing on intestacy
2	Property passes to the PRs on statutory trusts *(AEA 1925 s 33)*
3	Deduct funeral, testamentary and administrative expenses and debts
4	Set aside a pecuniary legacy fund
5	Work out who is entitled to the property (apply the statutory order of entitlement)
6	Consider whether the spouse/civil partner wishes to exercise his/her rights

Step 1   Discover the extent of the estate passing on intestacy

➤ Only property capable of passing by will can pass on intestacy.

Step 2   Property passes to the PRs on the statutory trusts

➤ Property passes to PRs on the statutory trusts *(AEA 1925 s 47)*.

➤ The terms of the trust dictate that the gift is construed as being:

◆ to those entitled within a class, in equal shares, *and*

◆ to all 'living' persons within the class, including any children *en ventre sa mere, and*

◆ on the death of a member of a class who was entitled on the intestate's death, to that beneficiary's issue in equal shares, *and*

◆ contingent on the beneficiary marrying *or* reaching the age of 18.

Note: if a contingency is not met, the failed interest is disregarded, and the distribution of the estate is reassessed as if the failed interest had never existed.

➤ The trustees have:

◆ powers of maintenance and advancement given by the *TA 1925 ss 31-32, and*

◆ (from 1 January 1997), power to sell.

  • Prior to 1 January 1997 trustees were under a duty to sell with a power to postpone sale and a direction that the deceased's 'personal chattels' should not be sold without a 'special reason' such as the payment of debts and administration expenses *(AEA 1925 s 33)*.

    ▪ When *TLATA* came into force on 1 January 1997 the duty to sell and convert ceased to apply *(TLATA 1996 Sch 2 para 5)*.

Step 3   Deduct funeral, testamentary and administrative expenses

Step 4   Set aside a fund from which to pay pecuniary legacies

| Step 5 | Work out who is entitled to property |

The statutory order of entitlement

➤ A surviving spouse/civil partner ('CP') takes priority over anyone else. Depending on the size of the estate, the spouse/CP may share an interest with one class of kinsmen (see the chart below); if one class exists those classes further down the line are excluded (*AEA 1925 s 46*).

➤ If there is no spouse/CP, blood kin take in the statutory order:

   a) issue, *then*

   b) parents, *then*

   c) brothers and sisters of whole blood, *then*

   d) brothers and sisters of half-blood, *then*

   e) grandparents, *then*

   f) uncles and aunts of whole blood, *then*

   g) uncles and aunts of half-blood, *then*

   h) *bona vacantia* goes to the Crown, the Duchy of Lancaster, or the Duke of Cornwall; there is discretion to provide for those for whom an intestate 'might reasonably have been expected to make provision'.

➤ For deaths on or after 1 January 1996, the spouse/civil partner is treated as not having survived the intestate if he or she dies within a period of 28 days beginning on the day of the intestate's death (*AEA 1925 s 46(2A)* as inserted by the *LR(S)A 1995 s 1*).

➤ *When a death occurs after EDP(FRLS)A 2011 comes into force, if a beneficiary dies without having reached the age of 18 and leaves issue, that beneficiary will be treated as having died immediately before the intestate (AEA 1925 s 47(4B)-(4D)).*

	Size of estate	Spouse/CP's entitlement	Others' entitlement
Spouse/ CP alone		Everything passing on intestacy	Nothing
Spouse/CP and issue	Estate under £250,000	Everything (including personal chattels)	
	Estate over £250,000	Personal chattels absolutely £250,000 statutory legacy* Life interest in half the residue	On the statutory trusts: ➤ half the residue, *and* ➤ interest in remainder of residue
Spouse/CP, no issue† but other kin	Estate under £450,000	Everything (including chattels)	Nothing
	Estate over £450,000	Personal chattels absolutely £450,000 statutory legacy* Half the residue absolutely	On the statutory trusts: ➤ half the residue
No spouse/CP			Everything on statutory trusts

† Issue: children and other descendants including adopted, legitimated and legitimised children

* Statutory legacy:
  a) this is paid free of tax and costs. It also includes interest from the date of death until the legacy is paid to the spouse/ civil partner
  b) the value of any personal chattels is not taken into account in establishing whether the estate is worth £250,000 or £450,000

NB: these figures (£250,000 and £450,000) for the statutory legacy apply only to deaths on or after 1 February 2009 (*FP(IS) O 2009*) (previously the relevant amounts were £125,000 and £200,000).

Disclaimer or forfeiture on intestacy (*AEA 1925 s 46A*)

➤ *When a death occurs after EDP(FRLS)A 2011 comes into force, if an interest in a residuary estate is disclaimed, or such an interest is precluded by virtue of the forfeiture rule in Forfeiture Act 1982, the individual who would have enjoyed that interest were it not for the disclaimer/forfeiture will be treated as having died immediately before the intestate.*

♦ *This is intended to preserve the position of a person who would either:*

a) *inherit as a result of a disclaimer, or*

b) *would otherwise be prevented from inheriting where a joint tenant forfeitures an interest in a residuary estate by murdering the intestate.*

Step 6	Consider whether the spouse/CP wish to exercise his/her rights

1 A spouse's/CP's right to redeem a life interest

➤ The spouse/civil partner may choose to convert the life interest into a lump sum.

Steps

1 The spouse/civil partner who wishes to convert a life interest into a lump sum must notify the PRs within 1 year of the date when the grant of representation is issued.

2 All those entitled to the remainder may, if they are *sui juris*, agree the value of the life interest in writing with the spouse/civil partner. Otherwise the sum is calculated according to *IS(IC)O 1977*.

3 The entitlement of other beneficiaries is recalculated.

4 IHT is recalculated and the spouse/civil partner bears any resulting charge.

2 A spouse/civil partner's right to appropriate the matrimonial or civil partnership home (*IEA 1952 s 5 and Sch II*)

➤ The spouse/CP can demand that PRs transfer the house to him/her as part of the inheritance to which he/she is absolutely entitled.

Steps

1 The spouse/civil partner must notify the PRs within 1 year of the date when the grant of representation is issued.

2 The house is valued at the time of appropriation, not death. If its value exceeds the spouse's/CP's entitlement, he or she can pay the difference to the estate as 'equality money'.

➤ If the spouse/CP is the sole surviving PR, then the President of the Family Division must be notified of an intention to invoke either of these statutory rights.

♦ This notification is done by lodging the notification together with the original grant at the Probate Registry so that this intention can be recorded on the grant.

D Probate

I   Overview of solicitor's role

II   Applying for a grant of representation

I   Overview of a solicitor's role

A solicitor's duty to PRs

1	Advise on succession and revenue law.
2	Prove the testator's will.
3	Administer the estate.
4	Prepare estate accounts.

How to carry out this duty

1   Take instructions directly from the PR.

2   Obtain the deceased's will (and ensure PRs each have a copy).

3   Attend to the deceased's wishes as regards cremation, organ donation, etc, in consultation with the PRs.

4   Secure property (ie: check an empty house is locked and insured, locate and safeguard documents of title to assets).

5   Attend to financial arrangements (ie: loans to support a family pending grant of probate or during the administration of the estate).

6   Obtain the death certificate.

7   Compile a list of the deceased's assets and liabilities. This list should be continuously updated during the administration of the estate, to show their state at any given time and what steps have been or are being taken with regard to them.

8   Discover details of all the beneficiaries (ie: ages and addresses).

9   Protect PRs from personal liability against unknown or missing creditors or beneficiaries (eg: place advertisements in good time for the purposes of *TA s 1925 s 27*, see p 195).

10 Prepare the oath and the HMRC account.

11 Obtain a grant and make office copies of the grant.

12 Collect and realise assets.

13 Pay debts.

14 Pay legacies.

15 Ascertain and distribute residue.

I   Administering property immediately after death

➤   The executor's first duty, after making suitable arrangements for a funeral, is to ascertain what assets and liabilities there are in the estate.

◆   Certain assets can be paid to someone who appears to be beneficially entitled to them without sight of a grant (which may take a little time to obtain) - this is a discretion to be exercised by whomever holds the assets, PRs cannot demand payment as of right.

Type of property	Comments
Salaries of public sector employees Some pensions National Savings bank accounts, TSB accounts National Savings certificates and premium bonds Building society and Friendly society accounts	The PRs can administer such property if (*AE(SP)A 1965*): ➤ payment is at the discretion of the trustees, *and* ➤ the asset is not worth more than £5,000, *and* ➤ the applicant appears to be beneficially entitled to the asset
Life assurance policy held on trust	A death certificate is needed to gain access to the proceeds of the policy The proceeds are paid to whomever was assigned the benefit of the policy, or in the case of a *MWPA* policy in favour of children, to the trustees who were appointed under the terms of the policy
Property held under a joint tenancy	A death certificate establishes a tenant's right to take through survivorship Only if a survivor murders another tenant will he not be entitled to the property
Chattels	Although a grant is theoretically necessary to prove title, in practice it is not usually necessary to produce one

●   These assets can be used to meet debts and to pay for funeral expenses and IHT.

●   National savings investments and British Government Stocks on the Bank of the England register can be used to pay IHT under the 'direct payment scheme'; funds can be transferred directly to HMRC to meet an IHT liability, although this can take up to 4 weeks (HMRC leaflet, *IHT 11*).

➤   The executors should write to institutions holding assets, quoting whatever details they possess about the assets and inquiring about:

a) the value of the asset(s) on the date of death (including accrued interest), *and*

b) the daily interest which is accruing on the asset(s), *and*

c) whether the institution holds any other assets on behalf of the deceased.

●   It is usual to *either* request a cheque for the sum due *or* to ask for the relevant papers needed to close the account.

●   The PRs should send appropriate evidence of their title, eg: to claim an insurance policy written into trust, send a certified copy of the trust instrument and any appointments/resignations of trustees plus a certified copy of the death certificate.

II   Applying for a grant of representation

➤ A PR's duty is (*AEA 1925 s 25* as amended *AEA 1971 s 9*): 'to collect and get in the real and personal estate of the deceased and administer it according to law'.

➤ A grant of representation is necessary to administer the rest of the deceased's estate as the executor(s) will need to be able to prove that he/they are entitled to sell or dispose of assets.

➤ The procedure for 'Swearing the oath' and 'Applying for the grant' is as follows:

Steps	
1	**Decide what sort of grant is appropriate.**
2	**Ascertain who is entitled to take a grant.**
3	**Ascertain who is entitled to take a grant.**
4	**Fill in the oath.**

Swearing/affirming the oath

➤ Executors complete the jurat before an independent solicitor with a current practicing certificate or commissioner for oaths (*not* an executor or connected with a firm acting for the PRs).

➤ If the oath is affirmed, rather than sworn, an executor does not need to hold a Bible/the New Testament and simply states 'I do solemnly sincerely and truly declare and affirm ...'

➤ Executors and a solicitor, or a commissioner for oaths, initial the will and any codicils.

Applying for the grant

➤ Send to the Probate Registry (using a District Registry may minimise publicity) with *form PA1*:

   ◆ the oath (*NCPR r 8*), *and*

   ◆ the will, *and*

   ◆ 2 A4 copies of the will (and any codicil), *and*

     ● If a will must be taken apart to copy it, a covering letter must be enclosed with the application informing the Probate Registry of that, and that the will has been restored to the same plight and condition that it was before it was copied and nothing of a testamentary nature was further attached or detached.

   ◆ the court fee, *and*

     ● £105, or free if the value of the net estate (assets less funeral expenses and debts) is £5,000 or less (see *form PA3* for a list of the probate registry's fees). Add to this the photocopy fee (£1) for each office copy of the grant of representation requested. (Work out how many copies to ask for by reference to the number of assets for which the grant will need to be produced.)

   ◆ a fee sheet showing how the fee was calculated *and*

   ◆ the HMRC account (unless the estate is 'excepted'.

➤ The Probate Registry usually issues the grant in 5 to 15 days.

➤ Where an estate is 'excepted', HMRC has 35 days after the grant is issued in which to demand the production of an account.

➤ If the PRs discover other assets, making it necessary to submit a corrective account, then they must send *form C4* to HMRC within 6 months of making this discovery.

| Step 1 | Decide what sort of grant is appropriate |

➤ A straightforward grant of probate *or* letters of administration is usually sought:

Grant	Circumstances	Effect of grant	PRs identified
Grant of probate	The executor appointed in a valid will is willing *and* able to act (even if the estate actually passes under the intestacy rules)	➤ It confirms the appointment made in the will ➤ It is conclusive evidence that the PRs have title to the estate *and* that the will is valid	In the will
Letters of administration with will annexed	The appointment of executors in the will fails as *either* it is invalid *or* they are unwilling to act	➤ It confers authority on the PRs ➤ It vests title to the estate in PRs	Following *NCPR r 20*
Simple administration	Total intestacy		Following *NCPR r 22*

➤ However, in certain circumstances, a different form of grant of representation will be appropriate:

Type of grant	Circumstances: when ...
Grant for the use and benefit of a person who is mentally incapacitated *NCPR r 35*	... a sole executor or only potential administrator is mentally incapacitated. Grant to a capable adult in the following order: a) adult authorised by the Court of Protection to apply for a grant b) lawful attorney of the incapacitated person, with registered enduring power of attorney c) the deceased's residuary legatee or devisee
Administration for the use and benefit of a minor *NCPR r 32*	.. a minor is the sole executor, or the only administrator in the category with highest priority. The grant is made to an adult, often the minor's guardian
Grants over specified property *NCPR r 53*	... a will appoints an executor in respect of particular property *or* the court exercises its discretion to make a grant over part of the estate (*SCA 1981 s 113*)
Grant *ad litem* *SCA 1981 s 116*	... an estate is a party to legal proceedings and there is no PR
Administration with litigation pending *SCA 1981 s 117*	... assets need safeguarding while a probate action takes place. This requires the consent of all parties to the action
Administration *ad colligenda bona* *NCPR r 52*	... a person with an interest in the estate seeks to ensure the collection and preservation of its property - this grant does not permit distribution, and ceases when a full grant is made
Attorney grants *NCPR r 31*	... a letter of administration is granted to the lawful attorney of someone who is entitled to a grant
Double grant of probate *	... power is reserved - it operates in tandem with the original grant
Cessate grant *	... a grant which was made for a limited time expires - it is a regrant to an executor of what remains of the estate
Grant *de bonis administrandum *	... a sole surviving PR dies so that the chain of representation is broken
* With applications for such grants submit *Form A5-C* to the probate registry (no need to first send *Form A5-C* to HMRC)	

Step 2	Ascertain who is entitled to take a grant

➤ Applicants for grants must satisfy the following criteria:

	Executors	Administrator
Mentally incapable	Not suitable (*NCPR r 35*)	
Renunciation (*NCPR r 37*)	If the executor has not 'intermeddled' with the estate (actively administered the estate) (*Re Stevens, Cooke v. Stevens* [1898] 1 Ch 162) he may renounce. When this is done he may not apply for a grant A renunciation must be in writing, signed, witnessed *and* filed at the probate registry	
Minor	Not suitable, until majority is reached when a cessate grant can be sought. If an adult is appointed, power can be reserved to a minor. If only a minor is appointed, parents or a guardian take letters of administration with the will annexed	Not suitable, until majority is reached, when a cessate grant can be sought. A parent or guardian can apply for a minor's 'use and benefit' (*NCPR r 32*); anyone entitled in the same degree takes in preference to a guardian (*NCPR r 27(5)*)
Former spouse/ civil partner	Not suitable, *unless* the will indicates an intention that, despite the divorce/dissolution, the appointment should stand (*WA 1837 s 15*)	Not suitable
Power reserved	Yes, if an appointee entitled in the same degree requests it. Notice must be given to all those entitled	No power may be reserved
Number needed	Up to 4 (reserve power if a future vacancy is likely)	At least 2 if there is a minority or life interest; unless the court permits one

NCPR r 20	*NCPR r 22*
➤ *NCPR r 20* allows the appointment of administrators if: ◆ the appointment is void, *or* ◆ the appointee is incapable.	➤ *NCPR r 22* sets out the entitlement to administer the estate on an intestacy.

NCPR r 20 flow:

a) Any executor
↓
b) A residuary legatee holding in trust for any other person
↓
c) A residuary legatee: a vested interest takes in priority to a contingent one, and those entitled to residue take priority over any entitled under a partial intestacy
↓
d) A PR of any residuary legatee, or of one entitled to residue under the intestacy rules, provided the deceased beneficiary had an absolute interest (eg: not a life interest)
↓
e) Any legatee, or creditor. A legatee of a vested interest takes priority over one entitled to a contingent interest
↓
f) A PR of any legatee (with an absolute interest) or creditor

A beneficiary under the will who is ...

a) a surviving spouse/civil partner
↓
b) children, or their issue if they are dead
↓
c) father and mother
If the couple are not married, there is a presumption the father is dead, unless they live together or the father is in contact with the child (*FLRA 1987 ss 18,21*)
↓
d) brothers and sisters of whole blood, or their issue if they are dead
↓
e) brothers and sisters of half-blood, or their issue if they are dead
↓
f) grandparents
↓
g) uncles and aunts of whole blood, or their issue if they are dead
↓
h) uncles and aunts of half-blood, or their issue if they are dead
↓
i) a creditor may apply, or the Treasury Solicitor claims the estate as *bona vacantia*

➤ An applicant for a grant under *NCPR r 20* or *r 22* must swear why those with priority are unable or unwilling to apply for the grant - this is known as 'clearing off'.

Step 3	Complete form *IHT 400* (unless the estate is 'excepted')

Step 4	Filling in the oath

Consider (and fill in or delete as appropriate) ...

... when preparing an oath for an executor

➤ details (in the top left hand corner) of the solicitor's firm lodging the oath.

➤ the deceased's name, plus any alias (and the reason for such an alias).

➤ the deceased's date of death and age at death. If the date of death is uncertain, the time when the deceased was last seen alive and the date on which the body was found are sworn.

➤ the deceased's last address and the address of the deceased when the will was made if this differs.

➤ whether any settled land was vested in the deceased.

➤ whether power is reserved and, if so, to whom.

➤ the gross and net value of the estate and whether it is 'excepted'.

◆ If an executor has renounced, ensure a Form of Renunciation is annexed to the oath.

... additionally when preparing an oath for an administrator with a will annexed

➤ if a minority arises under the estate, *or* the deceased at his death had an interest in land under a strict settlement, 2 administrators will be needed (one executor could have acted alone).

➤ details of the applicant's right under the *NCPR r 20* to seek a grant of representation:

a) an explanation of why an executor is not applying, ie: none was appointed, renunciation, or death, *and*

b) the applicant's capacity to take a grant - eg: 'residuary legatee and the devisee under the said will', 'specific legatee and devisee named in the said will'.

... additionally when preparing an oath for an administrator of an intestate

Marital status	Single	Married/CP	Divorced/Dissolved	Judicially separated	Annulled
	Bachelor/spinster	Married/CPed man/woman, or widow/er			Status before annulment

Fill in →

The court which implemented the divorce/dissolution, date of the order (if the court was outside England and Wales, provide an office copy of the decree)

That the deceased did not re marry/partner	That the separation continued until death

➤ Clear off those with a prior entitlement under *NCPR r 22* (but not those in the same category). Mention any renunciation and clear off using the following terms depending how the deceased died.

◆ Spouse/CP: abachelor/spinster, widow(er), single man/woman
◆ Children: without issue
◆ Parents

◆ Brothers, sisters/issue: (or) brother or sister of [whole/half] or issue thereof
◆ Grandparents: (or) grandparent
◆ Uncle, aunt/issue: (or) uncle or aunt of [whole/half] blood or issue thereof

➤ If a spouse/civil partner survives, and there are no issue qualifying for a share in the estate, the words 'or any other person entitled in priority to share in [his/her] estate by virtue of any enactment' remain - otherwise delete them.

➤ State the applicant's relationship to the deceased.

- Spouse/CP: lawful husband/widow/civil partner
- Child: son/daughter (whether or not parents were married at birth)
- Grandchild: grandson/daughter (state that the applicant's parents have died)
- Brother/Sister: brother/sister of [whole/half] blood
- Parent: father/mother
- Grandparent: grandfather/grandmother
- Cousin: cousin german of [whole/half] blood (state that the applicant's parents have died)

➤ State why the applicant is entitled to a share in the estate, eg: 'the only person entitled to the estate', 'one of the persons entitled to share in the estate'.

E Administration

I	Collecting in all the deceased's assets
II	Ensuring the estate meets its tax liability
III	Paying debts
IV	Paying legacies
V	Obtaining a discharge

I Collecting in all the deceased's assets

➤ A PR's duty is (*AEA 1925 s 25* as amended *AEA 1971 s 9*): 'to collect and get in the real and personal estate of the deceased and administer it according to law'.

➤ PRs should write to institutions holding the deceased's assets, enclosing an office copy of the grant together with any other appropriate documents (eg: building society pass-book if the account is to be closed, insurance policy) and requesting details of the assets.

◆ Ask for the office copies of the grant to be returned, to reduce costs.

➤ PRs and trustees have statutory powers, and may receive additional powers in the will.

PRs' statutory powers, rights and duties
Pay an agent: *TA 2000 s 32*.
Appropriate property in the estate amongst the beneficiaries (*AEA 1925 s 41*).
Insure the estate's assets: *TA 1925 s 19*.
PRs (and trustees) can **delegate the exercise of powers or discretions** for up to 1 year. ◆ This is useful if renunciation is impossible but the PR is going abroad, etc) (*TA 1925 s 25*). PRs can **employ agents to exercise 'delegable functions'** (*TA 2000 s 11*); these are any function other than: a) any function relating to whether or in what way any assets of the trust should be distributed, *or* b) any power to decide whether any fees or other payment due to be made out of trust funds should be made out of income or capital, *or* c) any power to appoint a person to act as trustee of the trust, *or* d) any power conferred by any other enactment or trust instrument which permits the trustees to delegate any of their functions or to appoint a person t act as a nominee or custodian.
Reimbursement of/payment of expenses: *TA 2000 s 31*.
Charging: *TA 2000 ss 28 -29*.
Apportionment: sell wasting assets (*Howe v. Dartmouth*), pay debts fairly (*Allhusen v. Whittell*), AA 1870 s 2.
Running a business: duty to run the business to maintain its value as an asset for sale.
Power and duties in respect of land forming part of the estate during the administration: ◆ In respect of estates arising due to deaths on or after 1 January 1997 when *TLATA 1996* came into force PRs have the same powers and duties as trustees of land, except that they will not be bound to obtain the beneficiaries' consent before selling land.
Power to invest (see p 175).
Power to appoint trustees who will be able to give the PRs valid receipt on behalf of a minor who is absolutely entitled (*TA 1925 s 42*).
Power to postpone distribution even if the will specifies payments within a time-frame (*AEA 1925 s 44*). If payment is delayed beyond a year after death, interest is payable from that date. If the testator specifies a date or contingency upon which payment is to be made, interest runs from that point. The rate of interest is 6% per annum, *or* as laid down in the will.

II   Ensuring the estate meets its tax liability

➤ PRs should complete a self assessment tax return for the deceased's income and capital gains from 6 April to his death. Any reliefs and allowances available for the full year may be claimed. Any liability or repayment forms part of the estate, and must be met or accounted for by the PRs during the administration.

➤ Throughout each tax year during the administration, the PRs must make tax returns on behalf of the estate.

1 Income tax

➤ This is chargeable on the deceased's income and is a debt due from the estate.

➤ Relief is available for interest on a loan taken out to pay IHT (*ITA 2007 ss 403-405*).

➤ Personal allowances are available for the tax year in which death occurs, but not for the remainder of the administration.

➤ The dividend ordinary rate (10%), dividend upper rate (32.5%), or dividend additional rate (42.5%) apply to company distributions. Interest is taxed at the savings rate (20%) and other income is subject to tax at the basic rate (20%) (*ITA 2007 s 463(1)*).

  ◆ If a beneficiary is entitled to income, PRs supply a certificate of deduction of tax (*Form 185 (Estate Income)*).

    • When a beneficiary prepares his self assessment he uses *Form 185 (Estate Income)* complete a self assessment (pages *SA 107*) and (if appropriate) reclaim tax (using *form R40*).

    • A beneficiary is liable for tax on the gross income (*IT(TOI)A 2005 Part 5 Ch 7*) .

2 Capital gains tax

➤ As death is not a disposal, no charge to CGT arises on death (*TCGA 1992 s 62(1)(b)*).

➤ The probate value becomes the base value (ie: rather than the original acquisition value) (*TCGA 1992 s 62(1)(a)*).

➤ Tax is due at the rate of 28% on chargeable gains realised during administration (*TCGA 1992 s 4(1AA)*).

  ◆ Entrepeneurs' relief is available (reducing tax due on a relevant gain to a 10% rate).

➤ The PRs are entitled to use an annual exemption (£10,600 for 2011/2012) (*TCGA 1992 s 3(7)*):

  ◆ for the year of death (*in addition* to the deceased's exemption accruing before his death), *and*

  ◆ for 2 subsequent years.

➤ Losses may be carried back 3 years and forward during the administration period, but not after it.

3 Loss relief for capital gains tax and inheritance tax

➤ PRs may opt either for:

  ◆ IHT loss relief at up to 40% (preferable if an estate is in the nil rate band/exempt), *or*

  ◆ CGT loss relief at 28% (advisable in most other circumstances).

Final adjustments

➤ PRs should retain sufficient assets to discharge any outstanding IHT liability, including provision for the payment of tax on instalment option property, and the need to meet any further liability from:

- ◆ LCTs or gifts with benefit reserved where the donee does not pay what he owes.

- ◆ newly discovered LCTs or PETs which the deceased made within 7 years of death, and which alter cumulation and tapering relief.

- ◆ valuations which are agreed with HMRC at a level different from the probate value.

- ◆ the discovery of assets or liabilities which were unknown on probate.

- ◆ any agreement with HMRC on the deceased's pre-death liability for income tax or CGT.

- ◆ sales which qualify for IHT 'loss relief' (see p 92).

- ◆ post-death variations or disclaimers.

Steps

1 **The PRs send a corrective account to the CTO.**

For minor adjustments the PRs may write a letter to the CTO, otherwise they complete a Form Cap D3, and send it to the CTO, who prepare a final assessment.

2 **The PRs send the CTO 2 copies of *Form IHT 30,* requesting a clearance certificate.**

3 **The CTO return the form with an endorsement.**

➤ The certificate discharges the PRs of liability and extinguishes any charge over the estate for unpaid IHT.

➤ Where instalments are outstanding, the discharge is partial: on their fulfilment PRs should seek a full certificate.

➤ The certificate provides only limited protection, as HMRC may re-open the account if:

a) there has been fraud or failure to disclose material facts, *or*

b) additional assets are later shown to have been included in the transfer, *or*

c) further tax becomes payable as a result of statutory amendments after issue of the certificate (*IHTA 1984 s 239(4)*).

III   Paying debts

➤   The rules depend on whether an estate will be **A Insolvent**, *or* **B Solvent**, after the payment of:

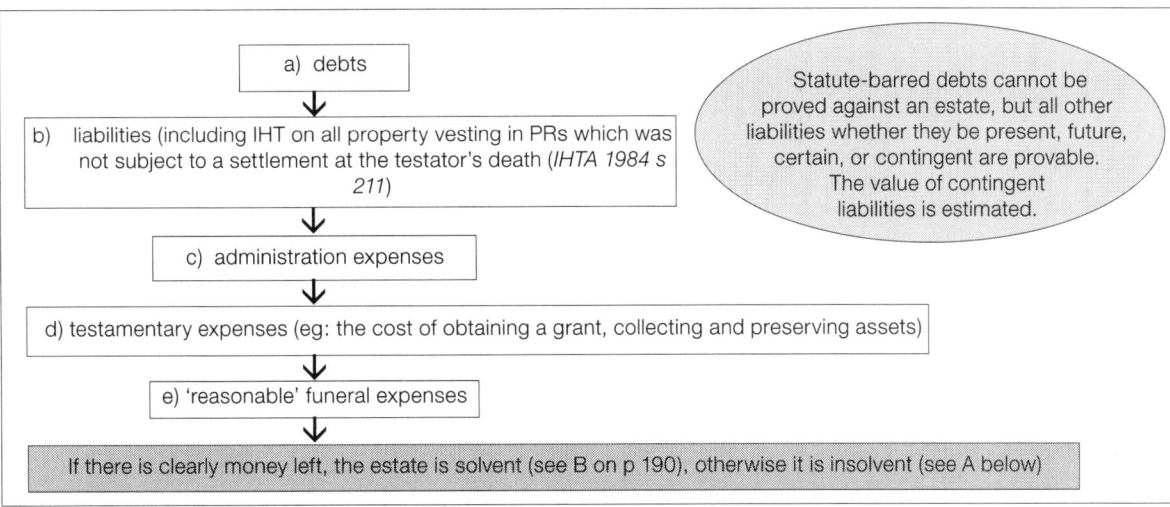

a) debts

b)   liabilities (including IHT on all property vesting in PRs which was not subject to a settlement at the testator's death (*IHTA 1984 s 211*)

Statute-barred debts cannot be proved against an estate, but all other liabilities whether they be present, future, certain, or contingent are provable. The value of contingent liabilities is estimated.

c) administration expenses

d) testamentary expenses (eg: the cost of obtaining a grant, collecting and preserving assets)

e) 'reasonable' funeral expenses

If there is clearly money left, the estate is solvent (see B on p 190), otherwise it is insolvent (see A below)

A   Insolvent estates (or where solvency is doubtful)

1   Secured creditors

➤ They have three options:

a)   sell the secured asset and seek to recover outstanding liability as unsecured creditors, *or*

b)   value the security and seek any outstanding balance as unsecured creditors, *or*

c)   simply rely on the fixed charge and collect the debt whenever the estate sells the security.

2   Unsecured creditors (*AIEDPO 1986*)

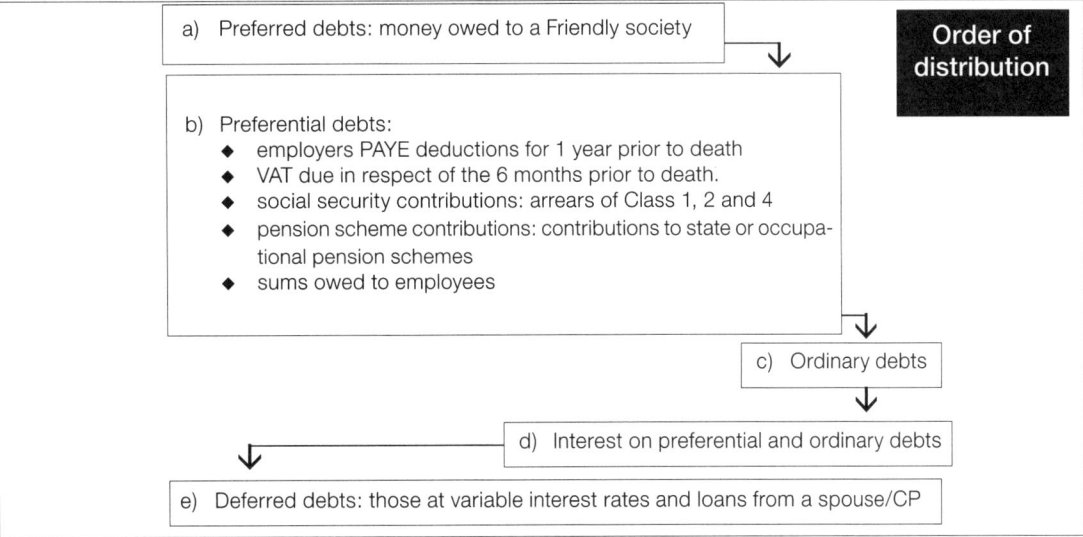

a)   Preferred debts: money owed to a Friendly society

Order of distribution

b)   Preferential debts:
   ◆   employers PAYE deductions for 1 year prior to death
   ◆   VAT due in respect of the 6 months prior to death.
   ◆   social security contributions: arrears of Class 1, 2 and 4
   ◆   pension scheme contributions: contributions to state or occupational pension schemes
   ◆   sums owed to employees

c)   Ordinary debts

d)   Interest on preferential and ordinary debts

e)   Deferred debts: those at variable interest rates and loans from a spouse/CP

➤ Debts of equal priority rank equally, and abate proportionately, if there are insufficient funds available.

B Solvent estates

1 **Property in the estate subject to any charge (*AEA 1925 s 35(1)*)**

➤ Mortgages, any charge imposed for unpaid IHT, or a debt in favour of a judgment creditor, is met by the property over which the charge is fixed.

➤ The will may override the statutory provisions by *either*:

a) a direction to 'pay debts including any mortgage charge on Whiteacre out of residue', *or*

b) expressing the gift to be 'free of mortgage'.

2 **Unsecured debts, funeral and testamentary expenses (*AEA 1925 s 34(1)*)**

➤ PRs first set aside a fund comprising undisposed of property from which they will later pay out pecuniary legacies. From this fund, they meet debts in the order dictated by the *AEA 1925 Sch I Part II*.

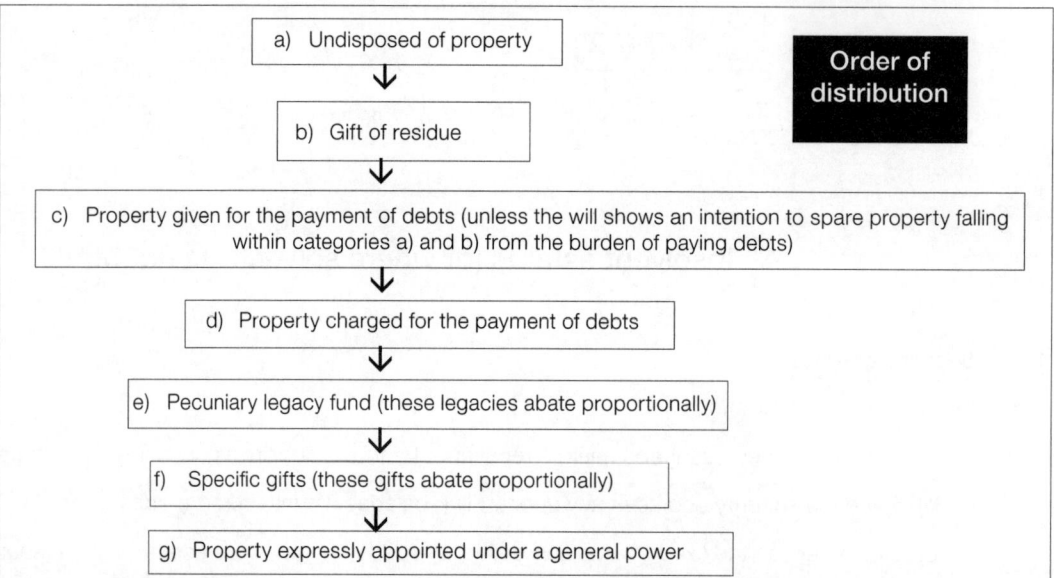

➤ Property passing under a will or intestacy bears the burden of debt equally. If there is no provision in the will, property which is undisposed of (ie: on a partial intestacy) is available first.

➤ The will may displace the statutory order by making:

a) a gift of residue 'subject to' the payment of debts, *or*

b) by charging property for this purpose and stating that property in a) and b) should not bear the liability.

IV Paying legacies

Transferring property to beneficiaries	
Property	**Method of transfer**
Personal chattels	An assent (written or oral) stating that the PRs have no further need of the items for the administration of the estate
National Savings certificates	Withdrawal or transfer forms
Shares	Stock transfer form; the grant will have to be produced
Premium bonds	These must be surrendered and the cash transferred to the beneficiary
Money in residuary estate	Cheque drawn on PRs' bank account
Land	A written assent signed by the PRs which names the person in whose favour it is made out (*AEA 1925 s 36(4)*). If the PRs are taking an indemnity covenant, the assent must be by deed. The assent should be endorsed on the original grant of representation; HM Land Registry has its own standard form of assent. *Either*: a) the PRs can register as proprietors, on producing the grant, and subsequently transfer the title to the beneficiary, *or* b) the PRs can supply the beneficiary with the assent and a certified copy of the grant so that he can apply for registration The Register is conclusive. Although it dispenses with the requirement for the grant to be endorsed, it is still good practice to obtain an endorsement

➤ The PRs should always obtain a valid receipt.

A Identifying the beneficiaries

1 Class gifts

➤ See p 173 for the rules governing the construction of these gifts.

2 *Wills Act 1837 s 33*

➤ Where a beneficiary dies a substitutional gift is implied in favour of the deceased beneficiary's children if the beneficiary was the testator's 'issue'.

3 Children

➤ References to 'children' are interpreted as follows (unless contrary intention is shown).

Statute	Effect	Protection of PRs
FLRA 1987 s 19(1)	For wills or codicils executed after 3 April 1988, a reference to a relationship is construed without regard to whether the relationship existed as a marriage/civil partnership Wills or codicils executed between 31 December 1969 and 4 April 1988 are construed similarly (*FLRA 1969 s 15*)	This offers PRs no protection The PRs should comply with the requirements of *TA 1925 s 27* (p 195)
ACA 2002 s 67	An adopted child is treated as the child of his adopted, rather than his natural parents An adopted child is deemed to have been born on the date of adoption Where more than one child is adopted on a day, then the actual order of their births dictates the order in which they are held to have been 'born' on the day of their adoption, but this maxim does not affect any reference to their ages (*s 69(2)*)	PRs are not under a duty to enquire into adoption. They are not liable if they distribute in ignorance of an adoption (*ACA 2002 s 72*) An adopted child may seek any property to which he is entitled from other beneficiaries
LA 1976 s 5(3)	A legitimated child is treated as a legitimate one *s 5(4)* duplicates *ACA 2002 s 69(2)*	*LA 1976 s 7*: this is a similar provision to the *ACA 2002 s 72*

B Paying different types of legacy

Specific legacies

➤ These gifts vest from death, so beneficiaries are entitled to income accruing from death.

➤ If the testator disposed of the property between making the will and dying, then the gift 'adeems' (ie: it fails). If the property's form has altered but it remains substantially the same (eg: a gift of shares in a company which has been taken over in return for shares in the company), the gift will not adeem.

➤ The beneficiary is responsible for costs incurred in preserving the asset between the death and transfer, unless the will states otherwise.

➤ The PRs supply *Form 185E* stating the gross income received; this enables a beneficiary to account to HMRC and meet whatever tax liability is owed as an individual.

➤ Where an asset is transferred directly to the legatee (rather than sold), the probate value serves as the 'base cost' at which the legatee is deemed to have acquired the asset (*TCGA 1992 s 62(4)*).

Pecuniary legacies

➤ Where the will is silent, the choice of which property to pay pecuniary legacies from is determined by different sets of rules, depending upon the circumstances.

a) **The gift of residue is valid** (ie: there is no partial intestacy)

The legacy is paid from personalty, unless one of 3 common law rules apply:

i) the will specifies a fund of realty and personalty from which pecuniary legacies should be paid - both types of property bear the burden of gifts proportionately (*Roberts v. Walker* (1830) 1 R & My 752).

ii) where a gift of realty does not distinguish realty from personalty, residuary realty can be used if personalty is insufficient (*Greville v. Brown* (1859) 7 HLC 689).

iii) the testator leaves realty specifically for the payment of pecuniary legacies.

b) **Partial intestacy and no express trust in the will**

A trust arises under the *AEA 1925 s 33(1)*. Pecuniary legacies are paid from undisposed of property (*s 33(2)* requires that *Sch I Part I (i)-(ii)* of the Act should be followed).

c) **Partial intestacy and an express trust in the will**

The *AEA 1925 s 33* institutes a trust under which pecuniary legacies are paid from money realised on the sale of undisposed of property. However, under *s 33(7)* the statutory trust is supplanted by the express trust in the will. There is conflicting authority as to whether *either*:

i) PRs should set aside a fund for the payment of pecuniary legacies in the order dictated by *AEA 1925 Sch II Part I (i)-(ii)* (*Re Midgley* [1955] Ch 576), *or*

ii) the common law rules (above) apply (*Re Taylor's Estate* [1969] Ch 245).

➤ If there are insufficient funds available, pecuniary legacies abate proportionately.

➤ Pecuniary legacies are payable 1 year after the testator's death. PRs are not under a duty to distribute before this period is up (*AEA 1925 s 4*).

➤ Interest is payable in the following circumstances:

a) when a pecuniary legacy is unpaid after a year, or after the passing of a named contingency, whichever occurs first, *or*

b) if the legacy is in satisfaction of a debt which the testator owed, *or*

c) the beneficiary is a child of the testator and no other fund exists for that child's maintenance, *or*

d) the beneficiary is a minor and the testator's intention was to provide for the child's maintenance.

F   Problems which can arise

I   Obtaining a grant and interpreting the will
II   A claim under the *I(PFD)A 1975*
III   Breach of duty by a PR
IV   A PR's death
V   Failure of a gift

➤   There are 5 areas in which difficulties are likely to arise (this list is not exhaustive!).

I   Obtaining a grant and interpreting the will

1   Someone objects to the issue of a grant (*NCPR r 44*)

➤   A caveat is lodged with the Probate Registry to prevent the issue of a grant.

2   A person entitled to take an oath fails to do so *or* fails to renounce

Citation to take or refuse a grant (*NCPR r 47*)

➤   When an executor has intermeddled, but not taken steps to acquire a grant within 6 months of the testator's death, then unless the executor can show good reason for his inaction, the citator can apply to court for an order allowing letters of administration to be issued under *NCPR r 20*.

➤   An applicant wishes to 'clear off' those with prior entitlement to a grant who have not applied for a grant.

3   A person entitled to a grant wishes to prove his right when another contests it

Citation to propound a will (*NCPR r 48*)

➤   To compel a named person with an interest in the estate (beneficiary or executor) to prove a will if they can.

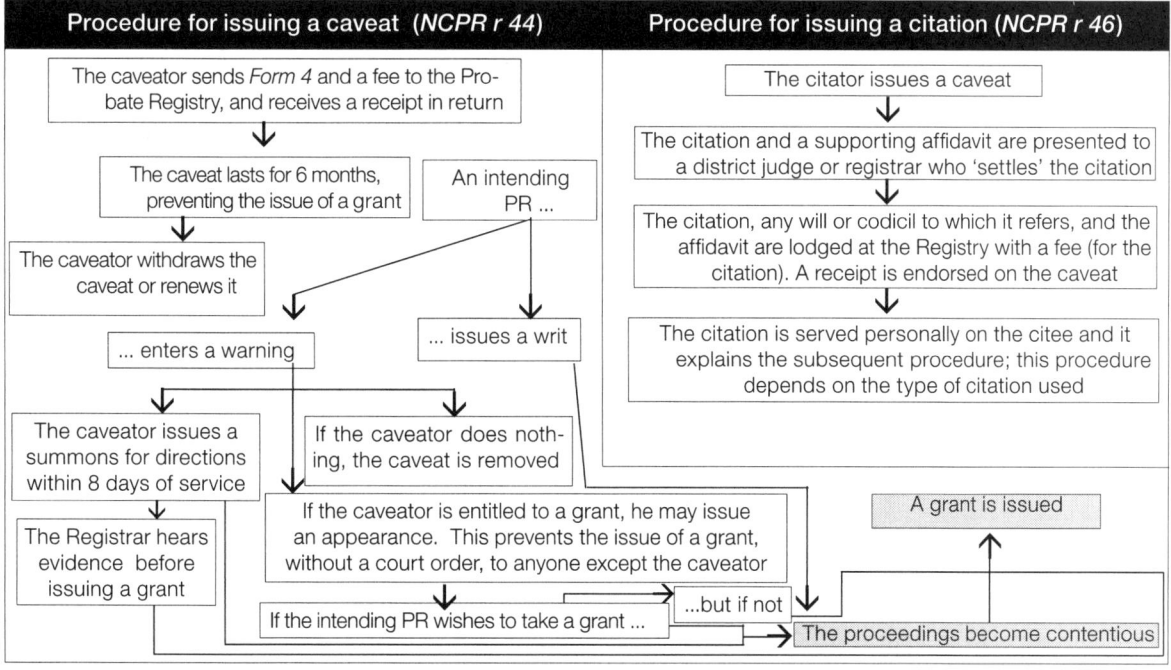

4   The Registrar requires additional evidence before issuing the grant

Affidavit of due execution (*NCPR r 16*)

➤ This is necessary if *either* an attestation clause is not present *or* is corrupt, *or* there is some doubt about the execution due to uncertainty about the testator's capacity or intention.

➤ The affidavit is sworn by witnesses to the execution of the will.

Affidavit as to knowledge and approval (*NCPR rr 13,16*)

➤ This is necessary if the testator was blind, *or* illiterate, *or* frail, *or* there were suspicious circumstances.

➤ The affidavit is sworn by a witness, *or* anyone who went through the will with the testator and can give first-hand factual evidence.

Affidavit of plight and condition (*NCPR rr 14,16*)

➤ This is necessary if there are *either* alterations to the will after its execution, *or* a mark suggesting that other documents were originally attached to the will, *or* signs of an attempt to revoke the will.

➤ An affidavit is sworn by anyone with relevant first-hand factual knowledge.

Lost will (*NCPR rr 15,16*)

➤ Such a will is presumed to be destroyed with the intention to revoke it.

➤ If this presumption can be rebutted, or evidence can be produced to show *either* that the will existed after the testator's death *or* that a copy (or reconstruction) of it is accurate, then the Registrar may grant probate on the production of an affidavit testifying to these facts.

5   The validity of a codicil is doubted

➤ The executor(s) should commence a probate action under *NCPR r 45*.

6   The interpretation of the will is uncertain

➤ PRs may seek clarification from the court by issuing a claim form - usually this is done through an application to the Chancery Division of the High Court, but the County Court has jurisdiction for claims with a value up to £30,000.

♦ The admission of extrinsic evidence is permitted if the will is a) meaningless, *or* b) *prima facie* ambiguous, *or* c) ambiguous in the light of evidence (other than evidence of the testator's intention) (*AJA 1982 s 21*).

♦ The court can rectify the will so as to carry out the testator's intentions, if the will's failure to do this is due to a clerical error *or* the draftsman's failure to understand the testator's instructions (*AJA 1982 s 20, NCPR r 55, CPR r 57.12, Re Segelman (deceased)* [1995] 3 All ER 676, ChD).

♦ The court can make an order authorising PRs to act as instructed by a barrister who has been practising for at least 10 years. The barrister can resolve matters of construction which are *not* disputed. This absolves the PRs of liability and, since the court does not hear any argument, saves the estate expense (*AJA 1985 s 48*, see *CPR r 64*).

II   A claim under the *I(PFD)A 1975*

➤ The *I(PFD)A 1975* allows close family (including a spouse or civil partner), dependants and co-habitees to seek provision from an estate when none is made under a will or the intestacy rules.

➤ Unless the value of the claim is clearly within the County Court's jurisdiction (ie: under £30,000), an application is made to either the Chancery Division or the Family Division of the High Court.

➤ The High Court and County Court procedure is governed by *CPR r 57.14-16*.

➤ The costs of pursuing litigation are considerable, and the defence will often send a 'Calderbank' letter to the claimant so that the claimant is liable for costs incurred after the letter.

III   Breach of duty by a PR

➤ The standard of duty is that of 'utmost good faith', except for professional trustees when it is higher.

 ◆ Liability is personal and unlimited (*Kennewell v. Dye* [1949] Ch 517).

 ◆ A breach of duty occurs if a PR fails to preserve the value of estate assets, *or* to distribute as required by the will and statute, *or* uses the estate's assets for the wrong purposes (eg: self-enrichment).

➤ Unless it is excluded by the trust instrument, a trustee is under a duty of care when exercising powers conferred under *TA 2000 ss 3, 8, 11, 16-17, 34* and in certain other situations (*TA 2000 s 1, Sch 1*).

> The duty is to exercise such care and skill as is reasonable in the circumstances, having regard in particular to any special knowledge that he has (or holds himself out as having) and (if he acts in the course of a business or profession) any special knowledge or experience that it is reasonable to expect of such a person.

➤ Likely claimants include the following.

 ◆ **Missing beneficiaries**

 • The PRs should advertise to locate them, but if this fails they should seek a 'Benjamin' order from the court (*Re Benjamin* [1902] 1 Ch 723) (see *CPR r 64*). This shields the PRs from liability, but it does not prejudice the claimant's (or his PRs') right to pursue assets from other beneficiaries of the estate.

 ◆ **Creditors who are unknown to the PRs**

 • The PRs should protect themselves by:

 a) advertising in the *London Gazette,* and in a local newspaper in the vicinity of land the deceased owned, as well as placing a notice anywhere else which is appropriate (*TA 1925 s 27*).

 ▪ An advertisement/notice must state a time period (of not less than 2 months from the date of the advertisement/notice) within which claimants may supply particulars of a claim; distribution should not begin until this period ends.

 b) searching HM Land Registry, the Central Land Charges Department and conducting local land searches to reveal any charges subsisting over land in the estate.

 • Creditors may pursue assets into the hands of the beneficiaries with a tracing action in equity.

 ◆ **Claimants under the *I(PFD)A 1975***

 • A PR should not distribute until 6 months after the grant of representation has been issued, thereafter there will be no personal liability under the *I(PFD)A 1975*, although the estate will be subject to any order which the court makes under its discretion to waive the limitation period.

 ◆ **Creditors who are unpaid after an 'unreasonable' delay**

 • PRs should pay pre-death debts with 'due diligence' (*Re Tankard* [1942] Ch 69).

 • PRs owe this duty to beneficiaries *and* creditors alike; any attempt to alter this duty by will is void.

 ◆ **Beneficiaries when debts are paid from the wrong property**

 • Where the interests of some beneficiaries are prejudiced, the doctrine of marshalling applies, so that their loss is made good from the rest of the estate.

 ◆ **Landlords**

 • Leaseholds (except statutory tenancies under the *Rent Acts*) vest in a PR in his 'representative' capacity, and *may* do so in a 'personal capacity' as a result of actual or constructive entry into possession (see table overleaf).

Liability	Release for PRs
In 'representative' capacity (*Re Bowes* (1887) 37 Ch D128)	
Under privity of estate: rent and breaches of covenant prior to death (to the extent that property is in their hands)	On the assignment, expiry or surrender of the lease
Under privity of contract: where the deceased was the original lessee Note: abolished for new leases granted on or after 1 January 1996 (*LT(C)A 1995 ss 1-5*)	a) PRs satisfy existing claims arising under the lease, *and* b) set aside money against any fixed or ascertained sums which the deceased had agreed in respect of the property, *and* c) assign it to a beneficiary or a purchaser (*TA 1925 s 26*)
In 'personal capacity' (*Re Owers, Public Trustee v. Death* [1941] Ch 389)	
Liable as assignees of the deceased's interest for: Covenants: liability is unlimited for any breach Rent: liability is limited to rent which the PRs actually receive, or would have done if they had acted with diligence	On the assignment, expiry or surrender of the lease, PRs can seek to protect themselves in one of 3 ways: a) taking out insurance, *or* b) seeking an indemnity from the beneficiaries, *or* c) creating an indemnity fund which is distributed to the beneficiaries once the liability has ended
Note: a landlord's remedies against beneficiaries are unaffected by any of this	

Relieving PRs of liability
Either a) by the court if the PR 'acted honestly and reasonably and ought fairly to be excused' (*TA 1925 s 61*),
or b) in the form of an indemnity from a beneficiary's interest in the estate when the court is shown the written consent of a beneficiary who has been fully informed of the breach (*TA 1925 ss 62, 68(1)*),
or c) where the beneficiary (being *sui juris*) who has been fully informed of the breach of trust (known as '*devestavit*') consents to it (*Walker v. Symonds* (1818) 3 Swan 1 at 64).

IV   A PR's death

➤ If a PR dies before a grant is issued, then his rights to the grant die with him.

➤ After a grant has been issued, one PR can administer the estate if the other PRs die: this is known as the chain of administration (*Flanders v. Clarke* (1747) 3 Atk 509).

➤ On the death of a sole surviving PR, the PR's executor steps into the deceased PR's shoes and shoulders all burdens and powers to administer the first testator's estate as well as the PR's estate (*AEA 1925 s 7*).

➤ Where a grant of probate or letters of administration are made to a deceased PR, and the chain of representation is broken, a grant *de bonis non administratis* is sought from the court in favour of whomever is entitled under *NCPR r 20* or *NCPR r 22* (Blackstone, *Commentaries* (14th ed), *506*).

V   Failure of a gift

➤ A gift can fail through Ademption, Lapse, Abatement, or under *CPA 2004*.

1   Ademption

➤ As a will 'speaks from death', property given in the will may not still form part of the estate on death. If the substance of the gift, rather than its form, has altered then the gift fails.

2   Lapse

a) joint tenants: if a tenant predeceases the testator, the remaining tenant(s) take the gift in full - the gift does not lapse unless they all predecease the testator.

b) tenants in common: if one tenant predeceases the testator, the gift as a whole lapses.

c) class: remains valid *unless* all members of a class have predeceased the testator.

d) witness: this lapses *unless* the witness's signature -supplemented those of 2 valid witnesses.

e) divorced spouse/civil partner under a dissolved civil partnership:

this lapses unless the will shows a contrary intention (*WA 1837 ss 18A, 18C*).

3   Abatement

➤ Where the estate is not able to meet all the legacies, and there is no contrary intention in the will, general legacies abate in equal proportions (*Re Whitehead* [1913] 2 Ch 56).

➤ Demonstrative legacies do not abate with general legacies, unless the fund out of which the demonstrative legacies are to be paid is insufficient to pay them all (*Roberts v. Pocock* (1748) 4 Ves 150).

➤ If the estate is unable to meet all its debts, specific legacies abate amongst themselves, otherwise they do not abate with general legacies.

4   Gift to civil partner and overlapping gift to issue

➤ Unless a contrary intention is shown, if the terms by which property is devised or bequeathed to a civil partner would give a civil partner an absolute interest in that property, and the same instrument purports to give an interest to the testator's issue, the gift to the civil partner is presumed to be absolute (*CPA 2004 Sch 4 para 5*).

Substitutional gifts

➤ A gift which adeems *or* lapses falls into residue, unless the will contains a valid gift over in favour of another beneficiary.

➤ *WA 1837 s 33* implies a substitutional gift to the testator's lineal descendants where the original gift was to the testator's children or remoter issue, and the intended donee predeceases the testator.

♦ There is no clear authority whether *WA 1837 s 33*:

a) saves a contingent gift if the original donee has not satisfied the contingency before dying, *or*

b) allows issue to take on satisfying the contingency specified for the original donee, *or*

c) applies to class gifts 'to children living at my death'.

♦ A will should therefore always provide an express substitutional provision in case the named beneficiary predeceases the testator - this avoids uncertainty and ensures that the testator's wishes are followed.

Disclaimer or forfeiture of a gift under a will (*AEA 1925 s 33A*)

➤ *When a death occurs after EDP(FRLS)A 2011 comes into force, if a gift in a will is disclaimed, or is precluded by virtue of the forfeiture rule in Forfeiture Act 1982, an individual who would have enjoyed that gift were it not for the disclaimer/forfeiture will be treated as having died immediately before the intestate.*

◆ *This is intended to preserve the position of a person who would either:*

a) *inherit as a result of a disclaimer, or*

b) *would otherwise be prevented from inheriting where a joint tenant forfeitures a gift by murdering the testator.*

Disputed wills - Law Society Practice Note (16 April 2009)

➤ A solicitor's duty of confidentiality to a testator continues after the retainer ends.

◆ A solicitor can generally only disclose information, prior to probate, with the consent of the executors (as the right to confidentiality passes to the testator's PRs).

- If a will is disputed a party to the dispute cannot claim privilege against another party to the dispute in relation to any communication previously made by the deceased to the solicitor.

- A court could subpoena a solicitor to disclose any information which is material to a dispute (*SCA 1981 s 122*) and the court can order pre-action disclosure of documents in order to dispose fairly of the anticipated proceedings or assist a dispute to be resolved without proceedings, or to save costs (*CPR r 31.16*).

- Where a dispute is more serious than the entering of a caveat, and a solicitor has such material information, the solicitor should make a statement of the evidence which he has available.

  - This evidence should relate to the circumstances in which (*Larke v Nugus* (2000) WTLR 1033, CA):

    a) the testator gave instructions for the will, *and*

    b) the will was executed.

  - The Law Society suggests that the quickest and easiest way of doing this, when there is no suggestion of negligence, is to supply a copy of the file to any person who has an interest in the dispute (even if the solicitor who is not acting) (para 3.1).

  - If the solicitor may have been negligent, the Law Society suggests the executors and beneficiaries should be informed that they may wish to take independent advice as to whether there was any negligence, and that the solicitor should immediately inform his insurers of the possible claim.

  - The Law Society indicates that where a solicitor does not disclose information promptly at any early stage, he/she may incur liability for the costs of the proceedings (eg: to the extent those proceedings could have been avoided if the information had been disclosed) (para 4).

➤ In order that an estate's assets can be safeguarded before a full grant of probate can be obtained, it may be appropriate (if agreement can be sought) for a solicitor (or another person) to apply for a temporary grant (*grant ad colligenda boni defuncti*).

CONVEYANCING

This chapter examines:

HM Land Registry plan colouring

➤ Red edging round a title.

➤ Green edging round land removed from a title.

➤ Blue shading over land subject to rights of way.

➤ Brown shading over land over which a registered title enjoys right of way.

➤ Green shading over areas of land within a title which do not form part of it.

It is not compulsory to adopt this scheme, but it is good practice to do so.

A   A chronological conveyance

The conveyance is divided into nine separate steps, outlined below.

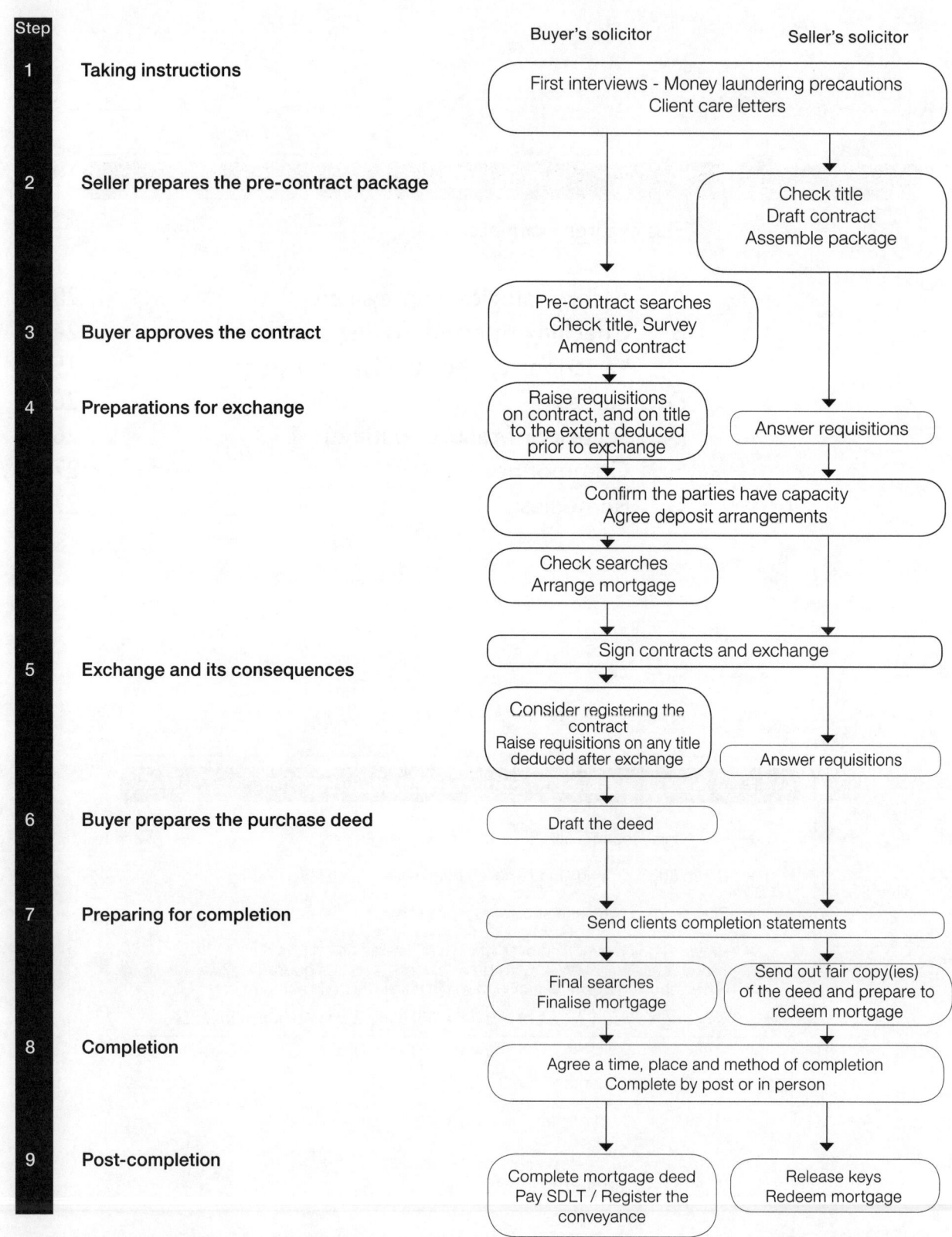

Step		Buyer's solicitor	Seller's solicitor
1	Taking instructions	First interviews - Money laundering precautions / Client care letters	
2	Seller prepares the pre-contract package		Check title / Draft contract / Assemble package
3	Buyer approves the contract	Pre-contract searches / Check title, Survey / Amend contract	
4	Preparations for exchange	Raise requisitions on contract, and on title to the extent deduced prior to exchange	Answer requisitions
		Confirm the parties have capacity / Agree deposit arrangements	
		Check searches / Arrange mortgage	
5	Exchange and its consequences	Sign contracts and exchange	
		Consider registering the contract / Raise requisitions on any title deduced after exchange	Answer requisitions
6	Buyer prepares the purchase deed	Draft the deed	
7	Preparing for completion	Send clients completion statements	
		Final searches / Finalise mortgage	Send out fair copy(ies) of the deed and prepare to redeem mortgage
8	Completion	Agree a time, place and method of completion / Complete by post or in person	
9	Post-completion	Complete mortgage deed / Pay SDLT / Register the conveyance	Release keys / Redeem mortgage

Step 1 — Taking instructions

I First interviews
II Post-interview formalities

I First interviews

With the seller

Seller's name, address, email and phone number(s) (mobile, etc): ....

Property address: ....

Estate agent's name and address: ....

Buyer's name and address: ....

Buyer's solicitor's name, address, telephone, fax, DX and email:...........................

Conflicts
➤ Is there a conflict of interest? There are special provisions regarding this in *SRA SCC Ch 3*.

Money laundering
➤ Comply with the *MLR 2007* and *PCA 2002* (see pp 21-22).

Finance
➤ *Proceeds:*

◆ will these cover the costs of sale, pay off any mortgage and/or fund another purchase?

◆ where should money be paid (bank details, account number)?

➤ *Deposit*:

◆ has a preliminary deposit been paid? (Take a copy of the receipt for the file.)

◆ has a deposit been agreed?

➤ *Taxation*: will CGT be payable?

➤ *Mortgage*: will this need to be redeemed? (Note the name(s) and address(es) of lender(s).)

➤ *Solicitor's fees*: explain what these will be.

Property
➤ *Tenure*: freehold or leasehold? Will there be a full or limited title guarantee?

➤ *Deeds*: if a client does not hold them, obtain the address of whoever does (eg: building society).

➤ *Contents*: ask the client to fill out a fittings and contents form [*TA 10*].

➤ *Property*: are restrictive covenants breached? Have planning and use regulations been obeyed?

➤ *Residents:* are there any third parties with rights to occupy the property?

Transaction
➤ *Completion*: when convenient, synchronisation? (ie: is the seller coordinating a purchase?)

➤ *Terms*: have any particular terms been agreed?

With the buyer

As for the seller plus -

Finance

➤ *Money*: can the client afford the acquisition, including the associated costs (eg: SDLT, legal fees, search fees, land registry fees, etc)?

➤ *Deposit*: will bridging finance be needed while an existing property is sold?

➤ *Mortgage*

◆ If acting for the lender, consider whether there is a conflict of interest (*SCC r 3.16-21*).

◆ Comply with *SCC r 9* if the firm has a relationship with a mortgage provider.

◆ Do not give advice outside *SFS(S)R 2001 r 3* unless regulated by the FSA.

Property

➤ *Intended use of the property*?

➤ *Survey*: the *caveat emptor* principle applies; the buyer chooses what sort of survey to have.

➤ *Location*: are plans or special searches necessary?

➤ *Insurance:* how will the buyer protect himself from exchange to completion?

Transaction

➤ *Who is buying the property*: is advice about co-ownership needed?

◆ For a joint tenancy the 'four unities' must be present - 'possession', 'interest', 'title' and 'time' (known as 'PITT'). If a joint tenant dies, the property passes to the survivor(s).

◆ A tenancy in common arises if the 'four unities' are not present, if severance is implied or stated in a conveyance or transfer, or under an equitable presumption. Tenants' share(s) pass by will or under the intestacy rules.

➤ *Client's present residence*: will it be sold, and/or will notice have to be given to a landlord?

II Post-interview formalities

➤ Write the client a letter summarising what was agreed at the meeting, what will happen next, what if anything the client needs to do, and the likely legal fees; complete an attendance note.

◆ Ask the seller to fill in a *Seller's Property Information Form* [*TA 6*] and *Additional Property Information Form* [*TA 11*] which should have been supplied at the interview, but may be enclosed with this letter.

◆ If instructions are obtained in person, *CP(DS)R 2000* should not apply.

➤ Write to the other party, explaining who the solicitor is acting for and how the solicitor can be contacted.

◆ Explain whether the solicitor intends to use the Law Society's *Standard Conditions of Sale* (5th ed) and follow the Law Society's *National Conveyancing Protocol* (the '**Protocol**').

● The 6th edition of the *Protocol* (2011) represents the Law Society's 'preferred practice' for solicitors acting for buyers and sellers in domestic conveyancing transactions.

● Members of the Law Society's 'Conveyancing Quality Scheme' ('**CQS**') are required to adopt the Protocol and the *Standard Conditions of Sale* (5th ed).

◆ The *Protocol* should only be used if the other party is represented by a solicitor or a licensed conveyancer.

➤ Write to the estate agents to inform of the instruction to act and to ask for a copy of their particulars. (These provide information about the property which it is useful to have on file.)

| Step 2 | Seller prepares the pre-contract package |

I   Check details of the seller's title
II   Draft the contract
III Energy performance certificate ('EPC')
IV   Assemble the pre-contract package

I Check details of the seller's title

➤ Find and trace the root of title (see pp 243-250).

Unregistered land	Registered land
➤ Obtain title deeds ◆ If a lender holds the deeds as security, the lender will usually release them in return for an undertaking from the solicitor that the lender will be paid first out of any proceeds of sale	➤ Obtain an official copy of the Register

II Draft the contract

➤ All contracts take a similar form, and will generally include 3 sections:

a) parties to the sale.

b) conditions of the sale.

c) memorandum of agreement.

➤ For the sake of convenience, the Law Society has produced Standard Conditions of Sale (5th ed., April 2011). Except where stated otherwise, these provide the model around which the following guide is based.

 ◆ Commonhold tenure is not addressed by the 5th ed. (although it was addressed by the 4th ed).

  • It is understood, somewhat bizarrely, that this is because of lack of space.

➤ When drafting a contract there are 3 layers of terms.

 ◆ The first layer is the open contract rules: these are terms which common law implies into contracts in the absence of any contrary intention between the parties.

 ◆ The second layer is the 'Standard Conditions of Sale' (*StC*): these form the backbone of the contract, and are found in small print on the inside pages of the Law Society's residential contract; they apply unless varied or excluded by the contract (*StC 1.1.4*).

 ◆ The third layer is the 'Special Conditions' (*SpC*): these override the *StCs*, and are found on the back page of the Law Society's contract.

➤ Check the accuracy of responses supplied by a seller against the title deeds in the solicitor's possession (a failure to do this could be a breach of *SRA SCC* as a failure to act in the client's best interests).

➤ A solicitor should:

a) be aware of the open contract rules, *and*

b) understand the effect of each *StC*, *and*

c) if a client's needs have not been catered for, draft a *SpC*.

➤ A member of the CQS and any solicitor who adopts the *Protocol* must use the 5th ed. of the *StCs*.

➤ The *Protocol* discourages the use of *SpCs* but recognises that amendments may be necessary to reflect land law or specific client instructions.   The obligation to act in a client's best interests takes priority over the *Protocol*.

Complete the *Standard Terms and Conditions*

Buyer's conveyancer Seller's conveyancer Law Society formula	This information does not form part of the contract. This information should be left blank on the draft contract, but should be added to the engrossment on exchange.
Date	Leave this blank on the draft; fill it in on the engrossed contract on exchange.
Seller	Seller's full name and address.
Buyer	Buyer's full name and address.
Property Freehold / Leasehold	Delete 'Freehold' or 'Leasehold' as applicable. **Plan** If a plan is required, the contract should state whether that plan is: a) 'for identification purposes only' - the verbal description of the property prevails, *or* b) 'as more particularly delineated on the plan'. The plan prevails if doubt arises. ◆ Note that HM Land Registry does not accept a plan 'for identification purposes only', and recommends a preferred scale of 1:1250-1:500 (urban property) and 1:2500 (rural property) (*Practice Guide 40*). ◆ Do not rely on the Land Registry plan - it is only a 'general boundary' unless fixed (*LRA 2002 s 60*) (for fixing boundaries, see *LRR 2003 rr 117-123*). The seller is not usually obliged to make a statutory declaration (*StC 4.4*), but where the physical extent of the property is uncertain the buyer should include a *SpC* providing that the seller does so. Include any appurtenances (easements and rights from which the title benefits).
Title number / Root of title	*Unregistered land*: describe the root of title eg: 'the conveyance dated . . between . . (1) and ... (2)' *Registered land*: the title number on the Property Register.
Specified Incumbrances	The seller should disclose: a) latent defects affecting the title to the property, *and* b) anything the seller does, or should, know about, *and* c) overriding interests in the property held by a third party, *and* d) the existence of any occupiers. The seller should disclose fully, as *StC 4.2.1* prevents the buyer raising questions about incumbrances at a later date, provided those incumbrances have been disclosed in the contract. The seller need *not* disclose physical defects apparent on inspection (*StC 3.1.2(b)* puts the buyer on notice of these) or the seller's mortgage (*StC 3.1.2(e)* ensures that the buyer will not take subject to this). A property is sold subject to incumbrances specified in the contract and discoverable by inspection of the property before the contract (*StC 3.1.2*). A buyer accepts the property in the physical state it is in on exchange unless the seller is building or converting the property (*StC 3.2.1*).

Title guarantee **(full / limited)**	Delete as appropriate and/or qualify by a *SpC* if appropriate. If this is left blank, the seller gives full title guarantee (*StC 4.6.2*). The *LP(MP)A 1994* implies covenants into a contract governing the disposition of land (whether or not for valuable consideration). A beneficial freeholder may give a full title guarantee: ◆ that the title is free of all charges, incumbrances and third party rights (*s 3(1)*). A trustee, fiduciary, PR or lender (*s 12*) may give a limited title guarantee: ◆ that no right or charge over the property has been granted to a third party since the last disposition for value (*s 3(3)*). NB: a trustee appointed to overreach an equitable interest will generally not give any title guarantee. A covenant for full or limited title guarantee affirms that: a) in all cases, in the purchase deed the disposer will: ◆ have the right to dispose of the property (*s 2(1)(a)*), *and* ◆ will at its own cost give the title he purports to give (ie: title which is sufficient to satisfy the Chief Land Registrar) (*ss 2(1)(b) and 2(2)*), *and* b) where a disposition is the mortgage of a property subject to a rentcharge, leasehold land or a commonhold unit, the borrower will fully and promptly perform all the obligations imposed by the rentcharge instrument, by the lease (on a tenant), or by the commonhold community statement (on a unit holder) (*LP(MP)A 1994 s 5*). NB: these covenants may be modified by deleting *SpC 2* and drafting an appropriate *SpC*.
Completion date	Under the open contract rules, this is in a 'reasonable time'. *StC 6.1.1* specifies that completion will occur 20 working days after the contract date and that time is not of the essence unless a notice to complete is served. If another date is envisaged insert that date here.
Contract rate	This is the rate of interest at which compensation is paid for delayed completion (*StC 7.2.2*). By default, the rate is 'The Law Society's interest rate from time to time in force' (*StC 1.1.1(e)*).
Purchase price	Fill this in as agreed. Note that *StC 1.4* provides that the purchase price and contents price are deemed to include VAT. Any other amount payable under the contract is exclusive of VAT. StC 1.4 is unlikely to be appropriate where the sale is to be partly standard rated (e.g. mixed use property).
Deposit	This is 10% of the total of the purchase price only (ie. not including any separate amount payable for contents) (*StC 2.2.1*). If the sum agreed differs, then fill in the agreed value here. *StC 2.2.5* provides that if before completion the seller agrees to buy another property in England and Wales as the seller's residence, the seller may use all or part of the deposit as a deposit for that transaction. The deposit will be held as 'agent' for the seller (rather than stakeholder). Draft a *SpC* if this StC 2.2.5 is not sufficient.
Contents price (if separate)	Fill this in as agreed (details are found on the *Fittings and Contents Form*), or delete *SpC 3*.

Balance	Add together the 'Purchase price' and the 'Contents Price', then subtract the 'Deposit'
	SDLT may be payable on the sale if the consideration exceeds £125,000 (residential land) or £150,000 (non-residential or mixed land); the value of contents is disregarded in working out how much (if any) SDLT is payable

Consider the *Special Conditions* which are pre-printed on the final page of the contract:

StC	*SpC 1*: provides that the StC are incorporated into the terms of the contract and that terms used in the contract have meaning given to them in the *StC*.
Title	*SpC 2*: this provides that the seller transfers the property with full or limited title guarantee as set out on the front page of the contract.
	If the seller will not transfer with full or limited title guarantee (e.g. because the seller is a trustee), this *SpC* should be deleted and replaced by a more appropriate *SpC*.
Fittings and Contents	*SpC 3*: if the sale includes contents or excludes fixtures, a *Fittings and Contents Form* should be attached to the contract.
	Delete *SpC 3* if it is not applicable.
Vacant possession	*SpC 4*: delete one of the alternative versions of *SpC 4*.
	If the property is subject to leases or tenancies, then insert the details here.
Completion time	*SpC 5*: if the seller has a related purchase the seller should specify a time for completion which is earlier than 2 pm.
	Delete *SpC 5* if it is not applicable.
Representations	*SpC 6*: this provides that only written representations (eg: replies to pre-contract enquires in *form TA 6*), made by a party to the contract or a conveyancer acting for a party to the contract, may be relied upon. It does not exclude liability for fraud or recklessness.
	This *SpC*, which is more likely to assist a seller (eg. by excluding representations made by an estate agent or orally by a seller at a viewing of the property), has been drafted as a *SpC* because an exclusion of liability that is not sufficiently prominent will not be effective (see eg: *Morgan v Pooley* [2010] EWHC 2447 (QB)).
Occupier's consent	*SpC 7*: any adults (other than the seller) occupying the property should sign the contract to confirm their agreement to the sale.
	A *SpC* should also be inserted in which such adults agree:
	<ul><li>not to register any rights in relation to the property, *and*</li><li>to cancel the registration of any such rights prior to completion.</li></ul>
	A child under the age of 18 should not (notwithstanding that its parents live in the property) have an equitable interest in that property provided the child has not paid anything towards the cost of the property.

Consider drafting further *Special Conditions*:

➤ Add further Special Conditions (including any to exclude or vary any *StCs*) after *SpC 7*.

➤ Note that if the Protocol has been adopted the use of further *SpCs* is discouraged except in limited circumstances.

➤ Further *SpCs* may be needed, eg:

Sale of part	If the sale only relates to part of the seller's property see p 257 below.

Additional seller obligations	Add an appropriate *SpC* if the seller is to provide a statutory declaration, or a defective title policy, or the seller is to carry out works to the property.

Retention	Add an appropriate *SpC* if there is to be retention. For example, where a sale relates to leasehold land the parties may agree that part of the sale proceeds will be retained pending final apportionment of service charge.

Sale subject to lease	Although *StC 3.3* applies, certain matters may need to be addressed by a *SpC*, eg: ◆ tenancy deposit issues. ◆ certain residential tenants enjoying rights of first refusal under the *LTA 1987*.

Management of the property	Any appropriate provisions which relate to the management of the property should be included (eg: see the Standard Commercial Conditions of Sale (2nd edition) for sample drafting).

Assignment of rights under the contract	*StC 1.5* prohibits an assignment of rights under the contract or a subsale. Disapply *StC 1.5.1* (assignments) and/or *1.5.2* (subsales) as appropriate if the buyer wishes to assign the benefit of its rights under the contract or require the seller to transfer the property to a person other than the buyer. If *StC 1.5* is retained, the buyer can contract to sell the property on to a third party, but the second transaction will have to be completed separately and subsequently and so SDLT may be paid twice: once by the buyer, and again by the person to whom the buyer sells the property.

Commonhold	*StC 9.3* of the 4th ed of the *StC* provided that a buyer of a commonhold unit is aware of, and is taken to accept, the terms of the *CCS* and memorandum and articles of association of the commonhold association. A commonhold association may give notice (known as a 'commonhold unit information certificate'; *form 9*) to a new unit holder requiring it to pay debts owed to the association by a former unitholder in respect of a unit; such a sum must be paid within 14 days of the date on which the notice is given to the new unitholder (*CCS para 4.7.5*). If payment is not made within this time, interest runs (*CCS para 4.7.6*); when payment is made the association's right to enforce payment against the old unit holder is deemed to be assigned to the new unitholder (*CCS para 4.7.7*). To avoid such a situation arising, insert a SpC that any such debt will be paid prior to completion (evidenced in a manner reasonably satisfactory to the buyer, eg: a certified copy of a receipt from the commonhold association).

Liability on covenants	*StC 4.6.4* makes the buyer indemnify the seller against all future breaches of obligations affecting the property (provided that the obligation was disclosed before exchange). The buyer's solicitor may try to include a *SpC* under which the seller indemnifies the buyer for any past breaches, *or* any which are current on the day of completion.

Insurance	**Common law**
	
	Common law passes risk to the buyer on exchange unless loss is due to the seller's lack of care.
	
	StC 5.1.6 expressly disapplies *LPA 1925 s 47*. *LPA 1925 s 47* provides that, subject to various conditions being fulfilled (including consent being obtained from an insurer), where money becomes payable under any policy of insurance maintained by a seller that money is, on completion, to be held or receivable by the seller on behalf of the buyer and paid by the seller to the buyer on completion, or so soon thereafter as the same shall be received by the seller.
	
	General rule - buyer risk (and impact of insurance proceeds on purchase price)
	
	StC 5.1.1 passes risk to the buyer on exchange.
	
	Seller's obligations with respect to insurance
	
	Under *StC 5.1.2* the seller is under no obligation to insure the property unless the contract provides that the seller should continue the existing insurance, *or* the property is let on terms under which the seller (as landlord or tenant) is obliged to insure the property.
	
	Where the seller is required to insure the property under *StC 5.1.2*, *StC 5.1.3* regulates the provision of this insurance; it provides that the seller must:
	
	a) do everything necessary to maintain the policy
	b) permit the buyer to inspect the policy (or evidence of its terms)
	c) in the event loss or damage occurs before completion:
	   i) pay to the buyer on completion any surplus (after repair or reinstatement) left over out of a payment received from the insurer, or
	   ii) if further payment is due from the insurer, on completion assign any rights to that payment to the buyer and hold any policy proceeds received in trust for the buyer
	d) cancel the policy on completion.
	
	The seller of a leasehold property, which is insured by a landlord (or other third party), is required to use reasonable efforts to ensure that insurance is maintained until completion. If loss is suffered before completion the seller must assign to the buyer on completion the seller's rights over policy monies (in such form as the buyer reasonably requires and at the buyer's expense) (*StC 5.1.4*).
	
	Usually it will be prudent for the seller to continue to insure until completion, and the buyer to insure from exchange. However, the buyer may wish to insert a *SpC* expressly obliging the seller to continue its insurance up to completion, eg: a buyer may want this to avoid the cost of organising its own policy.
	
	If the seller is obliged to continue its insurance where the property is leasehold or subject to leases (*StC 5.1.2(b)*), the buyer should consider adding a *SpC* requiring the seller to:
	
	  ◆ add the buyer as a joint insured, composite insured or note the buyer's interest on the policy.
	
	     ● Before agreeing to this the seller should check with its insurer whether this is feasible.
	
	  ◆ impose an obligation on the seller to make a claim on the seller's insurance if a loss occurs between exchange and completion.
	
	  ◆ increase the amount or extent of the cover.
	
	Unless the seller is required to insure the property (see *StC 5.1.2* above), if a loss is suffered and the payment received by the buyer under a policy effected by the buyer (or on the buyer's behalf) is reduced because of a policy effected by the seller (or on the seller's behalf), the purchase price for the property is abated by an amount equal to that reduction (this prevents a seller recovering from an insurance company and then being paid in full by the buyer) (*StC 5.1.5*).

Occupation by the buyer prior to completion	StC 5.2 sets out terms under which, with the seller's consent, the buyer may occupy the property prior to completion.
	If these terms are inappropriate, an alternative *SpC* should be drafted.

Void conditions	Conditions will be void that:
	◆ oblige a trustee to obtain consent from beneficiaries (*LPA s 42(1)*).
	◆ restrict the buyer's choice of solicitor (*LPA s 48*) - this is also a breach of *SRA SCC*.
	◆ require the buyer to pay for the stamping of improperly stamped documents - this is the seller's responsibility (*SA 1891 ss 14(4), 117*).

III   Energy performance certificate ('EPC')

➤ Unless a valid EPC is available, a seller of residential property must commission an EPC by instructing an energy assessor to prepare an EPC and either paying for the EPC or giving a clear undertaking to pay for it (*EPB(CI)(EW)R 2007, reg 5A(1)-(2)* inserted by *EPB(CI)(EW)(A)R 2010*).

➤ A person (e.g. an estate agent) is under a duty to ensure that an EPC has been commissioned before that person begins marketing the property (*EPB(CI)(EW)R 2007, reg 5A(3)*).

➤ The seller (of residential property) and its agent must make 'all reasonable efforts' to obtain an EPC within 28 days (*EPB(CI)(EW)R 2007, reg 5A(4)*).

   ◆ *The Government is expected to reduce this to 7 days.*

➤ An EPC may remain valid for ten years.

IV   Assemble the pre-contract package

Unregistered land	Registered land
Certified copies of documents which must be included in the title: ◆ Evidence of devolution on death - death certificate, assent, grant of representation ◆ Evidence of any change of name of an estate owner - marriage certificate, deed poll, etc ◆ Discharge of any legal mortgages ◆ Pre-root documents specifying restrictive covenants ◆ Memoranda endorsed on documents of title, eg: sale of part, assent to a beneficiary, severance of a joint tenancy ◆ Power of attorney (under which a document within the chain of title has been executed) **Include an Index Map search (so the buyer can see that the land has not been registered)**	*LRA 2002 s 67:* a) Copy of Register entries b) Copy of the file plan ◆ Evidence or an abstract if registered title is inconclusive about anything ◆ A copy or an abstract of any document mentioned on the Register *StC 4.1.2* ➤ Requires an official copy (rather than a copy) of an individual register, a plan referred to in an individual register, and any document referred to in a register and kept by the registrar ➤ a) and b) may *not* be excluded by a *Special Condition*

➤ 2 copies of the draft contract

➤ Evidence of any discharged equitable interests

➤ Details of equitable interests which will be overreached in the transaction

➤ Expired leases if the tenant is still in possession

➤ Other documents referred to in the contract, or in the seller's possession which may prove helpful to the buyer:

   ◆ copies of any relevant planning permission

   ◆ NHBC certificates (if the property is a new building)

   ◆ copies of any relevant insurance certificates or guarantees (eg: relating to roofing or damp course work)

   ◆ any necessary consents (eg: building regulation consents)

   ◆ any plans

   ◆ *Property Information Form [TA 6]*

   ◆ *Fixtures and Contents Form [TA 10]*

   ◆ if the property is a commonhold unit, copies of the commonhold community statement and the memorandum and articles of the commonhold association

   ◆ copies of any searches which the seller has made (these should not be relied on by the buyer, but they can provide the buyer with some comfort if a Bankruptcy search has been done against the seller (*Form K16*) showing that the seller is not subject to insolvency proceedings)

➤ Notification of the seller's target completion date(s)

➤ The seller's solicitor must complete a *CML Disclosure of Incentives Form* where mortgage finance is being obtained and:

   a) a property is new and has not yet been occupied, *or*

   b) an existing property has not yet been occupied in its current form (eg: it has been renovated or converted).

➤ A copy of this form must be given to the lender's solicitor/conveyancer, and (when requested) to the lender's valuer.

   ◆ This measure was introduced on 1 September 2008 to protect lenders from fraud; see also the Law Society's Practice Note 'Mortgage Fraud' (15 April 2009).

Step 3	Buyer approves the contract

I Make pre-contract searches
II Check the title documents supplied
III Investigate each document
IV Check the terms of any restrictive covenants
V Ensure there are no planning difficulties
VI Commission a survey
VII Check and amend the contract

I Make pre-contract searches

➤ For the searches necessary at this stage, see p 251.

II Check the title documents supplied

➤ The documents required are set out on pp 243-250.

➤ Questions to ask:

- ◆ is the root as described in the contract?

- ◆ is the chain unbroken since the root?

- ◆ are there any defects in title adverse to the buyer's interest?

III Investigate each document

A Registered land

➤ Check that the official copy of the register is correct and that priority periods have not expired, or are not about to expire.

- ◆ All land in England and Wales has been subject to compulsory registration from 1 December 1990.

- ◆ The *LRA 2002* allows Her Majesty to grant an estate in fee simple in absolute possession out of demesne land to Herself; such a grant is only treated as having been made if an application for registration is made. Certain other estates granted by Her Majesty must also be registered (*ss 79-85, LRR 2003 r 173*).

  - • Land held by the Crown in demesne does not subsist as an estate in land and so, prior to the *LRA 2002*, could not be registered.

➤ Check that any plans are accurate.

B   Unregistered land

➤   Start at the root, make written notes of omissions in the list of documents and of errors in the documents.

◆   Check:

- ◆ Requirement of registration

  - Do an Index Map search (if not supplied by the seller) to ensure there has been no conveyance or sale since the area became subject to registration.

- ◆ Searches

  - Were these done against all previous owners under the correct names for the correct periods?

  - Was completion for previous transfers within the priority period?

  - Will completion be within the priority period?

    ▪ If the answer to this question is 'no', the buyer should do a fresh search.

- ◆ Incumbrances

  - What are they?

  - Is there an unbroken chain of indemnity for covenants?

- ◆ Easements and rights

  - Do these follow the title?

  - Are there additions or subtractions?

- ◆ Description of property

  - Is this accurate?

  - Are plans provided where necessary?

- ◆ Dates

  - Do these form an unbroken chain from the root?

- ◆ Parties

  - Check the identities of the parties to conveyances

    ▪ Eg: names may have altered due to marriage or divorce; if so ask for documentary evidence to verify this.

- ◆ Acknowledgement for the production of earlier deeds

  - If needed, are the deeds present?

- ◆ Execution

  - Was this done by the correct parties in the correct form (ie: if positive covenants are present, did the buyers and the sellers both sign the conveyance)?

  - Were there any assents by deed (this imports consideration without which an assentee is not bound)?

  - Power of attorney: if used, was it valid? (A copy of the grant should be supplied.)

  - A receipt clause in a conveyance is evidence that a seller's lien was extinguished.

- ◆ Endorsements on deeds

  - If needed, are these present?

  - Are there adverse memoranda?

➤ Examine documents included in the abstract of title.

> ➤ Deeds must be in the correct form:
>
> *BEFORE 31 JULY 1990*
>
> - ◆ by an individual: signed, sealed, delivered as a deed. The seal must precede the signature. Delivery depends on intention; this is inferred from the signature and seal (*LPA s 73*).
>
> - ◆ by a company: sealed before a company secretary and a director (*LPA s 74*).
>
> *AFTER 31 JULY 1990 AND ON OR BEFORE 30 SEPTEMBER 2008*
>
> Clear on its face that it is a deed and delivered as a deed (*LP(MP)A 1989 s 1(2)(a)*):
>
> - ◆ by an individual: signed, signature witnessed and attested, or signed in his presence and at his command before 2 witnesses who attest the deed (*LP(MP)A 1989 s 1(3)*).
>
> - ◆ by a company: execution by affixing a seal, *or* by signature of a director and company secretary, or 2 directors if the document is expressed to be executed by the company. Execution and delivery are presumed if it is clear on its face that the document was intended as a deed (*CA s 36A(5)*).
>
> - ◆ by a LLP (formed under *LPA 2000*): as for a company, except signature is by 2 members.
>
> *AFTER 30 SEPTEMBER 2008*
>
> - ◆ *either* (*CA 2006 s 44*):
>
>   a) by a company affixing its seal, *or*
>
>   b) signed on behalf of a company by 2 'authorised signatories', *or*
>
>   - ■ An 'authorised signatory' is a director of the company, and in the case of a private company with a secretary, or a public company, the secretary (or joint secretary).
>
>   c) signed by a director in the presence of a witness who attests the director's signature.
>
>   - ■ If a person signs as director for more than one company, the capacity of each signature must be clear.
>
>   - ■ A deed is presumed to be executed on delivery, unless a contrary intention is shown (*CA 2006 s 46*)
>
> ➤ If an instrument was chargeable to stamp duty (eg: executed prior to 1 December 2003), it should be duly stamped or certified to be exempt from duty (and, in the case of a transfer of a fee simple, the grant of a lease for a term of 7 years or more, or the transfer of such a lease, have a PD stamp (*FA 1931 s 28*)).

IV   Check the terms of any restrictive covenants

1   Inform the buyer that the covenant exists.

2   Find out whether it:

   a)   affects the buyer's plans for the property, *or*

   b)   has been breached in the past (eg: by building work), *or*

   c)   adversely alters the property's value (a covenant preserving the character of the neighbourhood may actually enhance the value of a property, eg: if it was imposed by a developer and is rigorously enforced).

Validity

3   Does wording effectively annex the covenant to the land? If it does not, the covenant may be unenforceable.

4   If the covenant is post-1925, is it noted on the Charges Register, or as a Class D(ii) land charge?

   ➤   An unregistered covenant will be unenforceable.

5   If the covenant is valid, consider three options:

   a)   Insurance: the insurance company will normally need:

Options
if
valid

   • a copy of the document imposing the covenant, or its exact wording, *and*

   • details of past breaches, and a copy of any planning permission for development, *and*

   • the date of the covenant's imposition, *and*

   • the date of the covenant's registration, *and*

   • a description of the nature of the neighbourhood, *and*

   • steps taken to trace whoever has the benefit of the covenant.

   b)   Consent of the person with the benefit of the covenant to release/waive the covenant.

   c)   An application to the Upper Tribunal (Lands Chamber) to remove the covenant (*LPA s 24*): this is slow and expensive.

V   Ensure there are no planning difficulties

Check ...

a)   ... the date the property was originally built *and* the dates of subsequent additions or extensions.

b)   ... that any alterations within the last 4 years *either* had planning permission *or* did not need it (and that any covenants in a lease have been complied with).

c)   .. that any change of use over the last 10 years *either* did not need planning permission, *or* that it was granted (*and* that consent was granted by a landlord, if needed).

d)   ... whether building regulation consent was gained *and* complied with for work done in the past year.

e)   ... whether the property is a listed building *or* in a conservation area.

f)   ... whether a Unitary Development Plan, or a Structure or Local Plan affects the property.

Planning permission

1   A 'development' requiring permission (*TCPA 1990 s 55*) involves *either*:

    a) 'building, engineering, mining, in, on, over or under the land', *or*

    b) a 'material change' in use, (ie: not within same use class under *TCP(UC)O 1987*), *or*

    c) an alteration of a listed building, or demolition in a conservation area (*P(LBCA)A 1990 s 74*).

2   **Limited permission to develop without permission is available (*TCP(GPD)O 1995*) for:**

    a) maintenance work.

    b) internal work not affecting the exterior.

    c) use within the curtilage of a building for a purpose incidental to dwelling in the building.

    d) change of use within a use class, *TCP(UC)O 1987* (as amended): A1, most shops; A2, providing financial or professional services to the public; B1, use as an office outside A2.

    e) development within a general development order (*GPDO 1995* as amended, including in particular by *GPDO(A)(No.2)(E)O 2008*), or under a local authority's *Article 4* direction.

3   **Applications for planning permission**

    ➤ An applicant need not own land, but must tell the owner (*TCPA 1990 s 66*); if a development order requires it, it will be necessary to advertise the application in the local press (*TCPA 1990 s 65*).

    ➤ There are two main types of permission.

        a) **Outline permission:** matters which are 'reserved' must be approved within 3 years.

        Work must usually start within 2 years from approval being granted for matters 'reserved' (*TCPA 1990 s 91*).

        b) **Full permission:** no matters 'reserved'; work must usually begin in 3 years (*TCPA 1990 s 92*).

    ➤ Listed building consent

        This is required for altering listed buildings. It should only be granted after considering 'the building or its setting or any features of architectural or historic interest' (*P(LBCA)A 1990 s 72*).

    ➤ Conservation area consent

        This is required to demolish a building in a conservation area. It should only be granted after considering 'preserving or enhancing the appearance of the area' (*P(LBCA)A 1990 s 66*).

4   **Penalties/enforcement**

    ➤ An enforcement notice may be served up to 4 years after a breach if there are unauthorised building operations, or an unauthorised change of use to a use as a single dwelling house. Otherwise, a notice may be served within 10 years of any other breach (*TCPA 1990 s 172*).

    ➤ The local authority may issue:

        a) a stop notice (*TCPA 1990 s 183*): where an enforcement notice has been served, this compels builders to stop work or face criminal penalties.

        b) a temporary stop notice (*TCPA 1990 ss 171E-H*): where it thinks there has been a breach of planning control and it is expedient to stop the activity immediately.

        c) a breach of condition notice (*TCPA 1990 s 187A*): to compel compliance with a condition.

        d) completion notice (*TCPA 1990 ss 94-96*): to compel the recipient to complete work.

        e) a repair notice (*P(LBCA)A 1990 ss 47-48*): to protect a listed building; may be a prelude to compulsory purchase.

        f) a building preservation notice (*P(LBCA)A 1990 s 3*): to prevent demolition or alteration.

VI   Commission a survey

➤ There are 4 common types of 'survey' which a buyer can commission:

1   Valuation

✓ Cheap and fast.

✗ Very superficial, it only provides a guide as to whether a price appears fair in the present market.

2   Condition report (endorsed by the RICS from June 2011)

✓ Provides information on defects and is cheaper than a building survey.

✗ No valuation is given, and only suitable for relatively new and conventional properties.

3   House buyer's report and valuation

✓ This is more thorough than a valuation.

✗ A surveyor's duty is owed primarily to the lender. (With very 'low' priced property there is a duty to the buyer as well (*Smith v. Eric S. Bush* [1990] 1 AC 831).)

✗ A lender is primarily concerned with ascertaining the property's resale value, so the survey will not give the buyer a clear idea of any major works which will need doing in the future.

4   Full structural survey

✓ This is always relatively expensive and provides the most detailed information.

✓ If a property is unusual (eg: has its own drains in a remote location) special checks can be made.

✓ The surveyor owes the buyer a duty of care, and may be held liable in contract or tort.

◆ A survey is always advisable, but it should be considered particularly if:

- the property's construction is unconventional, *or*

- the property is in an unstable area, or likely to have structural problems (eg: mining area), *or*

- the property is not detached, *or*

- the property is of high value, *or*

- the property is over 100 years old, *or*

- a mortgage will provide only a small proportion (eg: under 75%) of the purchase price, *or*

- alterations or extensions are planned, *or*

- the property is not in good condition.

➤ Consider environmental liabilities and what action to take if contamination may be an issue.

◆ Compliance with a remediation notice issued by a local authority or the Environment Agency under *EPA 1990 Part IIA* may be prohibitively expensive; other relevant legislation includes *CL(E)R 2000*, *GR 1998* and the *PPC(EW)R 2000*. See also DETR *Guidance on Contaminated Land* (April 2000).

◆ If a person (a 'class A person') who causes or knowingly permits contamination cannot be identified, liability falls on an owner/occupier of land (including a lender in possession) (a 'class B person') and complex exclusion provisions deal with the transfer of liability.

- Make full enquiries, seek a specialist site investigation and consider where liability rests (under contract and the statutory exclusion provisions). It may be appropriate to require a seller to remedy contamination before completion, or to advise withdrawal from a transaction.

VII Check and amend the contract

Amending the contract

➤ Use red ink (and then green ink) to make amendments.

➤ Date alterations.

➤ Note on the contract 'Approved as drawn/amended on . . . [date].'

➤ Questions to ask

◆ Does the contract fulfil a client's instructions?

◆ Does it reflect what the buyer actually wants?

◆ Is it concise and unambiguous?

◆ Does it cater for the resolution of disputes?

◆ Does it describe the property accurately?

◆ Is a plan needed, and if so is one supplied to an adequate scale?

◆ Is the seller offering full title guarantee and if not, why not?

• If the answer to this final question is 'no', it is for the buyer to make a commercial judgment of the extent of any liability, the risk involved in the circumstances, and the likely impact on the property's resale value.

Competition Act 1998

➤ Prior to 6 April 2011 certain agreements relating to land were excluded from *CA 1998 Chapter I (Agreements affecting UK trade having the effect of preventing, restricting or distorting competition)* under the *CA 1998(LAER)O 2004* (repealed by *CA 1998(LAER)O 2010*). Since 6 April 2011, the *CA 1998 Chapter I* prohibition applies to all agreements.

➤ On 24 March 2011 the Office of Fair Trading issued guidance on the application of competition law to land agreements.

➤ The OFT guidance indicates that the *CA 1998 Chapter I* prohibition on an agreement which may affect trade in the UK and which has as its object or effect the prevention, restriction or distortion of competition within the UK is more likely to apply in the context of a land agreement where either:

a) competitors seek to restrict the use of land so as to share a market between them, *or*

b) a barrier is imposed so as to restrict access to a market.

➤ *CA 1998 Chapter II* prohibits an abuse of a dominant position where that abuse may affect trade in the UK. In the context of a land agreement this might include charging excessive above market or predatory rents, discriminating between tenants, limiting access to an essential facility (eg transport hub, utility distribution network, or sea port), or a restriction affecting the buying or selling of goods and services by the occupier of land.

➤ Large grocery retailers are also subject to regulation with respect to the imposition, enforcement and release of certain restrictive arrangements relating to land (*GMI(CL)O 2010*).

Step 4	Preparations for exchange

	I	Precautions regarding the parties
	II	Searches
	III	Insurance
	IV	Deposit
	V	Mortgage arrangements

I Precautions regarding the parties

1 Minors

➤ Provided that there is no restriction on the Register, the buyer may assume the seller is over 18.

➤ If land is held on trust *and* ...

... the trust instrument provides that a person should consent to any act of the trustees in relation to the land *and* that person is a minor, *then* ...

... a buyer is not prejudiced if this consent is not obtained.

- Trustees of land are under a duty to obtain consent from the minor's parent, or whoever has parental responsibility for him or is his guardian (*TLATA 1996 s 10(3)*).

➤ A contract may be repudiated during a minority or in a reasonable time of majority (*MCA 1987*).

◆ A conveyance to a minor used to operate like a contract to convey (*SLA 1925 s 27(1)*), but from 1 January 1997 a conveyance has operated as a declaration of trust over land in favour of the minor (a contract under *SLA 1925 s 27* now also operates as a trust) (*TLATA 1996 Sch 1, para 1*).

2 Married couples/Civil partners

➤ If the seller is married/a civil partner, a spouse/civil partner may have 'home rights' (*FLA 1996 ss 30-31*); these may be registered already *but* they can be registered (*form HR1*) at any time before completion.

◆ A spouse/civil partner should either be:

a) asked to execute a release before exchange, *or*

b) appointed as a trustee and made party to the contract. This ensures:

i) any equitable interest the spouse/civil partner may have is overreached, *and*

ii) binds the spouse/civil partner to vacate the property (*SpC 4*), *and*

iii) implies a term into the contract that the spouse will remove any *FLA* notice prior to completion.

■ Such a trustee would not usually give any title guarantee.

◆ A right registered under the *FLA 1996* can be removed (assuming land is registered) by submitting to the Registrar *form HR4* together with an official copy of:

- a court decree stating that the marriage/civil partnership has been terminated, *or*

- a court order ending the spouse/civil partner's home rights, *or*

- a death certificate (*FLA 1996 Sch 4, paras 4(1)(a)-(c), 5(1)*).

➤ See also (3) overleaf for land held on trust for sale, or (after 1 January 1997) under a trust of land.

3   Land held on trust

➤ If land is held on trust, pay to all the trustees (being 2-4) or a trust corporation (*LPA ss 2, 27*).

  ◆ If there is only one trustee (not being a trust corporation), a second trustee should be appointed *either*:

    a) before the contract is entered into, *or*

    b) after the contract is entered into (so that the seller can fulfil the covenants as to title).

  ◆ A second trustee appointed to satisfy *LPA ss 2, 27* may not be prepared to give any covenant as to title, but the original owner who holds subject to the trust may give full or limited title guarantee.

➤ If a sole owner is named as the proprietor on the Register, comply with any restriction to take free of any equitable interest.

➤ There may be a restriction on the Register regarding a joint tenancy.

  ◆ On the death of a tenant the legal estate vests in the survivor(s), *either*:

    a) execute a vesting assent in favour of a fully entitled survivor, *or*

    b) insist on the appointment of another trustee and pay the purchase money to them both.

      ▪ If a joint tenant murders his fellow tenant, the property does not pass on survivorship.

  ◆ If there is no restriction, assume that joint tenants hold absolutely; evidence of the deceased tenant's death (eg: death certificate) is needed (*LRR 2003 r 164*).

➤ From 1 January 1926, tenants in common and joint tenants held land under a trust for sale (under which they had a duty to sell land and a power to postpone sale). From 1 January 1997 land has been held by trustees under a trust of land (under which trustees have a power to sell land and a power to postpone sale).

  ◆ Trustees of land are under a duty to 'as far as is practicable, consult the beneficiaries of full age and beneficially entitled to an interest in possession in the land' (*TLATA 1996 s 11(1)*) (see the box on next page).

  ◆ A buyer of unregistered land who is not put on notice is not prejudiced by any limitation of the trustees' power to convey land, or their failure to consult beneficiaries (*TLATA 1996 s 16(1)*).

    ● A buyer who is on notice may take subject to the trust.

  ◆ A buyer of unregistered land is not (in any circumstances) prejudiced by any act of the trustees which contravenes any enactment or a rule of law or equity (*TLATA 1996 s 16(2)*).

  ◆ Trustees of unregistered land must, if the beneficiaries are absolutely entitled and of full age, execute a deed declaring that they are discharged from the trust. If they fail to do so, a court may order them to do so.

    ● A buyer may rely on such a deed, provided he is not on notice that the trustees erred in making the conveyance to the beneficiaries (*TLATA 1996 s 16(4)-(5)*).

Overview of the powers and duties of trustees of land

➤ Trustees have power to sell land and power to postpone sale (*TLATA 1996 s 4*).

◆ This power can be expressly excluded or modified in the trust instrument or will (*TLATA 1996 s 8*).

➤ For trustees' power to buy a legal estate in land (leasehold or freehold) anywhere in the United Kingdom, see *TA 2000 s 8*.

➤ Trustees of land, when exercising 'any function' relating to the land subject to the trust must:

a) 'as far as practicable' consult beneficiaries who are of full age and beneficially entitled to an interest in possession, *and*

b) give effect to the beneficiaries' wishes, so far as is consistent with the general interest of the trust. If the beneficiaries dispute among themselves, the trustees should have regard to the wishes of the majority (by reference to the value of their combined interests under the trust) (*TLATA 1996 s 11(1)*).

• This does not apply either to trusts which expressly exclude this requirement *or* to will trusts which arose before 1 January 1997 (*TLATA 1996 s 11(2)*).

• This only applies to trusts created before 1 January 1997, if such of the settlor(s) who are still alive and of full capacity execute(s) a deed making an irrevocable election that it shall apply (*TLATA 1996 s 11(3)-(4)*).

➤ If the beneficiaries are of full age and absolutely entitled the trustees may, having obtained their consent, partition land, convey it to them or mortgage it to pay the beneficiaries 'equality money' (*TLATA 1996 s 7*).

◆ This power can be expressly excluded or modified in the trust instrument (*TLATA 1996 s 8*).

➤ If beneficiaries are of full age and absolutely entitled to an interest in possession, the trustees may delegate, by power of attorney, any of their functions as trustees which relate to the land (*TLATA 1996 s 9*).

➤ Trustees may not act so as to prevent *any* person occupying land from remaining in occupation, or so as to make it likely that *any* person might cease to occupy land, unless that person consents, or the trustees obtain a court order under *TLATA 1996 ss 14-15*.

➤ A beneficiary's interest under a trust is no longer subject to the 'doctrine of conversion' under which land given to a beneficiary under trust for sale was deemed to be a gift of the proceeds from the sale of the land, and a beneficiary of a trust of money to be invested in land had an interest in the land rather than the cash. Land is now be treated as land, and personal property as personal property (*TLATA 1996 s 3*).

◆ This does not apply to a will trust if the testator died before 1 January 1997 (*TLATA 1996 ss 3(2), 18(3)*), but otherwise it applies to a trust irrespective of whether that trust arises or was created before or after that date (*TLATA 1996 s 3(3)*).

The rights of beneficiaries under trusts of land

➤ A beneficiary of a trust of land, who is absolutely entitled to an interest in possession under the trust may occupy the land if occupation is among the purposes of the trust, or the trustees hold the land so that it is available for occupation, provided the land is not unsuitable for occupation by that beneficiary (*TLATA 1996 s 12*).

➤ If 2 or more beneficiaries are entitled to occupy land held on trust, trustees:

♦ may not unreasonably exclude a beneficiary's right to occupy land, or restrict it with regard to:

- the purposes for which the land is held, *or*

- the settlor's intentions, *or*

- each beneficiary's circumstances, *but*

♦ may impose reasonable conditions on occupation, such as requiring a beneficiary to:

- pay outgoings or expenses in respect of the land, *or*

- assume any obligation in relation to the land or activities which take, or may take place on it (eg: comply with farming regulations, insure against a claim under the *OLA 1984*), *or*

- pay compensation to other beneficiaries whose entitlement to occupy the land has been restricted or excluded, *and*

- forgo another benefit under the trust to which the beneficiary would otherwise have been entitled (*TLATA 1996 s 13*).

➤ These provisions of *TLATA 1996* may *not* be excluded in the trust instrument and they apply to all trusts of land from 1 January 1997.

4 PRs

➤ PRs may become registered as proprietors of registered land by submitting the grant of probate to HM Land Registry (*LRR 2003 r 163*).

♦ **PR is registered:** the buyer should comply with any restriction on the Register.

♦ **PR is not registered:** the buyer should request a certified copy of a grant of probate and submit it with his application for registration.

➤ From 1 July 1995, one PR ceased to be able to bind the estate by contract. All the PRs who take a grant must be party to both the contract and the purchase deed (*LP(MP)A 1994 s 16*).

♦ Where there is a sole PR, the death certificate and the grant must be produced to show he acts alone.

➤ PRs do *not* need to seek consent from those interested in the administration of an estate before they sell land for the purposes of administration (*TLATA 1996 s 18*).

5 Companies (*LRR 2003 rr 181-185*)

➤ Lenders may insist that the Articles are checked to confirm that the company is acting within its powers, but a buyer should not be prejudiced if this is not done (*CA 2006 s 44*).

➤ Limitations on the power to purchase may be contained in a restriction on the Register.

6   **Charities (*LRR 2003 rr 176-180, Land Registry Practice Guide 14*)**

➤   If there is no restriction, no precautions are needed. Otherwise check:

a)   whether the transaction was authorised by statute or the deed governing the charity.

b)   whether the charity is an exempt charity (see *CA 1993 Sch 2* which lists exempt charities, eg: the trustees of the Royal Botanic Gardens (Kew), the Board of the British Library, Cambridge University, etc), and if the charity is not exempt either:

i)   the trustees can give a certificate in the purchase deed that they have complied with the provisions of *CA 1993 s 36* (to the extent applicable), *or*

CA 1993 s 36 (as amended by *ChA 2006*)

➤   No conveyance, transfer, lease or other disposition of land held on trust for a charity can take place unless:

a)   the trustees have obtained a written report on the proposed disposition from a qualified surveyor, *and*

b)   the property is advertised for the period, and as advised, by the surveyor, *and*

c)   the trustees are satisfied, having regard to the surveyor's report, that the terms of the disposition are the best that can be obtained, *and*

d)   prescribed words, indicating that the requirements of *CA 1993 s 36* have been complied with, are inserted in the contract and the purchase deed.

- When these words are included a buyer who acquires the property in good faith for money or money's worth can rely on the certificate as conclusive evidence that the trustees have the power to effect the disposition and have complied with the requirements of *CA 1993 s 36* (*CA 1993 s 37(4)*).

---

ii)   an order of the court or the Charity Commission has been obtained.

7   **Mental impairment**

➤   A contract or conveyance for value is binding unless one of the parties is unaware of the other's disability (*Hart v. O'Connor* [1985] 2 All ER 880), in which case it is voidable. A conveyance for no value involving someone of unsound mind is void.

➤   A deputy may deal with property with the court's consent (*MCA 2005 s 18(1)*); there will be no restriction on the Register unless the deputy is registered as the proprietor.

➤   If a trustee lacks capacity within the meaning of the *MCA 2005, and* ...

... all the beneficiaries are fully entitled *and* of full age, *and* ...

... nobody is willing and able to appoint a trustee to replace him under *TA 1925 s 36(1), then*

... the beneficiaries may issue a written direction to a deputy appointed for the trustee by the Court of Protection, the trustee's attorney under an enduring or lasting power of attorney registered under the *MCA 2005*, or a person authorised by the Court of Protection, requesting that person to appoint a replacement trustee (*TLATA 1996 s 20*).

◆   A buyer should ask to see a certified copy of any such direction together with the deed of appointment.

- Pre-contract enquiries should include a question as to whether a direction has been made, and requisitions on title could include a request for confirmation that none of the beneficiaries withdrew the direction before it was complied with under *TLATA 1996 s 21(1)*.

Undue influence (non commercial surety) (*Royal Bank of Scotland v Etridge* [2001] UK HL 44)

➤ The client and the solicitor should meet face to face without the principal debtor present.

◆ The solicitor's duty is to his client alone and he is concerned only with his client's interests.

◆ The solicitor must be alive to any potential conflicts of interest and if these inhibit or may inhibit his advice he must not act or continue to act (if already acting).

➤ The solicitor should explain the purpose of his/her involvement.

◆ The lender will rely on a solicitor's involvement to counter suggestions of:

a) lack of proper understanding of the transaction and its implications, *and*

b) influence or pressure by the principal debtor.

◆ The solicitor must obtain the client's confirmation to act and advise on the legal and practical implications of the transaction.

◆ The solicitor should obtain from the lender any information that he may need.

➤ Advice should depend on the circumstances of each case; the minimum requirements include:

a) explaining the documents and the consequences of signing them and ensuring that the client understands the worst case scenario such as the loss of a home and bankruptcy.

b) explaining the seriousness of the risks involved.

• The client should be told of:

i) the purpose of the loan, its amount and principal terms, *and*

ii) the possibility of the amount being increased, the terms being changed or a new facility being granted without notification, *and*

iii) the amount of the client's liability (if it is unlimited the client must be made aware of that fact) and the client's means of meeting the liability should be considered.

• The availability of other assets to meet repayments should be discussed as this enables the seriousness of the risk to be quantified.

c) indicating that the client has a choice as to whether to proceed or not - the decision to agree or not agree is the client's alone.

• Explanation of this choice may require a review of the client's current financial position including present indebtedness and current loan facilities.

➤ The client should be asked if he/she wishes to proceed.

◆ The client must indicate that he/she is content for the solicitor to confirm to the lender that the nature and effect of the documents have been explained.

◆ Instructions should be sought as to whether the terms of the documents should be negotiated.

• The solicitor should consider with the client the need to:

a) limit liability in terms of amount and/or time, *and*

b) limit the lender's ability to change terms, amounts etc without the client's prior approval, *and*

c) agree the order in which the lender will resort to available assets on enforcement to ensure that all other available assets are realised before resort is made to the client's assets.

➤ The Law Society has published guidance, 'Undue Influence - solicitors' duties post *Etridge*', and a model letter to send to a wife charging a home to secure a loan to a husband or his business (2002).

Powers of an owner of registered land under *LRA 2002*

➤ *LRA 2002*, unlike the *LRA 1925*, specifies the powers which an owner of registered land enjoys.

➤ An owner of a registered estate has the power to (*LRA 2002 s 23(1)*):

   a) make a disposition of any kind permitted by the general law in relation to the registered estate, *and*

   b) charge the estate at law with the payment of money.

➤ An owner of a registered charge has the power to (*LRA 2002 ss 23(2)-(3)*):

   a) make a disposition of any kind permitted by the general law in relation to that charge, other than:

      i) a transfer by way of mortgage, *or*

      ii) a sub-mortgage by sub-demise, *or*

      iii) a charge by way of legal mortgage, *and*

   b) charge at law with the payment of money indebtedness secured by a registered charge.

➤ A person who is the registered proprietor of a registered estate or charge, or entitled to be registered as proprietor of a registered estate or charge, may exercise an owner's powers (*LRA 2002 s 24*).

➤ A person's right to exercise an owner's powers is free from any limitation affecting the validity of a disposition, other than a limitation reflected by an entry on the register or imposed by, or under, the *LRA 2002* (*LRA 2002 s 26*).

   ◆ Charge certificates have been abolished and the importance of land certificates reduced; the registered owner is presumed to have unrestricted powers of disposition in the absence of any register entry.

II   Searches

➤ The buyer should check that these are all correct, and that exchange will occur before priority periods expire.

III   Insurance

➤ *StC 5.5.1* provides that a property is at the buyer's risk from exchange.

   ◆ See also the box relating to 'Insurance' on p 208.

➤ A buyer should ensure that suitable insurance cover is in place if the buyer is on risk from exchange.

IV Deposit

1 Where is the deposit coming from?

➤ Payment (unless the sale is by auction) is to be made (*StC 2.2.3-2.2.4*):

a) by electronic means from an account held in the name of a conveyancer at a clearing bank to an account in the name of the seller's conveyancer (or where *StC 2.2.5* applies because the desposit is being used for another transaction, to an account in the name of a conveyancer nominated by the seller's conveyancer and maintained at a clearing bank), *or*

b) by cheque drawn on a solicitor's or licenced conveyancer's client account to the seller's conveyancer (or, where *StC 2.2.5* applies, to a conveyancer nominated by the seller's conveyancer) .

◆ If a client account cheque is used the solicitor must be put in funds at least 5 working days in advance to ensure it clears (otherwise the *SAR 2011* may be breached).

➤ If payment is from a deposit account ensure that notice of withdrawal is given sufficiently early to avoid incurring an interest penalty *and* to make certain that the money is released for exchange.

➤ If bridging finance is required, arrange this in good time.

✗ A loan may be expensive.

✗ If the sale does not proceed liability must be discharged fast to prevent exorbitant interest payments.

2 How will the deposit be held?

➤ As agent for the seller

◆ This is the position under the general law unless the parties agree otherwise (or an auctioneer holds the deposit, in which case the auctioneer holds as stakeholder).

◆ *StC 2.2.5* permits a seller to use the deposit, or part of it, as a deposit on the purchase of a property in England or Wales as his residence, if the related purchase contract is entered into before completion (ie: of the contract for the seller's sale) and that related contract contains similar provisions to *StC 2.2.5-2.2.6*.

◆ A trustee is under a duty not to lose control of money held on trust, so if the seller is a trustee the seller's solicitor should hold the deposit as the seller's agent.

➤ As stakeholder (envisaged by *StC 2.2.6*)

◆ Unless the sellers are trustees *or* the seller wishes to use the deposit to buy another property (in accordance with *StC 2.2.5*), the seller's solicitor holds the deposit as stakeholder and is obliged to pay it to the seller on completion, together with accrued interest.

3 Where will the deposit be held?

➤ In a deposit account? This depends on whether interest penalties are imposed for short-term deposits and the feasibility of transferring money so it is available at need.

4 Interest on the deposit

➤ The solicitor must pay the client interest in accordance with *SAR 2011 r 22*.

➤ Estate agents must account to their client for interest over £500 (*EA(A)R 1981 r 7*).

➤ If money is held as stakeholder, interest should be paid to the seller on completion (*StC 2.2.6*).

5   **Troubleshooting**

➤ Deposit insurance: an insurance policy is advisable if it is feared the seller may abscond with the deposit.

➤ Buyer's lien: this attaches to the house for the amount of any deposit.

◆ The buyer can protect it with a notice (registered land) or a C(iii) charge (unregistered land).

➤ Estate agents must carry insurance against insolvency while holding a deposit (*EAA 1979 s 16*).

➤ If the cheque bounces this breaches a condition of the contract: the seller can treat the breach as repudiatory (*StC 2.2.2*), or allow the contract to continue. In either case he may sue for damages.

IV Mortgage arrangements

Types of mortgage			
Repayment		**Endowment**	**Pension**
Capital & Interest	Interest only		
➤ The borrower makes monthly repayments of interest *and* capital	➤ The borrower makes monthly repayments of interest only ➤ The borrower is responsible for repaying capital before the end of the mortgage term. It is vital for a borrower to make arrangements to fund the capital, but if this is done this type of mortgage can be very flexible and simple	➤ The borrower makes repayments of interest only ➤ An insurance policy is taken out on the borrower's life when the mortgage is granted, and this repays the capital when it matures ✓ When the policy matures any surplus is paid to the borrower ✓ The insurance policy on the borrower's life gives the lender extra security on a borrower's death	➤ These are linked with pension arrangements ✓ May be tax efficient for a higher rate tax payer
✗ On the borrower's death the debt falls due from the estate. ● if the estate is insolvent and property prices fall, the lender is left with a bad debt. ● A mortgage repayment policy insures against this occurring (a lender may insist on the borrower taking out such a policy)		✗ If the policy does not cover the loan, the borrower must make good the shortfall ✗ The mortgage cannot be transferred unless the whole sum is repaid	

Interest rates can be, for a period or for the whole term of a mortgage, either:

➤ fixed - interest is payable at a set rate (eg: 6%), *or*

➤ capped - the interest rate may vary, but will not exceed the 'cap' (eg: will not exceed 8%, but unlike with a fixed rate the borrower will benefit if the rate is below the cap by paying interest at the lower rate), *or*

➤ variable - the interest 'floats', usually in line with the rate set by the Bank of England under the *BEA 1998*.

➤ Ensure that:

♦ if there is more than one borrower, both borrowers are named on the mortgage offer.

♦ none of the borrowers is subject to undue influence.

♦ the firm has the necessary authorisation in relation to the mortgage and that the *FSMA 2000* is complied with.

♦ the borrower is aware of the repayments and can afford them (even, if the mortgage carries interest at a variable rate, when interest rates rise).

♦ the borrower knows the overall cost of the mortgage (eg: the lender may insist the property is insured under its own block policy *and* that the borrower pays for this).

♦ the buyer has enough money in hand, after moving expenses, to proceed with the purchase.

♦ retentions for repair work are not such as to prevent the borrower meeting his financial obligations. If the lender retains some of the capital until specified repairs have been done, this may cause additional financing difficulties.

● The seller may allow the buyer access before completion to carry out work the lender requires. The lender will then release the whole of the loan to enable the buyer to complete.

- any conditions attached to the mortgage are not too onerous. Explain the effect of any conditions to the client, eg the terms of the mortgage may:

  - prohibit the borrower letting part of the property without the lender's consent, *and/or*

  - require the borrower to repair or alter the property (can the borrower afford to comply?), *and/or*

  - impose penalties for early redemption (this is common if the lender offers the borrower favourable terms as an inducement to select a particular mortgage, eg: a low rate of interest for an initial period), *and/or*

  - oblige the borrower to give a full title guarantee to the lender in the mortgage deed (This may present difficulties if the borrower does not receive full title guarantee from the seller).

- any guarantee premium (also known as a 'mortgage indemnity') which the lender demands is satisfactory. Is this sufficient to protect the borrower if house prices fall below the purchase price (known as the 'negative equity' trap)? Is the premium expensive?

  - If acting for the lender, note that the lender will only be able to recover the difference between the correct valuation and the negligent one (ie: not the fall in market values), *South Australia Asset Management Corporation v. York Montague Limited* [1996] 3 All ER 365, HL.

- there is no conflict if the lender instructs the buyer's solicitor. (Comply with *SRA SCC IB 3.7*).

  - If acting for a lender check whether the lender's instructions follow the Council of Mortgage Lenders' *Lenders Handbook for England and Wales*. *Part 1* contains general instructions. *Part 2* comprises instructions for specific lenders. (This is available via the internet, see *www.cml.org.uk*.)

  - If a conflict of interest arises subsequently, the solicitor must cease acting, but he may not tell the other party the reason why as this would breach the duty of confidentiality.

- once a satisfactory offer has been made, the buyer accepts it within the time allowed.

- any arrangements with a lender are coordinated with the rest of the transaction: with a repayment mortgage, mortgage insurance can be taken out to enable the mortgage policy to be redeemed if the borrower dies.

- the borrower is aware of, and takes out, appropriate insurance policies (a lender may insist on this):

  a) Endowment policy - suitable only for an endowment mortgage, covers the borrower's life.

  b) Mortgage indemnity policy - provides protection when the loan is for a high percentage (eg: 80% or more) of the purchase price.

  c) Mortgage repayment policy - pays off the mortgage if the borrower dies prior to redemption.

  d) Mortgage payment protection policy - will pay amounts due under the mortgage while the borrower is unemployed.

  e) Building insurance - offers cover if the building is subject to subsidence, fire, flooding, storm damage, etc. If part of a property (eg: a flat) is subject to a policy taken out by the landlord for the whole building, a lender may be satisfied with the landlord's policy if that policy meets its requirements.

    - Risk moves to the borrower in accordance with common law or the contract.

If a borrower may default ...

➤ Mortgage possession claims are beyond the range of this book, but guidance can be found in the Law Society's practice note: 'Mortgage possession claims' (4 June 2009).

- This practice note offers guidance on the 'Pre-Action Protocol for Possession Claims based on Mortgage or Home Purchase Plan Arrears in Respect of Residential Property' (19 November 2008).

Step 5	Exchange and its consequences

    I   Exchange
    II   Consequences of exchange

I   Exchange

➤ The contract is signed.

- ◆ *Either* both parties sign one contract *or* they each sign identical copies (*LP(MP)A 1989 s 2*). For a contract to be binding under *s 2,* documents containing the terms of the contract must actually be exchanged (*Commission for the New Towns v. Cooper (Great Britain) Limited* [1995] 26 EG 129).

- ◆ The signatures need not be witnessed.

- ◆ A solicitor may sign, but should do so *either* under a power of attorney *or* with express written authority.

  - • Failure to obtain the proper authority may be a breach of warranty of authority (*Suleman v. Shahisavari* [1989] 2 All ER 460).

➤ Do not exchange without a client's express written authority to do so.

➤ Exchange using either *Formula A, B, or C* (see box below) via:

- ◆ telephone (make a file note of the time of the exchange), *or*

- ◆ post/DX (*StC 2.1.1*): a contract is made when it (or the last copy, if more than one) is posted, *or*

- ◆ personally (usually at the office of the seller's solicitors), *or*

- ◆ fax or email (*StC 1.3.3*): for messages required under one of the Law Society's *Formulae* (ie: not to exchange the contract itself). A fax must be confirmed with hard copies as soon as possible.

Formula A	Formula B	Formula C
When one solicitor holds both contracts	When each solicitor holds their client's contract	For a 'chain' of transactions Each solicitor holds their client's contract and exchange is by telephone

➤ After exchange has taken place:

- ◆ make an attendance note.

- ◆ notify the insurer of the property if appropriate (*StC 5.1.1* provides that the property is at the buyer's risk from exchange).

- ◆ inform client/lender.

- ◆ comply with undertakings given under the exchange *Formula* and deal with the deposit in accordance with the contract and the *SAR 2011*.

- ◆ if acting for the seller, write to any lender asking for confirmation of the amount required to redeem the mortgage on completion.

➤ consider registering the contract.

II   Consequences of exchange

➤   Any subsequent variation to the contract which is agreed between the parties must comply with the *LP(MP)A 1989 s 2* (see previous page) (*McCausland and Another v. Duncan Lawrie Limited*, The Times, 18 June 1996, CA).

1   Consider whether to register the contract

➤   This is advisable if:

a) the seller's good faith is doubted, *or*

b) a dispute arises, *or*

c) there are more than 2 months between exchange and completion, *or*

d) the seller delays completion beyond the contractual date, *or*

e) the transaction is a sub-sale.

   • Unregistered land: register the contract as a Class C(iv) land charge.

   • Registered land: enter a notice on the Register as a minor interest in the land.

2   Death of a party

➤   PRs are bound to complete a contract which the deceased entered into. This can cause difficulties for the estate as the buyer's death may lead to a revocation of the mortgage offer.

3   Seller's bankruptcy

➤   The seller's trustee in bankruptcy may complete with a redrafted purchase deed (the bankrupt is not party to the deed), or the trustee may disclaim the contract.

4   Requisitions

➤   Requisitions may not be raised:

a) on any title shown by the seller before the contract was made (*StC 4.2.1(a)*), *or*

b) with respect to (i) incumbrances specified in the contract, (ii) incumbrances discoverable by inspection of the property before the contract, (iii) incumbrances the seller did not and could not reasonably know about, (iv) incumbrances (other than mortgages) which the buyer knew about, (v) entries made before the date of the contract in any public register (except HM Land Registry, Land Charges Department or Companies House), or (vi) public requirements (*StC 4.2.1(b)*),

... *however* a buyer may raise requisitions in writing with respect to other matters within 6 working days of exchange, *or* when evidence of the seller's title is delivered to the buyer, whichever is later.

   • The seller replies within 4 working days; the buyer then has 3 working days within which to make written observations on the seller's replies (*StC 4.3.1*).

➤   Under common law the buyer accepts the seller's title on delivery of the draft purchase deed to the seller. Often the draft deed is submitted with requisitions on title.

➤   *Protocol 54* provides that the buyer should raise any additional requisitions on title immediately following exchange if permitted by the contract.

Step 6	Buyer prepares the purchase deed

1   Procedure

➤ At least 12 working days before completion the buyer sends the seller a draft of the transfer (*StC 4.3.2*): in practice one engrossment and a copy.

➤ The seller's solicitor replies with any queries within 4 working days of the draft being delivered to him (*StC 4.3.2*).

➤ The buyer must deliver an engrossment to the seller at least 5 working days before completion (*StC 4.3.2*).

◆ The buyer should prepare the SDLT return (*Protocol para 55*).

2   Form of the deed

➤ The transfer should be by deed (otherwise it will be void as a conveyance or grant) unless it is (*LPA s 52* as amended by the *LP(MP)A 1989 s 1*):

a) an assent by a PR, *or*

b) a disclaimer made in accordance with *IA 1986 ss 178-180* or *ss 315-319*, or not required to be evidenced in writing, *or*

c) a surrender by operation of law, including a surrender which may, by law, be effected without writing, *or*

d) a lease or tenancy or other assurances not required by law to be made in writing, *or*

e) a receipt other than falling within *LPA s 115*, *or*

f) a vesting order of the court or other competent authority, *or*

g) a conveyance taking effect by operation of law.

➤ Unregistered land: there is no prescribed form. *Form TR1* may be used.

➤ Registered land: use *Form TR1*.

3   Drafting

➤ The transfer should reflect the terms of the contract.

➤ Consideration: exclude contents; a separate receipt for these is given to the buyer on completion.

◆ VAT (if due) is included in the figure for consideration.

4   Parties

➤ All those whose consent to the transaction is necessary:

◆ a receiver or liquidator.

◆ a sub-purchaser on a sub-sale.

◆ a lender with a charge over unregistered land may *either* join a conveyance *or* give the buyer a separate deed of release.

● A lender with a charge over registered land will release the land using *Form DS1* or using a electronic discharge.

5 Signature

➤ The seller always signs the deed. The buyer signs the transfer if it contains a covenant or a declaration on his behalf.

➤ If an individual is incapable of signing, the transfer is read to him, and it can be signed on his behalf in the presence of 2 witnesses who attest his signature (*LP(MP)A 1989 s 1(2)-(3)*).

➤ An attorney signs *either* 'O by his attorney P' *or* 'P as attorney on behalf of O'.

➤ A company must comply with the requirements of *CA 2006 s 44* (see p 213).

➤ Pre-signed signature pages should not be used (*R (on the application of Mercury Tax Group and another) v HMRC [2008] EWHC 2721* and see guidance issued by The Law Society in February 2010: 'Execution of documents by virtual means').

◆ Where a deed (or a guarantee which does not need to be by deed) is to be executed, and the signatory is not present:

a) the complete deed should be emailed to the signatory, *and*

b) the signatory should print off the signature page, *and*

▪ Care should be taken to make it clear that a deed is not 'delivered' at this point (eg: the signatory should not date the document), unless delivery is actually intended.

c) the signatory should sign the signatory page, *and*

d) the signed signatory page should be scanned, and emailed to the signatory's solicitor, *and*

e) the solicitor should attach the scanned copy to the agreed form document.

▪ Applying this approach in the case of a guarantee is intended to prevent a guarantee being void as a result of non-compliance with the *Statute of Frauds 1677 s 4*.

6 Plans

➤ Attach these to the transfer.

➤ HM Land Registry requires parties to sign the plan if it is to accept its inclusion.

◆ Signing the plan is not compulsory for unregistered land, but it is advisable nonetheless.

◆ If a company seals the transfer, it should seal the plan as well (this need not be witnessed).

7 Witnesses (where necessary)

➤ For evidential reasons an independent party is preferable.

◆ A witness cannot be a party to the deed (*Seal v. Claridge* (1881) 7 QBD 516).

➤ 2 witnesses are required if a signature is by proxy.

8 Delivery

➤ A transfer is usually held 'in escrow' (ie: conditional upon completion, signed but not dated).

➤ Delivery is presumed to be the date of execution unless the contrary is shown (*CA 2006 s 46*).

➤ Receipt clause: this is sufficient discharge for the buyer (*LPA s 67*).

◆ A receipt clause authorises the buyer to pay consideration to the seller's solicitor (*LPA s 69*).

◆ A receipt is evidence, but not conclusive evidence, that the seller's lien over the property in respect of unpaid consideration is extinguished.

Step 7	Preparing for completion

1   **Seller's solicitor (and buyer's solicitor if necessary) should send a letter with an engrossed purchase deed**

➤ Explain:

◆ the purpose and contents of the purchase deed.

◆ any instructions for executing the deed and the date by which it should be returned to the solicitor.

◆ that the client should not date the purchase deed.

2   **Make final searches** (see p 252)

3   **Prepare and send completion statements to the clients**

➤ The seller's solicitor sends:

◆ the seller a statement of the sum due on completion, explaining how this was calculated, *and*

◆ the buyer 2 copies of the appropriate statement, together with any receipts if *either* the proceeds do not cover the price agreed *or* an apportionment is due (eg: in respect of a service charge), *or* for contents.

➤ The buyer's solicitor sends the buyer a statement giving:

◆ the sum needed to complete, explaining how this was calculated, *and*

◆ a statement of the mortgage, mentioning how much will be advanced and retained, *and*

◆ the amount due in disbursements (eg: search fees, SDLT, etc), *and*

◆ the solicitor's costs (plus VAT).

4   **Finalise arrangements with the lender** (if acting for a lender)

➤ Buyer's solicitor ...

... sends the buyer's lender a report on the title and requests a cheque/telegraphic transfer to cover the advance. Ensure that the cheque is paid in to client account at least 5 days before completion.

... prepares an engrossment of the mortgage deed.

... checks that all outstanding requisitions and enquiries have been satisfactorily answered, and advises the client of any remaining difficulties.

➤ Seller's solicitor ...

... gives an undertaking to the seller's lender to secure redemption of the mortgage in so far as monies come into the solicitor's hands, and seeks authority to act as the lender's agent to redeem the mortgage just before completion.

... verifies that the completion statement is correct.

... prepares a form of discharge of the mortgage, and if acting for a seller's lender, checks its instructions as to completion.

5   **Settle arrangements for completion**

➤ If completion is by post consider using the *Law Society's Code for Completion by Post* and (in any event) make preparations appropriate to the method of completion chosen.

◆ In 'exceptional circumstances' (eg: the amount to redeem a seller's mortgage exceeds the minimum level of solicitor's indemnity insurance (£2 million), or the lender is not a CML member), it is negligent for a buyer's solicitor to rely solely on an undertaking from the seller's solicitor to supply a *form DS1* following completion (*Patel v. Daybells* [2001] EWCA Civ 1229, CA).

Step 8	Completion

> The contract and the purchase deed do *not* merge on completion (*StC 7.3*).

   ◆ This ensures that a claim in contract is preserved after completion.

1   Time

> Completion takes place on the twentieth working day after exchange (*StC 6.1.1*), subject to any *SpC*.
> If completion takes place after 2 pm, it is deemed to occur on the following working day in which case an apportionment in respect of incomings and outgoings is made, and the buyer is obliged to compensate the seller by paying interest at the contract rate (*StC 6.1.2, 6.3 and 7.2*).

   ◆ No apportionment is made, and no compensation is due, if the sale is with vacant possession and the buyer is ready, able and willing to complete (*StC 1.1.3*), but does not pay until after 2 pm because the seller has not vacated the property (*StC 6.1.3*).

   ◆ Late completion on a Friday afternoon involves the buyer paying 3 days' interest.

2   Place

> At the seller's conveyancer's office, or any place which the seller may reasonably specify (*StC 6.2.2*).

3   Money

> Money is paid by direct transfer of cleared funds from an account held in the name of a conveyancer at a clearing bank and, if appropriate, by an unconditional release of a deposit held by a stakeholder (*StC 6.7*).

Usual methods of completion	
Postal	**Personal**
The buyer's solicitor and the seller's solicitor agree, preferably in writing, whether to use the Law Society's *Code for Completion by Post*.	The buyer's solicitor:
	◆ brings the deed, other relevant documents (see below) and a banker's draft for the balance of the purchase price. (A cheque is not good enough as only cash or an equivalent to cash is permitted by *StC 6.7*)
The buyer's solicitor usually sends the balance of the completion monies to the seller's solicitor by telegraphic transfer early on the morning of completion	
	The seller's solicitor:
See next page for the *Code* (as revised with effect from 1 April 2011)	◆ checks and signs 2 copies of the schedule of deeds (and retains one, giving the other to the buyer)

In the case of registered and unregistered land:
   ◆ the seller obtains a discharge for any mortgage, or gives an undertaking to discharge any mortgage.
   ◆ the buyer (on a personal completion) or the seller (on a postal completion) checks the purchase deed.
   ◆ the seller gives a receipt for money paid for contents.

For unregistered land: documents of title are checked against the epitome of title which the seller has supplied.

   ◆ If the seller sells as a PR, or on a conveyance of part, endorse a memorandum on the grant of representation or original conveyance of the whole respectively.
   ◆ If the seller will retain any of the documents (eg: sale of part, or trust instrument (*LPA s 45(9)*), the buyer's solicitor marks the abstract 'Examined against the originals at the office of .... on ...', and signs the abstract.
   ◆ If any of the documents of title are not handed over on completion, the seller agrees that (at the seller's expense) the seller will give (*StC 4.6.5*):
      a) a written acknowledgement of the buyer's right to production of that document, and
      b) (unless a fiduciary/lender has custody) a written undertaking for the document's safe custody.

Law Society's Code for Completion by Post (2011)

➤ A solicitor must expressly agree to adopt the *Code*, preferably in writing; such agreement is implied where the *Protocol* is used unless either solicitor states otherwise in writing (*para 1*).

◆ Any variation to the *Code* must be agreed in writing prior to completion (final *Note*).

◆ The seller's solicitor acts as agent for the buyer's solicitor at completion (without fee or disbursement) (*para 3*).

◆ Withdrawal by the seller's solicitor must be notified to the buyer no later than 4 pm on the working day prior to completion (or immediately, if the seller solicitor's authority to receive monies, is withdrawn after then) (*para 2*).

◆ References to a solicitor may apply equally to a licenced conveyancer (*para 14(ii)*).

◆ Any dispute as to the operation of the Code is to be referred to a single arbiter (*para 15*).

1 Before completion

➤ The buyer's solicitor uses 'reasonable endeavours' to ensure funds from the buyer/its lender are collected and transmitted to the seller's solicitor in good time on or before the day of completion (*para 4*).

➤ At least 5 working days before completion the seller's solicitor should provide the buyer's solicitor with replies to completion information and undertakings in the Law Society's standard form (*TA 13*), unless replies have been supplied to some other form of request for completion information submitted by the seller's solicitor (*para 5*).

➤ The seller's solicitor specifies in writing to the buyer's solicitor the mortgages, charges or financial incumbrances which will be redeemed or discharged on or before completion to the extent that these relate to the property, and the method of redemption or discharge (*para 6*).

➤ The seller's solicitor undertakes (*para 7*):

a) to have the seller's authority to receive the purchase money on completion, *and*

b) on completion to have the authority of the proprietor of each mortgage, charge or other financial incumbrance which has not yet been redeemed or discharged to receive the sum intended to repay it.

• The seller's solicitor undertakes that, notwithstanding a) and b), if he does not have the necessary authorities, he will advise the buyer's solicitor*:*

■ no later 4pm on the working day before the completion date that he does not have the authority referred to in a) and b), *or* immediately if authority is subsequently withdrawn, *and*

■ not to complete without the buyer's solicitor's instructions.

➤ The buyer's solicitor sends the seller's solicitor instructions as to (*para 8*):

i) documents to be examined and marked, *and*

ii) memoranda to be endorsed, *and*

iii) undertakings to be given*, and*

iv) deeds and documents (eg: relating to rents, deposits, keys) to be sent after completion to the buyer ('*para 8(iv) documents*'), *and*

v) consents, certificates or other authorities which may be required to deal with any restrictions on a Land Registry title to the property, *and*

vi) executed stock transfer forms relating to shares in any company directly related to the conveyancing transaction.

Law Society's Code for Completion by Post (2011) (continued)

➤ The buyer's solicitor remits to the seller's solicitor the completion amount (notified in writing by the seller's solicitor, or else as stated on the contract), and these funds are held to the buyer's solicitor's order (*para 9*).

◆ If telegraphic transfer is used the seller's solicitor reports receipt to the buyer's solicitor immediately upon becoming aware that the funds have been received.

2   Completion

➤ The seller's solicitor will complete (on receiving the completion monies, or a lesser sum if so agreed) unless (*para 10*):

a) the buyer's solicitor has notified (if possible in writing, or confirmed in writing) the seller's solicitor that the funds are to be held to the order of the buyer's solicitor, *or*

b) it has previously been agreed (if possible in writing, or confirmed in writing) that completion is to take place at a later time.

➤ The seller's solicitor undertakes when completing (*para 11*):

a) to comply any agreed completion arrangements and with any reasonable instructions with respect to the examination of documents etc under *para 8, and*

b) to redeem or obtain a discharge for any outstanding mortgages etc specified in *para 6, and*

c) that the seller's solicitor has identified the proprietor of each mortgage etc specified in *para 6* to the extent necessary for the purpose of the buyer's solicitor's application to HM Land Registry.

◆ Following *Angel Solicitors (a firm) v Jenkins O'Dowd & Barth* ([2009] EWHC 46 (Ch)) and *Clark v Lucas LLP* [2009] EWHC 1952 (Ch)), unless agreed otherwise, this undertaking includes confirmation that a satisfactory redemption statement has been obtained from any lender whose charge is to be redeemed (*Note 6*).

3   After completion

➤ The seller's solicitor undertakes (*para 12*):

a) to hold deeds and *para 8(iv)* documents to the order of the buyer's solicitor, *and*

b) as soon as possible and in any event:

● on the same day, to:

i)   confirm to the buyer's solicitor by telephone, fax or email that completion has occurred, *and*

ii) notify the seller's estate agent/keyholder that completion has taken place and authorise the agent/keyholder to make the keys available to the buyer immediately, *and*

● by the end of the working day after completion, to send written confirmation and (at the risk of the buyer's solicitor) the *para 8(iv)* documents by first class post or DX.

c) to notify the buyer's solicitor, in the case of a discharge by electronic means, as soon as any confirmation is received from the proprietor of a mortgage, etc that discharge has taken or is taking place.

Step 9	Post-completion

1   Seller's solicitor ...

... instructs the estate agent to release the keys.   Under *Protocol 64*, the solicitor should ensure the keys are released immediately and inform the buyer's solicitor when this has been done.

... deals with the proceeds of sale as instructed, and fulfils any undertakings (eg: to a lender).

... redeems the mortgage and (once the lender has redeemed the mortgage) sends the appropriate receipt to the buyer:

♦ Registered land: obtain *Form DS1.*

♦ Unregistered land: obtain a receipted mortgage deed.

... reports completion to the seller and sends the seller a bill.

2   Buyer's solicitor ...

... completes the mortgage deed (eg: add date of completion).

... fulfils any undertaking to repay bridging finance (eg: from a mortgage advance).

... obtains a SDLT certificate from HMRC.

♦ A SDLT certificate is obtained by submitting a land transaction return, a self assessment, and payment in respect of the SDLT payable to HMRC within 30 days of the effective date of the land transaction.

• If the consideration is contingent or uncertain and may fall to be paid more than 6 months after the effective date of the transaction, the purchaser can apply to defer payment of SDLT (*FA 2003 s 90*).

... applies to HM Land Registry to register the title and the mortgage, if appropriate (see next page).

♦ An application may be made for 'prejudicial' information to be excluded (*LRR 2003 r 136*, Form EX1).

... if the buyer is a company/LLP, any fixed charge must be registered at Companies House within 21 days.

... discharges any entries which have been registered at HM Land Registry or the Land Charges Department to protect the contract.

... checks the official copy of the Register, the official copy of the plan (where a plan has been created or amended by the application), and the title information document received from HM Land Registry.

♦ The title information document explains the reason for the issue of the official copy; it is provided for information purposes only.

... if the buyer has bought unregistered land from an attorney with a non-enduring power, or a power of attorney granted under *TLATA 1996 s 9*, he should advise the buyer to make a statutory declaration. If the buyer dies without doing so there will be a defect in the title where statute does not offer protection.

... if the property is a commonhold unit, give notice (on *Form 10*) to the commonhold association within 14 days of the buyer becoming entitled to be registered as a proprietor of the unit (*CCS para 4.7.8*, see p 273).

First registration

➤ If the 'requirement of registration' applies, the responsible estate owner (or his successor in title) must apply to be registered as proprietor of the registered estate (*LRA 2002 s 6(1)*).

The 'requirement of registration' (*LRA 2002 s 4* as amended by *LRA(A)O 2008*)

➤ The requirement of registration applies where there is:

a) a transfer (otherwise than by operation of law) of a qualifying estate for valuable or other consideration, by gift, or in pursuance of a court order, by means of a vesting assent, or giving effect to a partition of land subject to a trust of land, *or*

   - This does not include the assignment of a mortgage term or the assignment or surrender of a lease to the owner of the immediate reversion where the term merges on reversion.

b) the transfer of a qualifying estate:

   i) by a deed that appoints, or by virtue of *CA 1993 s 83* has effect as if it appointed, a new trustee or is made upon the appointment of a new trustee, *or*

   ii) by a vesting order under *TA 1925 s 44* upon the appointment of a new trustee

c) the grant out of a qualifying estate in land for a term of years absolute of more than 7 years from the date of the grant, and for valuable consideration, by gift or in pursuance of a court order (but not a grant to a person as a lender), *or*

d) the grant out of a qualifying estate in land for a term of years absolute to take effect in possession after the end of the period of 3 months beginning with the date of the grant, *or*

e) the creation of a 'protected first legal mortgage' of a qualifying estate, *or*

   - A 'first legal mortgage' is a mortgage which on creation ranks in priority ahead of any other mortgages and takes effect as a mortgage to be protected by the deposit of documents relating to the mortgaged estate.

f) the grant of a lease under the 'right to buy' legislation (*HA 1985 Part 5*) out of an unregistered legal estate in land, *or*

g) a disposal by a landlord which leads to a tenant no longer being a secure tenant (*HA 1985 s 171A*) (including by means of the grant of lease out of an unregistered legal estate in land).

➤ A 'qualifying estate' is an unregistered legal estate which is a freehold estate in land, or a leasehold estate for a term which, at the time of the relevant event, has more than 7 years to run.

First registration (continued)

➤ The period for registration is 2 months beginning on the date the relevant event occurs (although the Registrar has discretion to extend this period) (*LRA 2002 s 6(4)-(5)*, *LRR 2003 rr 21-38*).

◆ Send *Form FR1*, the correct fee, relevant documents and a list of documents (*Form DL1*)).

◆ A caution against first registration may, in limited circumstances, be entered on the cautions register (*LRA 2002 ss 15-22*, *LRR 2003 rr 39-53*, *Practice Guide 3*, use *Form CT1*) .

➤ If the requirement is not complied with the transfer, grant or creation becomes void as regards the legal estate (*LRA 2002 s 7(1)*).

◆ Title to the legal estate:

• (in the case of a transfer within a) or c) in the box on p 238) reverts to the transferor who holds on bare trust for the transferee (*LRA 2002 s 7(2)(a)*), *or*

• (in the case of a transfer within b) in the box on p 238) reverts to the person in whom it was vested immediately before the transfer (*LRA 2002 s 7(2)(aa)*).

◆ In the case of the grant of a lease or creation of a first protected mortgage, the grant or creation takes effect as a contract for valuable consideration to grant or create the relevant legal estate (*LRA 2002 s 7(2)(b)*).

◆ The transferee, grantee or mortgagor:

• is, on a retransfer, regrant or remortgage, liable to the other party for all proper costs of and incidental to retransfer, regrant or remortgage, *and*

• is liable to indemnify such a person in respect of any other liability reasonably incurred by that person because of the failure to comply with the requirement of registration (*LRA 2002 s 8*).

➤ Where the requirement of registration does not apply, an unregistered legal estate in land, a rentcharge, a franchise or a profit à prendre may be registered by a person who such an estate is vested in or who is entitled to have such an estate vested in him (*LRA 2002 s 3*).

➤ An application may not be made under *LRA 2002 s 3* in respect of a lease unless that lease was granted for a term of which more than 7 years are unexpired and the right to possession under the lease is not discontinuous.

Requirement to register certain dispositions of registered land

➤ A disposition of a registered estate, or a registered charge, which is required to be completed by registration does not operate at law until the registration requirements are met (*LRA 2002 s 27(1)*).

   ◆ The registration requirements also apply to dispositions by operation of law, other than a transfer on death or bankruptcy of an individual, a transfer on dissolution of a body corporate, or the creation of a legal charge which is a local land charge (*LRA 2002 s 27(5)*).

   ◆ The registration requirements (*LRA 2002 Sch 2*) are satisfied by the registration on the register of the transferee, grantee, or chargee (or a successor in title) as proprietor of the relevant legal interest (*LRA 2002 s 27(4)*).

Dispositions which are required to be completed by registration

➤ In the case of a registered estate these are (*LRA 2002 s 27(3)*):

   a) a transfer, *and*

   b) where the registered estate is an estate in land, the grant of a lease of a term of years absolute:

      i)   for a term of more than 7 years from the date of the grant, *or*

      ii) to take effect in possession after the end of the period of 3 months beginning with the date of the grant, *or*

      iii) under which the right to possession is discontinuous, *or*

      iv) in pursuance of the right to buy (under *HA 1985 Part 5*), *or*

      v)   where a landlord makes a disposal which leads to a person ceasing to be a secured tenant under *HA 1985 s 171A, and*

   c) where the registered estate is a franchise or manor, the grant of a lease, *and*

   d) the express grant or reservation of an interest within *LPA 1925 s 1(2)(a)* (ie: an easement or profit à prendre), other than an interest capable of registration under the *CRA 2006, and*

   e) the express grant or reservation of an interest within *LPA 1925 s 1(2)(b)/(e)* (ie: certain rentcharges or rights of entry exercisable over or annexed to a rentcharge), *and*

   f) the grant of a legal charge.

➤ In the case of a registered charge these are (*LRA 2002 s 27(3)*):

   a) a transfer, *and*

   b) the grant of a subcharge.

➤ Send to HM Land Registry, an application (*Form AP1*), transfer (*Form TR1*) and fee, *plus* (as appropriate):

   ◆ a discharge of a registered charge (*Form DS1*) (or indicate that the lender has discharged the charge by using an electronic discharge *e-DS1*).

   ◆ application to enter any relevant restriction (*Form RX1*) or notice (*Form AN1*).

   ◆ the new mortgage deed (and a certified copy).

   ◆ if the seller is a PR, a certified copy of the grant of representation.

   ◆ if the transfer was executed under a special power of attorney limited to the disposal the original power, *or* a certified copy of any other type of attorney.

   ◆ a SDLT certificate (*SDLT 5*), if needed.

Checking Identity

➤ In an attempt to combat an increase in fraud HM Land Registry now requires identity checks to be made (HM Land Registry, *Practice Guide 67 (Conveyancers), Public Guide 20 (Non-conveyancers)*); however identity evidence for a lender's attorney is not required for a *form DS1*, *form DS3* or a deed of substituted security.

➤ Confirmation of identity will be required in the following situations (although in some cases there may be exceptions such as where the true value of land is over £5,000):

◆ a transfer of a registered estate or registered charge, *and*

◆ a transfer or deed relating to the appointment or retirement of trustees, *and*

◆ a lease of a registered estate, *and*

◆ a legal charge, *and*

◆ a discharge of a registered charge in paper *form DS1*, *and*

◆ a release of a registered charge in *form DS3*, *and*

◆ a surrender of a registered lease, *and*

◆ an application for compulsory first registration where the deed inducing registration is dated on or after 10 November 2008.

◆ a voluntary application for first registration where title documents have been lost.

◆ an application to change the name of a registered proprietor.

● HM Land Registry may ask for proof of identity in other cases, and may extend its requirements to other types of application at short notice.

➤ If proof of identity is required, a conveyancer (eg: a solicitor), must either:

a) provide details of the conveyancers acting for any other relevant party (a transferor, transferee, landlord, tenant, borrower, lender, and an attorney acting for any of them), *or*

b) if a party is not legally represented either:

i) confirm that the conveyancer is satisfied that sufficient steps have been taken to verify the identity of each relevant party, *or*

● Confirmation of identity is not required in the case of certain parties, including a trustee in bankruptcy, liquidator and administrator as these parties will need to lodge evidence of their authority to act with any application.

● If it is not possible to confirm identity, the conveyancer must explain in a letter why this is the case; absence abroad will not usually be an acceptable reason (a foreign notary public or member of staff at a British embassy or consulate should provide verification in these circumstances).

ii) attach evidence of identity of each relevant party using *form ID1* (for an individual) or *form ID2* (for a company) and verify each relevant party's identity.

● Where an application is lodged in person, HM Land Registry is prepared to verify the identity of the person lodging the application (rather than a conveyancer doing so).

● A company's identity should not be verified without satisfactory evidence that the company exists, the individual representing it is authorised to act, and the company is indeed the registered proprietor of the land (or the person entitled to be registered as a proprietor of the land).

➤ Where proof of identity is required, and is not provided, an application will be rejected.

➤ Further guidance is provided by the joint Law Society and Land Registry Practice Note 'Property and Registration Fraud' (September 2010).

HM Land Registry - 'early completion' policy

➤ On 3 August 2009 HM Land Registry introduced a new policy with respect to the receipt of a multiple application for a discharge of an existing charge of whole accompanied by another application (*Land Registry Practice Bulletin 16*, April 2009).

➤ Under the 'old' practice, if proof had not yet been provided in relation to a discharge, HM Land Registry would raise a requisition and would normally 'stand over' the application for discharge during the requisition period if it appeared that the borrower was using its best efforts to obtain the proof of discharge, and retain the application until the necessary evidence had been provided.

◆ HM Land Registry would then register all the applications in the order in which the transactions to which they related had taken place (eg: the discharge, then a new transfer, than a new charge, etc).

◆ If the evidence was not provided, HM Land Registry would cancel not only the application for discharge but also the applications to register the transfer and new charge.

➤ Under HM Land Registry's 'new' policy, if proof has not yet been provided in relation to a discharge, it will reject the application for the discharge and will enter the other applications on the register as soon as possible.

◆ The rationale for this is that the interest of the buyer should not be jeopardised by a refusal to register the transfer due to delay in completing the discharge of the prior charge.

◆ It should be noted, however, that under the 'new' policy, if there is a restriction on the register in favour of the existing lender, HM Land Registry will requisition for evidence of discharge. If the requisition is not addressed, any part of the application (which, in the case of a restriction against any disposition, will be the entire application) affected by the restriction will be rejected.

◆ Where rejection is likely, the buyer should obtain a new priority search.

➤ For practical guidance on the issues this policy raises see the Law Society's practice note 'Land Registry Early Completion' (9 July 2009).

B Checking title and making searches

I   Unregistered title
II   Registered title
III Searches

I   Unregistered title

A Freehold title

Root of title
A valid title has a 'root' which may be (*LPA s 44*):

either a) a conveyance on sale, or legal mortgage at least 15 years old (this is preferable),

or   b) a voluntary assent or conveyance made after 1925,

and   it must be at the start of a chain which is uninterrupted up to the present day.

It is not necessary to look behind the root except for (*LPA s 45*):

➤   an abstract of a power of attorney under which an abstracted document was executed, *or*

➤   earlier documents referred to in an abstract, *or*

➤   a plan referred to in the abstract, *or*

➤   any limitation or trust over any part of property in an abstracted document, or any document creating a trust, or any limitation relating to a document forming part of the epitome.

Do an index map search to check there is no caution against first registration/C(iv) land charge.

Documents capable of forming title

1   Conveyance by trustees to themselves

➤ This may be a breach of trust, and is voidable unless ...

   a) ... there is *either*:

      i) a pre-existing contract to purchase land or an option or right of pre-emption in favour of a trustee or PR, *or*

      ii) a PR is a beneficiary under a will or intestacy, *or*

   b) ... the consent of the beneficiaries was obtained and all were *sui juris*, *or*

   c) ... the conveyance was sanctioned by the trust instrument, *or*

   d) ... the conveyance was executed under a court order.

2   **Conveyance by trustees of land**

➤ Prior to 1 January 1997 when *TLATA 1996* came into force land was held by PRs, trustees, tenants in common and joint tenants under a trust for sale. Subsequently, such land has been held under a trust of land by trustees who have a power to postpone sale and a power to sell land (*TLATA 1996 s 4*).

➤ A buyer takes free of any interests under a trust if he pays to 2 or more trustees, or a trust corporation (*LPA ss 2, 27*). A conveyance by an individual trustee needs further investigation.

◆ Valid receipt is not given if money is paid or receipt given by 1 person acting *either*:

a) as trustee and attorney for 1 or more trustees, *or*

b) as attorney for 2 or more trustees (*TDA 1999 s 7*).

➤ From 1 January 1997, a buyer of unregistered land does not take free of the trust (even if he pays to 2 trustees) if he is put on notice of any limitation of the trustees' power to convey *or* of their failure to take proper account of the beneficiaries' interests (*TLATA 1996 s 16*).

➤ Tenants in common

If only one tenant survives, the buyer should ask to see the death certificate, the grant of representation and the assent in favour of the tenant's successor under the will or intestacy.

➤ Joint tenants

A buyer can assume severance has not occurred if (*LP(JT)A 1964 s 1*):

a) no memorandum of severance is endorsed on the conveyance under which the joint tenants bought the property, *and*

b) no bankruptcy proceedings are registered against either joint tenant, *and*

c) the conveyance *either*:

i)   contains a recital that the seller is solely and beneficially entitled, *or*

ii) was executed pursuant to a contract for the sale of land dated before 1 July 1995, and the seller conveyed as 'beneficial owner'.

3   **Conveyance by PRs**

➤ If a grant is to 2 or more PRs, all must join the assent or conveyance.

➤ If only one PR survives, he can act alone.

◆ Check death certificate(s) to ensure the other PRs were deceased at the time of the transfer.

➤ An assent passes the property to a beneficiary under a will. It should:

◆ be in writing, *and*

◆ be to the beneficiary named, *and*

◆ be signed by all the surviving PRs, *and*

◆ if covenants are contained, be by deed (*AEA 1925 s 36(4)*).

➤ An assentee (or buyer) should demand an endorsement on the grant of representation, otherwise the trustees may subsequently defeat the assent by making a statement under the *AEA 1925 s 36* so that a subsequent buyer for value takes in priority to the assentee.

◆ A donee is not protected by statute against trustees defeating the assent in this manner.

4   **Voluntary dispositions below full market value**

➤ These may be revocable under *IA 1986* (see also *I(No 2)A 1994* for the position of a buyer who gives value to a seller where the seller has acquired land for a disposition which was below market value).

5   Conveyance from an attorney

➤ The buyer's position depends on the type of power of attorney which the seller has: ...

◆ ... if the seller uses a power of attorney (other than under an enduring/lasting power) the buyer takes clean title if the buyer acts in good faith without knowledge of revocation (revocation includes death) (*PAA 1971 s 4*).

● A buyer acquiring land from a seller under such a power is protected if (*PAA 1971 s 5(4)*) *either*:

a) the transaction occurred within 1 year of the power being granted, *or*

b) the buyer makes a statutory declaration within 3 months of completion (usually sent to the Land Registry with *Form AP1*) that he is ignorant of the revocation of the power.

▪ A buyer is protected if, within 3 months of the exercise of a trustee function, an attorney provides an 'appropriate statement' that at the time of exercise the donor had a beneficial interest in the property (*TDA 1999 s 2*).

◆ ... if the seller's attorney has an enduring power of attorney ('**EPA**') or lasting power of attorney ('**LPA**'), check with the Court of Protection/Public Guardian to ensure that the power was correctly registered.

◆ ... if a LPA is registered under *MCA Sch 1*, a buyer is protected if he has no knowledge either that a LPA was not created or of circumstances which would have terminated the donee's authority to act under that LPA (*MCA 2005 s 14(3)*, see also *s 14(4)*).

◆ ... if the seller's attorney is a beneficiary of a trust and has a power of attorney granted by a trustee under *TLATA 1996 s 9(1)*, the buyer is protected if he deals in good faith, having no knowledge of the power's revocation (eg: by the beneficiary ceasing to be entitled to an interest in possession (*TLATA 1996 s 9(4)*), and swears a statutory declaration to this effect within 3 months of completion of the purchase (*TLATA 1996 s 9(2)*).

➤ *TA 2000 s 11* enables a trustee to delegate delegable functions, see the 'Wills' Chapter.

◆ Delegation may be permitted by the trust instrument, by all the beneficiaries being *sui juris*, or *TA 1925 s 25* which permits delegation of powers and discretions in relation to land, the capital proceeds of land or income arising from land (subject to any prohibition in the trust instrument).

➤ Powers granted before 1 October 1971 are governed by *LPA ss 126-128*.

➤ It is no longer possible to make an EPA, but an EPA made before 1 October 2007 can be registered and may continue in force.

6   Conveyance from a lender

➤ Legal mortgages: if the lender sold under a power of sale there will be no receipt on a deed.

◆ For a building society mortgage receipted on or after 1 January 1987, valid receipt may be assumed if prescribed wording is present and the receipt is signed by an authorised person (*BSA 1986, Sch 4 para 2(3)*) (the receipt need not name the person making the payment to redeem the mortgage).

◆ For a building society mortgage receipted before 1 January 1987, or for a bank mortgage, ensure the receipt names the holder of the legal and equitable title as the payer of the debt. Otherwise, the receipt operates to transfer the mortgage (*LPA s 115*); so if a PR or a trustee redeems a mortgage, the receipt should state that no transfer is intended.

● If in doubt (or if the mortgage discharge post-dates the conveyance) make a land charge search against whoever bought from the borrower and ask for the title deeds from the lender/seller.

● If a property is sold under a lender's power of sale, check that the power had arisen.

Documents retained by the seller

➤ If a seller has at any time retained documents of title (eg: the original conveyance on a sale of part, or a trust instrument on sale by trustees), a conveyance may include (*LPA s 64*):

   a) an 'acknowledgement' entitling the buyer and any successor in title (but not a tenant paying rent) to demand whoever possesses the documents to produce them at the cost of the person making the request, *and*

   b) an 'undertaking' giving the buyer and any successor in title (but not a tenant paying rent) a remedy in damages if the documents are mislaid, or perish due to fire or undue care.

➤ A fiduciary (eg: lender, PRs, tenant for life, and trustee) is unlikely to have given an undertaking. If it has custody of documents, it may have given an acknowledgement.

Proving title

1   **Produce a sound root of title at least 15 years old**

   ➤ Include incumbrances not evidenced on the root, and which predate the root.

   ➤ A voluntary conveyance or assent will serve as a root provided it was made after 1925.

2   **Ensure that the root is sound**

   ➤ It should deal with *all* legal interests in the land.

   ➤ It should contain a recognisable description of the land.

   ➤ There are no elements which could cast doubt on the title.

3   **Produce an abstract, or an epitome of the title**

   ➤ List the documents comprising the root: these go to the buyer on completion (*StC 4.1.3, 4.6.5*).

   If the root is not sound consider whether defective title indemnity insurance is affordable and offers adequate protection

B Leasehold title

Proving title			
	Grant (lease)	**Grant (sub lease)**	**Assignment**
Open contract rules	No title is given if the lease is under 15 years	*LPA s 44*: a head lease and title root (eg: all assignments) going back at least 15 years	*LPA s 44*: the lease itself and all assignments going back at least 15 years
	No entitlement under *LPA s 44(2)* to call for deduction of freehold title		
StC 8.2.4.	If the lease will exceed 7 years, the seller provides everything necessary to give absolute title (ie: an epitome going back at least 15 years)		*StC 8.2.4* does not apply to assignments
Effect of a SpC?		To exclude *StC 8.2.4* if the head tenant never asked to see the freehold	To enable the buyer to check that the lease was validly granted *if* it was granted under 15 years ago (ie: right to call for head lease or evidence of reversionary title)

II   Registered title

A The 'Register'

➤ The Register is conclusive as to the proprietor of a registered estate in land (*LRA 2002 s 58*).

1   **Property Register *(LRR 2003 r 5)***

➤ This describes the property. The description does not exclude extraneous evidence from deeds, etc, unless the boundaries are 'fixed' by HM Land Registry at the proprietor's request.

➤ It gives details of:
  ◆ any mineral rights (*LRR 2003 rr 70-71*), *and*
  ◆ any rights from which the land benefits (*LRR 2003 rr 72-76*).

2   **Proprietorship Register *(LRR 2003 r 8)***

➤ This states, among other things, the class of title, the name of the proprietor, an address for service, indemnity covenants and positive covenants, and in the case of possessory title the name of the first registered proprietor (*LRR 2003 rr 64-65*).

3   **Charges Register *(LRR 2003 r 9)***

➤ This states, among other things, the date of the mortgage, the lender's name and an address for service on the lender.

Notices and restrictions

➤ A notice in respect of a registered estate or charge protects an interest (eg: a restrictive covenant) in registered land where an interest is intended to bind a person who acquires the land.

  ◆ No notice may be entered on the Register in respect of an excluded interest. An excluded interest is (*LRA 2002 s 33*):

  a) an interest under a trust of land, or a strict settlement under *SLA 1925*.

  b) a leasehold estate in land which is granted for a term of 3 years or less from the date of the grant and is not required to be registered.

  c) a restrictive covenant between lessor and lessee relating to demised premises.

  d) an interest capable of registration under *CRA 2006*.

  e) an interest in, or rights attached to, any coal, or coal mine, or rights under *CIA 1994*.

  ◆ An agreed notice in respect of home rights, an inheritance tax charge, an *ANLA 1992* notice, variation of a lease under *LTA 1987*, a public right or customary right can be entered on application (*LRA 2002 s 35, LRR 2003 rr 80-82, Form AN1* although for home rights *Forms HR1/HR2* are used).

  ◆ The Registrar may unilaterally enter a notice (*LRA 2002 s 35, LRR 2003 r 89, Form 83*).

  ◆ The Registrar may also enter a notice in respect of unregistered interests (*LRA 2002 s 37, LRR 2003 r 89*).

➤ A restriction regulates the circumstances in which a disposition of a registered estate or charge may be the subject of an entry on the Register (*LRA 2002 s 40*).

  ◆ To enter a restriction submit *Form RX1* (*LRA 2002 s 43, LRR 2003 rr 91-100*) and, eg: on the right to deal with land of a sole proprietor (*Form A*), trustees (*Form B*), PRs (*Form C*), a limited company, or a charity, etc (see *LRR 2003 Sch 1*).

➤ For a bankruptcy notice see *LRR 2003 r 165*, and for a restriction see *LRR 2003 r 166*.

Overriding interests under *LRA 2002*

➤ On required registration (ie: first registration) the following are binding (*LRA 2002 Sch 1*):

- ◆ a leasehold estate in land granted for a term not exceeding 7 years (not subject to the requirement of first registration under *LRA 2002 s 4*).

- ◆ an interest belonging to a person in actual occupation (except for an interest under *SLA 1925*).

- ◆ a legal easement or profit à prendre.

- ◆ a customary right or a public right.

- ◆ a local land charge.

- ◆ an interest in any coal, or a coal mine, or rights of any person under *CIA 1994 ss 38, 49, 51*.

- ◆ certain rights to mines and minerals created before 1925.

- ◆ a franchise.✶

- ◆ a manorial right.✶

- ◆ a right to rent reserved to the Crown on the granting of a freehold estate.✶

- ◆ a non-statutory right in respect of an embankment or sea/river wall.✶

- ◆ a right to payment *in lieu* of a tithe.✶

➤ On the making of a registrable disposition any right which would have been binding on first registration, *other than* (*LRA 2002 Sch 3*):

- ◆ a leasehold estate in land granted for a term not exceeding 7 years which is a registrable disposition.

- ◆ certain interests belonging to a person in actual occupation:

    i) under *SLA 1925, or*

    ii) the interest of a person of whom enquiry was made prior to the disposition who failed to disclose the right, *or*

    iii) an interest which belongs to a person whose occupation would not have been obvious on a careful inspection of the land at the time of the disposition and of which the person to whom the disposition is made does not have actual knowledge, *or*

    iv) a leasehold granted to take effect in possession after 3 months, which has not taken effect at the time of the disposition.

    - ◆ a legal easement or profit à prendre which is not registered under *CRA 2006 and*:

        i) is not within the actual knowledge of the person to whom the disposition is made, *and*

        ii) would not have been obvious on a reasonably careful inspection of the land.

- ◆ a PPP lease relating to transport in London (*LRA 2002 s 90*).

➤ *LRA 2002* preserves proprietary estoppel and mere equities (even if not noted on the Register) (*s 116*).

✶ These categories will cease to have effect at the end of the period of 10 years beginning on 13 October 2003 (*LRA 2002 s 117*).

NB: Transitional rules in *LRA 2002 Sch 12* govern the interaction of the new rules with the *LRA 1925*.

Rectification of the Register and state indemnity under *LRA 2002*

➤ The Registrar may rectify the Register if it is erroneous (*LRA 2002 Sch 4 para 5*).

➤ A person who suffers loss by reason of, eg: rectification of the Register, a mistake the correction of which would involve rectification, a mistake in an official search, a mistake in an official copy or the loss or destruction of a document lodged at the Registry for inspection or safe custody, is entitled to be indemnified by the Registrar (*LRA 2002 Sch 8*).

B Freehold title

There are three classes of freehold title

1   Absolute title (*LRA 2002 ss 9(2)-(3)*)

➤   Absolute title is (despite its name) still subject to interests which are the subject of a Register entry, unregistered interests (within *LRA 2002 Sch 1*) and interests acquired under *LA 1980* of which the proprietor has notice (*LRA 2002 s 11(4)*).

2   Possessory title (*LRA 2002 s 9(5)*)

➤   This title is subject to adverse interests subsisting, or capable of subsisting, at the date of first (or subsequent) registration.

3   Qualified title (*LRA 2002 s 9(4)*)

➤   The State indemnity excludes a specified defect in the title.

◆   The Registrar may upgrade a title after 12 years or when he is satisfied a different class of title is merited (eg: possessory title can be upgraded to absolute title) (*LRA 2002 ss 62-63, LRR 2003 rr 124-125*).

Proving title

LRA 2002 s 67

a)   A copy of Register entries.

b)   A copy of the filed plan.

➤   Evidence or abstract if the Register is inconclusive (for the fixing of boundaries, see *LRR 2003 rr 117-123*).

➤   Copy or abstract of any document mentioned on the Register (eg: a conveyance containing a restrictive covenant).

◆   Under *LRA 2002* a document kept by the Registrar referred to in the Register which is not an original is to be taken, as between the parties to a disposition, as correct and to contain all the material parts of the original document (*LRA 2002 s 120*).

◆   Note that a) and b) may *not* be excluded by a *Special Condition.*

StC 4.1.2

➤   Requires an official copy of items referred to in *LRR rr 134(1)(a)-(b),135(1)(a)* (ie: an individual register, a title plan referred to in an individual register, and any document referred to in the register of title and kept by the registrar).

➤   *LRA 2002 Part 8* provides for electronic conveyancing under which execution, communication to the Registrar and registration will take place simultaneously. Where electronic conveyancing takes place, the Register becomes conclusive as to as the priority of interests because creation and registration take place at the same moment in time.

➤   Where conveyancing does not take place electronically, the priority of any interest in registered land is determined by the date of creation (irrespective of whether the interest or disposition is registered) (*LRA 2002 s 28*), *unless* a disposition is made for valuable consideration in which case, on completion of that disposition, any preceding interest whose priority is not protected by registration is postponed to the registrable disposition (*LRA 2002 s 29*).

➤ Commonhold is a form of freehold title (*CLRA 2002 s 1*). Note, that if there is a transfer of a commonhold unit, there is also a transfer of an interest in a commonhold association. Consequently, a commonhold association should be notified; for a transfer by operation of law use *Form 12* (*CCS para 4.7.9*).

C Leasehold title

➤ In addition to absolute (*LRA 2002 s 10(2)*), qualified (*LRA 2002 s 10(5)*) and possessory title (*LRA 2002 s 10(6)*), there is a fourth class of leasehold title, 'good leasehold' title (*LRA 2002 s 10(3)*).

➤ The freehold reversion is unregistered, so the Registrar guarantees the lease only in so far as the grantor acted within his rights in granting the lease.

Proving leasehold title			
	Grant (lease)	Grant (sub lease)	Assignment
Open contract rules	As the Register is a public document it is possible to apply for an official copy of the Register		Under *StC 4.1.2* the seller must supply an official copy of the Register rather than just a copy
		There is *no* right to see the head lease	
StC 8.2.4.	Imposes an obligation to apply for an official copy of the register *StC 4.1.2* applies so a copy of an official copy of the register is insufficient	Imposes an obligation on the seller to produce an official copy of the Register and a copy of the head lease	*StC 8.2.4* does not apply. Insert a SpC requiring the assignee to produce an official copy of the Register showing absolute title. If the lease only carries good leasehold title, insert a *SpC* requiring the assignor to deduce satisfactory superior title (ie: absolute reversionary title, or a good root of title at least 15 years before the grant of the lease)

III   Searches

Checklist for making searches
1   Which searches are necessary?   Is the form being used the correct one?
2   If a plan is needed, are 2 correctly coloured copies attached and is the scale sufficiently large?
3   Have any additional questions been correctly entered on the form (eg: *CON29* Part II)?
4   Is the correct fee included with the form (telephone first to confirm the rate)?
5   Are the addresses of the property and that for the answers to the search correct?
➤ Make a file note when the search request is dispatched.
➤ Check the file and chase up any late responses with the relevant authorities.

Pre-contract searches			
Type of search	**Information**	**Protection**	**Application**
In all cases			
Enquiries of seller	The *Protocol* provides a standard form on which the seller lists fixtures, fittings and contents included in the sale	The seller can refuse to answer questions. Misrepresentation is the buyer's only protection	*Form SPIF (+ F&C)* There is a supplementary form for a tenant to fill in if a lease is being assigned
Local land charges	Information statute makes local authorities keep	Yes (*LLCA 1975 s 10*)	*Form LLC1*
Local authority	Information *not* required by statute: ➤ road schemes, *and* ➤ planning information, *and* ➤ smoke control orders, *and* ➤ imminent compulsory purchase orders	The authority, or water service company, is liable in negligence, subject to any exclusion clause on the search form	*Form CON29* Part I: for general queries Part II and additional enquiries: for specific matters, a charge is usually made for each item queried
Water service company	Water main and sewer records maintained by these companies under *WA 1989*		*Form CON29DW*
Coal Authority	Details of past, present and anticipated mineral extraction Check the Law Society's *Coal Mining Directory* for areas likely to be affected		*Form CON29M* is submitted to the surveyor at the Coal Authority's head office
Companies House	a) The company exists, *and* b) it has power to buy or sell land, *and* c) it is not in receivership, administration or liquidation, *and* d) that the land is not subject to a charge	None	Companies House search
Unregistered land			
Index Map	➤ Cautions against first registration ➤ Pending applications for registration		*Form SIM*
Land Charges Department	Incumbrances existing over unregistered land: a) easements and covenants affecting the land b) mortgages c) estate contracts d) occupation rights under *FLA 1996*	15 working day priority period	*Form K15* Search the names of all past and present title holders since 1926 (if known) for the period of their ownership of the estate. Search against any owner who made a voluntary disposition in the last 5 years. Search through pre-1973 counties as well as present day ones.
Registered land			
Official copies of the Register	Details of title and incumbrances at HM Registry (*LRA 2002 s 72, LRR 2003 rr 147-160*)		*Form OS3* non-priority search *Form OS1:* priority search (all) *Form OS2:* priority search (part) *Form PRD1:* produce docs
Index Map	List of registered titles within the relevant area		*Form SIM*
Law Society Search Validation Insurance Scheme			

➤ For residential properties selling for up to £500,000 (a premium is payable to take advantage of the scheme)
➤ The scheme covers the difference between the original market price of the property and its value with the adverse entry

Pre-completion searches		
Type of search	**Information**	**Application**
Unregistered land		
Land Charges Department	See p 251	
Registered land		
HM Land Registry search	See p 251. There is a 30 business day priority period	*Form OS1* whole of property *Form OS2* part of property
Land Charges Department	Details of *unregistered freehold* if a lease has good leasehold title	*Form K15* search against landlord's name
If acting in particular circumstances		
With a company involved in the transaction	Use this to check that: a) the company is not in receivership, administration or liquidation, *and* b) that the land is not subject to a charge	Companies House search
For a lender	Bankruptcy search against the buyer	*Forms K15* and *K16*
	If making a priority search against the Register, do so in the lender's name so the buyer is protected. Note that the lender is not protected if the search is done in the buyer's name	*Form OS1* for whole property *Form OS2* for part of property 30 business day priority period
When a grant of probate (or a certified copy) are not available	Check that a grant has been issued to the party concerned and is still valid	Principal Probate Registry
When a party will complete using an enduring power of attorney, or a lasting power of attorney	Check whether the power is registered, or registration is pending. An enduring power may only be used in limited circumstances (e.g. to maintain the donor or prevent loss to his estate) when registration is pending. A lasting power only becomes effective when it has been registered with the Public Guardian.	Probate Registry *Form EP4* / Office of the Public Guardian
If more than 3 months have passed since exchange	Repeat the Local Authority and Local Land Charges search	See p 251
If the contract is conditional on the results of subsequent searches		
House is under construction	Inspect the fabric to verify that it is satisfactory	Not applicable

Action if a pre-completion search shows an adverse entry

➤   Ascertain what the entry relates to.

➤   Contact the seller's solicitor and seek an undertaking that it will be removed prior to completion.

➤   If the search was at the Central Land Charges Department, apply for a copy of *Form 19* on which the entry was originally registered, to find out when (and by whom) it was registered.

➤   Keep client, lender and seller informed subject to the duty of confidentiality.

➤   Consider defective title indemnity insurance.

National Land Information Service ('NLIS')

➤ The NLIS allows certain searches to be carried out on the web.

◆ Data providers (eg: HM Land Registry) supply data to the NLIS hub and information is distributed from the NLIS hub by licensed channels (*www.searchflow.co.uk*, and *www.twpropertyinsight.co.uk*).

Searches

HM Land Registry and Land Charges Registry

➤	Home rights	*Form HR3*
➤	Official whole	*Form OS1*
➤	Index map search	*Form SIM*
➤	Official copies of the Register	
➤	Official copies of documents	
➤	Register view	
➤	Filed plan view	
➤	Daylist enquiry	
➤	ENDs enquiry	
➤	Computerised property description enquiry	
➤	Land charges search	*Form K15*
➤	Land charges bankruptcy	*Form K16*
➤	Land charges office copy	*Form K19*

Coal Authority

➤	Coal mining search	

Local authority

➤	Local land charges	*Form LLC1*
➤	Enquiries of a local authority	*Form Con 29*

Water service company

➤	Water mains and sewers	*Form Con 29DW*

➤ Both the NLIS and HM Land Registry accept requests for an electronic (rather than paper) official copy of a register of title, or title plan where the original is in electronic format; such an official copy is issued in 'pdf' format.

◆ A print from a 'pdf' will be an official copy, as will a forwarded 'pdf' file, provided in either case that the file has not been modified or corrupted.

◆ In determining whether an official copy is genuine, the HM Land Registry suggest asking: 'what does the document look like, and where did it come from?' (*Practice Guide 11*, December 2010).

Overview of HM Land Registry Electronic Services

➤ HM Land Registry's electronic services can be used by a qualified person who has entered into a network access agreement with HM Land Registry.

➤ Currently, electronic conveyancing is restricted to:

◆ an electronic discharge (e-DS1) (see p 255), *and*

◆ an electronic discharge (ED) (see p 255), *and*

◆ an electronic legal charge in standard form (e-CSF) (see p 255).

➤ HM Land Registry also accepts electronic lodgement of certain other applications via the Land Registry Portal (see below).

➤ On 30 June 2011 HM Land Registry announced that it had decided to postpone the introduction of full electronic conveyancing due to concerns over fraud, electronic signatures and the economic climate. Instead, HM Land Registry intends to offer a system whereby applications for most transactions affecting registered land can be lodged electronically.

Network Access Agreements

➤ There are 3 types of network access agreement (*LR(NA)R 2008 r 3*):

a) a 'full' agreement - this allows a subscriber to carry out network transactions.

b) a 'read only' agreement' - this allows a subscriber to retrieve information on the network.

c) a 'signature' agreement - this allows a subscriber to apply an electronic signature to a document and to retrieve information on the network (while not being a 'full' network access agreement).

➤ The criteria for entering into a full network access agreement are set out in *LR(NA)R 2008 Sch 1* and such an agreement must contain terms set out in *LR(NA)R 2008 Sch 2*.

◆ The types of person who can enter into a network access agreement with HM Land Registry include a solicitor, a licensed conveyancer, a barrister, a duly certified notary public and a registered European lawyer (*LR(NA)R 2008 Sch 1 para 1*).

◆ A subscriber must indemnify HM Land Registry for any loss and damage arising from the intentional, reckless or negligent misuse of the Land Registry network, breach of the network access agreement by the subscriber, negligent acts, errors or submissions by the subscriber or failure by the subscriber to establish his client's true identity (*LR(NA)R 2008 Sch 2 para 17*).

Electronic lodgement via the Land Registry Portal

➤ The following applications affecting the whole of a title can be lodged through the Land Registry Portal:

◆ to enter a restriction or a unilateral notice.

◆ on the death of a joint proprietor

◆ to cancel a caution, a notice, a unilateral notice, or a restriction.

◆ to change an address (eg for service), a name (on marriage/civil partnership, or deed poll), or a property description.

◆ to withdraw a caution, or a restriction.

◆ to enter a notice of home rights, or an agreed notice.

Electronic Conveyancing

1   Electronic legal charge in standard form

➤ The ability to create an electronic legal charge in standard form ('**e-CSF**') is facilitated by *LRA 2002 s 93*, and represents the first substantive step towards a system of electronic conveyancing.

◆ When an electronic legal charge is created, the Register is conclusive as to as the priority of interests because creation and registration takes place at the same moment in time.

➤ An electronic legal charge can be created over the whole of a registered estate in a single registered title.

◆ An e-CSF cannot be created in the context of a dealing prior to first registration, the grant of a legal charge by a body corporate, or where a charge is authenticated by a person other than the borrower (*LR(EC)R 2008 r 3(2)*).

➤ When an electronic legal charge is authenticated the borrower (or joint borrower):

a) must be registered as the proprietor of the registered estate that is charged, *or*

b) notice of an application to register that person as the registered proprietor (or joint proprietor) of the registered estate that is charged must be entered in the daily list (*LR(EC)R 2008 r 3(3)*).

➤ An electronic legal charge must:

a) be personally authenticated by the borrower (*LR(EC)R 2008 r 3(4)*), *and*

b) contain information set out or permitted by *LR(EC)R 2008 Sch 1*, *and*

c) be prepared using a procedure permitted by HM Land Registry (*LR(EC)R 2008 r 3(5)(a)*).

● A charge may be drafted automatically using an E-MD reference (*LR(EC)R 2008 r 3(6)*).

● Each electronic signature on a charge, and the certification of each such signature, must be made in accordance with the provisions of the network access agreement (*LR(EC)R 2008 r 3(5)(b)*).

➤ The Registrar sends the person who notifies it of a charge an acknowledgement stating the time and date when notification of the charge is received (*LR(EC)R 2008 r 4*).

2   Electronic discharge through HM Land Registry Portal

➤ An electronic form of discharge ('**e-DS1**') may be submitted by a corporate lender or its authorised agent through the portal and acts as both the evidence of discharge and an application to remove the charge from the register (*HM Land Registry Practice Guide 31*, January 2010, para 8).

➤ Once an e-DS1 has been submitted HM Land Registry issues an electronic acknowledgment to the user.

➤ An e-DS1 is often processed automatically so that the register is updated in a matter of seconds.

◆ However where, for example, there is a prior pending application against the title concerned, that prior application must be completed before a charge can be cancelled.

3   Electronic discharge by a lender using a virtual private network connected to HM Land Registry

➤ An electronic discharge ('**ED**') enables a lender to cancel a discharge of whole via a secure virtual private network (*HM Land Registry Practice Guide 31*, January 2010, para 7).

➤ A number of security features have been incorporated to ensure that only lenders can send EDs to HM Land Registry.

C Variations to the standard contract

I   Conditional contracts
II   Sale of part
III   New buildings

I Conditional contracts

➤ The terms and conditions must be clear and certain.

- ◆ If planning permission is needed:

  - • decide, if conditions are attached, what would entitle the buyer to rescind.   In particular, consider whether the buyer may rescind if:

    - ▪ planning permission is not granted within a specified period, *or*

    - ▪ a planning application is never submitted.

  - • settle who pays the fee for the application.

  - • agree whether the application for planning permission should be for outline or for full consent, and the form of application.

➤ The contract should deal with all these issues and it must state unambiguously:

- ◆ the precise event on which the contract is conditional.

- ◆ by what time any conditions must be fulfilled.

- ◆ the exact terms on which the party with the benefit of the condition may rescind.

➤ Ensure there are no loopholes, except the single express condition enabling a party to rescind.

II Sale of part

The transaction proceeds as normal (see p 200 for 'step' chronology), with these differences.

Step 1: Taking instructions

➤ Obtain the consent of any lender with a charge over the land.

- ◆ Unregistered land: the lender executes a deed of release, or is joined to the conveyance.

- ◆ Registered land: the part to be sold is released from the mortgage by the lender completing *Form DS3,* to which a plan will be attached.

Step 2: Seller prepares the pre-contract package

> ➤ There must be a scale plan, and a definition of the land sold and retained.

>> ◆ Registered land: use the title plan approved by HM Land Registry, or supply a plan which complies with the requirements of the *LRR 2003* (see further *Practice Guide 40*).

> ➤ Adapt the contract: draft any appropriate *Special Conditions.*

Protect the retained land from implied rights in favour of the plot disposed of	➤ Ensure that the sale does not include: any easement of way, light, or air which might interfere with, or restrict the free use of the retained land, for building or any other purpose. ➤ The transfer to the buyer should expressly exclude any such rights.
Impose new covenants	➤ These should be stated expressly. ➤ Covenants which are negative in substance are advantageous as they will run with the land. ➤ If covenants are to be enforceable against future owners they must be: a) expressly taken for the benefit of the retained land, *and* b) registered at HM Land Registry or the Land Charges Department.
Grant any easements in favour of the plot over the retained land	➤ These may be needed to gain access to the plot, or connect services to it.

Step 6: Buyer prepares the transfer

> ➤ Unregistered land: a professional drawn plan is advisable, though not essential.

>> ◆ Include in the transfer an acknowledgement that the seller has produced title deeds to the retained land and that they are in safe custody (*LPA s 64, StC 4.6.5*).

> ➤ Registered land: fill in the seller's title number on the purchase deed (*Form TP1*) and attach a title plan approved by HM Land Registry or a plan which complies with the guidelines in *Practice Guide 40*.

> ➤ If the land is a commonhold unit, the CCS must be updated using *form CM3* (*C(LR)R 2004 r 15*)

Step 7: Preparing for completion

> ➤ Registered land: make a pre-completion search on *Form OS2* attached to a plan.

Step 8: Completion

> ➤ Unregistered land

>> ◆ The buyer's solicitor marks the abstract or epitome as examined against the original.

>>> ● The seller's solicitor is required to provide an abstract or epitome as part of the pre-contract package and mark it as examined against the original under *Protocol 24(3)*.

>> ◆ A memorandum of sale is endorsed on the seller's most recent title deed (*LPA s 200*).

>> ◆ The seller's solicitor takes a note of any restrictive covenants which have been imposed, and keeps this with his documents of title.

Step 9: Post-Completion

> ➤ If the land is a commonhold unit, give notice (using *Form 11*) to the commonhold association of transfer of part of a unit within 14 days of the new owner becoming entitled to be registered a proprietor of that part of the unit (*CCS para 4.7.8*).

>> ◆ Use *Form CM3* to register the transfer at HM Land Registry (*C(LR)R 2004 r 15*).

III   New buildings

This is the same as for a freehold (see p 200 for 'step' chronology), with these additions:

Step 2: Seller prepares the contract

➤ The Law Society's form *TA 8* (New home information form) includes information which a developer or seller may wish to provide.

◆ If a property is incomplete, a predicted energy performance certificate may initially be provided. However, a full energy performance certificate and information relating to sustainability will be required once the property is 'physically complete'.

Step 3: Buyer approves the contract

➤ The contract is likely to be in a standard form which the developer wishes to use for the whole development.   It may be that the seller is consequently reluctant to negotiate terms which differ from the standard model.   Nonetheless, the buyer's solicitor must ensure that:

◆ any restrictive covenants to which the land is subject do not unduly restrict the buyer's use of the property and any new covenants to be imposed in the transfer are not too onerous.

◆ the seller undertakes to remedy any minor defects ('snagging') which emerge after completion within a specified time (and/or that the buyer is protected by an NHBC 'Buildmark' insurance policy).

◆ the seller undertakes to leave the property in 'ship-shape and Bristol fashion' and will:

• landscape the development appropriately.

• hand the property over in a neat state and remove all builder's rubble.

• erect suitable boundary fences.

◆ extra payments for fixtures and fittings (jacuzzis, washing machines, etc) are quantified.

◆ a plan is supplied with the contract and is accurate.

◆ a 'long stop' completion date is incorporated in the contract.   This should enable the buyer to rescind the contract if the work is unfinished after the time agreed. The seller may ask for completion to take place a certain number of days after work on the site is finished, in which case the buyer's solicitor should ensure that:

• the period before completion is long enough for pre-completion searches and site inspections by the buyer and his lender.

• the buyer has alternative accommodation while waiting for completion.

• the buyer has access to bridging finance for this period of time, and that the buyer is given enough notice of the works being completed for the lender to put the buyer's solicitor in funds.

➤ If the seller offers a financing package, ensure that the buyer is properly (by a permitted third party, if appropriate) advised on whether it is suitable for his needs.

➤ The seller may offer comfort in the form of an NHBC 'Buildmark' insurance policy, or a similar product. A 'Buildmark' policy protects the buyer and his successors in title against structural defects for 10 years after completion.   The buyer is insured against the builder's default, including its insolvency, for 2 years after completion.

◆ A lender may insist on such insurance cover.

➤ Examine a copy of any agreement between the developer and the highway authority under which the developer will put in roads and street lighting, and the authority will adopt them at a later stage (these agreements are authorised under *HA 1980 s 38*).   Ensure the agreement is backed by an adequate bond, in case the developer becomes insolvent before completing its obligations.

  ◆ Similar considerations apply to drains and sewers, and agreements with the water authority under *WIA 1991 s 104*.

  ◆ Ensure there are appropriate easements (eg: to use roads) so that the buyer will have a right of access prior to adoption.

  ◆ Note that if the bond is inadequate the buyer may have to pay for the works to be carried out or for adoption.

Step 9: Post-completion

➤ Ensure the buyer receives the following documentation, and that it is kept with the title deeds:

  ◆ an NHBC pack (if appropriate).   Return the tear-off form to the NHBC.

  ◆ a 'final certificate' from the local authority confirming that planning consent and building regulations have been complied with.

➤ Before 2 year cover under a 'Buildmark' policy against the builder's default runs out, advise the buyer to carry out a full structural survey to reveal any latent defects.

➤ If the property is a commonhold unit and no other units have yet been sold, the Register will indicate through a series of entries and restrictions on the Proprietorship Register that during a transitional period the rights and duties imposed by the CCS are not in force (as the title both to the common parts and every unit will be registered in the name of the original applicant for the land to be held as a commonhold).

  ◆ On the first unitholder becoming registered the CCS comes into force, the common parts are registered in the name of the commonhold association, and the entries on the Register relating to the transitional period will be removed.

D Leases

I   Drafting a lease - outline points
II   Management schemes
III   Procedure for granting a lease
IV   Procedure for assigning a lease
V   Obtaining a landlord's consent to an assignment or transfer
VI   Procedure for assigning a lease over a commonhold unit
VII   Procedure for selling a reversion

I Drafting a lease - outline points

1 Definitions section

2 Grant

➤ The premium, ie: the sum which the tenant pays the landlord for the grant of the lease (usually only if the lease is for a relatively long term).

➤ The term, ie: how long the lease lasts for.

➤ Starting date, ie: when the term runs from; this need *not* be the date of completion as the landlord may wish a batch of leases to start on the same day irrespective of when he finds tenants so as to ensure that the reversion dates are the same.

➤ Ground rent: this is often paid on the quarter days.

➤ Rent review: basis of calculation/frequency.

> **Quarter days**
>
> Lady Day: 25 March
> Midsummer Day: 24 June
> Michaelmas: 29 September
> Christmas: 25 December

2 Easements and reservations

3 Common parts

➤ Identify these, provide for their maintenance and repair. This is usually done through a periodic service charge.

4 Tenant's covenants

➤ To pay rent, repair, not to make alterations or improvements, not to change user, or alienate the lease (eg: by subletting the property without the landlord's consent).

5 Landlord's covenants: to insure and keep common parts in repair

6 Insurance

➤ This can be achieved in several ways, but contributions to a block policy taken out by the landlord (or management company) ensure tenants are covered for the same risks.

7 Cesser of rent

➤ Lease may provide that a tenant may cease to pay rent if a building is burnt down, or on specified events.

8 Forfeiture clause

➤ This states in what circumstances the landlord may regain possession. A court order is needed for an occupied dwelling (*PEA 1977 s 2*). On breach of covenant, a notice is usually served under the *LPA s 146*.

Flats: common law presumptions

a)   If the tenant is not responsible for something, then the landlord is presumed to be so.

b)   External walls are included in the demise, even if the landlord is responsible for repair.

c)   A flat includes the ceiling, at least to the underside of the floor joists to which the ceiling is attached.

d)   If the ownership of a roof is not expressly reserved by the landlord, the top floor tenant can occupy or alter it (eg: build extra stories).

e)   There is *no* presumption that internal boundary walls divide flats from each other or from common parts; therefore an accurate plan marking the extent of the flat, common parts and rights of way is essential.

II   Management schemes

These schemes govern how an estate is maintained; there are 3 types of scheme commonly used.

1   The landlord manages the estate either directly, or through an agent

✗ The landlord cannot walk away and wash his hands of day to day administration.

✗ Tenants are not given the freedom to organise things as they wish.

✗ Tenants do not have a contractual right to ensure their neighbours comply with their covenants. They rely on the landlord to police covenants which he has with each tenant.

2   Tenants covenant with each other by deed of covenant

✗ There is no co-ordination or general oversight - each tenant is on his own.

✗ Enforcement can be haphazard and difficult.

3   A management company is set up

✓ Enforcement by the company is practicable.

✓ The landlord is freed from the burden of administration.

✓ The landlord retains his investment in the reversion.

➤ There are 2 ways of setting up a private company (see the 'Business' Chapter): in both cases the landlord grants the lease and covenants to provide services. Then *either*:

   a)   at a later date, the management company can join the lease and the landlord irrevocably instructs the tenant to pay the service charge to the company in consideration of the company undertaking the service obligations, *or*

   b)   the landlord grants the company a concurrent lease of the block (effectively leasing the reversion). During the lease, the company becomes the tenant's landlord and provides the services specified in the lease', *or*

   c)   transfer of reversion to a management company (only if the reversion has no real value).

III   Procedure for granting a lease

This is the same as for a freehold conveyance (see p 200 for 'step' chronology), with these additions:

Step 2: Seller prepares the pre-contract package

➤ The landlord drafts the lease and the contract. He sends the buyer:

- ◆ proof of the freehold title (see pp 246 and 249), *and*

- ◆ if the lease is over a commonhold unit, a copy of the CCS and *Form 13* (notifying the tenant that it will be required to comply with the parts of the CCS which confer duties on him) (*CCS para 4.7.12*), *and*

- ◆ evidence that any lender with a charge over the land consents (if such consent is required as a term of the mortgage) to the grant of the lease and any alterations to the property, *and*

- ◆ a draft contract and a draft lease.

  - ● If the lease is a prescribed clause lease (*LRR 2003 r 58A*) granted on or after 19 June 2006, it must either begin with required wording (eg: landlord's title number, parties, premium, term etc.) set out in *LRR 2003 Sch 1A*, or that wording must appear after any front sheet.

Liability on covenants

➤ For leases granted on or after 1 January 1996 (other than under an agreement entered into, or a court order made before that date *or* assignments made by operation of law after that date) the tenant is released from covenants on any subsequent assignment (*LT(C)A 1995 s 5*).

➤ The landlord can protect his position by inserting a covenant that the tenant shall:

a) secure adequate references from a future assignee and other requirements relating to financial standing.

b) enter into an 'authorised guarantee agreement' under which the tenant agrees to guarantee the performance of any covenants by the assignee until the assignee makes another assignment (or the tenancy is assigned by operation of law) (*LT(C)A 1995 s 16*).

Step 3: Buyer approves the contract

➤ The buyer checks the freehold title.

➤ The buyer should also discover whether the lease is sufficiently marketable and whether it will remain so if the buyer envisages assigning the term before the lease expires.

- ◆ Banks and building societies are reluctant to lend money for leases of under 60 years.

Step 6: Landlord prepares the 'deed'

➤ The landlord sends a fair copy to the buyer at least 5 working days before completion (*StC 8.2.5*).

- ◆ Note that a lease for less than 3 years does not need to be by deed (*LPA s 53*) (or in writing (*LPA ss 52(2)(d), 54(2)*)).

Step 9: Post-completion

➤ Any SDLT payable should be paid and an SDLT certificate obtained for forwarding to HM Land Registry.

➤ In the case of a grant of a lease for exactly 7 years, which is not notifiable to HMRC, there is, strictly speaking, an obligation on the lessee to obtain a PD stamp from HMRC (*FA 1931 s 28*).

➤ If the lease is granted over a commonhold unit, notify (using *Form 14*) the commonhold association within 14 days beginning on the date the tenancy is granted (*CCS para 4.17.15*).

IV   Procedure for assigning a lease

This is the same as for a freehold conveyance (see p 200 for 'step' chronology), with these additions:

Step 2: Seller (ie: assignor) prepares the pre-contract package

➤ The seller should ensure that the contract contains an indemnity for the covenants.

◆ Prior to 1 January 1996 (at common law - but could be overridden by contract), *LPA s 77* provided for an indemnity where value was given for the estate in land.

◆ For leases granted on or after 1 January 1996 an indemnity is effectively provided for (*LT(C)A 1995, StC 4.6.4*).

➤ The seller should consider the relevant covenants as to title.

Covenants as to title	Where a disposition is made with full title or limited title guarantee, a leaseholder covenants that at the time of the disposition (*LP(MP)A 1994 s 4*): ◆ there is no breach of the tenant's obligations and nothing to render the lease liable to forfeiture, *and* ◆ the lease is subsisting. Note that StC 4.6.3 provides that the transfer of leasehold property is to contain a statement that the covenants implied by *LP(MP)A 1994 s 4* do not extend to any breach of the tenant's covenants relating to the physical state of the property

NB: these covenants may be modified by drafting an appropriate *SpC*

➤ The seller sends the buyer (ie: the assignee):

Pre-contract package

◆ the landlord's licence(s) permitting assignment (in the past and consent this time), *and*

◆ proof of leasehold title (unregistered title, see p 246; registered title, see p 250), *and*

◆ a copy of the original lease, *and*

◆ a *Leasehold Information Form* (*TA 7*) ('LIF') and a *Fitting and Contents Form* (*TA 10*) ('FCF'), *and*

◆ a copy of the insurance policy, and a receipt for the last premium payment, *and*

◆ a copy of the receipt for the last payment of rent and the service charge, *and*

◆ a lender's consent to the assignment (if required under the terms of a loan subject to which the property is charged).

Step 4: Preparations for exchange

➤ As well as checking the lease, the LIF/FCF, the contract, the consents and the seller's title, the buyer must ensure:

◆ any references the landlord requires are prepared, *and*

◆ a surety is found (if required by the lease).

Step 7: Preparing for completion

➤ The seller should take the necessary steps to obtain the landlord's consent.

   ◆ The apportionment of rent or service charge should be checked (this is governed by *StC 6.3*). The buyer should ask to see service charge accounts for recent years.

Step 9: Post-completion

➤ Any SDLT should be paid and an SDLT certificate obtained for forwarding to HM Land Registry.

➤ Send two copies of a notice of dealing to the landlord (and lender if appropriate) - the second copy to be receipted and returned.

➤ In the case of an assignment of a lease for exactly 7 years, which is not notifiable to HMRC, there is, strictly speaking, an obligation on the transferee to obtain a PD stamp from HMRC (*FA 1931 s 28*).

V   Obtaining a landlord's consent to an assignment or transfer

➤   A lease may prohibit assignment/transfer of the whole or part of the demised premises.

1   Qualified covenants **(ie: where the landlord covenants not to unreasonably withhold consent)**

      ➤   Consent may not be unreasonably withheld (*LTA 1927 s 19*).

      ◆   For leases granted on or after 1 January 1996 (except those granted under an agreement or court order dated before that date) ...

          ... over property which is *not* let as a private residence, ...

              ... the landlord shall not be regarded as acting unreasonably if he refuses to grant consent, or agrees to grant it subject to conditions, if the landlord cites a reason listed in an agreement with the tenant (eg: not to assign without securing for the landlord adequate references) (*LTA 1927 s 19A*).

      ➤   The landlord must respond within a 'reasonable' time, and must grant consent unless it is reasonable to withhold it (*International Drilling Fluids Ltd v. Louisville Investments (Uxbridge) Ltd* [1986] 1 EGLR 39).

      ◆   The landlord must send the tenant a notice giving any conditions attached to the consent or reasons for refusing it (*LTA 1988 s 1(3)*).

      ➤   The seller is responsible for seeking consent and using 'all reasonable efforts' to obtain it. If he fails, the buyer's remedy is rescission (*StC 8.3.2-3*).

      ➤   The landlord does not usually charge a premium, but he may ask the tenant to pay a reasonable administrative charge to cover his expenses.

      ➤   The licence is written, but it is not by deed unless it contains a covenant by the buyer (assignee).

      ◆   The landlord sends the seller a licence and retains a copy with his deeds of title.

2   **Absolute covenants prohibiting assignment**

      ➤   If the lease prevents assignment, a tenant who wishes to assign may be able to persuade the landlord to:

      a)   grant a deed of release from the covenant against assignment, *or*

      b)   vary the lease, *or*

      c)   give consent.

Transfer of part - leases granted after 1 January 1996

➤   The general rule is that the tenant ceases to be liable for the covenants given by the tenant, or to be entitled to the benefits of covenants given by the landlord, in respect of the part of the premises which he assigns (*LT(C)A 1995 s 5(3)*).

➤   If the performance of a covenant is not attributable to the tenant or the assignee, the parties can agree to apportion liability (*LT(C)A 1995 s 9*) provided that before or within 4 weeks of the assignment the parties serve a notice on the landlord detailing the assignment, their agreement and their request that he should be bound by the apportionment.

    ◆   If the landlord does not serve a notice objecting to the apportionment within 4 weeks of service on him, he is bound (if he does object, the parties may apply to the County Court for a declaration that it is reasonable for the apportionment to bind him) (*LT(C)A 1995 s 10*).

      •   A notice should comply with the *LT(C)A(N)R 1995*.

VI Procedure for assigning a lease over a commonhold unit

This is the same as for assigning any other lease, with these additions:

Step 2: Seller (ie: assignor) prepares the pre-contract package

➤ If the lease is over a commonhold unit, a copy of the CCS and *Form 15* (notifying the tenant that it will be required to comply with the parts of the CCS which confer duties on him) (*CCS para 4.7.16*).

Step 9: Post-completion

➤ If the lease is granted over a commonhold unit, notify (using *Form 14*) the commonhold association within 14 days beginning on the date the tenancy is granted (*CCS para 4.17.19*).

VII Procedure for assigning a reversion

This is the same as for a freehold conveyance (see p 200 for 'step' chronology), with these additions:

Step 2: Assignor (ie: landlord) prepares the pre-contract package

➤ The seller discloses the leases which have been granted over the property, together with details of the service charge accounts.

Steps 4 to 9: Assignor and assignee comply with the requirements of *LT(C)A 1995*

➤ The landlord may apply to be released from his covenants under the tenancy (*LT(C)A 1995 s 6(2)*), and a former landlord who immediately before the assignment was bound by a covenant under that tenancy may also apply for release (*LT(C)A 1995 s 7(2)*).

♦ The procedure involves service on the tenant of a notice before or within 4 weeks of the assignment, and an opposition procedure within 4 weeks of the date of service, similar to that set out in the box on p 265 (*LT(C)A 1995 s 8*).

➤ Any release of liability in respect of the landlord's covenants is accompanied by a loss of the benefit of the tenant's covenants.

➤ If the landlord only assigns the reversion in part and wishes to apportion liability in respect of non-attributable covenants which the landlord is obliged to perform, a procedure similar to that for tenants assigning part of the demised premises should be followed (*LT(C)A 1995 s 9(2)*).

♦ For this procedure, see the box on p 265. The only difference is that the application for the apportionment to become binding is served on the tenant(s) of the premises.

Gas safety

➤ A landlord (including a local authority, housing association, hostel owner, a private sector landlord, or landlord renting out a room or bedsit) who permits people to live in his property must ensure that there is maintained in a safe condition:

a) any relevant gas fitting, *and*

b) any flue,

... so as to prevent the risk of injury to any person in lawful occupation of the premises (*GS(IU)R 1998 r 36(2)*).

➤ A landlord may not delegate his duty to a tenant, must use a CORGI registered gas installer for the safety check and must leave a copy of that check with the tenant.

➤ Non-compliance is a criminal offence punishable, if the Health and Safety Executive take enforcement action under *HSWA 1974 s 37*, by imprisonment and/or an unlimited fine as well (if the landlord is a company) as disqualification for directors.

E   Security of Tenure (Outline)

There are 2 classes of tenancy which, on a new grant of a leasehold interest, may qualify for security of tenure by virtue of statute.

I	Residential tenancies
II	Commercial tenancies

I   Residential tenancies

The main features of assured and assured shorthold tenancies

➤ The tenant has some security of tenure. When the fixed term expires, a statutory periodic tenancy automatically arises (*HA 1988 s 5(2)*).

➤ The statutory periodic tenancy may be ended by:

a) a court order (*HA 1988 s 7*) (including a demotion order (*HA 1988 s 6A*)), *or*

b) action taken by a tenant at common law to end the tenancy (surrender, etc) (*HA 1988 s 5(2)*).

➤ A landlord may regain possession of property let on an assured shorthold tenancy by serving a notice under *HA 1988 s 21*.

> ➤ The RICS has published a voluntary Code of Practice for Service Charge Management of Residential Properties which may apply irrespective of how a tenancy is classified.

---

1   Is the tenancy an assured tenancy, or an assured shorthold tenancy?

Assured tenancy	Assured shorthold tenancy
Requirements (HA 1988 s 1(1)) ➤ dwelling house (includes a flat) ➤ let (ie: lease not a licence) ➤ as a separate dwelling (ie: at the time of the grant) ➤ to a tenant who is an individual (ie: not a company) and occupies the dwelling as its main or principal home Note: a dwelling has been held to be somewhere where 'all the major activities of life, particularly sleeping, cooking and feeding ...' take place (*Wright v. Howell* (1947) 92 Sol Jo26, CA)	➤ On or after 28 February 1997 the landlord serves a notice if an assured tenancy is *not* to be an assured shorthold (*HA 1988 s 19A*). ◆ A tenant who does not receive a notice under *s 19A* is entitled to request a written statement of the terms of the tenancy from the landlord (*HA 1988 s 20A*)

Exclusions from assured/assured shortholds (outline)

➤ Lease granted, or contract to grant a lease, dated before 15 January 1989
➤ Student lettings
➤ Lettings to homeless persons under *HA 1985 Part II*
➤ Properties of a high rent or rateable value (eg: over £100,000 per annum if granted on or after 1 October 2010 (*AT(A)(E)O 2010*), previously £25,000)
➤ Low rent properties (eg: under £1,000 per annum in the Greater London area if granted after 1 April 1990)
➤ Tenancies within the scope of the *LTA 1954 Part II*, or (in respect of assured shortholds) *HA 1988 Sch 2A*

267

2   Are there special terms which statute implies into the lease, or any other statutory regulation?

➤ There are controls on the calculation and payment of service charges (*LTA 1985 ss 18-30*).

◆ Tenants and landlords may ask the Residential Property Tribunal Service's leasehold valuation tribunal to assess whether a service charge is payable and the amount which is payable (*LTA 1985 s 27A*).

■ The tenant may challenge the landlord's choice of insurer or an excessive premium.

● The right to apply to a tribunal under *HA 1996 s 83* does not apply if a tenant:

a) agrees to or admits the service charge or insurance, *or*

b) is a party to an arbitration agreement which covers the dispute.

◆ If a property is let as a 'dwelling', a landlord may not be able to re-enter the property or forfeit the lease for non-payment of a service charge, unless:

● it is finally determined by (or on appeal from) a court or leasehold valuation tribunal, or by a tribunal under an arbitration agreement, that the service charge is payable by the tenant, *or*

● the tenant admits that the service charge is payable (*HA 1996 s 81*).

➤ Certain assured tenancies are subject to rent control provisions (*HA 1988 s 22*).

➤ For an assured shorthold tenancy entered into on or after 6 April 2007 any deposit made by a tenant must be protected by a rent deposit scheme; a landlord can chose either a 'custodial' scheme or an 'insurance' scheme (*HA 2004 ss 212-215* and *Sch 10* as amended by *H(TDS)O 2007*).

➤ A licence, granted by a local authority, is needed for a 'house in multiple occupation' (*HA 2004 Part 2*).

◆ It is a criminal offence for a landlord not to obtain such a licence (*HA 2004 s 72*).

➤ For *all* new residential leases of under 7 years granted to a new tenant (eg: not a former tenant or one in possession at the time of a grant), statute implies covenants that the landlord will:

a) keep the exterior and structure in repair, *and*

b) ensure installations for heating, water and space and those supplying water, gas, electricity and sanitation are kept in repair and proper working order (*LTA 1985 ss 11-14*).

3   Does the tenant have the right to buy the freehold, to a lease extension, or to manage?

➤ The tenant may have the right to buy the freehold, or extend the lease by up to 90 years (for a flat, *LRHUDA 1993*) or up to 50 years (for a house, *LRA 1967*) if the term of the lease is 21+ years.

➤ If, without 'reasonable excuse', a landlord fails to offer tenants first refusal on a disposal of his interest he commits a criminal offence punishable by a fine of up to £5,000 (*HA 1996 Sch 6*).

◆ This applies if the premises contain 2 or more flats more than half of which are rented (*LTA 1987, Part I*).

➤ Tenants may be entitled to manage if at least 2/3rds of the flats are let to tenants whose leases originally had a term of 21+ years and any non-residential part does not exceed 25% of the floor area (*CLRA 2002 ss 71-113*).

4   Can the landlord regain possession?

➤ The landlord commences proceedings by serving a notice on the tenant stating the ground(s) upon which he intends to take possession of the property (*HA 1988 s 8*). If *Ground 14A* (domestic violence) is relied on, the landlord's notice must meet additional requirements (*HA 1988 s 8A*).

◆ The notice period depends upon which ground of *HA 1988 Sch 2* the landlord relies upon.

➤ In addition, if the tenancy is an assured shorthold, the landlord may regain possession at the end of the term by serving a notice under *s 21* of the *HA 1988* giving at least 2 months' clear notice of his intention to take possession.

◆ If the tenant has not vacated when the notice expires, the landlord can start possession proceedings.

Are there grounds for a court order for possession? (*HA 1988 Sch 2*)

Assured tenancies

➤ If the landlord grants an assured tenancy on a fixed term basis, the landlord will only be able to regain possession during the fixed term if one of Grounds 2, 8, 10-15, or 17 apply and the tenancy provides for it to be ended on those grounds.

➤ When the fixed term of an assured tenancy ends, possession can be sought on any of the Grounds.

Mandatory 1-8	Ground 1*:	a) at some time before the tenancy began the property was the landlord's principal home, *or* b) the landlord seeks possession for himself or his spouse as a principal home *and* the reversion was not acquired for money or money's worth
	Ground 2*:	a lender under a pre-existing mortgage is exercising a power of sale
	Grounds 3-5*:	out of season holiday lettings, vacation lettings to students, lettings to ministers of religion
	Ground 6:	a) the landlord 'intends to demolish or reconstruct the whole or a substantial part of the dwelling, or carry out substantial building works ...', *and* b) the landlord did not acquire the reversion for money or money's worth, *and* c) possession is essential for the works (Varying the lease is unacceptable to the tenant or impractical)
	Ground 7:	death of a tenant. (A spouse's right to succession is unaffected by this ground (*HA 1996 s 17*))
	Ground 8:	rent arrears of 8 weeks if paid weekly, or 2 months if paid monthly, *when* notice is served *and* at the date of the hearing (plead Grounds 10 and 11 in the alternative) (amended by *HA 1996 s 101*) * The landlord must serve a notice stating that possession may be sought under the appropriate ground. This must be given 'not later than the beginning of the tenancy'
Discretionary 9-17	Ground 9:	the landlord offers 'suitable' alternative accommodation as defined in *HA 1996 Sch 2 Part III*
	Ground 10:	less than 3 months' rent is in arrears
	Ground 11:	persistent delay in paying rent
	Ground 12:	breach of tenancy clause which does not relate to rent
	Ground 13:	deterioration of the dwelling due to the tenant's neglect
	Ground 14:	the tenant or a person residing in or visiting the dwelling: a) is a nuisance or annoyance to anyone engaged in lawful activity in the vicinity, *or* b) is convicted for using the premises or allowing them to be used for illegal or immoral purposes, *or* c) commits an arrestable offence in the locality (see also *s 9A*)
	Ground 14A:	a) the occupiers are a married couple/CPs or living together as man and wife/CP, *and* b) one of the partners has left because of violence to him/herself or a child and is unlikely to return, *and* c) the landlord seeking possession is a 'registered social landlord' or a 'charitable housing trust' (inserted by *HA 1996 s 148*)
	Ground 15:	deterioration of furniture due to the tenant's conduct
	Ground 16:	the tenant's employment ends when the letting was a consequence of that employment
	Ground 17:	tenant's false statement, made knowingly or recklessly, induced the landlord to grant the lease (*HA 1996 s 102*)

Assured shorthold tenancies

➤ The grounds are the same as those for assured tenancies

➤ A landlord has a right to possession without using a Ground at any time after a fixed term comes to an end, or at any time during a contractual or statutory periodic tenancy, by giving 2 months notice under *s 21* of the *HA 1988*.

◆ Any order for possession will not take effect earlier than 6 months after the start of the original tenancy.

➤ If a landlord is a local housing authority, a housing action trust, or a registered social landlord it may apply to court for a secure tenancy to be terminated and replaced by a demoted tenancy if the tenant, or a person residing in or visiting the dwelling has engaged in, or threatened to engage in, antisocial behaviour or the use of premises for unlawful purposes (*HA 1996 s 82A*).

◆ *HA 1996 ss 144A-P* offer a procedure assist a landlord regain possession with respect to a demoted tenancy.

II   Commercial tenancies

> ### Commercial property leases
>
> ➤ An energy performance certificate must (save, for example, prior to demolition) be supplied on the letting (or sale or construction) of commercial property (*EPB(CI)(EW)R 2007*).
>
> ➤ The Law Society and the British Property Federation have endorsed a code of good practice (www.commercialleasecode.co.uk) which should be brought to the attention of landlords and tenants, especially if either are small businesses, before the grant of a lease.
>
>   ◆ If the industry does not voluntarily implement the Code to make the market more transparent, the Government may legislate on the conduct of rent reviews and alternative dispute resolution.
>
> ➤ The RICS has published a service charge Code for Commercial Properties (2nd ed.).

➤ The *LTA 1954 Part II* provides some security of tenure to tenants of commercial property by extending the term indefinitely after the date on which it would otherwise determine at common law (*LTA 1954 s 24(1)*).

1   Does the *LTA 1954 Part II* apply to the tenancy?

> ➤ If a lease to which the Act would otherwise apply is to be granted, the parties may wish to consider contracting out of the *LTA 1954*.
>
> ➤ If the parties wish to contract out, then either:
>
>   a) a landlord must serve a warning notice at least 14 days before a tenant is committed to a lease, and the tenant must sign a simple declaration stating that this has been done, *or*
>
>   b) the parties can agree less than 14 days before a tenant is committed to a lease, and the tenant must sign a statutory declaration before a solicitor that the tenant has received and read a warning notice and accepts its consequences (*LTA 1954 s 38A, RR(BT)(EW)O 2003 Schs 1-2*).

> ### Tenancies protected by the *LTA 1954 Part II*
>
> ➤ A tenancy is protected if it (*LTA 1954 s 23*):
>
>   a) is a tenancy (ie: not a licence), *and*
>
>   b) is of premises, *and*
>
>   c) is occupied by the tenant, *and*
>
>   d) is for the purposes of a business carried on by the tenant (or, by a company in which a tenant has a controlling interest, or if the tenant is a company a person with a controlling interest in the company) or for those and other purposes,
>
>   ... provided that it is not excluded for any reason, eg:
>
>   i) the tenancy is 'contracted out' under *LTA 1954 s 38A, or*
>
>   ii) it is an agricultural holding (*LTA 1954 s 43(1)(a)*), *or*
>
>   iii) it is granted by reason of employment (*LTA 1954 s 43(2)*), *or*
>
>   iv) it is for a term certain not exceeding 6 months (*LTA 1954 s 43(3)*) (a tenancy at will is not for a 'term certain' and is therefore excluded).

2   If the *LTA 1954* applies, how can the landlord regain possession, or a new lease be granted under the *LTA 1954*?

> ➤ The *LTA 1954* operates a system of notices (simplified in certain respects and extended by the *RR(BT)(EW)O 2003*), which must be served correctly and at the appropriate times.

➤ A *s 25* notice is served by a landlord who either:

a) wishes to regain possession, *or*

b) is not opposing renewal.

> ◆ To be valid a *s 25* notice must be:
>
> • served not less than 6 months and not more than 1 year before the date of termination, *and*
>
> • given to the tenant, *and*
>
> • specify the date of termination, *and*
>
> • demand action of the tenant (eg: vacate the premises, or enter negotiations for a new tenancy), *and*
>
> • *either:*
>
>   a) *if the landlord wishes to regain possession*: explain on which of the statutory grounds (*s 30(1)(a)-(g)*) the landlord will oppose the grant of a new tenancy, eg:
>
>   i) a breach of the tenant's repairing obligations.
>
>   ii) persistent delay in paying rent.
>
>   iii) other substantial breaches.
>
>   iv) the landlord can provide suitable alternative accommodation.
>
>   v) the landlord needs possession for letting or disposing of the property as a whole.
>
>   vi) the landlord intends to demolish or reconstruct the property.
>
>   vii) the landlord intends to occupy the premises for his business or as his residence, *or*
>
>   b) *if the landlord is not opposing renewal*: contain proposals for the terms of a new lease.
>
> • be in the correct form set out in the *LTA 1954 Part II (Notices) Regulations 2004*.

➤ A *s 26* request is served by a tenant who wants a new tenancy.

> ◆ A *s 26* request must:
>
> • specify a date for the new tenancy to begin which is not more than 1 year and not less than 6 months after the date specified in the notice (which cannot be earlier than, apart from this legislation, the date the tenancy would have come to an end by effluxion of time or by a notice to quit given by the tenant), *and*
>
> • contain proposals for the new lease (the amount of detail depends on the tenant's negotiating tactics, eg: whether the tenant wishes to tell the landlord early on exactly what he wants), *and*
>
> • be in the form set out in the *LTA 1954 Part II (Notices) Regulations 2004*.

3 Is the tenant entitled to any compensation on termination?

➤ If the landlord terminates the tenancy under grounds in *s 30(1)(e)-(g)*, then generally the tenant will be entitled to compensation, or if a tenant has been induced not to apply for renewal by misrepresentation or concealment, or a tenant's application is withdrawn for these reasons (*s 37*).

➤ If the tenant has made improvements to the property, he may be entitled to compensation under *LTA 1927 Part I*.

If a surrender is by agreement to surrender followed by a deed (rather than simply under a deed of surrender), a warning notice and declaration are required (see p 270) before entering into the agreement.

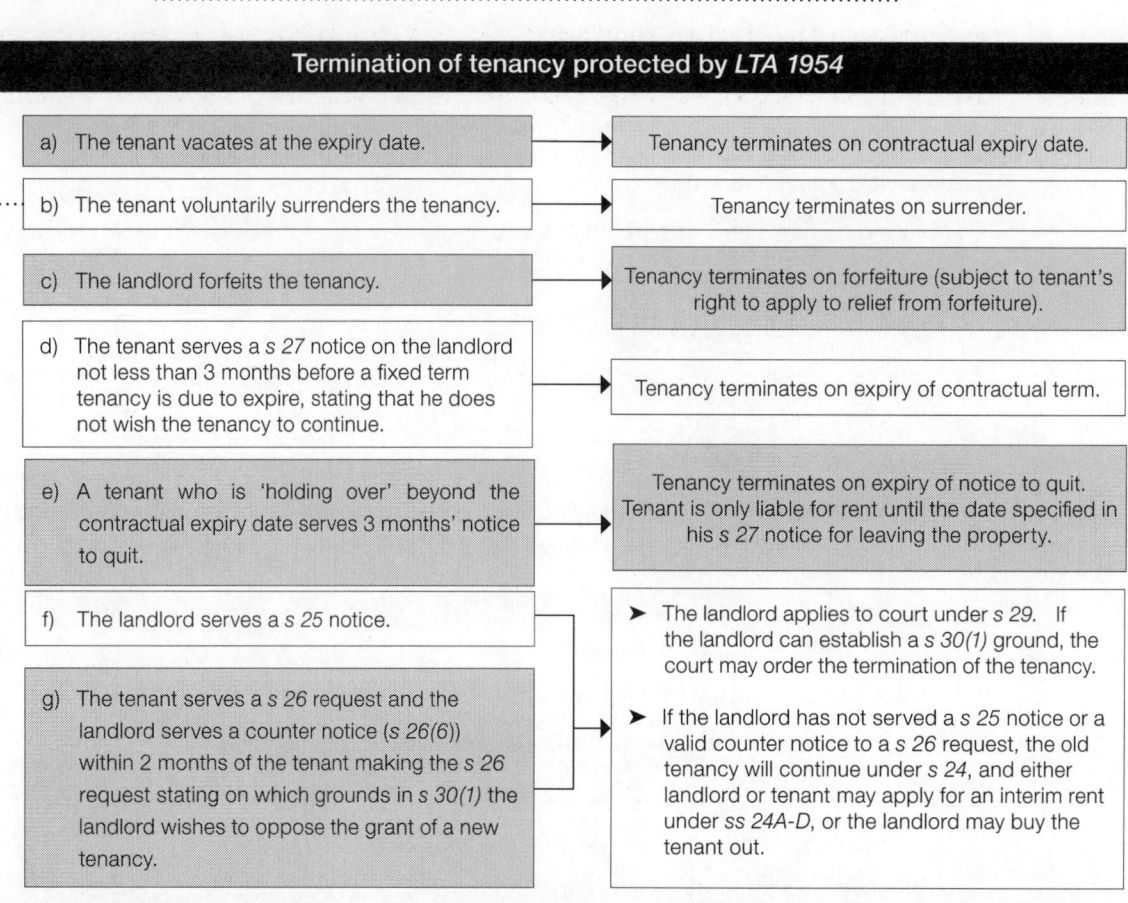

Termination of tenancy protected by *LTA 1954*

a) The tenant vacates at the expiry date. → Tenancy terminates on contractual expiry date.

b) The tenant voluntarily surrenders the tenancy. → Tenancy terminates on surrender.

c) The landlord forfeits the tenancy. → Tenancy terminates on forfeiture (subject to tenant's right to apply to relief from forfeiture).

d) The tenant serves a *s 27* notice on the landlord not less than 3 months before a fixed term tenancy is due to expire, stating that he does not wish the tenancy to continue. → Tenancy terminates on expiry of contractual term.

e) A tenant who is 'holding over' beyond the contractual expiry date serves 3 months' notice to quit. → Tenancy terminates on expiry of notice to quit. Tenant is only liable for rent until the date specified in his *s 27* notice for leaving the property.

f) The landlord serves a *s 25* notice.

g) The tenant serves a *s 26* request and the landlord serves a counter notice (*s 26(6)*) within 2 months of the tenant making the *s 26* request stating on which grounds in *s 30(1)* the landlord wishes to oppose the grant of a new tenancy.

➤ The landlord applies to court under *s 29*. If the landlord can establish a *s 30(1)* ground, the court may order the termination of the tenancy.

➤ If the landlord has not served a *s 25* notice or a valid counter notice to a *s 26* request, the old tenancy will continue under *s 24*, and either landlord or tenant may apply for an interim rent under *ss 24A-D*, or the landlord may buy the tenant out.

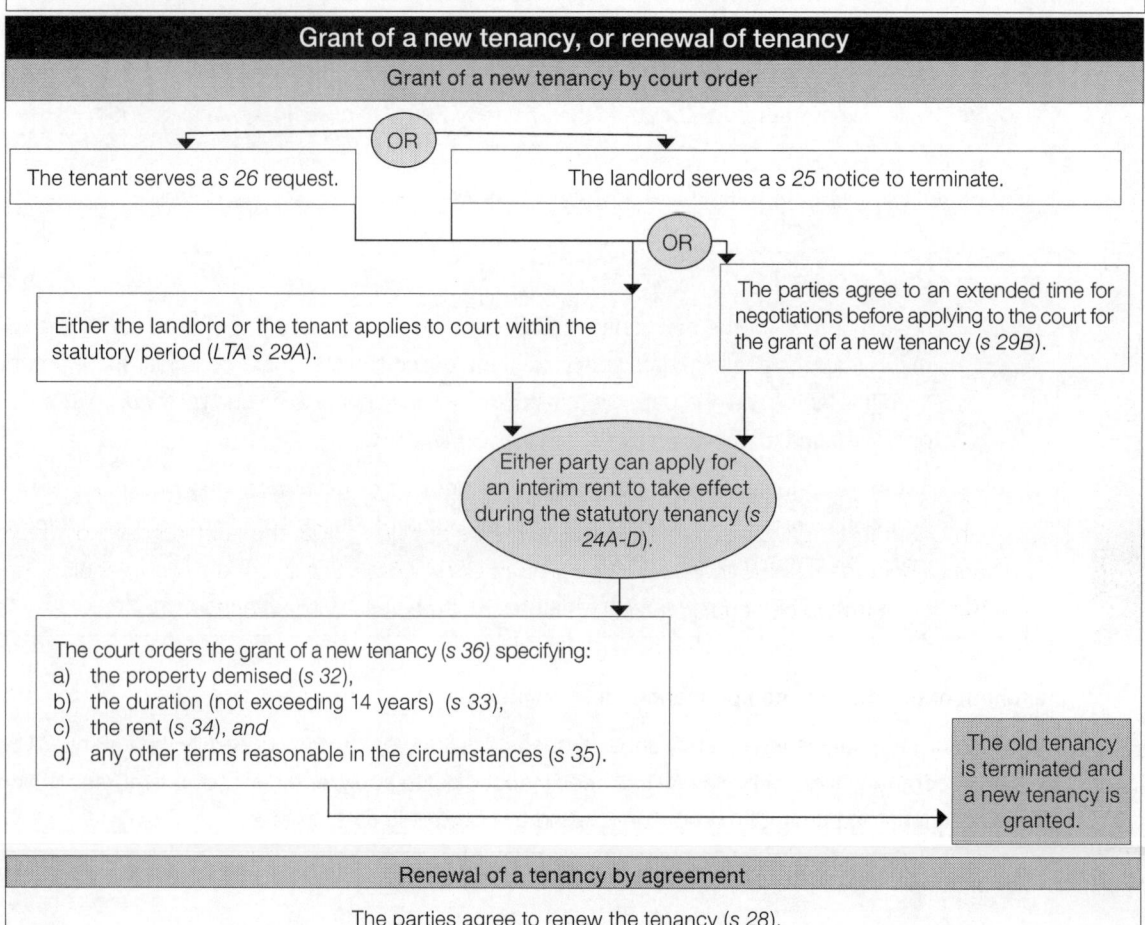

Grant of a new tenancy, or renewal of tenancy

Grant of a new tenancy by court order

The tenant serves a *s 26* request.   OR   The landlord serves a *s 25* notice to terminate.

OR

Either the landlord or the tenant applies to court within the statutory period (*LTA s 29A*).

The parties agree to an extended time for negotiations before applying to the court for the grant of a new tenancy (*s 29B*).

Either party can apply for an interim rent to take effect during the statutory tenancy (*s 24A-D*).

The court orders the grant of a new tenancy (*s 36)* specifying:
a)   the property demised (*s 32*),
b)   the duration (not exceeding 14 years) (*s 33*),
c)   the rent (*s 34*), *and*
d)   any other terms reasonable in the circumstances (*s 35*).

The old tenancy is terminated and a new tenancy is granted.

Renewal of a tenancy by agreement

The parties agree to renew the tenancy (*s 28*).

F Commonhold

➤ Commonhold is a new form of freehold tenure (*CLRA 2002 s 1*).

 ◆ An ownership interest in a commonhold property comprises both:

  a) ownership of a 'unit' within a development, *and*

  b) membership of a commonhold association ('**CA**'), a company limited by guarantee, which holds the common parts of a development and manages the development in accordance with a commonhold community statement ('CCS').

   • A unit is defined in a CSS in accordance with *CR 2004 r 9* and does not include the structure and exterior (unless the unit is a self-contained building).

   • A lease of a unit may not generally be granted for a term of more than 7 years (*CR 2004 r 11*).

➤ Commonhold is intended to offer a modern, transparent/flexible, and standardised alternative to leasehold.

 ◆ Eg: the CSS provides for the CA to insure (*CCS para 4.4*, *CLRA 2002 s 26(b)*) and repair/maintain (*CCS para 4.5*, *CLRA 2002 s 26(c)*) the common parts, and there are standard notifications (*CR 2004 Sch 4*) such as in respect of income a CA needs to raise by assessment (*Form 1*) and requesting payment of an assessment (*Form 2*).

 ◆ On registration of a commonhold development, any leasehold is extinguished (*CLRA 2002 s 9(3)(f)*).

➤ To register commonhold land:

Steps	
1	Incorporate a CA at Companies House using the form of Articles of Association set out in *CR 2004 Sch 1* and compliance with *CR 2004 rr 12-14*, *and*
2	Prepare a CCS in the form set out in *CR 2004 Sch 3* (*CR 2004 r 15*), and a plan of the development which is no larger than A0 size and is preferably 1/500 scale, based on an accurate survey (*HM Land Registry Practice Guide 60,* September 2009), *and*
3	Obtain the necessary consents (see *CLRA 2002 s 3* and *CR 2004 r 3*), broadly from those who have an interest in the property such as the registered proprietor of the freehold interest, or a chargee), *and*
4	Apply to HM Land Registry to register commonhold land using *Form CM1* (*C(LR) 2004 r 5*) plus:

  a) a certified copy of the CA's certificate of incorporation, *and*

  b) a certified copy of the CA's articles of association, *and*

  c) 2 certified copies of the CCS (future amendments must be made using *Form CM3*), *and*

  d) the consents referred to in 'step 3' above in *form CON1* (*C(LR) 2004 r 7*),

  e) a certificate given by the directors of the CA confirming that the articles of association comply with *CR 2004*, the CCS satisfies the requirements of *CLRA 2002*, the land is not land which cannot become commonhold land (specified in *CLRA 2002 Sch 2*, eg: a flying freehold), the CA has not traded or incurred liability which has not been discharged, *and*

  f) a statutory declaration from the applicant confirming that the required consents have been properly obtained, and giving details of any charge over part of a unit which is to be extinguished (*C(LR)R 2004 r 6*), *and*

  g) if an application is with unitholders (eg: an existing freehold or leasehold is being converted to commonhold, rather than there being a new development) *Form COV* which contains a request that *CLRA 2002 s 9* applies and lists the units (giving for each the name and address of the proposed unit holder or joint unit holders).

G   Remedies

I   Notice to complete
II   Compensation for delayed completion
III Contractual remedies

Vendor and purchaser application *(LPA s 49(1))*

➤ Under this section, either party may issue an application under *CPR 1998 Part 8* to resolve disputes connected with the transaction (but *not* one questioning the validity or existence of the contract itself).

➤ The court has summary jurisdiction to resolve such matters as:

a) the validity of a notice to complete.

b) whether the buyer is taking a clean title as promised in the contract.

c) whether a requisition on title is valid.

I   Notice to complete

➤ Initially time is not of the essence (*StC 6.1*), unless the contract is conditional.   It can be made of the essence if completion is delayed by serving a notice to complete.

➤ Time is 'of the essence' from the service of a notice to complete. Consequently, if completion does not occur when the notice specifies the party at fault commits a breach of contract.

  ◆ The innocent party may choose to terminate the contract after this breach and/or sue for damages.

  ◆ If the party who served the notice defaults, the recipient of the notice has a claim for breach. Consequently, a notice should only be served if you are sure you can complete.

1   At common law

➤ The notice must specify a 'reasonable' time for the new completion date.

➤ The party serving the notice must be ready, willing, and able to complete if the notice is to be valid.

2   *StC 6.8* displaces the common law rules

➤ The notice should state that it is served under this contractual provision.

➤ If a notice is served, the new completion date is set 10 clear days from the day of service.

➤ If the buyer has paid a deposit of under 10%, he must pay the full 10% on receipt of the notice.

➤ If the notice is ignored, the seller may rescind if he served the notice (*StC 7.4*), *or* the buyer may rescind if he served the notice (*StC 7.5*).

II Compensation for delayed completion

1 Delay due to the seller's fault (at common law)

➤ The seller pays outgoings on the property during the period of delay.

➤ The seller retains *whichever is less of*:

a) the interest on the purchase price which the buyer pays at the general equitable rate, *or*

b) the net income on the property.

2 Delay due to the buyer's fault (at common law)

➤ The buyer pays outgoings on the property.

➤ The buyer retains any income from the property.

➤ The buyer pays the seller interest on the balance at the general equitable rate.

3 *StC 7.2* (this overrides the common law regime)

➤ Whichever party causes the greater period of delay pays the other compensation at the contract rate.

➤ The sum on which interest is paid depends on which party is liable to pay compensation.

◆ The buyer's interest is calculated on the balance of the purchase price outstanding (ie: the deposit is deducted).

◆ The seller's interest is calculated on the purchase price.

➤ Interest runs for whichever is the shorter of:

a) the time between the contractual completion date and actual completion, *or*

b) the length of time during which the party liable to pay compensation was in default.

NB: compensation under *StC 7.2* is deducted from any damages a court subsequently awards.

III   Contractual remedies

Pre-completion	Post-completion
Action on the covenants for title	

For a list of the covenants implied by statute on, or after 1 July 1995, see p 205.

Before 1 July 1995, *LPA s 76(1)* implied into conveyances or transfers of land for value covenants which depended on the seller's capacity (as 'beneficial owner', 'fiduciary' or 'settlor'), and whether the interest concerned was freehold or leasehold.

➤   This action is *only* available *after* completion if the contract incorporates a non-merger clause similar to *StC 7.3*, otherwise the contract and the deed 'merge', removing the right to a remedy under the contract alone.

Rescission

➤ This restores the parties to their original position
➤ The claimant may seek an indemnity in the contract for any loss incurred
➤ The claimant may seek damages if:
  a) he is claiming rescission under *MA 1967 s 2(1)*, or
  b) rescission is due to the defendant's breach, *or*
  c) the claimant is seeking a declaration from the court that the defendant has committed a repudiatory breach of contract
➤ The claimant may *not* seek damages where obtaining rescission is the purpose of the action

The *StC* expressly reserve the right to rescind if:
a)   the seller makes a misrepresentation (an error of fact upon which the buyer relies in entering the contract) (*StC 7.1*), or
b)   the landlord does not grant a licence to assign (*StC 8.3*)

StC 7.1.2 lists rights on rescission *under the contract*:
a)   documents are returned to the seller, *and*
b)   the buyer pays for cancelling any entry on the Register to protect the contract, and (unless rescission results from a breach by the buyer) regains the deposit plus interest

Damages for breach of contract	Rectification

➤ Calculated on the principle in *Hadley v. Baxendale* (1854) 9 Exch 341:
  ◆ all loss arising naturally from the breach which the parties could reasonably have foreseen on entering the contract would result from the breach
	➤ This is an equitable remedy: the document is altered to reflect the parties' original intentions
	
	Either the parties agree,
	
	or the court grants the remedy at its discretion if:
	
	  ◆ *both* parties were mistaken, *or*
	  ◆ *one* party was mistaken *and* the other party was …
	    a) aware of the error and so is estopped from resisting rectification, *or*
	    b) fraudulent, *or*
	  ◆ only one party is party to the document
	
	Note:
	
	if both rescission and rectification are available, the court may let the claimant choose (*Solle v Butcher* [1950] 1 KB 671)

Specific performance	
➤ An equitable remedy in the court's discretion ➤ The court may award damages instead of granting specific performance (*SCA 1981 s 51*) ➤ The court may award damages as well as specific performance (*Johnson v Agnew* [1979] 1 All ER 883)	

➤   For dispute resolution between a commonhold association and a unitholder see *para 4.11* of the *CCS*.

BUSINESS

This chapter examines:

All tax aspects are dealt with in the 'Taxation' section of this book.

Right to establish a business (*TFEU: Article 49*)

➤   An EU citizen has a right to establish a business in any member state, provided that the requirements of national law regarding the running of that type of business are satisfied (ie: company, partnership, etc).

Right to provide services (*TFEU: Article 56*)

➤   There is a right for an EU citizen to provide services into any member state.

EU Services Directive (*Directive 2006/123/EC*)

➤ There are 4 main strands to uphold the rights in the 2 boxes above ('Rights'):

◆ **Simplification of administrative procedures:** Member States must examine their systems of regulation and authorisation. For service providers wishing to operate in other Member States, Member States must: i) have a legislative screening process, and ii) set up Points of Single Contact.

◆ **Upholding the Rights:** requirements on service providers must be non-discriminatory, necessary and proportionate.

◆ **Mutual assistance between regulatory bodies in different Member States to underpin the Rights:** Member States must ensure regulators co-operate across borders so service providers are properly supervised throughout the EU.

◆ **Limited rules harmonisation** (including rights for services recipients, information requirements and on removal of prohibitions on marketing of multi-disciplinary practices).

PSR 2009 - implements the EU Services Directive

➤ *Part 2* imposes requirements on service providers (SPs).
  ◆ SPs must communicate prescribed information about themselves and their services to recipients (*Regs 7-11*).
  ◆ SPs must handle complaints in a certain way (*Reg 12*).
➤ *Part 3* applies to the provision of services in the UK.
  ◆ A competent authority (CA) must not make access to or the exercise of a service activity subject to an authorisation scheme unless certain conditions are satisfied.
  ◆ There are many provisions about authorisations including the need to satisfy the conditions of non-discrimination, necessity and proportionality.
➤ *Part 4* relates to the freedoms of a SP established in another EEA state to provide a service in the UK from that state. Access to/exercise of a service activity must usually only be subject to requirements which respect the principles of non-discrimination, necessity and proportionality.
➤ *Part 5* concerns the rights of recipients of services.
  ◆ CAs are prohibited from restricting recipients' usage of services from other EEA states (*Reg 29*).
  ◆ CAs are prohibited from discriminating on the basis of recipients' nationality or place of residence, and from discriminating in their general conditions on the basis of recipients' place of residence (*Reg 30*).
➤ *Part 6* imposes duties on CAs.
➤ *Part 7* imposes information requirements on CAs.
➤ *Part 9* contains provisions relating to administrative cooperation between CAs in different EEA states.

A   Partnerships

I   Formation of a partnership
II   A written agreement for a partnership
III Obligations and liability of partners
IV   Dissolution of a partnership
V   After dissolution - distribution of assets
VI   Taxation: see 'Taxation' section

I   Formation of a partnership

➤ A partnership 'subsists between persons carrying on a *business in common* with a view to profit' (*PA s 1*).

➤ A partnership can come into existence orally, *or* by an agreement, *or* through a course of conduct.

➤ There is no limit on the number of partners allowed.

➤ However the partnership comes into existence, *CA 2006 ss 1192-1208* and *CBN(MP)R 2009* should be complied with.

> *CBN(MP)R 2009* **deals with restrictions relating to the registered name of a company and to business names.**
>
> ◆ Part 4 (about UK business names) deals with restrictions on names. There are lists of restricted words.
> ◆ Part 2 (about company names) lists characters that are permitted in the name (and consequently characters in lower case, ligatures, accents and other diacritical marks are not permitted in the name).

Business Names (applicable to partnerships, LLPs and companies) (*CA 2006 ss 1192-1208*)		
Section		**Content**
1192, 1200		➤ If the name is the partners' surnames (alone or with their initials), forenames or an 's' to show that there is more than one partner with a given name, then no restrictions apply.
1193-1194		➤ Words listed in *CLLPBN(SWE)R 2009* (eg: suggesting a connection with HM Government or a local authority or words linked to certain professions or the NHS) require specific approval from particular government bodies.
1197		➤ Rules may be made about names containing inappropriate indications of company type or legal form.
1198		➤ A person must not carry on business under a name that gives so misleading an indication of the nature of the business as to be likely to cause harm to the public.
1202-1204	Only applicable to individuals and partnerships (carrying on business under a business name)	➤ Unless a partnership of more than 20 partners, then the names of partners and the address for service of documents must appear both: a) on letters, orders, invoices, receipts and written demands for payment, *and* b) at the place of business to which suppliers and customers have access. ➤ These details must also be given to anyone who requests such information.
1206		➤ A contract with a third party who is prejudiced by the infringement will be unenforceable.
1205		➤ Breach of failure to disclose on business documents or at business premises is a crime.

II   A written agreement for a partnership

➤ A written agreement is safest to effect a partnership. Various matters are highlighted below which the draftsman may wish to consider. References are to the *Partnership Act 1890*, unless otherwise stated, and the Act will apply if the partnership agreement is silent on a particular matter.

1   **Commencement date:** an objective test based on *s 1*. The date stated in the agreement is not conclusive.

2   Name: the firm's name (and its trading name if this is different) which must comply with *CA 2006 ss 1192-1208* and *CBN(MP)R 2009* and *CLLPBN(SWE)R 2009* (see p 278).

3   **Financial input:** of each partner.

4   **Salaries:** if the agreement is silent, the partners will not be entitled to a salary (*s 24(6)*).

5   **Interest**

➤ Partners are entitled to interest at 5% on capital they advance in excess of their obligations under the terms of the partnership (*s 24(3)*).

➤ There is no entitlement to interest on capital until profits have been ascertained (*s 24(4)*).

6   **Capital profits or losses:** if the agreement is silent, these are shared equally (*s 24(1)*).

7   **Shares in profit derived from income:** if the agreement is silent, these are shared equally (*s 24(1)*).

8   **Drawings of money**

9   **Place and nature of business**

10 **Ownership of assets:** either i) by the partners privately, or ii) by partners on trust for all the partners.

11 **Work input**

➤ Full or part-time?

➤ Bar on the involvement of partners in other businesses during their membership of the partnership?

12 **Partners' roles**

➤ All the partners may manage the firm (*s 24(5)*), but this is inappropriate for 'sleeping' partners.

13 **Management**

➤ A simple majority prevails, unless otherwise stated (*s 24(8)*).

➤ Unanimity is required for i) changing the nature of the business (*s 24(8)*), ii) admitting new partners (*s 24(7)*), iii) changing the partnership agreement.

➤ If unanimity is required for anything else, put it in the contract.

14 **Duration of the partnership**

➤ i) At will, or ii) for a fixed term, or iii) for as long as a minimum of two partners remain.

➤ *PA s 26* provides that if no date is given, then if a notice of dissolution is given, it is effective immediately. To prevent this occurring inadvertently, a notice period should be specified.

15 **Death/bankruptcy/retirement:** if the agreement is silent, these dissolve a partnership (*s 33*).

16 **Expulsion of partners:** this is impossible without an express provision in the agreement (*s 25*).

17 **Paying for an outgoing partner's share.** Consider:

➤ either an *obligation* on (or an *option* for) the remaining partners to purchase the share.

➤ a method for valuing the share. Provide for professional valuation if the partners do not agree.

➤ a date on which payment falls due (a grace period allows those remaining to find new equity).

➤ whether an indemnity is included in the valuation.

18 **Restraint of trade on outgoing partners:** the clause must be 'reasonable' to be enforceable at common law (ie: with regard to time, geographical area, and whether the activity competes with the partnership).

19 **Income tax**

➤ An outgoing partner may be obliged to join the others in sending a tax election to HMRC.

➤ An outgoing partner should be indemnified against additional liability resulting from his election.

20 **Arbitration:** name an arbitrator in case of disputes between the partners (else recourse is to court).

III   Obligations and liability of partners

A   Generally

➤   Partners are bound to each other:

1   **in contract:** in accordance with the terms of the partnership agreement, *and*

2   **under the *PA ss 28-30* and a century of case-law as follows:**

   ◆   **Duty of utmost good faith:** partners are bound to each other by a set of duties that can collectively be called a duty of utmost good faith.

   ◆   Duty to render to each other true accounts and full information on all matters affecting the partnership (*s 28*).

   ◆   Duty to account for any benefit (eg: a transaction concerning the partnership made without the consent of the partnership) (*s 29*).

   ◆   Duty to account for the profits derived from any competing business (*s 30*).

➤   See also the effect of *C(ROTP)A 1999* on p 365.

B   Firm's liability

Recovery from the firm
➤   The firm is a group of persons who were partners at the time the cause of action arose (*PA ss 9, 17*).
➤   Recovery is possible from the partnership assets and also from partners personally.

➤   The firm may be liable:

1   **in tort:** for a partner's act or omission in the ordinary course of business, *or* an act with a partner's authority *(PA s 10)*.

2   **in contract:** for agreements made by a partner with, or with the partners', 'actual' or 'ostensible' authority.

   ◆   **Actual authority:** this can be expressly *or* impliedly given in the partnership agreement, or it may arise from a factual situation or a decision of the partners.

   ◆   **Ostensible authority:** 4 conditions must be satisfied (*PA ss 5-8*):

   subjective test
   - a)   the third party knows or believes he is dealing with a partner, *and*
   - b)   the third party is unaware that the partner was not actually authorised, *and*

   objective test
   - c)   the partner would usually be expected to be authorised to enter into such a transaction, *and*
   - d)   the firm's type of business is consistent with the nature of the transaction.

C Personal liability of a partner

1 **A partner to a third party**

➤ A partner is personally liable in contract (if he or the firm are party to the contract) and in tort.

◆ Liability is without limit for debts incurred while a partner (*PA s 9*).

◆ Liability does *not* cease on leaving the firm for obligations incurred while a partner (*PA s 17*).

2 **A partner to a partner**

➤ A partner acting outside his authority can be liable to the other partners for breach of warranty of authority.

3 **An ex-partner to a third party**

➤ Any partner is liable for obligations incurred *after* his departure from the partnership if there is:

a) **'holding out' that the ex-partner is a partner** (*PA s 14*) by:

i) a representation (oral/written/conduct) *either* by the ex-partner, *or* with his knowledge, *and*

ii) reliance on this representation by a third party,

or b) **failure to notify of leaving the partnership** (*PA s 36*).

◆ An ex-partner is liable *unless* notice of the change:

i) is given to all who have dealt with the firm recently. This protects against claims from previous customers.

ii) appears in the *London Gazette*. This protects against claims from future customers.

Note: i) and ii) do not apply on death or bankruptcy, so an estate is not liable for a firm's subsequent acts.

4 **A stranger to a third party**

➤ A stranger will be liable for an obligation if he has been 'holding out' that he is a partner (*PA s 14*):

i) by making a representation (oral/written/conduct) that he is a partner, *and*

ii) a third party relies on this representation.

D Limitation of personal liability

1 **By indemnity**

a) **No actual authority**

Where a partner has acted without actual authority, the other partners are entitled to an indemnity for any loss they suffer as a result of the unauthorised act.

Note: i) an indemnity will only protect the other partners if the indemnifier is solvent.

ii) the other partners will only be entitled to any indemnity if they act to mitigate their loss.

b) **Outgoing partner indemnity**

An outgoing partner may negotiate an indemnity from the remaining partners to protect himself.

2 **By novation**

➤ A 3-way agreement between a new partner, creditor and continuing partners by which the new partner takes on the outgoing partner's liability.

3 **By suitable acts**

➤ A leaving partner may try to limit liability by certain practical acts (see section 3b in Section C above).

◆ Eg. change the notepaper and the list of partners at the place of business, put suitable notices in relevant newspapers etc.

IV   Dissolution of a partnership

➤ The partnership agreement will usually make provisions for when a partnership may be dissolved. Where it does not (or there is no partnership agreement), the following list of 9 defaults will apply.

♦ **Always:** '5' below will apply even if a partnership agreement caters for the other situations.

♦ **Automatic termination:** '1', '3' and '6' will terminate the partnership automatically.

➤ A partnership may be dissolved by ...

1   ... expiry

➤ A 'fixed term' partnership terminates at the end of its term (*PA s 32(a)*).

➤ A partnership intended to achieve a single undertaking ends when that undertaking is attained (*PA s 32(b)*).

♦ If the partners continue acting in concert the agreement continues, but as a 'partnership at will'.

2   ... notice

➤ This is when any partner gives notice to the other(s) of his intention to dissolve the partnership.

♦ Notice may be effective immediately, or after a specified period (*PA s 32(c)*).

♦ Notice does not need to be written unless the partnership agreement is by deed (*PA s 26(2)*).

3   ... illegality

➤ When an event occurs that makes it unlawful to continue in partnership (eg: loss of a licence which is required for running the business) (*PA s 34*).

4   ... court order under *PA s 35*

➤ Regardless of what a partnership agreement may provide, the court has discretion to dissolve a partnership on one of the following grounds:

Either when a partner, other than the partner applying to court ...

s 35(b)   is rendered 'permanently' incapable of carrying out obligations under the agreement, *or*

s 35(c)   engages in conduct prejudicial to the partnership's business, *or*

s 35(d)   wilfully breaches the partnership agreement, or behaves in such a way that it is not reasonably practical for the other partners to continue the business,

or

s 35(e)   when the partnership can only be continued as a loss-making business, *or*

s 35(f)   when the court regards dissolution as 'just and equitable'.

5   ... a court order, or decision of a deputy appointed by the court, where a partner lacks mental capacity (*MCA 2005 ss 16(2), 18(1)(e)*)

➤ A decision to dissolve a partnership can be taken by a court, or a deputy (subject to restrictions in *MCA 2005 s 20*) appointed by the court, where this is in the 'best interests' (*MCA 2005 s 4*) of the partner and in accordance with the principles set out in *MCA 2005 s 1*.

6   ... death, bankruptcy (*PA s 33(1)*), retirement (*PA s 26*) or expulsion (*PA s 25*) of a partner

➤ These events dissolve the partnership.

7   ... charging order

➤ If a partner's share in the partnership assets is subject to an order for payment of a private debt (*PA s 23*), a creditor can seek a court order for the asset's sale; when this sale takes place, a purchaser gains a share in the asset without becoming party to the partnership.

➤ When an order is made, the other partners may give notice of dissolution to prevent a third party purchaser gaining title to the asset (*PA s 33(2)*).

8   ... disposal

➤ A partner may insist on the sale of the business as a whole or in parts (*PA s 39*).

9   ... winding up

➤ Any partner, except a bankrupt, can apply to the court for the appointment of a receiver (*PA s 38*).

V   After dissolution - distribution of assets

➤ Partners all have continuing authority to act on behalf of the partnership after its dissolution (*PA s 38*).

➤ On dissolution, every partner has a right to insist that the partnership property is used to pay the firm's debts (*PA s 39*).

➤ If a dissolution occurs, the business may be sold:

◆ as a going concern, *or*

◆ by breaking up the business and selling off the assets.

➤ The assets (or proceeds from sale of the assets) are distributed in the following order (*PA s 44*):

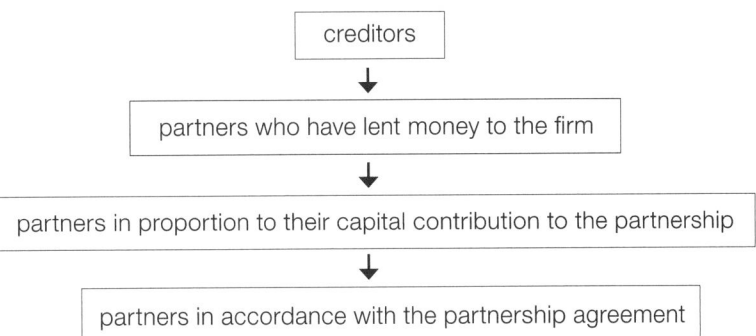

➤ When other partners continue the business, the outgoing partner is entitled to:

a) interest at 5% on that partner's share of the assets, *or*

b) whatever profit the court attributes to that partner's share of the partnership assets between the dissolution and the actual payment of his share (*PA s 42*).

➤ Where a partner dies, the entitlement under *s 42* to interest or ongoing profits is regarded as a debt owed to his estate from the date of his death (*PA s 43*).

VI   Taxation

➤ See the Taxation chapter: Income tax, CGT and IHT.

B Limited liability partnerships (LLPs)

I Formation of an LLP
II Membership of an LLP
III A written agreement for an LLP
IV Obligations and liability of an
LLP and its members
V Taxation - see 'Taxation' section

This section deals solely with an English law limited liability partnership (LLP) incorporated under LLPA 2000.

CA 2006 and LLP(ACA)R 2009

➤ Many provisions of *CA 2006* apply, with amendments, to LLPs.

◆ *LLP(ACA)R 2009* makes the relevant provisions of *CA 2006* apply.

◆ *LLP(ACA)R 2009* sets out what amendments are made to sections of *CA 2006* as they apply to LLPs.

I Formation of a limited liability partnership (LLP)

A What is an LLP?

What is an LLP?

➤ An LLP is not a partnership.

➤ An LLP is a new form of legal entity (*LLPA 2000 s 1(1)*). It is a legal person in its own right as a body corporate formed under the *LLPA 2000*.

◆ An LLP is a body corporate with unlimited capacity to act (eg: it can buy and sell property, sue and be sued and do anything which a natural person can do) (*LLPA 2000 s 1(3)*).

➤ LLPs offer:

a) limited liability to 'members' akin to that enjoyed by shareholders, *and*

● In a partnership, partners have unlimited liability. For partnership debts and obligations this liability is joint; for loss or damage from a wrongful act or omission (in the ordinary course of a partnership's business or with the authority of the partners) of partners in a partnership, it is joint and several.

b) the tax advantages of a partnership, as opposed to a company (ie: although the existence of the partnership may be important for computational purposes, prior to winding-up, an LLP or partnership is, unlike a company, transparent for tax purposes), *and*

● Income tax relief is not available for interest payable on a loan taken out by an individual to invest in an investment LLP (*ITA 2007 s 399*; see also p 105).

● The exemption from tax, otherwise accorded to a pension fund and a friendly society, do not apply if such an entity is a member of a property investment LLP whose business consists wholly or mainly of investing in land (*FA 2001 Sch 25*, and *FA 2004 s 186(2)*).

c) limited public disclosure to protect an LLP's creditors.

B Formation of an LLP

1 2 or more persons associated for carrying on a lawful business with a view to profit subscribe their names to an incorporation document (*LLPA 2000 s 2(1)(a)*).

2 Deliver to the Registrar (*LLPA 2000 ss 2(1)(b)-(c)*):

a) the incorporation document (or a copy of it), *and*

Incorporation document (*LLPA 2000 s 2*)

➤ The incorporation document must (*LLPA 2000 s 2(2)*):

- ◆ state the name of the LLP, *and*
- ◆ state whether the LLP's registered office is to be situated in England and Wales, in Wales, or in Scotland or in Northern Ireland, *and*
- ◆ state the address of the registered office, *and*
- ◆ give the required particulars of each of the persons who are members of the LLP on incorporation, *and*
  - ● The required particulars are those stated in the LLP's Register of Members and Register of Members' Residential Addresses.
- ◆ *either* specify which of those persons are to be designated members *or* state that every person who from time to time is a member of the LLP is a designated member.

---

b) a statement made by a solicitor engaged in the formation of the LLP or a subscriber to the incorporation document, that Step 1 has been complied with.

- ● It is an offence, punishable by a fine and/or imprisonment for up to 2 years to make this statement if a person knows it to be false or does not believe it to be true (*LLPA 2000 ss 2(3)-(4)*).

3 The Registrar, if satisfied that the requirements of *LLPA 2000 s 2* are complied with (*LLPA 2000 s 3(1)*):

- ◆ registers the documents delivered, *and*
- ◆ gives a certificate that the limited liability partnership is incorporated.
  - ● The certificate must state (*LLPA 2000 s 3(1A)*):
    - ▪ the name and registered number of the limited liability partnership, *and*
    - ▪ the date of its incorporation, *and*
    - ▪ whether the limited liability partnership's registered office is situated in England and Wales (or in Wales), in Scotland or in Northern Ireland.

Evidence that the LLP is incorporated

➤ The certificate is conclusive evidence that the requirements of *LLPA 2000 s 2* have been complied with and that the LLP is incorporated (*LLPA 2000 s 3(4)*).

Post formation (see also p 288): some practical things to think about...

➤ Any member who will be operating from home must fix a nameplate to that address.

➤ All stationery must bear the LLP name, incorporation number and registered office address.

➤ The normal accounting period runs from the date of incorporation to the last day of the month, 12 months later (but this can be changed or extended by using the relevant form).

➤ Accounts must be filed in accordance with companies legislation.

➤ Each LLP receives an annual accounts request (for HMRC purposes) - and results are made public through the annual registration process.

II   Membership of an LLP

➤ On the incorporation of an LLP, its members are the persons who subscribed their names to the incorporation document (other than any who have died or been dissolved) (*LLPA 2000 s 4(1)*).

➤ Any other person may become a member of a limited liability partnership by and in accordance with an agreement with the existing members (*LLPA 2000 s 4(2)*).

➤ A person may cease to be a member of an LLP (as well as by death or dissolution) (*LLPA 2000 s 4(3)*):

   ◆ in accordance with an agreement with the other members, *or*

   ◆ in the absence of agreement with the other members as to cessation of membership, by giving reasonable notice to the other members.

➤ A member of an LLP is not regarded for any purpose as employed by the LLP unless, if he and the other members were partners in a partnership, he would be regarded for that purpose as employed by the partnership (*LLPA 2000 s 4(4)*).

➤ For an LLP that carries on business without having at least 2 members and which does so for more than 6 months, any person who is a member of that LLP for any time after those 6 months and who knows that it is carrying on business with only 1 member, is liable (jointly and severally with the LLP) for the payment of the LLP's debts contracted during the period he was a member after those 6 months (*LLPA 2000 s 4A*).

➤ If a member of an LLP (*LLPA 2000 s 7*):

   ◆ ceases to be a member, *or*

   ◆ has died, *or*

   ◆ has become bankrupt or had his estate sequestrated or has been wound up, *or*

   ◆ has granted a trust deed for the benefit of his creditors, *or*

   ◆ has assigned the whole or any part of his share in the LLP (absolutely or by way of charge or security)

   THEN:.

   ◆ the former member, *or*

   ◆ his personal representative, *or*

   ◆ his trustee in bankruptcy or liquidator, *or*

   ◆ his trustee under the trust deed for the benefit of his creditors, *or*

   ◆ his assignee,

   MAY NOT interfere in the management or administration of any business or affairs of the LLP.

   NOTE: This does not affect any right to receive an amount from the LLP in that event.

Designated members (*LLPA 2000 s 8*)

➤ If the incorporation document specifies who are to be designated members (*LLPA 2000 s 8(1)*):

   ◆ they are designated members on incorporation, *and*

   ◆ any member may become a designated member by and in accordance with an agreement with the other members.

➤ A member may cease to be a designated member in accordance with an agreement with the other members (*LLPA 2000 s 8(1)*).

   ◆ If, at any time, there would otherwise be 0 or 1 designated members then every member is a designated member (*LLPA 2000 s 8(2)*).

➤ If the incorporation document states that every person who from time to time is a member of the LLP is a designated member, then every member is a designated member (*LLPA 2000 s 8(3)*).

➤ A person ceases to be a designated member if he ceases to be a member (*LLPA 2000 s 8(6)*).

➤ An LLP must ensure that where (*LLPA 2000 s 9*):

  a) a person becomes or ceases to be a member (or a designated member) that notice is delivered to the Registrar within 14 days, *and*

  b) there is a change in the particulars of a member as listed in the Register of Members or Register of Members' Residential Addresses, that notice is delivered to the Registrar within 14 days.

  - A notice delivered that relates to a person becoming a member/designated member must contain:

    a) a statement that the member/designated member consents to acting in that capacity, *and*

    b) when a person becomes a member, a statement of the particulars of the new member that are required to be included in the Register of Members/Register of Members' Residential Addresses.

  - Where an LLP gives notice of a change of a member's service address as stated in its Register of members and the notice is not accompanied by notice of any resulting change in the particulars contained in its Register of Members' residential addresses, then the notice must be accompanied by a statement that no such change is required.

  - Non-compliance is an offence by the LLP and every designated member, punishable by a fine not exceeding level 5 on the standard scale (currently £5,000 (*CJA 1982 s 37*)).

III   A written agreement for an LLP

➤ The mutual rights and duties of an LLP and its members may be governed by agreement between the members, or between the LLP and its members (*LLPA 2000 s 5(1)(a)*).

  ◆ If there is no agreement *LLPR 2001* resolve matters by applying (with suitable modifications) the law relating to partnerships (*LLPA 2000 s 5(1)(b)*). Partnership law does not apply generally, but only in accordance with default provisions set out in *LLPR 2001 rr 7-8*.

Default provisions for agreement between members (*LLPR 2001 rr 7-8*)

➤ All the members of an LLP are entitled to share equally in the capital and profits of the LLP (*r 7(1)*).
➤ The LLP must indemnify every member for payments made and personal liabilities incurred by him in:
  a)   the ordinary and proper conduct of the LLP's business, *or*
  b)   or about anything necessarily done for the preservation of the business or property of the LLP (*r 7(2)*).
➤ Every member may take part in the management of the LLP (*r 7(3)*).
➤ No member is entitled to remuneration for acting in the LLP's business or management (*r 7(4)*).
➤ No person may be introduced as a member or voluntarily assign an interest in an LLP without the consent of all existing members (*r 7(5)*).
➤ Any difference arising as to ordinary matters connected with the LLP's business may be decided by a majority of the members, but no change may be made in the nature of the LLP's business without consent of all members (*r 7(6)*).
➤ The LLP's books and records are to be available for inspection at the LLP's registered office or at such other place as the members think fit and every member of the LLP may when he thinks fit have access to and inspect and copy any of them (*r 7(7)*).
➤ Each member shall render true accounts and full information of all things affecting the LLP to any member or his legal representative (*r 7(8)*).
➤ If a member, without the LLP's consent, carries on any business of the same nature as and competing with the LLP, he must account for and pay over to the LLP all profits made by him from that business (*r 7(9)*).
➤ Every member must account to the LLP for any benefit derived by him without the consent of the LLP from any transaction concerning the LLP, or from his use of the LLP's property, name or business connection (*r 7(10)*).
➤ No majority of the members can expel any member unless a power to do so has been conferred by express agreement between the members (*r 8*).

➤ An agreement made before an LLP's incorporation between the subscribers may obligate an LLP (ie: it is not necessary to novate an agreement between the partners after incorporation) (*LLPA 2000 s 5(2)*).

IV   Obligations and liability of an LLP and its members

1   Obligations and liability of an LLP to third parties

➤ Every member is the agent of the LLP (*LLPA 2000 s 6(1)*). *But* an LLP is not bound by anything done by a member dealing with a person if (*LLPA 2000 s 6(2)*):

a) the member in fact has no authority to act for the LLP, *and*

b) the person knows that the member has no authority or does not know or believe the member to a member of the LLP.

- A former member of an LLP is regarded (in relation to any person dealing with the LLP) as still being a member of an LLP *unless* (*LLPA 2000 s 6(3)*):

   i)   the person has notice that the former member has ceased to be a member of the LLP, *or*

   ii) notice that the former member has ceased to be a member has been delivered to the Registrar.

➤ An LLP is liable to the same extent as a member if that member is liable to any person (other than another member of the LLP) as result of that member's wrongful act or omission in the course of the LLP's business or with its authority (*LLPA 2000 s 6(4)*).

➤ A document signed by 2 members of an LLP (or by 1 member whose signature is attested to by a witness) and which is expressed to be executed on behalf of the LLP has the same effect as if executed under the LLP's common seal (*CA 2006 s 44, LLP(ACA)R 2009 r 4*).

- A purchaser (in good faith for valuable consideration, including a lessee/mortgagee) may assume a document has been duly executed by an LLP if it purports to be signed by 2 members of the LLP (or by 1 member whose signature is attested to by a witness) (*CA 2006 s 44(4), LLP(ACA)R 2009 r 4*).

2   Obligations of an LLP which apply under *CA 2006* (as modified for LLPs by *LLP(AA)(ACA)R 2008* and *LLP(ACA)R 2009*)

By way of example, an LLP must ...	Source	Applicable by
... ensure the LLP's name appears outside its place of business	CA 2006 ss 82 C(TD)R 2008	LLP(ACA)R 2009 r 14
... ensure the LLP's place of registration, registered number and address of its registered office appear on its on its correspondence		
... keep accounting records	CA 2006 ss 386-389	LLP(AA)(ACA)R 2008
... prepare accounts (These are approved by the designated members and signed by designated members on behalf of the members)	CA 2006 ss 393-414	LLP(AA)(ACA)R 2008
... deliver accounts and any auditor's report to every member of the LLP and holder of its debentures not later than 9 months after the end of the accounting reference period or, if earlier, the date on which it actually delivers its accounts and the auditor's report on those accounts to the Registrar. ◆ Small and medium sized LLPs, like small companies, may submit less detailed accounts (*CA 2006 s 444, SLLP(A)R 2008, LMLLP(A)R 2008*)	CA 2006 s 423 CA 2006 s 425 CA 2006 s 442	LLP(AA)(ACA)R 2008
... deliver accounts, auditor's report and annual returns to the Registrar	CA 2006 s 441 CA 2006 ss 854-855A, 858	LLP(AA)(ACA)R 2008 LLP(ACA)R 2009 r 30
... register charges with the Registrar of Companies	CA 2006 s 860	LLP(ACA)R 2009 r 32
... have a Register of Members and Register of Members' Residential Addresses	CA 2006 ss 162-165	LLP(ACA)R 2009 r 18

3   Obligations and liability of members ...

<table>
<tr><td colspan="2" align="center">Obligations and liability of members ...</td></tr>
<tr><td colspan="2" align="center">... to the LLP</td></tr>
</table>

➤ Members owe an LLP a duty of good faith (akin to the fiduciary duty directors owe a company).

➤ There is no statutory duty of good faith between partners. However:

  ◆ If a member, without the consent of the LLP, carries on any business of the same nature as and competing with the LLP, he must account for and pay over to the limited liability partnership all profits made by him in that business (*LLPR 2001 r 7(9)*).

  ◆ Every member must account to the LLP for any benefit derived by him without the consent of the LLP from any transaction concerning the LLP, or from any use by him of the property of the LLP, name or business connection (*LLPR 2001 r 7(10)*).

<table>
<tr><td align="center">... to third parties</td></tr>
</table>

➤ The law is uncertain as to whether a third party who has suffered economic loss could successfully sue a member of the LLP.

  ◆ *Williams v National Life Health Foods Ltd* [1998] 1 WLR 830 suggests that the courts would consider whether:

    • the member assumed personal responsibility, *and*

    • the third party relied on that assumption, *and*

    • such reliance was reasonable.

<table>
<tr><td align="center">... in compliance with CA 2006 and IA 1986
(as modified for LLPs by LLPR 2001, LLP(AA)(ACA)R 2008, and LLP(ACA)R 2009)</td></tr>
</table>

➤ A designated member may commit an offence if an LLP is in default of its statutory obligations, eg: if annual accounts are not filed with 28 days of the return date (*CA 2006 s 858* by *LLP(ACA)R 2009 r 31*).

➤ The designated members must appoint auditors, otherwise the members may do so at a meeting convened for that purpose (*CA 2006 s 485* by *LLP(AA)(ACA)R 2008*).

➤ A member may be liable for wrongful trading (*IA 1986 s 214* by *LLPR 2001 Schedule 3*), or fraudulent trading (*CA 2006 s 993* by *LLP(ACA)R 2009 r 47*).

  ◆ The court may require a member to make a contribution if that member withdrew property within 2 years of the LLP being wound-up (*IA 1986 s 214A* as inserted by *LLPR 2001 Schedule 3*).

V   Taxation

➤ Prior to a winding-up, an LLP is essentially 'transparent', or 'look through', for tax purposes.

➤ See the Taxation chapter: Income tax and CGT. (For IHT see *IHTA 1984 s 267A*.)

C   Private companies limited by shares

I	Establishment	IV	Finance
II	Shareholders	V	Taxation
III	Directors		

All references in this chapter are to CA 2006, unless stated otherwise.

➤ This chapter ignores group and charity provisions.

➤ This book does not deal with the various special provisions on quoted companies or traded companies.

I   Establishment

Checks before establishing a company

➤ **Check 1:** search the index at Companies House to see if a desired name already exists (*s 66*).

➤ **Check 2:** do a trade mark search to see if the desired name already exists.

➤ **Check 3:** search local directories (eg: Yellow Pages, Thomson Local) to see if the desired name is already in use (to avoid passing off) (*s 69*).

2 methods of establishing a company

1: From scratch

Steps

1 Prepare the following (see also the next page for more detail):

1) Memorandum of Association (*s 8*)
2) Application for registration including: (*s 9*)
   ◆ A statement of capital and initial shareholdings (*s 10*)
   ◆ A statement of the company's proposed officers (*s 12*)
   ◆ A statement of the intended registered address (*s 9(5)a)*)
   ◆ Articles of Association (*s 9(5)(b)*)
3) A statement of compliance (*s 9(1)*)
4) Fee

File items 1 to 4 with the Registrar of Companies

See p 304 on how documents are sent to the Registrar

2 The Registrar registers the documents delivered to him if he is satisfied that the registration requirements of *CA 2006* have been complied with (eg: the name does not need approval under *CA 2006 Part 5*) (*s 14*). Registration is on the same day if submission is to the Central Registry (Cardiff) before 3 pm. Regional branches (London, Birmingham, Leeds, Edinburgh) also offer a same day service.

3 The Registrar issues the 'Certificate of Incorporation', bringing the company into existence as a legal person (*s 15*). A pre-incorporation contract is voidable. The company can only participate in a pre-existing agreement through a novation.

2: buy a shelf company

➤ A shelf company has already been incorporated and 'sits on the shelf'.

➤ The existing directors of the shelf company resign and members complete a stock transfer form.

➤ This costs around £350 and is fast and immediate. It is usual to change/ amend:

a) directors and secretary
b) shareholders
c) registered office
d) name
e) articles
f) share capital

➤ The purchased company comes with resignation letters from existing directors.

A The registration documents

1 Memorandum of association

➤ A memorandum of association is a memorandum stating that the subscribers (*s 8(1)*):

 ◆ wish to form a company under *CA 2006, and*

 ◆ agree to become members of the company and to take at least 1 share each.

➤ The memorandum must be in form in *C(R)R 2008* and must be authenticated by each subscriber (*s 8(2)*).

2 Application for registration

➤ The application for registration must (*ss (9(2), 9(4), 9(5)*):

 ◆ state the company's proposed name, *and*

 ◆ state if the company's registered office is to be in England or another part of the UK, *and*

 ◆ state if the members' liability is to be limited, and if so whether it is to be limited by shares, *and*

 ◆ state whether the company is to be a private or a public company, *and*

 ◆ contain a **statement of capital and initial shareholdings** which states (*s 10(2)*):

 • the total number of shares of the company to be taken on formation by the subscribers to the memorandum of association, *and*

 • the aggregate nominal value of those shares, *and*

 • for each class of shares:

 ▪ prescribed particulars of the rights attached to the shares, *and*

 ▪ the total number of shares of that class, *and*

 ▪ the aggregate nominal value of shares of that class, *and*

 • the amount to be paid up and the amount (if any) to be unpaid on each share (whether on account of the nominal value of the share, or by way of premium), *and*

 • certain information to identify subscribers to the memorandum (*s 10(3)*), *and*

 • for each subscriber to the memorandum (*s 10(4)*):

 ▪ the number, nominal value (of each share) and class of shares to be taken on formation (and if relevant for each class of shares (*s 10(5)*)), *and*

 ▪ the amount to be paid up and the amount (if any) to be unpaid on each share (whether on account of the nominal value of the share or by way of premium), *and*

 ◆ contain a **statement of the company's proposed officers** containing (*s 12*):

 • a consent by each person who will be a director or secretary (although if all partners in a firm are joint secretaries, consent may be by one partner on behalf of all), *and*

 • details of the person(s) who is/are to be the first director(s) and first secretary/joint secretaries together with the same details for each that are in the register of directors, register of directors' residential addresses and register of secretaries (*s 12*):

 ◆ contain a **statement of the intended address of the company's registered office**, *and*

 ◆ contain a copy of any proposed **articles of association** (to the extent that these are not supplied by the default application of 'model articles' (see p 293).

3 Statement of compliance

➤ This is a statement that the requirements of *CA 2006* as to registration have been complied with.

B A company's constitution

Constituents and status of a company's constitution

➤ A company's constitution includes (*ss 17, 29*):

'1' below
- the company's articles, *and*

'2' below
- any special resolution, *and*
- any resolution or agreement agreed to by all the members that, had it not been agreed by all the members, would not have been effective unless passed as a special resolution, *and*
- any resolution or agreement agreed to by all the members of a class of shareholders that, had it not been agreed by all that class, would not have been effective unless passed by some particular majority or otherwise in some particular manner, *and*
- any resolution or agreement that effectively binds all members of a class of shareholders though not agreed to by all those members.

➤ The constitution is a 'contract' between the company and its members, governing members' rights in their capacity as members of the company (*s 33(1)*).

1   Articles of Association (the 'regulations' governing a company's internal workings)

➤ A company may have 'model articles' (a default set) or bespoke articles specific to the company (*s 18*).

- If no articles are registered the model articles apply by default (*s 20(1)(a)*).

- If articles *are* registered, insofar as they do not exclude/modify the model articles, the model articles apply (*s 20(1)(b)*).

➤ **Form:** Must be in a single document and divided into paragraphs numbered consecutively (*s 18(3)*).

➤ **Alteration:** A company may amend its articles by special resolution (*s 21(1)*).

- **Formalities:** A company must send the Registrar a copy of the articles as amended not later than 15 days after any amendment takes effect else a criminal offence is committed (*ss 24, 26, 34, 35*).

➤ **Entrenchment:** The articles may contain rules (known as 'provisions for entrenchment' or 'PFE') saying that specified provisions of the articles may be amended/repealed only if certain conditions are met/procedures complied with, that are more restrictive than those of a special resolution (*s 22(1)*).

- *PFEs may only be made on formation or by later amendment of the articles agreed by all members (s 22(2)) [not yet in force] (CALLP(TPS)(A)R 2009).*

- PFEs do not prevent amendment of articles by agreement of all members or a court (*s 22(3)*).

- The company must always notify the Registrar if PFEs are added, amended or removed (*s 23*).

- If a company has a PFE and is required to send the Registrar a document evidencing an amendment to the articles - and it does amend the articles - it must also send a statement of compliance (*s 24*).

➤ **Objects:** Unless the articles specifically restrict the company's objects, they are unrestricted (*s 31(1)*).

- Companies with articles and memoranda filed under the previous *Companies Acts* will remain subject to any restrictions in them unless new articles are adopted or the old ones are amended.

2   Resolutions or agreements

➤ **Formalities:** A company must send the Registrar a copy of every resolution or agreement within 15 days after it is passed or made (*s 30*).

- For a resolution or agreement not in writing, a company must send the Registrar a written memorandum setting out its terms within 15 days after it is passed or made (*s 30*).

Summary of Model Articles for private companies limited by shares

MA	Subject matter
Directors	
3-6	Directors' powers and responsibilities
7-16	Decision-making by directors
17-20	Appointment of directors
Shares and distributions	
21-29	Shares
30-35	Dividends and other distributions
36	Capitalisation of profits
Decision-making by shareholders	
37-41	Organisation of general meetings
42-47	Voting at General Meetings
Administrative arrangements	
48	Means of communication to be used
49	Company seals
50	No right to inspect accounts/records
51	Provision for employees on cessation
Directors' indemnity & insurance	
52	Indemnity
53	Insurance

References in this Chapter to 'MA' are to the Model Articles

➤ The Model Articles are in *C(MA)R 2008 Schedule 1*.

This book assumes that a company has the MA in force and has not altered these

➤ The Model Articles (see table left) is a model set of articles that apply in the absence of other articles (unless specifically excluded).

➤ Despite the MA, special articles may be needed to:

◆ **empower directors to allot, or prohibit directors from allotting, shares:** if a company with more than 1 class of shares (*ss 550-551*) (see p 321).

◆ **empower directors to allot shares to whomever they wish:** lifting the statutory pre-emption rights of existing members to a pro rata allotment of newly issued shares (*s 567*).

● Directors can vote on such matters in certain circumstances (*MA 14*) (see p 321).

◆ **enable directors to vote on issues in which they have a personal interest.**

◆ **restrict members' right to transfer shares:** eg: in a small family company where the members are anxious to retain control of membership. *MA 26(5)* allows directors to refuse to transfer shares.

◆ **prevent removal of directors:** likely in small company. If a director holds shares, a *Bushell v Faith* clause is sensible as it multiplies his votes if a resolution proposes his removal. This provides some job security, but shareholders retain the right to remove directors by ordinary resolution (*s 168*).

Statutory books

➤ The statutory books must be kept by the company and constantly updated:
◆ Register of Members (*ss 113-121*) (see p 296), *and*
◆ Register of Directors (*ss 162-166*) (see p 306), *and*
● Register of Directors' Residential Addresses (*s 165*) (see p 306), *and*
◆ Register of Secretaries (*ss 275-279*) (see p 314), *and*
◆ Register of Debenture Holders (*ss 743-748*), *and*
◆ Register of Charges (*s 876*) (see pp 317 et seq), *and*
◆ Minute Books for board and general meetings (*ss 248 and 355*), *and*
◆ Accounting records (only after incorporation) (see pp 310 et seq), *and*
◆ Copies of directors' service contracts (only after incorporation) (see p 305).

C Registered office

➤ A company must maintain a registered office to which all communications/notices may be addressed (*s 86*).

Later alteration of a company's registered office (*s 87*)

➤ A company may change the address of its registered office by giving notice to the Registrar.

➤ The change takes effect when the notice is registered by the Registrar, but until the end of 14 days (starting with the date on which it is registered) a person may validly serve any document on the company at the address previously registered.

D Company name

➤ The name of a private limited company must (almost always) end with 'limited' or 'ltd' (*s 59(1)*).

➤ Existing company names are not permitted (*s 66*).

➤ A search of the Companies House Register and Trademarks Register checks if a name is in use.

♦ NB: There is no protection period after a search.

➤ An offensive name, or a name whose use would be a criminal offence, is forbidden (*s 53*).

➤ The following require written official approval (*s 54-56*): a name suggesting connection with HM Government or a local authority or any word /expression specified in regulations.

➤ There are restrictions on use of certain words, expressions, letters, characters, signs and symbols (*ss 54-57*).

Alteration of an existing company name

➤ A company may change its name (*s 77(1)*):

♦ **by special resolution** (*s 78*), *or*

• The company must give notice to the Registrar and forward a copy of the resolution to him.

  ▪ If the change of name is conditional on an event, the notice given to the Registrar of the change must specify that the change is conditional and state whether the event has occurred.

  ▪ If the notice states that the event has not occurred, the Registrar does not have to change the name until further notice. When the event occurs, the company must give notice to the Registrar stating that it has occurred.

♦ **by other means provided for by the company's articles** (*s 79*).

• The company must give notice to the Registrar together with a statement that the change of name has been made by means provided for by the company's articles.

➤ The Registrar will issue a new certificate after payment of the fee.

➤ The change of name:

♦ is advertised by the Registrar in the *Gazette* or other approved place (*ss 1077-1078*), *and*

• A third party is not fixed with notice until 15 days after the advertisement appears (*s 1079*).

♦ has effect from the date on which the new certificate of incorporation is issued (*s 81*).

➤ Within 12 months of a company registering its name, the Secretary of State may direct a company to change its name if it is the same as or, in the opinion of the Secretary of State, too like (*ss 67-68*):

♦ a name appearing at the time of the registration in the Registrar's index of company names, *or*

♦ a name that should have appeared in that index at that time.

➤ A person ('the applicant') may apply to a company names adjudicator to object to a company's registered name on the ground that it is (*ss 69-70*):

♦ the same as a name associated with the applicant in which the applicant has goodwill, *or*

♦ sufficiently similar to such a name that its use in the UK would be likely to mislead by suggesting a connection between the company and the applicant.

Business names and incorporation names

➤ A 'business name' is a trading name which a company may use in addition to its name of incorporation. It need not end with 'Limited', but should comply with *ss 1192-1208, CBN(MP)R 2009* and *CLLPBN(SWE)R 2009* (see p 278).

➤ Even if it uses a business name, the company must give the incorporation name and an address in the UK for serving documents:
- ◆ on all letters, orders, invoices, etc, *and*
- ◆ at all places of business to which customers have access, *and*
- ◆ to any member of the public who requests this information.

➤ The detailed regulations made under *s 82* are the *C(TD)R 2008*.

	Regulation	Requirement
Failure to comply with any regulation is a criminal offence (reg 10)	2	➤ All displays and disclosures required by these Regulations are to be in characters which can be read with the naked eye.
	3	➤ A company's registered name must be displayed at the registered office and other places at which records are kept for inspection. This does not apply to any company: ◆ which is "dormant" as defined in *s 1169*, or ◆ for which a liquidator, administrator or administrative receiver has been appointed; and the registered office/inspection place is also a place of business of that person.
	4	➤ A company's registered name must also be displayed at any location at which it carries on business. ◆ This applies to locations other than those referred to in regulation 3. ➤ Exceptions: ◆ any location which is primarily used for living accommodation, *or* ◆ the company is one where a liquidator, administrator or administrative receiver has been appointed and the location is also a place of business of that person, *or* ◆ any location at which business is carried on by a company where, for every director who is an individual, the registrar is prevented from disclosing to a credit reference agency the directors' residential addresses.
	5	➤ This sets out the manner in which a company is required to display its registered name. ➤ The name must be positioned so that it can easily be seen by any visitor to the premises. ➤ The name must also be displayed continuously unless a multiple occupation exception applies.
	6	➤ Every company must disclose its registered name on: ◆ its business letters, notices and other official publications, *and* ◆ its bills of exchange, promissory notes, endorsements and order forms, *and* ◆ cheques purporting to be signed by or on behalf of the company, *and* ◆ orders for money, goods or services purporting to be signed by or on behalf of the company, *and* ◆ its bills of parcels, invoices and other demands for payment, receipts and letters of credit, *and* ◆ its applications for licences to carry on a trade or activity, *and* ◆ all other forms of its business correspondence and documentation. ➤ Every company must disclose its registered name on its websites.
	7	➤ Every company must disclose on its business letters, its order forms; and its websites: ◆ the part of the UK in which the company is registered, *and* ◆ the company's registered number, *and* ◆ the address of the company's registered office, *and* ◆ if a limited company exempt from the obligation to use the word "limited" under *CA 2006 s 60*, the fact that it is a limited company.
	8	➤ Where a company's business letter includes the name of a director of that company, other than in the text or as a signatory, the letter must disclose the name of every director of that company.

The table title: ***C(TD)R 2008***

II Shareholders

A Joining a company (ie: becoming a member)

➤ Subscribers of the memorandum are deemed to have agreed to become members of the company (*s 112(1)*).

　◆ On registration these subscribers become members and are entered in the Register of Members (*s 112(1)*).

➤ Anyone who agrees can later become a member and is entered into the Register of Members (*s 112(2)*).

　◆ However, directors must enter a person into the Register, else the Register can be rectified (see below).

➤ A subsidiary cannot be a member of its holding company unless unusual circumstances apply (*s 136*).

Register of Members

➤ **Duty to keep a Register of Members:** Every company must keep a Register of Members which must state: the name, address, the dates on which the shareholder's membership of the company begins and ceases and the number of shares held by each member (by class if relevant) plus the consideration for the shares (*s 113(1)-(4)*).

　◆ Between acquisition and registration, the prospective member is beneficially entitled to the shares. Dividends voting rights of the existing registered member must be 'used' at the acquirer's direction.

➤ **1 member only:** If a company is formed with only 1 member there must be entered in the company's register of members the name and address of the sole member and a statement that the company has only one member. However, if the number of members of a limited company falls to 1 , when that happens there must be entered in the company's register of members the name and address of the sole member and a statement that the company has only 1 member and the date on which the company became a company having only 1 member (*s 123*).

　◆ If a company fails to do this, the company and every officer of it who is in default commits an offence and is liable to a fine and, for continued contravention, to a daily default fine (*s 123(4)-(5)*).

➤ **Rectification:** The court can order the register to be rectified if *either* (*s 125*):

　a) anyone's name is, without sufficient cause, entered in/omitted from the Register, *or*
　b) default is made/unnecessary delay takes place in showing anyone has ceased to be a member, *or*
　c) it is 'just and equitable' to do so (*Burns v Siemens Brothers Dynamo Works Ltd* [1919] 1 Ch 225).

B Shareholders' rights

Shareholders' rights

➤ Obligations between shareholders and the company are governed by the company's constitution (*s 33*).

➤ The articles may allow a member to identify someone who can exercise members' rights. They may specify that this applies to certain rights or all rights - except the right to transfer the shares (*s 145*).

➤ For a summary of shareholders' rights, see the chart on p 297.

➤ Shareholders may, by special resolution, direct directors to take/refrain from taking, specified action (*MA 4(1)*).

　◆ No such special resolution invalidates anything which the directors have already done (*MA 4(2)*).

➤ **Voting:** a shareholder can generally vote as he sees fit *unless*:

　a) individually, or together with other directors, he holds 50% or more of the shares: this prevents a member voting to permit an abuse of power in his capacity as a director, *or*

　b) a majority shareholder ignores 'equitable considerations'. A court may overrule a special resolution which disregards these 'equitable considerations' (*Clemens v Clemens Brothers Ltd* [1976] 2 All ER 268).

➤ All members holding ordinary shares have a right to attend and vote at a general meeting of the company.

All shareholders' rights		
Rights	Notes	Statute
Restrain an *ultra vires* act	Only before the act is done (after the company is bound). Remedy is an injunction	s 171
To a share certificate	Within 2 months of allotment/lodgement of share transfer. *Prima facie* evidence of title	ss 769/776
To a copy of annual accounts and reports for each financial year	In certain circumstances, there may only be a right to a summary financial statement. The company does not need to send anything to a person for whom the company does not have a current address	s 423 s 426 C(SFS)R 2008
To have a say in removing or appointing a director		s 168
To have a name on Register of Members To inspect this register free of charge		ss 113-116
To a dividend (if declared) (and a shareholder has a right to receive one)		MA 30
To vote on a written resolution (subject to the articles) (but see more detail on p 300)		s 284
To receive notice of general meetings		s 310
To attend and vote at general meetings (subject to the articles)		s 284
Ask court to call a general meeting	If a members' boycott prevents a quorum, a court can reduce the quorum needed	s 306
Inspect records of resolutions and meetings		s 358
Not to be unfairly prejudiced	Prejudice to rights as a member may be past, present, or future	s 994
To bring a derivative claim	Subject to the permission of the court	ss 260-264
Have a company wound up	Available if 'just and equitable' and the member has a 'tangible interest'. Not available if it prejudices someone unfairly.	IA 1986 s 122(g)
Members with a minimum of 90% of nominal value of shares with rights to attend/vote		
To call a general meeting on short notice	This may be raised to any figure up to 95% (but not above this) by the articles.	s 307
Members with a minimum of 10% of nominal value of shares with rights to attend/vote		
To prevent general meeting on short notice	This is the flip side of the 90% right (see above)	s 307
Members with a minimum of 10% of total voting rights		
To demand a poll vote at a general meeting	This may *not* be excluded by the articles other than in respect of the election of the chairman or an adjournment of the meeting	s 321
Members with a minimum of 5% of the paid up capital as carries the right of voting at general meetings		
To call a general meeting at any time	The procedure is set out on p 301	s 303 C(SR)R 2009
Members with a minimum of 5% of total voting rights		
Circulate written resolution	This may be lowered below 5% by the articles	s 292-294
Circulate a statement of not more than 1,000 words about anything in a proposed resolution to be dealt with at a meeting, or other business to be dealt with at that meeting	This may also be exercised by at least 100 members who have a right to vote and hold shares in the company on which there has been paid up an average sum, per member, of at least £100	s 314

Shareholders' agreement

➤ This binds members in matters beyond the scope of the articles and is used in practice to impose extra obligations on those concerned.

- ◆ It is a private document, and unlike the articles is not open to public inspection.

- ◆ It cannot be altered without the *unanimous* consent of all those who are party to it.

- ◆ It cannot override obligations under the articles or statute.

  - ● Many shareholders agreements provide that their terms prevail over the terms of a company's articles in the case of conflict.

- ◆ It provides a remedy in breach of contract - via an injunction or damages.

- ◆ Possible uses include:

  - ● to arrange for the sale of the business as a going concern to the company when a company is initially set up, *and/or*

    - ■ Eg: setting out the allotment of shares or the grant of debentures,

  - ● agreeing to appoint a particular managing director, chairman, director etc, *and/or*

  - ● joining a director, who is not a shareholder, to the agreement to enhance his job security by obliging the other signatories not to vote for his dismissal, *and/or*

  - ● agreeing to grant a particular member a service contract, *and/or*

  - ● binding the signatories to pursue a particular management policy - such matters are usually left to the board by the articles, and an agreement gives shareholders a direct influence on how the company is managed, *and/or*

  - ● agreeing to change the name of the company or to have some policy regarding this, *and/or*

  - ● pre-emption rights, where enshrining this in the articles would be too public an act, *and/or*

  - ● to allow a member to leave the company by obliging the other signatories to purchase the shares.

Methods to control the Board

➤ The shareholders may specifically want to control the board and may use the following methods:

- ◆ increasing the number required for a quorum at a general meeting, *and/or*

- ◆ appointing proxies when a shareholder is not at a general meeting, *and/or*

- ◆ preserving the balance of power (eg: by inserting entrenched provisions in the articles restricting the transfer of shares), *and/or*

- ◆ specifying in a shareholders' agreement a valuation and buy-out mechanism, *and/or*

- ◆ limiting in the articles the powers of the board, *and/or*

- ◆ limiting in the articles the board's powers to delegate powers, *and/or*

- ◆ replacing or amending the statutory pre-emption rights.

C Safeguards for shareholders

➤ Members have a cause of action in contract to enforce rights as members of the company (*s 33*).

  ◆ Relevant rights include rights to:

  a) a share of surplus capital on winding up.

  b) a lawfully declared dividend.

  c) vote at meetings.

  ◆ The liability of shareholders is limited to the amount invested in their shares.

  Note: a company can use *s 33* to compel members to fulfil contractual obligations (eg: pay for shares).

1   Shareholders' statutory actions: derivative claims (*ss 260-264*)

  ➤ General rule: members cannot sue in the company's name (*Foss v Harbottle* (1843) 2 Hare 461).

  ➤ However, a derivative claim may be brought for a cause of action arising from an actual or proposed act or omission involving negligence, default, breach of duty or breach of trust by a director.

  ◆ The court's permission is needed to continue a derivative claim (*s 261*).

  ◆ The action is 'derivative' as the claimant is pursuing a right which belongs to the company.

  ● *The company* is the claimant and *the company* is granted a remedy, not the member.

2   Shareholders' statutory actions: 'unfair prejudice' (*ss 994-996*)

  ➤ The member's rights as a shareholder include rights under statute, the constitution and any shareholders' agreement.

  ➤ Whether there is unfair prejudice is an objective test, so prejudice is viewed from the perspective of the 'reasonable bystander' (*Re R A Noble & Sons (Clothing) Ltd* [1983] BCLC 273).

  ◆ A shareholder cannot ordinarily complain of unfairness unless there has been a breach of the terms by which he had agreed that the company would be run (but this is tempered by equitable considerations). *s 994* depends on 2 features (*O'Neill v Phillips* [1999] 1 WLR 1092):

  ● the way in which a company is run is regulated by rules to which the shareholders agree, *and*

  ● this 'contract' is treated by equity as a contract of good faith.

  ➤ The court can make 'any order it thinks fit' (*s 996(1)*) and a non-exhaustive list of powers is given (*s 996(2)*). These include:

  ◆ authorising a member to bring a civil action in a company's name.

  ◆ restraining a company from an act, or compelling it to act so as to avoid the 'unfair prejudice'.

  ◆ providing for a member's shares to be purchased by other members or the company at a fair price.

  ➤ An action brought under *s 994* is not derivative, as the claimant is suing in his own right. Consequently, *the claimant* will receive a remedy if his plea is successful.

3   Petition to wind up the company (if 'just and equitable') (*IA 1986 s 122(g)*) (not covered in detail here)

Will the courts intervene?

➤ There is conflicting authority as to whether the courts will intervene wherever it is equitable if there is no precedent for them to do so (*Heyting v Dupont* [1964] 2 All ER 273, *Prudential Assurance Co v Newman Industries Ltd (No 2)* [1982] Ch 204).

➤ Previous cases where the courts have granted a minority shareholder a remedy include where:

  ◆ the company acted illegally.

  ◆ the company passed an ordinary resolution when a special resolution is needed.

  ◆ the majority shareholders 'defrauded' a minority member (*Clemens v Clemens Bros* [1976] 2 All ER 268).

D Resolutions

1 Types of resolutions generally

➤ There are 2 types of resolution: ordinary and special. They are voted by written resolution or at a meeting.

➤ An ordinary resolution is sufficient unless articles/statute require otherwise (s 281(3)).

Resolution	How voted	Majority needed
Ordinary	**Written resolution**	More than 50% of the total voting rights of eligible members. (NB: 50% blocks these - this is 'negative control') (s 282(2))
	At a meeting	**By show of hands:** more than 50% of the votes cast by those entitled to vote (s 282(3), C(SR)R 2009). **By poll:** more than 50% of total voting rights of members entitled to vote, who vote in person *or* by proxy, *or* in advance (s 282(4), C(SR)R 2009).
Special	**Written resolution** Not a special resolution unless stated to be proposed as a special resolution (s 283(3))	75% or more of the total voting rights of eligible members. (NB: 25.1% blocks these - this is 'blocking control') (s 283(2))
	At a meeting Not a special resolution unless the meeting notice included the text and specified the proposal as a special resolution (s 283(6))	**By show of hands:** 75% or more of the votes cast by those entitled to vote (s 283(4), C(SR)R 2009). **By poll:** 75% or more of total voting rights of members entitled to vote, who vote in person *or* by proxy, *or* in advance (s 283(5), C(SR)R 2009).

2 Written resolutions (ss 288-300)

➤ A written resolution has effect as if passed (as the case may be) by the company in a general meeting or by a meeting of a class of members of the company (s 288(5)).

➤ A resolution may be proposed as a written resolution by the directors or members (s 288(3)).

Proposed by directors (s 291)

➤ The company must send or submit a copy of the resolution to every eligible member by either of the following (or a mix of both):

♦ by sending copies at the same time (so far as reasonably practicable) to all eligible members in hard copy form, in electronic form or by means of a website, *or*

♦ if it is possible to do so without undue delay, by submitting the same copy to each eligible member in turn (or different copies to each of a number of eligible members in turn).

➤ The copy of the resolution must be accompanied by a statement informing the member how to signify agreement to the resolution and of the date by which the resolution must be passed if it is not to lapse.

Proposed by 5% of votes of members (ss 292-294)

➤ Members who wield 5% of voting rights (or less if specified in the articles) may require the company to circulate a written resolution (ss 292-294).

♦ This does not apply to resolutions that would, if passed, be ineffective (whether by reason of inconsistency with any enactment, the constitution or otherwise), be defamatory, be frivolous or vexatious.

♦ The members may require the company to circulate with it a statement of not more than 1,000 words on the subject matter of the resolution.

♦ The same rules for circulation apply as for circulation of a written resolution proposed by the directors, save that the copies must be sent not more than 21 days after a request from the relevant members for circulation.

♦ The expenses of the company must be paid by the members who requested the circulation of the resolution unless the company resolves otherwise.

➤ A proposed written resolution lapses if it is not passed before the end of (s 297):

♦ the period specified for this purpose in the company's articles, *or*

♦ if none is specified, the period of 28 days beginning with the circulation date.

➤ Written resolutions may *not* be used to dismiss *either* (s 288(2)):

♦ a director before the expiration of his period of office (s 168), *or*

♦ an auditor before the expiration of his period of office (s 510).

➤ **Voting** (unless Articles say otherwise) (ss 284(1), 285-287): for a company with a share capital, every member has 1 vote for each share or each £10 of stock held (and in any other case, every member has 1 vote) (see also p 302).

3   Resolutions at a meeting (ss 301-335)

4 ways a meeting can be called	
1 Directors	➤ The directors may call a general meeting of the company (s 302).

2
Directors
because the
members
request it
	➤ Members representing at least 5% of the paid-up capital of the company that carries the right to vote at general meetings of the company, may require directors to call a general meeting (s 303, C(SR)R 2009).
	   ◆ Any request (s 303(4)-(6)):
	      • must state the general nature of the business to be dealt with at the meeting, and
	      • may include the text of a resolution that may properly be moved and is intended to be moved at the meeting, and
	      • must not, if passed, be ineffective (whether by reason of inconsistency with any enactment or the constitution or otherwise), be defamatory, frivolous or vexatious, and
	      • may be in hard copy form or in electronic form, and
	      • must be authenticated by the person or persons making it.
	➤ Directors must call the meeting within 21 days from when the members require it (s 304).
	➤ Notice:
	   ◆ The meeting must be held on a date not more than 28 days after the date of the notice convening the meeting (s 304).
	   ◆ The notice must include notice of any resolution proposed by members who want the meeting (s 304).
	      • If the resolution is a special resolution the notice must state this (ss 283, 304(4)).

3
Members
because
directors
fail under 2
above
	➤ Directors' failure to call a meeting (s 305):
	   ◆ The members who requested the meeting or any of them representing more than 50% of the total voting rights of all of them may call a general meeting (s 305(1)).
	   ◆ The notice must include the text of a resolution to be moved at the meeting.
	   ◆ The meeting must be called for a date not more than 3 months from when the members required the directors to call the meeting.
	   ◆ The meeting must be called in the same manner, as nearly as possible, as that in which meetings are required to be called by directors.
	   ◆ Any reasonable expenses incurred by the members requesting the meeting by reason of the failure of the directors duly to call a meeting must be reimbursed by the company.

4
The court
	➤ The court may order a meeting if it is impracticable (s 306):
	   ◆ to call a meeting of a company in any manner in which meetings of that company may be called, or
	   ◆ to conduct the meeting in the manner prescribed by the company's articles or CA 2006.
	➤ The meeting may be called, held and conducted in any manner the court thinks fit (s 306).

Meeting	Notice	
General meeting (private company) (s 307(1))	at least 14 clear days	If an adjourned meeting is continued more than 14 days after adjournment, the company must give at least 7 clear days' notice of it (ie: excluding the day of the adjourned meeting and the day on which the notice is given) (MA 41(5))
AGM (public company) (s 307(2))	at least 21 clear days	
EGM (public company) (s 307(2))	at least 14 clear days	
General meetings where (s 312): a) special resolutions are proposed, or b) there is a resolution to remove a director or an auditor (s 168, s 510)	➤ 28 days' notice must be given to the company of the intention to move a resolution requiring special notice (s 312). ➤ Where it is not practicable for the company to give members notice of such a resolution at the same time as it gives notice of the meeting at which the resolution is to be moved, the company must give at least 14 days' notice either by newspaper advertisement (or other manner allowed by the articles) (s 312).	
Shorter notice for a private company		
➤ A general meeting may be called by shorter notice if 90% (or a higher percentage specified in the articles - but not more than 95%) of the members having a right to attend and vote at the meeting say so (s 307(4)-(5)).		

Notice of a general meeting

➤ May be given in hard copy or electronic form or by a website (or a mixture of all) (*s 308*).

➤ Must state time, date, place of meeting and (subject to articles) general nature of business (*s 311*).

➤ Must state the rights to appoint a proxy (*s 325*).

> A members' statement (see bottom row in box on p 297) must be at the company at least 1 week before the meeting (*s 314(4)*).

➤ See rules on special resolutions (see p 300).

➤ Accidental failure to give notice to anyone of a general meeting or a resolution to be moved is ignored unless the articles say otherwise except for (*s 313*):

◆ notices of any meetings called by members, *or*

◆ notices of an AGM called by members of a public company.

➤ **Recipients and service:** Notice is sent in writing to all directors and members (including all entitled to a share in consequence of death/bankruptcy of a member) (*s 310*). (Subject to articles).

➤ Adjourned meetings: If the continuation of an adjourned meeting is to take place the company must give notice of it (*MA 41(5)*):

◆ to the same people to whom notice of general meetings is required to be given, *and*

◆ containing the same information as a regular general meeting notice.

Voting at meetings (unless articles say otherwise) (*ss 284-287, C(SR)R 2009*)

➤ Voting is *either* on a show of hands *or* by poll.

◆ Voting is by a show of hands unless a poll is taken in accordance with the articles (*MA 42*).

On a vote on a show of hands	On a vote on a poll
◆ Every member present in person has 1 vote (*s 284(2)*). • Every proxy present who has been duly appointed by at least 1 member entitled to vote on the resolution has 1 vote (unless the articles say otherwise) (*s 285(1)*). • BUT a proxy has 1 vote for and 1 vote against (unless the articles say otherwise) if (*s 285(2)*): ■ the proxy has been duly appointed by more than 1 member entitled to vote on the resolution, *and* ■ the proxy has been instructed by 1 or more of those members to vote for the resolution and by 1 or more other of those members to vote against it.	◆ Every member has 1 vote for each share or each £10 of stock held by that member (*s 284(3)*). • All or any of a member's voting rights may be exercised by 1 or more appointed proxies (*s 285(3)*). ■ If a member appoints more than 1 proxy, the proxies, taken together, may not exercise more extensive voting rights than could be exercised by the member in person (*s 285(4)*). • For a resolution required or authorised by an enactment, if a private company's articles say that a member has a different number of votes when it is passed as a written resolution and when it is passed on a poll taken at a meeting, then the provision about how many votes a member has in relation to the resolution passed on a poll is void and a member has the same number of votes for the resolution when it is passed on a poll as the member has when it is passed as a written resolution (*s 285A*). ◆ A poll vote can be demanded by (*MA 44(2)*): • the chairman, *or* • the directors, *or* • 2 or more people having the right to vote on the resolution, *or* • members or proxies representing not less than one tenth of the total voting rights of all the shareholders having the right to vote on the resolution. ◆ If votes are equal, the resolution is defeated. • The articles may allow for a chairman's casting vote however.

➤ Nothing in this box (apart from the articles) restricts the effect of (*s 284(5)*): the exercise of rights by nominees (*s 152*), voting by proxy (*s 285*), exercise of voting rights on poll (*s 322*), voting on a poll: votes cast in advance (*s 322A*), or the representation of corporations at meetings (*s 323*).

Members who: i) have at least 5% of the total voting rights, *or* ii) are at least 100 members who have a right to vote and hold shares in the company on which there has been paid up an average sum, per member, of at least £100 ... may require the company to circulate, to members entitled to receive notice of a general meeting, a statement of not more than 1,000 words about anything in a proposed resolution to be dealt with at that meeting, or other business to be dealt with at that meeting (s 314).

Procedure at meetings (ss 318-335)

➤ **Quorum** (s 318):

  ◆ For 1 member companies: 1 person (member/proxy/corporate rep) present is a quorum.

  ◆ In any other case: 2 persons (members/proxies/corporate reps) present are a quorum (unless the articles say otherwise).

    ● 2 or more proxies/corporate reps of the same member do not count towards a quorum.

  ◆ If there is no quorum, no business is allowed other than the appointment of a chairman (MA 38).

  ◆ If there is no quorum within half an hour of the time of the meeting start time (or if during a meeting a quorum ceases to be present), the chairman of the meeting must adjourn it (MA 41(1)).

➤ **Chairman** (ss 319, 328):

  ◆ A chairman runs meetings. If director-appointed, he must chair where he is present and willing to do so (MA 39(1)).

    ● If no chairman has been appointed (or if he has but is not willing to chair the meeting) (or if the chairman is not present within 10 minutes of the meeting start time) the directors (or if none present, the meeting) must appoint a director/shareholder to chair, and his appointment must be the first business of the meeting (MA 39(2)).

  ◆ A member/proxy may be elected to be the chairman by a resolution passed at the meeting.

    ● This is subject to anything in the articles stating who may or may not be chairman.

➤ **Polls** (ss 321-322, s 322A, C(SR)R 2009)

  ◆ The articles may *not* exclude the right to demand a poll, save with respect to the election of the chairman, *or* adjournment of the meeting.

  ◆ The articles may *not* be altered to raise the threshold for requesting a poll above a top limit of *either* 5 members, *or* members with more than 10% of the total voting rights/paid up capital (s 321(2)).

  ◆ A member need not use all his votes or cast all the votes he uses in the same way.

  ◆ A company's articles may, for resolutions on a poll taken at a meeting, allow votes cast in advance.

    ● For a traded company any such provision may be made subject only to such requirements and restrictions as are necessary to ensure the identification of the person voting and proportionate to the achievement of that objective. .

    ● Any provision of a company's articles is void if it would have the effect of requiring any document casting a vote in advance to be received by the company or another person earlier than:

      ■ 24 hours before the time appointed for the taking of the poll (for a poll taken more than 48 hours after it was demanded), *or*

      ■ 48 hours before the time for holding the meeting or adjourned meeting (for any other poll).

    NOTE: No account is to be taken of any part of a day that is not a working day

➤ **Proxies** (ss 324-331):

  ◆ A member may appoint another person as his proxy to exercise all or any of his rights to attend and to speak and vote at a meeting of the company (s 324(1)).

  ◆ A proxy must vote in accordance with any instructions given by the member by whom the proxy is appointed (s 324A, C(SR)R 2009).

  ◆ A member may appoint more than 1 proxy, provided each proxy exercises the rights of different share(s), or (as the case may be) to a different £10 multiple of stock held by him (s 324(2)).

  ◆ Any provision of the company's articles is void in so far as it would have the effect of requiring any appointment (or document) to be received by the company/anyone else earlier than the following time (s 327 (2)) (and no account is taken of any day which is not a working day (s 327(3))):

    ● (for a meeting/adjourned meeting) 48 hours before the time for holding it (s 327(2)(a)), *or*

    ● (if a poll is taken more than 48 hours after demanded), 24 hours before the poll (s 327(2)(b)), *or*

    ● *(if a poll is taken 48 hours or less after it was demanded), the time it was demanded [s 327(2)(c) not yet in force].*

➤ **Attendance and speaking by directors and non-shareholders** (MA 40)

  ◆ Directors may attend and speak at general meetings, even if they are not shareholders.

  ◆ The chairman may permit people who are not shareholders (or otherwise entitled to exercise the rights of shareholders at general meetings) to attend and speak at a general meeting.

➤ **Adjournments:** When adjourning a meeting, the chairman must (MA 41(4)):

  ◆ either specify the time and place to which it is adjourned, or state that it is to continue at a time and place to be fixed by the directors, *and*

  ◆ comply with any directions as to time and place of any adjournment given by the meeting.

Amendments to resolutions (MA 47)

➤ An ordinary resolution to be proposed at a general meeting may be amended by ordinary resolution if:

  ◆ notice of the proposed amendment is given to the company, in writing, by a person entitled to vote at the general meeting at which the resolution is to be proposed, no less than 48 hours before the meeting is to take place (or at such later time as the chairman of the meeting may determine), *and*

  ◆ the proposed amendment does not, in the reasonable opinion of the chairman of the meeting, materially alter the scope of the resolution.

➤ A special resolution to be proposed at a general meeting may be amended by ordinary resolution, if:

  ◆ the chairman of the meeting proposes the amendment at the general meeting at which the resolution is to be proposed, *and*

  ◆ the amendment does not go beyond what is necessary to correct a grammatical or other non-substantive error.

➤ If the chairman of the meeting, acting in good faith, wrongly decides that an amendment to a resolution is out of order, the chairman's error does not invalidate the vote on that resolution.

Special rules for class meetings (s 334)

➤ Members do not have power to require directors to call a class meeting.

➤ The court does not have power to order a meeting.

➤ There are special provisions about class meetings where class rights will be varied.

4   After a resolution has been passed

After a shareholders' resolution has been passed

Steps

1 Comply with the filing formalities (s 30) (see p 292).

  ◆ A sole member must provide the company with written notice of his resolution, otherwise although its validity is unaffected, the member will be liable for a fine (s 357).

2 Write up the minutes (s 355).

3 The board must meet and resolve to carry out any act which the shareholders have authorised *if* the shareholders wish to use this authority - but they are not compelled to do so.

Public notice of receipt of certain documents (ss 1077-1079, 1144)

➤ Documents or information to be sent/supplied to a company or sent by/supplied by a company must be sent in hard copy or electronic form.

➤ The Registrar must publish in the Gazette notice of the receipt of any of the documents listed in the box below.

➤ The notice must state name and registered number of the company, a description of document and the date of receipt.

  ◆ The Registrar need not publish before the date of incorporation of the company to which the document relates.

➤ A third party is not fixed with notice until 15 days after the advertisement appears.

◆ The memorandum and articles. ◆ Any amendment of the articles (including every resolution/agreement required to be embodied in or annexed to copies of the articles). ◆ After any amendment of the articles, the text of the articles as amended. ◆ Any notice of a change of the company's name. ◆ The statement of proposed officers required on formation of the company. ◆ Notification of any change among the directors.	◆ Notification of any change in the particulars of directors required to be delivered to the Registrar. ◆ Annual accounts and reports required to be delivered to the Registrar. ◆ The annual return. ◆ Notification of any change of the registered office. ◆ Copy of any winding-up order. ◆ Notice of the appointment of liquidators. ◆ Order for the dissolution of a company on winding up. ◆ Return by liquidator of the final meeting on a winding up.

III   Directors

A   Powers

➤ The directors are responsible for the management of the company's business, for which purpose they may exercise all the powers of the company (subject to the articles) (*MA 3*).

➤ The acts of a person acting as a director are valid notwithstanding that it is afterwards discovered (*s 161*):

- ◆ that there was a defect in the person's appointment, *or*

- ◆ that the person was disqualified from holding office, *or*

- ◆ that the person had ceased to hold office, *or*

- ◆ that the person was not entitled to vote on the matter in question.

B   Appointment

1   Methods of appointment of directors

➤ The first directors are named in the statement of proposed officers in the application for registration (*s 12*). They take office on incorporation.

➤ Thereafter they are appointed by the directors' decision or directly by ordinary resolution (*MA 17(1)*).

- ◆ Each prospective director must sign a consent which is filed at Companies House.

- ◆ In any case where, as a result of death, the company has no shareholders and no directors, the personal representatives of the last shareholder to have died have the right, by notice in writing, to appoint a person to be a director (*MA 17(2)*).

➤ A director will need to possess 'qualification shares' to join the board if a special article requires this.

2   Requirements for directors

➤ A private company must have at least 1 director (*s 154(1)*).

➤ A company must have at least one director who is a natural person (i.e. an individual) (*s 155(1)*).

➤ A person may not be appointed a director unless he is at least 16 years old (*s 157(1)*).

- ◆ However, if appointed in breach the liability of such person is unaffected (*s 157(5)*).

➤ A director may need to possess 'qualification shares' to join the board if the articles requires this.

3   Service contracts

➤ When the board is about to discuss a director's contract, the director must avoid conflicts of interests and make a declaration (*s 177*) (see p 308).

- ◆ See restrictions on a director counting towards a vote or quorum on an authorisation vote (see p 308).

- ◆ A members' resolution or the articles may also restrict the quorum in other ways in this instance.

➤ Members must consent by ordinary resolution for contracts over 2 years, otherwise the fixed-term clause is void and the agreement becomes terminable at 'reasonable notice' (*ss 188-189, 281(3)*).

➤ All directors' service contracts must be available for inspection by members (free of charge) at the registered office until at least 12 months after they expire *(ss 228-229)*.

- ◆ Members also have rights to be provided with a copy of a service contract *(ss 228-229)*.

4   Shadow director

➤ A shadow director is any person (ie: even a legal person such as a company) in accordance with whose directions or instructions the directors of a company are accustomed to act (*s 251*).

Register of Directors and Register of Directors' Residential Addresses (ss 162-167, 1088)

➤ A company must keep a register of its directors with the following details (s 162(1)):
- ◆ **Individuals:** name (and former names), a service address (may be stated as 'The company's registered office'), the country/state/part of the UK in which he is usually resident, nationality, occupation (if any) and date of birth (s 163).
- ◆ **Businesses:** corporate/firm name, registered/principal office, legal form of the company/firm and law by which it is governed (and, if applicable, the register in which it is entered and its registration number in that register) (s 164).

➤ The register must be kept available for inspection at the registered office (s 162(3)).

➤ The register must be open for inspection by any member for free, and by anyone else for a fee.

➤ A company must keep a register of directors' residential addresses (s 165).
- ◆ If a director's usual residential address is the same as his service address (as stated in the register of directors), the register reflects that. (This does not apply if his service address is stated to be 'The company's registered office').
- ◆ Addresses may be kept from public inspection if an application is made for a good reason (s 1088).
  - There are also other protections against disclosure of directors' residential addresses to entities other than the public in certain circumstances (ss 240-246 and C(DA)R 2009).

➤ **Changes:** The Registrar must be notified of any change and the date of any change, within 14 days of a person becoming/ ceasing to be a director (or any change in the register of directors / register of directors' residential addresses) (s 167).

C   Loss of office

1   Events on loss of office

➤ A director may, depending on his contract, simultaneously lose any executive office.
- ◆ A director may claim for wrongful or unfair dismissal, or redundancy.
- ◆ A director may be entitled to compensation under his contract.

➤ The board and officers:
- ◆ file the relevant form at Companies House, *and*
- ◆ delete the director from the register of directors, *and*
- ◆ cease to be required to make the contract available at the registered office 1 year after the director's service contract terminates or expires (s 299).

2   *Companies Act 2006 s 168:* removal by members

Steps	
1	The members have the right to remove a director at any time by ordinary resolution at a general meeting notwithstanding anything in any agreement between the company and that director (s 168(1)).
2	Members contemplating seeking the dismissal of a director should check the director's service contract to ascertain what compensation and/or damages may be due under it (s 168(5)).
3	A member gives 'special notice', leaving a formal notice at the registered office at least 28 days before a general meeting. (If one is called in this period (ie: less than 28 days after this special notice), the notice is deemed to have been properly given) (s 168(2), s 312)
4	On receipt of the 'special notice', the company must immediately inform the director concerned (s 169(1)).
5	If the board does not call a meeting the member may be able to call a meeting if he has sufficient rights (see the box on p 301 called '4 ways a meeting can be called').
6	The director has a right to make a written representation (of reasonable length) to members as well as speak at the meeting (even if he is not a member) (s 169(2)-(6)).
7	If there is a *Bushell v Faith* provision (see p 307) in the articles and the resolution concerns a director's employment, his votes will increase in proportion to the size of his shareholding.

- ◆ Where the director has enough shares to defeat an ordinary resolution removing him from the board, consider passing a special resolution to remove this article.
- ◆ If there is an entrenched provision in the articles protecting the director this cannot be changed without following the set procedure for this in the articles.

3   Disqualification

a) *MA 18*

➤ A person ceases to be a director as soon as:

◆ he ceases to be or is prohibited from being a director by *CA 2006* or by law, *or*

◆ a bankruptcy order is made against him, *or*

◆ a composition is made with his creditors generally in satisfaction of his debts, *or*

◆ a registered medical practitioner who is treating that person gives a written opinion to the company stating that that person has become physically or mentally incapable of acting as a director and may remain so for more than 3 months, *or*

◆ by reason of his mental health, a court makes an order which wholly or partly prevents him from personally exercising any powers or rights which he would otherwise have, *or*

◆ a notification is received by the company that he is resigning or retiring from office as director takes effect in accordance with its terms.

b) *Company Directors' Disqualification Act 1986*

➤ Disqualification may last from 2 to 15 years, depending on the director's previous conduct and the nature of the offence (*CDDA 1986* and *Re Sevenoaks Stationers (Retail) Ltd* [1991] Ch 164).

➤ Disqualification is imposed for:

◆ being convicted of an indictable offence in connection with the promotion, formation, management, liquidation or striking off of a company with the receivership of a company's property or with his being an administrative receiver of a company (*CDDA 1986 s 2*), *or*

◆ persistent default over filing with the Registrar of Companies (*CDDA 1986 s 3*), *or*

◆ fraudulent trading (*CDDA 1986 s 4*), *or*

◆ general misconduct in relation to a company which has become insolvent (*CDDA 1986 s 6*), *or*

◆ where a company is insolvent, and the director's conduct during the insolvency makes the director unfit to hold office (*CDDA 1986 s 10*).

Protecting a director's position

➤   To protect his position, a director might try to:

◆ have a *Bushell v Faith* clause in the articles. Where the director is also a shareholder, this multiplies the director's voting power at a general meeting at which his dismissal is on the agenda.

◆ entrench a provision in the articles protecting him which cannot be changed without going through a pre-defined procedure set out in the articles.

◆ hold over 25% of the voting shares or over 50% to control the board's composition.

◆ hold a debenture which is conditional on the lender remaining a director.

◆ ensure damages are due under a service contract if the director is removed.

◆ if he is not the chairman, remove the chairman's casting vote (especially if there are only 2 directors on the board).

◆ set the quorum at a general meeting (or a board meeting) at a level to protect himself.

◆ if he is a shareholder and there is a shareholders agreement, he can contractually protect himself in that agreement.

D   Directors' duties

The statutory fiduciary duties owed to the company	
Duty to act within powers (s 171)	➤ A director must act in accordance with the company's constitution. ➤ A director must only exercise powers for the purposes for which they are conferred. ➤ It is generally thought that an ordinary resolution can absolve a director of liability as long as there is no fraud on the minority (although the law is unclear).

Duty to act in the way he considers, in good faith, would be most likely to promote the success of the company (s 172)	➤ '... promote the success of the company': this must be for the benefit of the members as a whole (unless the company is insolvent when the interests of creditors are put first).
	➤ A director must have regard (amongst other matters) to the:
	  ◆ likely consequences of any decision in the long term, *and*
	  ◆ interests of the company's employees, *and*
	    • Employees do not have the right to enforce this.
	  ◆ need to foster the company's business relationships with suppliers, customers and others, *and*
	  ◆ impact of the company's operations on the community and the environment, *and*
	  ◆ need to act fairly as between members of the company, *and*
	  ◆ desirability of the company maintaining a reputation for high standards of business conduct.

Duty to exercise independent judgment (s 173)	➤ There is no breach if a director acts as authorised by the company's constitution. ➤ There is no breach if a director acts in accordance with an agreement entered into by the company that restricts the future exercise of discretion by its directors.

Duty to avoid conflicts of interest (s 175)	➤ This means avoiding a situation in which a director has, or can have, a direct or indirect interest that conflicts, or possibly may conflict, with the interests of the company.
	  ◆ Applies particularly to exploitation of property, information or opportunity (and it is immaterial whether the company could take advantage of the property, information or opportunity).
	➤ This duty does not apply to a conflict of interest arising in relation to a transaction or arrangement with the company. However, interests in proposed transactions/arrangements must be declared under s 177 (below) and existing transactions/arrangements must be declared under s 182 (below).
	  ◆ The board may authorise most conflicts arising from third party dealings by the director (eg: personal exploitation of corporate resources and opportunities).
	    • Board authorisation is effective only if the conflicted director has not taken part in the decision or the decision is valid even without the participation of the conflicted director.
	    • Board authorisation is only effective if nothing in the constitution invalidates it.
	  ◆ Member authorisation is permitted (s 180(2)).
	➤ This duty is not infringed if the situation cannot reasonably be regarded as likely to give rise to a conflict of interest.
	➤ This duty also applies after a director ceases to be a director (as regards the exploitation of any property, information or opportunity of which he became aware at a time when he was a director) (s 170(2)).

Duty not to accept third party benefits due to: his status or doing/not doing anything as director (s 176)	➤ 'Third party' means a person other than the company/person acting on behalf of the company. ➤ Benefits from a person by whom the director's services are provided to the company (eg: his service company) are not regarded as conferred by a third party. ➤ There is no breach for accepting a benefit which cannot reasonably be regarded as likely to give rise to a conflict of interest. ➤ No board authorisation is permitted. ➤ Member authorisation is permitted (s 180(2)). ➤ This duty also applies after a director ceases to be a director (as regards things done or omitted by him before he ceased to be a director) (s 170(2)).

Duty to declare interest in *proposed* transaction or arrangement with the company (s 177)	Duty to declare interest in *existing* transaction or arrangement with the company (ss 182-187)

➤ The declaration must be made before the company enters into the transaction or arrangement.
➤ The declaration may be made by several methods.
⊙➤ The nature and extent of the interest must be declared.
⊙➤ No declaration is required if:
  ◆ there is only 1 director, *or*
  ◆ it cannot reasonably be regarded as likely to give rise to a conflict of interest, *or*
  ◆ (or to the extent that) the other directors are already aware of it or reasonably ought to be, *or*
  ◆ (or to the extent that), it concerns terms of his service contract that have been or are to be considered by a meeting of the directors.
	➤ No declaration is needed if or to the extent that the interest has been declared under s 177 (see left)
	➤ Duty: Where a director is in any way, directly or indirectly, interested in a transaction or arrangement that has been entered into by the company, he must declare the nature and extent of the interest to the other directors as soon as reasonably practicable (s 182).
	  ◆ **Failure to declare is a criminal offence.**
	  ◆ The declaration must be made at a directors' meeting (s 182) or by the affected director sending a notice in writing to the other directors (s 184) or by giving general notice at a directors meeting (s 185).
	  ◆ The third and fourth arrow points for a s 177 declaration also apply here (follow the arrows).

| The statutory duty to exercise reasonable care, skill and diligence (s 174) |

➤ The care, skill and diligence that would be exercised by a reasonably diligent person with:

   ◆ the general knowledge, skill and experience that may reasonably be expected of a person carrying out the functions of a director in relation to the company (ie: an objective test), and

   ◆ the general knowledge, skill and experience that the director has (ie: a subjective test).

E Restrictions on directors

1 **Service contracts** (ss 188, 189, 228, 229, 281(3))

   ➤ These may not exceed 2 years, unless approved by members' ordinary resolution (see p 305).

   ➤ Shareholders have a right to inspect service contracts (see p 305).

2 **Substantial property transactions** (ss 190-196, 281(3))

   ➤ Director transactions with the company are forbidden (unless approved by members' ordinary resolution or conditional on member approval) if a non-cash asset is of 'substantial value'.

   ◆ 'substantial value' means:

      a) the asset is over £5,000 and exceeds 10% of the company's asset value as shown in the latest statutory accounts (or if no statutory accounts, 10% of the called-up share capital), or

      b) the asset exceeds £100,000.

      ● The value of assets forming part of an arrangement or series are aggregated.

      ● Payments under a director's service contract and payments for loss of office are excluded.

   ➤ If members' approval is not gained, the contract is voidable.

   ➤ Any director involved must indemnify the company for any loss/damage and account to it for any profit.

3 **Restriction on loans to directors and related matters** (ss 197, 204-209, 213, 281(3))

   ➤ These are forbidden subject to the following exceptions:

   ◆ expenditure on company business (if it aggregates to £50,000 or less).

   ◆ expenditure on personally defending certain proceedings (in connection with any alleged negligence, default, breach of duty or breach of trust by the director in relation to the company), regulatory actions or investigations related to the company.

   ◆ minor loans (if they aggregate to £10,000 or less) (if made to the director or connected persons),

   ◆ the company is in the business of money-lending.

   ➤ If members' approval is not obtained, the contract is voidable.

   ➤ Not a criminal offence: to make such loans but the prior restrictions have often been ignored in practice.

   ➤ The company has redress (for profit or losses accruing to the company due to the transaction) against a director who receives the loan and against directors who authorised it (s 213).

4 **Payments for loss of office** (ss 215-222)

   ➤ Payments for loss of office (eg: a 'golden handshake') must have prior approval of members by ordinary resolution, otherwise such payments are held on trust by the recipient and must be repaid.

   ◆ Exception: small payments or small values (ie: £200 or less) are allowed.

   ➤ Redundancy payments, unfair dismissal compensation, damages for breach of contract are unaffected.

5 **Contract with a sole member who is a director (not in the ordinary course of business)** (s 231)

   ➤ The contract must be written or the terms should be set out in a memorandum or in the minutes of the first board meeting after the contract is made.

   ➤ It is a criminal offence not to comply.

F Directors' responsibilities related to accounts and reports

1 Accounting records

➤ The directors of a company must ensure that the company keeps adequate accounting records (*s 386*).

➤ The accounting records must (*ss 388(1), 388(4)*):

◆ be kept for at least 3 years from the date on which they are made, *and*

◆ be kept at its registered office or such other place as the directors think fit, *and*

◆ at all times be open to inspection by the company's officers.

2 Annual accounts

➤ **Duty to prepare:** The directors must prepare company 'individual accounts' for each financial year (*s 394*) containing a balance sheet as at the last day of the financial year and a profit & loss account (*s 396*).

➤ **Content:** The accounts must give a true and fair view of the assets, liabilities, state of affairs, financial position and profit/loss (*ss 393, 396(2)*).

◆ The annual accounts must be approved by the board and must be signed by a director on behalf of the board (on the balance sheet within the accounts) (*s 414*).

◆ The accounts must contain a statement that there is no relevant audit information of which the auditors are unaware, and that the director has taken all steps which ought to have been taken to make himself aware of such information and to establish that the auditors are so aware.

● A director commits a criminal offence if this statement is false (*s 418*).

◆ Accounts may be less detailed for small/medium companies (*ss 382, 383, 444, 445, 465, 466*).

● If the accounts are prepared in accordance with the small companies regime, the balance sheet must contain a statement to that effect in a prominent position above the signature (*s 414(3)*).

◆ The accounts must comply with *LMCG(AR)R 2008* and *SCG(ADR)R 2008*.

➤ **Filing and informing:** The accounts must be filed with the Registrar within 9 months after the end of the accounting reference period (*s 442(2)*).

◆ By that time, (or, if earlier, the date on which it actually delivers its accounts/reports to the Registrar), a company must send a copy of its annual accounts/reports for each financial year to (*s 423-424*):

● every member of the company, *and*

● every holder of the company's debentures, *and*

● every person who is entitled to receive notice of general meetings.

◆ If the relevant accounting reference period is the company's first and is a period of more than 12 months, the period for filing the accounts with the Registrar, is the later to expire of (*s 442(2)*):

● 9 months from the first anniversary of the incorporation of the company, *or*

● 3 months after the end of the accounting reference period.

3 Directors' report

➤ The directors must submit a report for each financial year (*s 415*) which must contain (*s 416-417*):

◆ the names of the persons who, at any time during the financial year, were directors, *and*

◆ the principal activities of the company in the course of the year, *and*

◆ (except if entitled to the small company exemption) any amount the directors recommend should be paid as dividend, *and*

◆ (except if entitled to the small companies exemption) a business review being a fair review of the business of the company and a description of the principal risks and uncertainties facing the company.

➤ The form of the report must comply with *LMCG(AR)R 2008* and *SCG(ADR)R 2008*.

➤ The report must be approved by the board and signed on its behalf by a director or secretary (*s 419(1)*).

➤ If the report is prepared taking advantage of the small companies exemption, it must contain a statement to that effect in a prominent position above the signature (*s 419(2)*).

➤ Any separate corporate governance statement must be approved by the board and signed on behalf of the board by a director or the secretary of the company (s 419A) (CA(A,R,A)R 2009 para 2).

➤ **Filing and informing:** as per 'Annual accounts' (above).

4   **Annual return** (ss 854, 855, 855A, 856, 856A, 856B and CA(ARSA)R 2008)

➤ Every company must deliver to the Registrar successive annual returns.

➤ This must be made up to a date not later than the company's return date, being:

   ◆ the anniversary of the company's incorporation, *or*

   ◆ if the last return was made up to a different date, the anniversary of that date.

➤ The return must be delivered to the Registrar within 28 days after the date to which it is made up.

➤ The return shows: the address of the registered office, type of company and principal business activities, certain details of directors and company secretary (if any), certain details about share capital and shareholders.

Auditors

➤   A company's accounts must be audited unless exempt as a small company (below) or dormant (s 475).

   ◆ The auditor must be a certified or chartered accountant who is independent of the company (ss 1209-1238).

➤   **Appointment:** Auditors must be appointed for each financial year by the directors or members by ordinary resolution (s 485).

   ◆ Exception: if the directors reasonably resolve otherwise on the ground that audited accounts are unlikely to be required.

➤   **Time:** (Other than for the first financial year), the appointment must be within 28 days of the earlier of (s 485(2)):

   ◆ the end of the time allowed for sending out the annual accounts/reports for the previous financial year (see p 310), *or*

   ◆ the day on which the annual accounts/reports for the previous financial year were actually sent out.

➤   **Re-appointment:** Where no auditor has been appointed by the end of the relevant period, any auditor in office immediately before that time is deemed to be re-appointed at that time, *unless* (s 487(2)):

   ◆ he was appointed by the directors, *or*

   ◆ the articles require actual re-appointment, *or*

   ◆ the deemed re-appointment is prevented by the members (see below), *or*

     ● Members representing at least 5% (or any lower amount specified in the articles) of the total voting rights of all members who would be entitled to vote on a resolution that the auditor should not be re-appointed may serve notice that the auditor shall not be re-appointed (s 488).

   ◆ the members have resolved that the auditor should not be re-appointed, *or*

   ◆ the directors have resolved that no auditors should be appointed for the relevant financial year.

➤   **Removal:** Members can remove the auditor at any time by an ordinary resolution at a general meeting (s 510). The procedure is the same as for the removal of a director (see p 306) (ss 511-521).

   ◆ The Registrar must be notified of the resolution removing the auditor within 14 days (s 512).

The need for an auditor in a small company (ss 476, 477)			
Balance sheet	Over £3.26 million	Any	£3.26 million or less
Turnover	Any	Greater than £6.5 million	£6.5 million or less
Need for an auditor?	✓	✓	✗

Shareholders with at least 10% of the nominal value of the issued share capital (or a class of it) can insist on an audit

G Directors' decisions and board meetings

Directors' decisions

➤ The directors may make any rule which they think fit about how they take decisions, and about how such rules are to be recorded or communicated to directors (*MA 16*) ... subject to the articles.

➤ **General rule:** Directors' decisions must be either unanimous or a majority decision (*MA 7(1)*).

 ◆ **Exception:** If a company has 1 director and nothing in the articles requires it to have more than 1 director, directors may take decisions ignoring anything in the articles about directors' decision-taking (*MA 7(2)*).

➤ **Unanimous decision:** The directors take a unanimous decision when they all indicate to each other by any means that they share a common view on a matter (*MA 8(1)*).

 ◆ A unanimous decision may take the form of a written resolution, copies of which have been signed by each eligible director or to which each eligible director has otherwise indicated agreement in writing (*MA 8(2)*).

  ● An eligible director is one who would have been entitled to vote on the matter if it had been proposed as a resolution at a directors' meeting (*MA 8(3)*).

 ◆ A unanimous decision may only be made under *MA 8* if the eligible directors would have formed a quorum at such a meeting (*MA 8(4)*).

Calling a directors' meeting (ie: a board meeting) *(MA 9)*

➤ Any director may call a directors' meeting by giving notice of the meeting to the directors or by authorising the company secretary (if any) to give such notice. (*MA 9(1)*).

➤ **Notice of any directors' meeting:**

 ◆ must indicate (*MA 9(2)*):

  ● its proposed date, time and subject matter, *and*

  ● where it is to take place, *and*

  ● if it is anticipated that directors participating in the meeting will not be in the same place, how it is proposed that they should communicate with each other during the meeting, *and*

 ◆ need not be given in writing (*MA 9(3)*), *but*

 ◆ need not be given to directors who waive their entitlement to notice of that meeting, by giving notice to that effect to the company not more than 7 days after the date on which the meeting is held (*MA 9(4)*).

  ● Where such notice is given after the meeting has been held, that does not affect the validity of the meeting, or of any business conducted at it.

  ● Oral notice is sufficient.

Participation in a directors' meeting (ie: a board meeting) *(MA 10)*

➤ Subject to the articles, directors participate in a directors' meeting (or part of it) when:

 ◆ the meeting has been called and takes place in accordance with the articles, *and*

 ◆ they can each communicate to the others any information or opinions they have on any particular item of the business of the meeting.

➤ In determining whether directors are participating in a directors' meeting, it is irrelevant where any director is or how they communicate with each other.

➤ If all the directors participating in a meeting are not in the same place, they may decide that the meeting is to be treated as taking place wherever any of them is.

1   **Quorum for majority decisions** (*MA 11*)

➤ At a directors' meeting, unless a quorum is participating, no proposal is to be voted on (*MA 11(1)*).

◆ Exception: a proposal to call another meeting (*MA 11(1)*).

➤ Quorum is 2 unless changed by the directors - but it cannot be changed to less than 2 (*MA 11(2)*).

➤ If the quorum is lacking, the directors must not take any decision other than a decision to appoint further directors, *or* to call a general meeting to enable the shareholders to appoint further directors (*MA 11(3)*).

2   **Chairing of directors' meetings** (*MA 12*)

➤ The directors may appoint a director to chair their meetings: this person is known as the chairman.

➤ The directors may terminate the chairman's appointment as chairman at any time.

➤ If the chairman is not participating in a directors' meeting within 10 minutes of the time at which it was to start, the participating directors must appoint one of their number to chair it.

3   **Voting and the casting vote** (*MA 13*)

➤ Usually, there is 1 vote per director (although the *MA* do not specify this).

➤ The *MA* call for voting by majority or unanimity. Usually, resolutions are passed by a simple majority.

➤ If votes for and against a proposal are equal, the chairman or other director chairing has a casting vote.

◆ This does not apply if, in accordance with the articles, the chairman or other director is not to be counted in the decision-making process for quorum or voting purposes.

4   **Conflicts of interest** (*MA 14* and see also p 308)

➤ If a proposed directors' decision concerns an actual/proposed transaction/arrangement with the company in which a director is interested, that director can't be counted for voting or quorum purposes.

◆ Exception:

● the company by ordinary resolution disapplies the provision of the articles which would otherwise prevent a director from being counted as participating in the decision-making process, *or*

● the director's interest can't reasonably be regarded as likely to give rise to a conflict of interest, *or*

● the director's conflict of interest arises from:
  ■ a guarantee given, or to be given, by or to a director in respect of an obligation incurred by or on behalf of the company or any of its subsidiaries, *or*
  ■ subscription, or an agreement to subscribe, for shares or other securities of the company or any of its subsidiaries, or to underwrite, sub-underwrite, or guarantee subscription for any such shares or securities, *or*
  ■ arrangements where benefits are made available to present/former employees/directors of the company/subsidiaries which do not provide special benefits for directors/ former directors.

➤ If a question arises at a meeting of directors (or of a committee of directors), as to the right of a director to participate for voting or quorum purposes, the question may, before the end of the meeting, be referred to the chairman. His ruling is final and conclusive (except in respect of the chairman).

◆ If the question is about the chairman's right to participate, this must be decided by a directors' decision at that meeting. The chairman cannot participate for voting or quorum purposes in this decision.

5   **Records of decisions to be kept** (*s 248* and *MA 15*)

➤ The directors must ensure that the company keeps a written record of every unanimous or majority decision taken by the directors for at least 10 years from the date of each decision recorded.

◆ It is a criminal offence to fail to keep board meeting minutes for 10 years from the date of the meeting.

First board meeting

Consideration may be given to the following:

1   Declaring interests

2   Electing a chairman / managing director / any directors with special responsibility.

3   Appointing further directors and/or a secretary.

4   Approving the cost of formation: the company may reimburse subscribers by a novation contract.

5   Adopting a business name.

6   Opening a bank account and approving bank mandates.

7   Ordering stationery complying with the requirements in s 82, to state the company name, its place of registration and registered number, the address of its registered office.

   ◆   This information should also be displayed at any place where the company conducts business.

8   VAT registration with HMRC.

9   PAYE and National Insurance obligations: contact the local tax office.

10   Insurance: Ensure all the company's assets/ necessary insurance policies are in its own name.

11   Appointing an auditor.

12   By default, the accounting reference date is fixed by statute as the last day of the month in which the anniversary of incorporation falls (s 391(4)). This may be changed later by submitting a form under s 392.

13   Perhaps adopting a company seal (s 45).

14   Awarding directors' service contracts.

   ◆   If the contract is for over 2 years, the board must resolve to seek shareholders' approval (s 188).

15   Allotting/Transferring shares and issuing share certificates.

16   Whether to call a general meeting to obtain authority from shareholders to deal with relevant matters.

17   Issuing debentures.

H   The company secretary

➤   A private company is not required to have a company secretary (s 270(1)). If a company has none:

   ◆   anything authorised or required to be given or sent to or served on, the company by being sent to its secretary:

      ●   may be given or sent to, or served on, the company itself, *and*

      ●   if addressed to the secretary is treated as addressed to the company, *and*

   ◆   anything else required or authorised to be done by or to the secretary may be done by or to:

      ●   a director, *or*

      ●   a person authorised generally or specifically in that behalf by the directors.

➤   A company must keep a register of its secretaries (s 275(1)).

➤   Anything requiring or authorising something to be done by or to a director and secretary is not satisfied by being done by or to the same person acting both as director and, or in place of, the secretary (s 280).

➤   The secretary has ostensible authority (and probably actual authority) to act in administrative matters (*Panorama v Fidelis* [1971] 2 QB 711). This includes keeping the statutory books.

➤   The first secretary (if any) is named in the statement of proposed officers in the application for registration and takes office on incorporation (s 12).

I Directors' liability

➤ **On the hook:** A provision (in the articles, in a contract or otherwise) attempting to exempt/indemnify a director against liability for negligence, default, breach of duty or breach of trust by him is void (*s 232*).

  ◆ This does not apply to lawful provisions in the articles for dealing with conflicts of interest.

  ◆ However, directors may obtain Qualifying Third Party Indemnity Provisions (QTPIPs) and Qualifying Pension Scheme Indemnity Provisions (QPSIPs) (*ss 232-237*). (A director can purchase insurance.)

    ● The company must retain QTPIPs/QPSIPs for at least 1 year after expiry. They can be viewed by shareholders (*s 238*).

➤ **Ratification of acts of directors** (*s 239*):

  ◆ Shareholders can generally ratify acts of directors by ordinary resolution, subject to the articles.

  ◆ No reliance is allowed on the votes in favour by the director or any connected person.

  ◆ If the ratification decision is taken by written resolution the director (and connected persons) may not take part in the written resolution procedure.

    ● The company need not send such a director a copy of the written resolution, and that director (and connected persons) are not counted among votes required for the written resolution to be passed.

  ◆ If the ratification decision is taken at a general meeting, those members whose votes are to be disregarded may still attend that meeting, take part in that meeting and count towards the quorum for that meeting (if their membership gives them the right to do so).

➤ **Liability:** Generally, a director is *not* personally liable, although *exceptions include* if he ...

  ◆ ... breaches a statutory, or other, duty (see p 308).

  ◆ ... **gives a personal guarantee or enters into other personal obligations:** This will occur in a small company where the banks insist on a personal guarantee to back loans.

  ◆ ... **acts while disqualified:** He will be liable for all debts the company incurs during this period.

  ◆ ... trades 'fraudulently' (*IA s 213*) (see p 347).

    ● This means the director is knowingly party to fraudulent trading.

    ● An action under *IA s 213* is only possible during liquidation, when the liquidator may petition the court for the director to contribute to the company's assets.

  ◆ ... trades 'wrongfully' (*IA s 214*) (see p 347).

    ● The director knows or ought to know that the company's insolvency is likely, *and*

    ● he fails to act to minimise the loss of creditors, *and*

    ● he may be required to contribute to the company's assets during liquidation.

  ◆ ... breaches a warranty of authority.

    ● The director purports to act for the company, but acts *ultra vires*.

    ● If the director has ostensible authority, the company is bound.

> *s 1157:* a court may excuse a director either wholly or partly from liability if it is fair to do so

Ultra vires acts (ie: acts beyond what the company's constitution permits)		
Company acts *ultra vires* (*s 39*)	➤ The company is bound provided its agent had actual or ostensible authority to act (see p 366). ➤ The directors are liable for any breach of duty (see pp 308 et seq).	

Agent acts *ultra vires*, but within the company's power (*s 40*)	➤ **Board of directors:** power to bind company (and to authorise others to do so) is unfettered.
	  ◆ A company is bound against a third party acting in good faith.
	  ◆ Members can generally ratify directors' acts with an ordinary resolution, subject to the articles.
		see pp 305 and 316 for the validity of directors' acts notwithstanding a problem

Agent (eg: unauthorised director or company secretary)	➤ If the agent has 'ostensible' authority the company is bound. ➤ Members can generally ratify the act with an ordinary resolution, subject to the articles.	

➤ Companies House is a public register but third parties are not fixed with constructive notice of the constitution (*s 40(2)*).
➤ An agent/director will not be subject to penalty unless the company incurs a loss due to their actions.

Instructions for use of this box:
Read it from left to right
- grey areas indicate a choice that has to be made depending on circumstances or facts which may (or may not) be true
- non-grey areas indicate consequences that automatically flow from whatever is on the left

IV = *intra vires*
UV = *ultra vires*

Party	Act	Actual authority?	Apparent authority?	Company bound?	Ratification?	Director liable?
Board	*intra vires*	✓ (always for IV)	✓ (Board always has this)	✓ (ss 39-40)	Ratification by the Board if within the Board's power, else ratification by an appropriate resolution at a GM (unless a fraud on the minority)	✗
	ultra vires	✗ (always for UV)	✓ (Board always has this)	✓ (ss 39-40)	An ordinary resolution is needed to ratify a UV act (or a special resolution if changing the articles)	✓
Single Director	*intra vires*	✓	✓ (must be if Board has actual authority)	✓	Ratification by the Board if within the Board's power, else ratification by an appropriate resolution at a GM (unless a fraud on the minority)	✗
		✗	✓	✓	Ratification by the Board if within the Board's power, else ratification by an appropriate resolution at a GM (unless a fraud on the minority)	✓
		✗	✗	✗ No because it is not an act done with the authority of the Board ss 39-40 do not apply	Ratification by the Board if within the Board's power, else ratification by an appropriate resolution at a GM (unless a fraud on the minority)	✓
	ultra vires	✗ (always for UV)	✓	✓	An ordinary resolution is needed to ratify a UV act (or a special resolution if changing the articles)	✓
			✗	✗ No because it is not an act done with the authority of the Board ss 39-40 do not apply		✓
Unauthorised agent	*intra vires* or ultra vires	✗	✗	✗	✗	Not applicable

IV Finance

➤ This section examines 2 methods by which companies raise money: by loans and by shares.

A Debentures

➤ Directors and a lender take the following steps to grant a debenture:

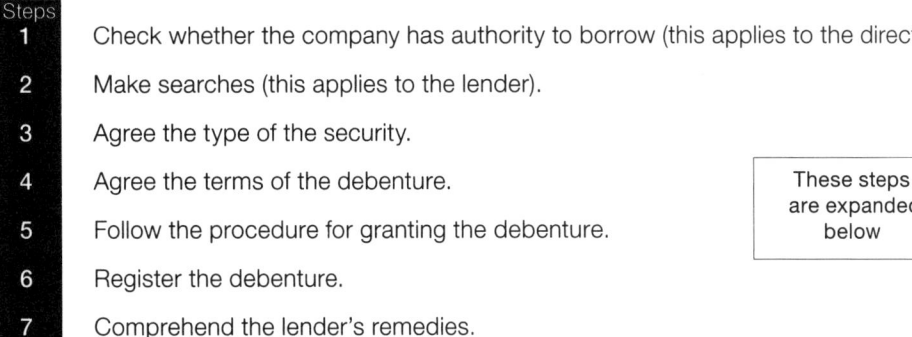

Steps	
1	Check whether the company has authority to borrow (this applies to the directors).
2	Make searches (this applies to the lender).
3	Agree the type of the security.
4	Agree the terms of the debenture.
5	Follow the procedure for granting the debenture.
6	Register the debenture.
7	Comprehend the lender's remedies.
8	Redeem the debenture.

> These steps
> are expanded
> below

1   Check whether the company has authority to borrow (this applies to the directors)

➤ A company's constitution generally allows borrowing unless it states specifically that this is limited.

 ◆ NB: Companies have unlimited objects unless the articles contain specific restrictions.

 • For pre-*CA 2006* companies, restrictions in the memorandum are deemed to be part of the articles. Therefore, rather than checking for powers, the check needs to be for restrictions.

2   Make searches (this applies to the lender)

➤ The lender should make a search of the Charges Register at Companies House which lists the date on which any charge was created, the amount of the security, the property subject to the charge and the holder of the charge.

 ◆ If these particulars are given incorrectly on the Register, then registration is void against an administrator, liquidator or purchaser for value.

➤ The lender should also check at Companies House to ensure that:

 ◆ the directors have power to borrow. (He should inspect the constitution but see also under '1' above.)

 • Although this is sensible, it is not *necessary,* as *s 39(1)* says that the company has power ostensibly and a third party does not need to check whether it *actually* has such power.

 ◆ the directors have been properly appointed - a lender should inspect the forms of appointment at Companies House which will confirm the authorisation of particular individuals to act.

 ◆ the property is not already subject to a prior charge on the Charges Register.

 Note: the lender should ask the holder of a floating charge for a 'letter of non-crystallisation', stating that the charge has not crystallised.

➤ The lender should search HM Land Registry and the Land Charges Department. Both keep records of charges over land. A 'purchaser' for value is only fixed with notice of charges which appear on *these* registers, irrespective of whether the charge is also registered at Companies House.

3   Agree the type of security

a) **A fixed charge** is a charge over specified property. It prevents the company disposing of that asset without the debenture holder's agreement.

b) **A floating charge** hangs over a class of property. The company may dispose of the property in the class without the debenture holder's agreement. If an event specified in the debenture occurs, the charge 'crystallises' and the property in the class becomes 'fixed'. At this point the rules for a fixed charge apply. Examples of when a charge may crystallise include when:

   ◆ a winding up petition is presented to a court, *or*

   ◆ there is a members' resolution to voluntarily wind up the company, *or*

   ◆ an administration order is made against the company, *or*

   ◆ any other event specified in the debenture occurs.

c) **A personal guarantee** may be required from the directors, in which case they will be personally liable if the company defaults.

   ◆ The director concerned must be sure to comply with his statutory fiduciary duties and make relevant declarations when the loan is discussed (see p 308).

4   Agree the terms of the debenture

➤ **Repayment date:** on a fixed date *or* on the occurrence of a specified event.

➤ **Interest:** when payable and how the rate will be calculated.

➤ **Conditions:** if the charge is a floating one, the lender will impose a condition preventing the subsequent creation of a fixed charge over the property as this would take priority over the floating charge on liquidation.

   ◆ The company is responsible for registering this prohibition.

➤ **Power to appoint a receiver and an administrative receiver:** to be exercised if the company defaults on interest or capital repayments.

   ◆ **A receiver** has power to sell assets (and it is usual to have power to appoint one for a fixed charge).

     ● A receiver should be expressly empowered to:

       ▪ sell assets, *and*

       ▪ manage the company, *and*

       ▪ take legal proceedings in its name.

   ◆ **An administrative receiver** has management powers (and it is usual to have power to appoint one for a floating charge).

➤ **Any other powers:** eg: power to sell the security, power to run the business, etc.

5   Follow the procedure for granting the debenture

➤ The board resolves to grant the debenture.

➤ 2 directors sign the debenture.

6   **Register the debenture as a charge** (*ss 860, 870, 874*)

➤ Register the charge at Companies House and pay the fee.

◆ If appropriate, register it also with HM Land Registry or the Land Charges Department.

➤ It is the company's duty to register the charge, but anyone interested in it may do so.

◆ The security of an *un*registered charge is void against (*s 874(1)*):

● an administrator,

● a liquidator,

● a creditor of the company - the creditor ranks as an unsecured creditor,

● a person who has registered a proprietary right or interest in the property subject to the charge.

◆ A second charge which is registered, takes precedence over a first unregistered charge.

➤ The debenture should be registered at Companies House within 21 days starting with the day after the charge was created (*s 870(1)*).

◆ *CA 2006* requires the registration of 'prescribed particulars' of the charge and the instrument of the charge at Companies House.

➤ Late registration

◆ Either seek leave of the court for late registration (*s 873*) or take out a fresh charge.

➤ Incorrect registration

◆ Corrupted register entries do not offer protection so the lender should check a copy of the entry.

◆ Errors can be corrected (*s 873*). Although alterations are not retrospective, the court can order that the alteration should be valid if it does not prejudice a third party.

7   **Comprehend the lender's remedies**

➤ If remedies are required, then appoint an administrative receiver.

◆ An administrative receiver should notify the following of his appointment: the company, creditors and the Registrar (*IA s 46*).

8   **Redeem the debenture**

➤ The company sends a memorandum of discharge to the Registrar (*s 872*).

➤ The lender endorses a receipt for repayment on the debenture.

B Shares

1   **Share capital**

Money from an issue of shares
➤ The company can use the money raised from the sale of shares as it sees fit.
➤ A share must have a fixed nominal value (*s 542*).
➤ If the company receives money for a share above the nominal value, the extra consideration is paid into a share premium account (*s 610*).
➤ A company may not allot a share at a discount. If it does receive money for a share below the nominal value, the shareholder must pay the company a sum equal to the discount in the share plus interest (*s 580*).

1   **Transfer and transmission of shares**

a) Transfer of shares

> **Steps**

1   The donor or vendor completes and signs a stock transfer form.

➤ If the shares are partly paid, the transferee also signs the form.

➤ Stamp duty/SDRT may be payable - see the 'Taxation' chapter of this book.

2   The transferee sends the stock transfer form to the company (*s 770*).

3   The company amends the Register of Members and issues a certificate in the transferee's name within 2 months (*s 771*).

➤ The directors may refuse to register the transfer. If they do refuse, the instrument of transfer must be returned to the transferee with the notice of refusal unless the directors suspect that the proposed transfer may be fraudulent (*MA 26(5)*).

♦ The directors must give reasons for any refusal (*s 771(2)*).

♦ Circumstances where directors may want to refuse to register a transfer include:

a) the shares are partly paid and the directors do not approve of the transferee, *or*

b) the company has a lien over the shares, *or*

c) there is a procedural irregularity such as:

• the transfer is not lodged at the registered office with the share certificate, *or*

• the transfer relates to more than one class of share.

♦ The directors must decide as soon as practicable and always within 2 months (*s 771*).

♦ If the directors refuse, and they are acting *ultra vires, or* the transferee shows they are acting in bad faith, the court will order the register to be rectified.

♦ If the directors validly refuse to transfer shares, this does not entitle the transferee to seek damages or rescission of the contract to purchase the shares. In such a case:

• the transferor remains the legal owner of the shares and holds them on trust for the transferee.

• the transferor receives notice of resolutions and general meetings, and he may both vote and receive dividends, but he must act as the transferee instructs.

4   The company records the transfer on the annual return.

b) Transmission of shares

➤ Transmission of shares occurs when a member dies.

➤ Shares vest automatically in personal representatives (PRs) or trustees in bankruptcy by operation of law.

♦ However, although the PRs or trustees control the beneficial interest, they are not members of the company and so cannot vote or receive dividends. They can either:

i) elect for registration as members in their own right (*ss 773-774*), *or*

ii) nominate a transferee (ie: transfer the shares to a beneficiary or creditor who can then apply for registration as a member).

➤ The company behaves in accordance with *MA 27-29*.

2 Increasing share capital (issue of new shares: allotment) (*s 617*)

Steps

1 A board meeting resolves to allot shares. The directors have the power to do this, provided:

- if a private company with only 1 class of shares, nothing in the articles prohibits this (*s 550*), *or*

- otherwise, the articles or an ordinary resolution authorises it (*s 551*). Authorisation must:

  - state the maximum amount of shares that may be allotted under it, *and*

  - specify a date on which the authority expires, which must be not more than 5 years from:

    - for authorisation in articles at the time of incorporation, the date of incorporation, *or*

    - otherwise, the date on which the resolution is passed.

2 A general meeting is called to obtain shareholders' approval if:

a) the directors lack authority to allot shares under *s 551* (as above).

  - A resolution of a company to give, vary, revoke or renew authorisation under *s 551* may be an ordinary resolution, even though it amends the company's articles (*s 551(8)*).

b) the directors wish to suspend pre-emption rights under *s 561*.

s 561
➤ The company must offer existing ordinary shareholders shares on a pro rata basis for 14 days. After that, any shares not allotted can be taken by third parties (but not on terms more favourable than those offered to shareholders) (*s 562(5)*, *C(SCACOS)R 2009*).
➤ The articles may remove/alter the need for pre-emption rights or any rules associated with them (*s 567*).

- The directors will want to disapply *s 561* rights where (*ss 567-568*):

  - the consideration is wholly in cash, *or*

  - the directors do not intend to offer existing members the chance to take up their pro rata entitlement (*either* because members are unlikely to do so, *or* because the directors wish to broaden the company's membership), *or*

  - the directors do not wish to keep the share offer open for 21 days.

Suspending pre-emption rights: 3 methods (*ss 569-571*)
1 The directors of a private company with only 1 class of shares may be given power by the articles (or by a special resolution of the company) to allot equity securities of that class as if there were no right of pre-emption.
2 Directors of any type of company may be generally authorised by the articles (or by a special resolution) but this authorisation only lasts for as long as the authority under *s 551* lasts.
3 Members may pass a special resolution. This must not be proposed unless it is recommended by the directors. Before the resolution is proposed, the directors make a written statement setting out the reasons for making the recommendation, the amount to be paid to the company for the equity securities to be allotted and the directors' justification of that amount. The statement must, if the resolution is proposed: ◆ as a written resolution, be sent/submitted to every eligible member at or before the time at which the proposed resolution is sent/submitted, *or* ◆ at a general meeting, be circulated to the members entitled to notice of the meeting with that notice.

3 File with the Registrar all relevant resolutions mentioned on this page (*s 30, s 551(9)*).

4 A company must register an allotment of shares in the company's register of allotments as soon as practicable and in any event within 2 months after the date of the allotment (*s 554(1)*).

5 A company must register at Companies House a return of allotment within 1 month of making the allotment (*s 555(2)*).

6 The board resolves to seal share certificates.

3   **Reducing share capital - 3 methods**

a) **Reduce share capital** (*ss 641-651*)

➤ This requires a special resolution and *either*: i) a solvency statement, *or* ii) the court's consent.

➤ The company can (*s 641(3)*):

◆ cancel/reduce further liability on partly paid shares, *or*

◆ repay any paid-up share capital in excess of the company's wants, *or*

◆ cancel paid-up share capital that is lost or unrepresented by available assets. (This does not prejudice creditors as it merely represents an admission of losses that have been incurred.)

b) **Buy back its own fully paid ordinary shares which have been issued** (*s 690*)

➤ Repurchased shares are effectively cancelled.

➤ It is only possible to buy back ordinary shares if:

◆ the articles do not prevent this (*s 690(1)(b)*), *and*

◆ the members pass a special resolution to do so (the shares affected carry no voting rights), *and*

• the contract must be sent with the proposed resolution (for a written resolution) (*s 696(2)*), *or*

• the contract must be available for at least 15 days before a general meeting voting on the resolution and at the general meeting itself (*s 696(2)*).

◆ the company has money available which will be from one of the following sources:

Conditions for buy-back of shares

i)   distributable profits ('in reserves') (*s 692(2)(a)(i)*), *or*

ii)   an issue of shares (*s 692(2)(a)(ii)*), *or*

iii) capital (*s 710*), but only if:

■ shareholders pass a special resolution approving the use of capital (the shares affected carry no voting rights) (*s 716*), *and*

■ creditors are notified through a notice in the Gazette (*s 719*), *and*

■ the directors make a statement about the company's solvency for the next year backed up by an auditor's report (*s 714*).

◆ the contract must be available at the registered office for 10 years after it is concluded (*s 702*).

➤ A form is sent to the Registrar stating the number of shares bought and the nominal value of the shares (*s 707*).

➤ Note: a) if the directors erroneously make a solvency statement, they may be personally liable together with the purchaser of the shares to compensate the company's creditors.

b) a vendor shareholder cannot vote at the meeting.

c) **Redeem redeemable shares** (*s 684*)

➤ The company can buy back this type of share if:

i)   the shares are fully paid up (*s 686(1)*), *and*

ii)   the company has already issued non-redeemable shares, *and*

iii) nothing in the articles prevents the company from doing so.

➤ Directors may determine the terms, conditions and manner of redemption if authorised by (*s 685*):

◆ the company's articles, *or*

◆ a resolution of the company (which may be an ordinary resolution, even though it amends the company's articles).

➤ The redemption may be out of capital as per a buy-back (*s 710*) above (*s 687(1)*).

4   **Dividends**

➤ The company may by ordinary resolution declare dividends (*MA 30(1)*).

➤ The directors may decide to pay interim dividends (*MA 30(1)*).

   ◆ If the company's share capital is divided into different classes, no interim dividend may be paid on shares carrying deferred or non-preferred rights if, at the time of payment, any preferential dividend is in arrears (*MA 30(5)*).

➤ A dividend must not be declared unless the directors have made a recommendation as to its amount (*MA 30(2)*).

   ◆ Such a dividend must not exceed the amount recommended by the directors (*MA 30(2)*).

➤ No dividend may be declared or paid unless it is in accordance with shareholders' respective rights (*MA 30(3)*).

➤ A dividend must be paid by reference to each shareholder's holding of shares on the date of the resolution or decision to declare or pay it, unless (*MA 30(4)*):

   ◆ the shareholders' resolution to declare the dividend specifies otherwise, *or*

   ◆ a directors' decision to pay the dividend specifies otherwise, *or*

   ◆ the terms on which shares are issued specify otherwise.

➤ The directors may pay at intervals any dividend payable at a fixed rate if it appears to them that the profits available for distribution justify the payment (*MA 30(6)*).

➤ If the directors act in good faith, they do not incur any liability to the holders of shares conferring preferred rights for any loss they may suffer by the lawful payment of an interim dividend on shares with deferred or non-preferred rights (*MA 30(7)*).

➤ The directors consider the payment of a 'final' dividend after the accounts have been completed (*s 836*).

➤ The accounts for the calculation of a final 'dividend' must be the last set for the financial year, prepared as per *s 396* (ie: audited, filed with the Registrar, etc) (see p 310).

➤ At any time during an accounting period, the directors can decide to declare an 'interim' dividend. For the payment of an 'interim' dividend, the company can prepare 'interim' accounts (*s 838*).

➤ Dividends can only be paid if there are 'profits available' (*s 830(1)*).

   ◆ There are 'profits available' if the undistributed trading profit accumulated during the past year and previous years exceeds the total amount of debts fallen due over the past year and previous years (*s 830(2)*).

   ◆ There are some additional statutory rules about what can be counted as 'profit' and 'losses'.

➤ Members can sue the company for unpaid 'final' dividends as a debt which is owed to them from the date when the dividend was declared. There is no debt action for unpaid 'interim' dividends as members may not expect these as of right until the money is actually paid to them.

➤ Members knowingly in receipt of dividends paid when there are insufficient 'profits available' must refund the money to the company (*s 847*).

Note on taxation (CTA 2010 ss 1033-1048)

➤ Money received by an individual from the company is usually classified as a dividend or distribution subject to income tax as savings and investment income (IT(TOI)A 2005 Part 4).

➤ However, on a redemption, repayment or purchase of shares by an unquoted trading company, or the unquoted holding company of a trading group, an individual is treated as having made a disposal for capital gains tax purposes rather than having received income if:

a) the owner of the shares is resident and ordinarily resident in the UK during the year of assessment in which the transaction occurs (CTA 2010 s 1034(1)-(2)), and

b) has possessed the shares for 5 years (CTA 2010 s 1035), and

c) the sale 'substantially' reduces his holding or that of his associates (partners, close relatives, etc) (CTA 2010 ss 1037, 1040-1043),

... and the transaction was either:

'wholly or mainly for the purposes of benefiting a trade carried on by the company' and not 'to enable the owner of the share to participate in a company's profits without receiving a dividend or for the avoidance of tax' (CTA 2010 s 1033(2)),

... or i) the money received is applied to pay IHT within 2 years of death, and

ii) the IHT arises on death, and

iii) undue hardship would arise if the company did not repurchase the shares (CTA 2010 s 1033(3)).

C   Comparison of shareholding and debenture holding

	Shareholder	Debenture holder
Control	✓ Investor may vote to influence running of the company	✗ Lender usually has no right to vote
Income	✗ Dividends not paid unless company makes a profit	✓ Interest and payment dates guaranteed. If insufficient profits available, interest paid from capital
Security	✗ Capital not repaid unless the company buys back its own shares or issues redeemable shares ✓+✗ Value of capital may fluctuate - up (or down!)	✓ Capital repaid on a predetermined date or when the debenture holder demands it ✓ Capital sum normally stays set at loan amount ✗ Capital sum will not appreciate
	✗ Capital not returned if company insolvent on winding up	✓ Capital recovered on insolvency if debenture is secured
Marketability	✗ Articles may restrict transfer of shares	✓ Debenture can be sold to anyone
Tax	✗ Dividends not tax deductible	✓ Interest on the loan may be deductible as a debit on a 'loan relationship' (see p 123)

V   Taxation

➤ See the 'Corporation Tax' section.

Summary of company procedure

Transaction	Authority	Resolution	Internal procedures	External procedures
Appoint directors for at least 2 years	s 188	Ordinary	◆ If appointment is by a written resolution: • Contract must be sent with proposed resolution ◆ If appointment is by a resolution at a meeting: • Contract is kept at the registered office for 15 days before the meeting and must be at the meeting itself	
Increase share capital (ie: allot new shares) if not a private company with 1 class of shares	s 551	Ordinary		File resolution
Remove statutory pre-emption rights	ss 569-571	Special		File resolution
Change company name	s 78	Special		File resolution
Select business name		Board resolution	Alter stationery/website as appropriate	
Change articles	s 21	Special		File amended articles and resolution
Change entrenched provision in the articles	s 22	Depends	Any procedure to change an entrenched provision must be followed	File amended articles and resolution
Remove a director	s 168	Ordinary	This resolution can only be passed at a general meeting (not by a written resolution). Complainant member gives 'special notice', leaving a formal notice at the registered office at least 28 days before a general meeting. (If a meeting is called in this period (ie: less than 28 days after this special notice), then notice is deemed to have been given). On receipt of the 'special notice', the company should immediately inform the director concerned. If the board does not call a meeting, the member may be able to call a meeting if he has sufficient rights (see p 301). A director can make a written representation which the board circulates to members. Alter the Register of Directors	File appropriate form for removal of a director
Remove an auditor	s 510	Ordinary	Special notice rules and procedure as for the removal of a director	Notify Registrar of resolution removing auditor within 14 days
Reduce share capital	ss 641-651	Special		File resolution and obtain the court's consent or file resolution and solvency statement
Sanction a 'substantial property transaction'	s 190	Ordinary		

Transaction	Authority	Resolution	Internal procedures	External procedures
Payment to a director for loss of office	ss 215-222	Ordinary	◆ If approval is by a written resolution: • Memorandum of proposed payment must be sent with proposed resolution ◆ If appointment is by a resolution at a meeting: • Memorandum of proposed payment is kept at the registered office for 15 days before the meeting and must be at the meeting itself	
Repurchase ordinary shares	ss 690-692	Special	Update Register of Members	File resolution + form (no. of shares + nominal value)
Approve dividend	MA 30	Ordinary		
Absolve liability for *ultra vires* act		Special		File resolution
Grant indemnity for *ultra vires* act		Special		File resolution
Absolve liability for exceeding actual authority		Ordinary		
Issue of a debenture		Board resolution	The board resolves to take out the loan. Execute the debenture properly. Update Register of Charges	File form at Companies House within 21 days. Charges over land should be registered with the Land Charges Department or HM Land Registry
Redemption of a debenture		Board resolution	Lender endorses receipt on the debenture Update Register of Charges	File statutory declaration and memorandum of satisfaction that the debt has been repaid
Voluntary winding up - company is insolvent	IA s 84	Special	see p 345	File resolution
Winding up - company is solvent	IA s 84	Special	see p 345	File resolution
Approve voluntary arrangement	IR 1986 rr 1.19-1.20	50% (in value) of members who are present (in person or by proxy) and voting, *and* 75% or more (by value) of unsecured creditors whc are present (in person or by proxy) and voting	see p 343	
Move registered office	s 87	Board resolution		File appropriate form

Note: a) the table assumes that the *MA* are in force and have not been amended.

b) every members' resolution which is passed concerning the company's management will need a separate board resolution if it is to be executed.

c) written resolutions are an acceptable alternative to members' resolutions passed at meetings in all cases except removal of a director or auditor.

D Public companies

References in this section apply to the Companies Act 2006, unless stated otherwise.

I	UK PLCs
II	European Public Limited Liability Companies (SEs)

➤ This book does not deal with the various special provisions on quoted companies or traded companies.

I UK PLCs

Advantages associated with UK plcs

✓ Shares/debentures may be offered to the public. (It is a criminal offence for a private company to do this (s 755).)

✓ To have the commercial respectability of the 'plc' suffix.

✓ The company may apply for listing of its securities if it meets certain requirements.

Extra stringencies associated with UK plcs

✘ Costs of changing name on memorandum and stationery.

✘ More administrative requirements.

✘ A public company (even if not listed) is subject to the City Code on Takeovers and Mergers.

   ◆ This can cause problems for a sale of the company, particularly if there is a restricted shareholder base.

✘ Minimum of 2 directors (s 154). Private companies can have 1 director (s 154).

✘ Must have a company secretary (s 271) who must have certain qualifications (s 273).

✘ Must hold annual general meetings (s 336).

✘ The company must call a general meeting if 'net assets' fall to 50% or less of the share capital (s 656).

✘ Must lay accounts before general meetings (s 437).

✘ Provisions allowing small/medium companies to file abbreviated accounts do not apply (s 384, s 467).

✘ Must appoint auditors annually (s 489).

✘ May not use the statutory procedure permitting written resolutions to conduct business (s 288).

✘ Cannot allot shares until 25% of the nominal value and the whole of any premium has been paid up (s 586).

✘ Usually, may not issue shares for a non-cash consideration unless it first obtains an expert's valuation and report about such non-cash consideration (ss 593-595).

✘ Restrictions on ability to pay dividends - rules for distributions are much stricter (ss 829-853).

✘ There is an absolute bar on financial assistance to buy shares (s 678).

✘ The company needs a special resolution, or article to disable statutory pre-emption rights (ss 570-573). (A private company may do this in its articles (s 567).)

✘ A plc may not redeem or purchase shares from capital (s 709).

✘ 6 months to file accounts and reports after accounting reference period ends (private companies have 9) (s 442(2)).

✘ For listed companies: the UK Corporate Governance Code must be complied with.

Conversion to a plc
Requirements

1 Issued share capital is a minimum of £50,000 (or 57,100 euros) (*ss 761, 763, C(AM)R 2008* and *C(AM)R 2009*).
2 At least 25% of the share capital is fully paid to the nominal value and the whole of any premium (*s 91*).
- For most types of share, where a share (or any premium payable on such a share) has been paid up wholly or partly in consideration of an undertaking given by any person that someone should do work or perform services for the company or a third party, that undertaking must have been performed or discharged (*s 91*).

Procedure
(*CA 2006 ss 90-96*)

Steps

1 Pass a special (or written) resolution to re-register as a plc.
2 Adopt articles suitable for a public company.
- This is usually done by adopting a new set of articles appropriate for a public company rather than through changes to the existing articles.
- If a company will want to be admitted to the Official List soon, it generally disapplies the whole of the *Model Articles* and adopts long form articles complying with the Listing Rules.
3 Send to the Registrar within 15 days of the resolution being passed:
- a copy of the special resolution, *and*
- a copy of the new memorandum and articles.
4 Apply for registration as a plc on the correct form + the fee, together with:
- a copy of the special resolution (unless already sent), *and*
- a statement *of* the company's proposed name on re-registration, *and*
- for a company without a secretary, a statement of:
  - the company's proposed secretary with the same details that will go into the register of secretaries, and
  - a consent by the person named as secretary to act as such.
- a written statement by the auditors that, in their opinion, the balance sheet (which must be prepared as at a date not more than 7 before) shows that the amount of the company's net assets was not less than the aggregate of its called up share capital, *and* the balance sheet with an unqualified report by the company's auditors, saying as above, *and*
  - The unqualified report must state that the balance sheet has been properly prepared in accordance with *CA 2006* and gives a true and fair view of the state of the company's affairs.
- A valuation report (if applicable) on any shares allotted as fully or partly paid up for non-cash consideration between the balance sheet date and the date on which the resolution to re-register was passed, *and*
- A 'statement of compliance' stating that:
  - the resolution was passed on the date specified in the form, *and*
  - so far as they are applicable, provisions about valuation of report (see above) have been satisfied, *and*
  - the requirements relating to minimum capital have been satisfied, *and*
  - there has been no change in the company's financial position between the relevant balance sheet date and the date of application for re-registration causing its net assets to be reduced to less than the sum of its called-up share capital and undistributable reserves, *and*
- If the private company has no secretary at all (or a suitable secretary), the correct forms of appointment.
5 The Registrar issues a certificate of incorporation as a plc.
6 The Registrar notifies the amendment of the memorandum and articles in the London Gazette (*ss 1077(1)(a), 1078(2)*).

II   European Public Limited Liability Companies (SEs)

➤ On 8 October 2001, the European Council created a legal form of European Company known as the Societas Europaea (SE) which became law throughout the EU on 8 October 2004.

- This was over 30 years after negotiations for the creation of a European company were initiated!

➤ Sources of law:

- At the EU level: Euro Regulation 2157/2001 and Directive 2001/86/EC.
- At the UK level: implemented by *EPLLCR 2004*.

Rules applicable to a Societas Europaea

➤ **Objectives of an SE:**

◆ to create a European company with its own legislative framework which allows companies incorporated in different Member States to merge or form a holding company or joint subsidiary, while avoiding the legal and practical constraints arising from the existence of multiple legal systems, *and*

◆ to involve employees in the SE and recognise their place and role in the company.

● This does not mean participation in day-to-day decisions (which are a matter for the management) but participation in the supervision and strategic development of the company.

● Several models of participation are possible:

a) a model in which the employees form part of the supervisory or administrative board, *or*

b) model in which the employees are represented by a separate body, *or*

c) other models to be agreed between the management or administrative boards of the founder companies and the employees or their representatives in those companies (levels of information and consultation being the same as in (b).

● Employees' representatives must be provided with financial and material resources and other facilities to enable them to perform their duties properly.

➤ **Formation:** there are 4 ways of forming an SE:

◆ merger (available only to public limited companies from different Member States), *or*

◆ formation of a holding company (available to public and private limited companies with their registered offices in different Member States or having subsidiaries or branches in Member States other than that of their registered office), *or*

◆ formation of a joint subsidiary, *or*

◆ conversion of a public limited company previously formed under national law.

➤ **Registration (and liquidation):** must be disclosed for information purposes in the Official Journal of the European Communities. Every SE must be registered in the State where it has its registered office, in a register designated by the law of that State.

➤ **Registered office:** must be where the SE has its central administration (ie: its true centre of operations).

◆ The SE can easily transfer its registered office within the EU.

➤ **Minimum capital:** 120,000 euros (unless the registered office is in a Member State where national law requires a larger capital for companies exercising certain types of activity).

➤ **Annual accounts:** the SE must draw up annual accounts comprising the balance sheet, the profit & loss account (and notes to accounts), and an annual report giving a fair view of the company's business and of its position (consolidated accounts may also be required).

➤ **Tax:** the SE is treated the same as any other multinational (ie: it is subject to the tax regime of the national legislation applicable to the company and its subsidiaries). SEs are subject to taxes and charges in all Member States where their administrative centres are situated. NB: SE tax status is not perfect because there is no tax harmonisation at the European level and the UK tax rules are complex.

➤ **Company rules:** must provide for general meeting of shareholders and for either a management board and a supervisory board (2 tier system) or an administrative board (1 tier system).

◆ 2 tier system: management by a management board whose members have power to represent the company in dealings with third parties and in legal proceedings. They are appointed and removed by the supervisory board. No person may be a member of both the management board and the supervisory board of the same company at the same time.

◆ 1 tier system: management is by an administrative board whose members have the power to represent the company in dealings with third parties and in legal proceedings. Powers of management may be delegated to one or more of its members.

➤ The following require authorisation of the supervisory board or the deliberation of the administrative board:

◆ any investment project requiring an amount more than the percentage of subscribed capital, *and*

◆ the setting-up, acquisition, disposal or closing down of undertakings, businesses or parts of businesses where the purchase price or disposal proceeds account for more than the percentage of subscribed capital, *and*

◆ the raising or granting of loans, the issue of debt securities and the assumption of liabilities of a third party or suretyship for a third party where the total money value in each case is more than the percentage of subscribed capital, *and*

◆ the conclusion of supply and performance contracts where the total turnover provided for is more than the percentage of turnover for the previous financial year.

● The percentage is to be determined by the Statutes of the SE but may not be less than 5% nor more than 25%.

E   Converting businesses

┌─────────────────┐
│   │ ✓ A shaded box indicates that a point also applies to
└─────────────────┘   an LLP incorporated under the *LLPA 2000*

Converting sole trader to partnership	Converting a partnership to a company/LLP
Formalities	

➤ Draw up a partnership agreement
➤ Decide on the ownership of capital assets, which can be:
  ◆ leased or licensed to the firm
  ◆ owned by the partners jointly - this requires a transfer or conveyance
  ◆ held on trust by a partner for all the partners
➤ Comply with rules on business names (*CA 2006 ss 1192-1208* and *CBN(MP) R 2009*- see p 278)
	➤ Purchase or create a company/LLP
	➤ Observe the formalities for board and shareholder meetings
	➤ Draw up a contract for sale of the business:
	  ◆ listing the assets being sold, consideration and method of payment
	  ◆ stating the company's acceptance of the seller's title to assets
	  ◆ recording the company's acceptance of stock in its current condition
	  ◆ apportioning the value of assets
	  ◆ providing an indemnity from the company in respect of business liabilities.
	➤ Comply with rules on business names (*CA 2006 ss 1192-1208, CBN(MP) R 2009* and *CLLPBN(SWE)R 2009*- see p 278) and *CA 2006 ss 53-81* (see p 294 et seq)

Income tax	
	➤ The seller may incur a 'balancing charge' on the sale of capital assets (*CAA 2001 s 61/IT(TOI)A 2005 s 242*). If the ex-partners are controlling shareholders, then they and the company may elect for the company to inherit the business's writing down allowance (there are 2 years in which to make this election) (*CAA 2001 s 266*) If this election is made, no 'balancing charge' is deemed to arise on the discontinuance of trade by the partnership (*CAA 2001 s 267(2)*) ➤ Unrelieved trading losses can be carried forward and offset against any salary or dividends paid by the company to the vendor, as long as shares in the company provided most of the consideration for the sale (*ITA 2007 s 86*)
Capital taxation	

➤ A sole trader going into partnership may be disposing of chargeable assets. Consider:
  ◆ annual exemption
  ◆ hold-over relief on a *gift*
  ◆ entrepreneurs' relief
	➤ Insofar as shares are consideration for the transfer of assets, gains can be 'rolled-over' (*TCGA 1992 s 162*) into shares on condition that all the business's assets (except cash) are sold to the company and that the shares issued by the company qualify for the EIS (*TCGA 1992 ss 150-150C, Sch 5B*). This has disadvantages:
	  ◆ any subsequent gain may be liable to double taxation
	  ◆ assets transferred to the company are available to creditors if it becomes insolvent, and so might not be recoverable

SDLT	
➤ SDLT is less likely to be applicable as title to assets may not be transferred	➤ SDLT may be due on an instrument transferring or agreeing to transfer an interest in UK land, see pp 156 et seq, in Taxation, Section L Stamp duty land tax ('SDLT') ◆ There is an exemption for a transfer to an LLP within 1 year of incorporation (*FA 2003 s 65*)
VAT	
➤ If the company is not registered *before the sale,* the seller must charge VAT unless the business is transferred as a going concern (*VATA s 49*)	
Employees	
Transfer of Undertakings (Protection of Employment) Regulations 2006 ➤ When the business is taken over, the employees retain all the rights they enjoyed previously	

F   Choice of business medium

Note on shaded boxes in this chapter
A shaded box on this page indicates that a point applies to an LLP incorporated under the *LLPA 2000*
A shaded box on the next page indicates that a point applies to a partner in an LLP (also under the *LLPA 2000)*

➤ The choice of business medium determines how a business is financed and run.

➤ Issues that concern clients include:

   ◆ the different liabilities assumed by sole traders or partners (as opposed to shareholders).

   ◆ the amount of statutory control over the business.

   ◆ how easily profits may be extracted from the business.

   ◆ working out what tax is payable by the business and what tax is payable by the individuals involved (although this depends on whether they are sole traders, directors or shareholders.)

➤ As a general rule:

   ◆ Partnerships are better initially when profits are low (because of lower running costs and start-up relief).

   ◆ Companies are usually better initially when profits are expected to be higher.

	Sole trader or partnership	Company
	General matters	

Personal liability for debts	✘ Unlimited liability
	✘ A partner and a sole trader are personally liable for debts the business incurs
	
	Note:
	A novation agreement or an indemnity only protects if the guarantor is solvent
	
	NB: Under the self assessment regime, partners are in most cases no longer jointly and severally liable for income tax
		✔ Limited liability
		✔ Members are only liable to the extent of the fully paid up value of the shares
		➤ Directors are not personally liable *unless* they:
		   ◆ give a personal guarantee
		   ◆ breach their fiduciary duty to the company
		   ◆ trade wrongfully or fraudulently (*IA 1986 ss 213-214*)
		   ◆ breach certain statutory administrative requirements
		   ◆ sign a document giving an incorrect company name

Finance	✘ Can only create fixed charges ✘ A new partner is liable for future debts	✔ Can create a qualifying floating charge ✔ A new investor in shares only incurs limited liability
Management	✔ Flexibility: the business can be organised as the participants wish ✘ All partners have apparent authority to bind the firm	✔ Management is largely divorced from capital investment ✔ Shareholders have no authority to act for the company
Status		✔ Often seen by clients as more substantial and 'solid'

Setting-up and initial cost	✔ Theoretically free as acting in a certain way is enough to start a partnership
	✘ For a partnership, an agreement ought to be drawn up, so in practice this is not a viable 'short-cut'
		✘ Many statutory requirements must be fulfilled:
		   ◆ the formalities at start-up, *and*
		   ◆ the ongoing formalities

Statutory control	✔ This is minimal	✘ The inconvenience of maintaining the required registers, minutes, annual returns, etc
		✘ The expense of professional advice to ensure compliance with statutory requirements
		✘ Restrictions on certain activities:
		   ◆ purchase and redemption of its own shares
		   ◆ paying dividends solely out of 'available' profit as defined by *CA 2006 ss 829-830*

Publicity	✔ Need reveal only the partners' names and their addresses for the service of documents	✘ Information filed at Companies House is open to public inspection. This includes annual accounts but for smaller companies, a profit & loss account does not have to be filed; nor is there a need for an audit (see p 311)

Sole trader or partnership	Company	Director
Income tax / National insurance contributions		
✔ Expenses are more generous: anything 'wholly and exclusively for the purposes of the trade'		✔ Expenses: 'wholly, exclusively and necessarily in the performance of an employee's duties'
£0- £35,000 at 20% £35,000-£150,000 at 40% £150,000+ at 50% ✘ Income profit £35,000+ at 40%, and £150,000+ at 50% not 20%-27.5%	£0 - £300,000 at 20% £300,001- £1,500,000 at 27.5% £1,500,000+ at 26% ✔ Reinvestment is easier if profit is taxed in the 20% band	£0- £35,000 at 20% £35,000-£150,000+ at 40% £150,000+ at 50%
✔ Start-up relief over first 4 years ✔ Losses can be set against an individual's income or gains from other sources	Check whether *IT(EP)A 2003 ss 49-56* apply (see p 104)	
✘ A sole trader/partner pays Class 4 contributions related to profit and Class 2 contributions at a flat rate ✔ Neither Class 4 or 2 qualify for tax relief, but Employer secondary Class 1 contributions (13.8%) do not apply to a sole trader's or partner's earnings. ✘ Benefits are poorer than for employees	✔ A company may claim tax relief on secondary national insurance contributions	✘ No tax relief on national insurance contributions ✔ Benefits are more generous than for a self-employed person
✔ Income tax relief may be claimed in respect of interest on a loan to buy into a partnership/LLP (*ITA 2007 ss 383, 398*)	✔ Income tax relief may be claimed in respect of interest on a loan to buy shares (see p 165)	

Sole trader or partner	Director/Shareholder	Company
Capital gains tax		**Corporation tax**
	✔ Annual exemption and entrepreneurs' relief	✘
✔ Roll-over relief on replacement of 'qualifying assets'	✔ Roll-over relief on replacement of 'qualifying assets' *if* the company is a personal trading company	✔
✔ Hold-over relief on a gift of business assets	✔ Hold-over relief on a disposal of assets used by the company (other than shares) not at arm's length provided the company is a personal trading company	✘
Double taxation		
✔ A trader or partner only pays CGT once	✘ Company: pays corporation tax on gains (subject to reliefs or the substantial shareholding exemption). Shareholder: pays CGT on corresponding rises in share value ✔ This can be alleviated or prevented if a company distributes capital profit ✘ An asset-owning shareholder who licenses/leases to the company is only taxed once	
Inheritance tax		
✔ Business property relief ✔ Instalment option: always available on business assets	✘ Business property relief is not always available, see p 166 ✘ The instalment option is only available if *either* the transfer concerns a controlling holding *or* other conditions exist	Generally not applicable (unless a close company, etc)

G Insolvency

All references in this section are to the Insolvency Act 1986, unless stated otherwise.
A general outline only is presented below.

I	Personal insolvency
II	Partnership insolvency
III	LLP insolvency
IV	Corporate insolvency
V	A note on statutory demands
VI	Cross-border EU insolvency

I Personal insolvency

A Alternatives to bankruptcy

➤ At present, the main alternative to bankruptcy is an 'IVA' (ie: individual voluntary arrangement).

◆ Other alternative remedies are proposed by *TCE 2007*.

1 IVA (*ss 252-263G*)

➤ The debtor may choose to apply for a moratorium (called an 'interim order'). In return, the debtor agrees to a voluntary repayment plan (*s 252*).

◆ During the period of this interim order:

● no bankruptcy petition relating to the debtor may be presented or proceeded with, *and*

● no landlord or other person to whom rent is payable may exercise any right of forfeiture by peaceable re-entry in relation to premises let to the debtor in respect of a failure by the debtor to comply with any term or condition of his tenancy of such premises, except with the leave of the court, *and*

● no other proceedings, and no execution or other legal process, may be commenced or continued and no distress may be levied against the debtor or his property except with the leave of the court.

➤ A resolution for a voluntary arrangement must be passed by a majority of at least 75% (by value) of the creditors present in person or by proxy. The resolution binds every unsecured creditor (but if an unsecured creditor did not have notice of the meeting, he may apply to the court for relief) (*s 262*).

➤ A debtor may enter a voluntary arrangement at any time before a bankruptcy petition by the debtor is pending (*s 253(5)*).

➤ A voluntary arrangement may take the form of a 'composition', ie: the creditor and debtor agree the payment of a lesser sum in full satisfaction of the claim. Alternatively, it can take the form of a 'scheme of arrangement' which can be on any terms acceptable to the parties (eg: sale of assets, etc).

Pros and cons of an IVA	
✓ Avoids stigma and disability of bankruptcy.	✗ The supervisor of the voluntary arrangement does *not* have power to set aside transactions.
✓ Cheaper and quicker.	
✓ Creditors retain the option of petitioning the court if a debtor defaults.	✗ Creditors may not get paid in full.

1 The debtor appoints a qualified person such an insolvency practitioner known as a 'nominee' to investigate his finances (*s 253*).

2 The debtor prepares a proposal for the intended nominee setting out (*IR 1986 rr 5.2-5.3*):

i) his assets, liabilities and the terms of the IVA (this is what is actually known as the 'proposal'), *and*

ii) a short explanation why, in his opinion, a voluntary arrangement is desirable, *and*

iii) reasons why the creditors may be expected to concur with such an arrangement.

3 The proposal is sent to the intended nominee, who then decides whether to act as nominee (*IR 1986 r 5.4*).

4 If the debtor has not already delivered a statement of affairs to the nominee, then shortly after sending the proposal, the debtor must send to the nominee a statement of affairs containing particulars of his creditors, debts, other liabilities, assets and other information as may be prescribed (*IR 1986 r 5.5*).

5 The debtor may choose to apply for an interim order (the moratorium described above). This usually lasts for 14 days but can be extended (*ss 255(6), 256(4)*).

6 The nominee prepares a report on the proposal to the court including whether a creditor's meeting should be held (and giving the nominee's opinion on whether the proposal has a reasonable prospect of being approved and implemented (*s 256(1)*).

7 The court considers whether, based on the nominee's recommendation, a creditors' meeting is necessary to obtain their approval (*s 258*).

- ◆ **If an interim order has been made:** If a meeting is necessary, then during the period of the interim order, creditors can examine the proposed voluntary arrangement.

- ◆ **An interim order has not been made or applied for:** If a meeting is necessary, then creditors can examine the proposed voluntary arrangement (*ss 256A-258*).

- ◆ 75% or more (by value) of creditors present and voting (in person or by proxy) at the meeting must agree to the IVA (*IR 1986 r 5.23*).

8 Provided that consent is obtained, a bankruptcy order is avoided, and the nominee is appointed as the debtor's 'supervisor' to ensure the IVA is carried out in accordance with its terms (*s 263*).

False representations by the debtor (*s 262A*)

➤ The debtor commits an offence if, for the purpose of obtaining the approval of creditors to a proposal, he makes any false representation or fraudulently does, or omits to do, anything.

➤ This applies even if the proposal is not approved.

➤ This offence carries a penalty of imprisonment or a fine, or both.

Fast-track procedure (*s 263A*)

➤ The debtor can use a fast-track procedure to make an IVA if:

- ◆ the debtor is an undischarged bankrupt (ie: this is a post bankruptcy IVA), *and*

- ◆ the official receiver is specified in the proposal as the nominee in relation to the voluntary arrangement, *and*

- ◆ no interim order has been made.

2   **Debt relief orders** (ss 251A-251X, Schedule 4ZA and Schedule 4ZB, all inserted by TCE 2007 s 108)

➤ Many remedies are not accessible to an individual with problems paying debts because:

◆ there is a need to pay a fee to access the remedy, and/or

◆ there is a need for assets or funds to distribute to creditors on a regular basis (eg: an IVA or a non-statutory debt management plan).

➤ A Debt Relief Order (DRO) is a procedure that enables some individuals who meet specified criteria (ie: relatively low liabilities, no realisable assets and little or no disposable income) to make an application for a DRO to seek relief from certain debts.

◆ A DRO is made administratively by official receivers (who operate the scheme via approved experienced debt advisers who advise the applicant). It does not routinely need any court intervention.

◆ A DRO (which can only be applied for online on payment of a low administration fee).

◆ A DRO prevents creditors from enforcing debts (the debtor is discharged from the debts after 1 year).

● Creditors are notified of the making of an order and have a right to make objections on certain grounds if they believe the order should not have been made.

◆ While a DRO is in force, the debtor is under the same restrictions and obligations as in bankruptcy and the debtor will be subject to prosecution if his conduct in the insolvency is found to be culpable.

➤ There is a right of appeal to the court for both the debtor and any creditors who are dissatisfied with the way the official receiver has dealt with the case.

➤ **Debt relief restrictions orders:** may be made in respect of a debtor who is subject to a DRO where (broadly) the debtor's conduct in relation to his insolvency is found to be culpable. Schedule 4ZB (inserted by TCE 2007 Schedule 19) sets out who may apply and possible grounds for obtaining this order.

◆ Such orders last 2 to 15 years and are intended to protect the public from a culpable debtor. A debtor subject to an order is under the same disabilities as those imposed by the original DRO (eg: he will not be able to obtain credit beyond the prescribed amount without disclosing his status).

Other proposed changes under TCE 2007 (ss 106-107 and 109 to 133) [not yet in force]
Administration Orders and Enforcement Restriction Orders
➤ *Administration Orders (AOs) are a court-administered debt management scheme for those with multiple debts totalling no more than £5,000, one of which must be a judgment debt (CCA 1984 ss 112-117).*
➤ *Enforcement Restriction Orders are another statutory debt-management scheme.*
➤ *TCE 2007 ss 106-107 amends CCA 1984 Part 6 inserting new ss 117A-117X by: i) increasing the debt ceiling for AOs and ii) properly time limiting AOs and iii) providing a better version of EROs.*
Debt Management Schemes
➤ *Existing providers of debt management advice and assistance do not have the power:*
◆ *to compel creditors to keep to the terms of a debt repayment plan (ie: to make creditors accept the planned repayments without their taking enforcement action), or*
◆ *to compose debts that cannot be repaid within a reasonable period (ie: to force a write off of a proportion of the debts where a debtor complies generally but simply cannot repay the full amount) as an incentive for the debtor to maintain the required repayments.*
➤ *TCE 2007 ss 109-133 allows approved service providers to use the powers above to operate Debt Management Schemes (DMSs) for individual debtors. They also enable scheme operators to exercise powers to compel creditor participation by preventing enforcement action but allow creditors a right of appeal).*

B Bankruptcy

Steps

1 A petition is made to a court with insolvency jurisdiction, by any of the following:

a) **Creditor (1)** (*s 267*) ...

   i) ... who is owed £750 or more, *and*

   ii) the debt is for a liquidated sum payable now, or at a certain future time, and is unsecured, and

   iii) the debtor is unable to pay or has no reasonable prospect of doing so.

       ◆ The evidence for this is:

          • 1) there is evidence of the debtor's failure to comply with a statutory demand within 3 weeks, *and*

             2) there is no outstanding application to set aside a statutory demand.

       or • the debtor has failed to satisfy execution of a judgment debt.

b) **Creditor (2)** ... who is bound by a voluntary arrangement where the debtor has not complied with the arrangement, or the debtor has entered the scheme giving misleading information.

c) **Debtor** ... with a statement of affairs showing that he is unable to pay his debts (*s 272*).

2 A bankruptcy order is made at a court hearing (at least 14 days must elapse between service of the petition and the hearing), or the court may appoint an insolvency practitioner to investigate the possibility of an IVA. A bankruptcy order will be entered into the public register of bankruptcy orders.

3 The courts appoints an official receiver (*s 287*) until the bankrupt's estate vests in the trustee in bankruptcy.

  ◆ If a creditor began the action, the debtor has 21 days to submit a statement of affairs (*s 288*).

4 A creditors' meeting is held at the official receiver's discretion *or* if 25% of creditors (by value) request it (*s 294*).

5 A trustee in bankruptcy is appointed by the creditors at the meeting, *or* if no meeting is called or no appointment is made by creditors, the official receiver will act as the trustee in bankruptcy (*s 293*).

6 The bankrupt's property vests in the trustee (see chart opposite '*Property vesting in the trustee*') (*s 306*).

7 The function of the trustee is to get in, realise, and distribute the bankrupt's estate to satisfy the creditors (see chart opposite for '*Trustee's powers to gather assets*').

8 A bankrupt is discharged from bankruptcy at the end of the period of **1 year** beginning with the date on which the bankruptcy commences (*s 279*).

  ◆ However, the court may extend this if the bankrupt has failed or is failing to comply with an obligation in the relevant legislation.

  ◆ The one year discharge period may be reduced if the Official Receiver files a notice stating that further investigation into the bankrupt's conduct and affairs is unnecessary, or has been concluded.

9 When the bankruptcy order is discharged, the discharge (*s 281*):

  ◆ releases the bankrupt from all the bankruptcy debts, but has no effect on the functions (so far as they remain to be carried out) of the trustee of his estate,

  ◆ does not affect the right of any secured creditor of the bankrupt to enforce his security for the payment of a debt from which the bankrupt is released,

  ◆ does not release the bankrupt from any bankruptcy debt which he incurred connected with fraud,

  ◆ does not usually release the bankrupt from any liability to pay damages for negligence, nuisance or breach of a statutory, contractual or other duty or damages for personal injuries to any person,

  ◆ does not release any person other than the bankrupt from any liability.

Property vesting in the trustee in bankruptcy

Property retained by the bankrupt	Property vesting in the trustee
➤ Any right which is purely personal, rather than proprietary ➤ Tools of a trade, vehicle (s 283(2)) ➤ Bankrupt's and family's furniture, bedding and clothing (s 283(2)) Note: the above might be replaced by functional cheaper versions ➤ Trust property eg: trust property held for a minor	➤ All other property Note: Where the debtor's property is an interest in a dwelling-house which at the date of the bankruptcy was the sole or principal residence of the bankrupt, the bankrupt's spouse or a former spouse of the bankrupt, then at the end of the period of 3 years (beginning with the date of the bankruptcy) that interest ceases to be comprised in the debtor's estate and vests in the debtor (without conveyance, assignment or transfer). However, this does not apply if during that 3 year period, the trustee realises that interest, applies for an order for sale of that dwelling-house or applies for an order for possession of the dwelling-house (s 283A). ◆ If the house if of low value (defined in secondary legislation) the trustee will not be granted an order for sale of the property (s 313A).

➤ Initially the bankrupt can usually continue to occupy the family home *if either*: (ss 336-338)

    a) a spouse has a right of occupation under the *FLA 1996, or*

    b) the bankrupt is living with minors and therefore has a right of occupation under the *FLA 1996*

➤ During the first year a possession order is unlikely to be granted as the needs of the children are paramount

➤ After 1 year, an order for possession will probably be granted as the creditors' interests now become paramount

Trustee's powers to gather assets

Transaction	Time of transaction	Defence	Effect
At an undervalue (ss 339, 341)	With an unconnected person ➤ Within 5 years prior to bankruptcy, *and* the debtor is insolvent at the time or became so as a result of the transaction		All such property is 'reclaimed' under a court order by the trustee, and distributed to the creditors
	With an associate ➤ Within 2 years prior to bankruptcy	a) The debtor was not insolvent at the time, *or* b) the debtor did not become insolvent as a result of the transaction	
To create a preference (ss 340-341)	With an unconnected person ➤ Within 6 months prior to bankruptcy, *and* the debtor was insolvent at the time or became so because of the transaction, *and* the debtor intended to prefer, *and* the creditor was thus put in a better position	The debtor did not intend to prefer, or pressure was exerted to prefer	
	With an 'associate': ➤ Within 2 years prior to bankruptcy, *and* the debtor was insolvent at the time or became so due to this transaction (presumed), *and* the creditor was put in a better position as a result (presumed)	a) The debtor was not insolvent at the time, *or* b) the debtor did not become insolvent as a result of the transaction The debtor did not intend to prefer, or pressure was exerted to prefer	
At an undervalue to defraud creditors (s 423)	No time limit		

➤ 'Onerous' contracts or property - if an interested third party serves notice, a trustee must disclaim the contract or property within 28 days, otherwise he loses this right to disclaim and will be deemed to have adopted any contract (ss 315-316)
    ◆ Third parties who lose from a disclaimed contract claim loss from the bankrupt's estate

➤ Any disposition made between the day of presentation of the petition and the vesting of the bankrupt's estate in the trustee is void unless the court consents (s 284)

A trustee is *not* entitled to pursue:

➤ sale proceeds from a fully enforced judgment order obtained before the bankruptcy order was made (s 346)

➤ goods which, before a bankruptcy order was made, a landlord has distrained for up to 6 months arrears of rent (s 347)

Disabilities (ie: things the bankrupt may not do)
➤ **BROs: *s 281A* and *Sch 4A* set out the rules for bankruptcy restrictions orders (BROs) which impose restrictions on bankrupts who abuse the system or whose conduct has been dishonest or otherwise culpable, either before or after bankruptcy. BROs run for 2 to 15 years.**
➤ It is a criminal offence to take credit above £250 without disclosing the bankruptcy or to trade under a non-bankrupt name without disclosing the bankrupt name (*s 360*).
➤ A bankrupt may not retain membership of a partnership (the consequences of becoming a bankrupt while a partner) depend on the partnership agreement.
➤ A bankrupt may not retain directorships (*CDDA 1986 s 11*).

Order of distribution

1 **Secured creditors:** they realise their security and account to the trustee for any surplus. If the security is not sufficient to discharge the whole debt, they are treated as unsecured creditors for the balance

2 **Bankruptcy expenses and costs**

3 **Preferential debts:** these rank equally and abate equally (*ss 328, 386, Schedule 6*)
  ◆ Employee wages owed for the final 4 months prior to the bankruptcy order (subject to an individual maximum)
  ◆ Holiday pay which is owed to employees

4 **Unsecured creditors:** these rank equally and abate equally   *Any surplus after paying these 5 sets of creditors goes to the bankrupt*

5 **Postponed creditors** (eg: loan between spouses)

(left margin: Order ↓)

False representations by the bankrupt (*s 356*)
➤ The bankrupt is guilty of an offence if he makes any material omission in statements about his affairs.
➤ The bankrupt is guilty of an offence if:
◆ knowing or believing that a false debt has been proved by any person under the bankruptcy, he fails to inform the trustee as soon as practicable, *or*
◆ he attempts to account for any part of his property by fictitious losses or expenses, *or*
◆ at any meeting of his creditors in the 12 months before petition or (whether or not at such a meeting) at any time in the initial period, he did anything which would have been an offence under the bullet above if the bankruptcy order had been made before he did it, *or*
◆ he has made a false representation or fraud to obtain the consent of any creditors to an agreement with reference to his affairs or to his bankruptcy.

II   Partnership insolvency

Insolvent Partnerships Order 1994, IA 1986

➤ The parts of the *IA* regarding company voluntary arrangements and administration apply to partnerships.

➤ The partnership is treated as an unregistered company even though a partnership is not a legal person in its own right. There are different treatments for creditors' and members' winding up petitions.

➤ The law of bankruptcy does not apply to the firm but individual partners may be subject to bankruptcy orders, whereupon the official receiver becomes trustee.

➤ A modified form of moratorium applies to partnerships with similar criteria to small companies, see p 344.

III   LLP insolvency

➤ The *IA 1986* applies to an LLP broadly as it does to a company.

  ◆ *LLPR 2001 r 5* and *Sch 3* apply the *IA 1986* (with appropriate modifications) to LLPs.

IV Corporate insolvency

A Alternatives to liquidation

➤ There are 3 main alternatives to liquidation:

1 The company is declared defunct.

2 The company goes into administration (or very rarely an administrative receiver is appointed).

3 A voluntary arrangement is made.

---

1 **The company is declared defunct** (*CA 2006 s 1000*)

➤ The company ceases trading.

➤ The Registrar of Companies can act on his own initiative to strike off the company.

➤ The Registrar must advertise his intention to strike off the company.

➤ For up to 20 years, a prejudiced member or creditor may apply for the company to be restored.

➤ The liability of every director, managing officer and member of the company continues, and may be enforced as if the company had not been dissolved (*CA 2006 s 1000(7)*).

---

2 **The company goes into administration (or very rarely an administrative receiver is appointed).**

Paragraph numbers in this sub-section refer to paragraphs in IA 1986 Sch B1, unless otherwise stated.

a) **What an administration is - and its purpose**

➤ Administration is a procedure where a company that is, or is likely to become, insolvent can be reorganised or have its assets realised for the benefit of creditors.

➤ When a company goes into administration, an insolvency practitioner takes over the control of the company's affairs from its directors to achieve one of the aims set out below.

◆ The procedure is governed by *IA 1986 Schedule B1* and *IR 1986 Part 2*.

➤ **Primary Aim:** to rescue the company (as opposed to the business that the company carries on) so that it can continue trading as a going concern (*para 3(1)(a)*).

◆ If this is not achievable, there are 2 secondary aims for which a company can go into administration:

● **Secondary Aim 1:** To achieve a better result for the company's creditors as a whole than would be likely if the company were put into liquidation (*para 3(1)(b)*), *or*

● **Secondary Aim 2:** To realise the company's property to make a distribution to the company's secured or preferential creditors (*para 3(1)(c)*).

➤ Administration must be completed within 1 calendar year unless the creditors or the court agree an extension (*para 76*) but, in practice, many companies remain in administration for more than 1 year.

b) **Nature of administration**

➤ Whether or not appointed by the court, an administrator is an officer of the court (as well as an agent of the company) and can only be appointed if qualified to act as an insolvency practitioner.

➤ An administrator may not be appointed if the company is already in administration.

➤ A company cannot go into administration if:

◆ a resolution for voluntary winding-up has been passed (*para 8(1)(a)*), *or*

◆ a winding-up order has been made (subject to an application by the liquidator or a floating charge holder) (*para 8(1)(b)*).

c) **Appointment of administrator**

➤ Administrators can be appointed by court order or by holders of floating charges and companies or their directors **without a court hearing** (*paras 14-34*).

i. **Appointment by court** (*paras 10-13*)

➤ A company or its directors, or one or more creditors of a company (which could include a floating charge holder) can apply to court for an administration order.

➤ The court may only make an order if it is satisfied that the company is, or is likely to become, unable to pay debts and that an order is reasonably likely to achieve an objective/the purpose of administration.

➤ Once an administration application has been made, the applicant must notify anyone who has appointed, or can appoint, either an administrative receiver or an administrator (*para 12(2)*). The application for administration cannot be withdrawn without the permission of the court (*para 12(3)*).

➤ On hearing an administration application, the court may either make the order, dismiss the application or make any other appropriate order (*para 13*).

ii. **Appointment by the holder of a floating charge** (*paras 14-21*)

➤ Floating charge holders can appoint an administrator of their choosing, provided that:

♦ the floating charge on which the appointment relies is enforceable, *and*

♦ the floating charge holder has given notice to the holder of any superior floating charge, *and*

♦ the company is not in liquidation, *and*

♦ neither an administrative receiver nor administrator is already in office.

➤ Before the administrator takes office, the floating charge holder must file a notice of appointment with the court identifying the administrator and including a statement of consent from the administrator. He must also attach a statutory declaration by the floating charge holder stating that he has a qualifying floating charge over the whole or substantially the whole of the company's property and that this is or was enforceable on the date of the appointment.

iii. **Appointment by company or directors** (*paras 22-34*)

➤ A company or its directors can only appoint an administrator if:

♦ the company has not been in administration (instigated by the company or directors) nor subject to a moratorium in respect of a failed CVA in the previous 12 months, *and*

♦ the company is or is likely to become unable to pay its debts, *and*

♦ there is no outstanding winding-up petition/application for administration, *and*

♦ the company is not in liquidation, *and*

♦ there is no administrator or administrative receiver in office.

➤ A 'notice of intention to appoint' must identify the proposed administrator (*para 26(3)*).

➤ Once the 'notice of intention to appoint' is sent to the floating charge holder and filed at court, an interim moratorium commences (*para 44(2)*).

➤ During the notice period, a floating charge holder entitled to appoint an administrator may either agree to the proposed appointment or appoint their choice of administrator (*para 14*).

♦ The company or directors must give floating charge holders at least 5 business days' notice in writing of their intention to appoint an administrator in this way (*para 26*).

♦ The 'notice of intention to appoint' must also be filed with the court and accompanied by a statutory declaration, stating that the application meets the relevant criteria.

◆ If the floating charge holder consents to the company's/directors' nominee or does not respond to the notice within 5 business days, the company/directors must make the appointment no more than 10 business days after filing their 'notice of intention to appoint' (*para 28(2)*). If out of time, the interim moratorium ceases to have effect and an administrator cannot be appointed.

➤ If there is no floating charge holder, the company/directors file the 'notice of appointment' at court together with a statutory declaration stating that the application meets the relevant criteria.

➤ A 'notice of appointment' must attach a statement from the administrator: a) consenting to act and b) stating that the purpose of administration is reasonably likely to be achieved. After this, the administrator is automatically appointed and takes office once the 'notice of appointment' and attached documents are filed at court. The company or directors then notify the administrator of their appointment.

➤ If, for whatever reason, the administrator's appointment is discovered to be invalid, the court may order the person who made the appointment to indemnify the administrator against liability (*para 34*).

d) Functions of the administrator

➤ On appointment, an administrator must take custody or control of all company property (*para 67*).

➤ The administrator may do anything necessary or expedient for the management of the affairs, business and property of the company (including removing or appointing a director (*paras 59, 61*).

➤ The administrator may make a distribution:

◆ to secured creditors and preferential creditors without permission of the court (*para 65*).

◆ to unsecured creditors with the permission of the court (*para 66*).

◆ if he thinks that the payment is likely to assist in achieving the purpose of administration (*para 66*).

➤ The administrator may dispose of property subject to a floating charge (as created), as if the property were unencumbered, without the consent of the floating charge holder. However, the floating charge holder has first call on the proceeds of sale (*para 70*).

➤ The court may give the administrator power to override the rights of the holder of a fixed security over the company's property and power to dispose of the property in question as if it were owned by the company. However, the holder of the fixed security has first call on the proceeds of sale (*para 71*).

e) Effects of the administration

➤ Any outstanding winding-up petitions are dismissed (unless the administration is because a floating charge holder has appointed an administrator, when any winding-up petition is suspended) (*para 40*).

➤ If an administrative receiver (AR) is in office, the court dismisses an administration application unless the AR's appointee or the court thinks the appointee's security may be set aside (*para 39*).

➤ An AR (and a receiver if asked by the administrator) must vacate office (*para 41*).

➤ Once in administration (ie: an administration order is made or administrator appointed), a moratorium starts from the filing date of the administration application/notice of intention to appoint. Then:

◆ no resolution cannot be passed, or order made, to wind up the company (*paras 42 and 43*).

◆ no steps can be taken by creditors to enforce their rights without the consent of the administrator or the permission of the court (*para 43*).

◆ every business document issued by the company or the administrator must identify the administrator and state that the affairs, business and property are being managed by him (*para 45*).

➤ Usually, the administration leads to the sale of the company's assets under *para 3(1)(b)* and may lead to a better result for the company's creditors than immediate liquidation eg: the company may be able to continue trading thus allowing a greater value for the assets as part of a sale on a going concern basis.

f) **Procedure**

Steps	
1	The administrator is appointed and sends notice of the appointment (*paras 45-48*): ◆ to the company and its creditors as soon as is reasonably practicable, *and* ◆ to the Registrar of Companies within 7 days of the appointment.
2	By notice, the administrator requires a company representative to give a statement of affairs within 11 days of receipt of the notice. The statement must be verified by a statement of truth and give details of the company's property, debts and liabilities, and the details of each creditor and their security.
3	As soon as reasonably practicable (and in any event within 8 weeks of the administration starting) the administrator must make proposals to achieve administration purpose. He sends them to: ◆ the Registrar of Companies, *and* ◆ the company's creditors (with an invitation to an initial creditors' meeting, which must be held as soon as reasonably practicable and in any event, within 10 weeks of the administration commencing), *and* ◆ every member of the company (by publishing a notice). If the administrator does not consider it reasonably practicable to rescue the company and/or achieve a better result for creditors than on a winding-up, his statement must state why (*para 49*).
4	The administrator presents the proposals at the initial creditors' meeting. ◆ If the administrator thinks that the company can be rescued as a going concern, he puts the proposal to the creditors who decide whether to accept an arrangement (eg: a CVA), reject the proposals or, if the administrator himself consents, amend the proposals. ◆ If company rescue is not reasonably practicable or would not get the best outcome for creditors, the administrator explains why. He puts a proposal to the creditors to achieve a better result for the company's creditors as a whole. The creditors vote on whether to accept, modify or reject the proposal. ◆ The administrator does not call a meeting of the creditors where it is thought there will be no funds available from the insolvent estate for unsecured creditors or where he thinks there are funds to pay all creditors in full. However, within a set period, such a meeting may be requisitioned by creditors whose debts amount to at least 10% of the total company debts (*para 52*).
5	The administrator's statement of proposals may not include (*para 73*): ◆ a proposal that affects the right of a secured creditor to enforce his security without his consent, *or* ◆ an action resulting in a preferential debt being paid other than in priority to a non-preferential debt.
6	Only a creditors' meeting may modify the administrator's proposals (*para 54*). ◆ The administrator cannot subsequently make any substantial revisions to the proposals without first obtaining the agreement of the creditors.
7	After the conclusion of the initial creditors' meeting (and any subsequent meeting), the administrator reports any decision taken to the court and the Registrar of Companies.
8	If the creditors fail to approve the proposals, the court may provide that the administrator's appointment ceases, adjourn the hearing conditionally or unconditionally, make an interim order, make an order on a suspended petition for winding up or any other appropriate order (*para 55*).

Note: All time periods in Steps 3 and 4 can be extended with the permission of the court or with the consent of the creditors.

A note on debentures and administrative receivers

➤ Debentures historically allowed a debenture holder to appoint an administrative receiver if he was not paid sums owed under the debenture, provided the holder had security over substantially the whole of the assets of the company. *IA 1986* (by *EA 2002)* now prohibits appointing an administrative receiver except in very limited circumstances - and administrators are nowadays appointed instead.

Pre-pack administrations

➤ If the sale of a company's assets is agreed before going into administration and the sale is then completed immediately after the start of the administration, this is known as a 'pre-pack administration'.

Advantages	Disadvantages
◆ Pre-packs lead to a quick and smooth transfer of a business. ◆ Pre-packs are faster than normal administration, so the costs of the administration process can be reduced (ie: a better return for creditors). ◆ Pre-packs minimise the erosion of supplier/ customer/ employee confidence often seen in insolvency proceedings. ◆ Pre-packs save more jobs than a normal administration. ◆ Pre-packs may work where no funding is available, as the administrator cannot trade the business through a normal administration. (The alternative would be liquidation and the immediate cessation of the company's business.) ◆ Pre-packed companies are (by definition) insolvent so unsecured creditors are unlikely to recover all their money anyway. When unsecured creditors lose out in a pre-pack, it is not necessarily as a result of the pre-pack process but the company's underlying financial difficulties.	◆ There is a lack of transparency. Unsecured creditors often do not realise a pre-pack is going to happen and have no opportunity to protect their interests by voting on the pre-pack proposal. (Secured creditors must be involved because they need to consent to the release of their security.) ◆ There is a lack of accountability. Administrators involved in pre-packs do not need prior approval from the court or creditors in the same way as they do in a normal administration. ◆ Pre-packs do not maximise returns for unsecured creditors. Businesses which are sold by pre-pack are usually sold with limited marketing compared with a normal administration. It is impossible for the proposed administrator to test the market fully because of the risk of the company's financial difficulties being leaked, which could destroy the value of the business. ◆ Pre-packs are similar to the outlawed practice of creating "phoenix" companies (ie: where the management of a company put it into liquidation and then the same business re-emerges trading as a new "phoenix" company, but without the debts of the old company). Creditors are most suspicious about pre-packs when the business is sold back to the original owners. (Under the pre-pack guidelines, administrators have to disclose to creditors the name of the buyer and whether there is any connection between the buyer and the company). ◆ The proposed administrator is often introduced to the company by its directors in the context of a proposal that the business and/or assets of the company be sold back to them. If he wants to be appointed as the company's administrator, he will have an inherent preference for the proposed pre-pack - leading to a conflict of interest. ◆ A pre-pack doesn't subject the company to a restructuring, which is often necessary if the business is to survive in the long term.

3 **A voluntary arrangement is made** (*ss 1-7*) ie: a company voluntary arrangement ('CVA')

Aim: for the company to agree on a binding plan to repay debts so the company can survive.

Steps	
1	If it is a 'small company', it may apply for a moratorium on actions against it (*Sch A1*).
2	The directors draft a proposal for a composition or scheme of arrangement.
3	An authorised person (eg: an insolvency practitioner), called a 'nominee', reports to the court, stating whether in his opinion the proposal has a reasonable prospect of being approved/ implemented and whether meetings of shareholders and creditors should be held to consider the proposal. Unless the court directs otherwise, meetings of shareholders and creditors are held. ◆ Consent must be obtained from more than 50% (in value) of the members who are present (in person or by proxy) and voting, and 75% or more (by value) of the unsecured creditors who are present (in person or by proxy) and voting (*IR 1986 rr 1.19-1.20*). ◆ However, a decision by the creditor's meeting to approve the CVA prevails over a member's meeting to reject the CVA, subject to a right by a member to challenge this in court (*s 4A*).
4	If approved, this approval is reported to the court.
5	The 'nominee' now becomes the 'supervisor' and carries out the CVA.

➤ Consequences:

   ◆ A CVA binds every creditor who had notice of, and was entitled to attend and vote at the meeting.

   ◆ It is *not* binding on secured creditors unless they agree to be bound by the arrangement.

   ◆ If the company defaults, creditors or members can petition to have the company wound up.

CVA 'small' company moratorium (*IA 1986 Sch A1*)

➤ A 'small company' may apply for a moratorium by filing certain documents with the court.

   ◆ A small company has at least 2 of 3 conditions applicable to it in the year ending with the date of filing, or in the financial year of the company which ended last before that date (*CA 2006 s 382*):
   a) turnover is not more than £6.5 million,
   b) the balance sheet total is not more than £3.26 million,
   c) there are not more than 50 employees.

   ◆ A small company cannot apply for a moratorium if:

      ● the company is in administration, *or*

      ● the company is being wound up, *or*

      ● there is an administrative receiver of the company, *or*

      ● a voluntary arrangement has effect in relation to the company, *or*

      ● there is a provisional liquidator of the company, *or*

      ● a moratorium has been in force for the company at any time during the period of 12 months ending with the date of filing, *and*
         i)   no voluntary arrangement had effect at the time when the moratorium came to an end, *or*
         ii) a voluntary arrangement in force at any time in that period came to an end prematurely, *or*

      ● an administrator held office during 1 year before the filing date, *or*

      ● it is a holding company of a group which does not qualify as a small/medium-sized group, *or*

      ● on the filing date, it is a party to a capital market arrangement (where under the issue of a capital market investment a party has incurred a debt of at least £10 million), *or*

      ● it is a project company for a public-private partnership project, and includes step-in rights, *or*

      ● on the date of filing, it has incurred a liability under an agreement of £10 million or more.

➤ **The moratorium starts** when certain documents are filed with the court.

➤ **The moratorium ends** at the earlier of 28 days after it begins or at the end of the day on when the CVA meetings are first held (or, if the meetings are held on different days, the later of those days). A meeting to establish a CVA may extend the moratorium for a further 2 months from the CVA meeting.

➤ **While the moratorium is in force:**

   ◆ no petition may be presented for the winding up of the company, *and*

   ◆ no meeting of the company may be held except with the nominee's consent or leave of the court and subject (where the court gives leave) to such terms as the court may impose, *and*

   ◆ no resolution may be passed or order made for the winding up of the company, *and*

   ◆ no petition for an administration order in relation to the company may be presented, *and*

   ◆ no administrative receiver of the company may be appointed, *and*

   ◆ no administration application may be made or administrator appointed, *and*

   ◆ no landlord may exercise a right of forfeiture by peaceable re-entry for premises let to the company (if the company has failed to comply with any term/condition of its tenancy of such premises), except with the leave of the court, *and*

   ◆ nothing else may be done to enforce security over the company's property, or to repossess goods in its possession under any hire purchase agreement, except with the leave of the court, *and*

   ◆ no other proceedings or execution or other legal process may be started or continued, and no distress may be levied, against the company or its property except with the leave of the court, *and*

   ◆ there are special rules relating to an uncrystallised floating charge (not dealt with here), *and*

   ◆ security granted by the company may only be enforced if, at the time it was granted, there were reasonable grounds for believing that it would benefit the company, *and*

   ◆ business correspondence must carry a statement of the nominee's name and that the moratorium is in force (but if not done transactions are still enforceable by third parties), *and*

   ◆ the company may not obtain credit of £250 or more from a person who has not been informed that a moratorium is in force, *and*

   ◆ there are several other restrictions on what the company may do during this time.

B Liquidation

1 Voluntary liquidation

Sometimes a company may be wound up following criteria laid down in the articles (eg: to enable the shareholders to extract their capital). Otherwise it may be wound up after a special resolution has been passed, or after an extraordinary resolution has been passed due to its perceived liabilities.

Steps

1 The directors prepare a statement of affairs.

2 Either (a) or (b) will apply below depending on whether the company is solvent or insolvent.

a) The company is *solvent.* This is known as a members' voluntary liquidation since the members will control the winding up of the company.

The directors make a statutory declaration that the company will be able to pay its debts, including interest, within a period not exceeding 1 year (and this must be done within 5 weeks prior to passing a resolution to wind up the company) (*s 89*). They summon a general meeting (*s 89*) at which the members may:

  i) pass a special resolution to wind up the company (*s 84*), and advertise the fact in the *Gazette* within 14 days of the resolution being passed (*s 85*), and

  ii) pass an ordinary resolution to appoint a liquidator (*s 91*).

or:

b) The company is *insolvent.* This is known as a creditors' voluntary liquidation. It is not a remedy available to creditors, but rather it is a procedure supervised by creditors.

The members pass an extraordinary resolution to wind up the company (*s 84*), and the resolution is advertised in the *Gazette* (*s 85*). Separate meetings are held for creditors and members to appoint a liquidator - generally all meetings are held on the same day.

  ♦ The creditors should meet within 14 days of the members' general meeting (*s 98*), where they are shown a statement of affairs by the directors (*s 99*).

  ♦ The creditors may appoint a liquidator.

  ♦ The creditors' choice of liquidator takes priority over that of the members (*s 100*).

3 The liquidator advertises his appointment and notifies the Registrar of Companies (*s 109*).

4 The liquidator has the same powers and duties as for a compulsory insolvency (see p 347).

5 After the company's assets have been distributed, the liquidator makes final reports prior to dissolution to a meeting of members (members' voluntary winding up)(*s 94*), *or* to meetings of members and creditors (creditors' voluntary liquidation)(*s 106*).

6 The liquidator sends the final return to the Registrar of Companies (*ss 94(3),106(3)*).

7 The Registrar dissolves the company 3 months after receiving the liquidator's final return (*s 201*).

2   **Compulsory liquidation** (for unsecured creditors. Secured creditors usually have more specific remedies, eg: appointing an administrative receiver or receiver)

Steps	
1	A creditor *or* the company petitions the Chancery Division of the High Court on one of 7 statutory grounds (*ss 122 (a)-(g)*) (eg: the company is unable to pay its debts).

♦ The company is *presumed* to be unable to pay its debts if:

• a statutory demand has been served by a creditor (minimum debt of £750) and is outstanding for 3 weeks, *or*

• execution has been issued for an unsatisfied judgment debt.

♦ If this presumption does not arise, insolvency must be shown to the court by taking into account actual, prospective and contingent liabilities. |
| 2 | The court has discretion to grant a winding up order (*s 125*). |
| 3 | The court appoints an official receiver. He is the liquidator until another is appointed (*s 136*). He:

♦ takes the board's powers and is obliged to alter the company's notepaper so that the insolvency is apparent to third parties (*s 188*).

♦ advertises his appointment in the *Gazette*.

♦ notifies the Registrar of Companies and the company itself of his appointment. |
| 4 | The directors present a statement of affairs to the official receiver (or liquidator) within 14 days of the order. He reports to the court on the reasons and causes for the failure, and generally the position, dealings, etc, of the company, and any suspicious circumstances (*ss 131-132*). |
| 5 | The receiver calls separate members' and creditors' meetings, and may nominate an alternative liquidator to the official receiver (*s 136(5)*).

♦ The official receiver *must* call a creditors' meeting if 25% (by value) request it (*s 136(5)*).

♦ The creditors' nomination as liquidator takes priority. |
6	The liquidator takes the board's powers and collects in all property of the company (see *'Liquidator's powers to recover assets'* on p 347) (Powers are listed in *Sch 4*).
7	The liquidator distributes assets (see below for the *'Order of distribution'*).
8	After distribution, the liquidator notifies the Registrar of Companies, who dissolves the company 3 months later (*s 202*).
9	The liquidator makes a final report to the creditors' and the members' meetings (*s 146*).

Distribution	Order of distribution
➤ Property does NOT vest in the liquidator (as he is the company's agent), but he is under a duty to take it all into his possession.

➤ Legal proceedings against the company cannot proceed without leave of court. Leave will be refused, for example, if it gives a creditor a chance to 'promote' himself from an unsecured position. | 1 Liquidator's expenses incurred during the winding up

↓

2 Preferential creditors (*s 175*)

↓

3 Floating chargees (in order of charge registration)

↓

4 Ordinary unsecured creditors

↓

5 Members of the Company

BUT see the caveat on the left: |

C A V E A T
➤ Where a floating charge relates to a company which has gone into liquidation/ is in administration, the liquidator/administrator must make some of the company's net property (maximum £600,000) available for the satisfaction of unsecured debts in preference to the proprietor of a floating charge (*s 176A*), *unless*

♦ the company's net property is less than £10,000, *or*
♦ the liquidator/administrator thinks that the cost of making a distribution to unsecured creditors would be disproportionate to the benefits, *or*
♦ the court orders otherwise.

➤ The amount of net property to be made available for unsecured debts is 50% of the first £10,000 of net property and 20% of net property in excess of £10,000 (*IA(PP)O 2003*).

Liquidator's (and administrator's for *ss 238, 239, 423*) powers to recover assets

Transaction	Requirements	Defence	Effect
At an undervalue (*s 238*)	Within 2 years prior to the insolvency + the company was insolvent at the time or became so as a result of this transaction (presumed if with a connected person)	A bad bargain was: ➤ in good faith ➤ on reasonable grounds ➤ for genuine commercial reasons	He can set aside the transaction. (It is actually more complicated than this, but it holds true in general terms)
To create a preference (*s 239*)	Within 6 months prior to the onset of insolvency + the company was insolvent at the time or became so as a result of this transaction + voluntary act + desire to prefer + creditor put in a better position as a result		
	Within 2 years prior to the onset of insolvency for a transaction with a 'connected person' + insolvent at the time or became so as a result of this transaction + voluntary act + creditor put in a better position as a result	Pressure was exerted on the company (no desire to prefer)	
At an undervalue to defraud creditors (*s 423*)	An attempt to put assets beyond the reach of the person making, or who at some time, may make a claim, or otherwise prejudicing the interests of such a person	None	
Fraudulent trading (*s 213*)* Criminal offence CA 2006 s 993	➤ A positive act ➤ The business has been carried on with intent to defraud creditors or for a fraudulent purpose	No such intention	The court will require an offender to contribute to the company's assets insofar as it thinks it proper in the circumstances
Wrongful trading (*s 214*)*	➤ A director knew, or ought to have concluded that there was no reasonable prospect of the company avoiding insolvency; *and* ➤ did not take every step he ought to have taken to minimise loss to creditors	On becoming aware, he took every step that a reasonably diligent person would have, to minimise loss to creditors	

* The liquidator alone can seek an order under these sections

Charges

Fixed charge: is void against the liquidator if unregistered (or registered after 21 days of charge creation) (*CA 2006 s 870*)

Floating charge: is void against the liquidator if:
♦ unregistered (or registered after 21 days of creation of the charge) (*CA 2006 s 870*), *or*
♦ (except to the extent of the value of consideration provided to the company in money or money's worth at the same time, or after the creation of the charge):
  ● (if in favour of a connected person) the charge was created within 2 years of liquidation, *or*
  ● (if in favour of an unconnected person):
    i) the charge was created within 1 year of liquidation, *and*
    ii) the charge was created at a time when the company was insolvent or became insolvent as a result (*IA s 245*).

A liquidator may not pursue sale proceeds of a fully enforced judgment order obtained before the bankruptcy order. If the order is not fully enforced, the sheriff will transfer any seized goods to the liquidator (*s 183*)

A liquidator may set aside 'onerous contracts', or disclaim 'onerous property', provided he replies to any inquiry by an interested third party within 28 days (*s 178*). 'Onerous' means that it is a drain on the company's assets or cash flow

V   A note on statutory demands

➤ A statutory demand is a powerful creditor weapon because it obviates the need for court proceedings.

   ◆ A debtor's failure to comply for 3 weeks can become the basis of a bankruptcy/insolvency petition.

➤ It is not a court document so the creditor must serve it and prove service.

➤ *IR 1986* (*r 6*) set out the detailed requirements.

VI   Cross-border EU insolvency

➤ EC *Regulation 1346/2000* has direct effect. In the UK it is implemented by *I(A)R 2002*, amending *IR 1986*.

   ◆ It is intended to improve the efficiency and effectiveness of insolvency proceedings with an EU cross-border element without harmonisation. It sets out a framework for the different EU insolvency systems.

➤ There are 2 types of insolvency proceedings:

   ◆ Main proceedings

     ● These can be opened in the member state where the debtor has its 'centre of main interests'. There is no complete definition of this expression but for a company there is a rebuttable presumption that this is the place of the registered office. However, the Regulation provides that the centre of main interests should correspond to the place where the debtor conducts the administration of his interests on a regular basis and is therefore ascertainable by third parties.

     ● The legal effects of main proceedings must be recognised in all other member states and the officeholder appointed in the main proceedings must be recognised, and will be able to exercise his powers, in other member states without the need for a further court order.

   ◆ Secondary (or ancillary) proceedings

     ● These can be opened by either the officeholder in the main proceedings, or any person or authority authorised to do so in the member state in which the application is made, in any territory where the debtor possesses an 'establishment'.

     ● Secondary proceedings are limited in scope to assets in the member state where they are opened. In limited cases, such proceedings may be opened before main proceedings - they are then called 'territorial proceedings', eg: if local creditors request it or where main proceedings cannot be opened under the law of the member state where the debtor has his main centre of interest.

➤ **UK insolvency proceedings that will be recognised:**

   ◆ Main proceedings (*Annex A*): In the UK: winding up by or subject to the supervision of the court, creditors' voluntary winding up (with confirmation by the court), administration, voluntary arrangements under the insolvency legislation and bankruptcy.

   ◆ Secondary proceedings (*Annex B*): In the UK: winding up by or subject to the supervision of the court, creditors' voluntary winding up (with confirmation by the court) and bankruptcy.

   NB: Receivership and administrative receivership are not listed as a main or secondary proceeding for the UK as they are considered a self-help remedy for the secured creditor.

➤ **Choice of law:** The general rule is that the law of the member state in which proceedings are opened will generally determine all the effects of those proceedings including the conditions for opening the proceedings, their conduct and closure. There are exceptions to this, eg: rights in rem and set-off rights.

H Competition and trading

I   Merger control law

A European merger control

➤ *Merger Control Regulation 139/2004* came into force on 1 May 2004 and provides for a system of merger control for mergers with a 'Community dimension'. The Commission has sole jurisdiction for this.

- ◆ 'Community dimension' is assessed by minimum bounds for worldwide turnover, Community-wide turnover, and in some cases, national turnover (*Article 1*).

- ◆ Purely national mergers are excluded but may be subject to national legislation.

➤ The Commission must evaluate such concentrations to see if they are compatible with the common market (*Article 2*).

➤ **Notification:** Concentrations with a Community dimension must be notified to the Commission prior to their implementation and following the conclusion of the agreement, the announcement of the public bid, or the acquisition of a controlling interest (*Article 4*).

- ◆ Notification may also be made where the undertakings concerned demonstrate to the Commission a Community dimension and a good faith intention to conclude an agreement or, in the case of a public bid, where they have publicly announced an intention to make such a bid.

➤ **Publication:** The Commission must publish the notification, the names of the undertakings concerned, their country of origin, the nature of the concentration and the economic sectors involved (*Article 4*).

➤ **Decision:** The Commission must examine the notification as soon as it is received and publish a decision within 25 working days as set out below (*Articles 6* and *10(1)*).

- ◆ Where it finds that the concentration notified is not within scope, it publishes a decision saying so.

- ◆ Where it finds that the concentration notified, although within scope, does not raise serious doubts as to its compatibility with the common market and it decides not to oppose it, it publishes a decision saying that it is compatible with the common market.

  - An indication that a concentration will not impede competition is if the market share of the undertakings does not exceed 25% either in the common market or in a substantial part of it (*Recital 32*).

- ◆ Where it finds that the concentration notified falls within scope and raises serious doubts as to its compatibility with the common market, it may initiate negotiation with the parties who have a chance to modify the proposal or agree to conditions. These negotiations are closed by a decision as above.

➤ The implementation of concentrations should be suspended until a final decision of the Commission has been taken but it is possible to derogate from this suspension on rare occasions (*Recital 34*).

➤ In certain circumstances, the Commission can refer a case to a relevant Member State (*Article 9*).

➤ The Commission has wide powers to request information and to mount inspections (and ask Member States to help) (*Articles 11-13*) and to impose fines and penalties (*Articles 14-15*).

B   UK Merger control

➤ *EA 2002 Pt 3* (*ss 29-130*) sets out the UK's regime for merger control (except for control of newspaper mergers). The main provisions about mergers provide for:

- ◆ final decisions to be taken by the Office of Fair Trading (OFT) and Competition Commission (CC).

- ◆ a new test of whether a merger will result in a substantial lessening of competition.

- ◆ discretion for the competition authorities to clear a merger or allow it to proceed with less stringent competition remedies in circumstances where, notwithstanding an expected substantial lessening of competition, they expect it to result in defined types of customer benefit.

- ◆ the Secretary of State may decide mergers which raise defined public interest considerations.

- ◆ a two-stage approach to merger control.

  - ● The OFT will carry out the first stage investigation to decide whether a CC reference is required.

  - ● The CC will carry out the second stage, in-depth investigation where necessary.

- ◆ a system of voluntary rather than compulsory pre-notification of mergers.

- ◆ statutory maximum timetables for competition authorities to reach final decisions for both first and second stage investigations.

- ◆ a UK-based turnover test to determine whether a merger is subject to merger control procedures.

➤ The European Commission has sole jurisdiction for mergers with a 'Community dimension' (see p 349).

➤ Enforcement powers of the OFT and CC before, during and after a merger reference are in *EA 2002 ss 71-95*.

➤ Enforcement takes 2 forms: undertakings and orders.

- ◆ Undertakings are given voluntarily by one or more of the parties to a merger. Once accepted by the relevant authority, these become legally binding and enforceable in the courts.

- ◆ Orders are made by the authorities and prohibit the parties specified in the order from doing something or specify that they must take certain action.

➤ Before and during a reference, undertakings and orders seek to prevent any action being taken that might prejudice the eventual outcome of the merger inquiry.

Cross-border mergers of limited liability companies

➤ *C(CBM)R 2007* implements *Directive 2005/56/EC* on cross-border mergers of limited companies.

➤ *C(CBM)R 2007* sets out a framework for a cross-border merger, ie: a merger by absorption, a merger by absorption of a wholly-owned subsidiary or a merger by formation of a new company.

- ◆ The merger must involve at least 1 company formed and registered in the UK and at least 1 company formed and registered in an EEA State other than the UK.

II   EU competition law

TFEU Article 101: restriction or distortion of competition

➤ This article prohibits agreements, decisions and concerted practices ...

- ◆ ... between undertakings or associations of undertakings ...

- ◆ ... which have as their object *or* effect ...

- ◆ ... prevention, restriction or distortion of competition within the EU.

➤ Such agreements are void. However, *TFEU Article 101(2)* would permit severance of an offending term if national law permits this. (English law does permit this.)

Avoiding infringement of *TFEU Article 101*

➤ **Agencies** (guidelines to *Regulation 330/2010* at *http://ec.europa.eu/competition/antitrust/legislation/ guidelines_vertical_en.pdf*, see also p 365.) There is generally no infringement if:

♦ the principal and agent are pursuing the same economic interest, *and*

♦ the agent does not take the financial/commercial risk and does not act independently of the principal.

➤ **Agreements between parents and subsidiaries**

♦ These are *usually* treated as one 'undertaking', and therefore are not caught by *TFEU Article 101*.

➤ **Agreements of 'minor importance' (which are not 'black-listed' agreements)**

♦ Agreements under Commission Notice (*2001/C 368/07 - Dec 2001*) do not infringe *TFEU Article 101*.

le: where the parties' combined share of the relevant market does not exceed 10% (for horizontal agreements) or 15% (for vertical agreements) of the total market in the agreement area.

♦ The Notice also contains guidelines for national courts.

♦ The Commission is not bound by the Notice, but compliance with it will avoid heavy fines.

➤ **Block exemptions**

♦ These allow parties to certain types of agreement to include anti-competitive/*TFEU Article 101* infringing provisions in their agreements. However, they will be permitted, if the agreement is drafted strictly in accordance with a block exemption. Block exemptions list forbidden 'black' clauses (eg: export bans) which must be avoided and permitted 'white' clauses (eg: certain territorial restrictions).

♦ Examples of block exemptions are:

● *Regulation 330/2010* - vertical agreements (see also p 367)

● *Regulation 1217/2010* - research and development agreements

● *Regulation 1218/2010* - specialisation agreements

horizontal agreements

● *Regulation 772/2004* - new technology transfer

➤ **Notification to the Commission:** this protects against fines in respect of the period from the date of notification until the Commission's 'first adverse reaction' (ie: possibly before its final ruling).

♦ The Commission then has 3 options:

a) **Negative clearance:** a declaration that *TFEU Article 101* is not infringed.

b) **Individual exemption:** granted under *TFEU Article 101(3)* if the agreement can be justified because it will 'contribute to the improvement of production or distribution of goods, or to promoting technical or economic progress, while allowing consumers a fair share of the resulting benefit'. An exemption binds the Commission, but few are granted and the process is lengthy.

c) **Comfort letter:** a non-binding reassurance that *either TFEU Article 101* is not infringed, *or* a block exemption covers the agreement, *or* the Commission is closing its files for the moment.

TFEU Article 102: abuse of a dominant position

➤ This article prohibits abuse by one or more undertakings of a dominant position ...

- ◆ ... within the EU or a substantial part of it ...

- ◆ ... which may affect trade between member states.

➤ A market share of 40% or more is a good indication that an undertaking is dominant in a market.

- ◆ Markets can be defined widely or narrowly (eg: passenger aircraft or commuter aircraft).

- ◆ A market is evaluated:

  - • geographically, *and*

  - • by product market.

    - ▪ The test is 'what other product, if any, can be substituted for the product in question, given the nature of it, its price and its intended use?' (*United Brands v Comm.* [1978] ECR 207).

Avoiding infringement of *TFEU Article 102*

➤ If dominant in the market, an undertaking should not abuse its position.

➤ The European Commission ('Commission') can grant negative clearance. This is a declaration that an agreement does not contravene *TFEU Article 102*.

- ◆ This is the only option open to an undertaking to avoid infringement.

III   UK competition law

A   The Office of Fair Trading (OFT)

➤ The OFT has the function of (*EA 2002 ss 6-8*):

- ◆ making the public aware of the ways in which competition may benefit consumers in, and the economy of, the United Kingdom; and

- ◆ giving information or advice in respect of matters relating to any of its functions to the public.

- ◆ making proposals or giving other information or advice on matters relating to any of its functions to any Minister of the Crown or other public authority.

- ◆ promoting good practice in the carrying out of activities which may affect the economic interests of consumers in the United Kingdom.

➤ The OFT is the enforcing body under the *CA 1998*.

- ◆ Appeals from the OFT are to the Competition Commission.

B   Common law restraint of trade doctrine

➤ The restraint of trade doctrine prevents restrictive covenants being enforceable *unless*:

- ◆ they are reasonably limited as to time, space and scope, *and*

- ◆ they are reasonably necessary in the context of the whole agreement.

C   *Competition Act 1998*

➤ *CA 1998 s 60:* UK competition authorities must ensure there is no inconsistency with European competition law and must have regard to any statement/decision of the EU Commission.

CA 1998: The Chapter I prohibition

➤ This is modelled on the European *TFEU Article 101* regime but certain EU principles are not relevant eg: EU market principles and objectives.

➤ The Chapter I prohibition prohibits agreements, decisions and concerted practices between undertakings or associations of undertakings which have as their object *or* effect prevention, restriction or distortion of competition within the UK.

➤ Such agreements are void (but offending terms may be severed).

➤ Some agreements are not caught, eg: mergers, land agreements etc.

Avoiding infringement of the Chapter I prohibition

➤ **Outside scope:** Generally, the OFT says there is no 'appreciable effect' if the parties' combined share of the relevant market is not greater then 25%.

◆ A market share of less than 25% will have 'appreciable effect' if the agreement fixes prices, sets minimum resale prices or is part of a network of agreements that have a cumulative effect.

➤ **"Small agreements":** There is limited immunity for 'small agreements' (ie: all agreements between undertakings where their combined applicable turnover does not exceed £20 million) (*CA(SACMS)R*).

➤ **Exemptions: 2 types:**

◆ **Block exemptions** made by the OFT, which must be an agreement that (*CA 1998 ss 6, 9*):

• contributes to:
- improving production or distribution, *or*
- promoting technical or economic progress,

while allowing consumers a fair share of the resulting benefit, *and*

• does not:
- impose on the undertakings concerned restrictions which are not indispensable to the attainment of those objectives, *or*
- afford the undertakings concerned the possibility of eliminating competition in respect of a substantial part of the products in question.

◆ **EU exemptions or decision** (ie: EU block exemptions/decision, p 351) (*CA 1998 ss 10-11*).

➤ **Notification to the EU Commission** (see p 351): this gives immunity from fines in *CA 1998* but infringements may still be investigated by OFT.

CA 1998: The Chapter II prohibition

➤ This is based on *TFEU Article 102* but certain EU principles are irrelevant eg: EU market principles/objectives.

➤ The Chapter II prohibition provides that any conduct on the part of one or more undertakings which amounts to the abuse of a dominant position in a market is prohibited if it may affect trade within the UK.

◆ A market share of 40% or more is a good indication that an undertaking is dominant in that market.

• Markets can be defined widely or narrowly (eg: passenger aircraft or commuter aircraft).

• A market is evaluated:
- geographically, *and*
- by product market.

Avoiding infringement of the Chapter II prohibition

➤ If dominant in the market, an undertaking should not abuse its position.

➤ **Minor conduct:** There is limited immunity from penalty for conduct of minor significance (ie: conduct by an undertaking whose applicable turnover does not exceed £50 million) (*CA(SACMS)R*).

IV   Enforcement of competition law

Enforcement of EU competition law (*Regulation 1/2003*)

Art	
2	**Burden of proof:** In national or EU proceedings, the burden of proof is on the party alleging infringement. An undertaking claiming an *TFEU Article 101(3)* exemption bears the burden of proof of it.
3	**Relationship of national/EU law:** There must be simultaneous enforcement of national and EU in the competition law area but Member States may have national law which is stricter than EU law.
5/6	**National powers:** National competition authorities and courts can apply *TFEU Articles 101 & 102*.
7	**Finding infringement:** Where the Commission finds infringement, it may require undertakings concerned to end the infringement. It may impose on them any behavioural (this is preferred) or structural remedies which are proportionate to the infringement and necessary to end the infringement.
8	**Interim measures:** In urgent cases (ie: risk of serious and irreparable damage to competition), the Commission may order interim measures, on the basis of a prima facie finding of infringement.
9	**Commitments:** The Commission may accept a commitment from an undertaking to meet the Commission's concerns instead of making a finding of an infringement.
11	**Cooperation:** The Commission and the competition authorities of the Member States apply the EU competition rules in close cooperation (including by exchanging information)
13	**Suspension/termination of proceedings:** Where competition authorities of 2 or more Member States act against the same agreement, any of them may suspend the proceedings or reject the complaint on the grounds that another is dealing with it. The Commission may also reject a complaint on the ground that a competition authority of a Member State is dealing with the case and vice versa.
16	**Uniformity of legal application:** National courts cannot rule on agreements, decisions or practices so as to be inconsistent with a decision adopted or contemplated by the Commission.
17-19	**Investigations:** Where circumstances suggest that competition may be restricted/distorted within the EC, the Commission may conduct an inquiry into a particular sector of the economy or into particular types of agreement across various sectors. In that inquiry, the Commission may request undertakings concerned to supply information, carry out inspections and interview any person who consents to be interviewed to collect information relating to the subject matter of the investigation.
20-21	**Inspection:** The Commission has wide powers of inspection, including powers to: ◆ enter premises, land and means of transport of undertakings (and also the homes of directors and staff if there is reasonable possibility that important evidence is actually kept there), *and* ◆ examine books and records related to the business, irrespective of the medium of storage, *and* ◆ take or obtain in any form copies of or extracts from such books or records, *and* ◆ seal business premises, books or records during and to the extent necessary for inspection, *and* ◆ ask any representative or member of staff for explanations on facts or documents relating to the subject-matter and purpose of the inspection and to record the answers.
22	**Member State investigations:** Member State competition authorities may in their own territory carry out any inspection under national law on behalf of the competition authority of another Member State.
23	**Penalties imposable by the Commission:** An undertaking may be fined a maximum percentage of its total turnover in the preceding business year as follows: ◆ For intentionally or negligently giving incorrect/misleading information: maximum 1%. ◆ For infringing *TFEU Article 101/102*: maximum 10%.

The Commission applies a publicly-declared fining policy within these limits (last updated June 2006, see http://ec.europa.eu/comm/competition/antitrust/legislation/fines.html). In fixing the fine, regard is had to the gravity and duration of any infringement

Enforcement of competition law by the OFT in the UK (*CA 1998 s 25*)

➤ The OFT may conduct an investigation if there are reasonable grounds for suspecting that:

◆ there is an agreement which:

● may affect trade within the United Kingdom, *and*

● has as its object or effect the prevention, restriction or distortion of competition within the UK, *or*

◆ there is an agreement which:

● may affect trade between Member States, *and*

● has as its object or effect the prevention, restriction or distortion of competition within the EU, *or*

◆ the Chapter II prohibition has been infringed, *or*

◆ the prohibition in *TFEU Article 102* has been infringed, *or*

◆ at some time in the past, there was an agreement which at that time:

● may have affected trade within the UK, *and*

● had as its object or effect the prevention, restriction or distortion of competition within the UK, *or*

◆ at some time in the past, there was an agreement which at that time:

● may have affected trade between Member States, *and*

● had as its object or effect the prevention, restriction or distortion of competition within EU.

➤ The OFT has sweeping powers of investigation and enforcement similar to those of the European Commission (see p 354) but also backed by criminal sanction (*CA 1998 s 26*).

➤ The OFT must make a decision as to whether infringement of EU or UK Competition law has occurred. It can also accept commitments from persons to take certain action so as to avoid a finding of infringement (*CA 1998 ss 31-31E*).

➤ The OFT has power to give such directions as it sees fit to end any infringement (enforced by courts).

◆ The OFT can also give interim measures directions, pending the completion of an investigation.

➤ Fines imposed by the OFT for infringements of competition law may be up to 10% of an undertaking's turnover during the preceding year (*CA 1998 s 36* and *CA(DTP)O 2000*).

◆ For infringements of the Chapter I prohibition only, there is immunity for 'small' agreements and for infringements of the Chapter II prohibition only, there is immunity for 'conduct of minor significance', but not, in either case if the agreement or conduct is in respect of price fixing (*CA 1998 ss 39-40*).

◆ The amount of the fine depends on the seriousness of the abuse, the party's position in the market, the size of the offender, and any mitigating factors such as co-operation with the OFT.

◆ An undertaking may appeal against the OFT's ruling to the Competition Commission.

➤ If there is any overlap between European penalties and those which the OFT seeks to impose, the OFT must take the European penalties into account so there is no 'double jeopardy'.

➤ *EA 2002 ss 188-202* provide for criminal offences for individuals who dishonestly engage in cartel agreements. These operate alongside (but are narrower than) the existing regime that imposes civil sanctions on undertakings that breach the competition provisions of *CA 1998*.

V   Free movement of goods

TFEU: *Articles 34 and 35*

➤ *Articles 34* and *35* prohibit quantitative restrictions on imports and exports and all measures having equivalent effect.

   ◆ 'Equivalent effect' means 'all trading rules enacted by member states that are capable of hindering, directly, or indirectly, actually or potentially, intra-community trade' (*Procureur du Roi v Dassonville* [1974] ECR 837).

   ◆ The measure must have some discriminatory effect (ie: putting imports at a disadvantage (*Re Keck and Mithouard* (Joined Cases C-267/91 and C-268/91) [1993] ECR I-6097; [1995] 1 CEC 298).

      ● Before *Keck* it had been held that some marketing provisions had infringed *Article 34*. *Keck* seems to say that rules about selling arrangements/marketing probably do not come within *Article 34* and so it is not clear how the courts will treat such rules now.

   ◆ *Article 34* applies not only to the official laws of the state, but also when the state acts through another undertaking or 'bodies established or approved by an official authority' (*Re Peter Vriend* [1980] ECR 327, *Commission v Ireland* [1982] ECR 4005).

   ◆ The effect can be indirect and need not be the main purpose of the legislation (*Torfaen Borough Council v B & Q plc* [1989] ECR 765) (one of the Sunday trading cases), and it includes bureaucratic procedures (*Rewe-Zentralfinanz GmbH v Landwirtschafiskammer* [1975] ECR 843).

   ◆ Discrimination against national goods is allowed since *Article 34* is not meant to give a level playing-field, but rather to avoid discrimination against imports (*Nederlandse Bakkerij Stichting v Edah BV* [1986] ECR 3359).

Two classes of exception to *Article 34*

1   Rule of reason (if both domestic and imported products are affected)

➤ National legislation for 'fiscal supervision, the protection of public health, the fairness of commercial transactions and the defence of the consumer' (*Rewe-Zentral AG v Bundesmonopolverwaltung fur Branntwein (Re Cassis de Dijon)* [1979] ECR 649), and the protection of the environment (*Commission v Denmark* [1989] CMLR 619) will not infringe *Article 34*.

➤ The 'rule of reason' test. Is the restriction ...
   a)   ... justifiable under EU law, *and* ...
   b)   ... in proportion to its declared aim? (ie: is the effect 'direct, indirect or merely speculative' and does it 'impede the marketing of imported products more than the marketing of national products' (*Stoke-on-Trent City Council v B & Q plc* [1993] 1 All ER 481))?

2   *Article 36*

➤ Certain laws will escape the prohibition of *Articles 34* and *35*. Such laws must be:

   ◆ to uphold public morality in a state (*R v Henn & R v Darby* [1979] ECR 3795 (pornography import)), *or*

   ◆ on grounds of public policy, *or*

   ◆ to maintain public security (internal and external), *or*

   ◆ to protect public health, *or*

   ◆ to protect national treasures, *or*

   ◆ to protect intellectual property rights

| **BUT** such laws must not *either:* |
| a)   constitute a means of arbitrary discrimination, *or* |
| b)   be a disguised restriction on trade between member states. |

VI   Sale of goods / supply of services

A   Terms implied by statute and regulation (generally)

➤   Terms may be implied by the 3 statutes listed in the following table where a contract for sale or supply of goods and/or services (*SGA s 55*) is silent as to certain matters.

➤   Other legislation also mandates certain rules in contracts (eg: *LPCD(I)A 1998* and *CP(DS)R 2000*).

Term	SGA 1979 amended by SSGA 1994/5	SGSA 1982 amended by SSGA 1994			SG(IT) A 1973	When a term is implied into a contract *and* a few details as to the nature of the term
	Contract for sale of goods	Contract for hire	Contract for transfer of goods / Contract for work + materials	Contract for services	Contract for hire purchase	
Description	s 13	s 8	s 3		s 9	Goods/services must correspond with description (if sold by description)
Satisfactory quality	s 14(2) s 14(2A)	s 9(2) s 9(3)	s 4(2) s 4(3)		s 10(2)	Implied when dealing in the course of seller's business. Not applicable to: a) defects shown to the customer, *or* b) defects which the customer's examination ought to have revealed
Fitness for purpose	s 14(3)	s 9(4) s 9(5)	s 4(4) s 4(5) s 4(6)		s 10(3)	On a consumer sale, seller is liable for public statements made by the seller or producer regarding the subject of the sale
Title	s 12	s 7 (Possession)	s 2		s 8	Always implied
Price	s 8					See p 358
Payment	s 10					See p 358
Ownership	ss 16-18					See p 358
Risk	s 20					See p 359
Delivery	s 29					See p 359
Sample	s 15	s 10	s 5		s 11	Always implied on a sale by sample
Reasonable care and skill				s 13		Implied when dealing in the course of the seller's business
Within reasonable time				s 14		Implied when dealing in the course of the seller's business. Not applicable if the time is fixed by contract, or is left to be agreed in the manner set out in the contract, *or* is determined by a course of dealing between the parties
Reasonable charge				s 15		Always implied. Not applicable if charge is fixed by contract, or is left to be agreed in the manner set out in the contract, *or* is determined by a course of dealing between the parties

B Sale of Goods Act 1979

➤ When a sale of goods contract is formed, sometimes not all terms that are supposed to be included, are in fact included. The following defaults only apply where the contract does not make provision.

		Sale of Goods Act 1979		
s	**Area**	**Content**		
		Formation of the contract		
2	Definition	A contract for sale of goods is a contract by which the seller (S) transfers or agrees to transfer the property in goods to the buyer (B) for a money consideration, called the price		
8	Price	Where price is not agreed, or determined by fact, B must pay a reasonable price		
10	Time of payment	Not of the essence Note: other stipulations as to time depend on the terms of the contract		
15	Sale by sample	2 implied terms: ◆ the bulk corresponds with the sample in quality ◆ the goods are free from any defect not apparent on a reasonable examination of the sample		
		Effect of the contract		
16 17 18	Ownership	Ownership passes when the parties intend it to pass ◆ If the parties do not express an intention as to when ownership passes, the time it does pass depends on the type of contract:		

Rule	**Type of contract**	**Ownership passes**
1	Unconditional contract for specific goods in a deliverable state	When the contract is made
2	Contract for specific goods to be put into a deliverable state	When they are in a deliverable state and B is told of this
3	Contract for specific goods where something must be done to ascertain the price	When the price is set and B is told what it is
4	Goods on approval for sale and return	When *either*: ◆ B indicates his acceptance of the goods to S, *or* ◆ B's conduct implies that he accepts the sale transaction *or* ◆ B retains the goods beyond a reasonable period (or agreed time) without rejecting them
5	Unascertained goods	When goods are available and unconditionally appropriated to the contract (ie: ascertained)

Specific goods: 'goods identified and agreed on at the time the contract of sale is made' (*SGA s 61(1)*)

19	Reservation of title
	
	Note: the importance of retention of title clauses is manifest on insolvency; their purpose is either to recover goods when a business becomes insolvent, or failing that, to put the debtor in a strong position in negotiations with the receiver
		◆ S may reserve title to 'specific goods' or those 'appropriated to the contract' by a 'retention of title clause'
		◆ There are 3 types of these clauses, known collectively (and confusingly!) as '*Romalpa*' clauses.
		  a) Retention of title clause: title is reserved until payment is received
		  b) 'All moneys clause': title does not pass until *all* moneys owing to S, whether under this contract or any other contract, are paid
		  c) A true '*Romalpa*' clause: title is retained in the goods, and S is permitted to trace the purchase price into the hands of a third party to whom the goods are sold
		  • a) and b) are generally upheld by the courts
		  • c) succeeded on particular facts once when a fiduciary relationship was found between S and B (*Aluminium Industrie v Romalpa Aluminium Ltd* [1976] 2 All ER 552). Attempts to copy it have failed and the Courts construe c) as an unregistered (ie: void) charge
		◆ To stand a chance of being effective (ie: to stand a chance of being construed as more than just a charge that is void and being construed instead as a right to repossession) a clause should:
		  • reserve full *legal* title to the goods (equitable and/or beneficial title are insufficient), *and*
		  • entitle the seller to enter the buyer's property to inspect and repossess the goods, *and*
		  • oblige the buyer to store the goods separately, or label them, so they can be identified as being appropriated to the contract

	**Sale of Goods Act 1979 (cont.)**
s	**Area**	**Content**
	Effect of the contract (cont.)
20	Risk	◆ Goods are at the risk of S unless property is transferred to B ◆ If property has been transferred to B, goods are at B's risk whether delivery has been made or not ◆ If goods are delayed due the fault of one party, the goods are at the risk of the party at fault NB: On a consumer sale, goods are at S's risk until delivered to the consumer
20A	Undivided shares in bulk	When goods within a bulk become identified *and* the price has been paid for the goods in the bulk, *then* ◆ property in undivided share is transferred to B, *and* ◆ B becomes an owner in common of the bulk
21	Capacity to pass property	One cannot give what one does not have - *nemo dat quod non habet.* (Exceptions include factors, S in possession after sale, and motor vehicles (*HPA 1964 s 27(5)(a)*)
	Performance of the contract
27 28	Duties	S must deliver the goods and B must accept and pay for the goods Delivery and payment are concurrent (ie: cash on delivery)
29 31	Delivery	**Place of delivery:** S's place of business (or if not, his residence) Note: if goods are specific goods and they are known to be at another place, delivery is at that other place Note: delivery to an independent carrier is counted as delivery to B **Delivery time:** S must send the goods within a reasonable time and at a reasonable hour
30	Wrong quantity delivered	**Smaller quantity than expected:** B may reject all the goods (unless he is not a consumer and the shortfall is only slight) B may accept all the goods. If so, he must pay for them at the contract rate **Larger quantity than expected:** B may accept the right quantity and reject the excess B may reject the whole (unless he is not a consumer and the excess is only slight) B may accept all the goods. If so, he must pay for them at the contract rate
31 34 35 35A 36	Acceptance ?	**B accepts the goods by:** ◆ intimating to S that he accepts, *or* ◆ after the goods have been delivered, acting in a manner inconsistent with the ownership of S **B rejects the goods:** ◆ B has a right to reject the goods if he has not had a reasonable opportunity to examine the goods (this cannot be waived if B is a consumer) ◆ B has a right to reject part of the goods ◆ B is not bound to return rejected goods ◆ B does not have to accept the goods if they unexpectedly arrive in instalments
41 42 44 45	Unpaid seller	**An unpaid seller, if he has received no payment, or tender of payment may:** ◆ have a lien on the goods or part of them for the price, *or* ◆ (if B is insolvent) stop the goods in transport, *or* ◆ (if the goods are perishable and S informs B he has not been paid) re-sell the goods
	Remedies
48A 49 50 15A	Things go wrong	**Remedies for S** ◆ **Property has passed and S has received no payment** - S sues for the price ◆ **Property has passed and payment time has passed without payment** - S sues for the price ◆ **B wrongfully refuses to accept the goods** - S sues for damages and losses 'directly and naturally' flowing from B's breach of contract **Remedies for B** ◆ **S does not deliver** - B sues for damages and losses 'directly and naturally' flowing from S's breach of contract ◆ **S breaches a warranty** - B sues for damages NB: if S breaches *ss 13-15* (see p 357) and B is a non-consumer, and the breach is slight, this may be treated as a breach of warranty NB: if B is a consumer and goods do not conform to contract at time of delivery, B may require S to repair or replace the goods (unless impossible or disproportionate, in which case B can require a reduction in the purchase price or a rescission of the contract). A defect discovered within 6 months after delivery is presumed to have been there at the time of delivery unless shown otherwise by S

C Other statutory rules and regulations

➤ Many specific industries have their own rules and regulations e.g. food labelling for supermarkets.

   ◆ However there are many of general application too.

Late Payment of Commercial Debts (Interest) Act 1998

➤ *LPCD(I)A 1998* gives a creditor a statutory right to claim interest on debts paid late (*s 1*) in contracts for the sale/hire of goods/services where purchaser and supplier both act in the course of business.

   ◆ 'Business' includes professions and government departments or local/public authorities.

   ◆ Exempt contracts include consumer credit agreements, mortgages, charges or security (*s 2*).

   ◆ Interest starts to accrue on (*s 4*):   *either*   the day after the contractual date for payment,

                              or if none, 30 days from the later of:

   - delivery of the invoice for payment, *or*

   - delivery/performance of the relevant goods/services .

   ◆ The interest rate is 8% above the official dealing rate in force on 30 June (for interest starting between 1 July - 31 December) or 31 December (for interest starting between 1 January - 30 June).

   ◆ There are slightly different rules for advance payments (not dealt with here).

➤ Once interest starts to accrue, the supplier is entitled to a fixed sum (in addition to the statutory interest on the debt) which is specified in *s 5A(2)*.

➤ Contracting-out of *LPCD(I)A 1998* before the debt is created is not permitted unless there is a substantial contractual remedy for late payment in the contract *(s 8)*.

The Business Protection from Misleading Marketing Regulations 2008

Part	➤ *BPMMR 2008* implements Directive 2006/114/EC concerning misleading and comparative advertising.
1	➤ Prohibits advertising which misleads traders.
	➤ Sets out the conditions under which comparative advertising (ie: advertising which identifies a competitor or a competitor's product) is permitted.
	➤ Requires code owners (ie: traders and bodies responsible for codes of conduct or monitoring compliance with such codes) not to promote misleading advertising and comparative advertising which is not permitted.
2	➤ Provides for criminal offences and defences that apply where a trader engages in misleading advertising.
3	➤ Places a duty to enforce the Regulations on the OFT and local weights and measures authorities.
	◆ They are given the power to take proceedings for an injunction to secure compliance with *BPMMR 2008*.
4	➤ Gives the enforcement authorities powers to investigate whether there has been a breach of *BPMMR 2008* including a power to make test purchases and powers to enter premises with or without a warrant.

Consumer Protection (Distance Selling) Regulations 2000

Reg	➤ There are many types of distance sales, including those made over the Internet. *CP(DS)R 2000* implements (most of) Euro Directive 97/7/EC on the protection of consumers in relation to distance contracts.
	◆ *FS(DM)R 2004* implements Euro Directive 2002/65/EC on the distance marketing of consumer financial services (ie: services of a banking, credit, insurance, personal pension, investment or payment nature which the FSA/OFT do not regulate under their existing regulatory structures). For these things, it contains similar provisions to *CP(DS)R 2000*.
4	➤ *CP(DS)R 2000* applies to contracts for goods or services to be supplied to a consumer where the contract is made exclusively by means of distance communication (ie: any means used without the simultaneous physical presence of the consumer and the supplier.
5	◆ *CP(DS)R 2000* do not apply to 'excepted contracts' ie: contracts:
	• for the sale an interest in land except for a rental agreement, *or*
	• relating to financial services, *or*
	• concluded by means of an automated vending machine or automated commercial premises, *or*
	• concluded with a telecommunications operator through a public pay-phone, *or*
	• concluded at an auction.
6	◆ Most of *CP(DS)R 2000* do not apply to contracts for the supply of groceries by regular delivery or contracts for the provision of accommodation, transport, catering or leisure services.
19	➤ The contract must be performed within 30 days, subject to agreement between the parties. If the supplier cannot supply the goods/services ordered, he may offer substitutes if set conditions are met.
26-27	
	➤ The OFT must consider complaints about a breach of *CP(DS)R 2000*.

Consumer Protection (Distance Selling) Regulations 2000 (continued)

Reg 7

➤ In good time **prior to the conclusion of the contract** the supplier must:

◆ provide to the consumer the following information in a clear and comprehensible manner:

- the supplier's identity and, if the contract requires advance payment, the supplier's address, *and*
- a description of the main characteristics of the goods or services, *and*
- the price of the goods or services including all taxes and delivery costs where appropriate, *and*
- the arrangements for payment, delivery or performance, *and*
- the existence of a right of cancellation (except in the exceptional cases - see below), *and*
- the cost of using the means of distance communication, if not at the basic rate, *and*
- the period for which the offer or the price remains valid, *and*
- where appropriate, the minimum duration of the contract, in the case of contracts for the supply of goods or services to be performed permanently or recurrently.

◆ inform the consumer if he proposes that, if the goods/services ordered by the consumer are unavailable, he will provide substitutes of equivalent quality and price, *and*

◆ inform the consumer that the cost of returning any such substitute goods to the supplier in the event of cancellation by the consumer will be met by the supplier.

8

➤ The supplier must confirm in writing, or on other durable medium available and accessible to the consumer, most of the information already given **and** some additional information, eg:

◆ conditions and procedures relating to the cancellation rights, including:

- where the consumer must return the goods for a cancellation, notification of that fact, *and*
- information as to whether the consumer or supplier is responsible for the cost of return if the consumer cancels the contract, *and*
- in a services contract, information of how the right to cancel may be affected by the consumer agreeing to performance of the services starting before the end of the cooling-off period.

◆ information on after-sales services/guarantees), *and*

◆ conditions for exercising any contractual right to cancel, where the contract is of an unspecified duration or a duration exceeding 1 year.

10-12

➤ There must be a 'cooling off period' so the consumer can cancel the contract by giving notice of cancellation. The effect of this notice is that the contract is treated as if it had not been made.

◆ If the supplier gives the specified information on time, the cooling-off period is 7 working days from: i) (for services) the day after the date of the contract, *or* ii) (for goods) the day after the date of delivery.

◆ If the supplier fails to supply the required information, the cooling-off period is extended by 3 months (but if the performance of a services contract has begun with the consumer's agreement before the expiry of the cooling-off period and the supplier has not supplied information, different rules apply).

◆ If the supplier complies with the information requirement later than he should have done but within 3 months, the cooling-off begins from the date he provided the information.

13

➤ There is no cancellation right (unless the parties agree) if the contract is for the supply of:

◆ services, if performance of the contract has begun with the consumer's agreement either before the end of the cancellation period or after the supplier has supplied information (see above), *or*

◆ goods/services where price depends on financial market fluctuations outside the supplier's control, *or*

◆ goods made to the consumer's specifications or clearly personalised or which by reason of their nature cannot be returned or are liable to deteriorate or expire rapidly, *or*

◆ audio or video recordings or computer software if they are unsealed by the consumer, *or*

◆ newspapers, periodicals or magazines, *or*

◆ gaming, betting or lottery services.

14

➤ If the consumer cancels, the consumer must be reimbursed within a maximum of 30 days.

15

◆ If the consumer cancels the contract, a related credit agreement is automatically cancelled.

17

◆ On cancellation, the consumer must restore goods to the supplier if he collects them, but meanwhile the consumer must take reasonable care of them. The consumer does not have to return goods but if he breaches a requirement under the contract, he must pay the supplier's recovery costs.

21

➤ If the consumer's payment card is used fraudulently, he may cancel the payment. If the payment has already been made, he is entitled to a re-credit or to have all sums returned by the card issuer.

The Consumer Protection from Unfair Trading Regulations 2008

➤ *CPUTR 2008* implement Directive 2005/29/EC concerning unfair business-to-consumer commercial practices.

➤ Sets out the prohibition on unfair commercial practices.

- ◆ Generally, a commercial practice is unfair if (*reg 3(3)*):
  - it contravenes the requirements of professional diligence, *and*
  - it materially distorts or is likely to materially distort the economic behaviour of the average consumer with regard to the product.

- ◆ A commercial practice is unfair if it is a misleading action under *reg 5, or* it is a misleading omission under *reg 6, or* it is aggressive under *reg 7* (*reg 3(4)*).

- ◆ Commercial practices which are in all circumstances considered unfair are listed in Schedule 1. Eg:
  - Claiming to be a signatory to a code of conduct when the trader is not.
  - Displaying a trust mark, quality mark or equivalent without having obtained the necessary authorisation.
  - Claiming that a trader (including his commercial practices) or a product has been approved, endorsed or authorised by a public or private body when the trader, the commercial practices or the product have not or making such a claim without complying with the terms of the approval, endorsement or authorisation.
  - Bait advertising and 'bait and switch' (ie: making an invitation to purchase products at a specified price and then refusing to show the advertised item to consumers, *or* refusing to take orders for it or deliver it within a reasonable time, *or* demonstrating a defective sample of it; ... with the intention of promoting a different product.
  - Falsely stating that a product will only be available for a very limited time, or that it will only be available on particular terms for a very limited time, in order to elicit an immediate decision and deprive consumers of sufficient opportunity or time to make an informed choice.
  - Stating or otherwise creating the impression that a product can legally be sold when it cannot.
  - Presenting rights given to consumers in law as a distinctive feature of the trader's offer.
  - Using editorial content in the media to promote a product where a trader has paid for the promotion without making that clear in the content or by images or sounds clearly identifiable by the consumer.
  - Making a materially inaccurate claim concerning the nature and extent of the risk to the personal security of the consumer or his family if the consumer does not purchase the product.
  - Promoting a product similar to a product made by a particular manufacturer to deliberately to mislead the consumer into believing that the product is made by that same manufacturer when it is not.
  - Establishing, operating or promoting a pyramid promotional scheme.
  - Claiming that products are able to facilitate winning in games of chance.
  - Falsely claiming that a product is able to cure illnesses, dysfunction or malformations.
  - Passing on materially inaccurate information on market conditions/possibility of finding the product intending to induce the consumer to acquire the product at conditions less favourable than normal market conditions.
  - Describing a product as 'gratis', 'free', 'without charge' etc. if the consumer has to pay anything other than the unavoidable cost of responding to the commercial practice and collecting or paying for delivery of the item.
  - Including in marketing material an invoice or similar document seeking payment which gives the consumer the impression that he has already ordered the marketed product when he has not.
  - Falsely claiming or creating the impression that the trader is not acting for purposes relating to his trade, business, craft or profession, or falsely representing oneself as a consumer.
  - Creating the impression that the consumer cannot leave the premises until a contract is formed.
  - Conducting personal visits to the consumer's home ignoring the consumer's request to leave or not to return, except in circumstances and to the extent justified to enforce a contractual obligation.
  - Making persistent and unwanted solicitations by telephone, fax, e-mail or other remote media except in circumstances and to the extent justified to enforce a contractual obligation.
  - Requiring a consumer who wishes to claim on an insurance policy to produce documents which could not reasonably be considered relevant as to whether the claim was valid, or failing systematically to respond to pertinent correspondence, in order to dissuade a consumer from exercising his rights.
  - Including in an advertisement a direct exhortation to children to buy advertised products or persuade their parents or other adults to buy advertised products for them.
  - Inertia selling: Demanding immediate or deferred payment for or the return or safekeeping of products supplied by the trader, but not solicited by the consumer (subject to limited exceptions).
  - Explicitly saying that a consumer does not buy the product/service, the trader's job will be in jeopardy.
  - Creating the false impression that the consumer has already won, will win, or will on doing a particular act win, a prize or other equivalent benefit, when there is no prize or other equivalent benefit, or taking any action to claim the prize or other equivalent benefit subject to the consumer paying money or incurring a cost.

➤ Breaches of the prohibition on unfair commercial practices are criminal offences (subject to limited exceptions).

- ◆ There are provisions for defences of due diligence and innocent publication of advertisements.

➤ The OFT has a duty to enforce the Regulations.

Consumer guarantees

➤ Under *SSGCR 2002 r 15*, if goods are sold to a consumer with a consumer guarantee, the consumer guarantee takes effect at the time the goods are delivered as a contractual obligation owed by the guarantor under the conditions set out in the guarantee statement and the associated advertising.

➤ A guarantee must be in plain intelligible language and state duration, territorial scope and guarantor's name & address.

D Exclusion clauses

➤ A clause which successfully excludes or limits liability must have overcome certain hurdles:

1 Common law rules

➤ **Incorporation:** the clause must be properly incorporated into the contract (ie: reasonable steps must be taken to draw the term to the promisee's attention).

➤ **Construction:** the clause must cover the breach which occurs.

➤ **Particular common law rules:** the *'contra proferentem'* rule - any ambiguity in a term of the contract is interpreted against the party attempting to rely on the exclusion.

2 Some statutory/regulatory rules - background

➤ Certain rules cannot be contracted out of. For example, the *CP(DS)R 2000, the Unfair Contract Terms Act 1977 ('UCTA')* and *the Unfair Terms in Consumer Contracts Regulations 1999 ('UTCC')*.

➤ *CP(DS)R 2000* has been dealt with on pp 360 et seq.

➤ *UCTA* has been in English law since 1977. *UTCC* on the other hand, is a relatively recent development and is based on a European directive.

   ◆ There are 3 problems with having these 2 sources of legislation:

   a) There is a degree of overlap because:

   • *UCTA* covers exclusion and limitation of liability clauses in business and consumer contracts.

   • *UTCC* covers unfair terms in consumer contracts which have not been individually negotiated.

   ■ An 'unfair term' is a term which is contrary to the requirement of good faith and causes a significant imbalance in the parties' rights/obligations to the detriment of the consumer.

   b) Key concepts such as 'consumer' are defined differently in both pieces of legislation.

   c) The list of contracts exempted from each legislative regime is different and must be checked.

UCTA and *UTCC*

➤ Where there is a **consumer contract** containing an **unfair exemption clause**, there is an overlap between the *UCTA* and *UTCC* and both must be checked against the contract.

   ◆ The procedure is as follows:

Steps	
1	Check definitions in *UCTA*
2	Check *UCTA* (see box on p 364)
3	Tighten the contract to comply with *UCTA*
4	Check definitions in *UTCC*
5	Check *UTCC* (if a consumer contract) (see box on p 364)
6	Tighten the contract to comply with *UTCC*

➤ *UCTA* does not apply to International Supply Agreements (*UCTA 1977 s 26*).

Step 2: *Unfair Contract Terms Act 1977*: contents

	Attempted exclusion		Effect
s 2	a) The common law duty of care, *or* b) liability under the *Occupiers Liability Act 1957*		Void for death *or* personal injury Valid for other loss if the clause satisfies the requirement of reasonableness'
s 3	General exclusion of liability NB: This section is only applicable if one party 'deals as a consumer' and/or uses the other's standard written terms ➤ Covers 2 parties dealing in business ➤ Not applicable to implied terms		Entitles the promisor to offer performance of the contract 'substantially different from that which was reasonably expected of him', subject to the 'requirement of reasonableness'
s 6	*SGA* or *SG(IT)A* implied terms:	◆ Description, satisfactory quality, fitness for purpose, sample	Exclusion is void against purchaser 'dealing as a consumer', but otherwise it is valid if it satisfies the 'requirement of reasonableness'
		◆ Title	Always void
s 7	Where possession or ownership of goods passes under a contract which is not a sale of goods or hire purchase contract, ◆ any term implied by law, *or* ◆ SGSA s 2 (Title), *or* ◆ right to transfer goods		◆ Exclusion is void if a party is dealing as a consumer, otherwise a clause is valid subject to satisfying the 'requirement of reasonableness' ◆ SGSA s 2 (Title) is not excludable ◆ Subject to 'requirement of reasonableness'

Requirement of reasonableness (*s 11*) is ...

'... a fair and reasonable [term] ... having regard to the circumstances which were, or ought reasonably to have been, known to or in the contemplation of the parties when the contract was made'

➤ Although the guidelines exist in *Schedule 2* to define reasonableness, they are only obligatory for *ss 6-7*. Nevertheless, the courts frequently use them in other cases too. They include:
   ◆ the customer's knowledge
   ◆ the bargaining position of the parties
   ◆ whether the contract involved the customer making a special order

Step 5: *Unfair Terms in Consumer Contracts Regulations 1999*: contents

Section	Breakdown of the section
r 3	Interpretation clause. Includes the definition of: ◆ seller/supplier (any natural/legal person acting for purposes relating to his trade, business or profession), ◆ consumer (any natural person acting for purposes outside his trade, business or profession - different to *UCTA*)
r 4	Regulations apply to unfair terms in contracts between a seller/supplier and a consumer *but* subject matter of the contract and price are not tested for fairness (*r 6(2)*)
r 5	Key concept of an 'unfair term' which is a term 'contrary to . . . good faith [which] causes a significant imbalance in . . . rights . . . to the detriment of the consumer'
r 6	To see if a term is unfair, it must be looked at in context at the time it was made
r 7	Terms must be in plain, intelligible language; if not, the term will be construed in the consumer's favour
r 8	Unfair terms do not bind a consumer.
r 10-15	The OFT considers any complaints made and has various powers
Schedule 2	Examples of unfair terms

➤ The OFT has published a bulletin covering the following topics:
   ◆ the most common unfair terms in consumer contracts
      eg: ● entire agreement clauses
            ● penalty clauses
            ● variation of price clauses
   ◆ terms that have been successfully excluded after OFT intervention
      eg: ● 'The Council accepts no liability for loss or damage to cars parked in this car park ... howsoever caused.'

I Commercial agreements

I Third party rights in contracts
II Agency agreements
III Distribution agreements
IV Choosing the right type of agreement
(Agency, Distribution, Franchise or Licence?)

I Third party rights in contracts

➤ Under *C(ROTP)A 1999,* if a contract is made with the purpose of conferring a benefit on a third party, under certain circumstances that person has a right to sue for breach of contract.

II Agency agreements

A 3 types of agency

3 types of agency		
Classical sales agency	P authorises A to enter into contracts with C on behalf of P	P → A ↓ C Note: in this chapter P=Principal A=Agent C=Customer
Marketing agency	P authorises A to introduce customers (C) to P	P → A ↓ C
Note: a del credere agent guarantees C's performance for an additional commission		

B Legislative rules

Commercial Agents (Council Directive) Regulations 1993	
Affects all commercial agents operating in the UK after 1 January 1994	*Regulation*
◆ oblige the principal and the agent to exchange certain information	*3-4*
◆ govern the amount of commission paid to an agent and the method of payment	*6-12*

◆ provide for compensation to be paid to the agent on termination especially where:
a) the agent has been deprived of commission which proper performance of his duties would have procured for him, while the principal retains substantial benefits linked to the agent's activities, *or*
b) the agent has been unable to amortise the costs and expenses that he had incurred in the performance of the contract on the principal's advice
◆ give the parties a choice between an indemnity or compensatory arrangement on termination
   ● Where no preference is expressed, the agent will be entitled to compensation (*rr 17-18*)
   ● The right to damages, as well as an indemnity (linked to the fruits of the agent's efforts), is preserved
	13-19

◆ renders any attempt to restrain an agent's trade after termination void, unless it: a) is contained in a written agreement b) defines a geographical area where the agency operates *or* the area in which customers are situated c) ceases no more than 2 years after termination	*20*
Note a) agencies in other EU member states may be governed by a version of the *Regulations* enacted in accordance with that state's laws. Complicated questions of jurisdiction and applicable law determine which courts (UK or foreign) will enforce which set of legislation (UK, local state or EU directive) b) certain classes of agent, such as unpaid agents, insolvency practitioners and those whose 'activities as agents are considered to be secondary' are excluded from the *Regulations*	

C The law of agency: basic principles

➤ An agency agreement can be oral or written, express or implied.

1 **Authority**

➤ **Actual authority:** this can be given expressly *or* impliedly.

➤ **Ostensible authority.** Four conditions must be satisfied (*PA ss 5-8*):

subjective test
a) C knows or believes he is dealing with A, *and*

b) C is unaware that 'A' is not actually authorised, *and*

objective test
c) 'A' would usually be expected to be authorised to enter into such a transaction, *and*

d) P's type of business is consistent with the nature of the transaction.

2 **Liability**

➤ **When A is authorised to act**

◆ P is liable for A's acts.

◆ A is not liable unless the contrary is agreed, expressly or implicitly, by A and P or A and C.

➤ **When A is *unauthorised* to act**

◆ Generally, P is not liable to C for A's acts.

◆ If A has ostensible authority, but has exceeded his actual authority, P will be liable and A may be liable to P and C for breach of warranty of authority.

3 **Ratification of A's acts**

➤ P can 'ratify' (ie: agree to be bound by) **a contract by an unauthorised A if:**

a) C could identify P when the contract was agreed, *and*

b) P has contractual capacity at the date of the contract and the date of ratification, *and*

c) the act is capable of ratification (ie: not illegal), *and*

d) ratification occurs within a reasonable time.

4 **Non-disclosure of agency**

➤ **If A does not disclose his agency, P can always intervene *unless*:**

a) the contract between A and C, expressly or impliedly excludes an agency, *or*

b) C wished to contract with A, *or*

c) the 'personality' of the parties is central to the contract.

5 **Termination**

➤ The agency agreement can be terminated by *either* A *or* P at any time subject to the contract.

➤ If P who is a debtor gives a creditor authority to act as an agent, then while the debt remains outstanding, the agency is irrevocable (*Greer v Downs Supply Co* [1927] 2 KB 28).

➤ The contract is terminated by the death or mental incapacity of A or P, but A is protected if he acts in ignorance of P's incapacity (*PAA 1971 s 5(1)*).

6 **Payment**

➤ Payment to A by C does not discharge a debt owed to P by C unless *either* A has authority (actual or apparent) to receive the payment, *or* P is undisclosed.

➤ Payment by P to A does not discharge a debt owing to C unless C misleads P into thinking that the money is to reimburse A for money already paid to C.

III Distribution agreements

A Types of distribution agreement

➤ Distribution agreements with anti-competitive provisions may infringe European/UK competition law. Eg:

1 **Exclusive distribution** - distributor alone may distribute supplier's goods in a particular territory, but supplier may still make passive sales in the territory.

2 **Sole distribution** - as in 1, but supplier can actively sell within the 'exclusive territory'.

3 **Selective distribution** - supplier attempts to retain control over the sales that his distributor makes.

4 **Exclusive purchasing** - distributor promises to buy goods from a sole supplier for an 'exclusive territory'.

B Relevant law

black clauses
white clauses

➤ See pp 350 et seq for relevant law and possible ways to avoid infringement.

Block Exemption Regulation (BER) covering vertical agreements (*Regulation 330/2010*)

➤ Vertical agreements are agreements or concerted practices entered into by 2 or more undertakings each of which operates at a different level of the production or distribution chain, which relate to the conditions under which the parties may purchase, see or resell certain goods or services (*Art 1(a)*).

➤ If a vertical agreement has a 'vertical restraint' (ie: something which infringes *TFEU Article 101(1)*) it should be illegal but the block exemption permits it (*Art 2*). The exemption only applies if:

 ◆ no undertaking involved (together with connected undertakings) has a turnover of more than €50 million (*Art 2(2)*), *and*

 ◆ the market share held by the supplier does not exceed 30% of the relevant market on which it sells the contract goods or services and the market share held by the buyer does not exceed 30% of the relevant market on which it buys the contract goods or services (*Art 3(1)*).

➤ The exemption does not apply to vertical agreements which, directly or indirectly, in isolation or in combination with other factors under the control of the parties, have as their object a restriction (*Art 4*):

 ◆ on the buyer's ability to determine its sale price (even though the supplier may impose a maximum sale price or recommend a sale price, provided that it does not amount to a fixed or minimum sale price due to pressure), *or*

 ◆ on active or passive sales to end users by members of a selective distribution system operating at the retail level of trade, without prejudice to the possibility of prohibiting a member of the system from operating out of an unauthorised place of establishment, *or*

 ◆ on cross-supplies between distributors within a selective distribution system, including between distributors operating at different level of trade, *or*

 ◆ agreed between a supplier of components and a buyer who incorporates those components, of the supplier's ability to sell the components as spare parts to end-users or to repairers or other service providers not entrusted by the buyer with the repair or servicing of its goods, *or*

 ◆ on the territory into which, or of the customers to whom, the buyer may sell the contract goods or services.

 NB: the following restrictions *are* allowed - restrictions on:

 • active sales into the exclusive territory or to an exclusive customer group reserved to the supplier or allocated by the supplier to another buyer, where such a restriction does not limit sales by the customers of the buyer.

 • sales to end users by a buyer operating at the wholesale level of trade.

 • sales to unauthorised distributors by the members of a selective distribution system.

 • the buyer's ability to sell components, supplied for the purposes of incorporation, to customers who would use them to manufacture the same type of goods as those produced by the supplier.

➤ The exemption does not apply to the following direct or indirect obligations contained in vertical agreements (*Art 5*):

 ◆ a non-compete obligation which is indefinite or exceeds 5 years, *or*

 • Note: If it is tacitly renewable beyond 5 years, it is deemed to have been concluded for an indefinite duration.

 • Note: The 5 year time limitation does not apply where the contract goods/services are sold by the buyer from premises/land owned by the supplier (or leased by the supplier from a third party unconnected with the buyer) - as long as the non-compete does not exceed the period of occupancy by the buyer of the premises /land.

 ◆ an obligation forbidding members of a selective distribution system from selling brands of competing suppliers, *or*

 ◆ an obligation forbidding the buyer, after termination of the agreement, from manufacturing, purchasing, selling or reselling goods or services, unless such an obligation:

 • relates to goods or services which compete with the contract goods or services, *and*

 • is limited to the premises and land from which the buyer has operated during the contract period, *and*

 • is indispensable to protect know-how transferred by the supplier to the buyer

 • has its duration limited to 1 year after agreement termination (without prejudice to the possibility of imposing a restriction which is time unlimited on the use/disclosure of know-how which has not entered the public domain).

Useful documents on the interpretation of the Regulation:
▲ Guidelines: http://eur-lex.europa.eu/LexUriServ/LexUriServ.do?uri=OJ:C:2010:130:0001:0046:EN:PDF
▲ Commission FAQs: http://europa.eu/rapid/pressReleasesAction.do?reference=MEMO/10/138

IV Choosing the right type of agreement

	Agency agreement	Distribution agreement
Supervision	This depends on the type of agency: **classical sales agency:** requires more supervision over the agreement **marketing agency:** requires less supervision over the agreement ✗	There is no need for day to day supervision, and the principal specifies any detailed requirements in the agreement. These are preferable if the principal wishes to deal in a new geographical market with minimum expense and inconvenience ✓
Goods	Suitable for goods which are ordered on a 'one-off' basis to a customer's individual specification	Suitable for standard ranges of goods which do not require specialist after-sales support
Prices	➤ The supplier sells directly to the retailer ➤ The supplier controls the price ➤ The agent takes commission ✓	➤ The supplier sells to the distributor who marks up the resale price ➤ The supplier can 'recommend', but cannot control the price as *TFEU Article 101* and *CA 1998* prohibit price-fixing ✗
Risk	P takes the risk, A gets the commission ✗	The distributor takes the risk ✓
Marketing	The supplier retains tight control over marketing ✓	The supplier has less say; the distributor has more freedom of action ✗
Enforcing contracts	This is difficult as the supplier sells to many customers ✗	This is straightforward as there is only one buyer - the distributor ✓
Liability	This depends on the type of agency: **classical sales agency:** the principal is directly liable in contract to customers **marketing agency:** the agent has no actual authority to act on the principal's behalf ✗	The principal is only liable in contract to the distributor The principal may be liable to consumers under the *CPA 1987* or *GPSR 2005* ✓
Protection of a territory	As a principal and agent are separate undertakings, the agent can be given an 'exclusive territory' ✓	**Passive sales** cannot be banned (*either* those by a distributor outside his territory, *or* by a supplier within the territory) **Active sales** by either party in contravention of an 'exclusive territory' can usually be banned ✗
TFEU Article 101 problems	Usually non-applicable as principal and agent are counted as one undertaking ✓	This can be a problem, unless use is made of a block exemption ✗
Taxation	An overseas business trading through an agency in the UK may be subject to corporation tax	This depends on the agreement's wording, and the extent of the principal's presence in the UK
Compensation	The agent may seek compensation for termination under *CA(CD)R 1993* ✗	The only remedies are those usually available in contract and tort ✓

✓ advantage	✗ disadvantage

Franchise

➤ These are suitable vehicles for exploiting a 'business format' (eg: Pizza Hut)

   ◆ The franchisor can control closely many aspects of the product, and thus protect and foster his goodwill without incurring the capital costs of expanding in new markets

   ◆ The franchisee also benefits from the accumulated goodwill. He contributes his own capital. His freedom to innovate is rather limited by the franchise

Licence

➤ These enable the exploitation of intellectual property rights by permitting a third party to use a process, or manufacture a product

   ◆ The licensor is spared the difficulties and capital investment involved in manufacture

   ◆ A licence (possibly combined with a distribution agreement) may be vital where national laws insist that products are manufactured within a given area

This chapter examines:

Note: use this chart as a 'map' to sections 'B' to 'I'

The tracks

Rules of the court

➤ Rules of court procedure are governed by the **Civil Procedure Rules** (*CPR*) (exceptions are in *r 2.1*).

 ◆ Definitions of terms in the *CPR* are listed in *r 2.3* and also in a glossary at the back.

 ◆ Each *Part* contains rules - notation is as follows: eg: *Part 7 r 7.2(2)* refers to rule 7.2(2) in *Part 7*.

 ◆ Each *Part* is supplemented by practice directions - we use notation as follows: *eg: PD7A: 8.2* refers to paragraph 8.2 in the Practice Direction that supplements *Part 7*.

 ◆ *Costs PD:* refers to the Practice Direction on Costs (on *Parts 43-48*).

➤ For some purposes, some of the old rules that existed prior to the CPR are retained.

 ◆ For the High Court, these are the Rules of the Supreme Court (*RSC*) now in *Schedule 1* to the *CPR*.

 ◆ For the county courts, these are the County Court Rules (*CCR*) now in *Schedule 2* to the *CPR*.

A   First steps

Is the claim viable?			
CONTRACT	**TORT**		
	NEGLIGENCE	**PERSONAL INJURY**	**LATENT DAMAGE**

1   Is the defendant worthy of attention?

Is the defendant i) traceable and ii) solvent?

2   How strong is the claimant's case?

Does the evidence i) show all the elements required in law, *and* ii) prove these elements on the balance of probabilities?

3   Has the limitation period expired? (*LA 1980*)

CONTRACT	NEGLIGENCE	PERSONAL INJURY	LATENT DAMAGE

6 years from the breach of contract (*s 5*)	6 years from when the damage occurs (*s 2*)	3 years from (*s 11*):
		 a) the date of the accident, *or*
		 b) the date of knowledge that (*s 14*):
		     i) the injury is significant enough for proceedings +
		     ii) an injury is due to the defendant's fault +
		     iii) the defendant's identity becomes known
			Either:
			 a) 6 years from the date on which the cause of action accrues (*s 14A*), *or*
			 b) (if later than a)), 3 years from the date that a claimant could start proceedings because a claimant now has:
			    i) the knowledge* required for bringing an action, *and*
			    ii) a right to bring such an action (ie: recovery from a defendant seems realistic)
			 (**NB**: it must not be more than 15 years from the date of the breach)
			 *Knowledge means knowledge of the facts such that an action may be brought eg: the identity of the defendant and that the damage was due to the defendant's fault, etc

For death and personal injury, the court has discretion to override the limitation period (*s 33*)

4   What damages are available?

CONTRACT	NEGLIGENCE	PERSONAL INJURY

Generally
 Loss which flows naturally from the breach
 	
 Loss which was within the reasonable contemplation of the parties at the time the contract was made
 	
 There is a duty on the claimant to mitigate loss
 	
 Debt claims
 If the action is a claim for debt, the one claiming the sum outstanding does not have the duty to mitigate his loss, which applies to all other types of damages
	Direct loss and consequential loss which is a reasonably foreseeable consequence of the negligence
	
	 Note: It is doubtful whether pure economic loss can be recovered
		a) **Special damages:** liquidated claims for actual financial loss up to the date of the trial
		 b) **General damages:** unliquidated, compensating for:
		    i) past and future non-financial loss, *and*
		    ii) future financial loss
		 c) ***SS(RB)A 1997*:** if the claimant receives state benefits:
		    i) the defendant obtains a certificate of recoverable benefits from the Department for Work and Pensions (DWP) Compensation Recovery Unit (CRU)
		    ii) the defendant is obliged to pay to the CRU the *full* amount of certain benefits listed which have been paid to the injured person

iii) where part of the compensation payment itself from the defendant to the claimant is in respect of a particular kind of loss, (loss of earnings, cost of care, loss of mobility) and benefits have been paid to the claimant for this kind of loss, the defendant may deduct the relevant benefits from the compensation payment (ie: the claimant is paid damages net, less the sum due to the DWP which the defendant forwards to the CRU within 14 days of the claimant receiving compensation)

NB: No deductions are possible for pain and suffering ie: the victim keeps all the damages for pain and suffering.

d) ***DA 1996 (CPR rr 41.4 - 41.10)*:** a court awarding damages for future pecuniary loss may, on its own, order that damages are wholly or partly to be as periodical payments. For other personal injury damages, a court may only order that damages are to take the form of periodical payments if the parties consent. But a court may not make an order for periodical payments unless satisfied that the continuity of payment under the order is reasonably secure

5   Does the claim carry interest?

CONTRACT	NEGLIGENCE	PERSONAL INJURY	LATENT DAMAGE

Interest is given from:
 a) the date when the action arose to judgment *or*
 b) date of payment (if sooner) *either*
    i) at the contract rate, *or*
    ii) at a court's discretion (unlikely to exceed the judgment debt rate)
 	
 Debt claims
 High Court: 8% from final judgment date
 County Court: see rules on p 470
	At the Court's discretion	**Judgment for a sum ...**
		 a) ...**over £200**: a court must award interest (but will not do if it has a special reason (*SCA 1981 s 35A*)
		 b) ...**£200 or less**: at the court's discretion
		
		 The rate is usually:
		 i) 0% for future loss of earnings
		 ii) 2% from the service of the claim form to the trial, for pain, suffering and loss of amenity
		 iii) half the court's average Special Account average rate from the accident to the start of trial for 'special damages'
			At the Court's discretion

6   What other remedies are possible?

Eg: possession orders, injunctions, etc.

A   Consider 10 alternatives to issuing proceedings

1   Negotiation

➤ This is always better than litigation and should normally be conducted 'without prejudice'.

2   Alternative dispute resolution (ADR)

➤ It is the duty of a solicitor to put the possibility of ADR to the client.

◆ See also the Practice Direction on Pre-Action Conduct provisions and effect on costs (p 373).

◆ 'All members of the legal profession should now routinely consider with their clients whether their disputes are suitable for ADR.' (per Dyson LJ in *Halsey v Milton Keynes NHS Trust* [2004] EWCA 576).

◆ There are many types of ADR, eg: mediation, neutral evaluation, expert determination, etc.

➤ In mediation, a third party mediates and the mediation may or may not be binding.

◆ If no binding agreement is reached, then arbitration or litigation is possible later.

➤ ADR is usually quicker, cheaper and less destructive of the parties' relationship than litigation.

3   Motor Insurers' Bureau ('MIB') (see www.mib.org.uk)

➤ The MIB was established in 1946 and administers a guarantee fund through 2 agreements between the MIB and the government. There 2 schemes are updated periodically:

Victims of *uninsured* drivers (agreement of 13 August 1999, as amended on 7 November, 2008)	Victims of *untraced* drivers (agreement of 7 February 2003, as amended on 30 December, 2008 and 15 April, 2011)
Commence proceedings ↓ Give notice in writing to MIB of the date of Claim Form service by the first to occur of: a) **7 days after:** ◆ the date when the Claimant receives notice from Court that service of the Claim Form or other originating process has occurred, *or* ◆ the date when the Claimant receives notice from the Defendant that service of the Claim Form has occurred, *or* ◆ the date of personal service, *or* b) **14 days after:** ◆ the date when service is deemed to have occurred according to the CPR. ↓ Give copies of relevant documents to MIB within 14 days of starting proceedings ↓ If 7 days after final judgment against the Defendant driver the claim is not satisfied, the MIB will meet the claim together with costs ↓ Judgment must be assigned to the MIB so it may try and recover from the insured driver	The death or injury must not have been caused deliberately by the untraced driver ↓ Give notice to the police within: **14 days** of the accident for death and bodily injury, *and* **5 days** of the accident for property damage or, in either case, as soon as reasonably possible ↓ Notify the MIB by letter within: (1) **the tort claim period** (ie: 3 years (*LA 1980 s 11*)) of the accident for death/bodily injury claims, but (2) **9 months** of the accident for property damage claims ↓ The MIB itself investigates the merit of the claim (Negligence *must* be proved) ↓ The MIB will cover death, bodily injury, damage to property and there is no need to prove these costs. (Note: the MIB will award the same heads of damages that a court would)
	Appeals against the amount of damages is by arbitration
	An accelerated process may be available allowing the Claimant and MIB to reach a compromise (with no full investigation). If there is a disagreement, a full investigation is carried out.
Any property damage over £1 million is not covered	1) Any property damage over £1 million is not covered. 2) Where a vehicle is identified, there is no excess. 3) Where a vehicle is unidentified, property damage (and property related damage) is paid for if there has been a "significant" injury but is subject to a £300 excess.
◆ The MIB pays to the CRU money owed to NHS trusts and hospitals (*RT(NC)A 1999*).	

There are other 7 day limit dates to notify various documents too

4   **Statutory demand:** see p 348.

5   **Insurance (motor accidents)**

➤ The decision how to claim depends on the type of insurance policy concerned:

    a) **Compulsory risks** (required by *RTA 1988*). Such insurance covers ...

       ◆ ... death or injury to any other person, *and*

       ◆ ... property damage up to £250,000, excluding damage to the insured vehicle and its contents, *and*

       ◆ ... the cost of emergency hospital treatment.

    b) **Third party, fire and theft.** Such insurance additionally covers...

       ◆ ... the insured against these risks.

    c) **Comprehensive.** Such insurance additionally covers...

       ◆ ... damage to the insured's vehicle and limited compensation for a driver's injuries.

➤ Claims against the insured's own insurance (*only* if the policy is 'comprehensive').

    ◆ A 'no-claims' bonus may be lost, increasing the premium payable on the policy in the future.

    ◆ The insured may have to pay an 'excess' as a contribution to damages.

    ◆ The insurance company may insist that the insured lends their name to any legal proceedings.

    ◆ If the other party has 'comprehensive' insurance, the companies may agree between themselves to cover the costs of their own insured - the claimant has no control over the settlement they reach. This is called 'knock for knock'.

    ◆ The claimant may also choose to proceed against the other party or their insurer's for any *un*insured losses, eg: the amount of the excess *or* loss of any discount given by a no claims bonus.

➤ Claims against the other party's insurance.

    ◆ Provided the claimant serves a notice on the defendant's insurers within 7 days of commencing proceedings, he can recover damages from them, even if they are entitled to avoid *or* cancel the policy (*RTA 1988 ss 151-152*).

➤ Insurance is not necessarily an alternative to proceedings in the courts because of subrogation of rights - the insurer may still bring the action, leading to litigation.

6   **Criminal Injuries Compensation Authority**

➤ The Criminal Injuries Compensation Authority was set up in 1964 to award, *ex gratia*, compensation to the victims of crime. Awards are normally small but in some severe cases may be substantial.

➤ There is a fixed scale of awards (see *CICA 1995*). The absolute maximum it may award is £500,000.

7   **Criminal compensation order** (*PCC(S)A 2000 ss 130-134*)

➤ This is available for personal injury losses or damage following a criminal offence (other than loss due to accident arising out of there being a personal motor vehicle on a road). Compensation may be payable for damage which is not covered by the MIB.

    ◆ Magistrates' Court: fine up to £5,000 for each offence.

    ◆ Crown Court: fine unlimited, taking account of the defendant's means.

8   **Arbitration under *Arbitration Act 1996***

➤ This may or may not be cheaper and faster than litigation depending on the circumstances. Procedure is governed by *Arbitration Act 1996* (not covered here). It is binding, with appeal to the courts.

9   **Trade schemes**

➤ These are operated by various trade and professional bodies and include Royal Institute of Chartered Surveyors (RICS) and the Association of British Travel Agents (ABTA).

10 **Application in a foreign jurisdiction** - (*CJJA 1982 & PIL(MP)A 1995*) NB: See also p 468.

➤ A person domiciled in the UK, or a company based in the UK, may sue in the UK.

➤ The rules are complicated but in general, usually a UK claimant may sue abroad if:
   ◆ for contractual claims: *either* the defendant is domiciled abroad, *or* the cause of action arose abroad, *or* a foreign law or jurisdiction is stipulated in the contract.
   ◆ for tortious claims: *either* the tort occurred abroad, *or* the damage was suffered abroad.

NB: Consider the costs and remedies, and the likelihood of enforcement in foreign jurisdictions.

NB: Consider whether alternatives are available eg: arbitration.

B   How will the client finance the action?

➤ The client may be eligible for legal aid. If not, the solicitor should:

a) explain that the client is responsible for all the solicitor's costs and that if the case is lost he may have to pay the other side's costs. Even if the client is successful, costs are at the court's discretion and will not be awarded to the client automatically, the client will have to meet any shortfall, *and*

b) ask the client for a 'payment on account' to finance preparatory work, expert's reports, etc.

➤ A CFA should also be considered where appropriate.

C   Is there a relevant pre-action protocol?

➤ Pre-action protocols are intended to improve pre-action contact between the parties, to ease exchange of information between the parties and to allow both sides to more fully investigate a claim at an earlier stage. All this is to encourage early settlement.

➤ The extent to which a party has (or has not) complied with any relevant pre-action protocol, is one of the factors a Court will consider when making orders as to costs (see p 461) and sanctions (see p 381) and giving directions to manage proceedings (see p 440 and p 442).

➤ There are currently 11 pre-action protocols for:

1) possession claims based on Mortgage or Home Purchase Plan Arrears (Residential Property)

2) personal injury claims (if likely to be allocated to the fast track)	6) housing disrepair cases	10) defamation
3) low value personal injury claims in Road Traffic Accidents	7) resolution of clinical disputes	11) judicial review
4) possession claims based on rent arrears	8) professional negligence	
5) construction and engineering disputes	9) disease and illness claims	

PD on Pre-Action Conduct - generally

➤ This PD contains rules of general application in all cases. It is intended:
   ◆ to enable parties to settle the issue between them without the need to start proceedings, *and*
   ◆ to support the efficient management by the court and the parties if proceedings cannot be avoided.
➤ It describes the conduct the court normally expects of the prospective parties before the start of proceedings.
➤ The court may ask the parties to explain what steps were taken to comply prior to the start of the claim. Where there has been a failure of compliance by a party the court may ask that party to provide an explanation (*para 4.2*).
   ◆ When considering compliance the court will (*para 4.3*):
      • be concerned about whether the parties have complied in substance with the relevant principles and requirements (and is not likely to be concerned with minor or technical shortcomings), *and*
      • will consider the proportionality of the steps taken compared to the size and importance of the matter, *and*
      • take account of the urgency of the matter.
         ■ If a matter is urgent, the court will expect the parties to comply only to the extent that it is reasonable to do so.
   ◆ Non-compliance examples (*para 4.4*):
      • not providing sufficient information to enable the other party to understand the issues, *or*
      • not acting within time limits in a relevant pre-action protocol, or, if no time limit applies, within a reasonable period, *or*
      • unreasonably refusing to consider ADR, *or*
      • without good reason, not disclosing documents requested to be disclosed.
➤ **Sanctions:** Courts look at overall effects of non-compliance on other parties in deciding whether to impose sanctions (*para 4.5*).
➤ **Sanctions examples** (*para 4.6*): staying proceedings; ordering a party at fault to pay costs (even on the small claims track); ordering a party at fault to pay costs on an indemnity basis; removing interest or awarding interest at a higher rate (not exceeding 10% above base rate).

PD on Pre-Action Conduct
(Requirements in all cases except if a pre-action protocol overrides)

➤ Documents provided by one party to another in the course of complying with this PD (or any relevant pre-action protocol) must not be used for any purpose other than resolving the matter, unless the disclosing party agrees in writing (*para 9.2*).

➤ Where a party enters into a funding arrangement, that party must inform the other parties about this arrangement as soon as possible and in any event either within 7 days of entering into the funding arrangement concerned or, where a claimant enters into a funding arrangement before sending a letter before claim, in the letter before claim. (*para 9.3*)

➤ Where the evidence of an expert is necessary the parties should consider how best to minimise expense. Guidance on instructing experts is in Annex C of the PD (*para 9.4*).

PD on Pre-Action Conduct
(In all cases not subject to a pre-action protocol)

➤ Unless the circumstances make it inappropriate, before starting proceedings the parties should (*para 6.1*):

◆ exchange sufficient information about the matter to allow them to understand each other's position and make informed decisions about settlement and how to proceed, *and*

◆ make appropriate attempts to resolve the matter without starting proceedings, and in particular consider the use of an appropriate form of ADR to do so.

➤ The parties should act in a reasonable and proportionate manner in all dealings with one another. In particular, the costs incurred in complying should be proportionate to the complexity of the matter and any money at stake (*para 6.2*).

◆ The parties must not use this PD as a tactical device to secure an unfair advantage or to generate unnecessary costs.

➤ Before starting proceedings (*para 7.1*):

◆ the claimant should set out the details of the matter in writing by sending a letter before claim to the defendant, *and*

◆ the defendant should give a full written response within a reasonable period (preceded, if appropriate, by a written acknowledgment of the letter before claim).

  • What is a 'reasonable period of time' will vary depending on the matter (*para 7.2A*). But generally:

   ■ the defendant should send a letter of acknowledgment within 14 days of receipt of the letter before claim (if a full response has not been sent within that period), *and*

   ■ where the matter is straightforward (eg: an undisputed debt), then a full response should normally be provided within 14 days, *and*

   ■ where a matter requires the involvement of an insurer or other third party or where there are issues about evidence, then a full response should normally be provided within 30 days, *and*

   ■ where the matter is particularly complex (eg: requiring specialist advice), then longer than 30 days may be appropriate, *and*

   ■ longer than 90 days to provide a full response will only be considered reasonable in exceptional circumstances.

➤ See the provisions of Annex A which apply (see p 375).

PD on Pre-Action Conduct - Annex B

➤ Annex B sets out the specific information that should be provided in a debt claim by a claimant who is a business against a defendant who is an individual.

◆ It lists information to be provided. The claimant should:

  • provide details of how the money can be paid (for example the method of payment and the address to which it can be sent), *and*

  • state that the defendant can contact the claimant to discuss possible repayment options, and provide the relevant contact details, *and*

  • inform the defendant that free independent advice and assistance can be obtained from organisations including those listed in the table below.

PD on Pre-Action Conduct - Annex A

➤ Annex A: sets out detailed guidance on a pre-action procedure likely to satisfy the court in most circumstances where no pre-action protocol applies and where the claimant does not follow any statutory or other formal pre-action procedure.

➤ **Claimant's letter before claim:** This should give concise details about the matter to enable the defendant to understand and investigate the issues without needing to request further information (*para 2.1*). The letter should include (*para 2.1-2.2*):

◆ the claimant's full name and address, *and*

◆ the basis on which the claim is made (i.e. why the claimant says the defendant is liable), *and*

◆ a clear summary of the facts on which the claim is based, *and*

◆ what the claimant wants from the defendant, *and*

◆ if financial loss is claimed, an explanation of how the amount has been calculated, *and*

◆ details of any funding arrangement, *and*

◆ a list of the essential documents on which the claimant intends to rely, *and*

◆ the form of ADR (if any) that the claimant considers the most suitable and invite the defendant to agree to this, *and*

◆ the date by which the claimant considers it reasonable for a full response to be provided by the defendant, *and*

◆ identify and ask for copies of any relevant documents not in the claimant's possession which the claimant wants to see.

➤ Unless the defendant is known to be legally represented the letter should (*para 2.3*):

◆ refer the defendant to this PD and draw attention to the court's powers to impose sanctions for failure to comply, *and*

◆ inform the defendant that ignoring the letter before claim may lead to the claimant starting proceedings and may increase the defendant's liability for costs.

➤ **Defendant's acknowledgment of the letter before claim:** Where the defendant is unable to provide a full written response within 14 days of receipt of the letter before claim the defendant should, instead, provide a written acknowledgment within 14 days which:

◆ should state whether an insurer is or may be involved, *and*

◆ should state the date by which the defendant (or insurer) will provide a full written response, *and*

• If longer than the period stated in the letter before claim, the defendant should give reasons why (*para 3.3*).

◆ may request further information to enable the defendant to provide a full response.

➤ If the defendant (or insurer) does not provide either a letter of acknowledgment or full response within 14 days, and proceedings are subsequently started, then the court is likely to consider that the claimant has complied (*para 3.4*).

➤ Where the defendant is unable to provide a full response within 14 days of receipt of the letter before claim because the defendant intends to seek advice then the written acknowledgment should state (*para 3.5*):

◆ that the defendant is seeking advice, *and*

◆ from whom the defendant is seeking advice, *and*

◆ when the defendant expects to have received that advice and be in a position to provide a full response.

➤ A claimant should allow a reasonable period of time of up to 14 days for a defendant to obtain advice (*para 3.6*).

➤ **Defendant's full response:** The defendant's full written response should (*para 4.1*):

◆ accept the claim in whole or in part, *or*

◆ state that the claim is not accepted.

➤ Unless the defendant accepts the whole of the claim, the response should (*para 4.2*):

◆ give reasons why the claim is not accepted, identifying which facts and which parts of the claim (if any) are accepted and which are disputed, and the basis of that dispute, *and*

◆ state whether the defendant intends to make a counterclaim against the claimant (and, if so, provide information equivalent to a claimant's letter before claim), *and*

◆ state whether the defendant alleges that the claimant was wholly or partly to blame for the problem that led to the dispute and, if so, summarise the facts relied on, *and*

◆ state whether the defendant agrees to the claimant's proposals for ADR and if not, state why not and suggest an alternative form of ADR (or state why none is considered appropriate), *and*

◆ list the essential documents on which the defendant intends to rely, *and*

◆ enclose copies of documents requested by the claimant, or explain why they will not be provided, *and*

◆ identify and ask for copies of any further relevant documents, not in the defendant's possession and which the defendant wishes to see.

➤ If the defendant (or insurer) does not provide a full response within the period stated in the claimant's letter before claim (or any longer period stated in the defendant's letter of acknowledgment), and a claim is subsequently started, then the court is likely to consider that the claimant has complied (*para 4.3*).

➤ If the claimant starts proceedings before any longer period stated in the defendant's letter of acknowledgment, the court will consider whether or not the longer period requested by the defendant was reasonable (*para 4.4*).

➤ **Claimant's reply:** The claimant should provide the documents requested by the defendant within as short a period of time as is practicable or explain in writing why the documents will not be provided (*para 5.1*).

◆ If the defendant has made a counterclaim the claimant should provide information equivalent to the defendant's full response (*para 5.2*).

➤ **Taking Stock** (*para 6*): If having completed the Annex A procedure, the matter has not been resolved, then the parties should undertake a further review of their respective positions to see if proceedings can still be avoided.

After the first client meeting

1   Write to the client confirming instructions.

2   Consider possibilities for settlement. Discuss possible approaches with the client to avoid litigation.

3   Take some general statements from the client and witnesses to get a 'feel' for the case.

4   Make a site visit, if relevant, as soon as possible and take appropriate photographs, etc.

5   Consider whether experts may be needed and prepare possible names (see p 458).

6   Research any relevant law.

7   Road traffic accident cases only

   ◆ Write to the Chief Superintendent requesting a copy of the police accident report.

   ◆ Obtain a certificate of conviction from the court (if appropriate).

   ◆ Serve a *s 151/s 152* notice on the defendant's insurers before issuing proceedings or within 7 days after issuing proceedings.

8   Personal injury cases only:

   ◆ Comply with the relevant pre-action protocol. Prepare the calendar with appropriate reminders.

   ◆ Write to the client's employer for details of gross and net salary over the 26 weeks prior to the accident, the employee's prospects and details of the employment contract.

   ◆ Write to the Her Majesty's Revenue and Customs (HMRC) to claim a tax rebate (if appropriate).

   ◆ Notify the Compensation Recovery Unit (CRU) within 14 days of receiving a letter before action.

9   Send a letter before action to the defendant stating:

   a) for whom the solicitors are acting, *and*

   b) the factual circumstances by which the claim has arisen, *and*

   c) the action the solicitors are preparing to take, *and*

   d) brief details of any loss, injury or damage.

   ◆ The letter should demand either settlement *or* a response within 7 to 14 days, failing which proceedings will be issued. The letter should warn that any claim will include interest and costs.

10   Negotiate or propose some other means of reaching a settlement (eg: ADR or *Part 36* - see p 429)

   ◆ Before proceedings are issued the solicitor has no implied authority to settle.

   ◆ After proceedings have been issued the solicitor has implied authority to settle; however, the client's express authority should always be sought (ideally in writing).

   ◆ Negotiations should normally be conducted 'without prejudice' so that nothing in the negotiations will be admissible in court.

11   Consider drawing up formal 'Instructions to Counsel' and arranging a conference (see p 456).

12   Consider forcing the potential defendant or a third party to give information by applying for an order for pre-action disclosure (see p 444)

   ◆ Ask the defendant to co-operate by letter. This should save the claimant costs.

   ◆ An order can be made against *anyone* who holds property central to the case.

   ◆ An order might permit: photography, detention and custody, inspection, testing, and sampling.

Overview of proceedings (early stages)

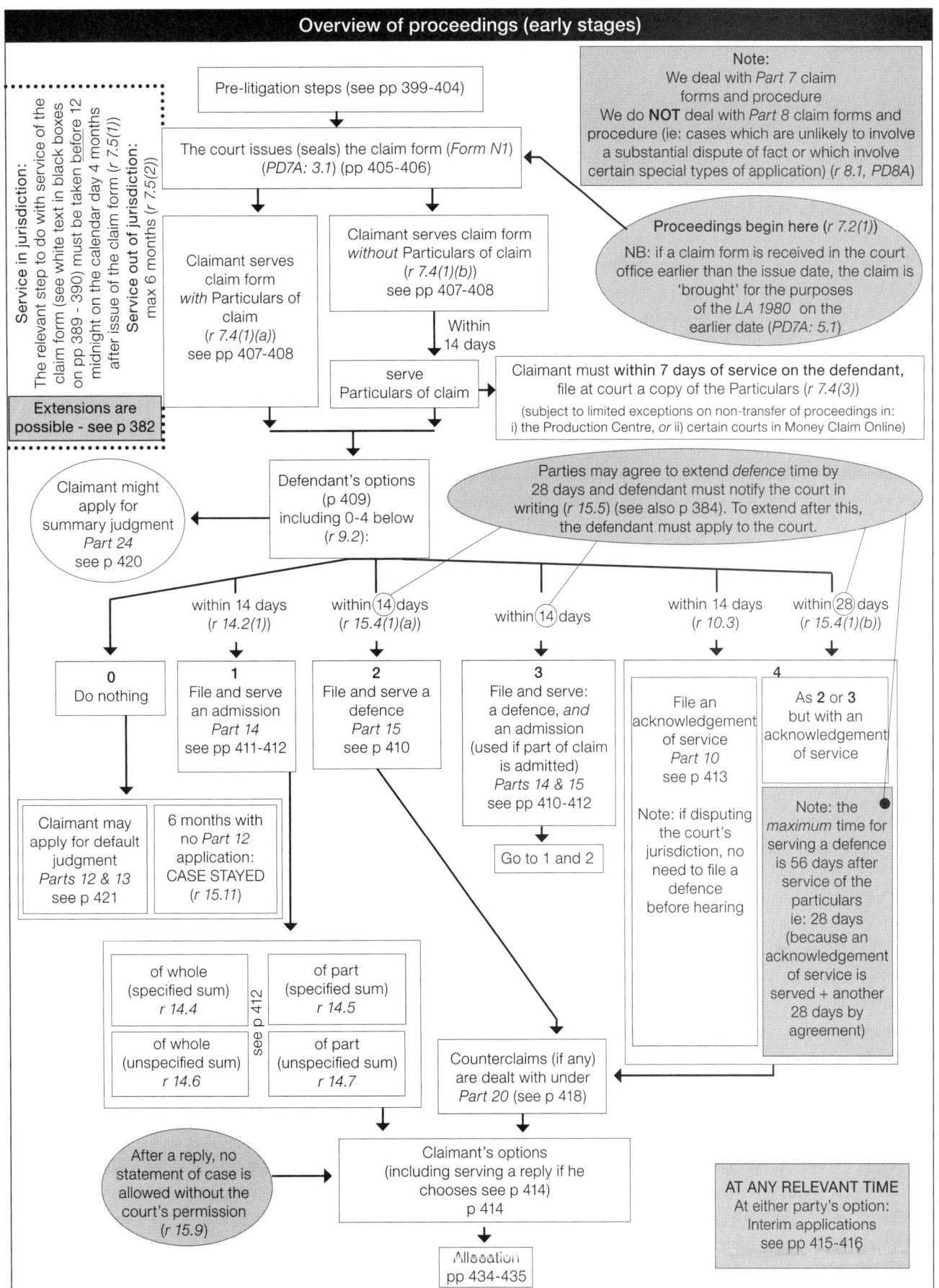

Pre-litigation steps (see pp 399-404)

The court issues (seals) the claim form (*Form N1*) (*PD7A: 3.1*) (pp 405-406)

Note:
We deal with *Part 7* claim forms and procedure
We do **NOT** deal with *Part 8* claim forms and procedure (ie: cases which are unlikely to involve a substantial dispute of fact or which involve certain special types of application) (*r 8.1, PD8A*)

Service in jurisdiction:
The relevant step to do with service of the claim form (see white text in black boxes on pp 389 - 390) must be taken before 12 midnight on the calendar day 4 months after issue of the claim form (*r 7.5(1)*)
Service out of jurisdiction: max 6 months (*r 7.5(2)*)

Extensions are possible - see p 382

Claimant serves claim form *with* Particulars of claim (*r 7.4(1)(a)*) see pp 407-408

Claimant serves claim form *without* Particulars of claim (*r 7.4(1)(b)*) see pp 407-408

Proceedings begin here (*r 7.2(1)*)
NB: if a claim form is received in the court office earlier than the issue date, the claim is 'brought' for the purposes of the *LA 1980* on the earlier date (*PD7A: 5.1*)

Within 14 days

serve Particulars of claim

Claimant must **within 7 days of service on the defendant,** file at court a copy of the Particulars (*r 7.4(3)*)
(subject to limited exceptions on non-transfer of proceedings in: i) the Production Centre, *or* ii) certain courts in Money Claim Online)

Claimant might apply for summary judgment *Part 24* see p 420

Defendant's options (p 409) including 0-4 below (*r 9.2*):

Parties may agree to extend *defence* time by 28 days and defendant must notify the court in writing (*r 15.5*) (see also p 384). To extend after this, the defendant must apply to the court.

within 14 days (*r 14.2(1)*)

within (14) days (*r 15.4(1)(a)*)

within (14) days

within 14 days (*r 10.3*)

within (28) days (*r 15.4(1)(b)*)

0 Do nothing

1 File and serve an admission *Part 14* see pp 411-412

2 File and serve a defence *Part 15* see p 410

3 File and serve: a defence, *and* an admission (used if part of claim is admitted) *Parts 14 & 15* see pp 410-412

File an acknowledgement of service *Part 10* see p 413

Note: if disputing the court's jurisdiction, no need to file a defence before hearing

4 As **2** or **3** but with an acknowledgement of service

Note: the *maximum* time for serving a defence is 56 days after service of the particulars ie: 28 days (because an acknowledgement of service is served + another 28 days by agreement)

Claimant may apply for default judgment *Parts 12 & 13* see p 421

6 months with no *Part 12* application: CASE STAYED (*r 15.11*)

Go to 1 and 2

of whole (specified sum) *r 14.4*

of part (specified sum) *r 14.5*

see p 412

of whole (unspecified sum) *r 14.6*

of part (unspecified sum) *r 14.7*

Counterclaims (if any) are dealt with under *Part 20* (see p 418)

After a reply, no statement of case is allowed without the court's permission (*r 15.9*)

Claimant's options (including serving a reply if he chooses see p 414) p 414

AT ANY RELEVANT TIME
At either party's option: Interim applications see pp 415-416

Allocation pp 434-435

B Court matters applicable throughout litigation

I General powers of the court
II Provisions as to time
III Documents for court
IV Statements of case
V Statements of truth
VI Service of documents

I General powers of the court

A The court's overriding objective

The court's overriding objective in applying the *CPR* (*r 1*)

➤ The *CPR* are a procedural code with the overriding objective of enabling the court to deal with cases justly.

◆ 'justly' means:

a) ensuring that the parties are on an equal footing, *and*

b) saving expense, *and*

c) dealing with the case in ways which are proportionate:

i) to the amount of money involved, *and*

ii) to the importance of the case, *and*

iii) to the complexity of the issues, *and*

iv) to the financial position of each party, *and*

d) ensuring that a case is dealt with expeditiously and fairly, *and*

e) allotting to a case an appropriate share of the court's resources, while taking into account the need to allot resources to other cases.

➤ The court must seek to give effect to the overriding objective when it:

◆ exercises any power given to it by the *CPR, or*

◆ interprets any rule.

➤ The parties are required to help the court to further the overriding objective.

➤ The court must further the overriding objective by actively managing cases.

Decisions under pre-*CPR* cases

➤ Decisions under pre-CPR rules will not be followed, even on identical wording (*Biguzzi v Rank Leisure* [1999] 1 WLR 1926). However, thought processes underlying decisions under pre-CPR rules will not be thrown out (*UCB Corporate Services v Halifax (SW) Ltd* [1999] CPLR 691) and in practice *are* often followed.

B Case management powers

The court's general powers of case management (r 3.1)

➤ The court has these additional general powers of management (unless a rule provides otherwise):

- ◆ to extend or shorten the time for compliance with any rule, practice direction or court order (even if an application for extension is made after the time for compliance has expired),

- ◆ to adjourn or bring forward a hearing,

- ◆ to require a party or a party's legal representative to attend the court,

- ◆ to hold a hearing and receive evidence by telephone or by using any other method of direct oral communication,

- ◆ to direct that part of any proceedings (eg: a counterclaim) be dealt with as separate proceedings,

- ◆ to stay the whole or part of any proceedings or judgment either generally or until a specified date or event,

- ◆ to consolidate proceedings,

- ◆ to try 2 or more claims on the same occasion,

- ◆ to direct a separate trial of any issue,

- ◆ to decide the order in which issues are to be tried,

- ◆ to exclude an issue from consideration,

- ◆ to dismiss or give judgment on a claim after a decision on a preliminary issue,

- ◆ to order any party to file and serve an estimate of costs,

- ◆ to take any other step or make any other order for the purpose of managing the case and furthering the overriding objective.

➤ When the court makes an order, it may:

a) make it subject to conditions, including a condition to pay a sum of money into court, *and/or*

b) specify the consequence of failure to comply with the order or a condition.

➤ A power of the court under the *CPR* to make an order includes a power to vary or revoke the order.

The court's powers to make an order of its own initiative (r 3.3)

➤ Except where a rule or some other enactment provides otherwise, the court may exercise its powers on an application or of its own initiative (*Part 23*).

- ◆ Where the court proposes to make an order of its own initiative it *may* (but does not have to) give any person likely to be affected an opportunity to make representations.

  - ● If it does so it must set the time by and the manner in which the representations must be made.

  - ● It must give each party likely to be affected by the order at least 3 days' notice of the hearing.

➤ A party affected by the order may apply to have it set aside, varied or stayed. Such an application:

a) must be made within such period as may be specified by the court, *or*

b) if the court does not specify a period, must be made not more than 7 days after the date on which the order was served on the party making the application.

➤ If the court of its own initiative strikes out a statement of case or dismisses an application, and it considers that the claim or application is totally without merit:

a) the court's order must record that fact, *and*

b) the court must at the same time consider whether it is appropriate to make a civil restraint order.

C Power to strike out a statement of case (r 3.4)

	Striking out a statement of case	
Grounds *(r 3.4(2))*	**1** A statement of case (or part of a statement of case) discloses no reasonable grounds for bringing or defending a claim (*r 3.4(2)(a)*), *or* Eg: the particulars of claim set out no facts indicating what the claim is about, or are incoherent and make no sense, or do not disclose no legally recognisable claim against the defendant (*PD3A: 1.4*) Eg: a defence consists of a bare denial, sets out no coherent statement of facts, or those facts (being coherent) would not even if true amount in law to a defence (*PD3A: 1.6*) *or* **2** A statement of case (or part of a statement of case) is an abuse of the court's process or is otherwise likely to obstruct the just disposal of proceedings (*r 3.4(2)(b)*), *or* Eg: a claim is vexatious, scurrilous, or obviously ill-founded (*PD3A: 1.5*). *or* **3** There has been a failure to comply with a rule, practice direction or court order (*r 3.4(2)(c)*)	

	Striking out a claim (*PD3A: 2*)	Striking out a defence (*PD3A: 3*)
Procedure (if court acts of its own volition on grounds set out in *r 3.4(2(a)(-(b))*	➤ A court officer must issue a claim form, but before returning the form to the claimant or taking any step to serve it on the defendant, the officer may consult a judge if the officer believes that there may be grounds for the claim to be struck out. ➤ The judge may make an order of his own initiative to ensure that the claim is disposed of or proceeds in a way which accords with the rules: this includes an order that: ◆ the claim be stayed until further order, *or* ◆ the claim form be retained by the court and not served until the stay is lifted, *or* ◆ no application by the claimant to lift the stay be heard unless the claimant files other documents (eg: a witness statement).	➤ A court officer may consult a judge if the officer believes that there may be grounds for the defence to be struck out. ➤ The judge may *either*: ◆ make an order of his own initiative (eg: striking out the defence or extending the time for the defendant to file a defence), *or* ◆ make an order under for further information *r 18.1* (see p 422)
	➤ A court may exercise its powers under *r 3.4(2)* at any time of its own volition ➤ If a judge acts of his own volition, he may decide to hold a hearing before making an order	

Order to strike out	➤ The court may make any consequential order it considers appropriate (*r 3.4(3)*) ➤ If a claimant's statement of case (or part of it) is struck out, *and* ... the claimant has been ordered to pay costs to the defendant, *and* ... before the claimant pays those costs, he starts another claim against that defendant arising out of facts which are substantially the same as those relating to the struck out claim, ... the court may on the defendant's application stay the second claim until the costs of the struck out claim have been met (*r 3.4(4)*).	If the court strikes out a claimant's statement of case and it considers that the claim is totally without merit: a) the court's order must record that fact; *and* b) the court must at the same time consider whether it is appropriate to make a civil restraint order.

Judgment without trial after striking out
(r 3.5)
	➤ If a party's statement of case (or part of its statement of case) is struck out as a term of a court order and that party does not comply with that order, *then* ...
	Either...
	    ... if the order relates to the whole statement of case, a party may obtain costs by filing a request for judgment *provided that* if the party wishing to obtain judgment is the claimant, the claim is for:
	    ● a specified amount of money, *and/or*
	    ● an amount of money to be decided by the court, *and/or*
	    ● delivery up of certain goods where the claim form gives the defendant the alternative of paying their value
	OR
	    ... a party must make an application under *Part 23* (see p 415) if he wishes to obtain judgment.
	
	➤ A party may apply within 14 days after receiving a judgment under *r 3.5* to have that judgment set aside (*r 3.6(1)-(2)*).
	➤ The court must set aside judgment if the right to enter judgment had not arisen at the time when judgment was entered (*r 3.6(3)*).
	➤ If an application to set aside is made for any other reason, *r 3.9* applies (*r 3.6(4)*)	

D Sanctions: powers and procedure

➤ Where a party has failed to comply with a rule, *PD* or court order, any sanction for failure to comply has effect unless the party in default applies for and obtains relief from the sanction (*r 3.8(1)*).

➤ Where the sanction is the payment of costs, the party in default may only obtain relief by appealing against the order for costs (*r 3.8(2)*).

Sanctions for non-payment of certain fees (*r 3.7, 3.7A, PD3B*)

➤ A fee is usually payable by a claimant:

    a) ◆ on filing the allocation questionnaire, *or*

       ◆ if a claimant is not required to file an allocation questionnaire,

  and b) ◆ on filing the pre-trial checklist, *or*

       ◆ if a claimant is not required to file a pre-trial checklist,

  and c) ◆ for certain hearings.

➤ A court fee may be payable by a counterclaimant in respect of a counterclaim.

➤ If the fee is not paid (or no remission has been applied for), the court will serve a notice on the claimant/counterclaimant specifying the date by which the claimant/counterclaimant must pay.

➤ After the notice, if the claimant/counterclaimant does not pay the fee (or make an application for full or part remission of the fee) by the date specified in the notice:

◆ the claim/counterclaim will automatically be struck out without further order of the court (and the court sends the other party a notice of this), *and*

◆ a claimant (only) will be liable for the defendant's costs (unless the court orders otherwise), *and*

◆ any interim injunction which the court granted may cease to have effect 14 days after the date on which the claim is struck out (see *r 25.11*).

Sanctions for non-compliance with case management directions (*PD28: 5, PD29: 7*)

➤ Where a party has failed to comply with a case management direction, any other party may apply for an order to enforce compliance or for a sanction to be imposed or both of these.

➤ A party applying for such an order must not delay and must first warn the other side of his intention.

➤ The court may take any such delay into account when it decides whether to make an order imposing a sanction or whether to grant relief from a sanction imposed by the rules or any *PD*.

◆ Postponement of a trial is a last resort and will be for the shortest time possible. The court may require a party *and* his legal representative to attend where such an order is sought. Other than in exceptional circumstances, the court will not allow failure to comply with directions to lead to postponement. The court will assess steps each party should take to prepare for trial, directs those steps be taken in the shortest possible time and impose a sanction for non-compliance.

◆ The court will not postpone any other hearing without a very good reason, and the failure of a party to comply on time with directions previously given will not be treated as a good reason.

Civil restraint orders (*r 3.11, PD3C*)

➤ If a party issues 2 claims/makes 2 applications totally without merit, the court may make **a limited civil restraint order** (ie: stopping him from making further applications in current proceedings), *or*

➤ If a party persistently issues claims or makes applications totally without merit, the court may make **an extended civil restraint order** (ie: stopping him from issuing certain claims or making certain applications in specified courts), *or*

➤ If a party issues claims or makes applications in spite of an extended civil restraint order, the court may make **a general civil restraint order** (ie: stopping him from issuing any claim or making any application in specified courts).

Obtaining relief from sanctions (r 3.9)

➤ On an application for relief from sanctions (which must be supported by evidence) the court will consider all the circumstances including:

- ◆ the interests of the administration of justice,
- ◆ whether the application for relief has been made promptly,
- ◆ whether the failure to comply was intentional,
- ◆ whether there is a good explanation for the failure,
- ◆ how much a party in default has complied with other rules, *PD*s, court orders, pre-action protocols,
- ◆ whether the failure to comply was caused by the party or his legal representative,
- ◆ whether the trial date or the likely trial date can still be met if relief is granted,
- ◆ the effect which the failure to comply had on each party,
- ◆ the effect which the granting of relief would have on each party.

II   Provisions as to time

Provisions as to time (rr 2.8-2.11)

➤ **days:** time expressed in the *CPR* as a number of days means clear days.
- ◆ **'clear days'** do not include:
  - a) the day on which the period begins, *and*
  - b) (if the end of the period is set by reference to an event), the day on which that event occurs.
- ◆ Where the specified period is 5 days or less *and includes* a Saturday or Sunday; *or* a Bank Holiday, Xmas Day or Good Friday; then that day does not count.

➤ **month:** 'month' in any judgment, order, direction or other document, means a calendar month.

➤ **time limits (1):** Where the court gives a judgment, order or direction with a time limit, the last date for compliance must, wherever practicable:
- ◆ be expressed as a calendar date, *and*
- ◆ include the time of day by which the act must be done.

➤ **time limits (2):** Where the date by which an act must be done is inserted in any document, the date must, wherever practicable, be expressed as a calendar date.

Time limits may be varied by the parties (r 2.11)

➤ Unless the court orders otherwise, any time limits specified by the *CPR* or by the court for a person to do any act may be varied by the written agreement of the parties.
- ◆ Exceptions are:
  - • any sanctions imposed have effect unless defaulting party obtains relief, *or*
  - • when the *CPR* specifies the sanctions for failure to comply with a fixed time (r 3.8(3)), *or*
  - • variation of the times in a case management timetable for fast track and multi-track, *or*
  - • time limits for an appeal to the Court of Appeal (see p 478).

Extension of time for serving a claim form (r 7.6)

➤ The claimant may apply for an order extending the period for compliance with *r 7.5* (relevant steps to be taken to serve the claim form, see p 377 and pp 389-390)).

➤ Generally, an application to extend the time must be made:
- ◆ within the period specified by *r 7.5* (see p 377 and pp 389-390)), *or*
- ◆ if an order is made to extend then within the period for service specified in the order.

➤ If the claimant applies for an order to extend the time after time periods in the previous arrow bullet, then the court may make such an order only if the claimant has acted promptly in making the application and:
- ◆ the court has failed to serve the claim form, *or*
- ◆ the claimant has taken all reasonable steps to comply with *r 7.5* but has been unable to do so.

➤ The application to extend must be supported by evidence and may be made without notice.

III   Documents for court

Documents for court (r 5.2, 5.3)

➤ A document should be legible, duly authorised and must not be unsatisfactory for a similar reason.

➤ If a document must be signed, it may be manual, printed by computer or another mechanical means.

➤ Every document prepared by a party for filing or use at the court:

<table>
<tr>
<th>must be (PD5A: 2.2):</th>
<th>may be filed at court by fax (in which case a hard copy must not be sent) (PD5A: 5.3) BUT:</th>
</tr>
<tr>
<td>
<ul>
<li>(unless impracticable) on A4 paper of durable quality having a margin not less than 3.5 cm wide, and</li>
<li>fully legible and should normally be typed, and</li>
<li>where possible, bound securely so as not to hamper filing or otherwise each page should be endorsed with the case number, and</li>
<li>so that pages have consecutive numbering, and</li>
<li>divided into numbered paragraphs, and</li>
<li>such that all numbers, including dates, are expressed as figures, and</li>
<li>give in the margin the reference of each document mentioned that has already been filed.</li>
</ul>
</td>
<td>
<ul>
<li>Faxes should not be used to send letters or documents of a routine or non-urgent nature.</li>
<li>If a fax is sent after 4pm, it is treated as filed the next day that the court office is open.</li>
<li>The following documents may not be faxed unless there is an unavoidable emergency:
<ul>
<li>documents that attract a fee (and the nature of the emergency must be explained in the fax together with an undertaking to make payment), or</li>
<li>a document relating to a hearing less than 2 hours ahead, or</li>
<li>trial bundles or skeleton arguments.</li>
</ul>
</li>
</ul>
</td>
</tr>
</table>

Electronic working generally (r 5.5, r 7.12, PD5C)

➤ The CPR allow for the possibility of starting a claim by requesting the issue of a claim form electronically (r 7.12) and for the filing and sending of documents electronically (r 5.5).

➤ *PD5C* sets out a complete scheme for electronic working.

Electronic communication and filing of documents (r 5.5, PD5B)

➤ Definitions:

◆ A court or court office which has published an email address for the filing of documents on the Court Service website www.courtservice.gov.uk is a 'specified court'.

◆ A document listed on the Court Service website as a document that may be sent to or filed in a specified court by email is a 'specified document'.

➤ Rules:

◆ A party to a claim in a specified court may send a specified document to the court by email.
  ● But a party must not use email to take any step in a claim for which a fee is payable.

◆ The email message must contain the name, telephone number and email address of the sender and should be in plain text or rich text format rather than HTML.

◆ Correspondence and documents may be sent as text in the email body or as attachments, except for documents required to be in a practice form (which must be sent as attachments).
  ● Note: Court forms may be downloaded from the Court Service website.
  ● Attachments must be sent in a format supported by the software used by the specified court to which it is sent. The format or formats which may be used in sending attachments to a particular specified court are listed on the Court Service website.
  ● The length of attachments and total size of email must not exceed the maximum which a particular specified court has indicated that it can accept on the Court Service website.

◆ Where proceedings have been commenced, the subject line of the email must contain:
  ● the case number, *and*
  ● the parties' names (abbreviated if necessary), *and*
  ● the date and time of any hearing to which the email relates.

Online forms service (PD5B: 6)

➤ Some courts run an 'online forms service' which is a service available at www.courtservice.gov.uk.

   ◆ The service contains certain documents which a user may complete online and then submit electronically to a specified court.

➤ A party to a claim in a specified court may send a specified document to the court using the online forms service.

➤ A party may use the online forms service to take a step in a claim for which a fee is payable.

   ◆ The fee must be paid, using the facilities available at the online forms service, before the application, or other document attracting a fee, is forwarded to the specified court.

➤ The online forms service assists a user in completing a document accurately but the user is responsible for ensuring that the rules and practice directions relating to the document have been complied with.

➤ Transmission by the service does not guarantee that the document will be accepted by the court.

General rules about filing of documents electronically (PD5B: 8)

➤ Where a party files a document electronically, he must not send a hard copy of that document to the court.

➤ A document is not filed until the transmission is received by the court, whatever time it is shown to have been sent.

   ◆ The time of receipt of a transmission will be recorded electronically on the transmission as it is received.

   ◆ If a transmission is received after 4pm, the transmission is treated as received and any document attached to the transmission is treated as filed, on the next day the court office is open.

➤ The court will normally reply by email where the response is to a message transmitted electronically *and* the sender has provided an e-mail address.

➤ Parties are advised *not* to transmit electronically any correspondence or documents of a confidential or sensitive nature, as security cannot be guaranteed.

➤ If a document transmitted electronically requires urgent attention, the sender should contact the court by telephone.

Statement of truth in documents filed electronically (PD5B: 9)

➤ Where a party wants to file a document electronically with a statement of truth, that party should retain the document with the original signature and file with the court a version of the document satisfying 1 of the following:

   ◆ the name of the person who has signed the statement of truth is typed underneath the statement, *or*

   ◆ the person who has signed the statement of truth has applied a facsimile of his signature to the statement in the document by mechanical means, *or*

   ◆ the document that is filed is a scanned version of the document containing the original signature to the statement of truth.

IV   Statements of case

A   Statements of case generally

Statements of case

➤   Statements of case are documents that each party produces, containing formal statements of case.

◆   Statements of case focus the parties and the court on the pertinent issues.

➤   A subsequent statement of case must not contradict or be inconsistent with an earlier one.

◆   eg: a reply to a defence must not bring in a new claim. Where new matters arise, the appropriate course may be to seek the court's permission to amend the statement of case (*PD16: 9.2*).

➤   Time limits for service are often (and usually) extended by agreement between parties (see p 382).

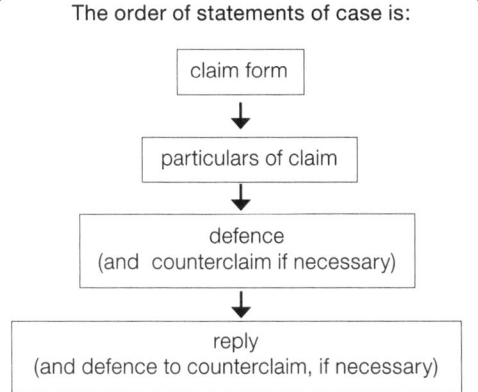

The order of statements of case is:

claim form

↓

particulars of claim

↓

defence
(and counterclaim if necessary)

↓

reply
(and defence to counterclaim, if necessary)

Drafting tip

◆   A typical claim is structured using the formulation: DUTY
↓
BREACH
↓
LOSS

Every statement of case must be headed
with the title of the proceedings stating (*PD7A: 4.1*):

◆   the claim number of the proceedings
◆   the court or Division in which they are proceeding
◆   the full name of each party
◆   each party's status in the proceedings (ie: claimant/defendant)

Where there is more than 1 claimant and/or more than 1 defendant, the parties should be described in the title as follows (*PD7A: 4.2*):

(1)   AB
(2)   CD
(3)   EF
                    Claimants
(1)   GH
(2)   IJ
(3)   KL
                    Defendants

Clinical negligence practice tip

◆   The words 'clinical negligence' should appear at the top of every statement of case (*PD16: 9.3*).

6 practice rules for statements of case

1   State all material facts

2   State facts relevant to the action

3   State facts, not evidence

◆   One exception to this rule is criminal convictions (see p 407)

4   Refer to any point of law on which the claim/defence is based (*PD16: 13.3*)

5   Give the name of any witness a party proposes to call (*PD16: 13.3*)

6   Attach to or serve with the statement of case a copy of any document which is necessary to the claim/defence (including any expert's report) (*PD14: 16.3*)

7   If exceptionally a statement of case exceeds 25 pages (excluding schedules) an appropriate short summary must also be filed and served (*PD16: 1.4*).

B Amendments to statements of case

➤ Amendments generally take effect retrospectively from the date of the original document.

➤ Limited amendments only are allowed (see box below) if:

♦ the limitation period has expired, or

♦ parties are to be amended.

➤ In practice, amendments are often agreed (subject to costs). However, a party applying

for an amendment will usually be responsible for the costs of and arising from the amendment.

> If a party has amended his statement of case where permission of the court was not required, the court may disallow the amendment (r 17.2)

What to do when amending

➤ Any amended statement of case (and its court copy) must be endorsed as follows (PD17: 2.1):
♦ *where the court's permission is required:*
'Amended [Particulars of Claim *or other*] by Order of [Master .....][District Judge .... *or other*] dated......'
♦ *where the court's permission is not required:*
'Amended [Particulars of Claim *or as may be*] under CPR [rule 17.1(1) or (2)(a)] dated...........' (see box below).
➤ The statement of case in its amended form need not show the original text, but the court may direct that the amendments should be shown *either* (PD17: 2.2):
♦ by coloured amendments, either manuscript or computer generated, *or*
♦ by use of a numerical code in a monochrome computer generated document.
➤ Where colour is used, the text to be deleted should be struck through in colour and any text replacing it should be inserted or underlined in the same colour (PD17: 2.3).
♦ The order of colours for successive amendments is: red, green, violet and yellow (PD17: 2.4).
➤ All amendments must carry a statement of truth (see p 388).

Amending before service	Amending after service
♦ A statement of case may be amended any time before service of it on any other party (r 17(1)).	♦ After service, a party may amend a statement of case only: • (r 17.1(2)(a)): with written consent of all other parties, *or* • (r 17.1(2)(b)): with the permission of the court (but subject to substitution of parties and limitation rules below). ♦ The court may give consequential directions (r 17.3)).

♦ Procedure (PD17: 1):

Steps

1 Usually the court will hold a hearing unless the parties agree otherwise between themselves.

2 When making an application to amend a statement of case, the applicant should file with the Court:
a) the application notice *and* b) a copy of the statement of case with proposed amendments.

3 Where permission to amend is given, the applicant, within 14 days of the date of the order (or other period directed by the court), must file with the court the amended statement of case.

4 If the substance of the statement of case is changed by reason of the amendment, the statement of case should be re-verified by a statement of truth.

5 The amender should serve a copy of the order and the amended statement of case on every party to the proceedings, unless the court orders otherwise.

> **NB:** if changing the parties use the procedure steps on the next page instead

---

Amending after limitation expiry

➤ After a limitation period has expired, the only amendment a court may allow is one (r 17.4):
♦ whose effect is to add/substitute a new claim, *but only if* the new claim arises out of the same (or substantially the same) facts as a claim in respect of which the party applying for permission has already claimed a remedy, *or*
♦ to correct a mistake as to the name of a party, *but only if* the mistake was genuine and not one which would cause reasonable doubt as to the identity of the party in question, *or*
♦ to alter the capacity in which a party claims if the new capacity is one which that party had when the action started or has since acquired.

➤ The court may add/substitute a party only if (r 19.5(2)):
♦ the relevant limitation period was current when the proceedings were started, *and*
♦ a) the new party is to be substituted for a party who was named in the claim form in mistake for the new party, *or*
b) the claim cannot properly be carried on by or against the original party unless the new party is added or substituted as claimant or defendant, *or*
c) the original party has died or is under a bankruptcy order and his interest/liability has passed to the new party.
Note: For personal injuries, the court may add/substitute a party where it directs that (r 19.4) LA 1980 ss 11-12 does not apply to the claim by/against the new party or the issue of whether those sections apply shall be determined at trial.

Adding or substituting a party (after service)

The court may (r 19.2):

- **Add** a party if:
  a) it is desirable to add the new party so that the court can resolve all the matters in dispute in the proceedings, *or*
  b) there is an issue involving the new party and an existing party which is connected to the matters in dispute in the proceedings, and it is desirable to add the new party so that the court can resolve that issue

- **Substitute** a party if:
  a) the existing party's interest or liability has passed to the new party, *and*
  b) it is desirable to substitute the new party so that the court can resolve the matters in dispute

  Note: To substitute a party, an application may be made without notice (r 19.4)

Procedure for adding/substituting parties (r 19.4):

Steps	
1*	An application for permission to amend may be made by: a) an existing party, *or* b) a person who wishes to become a party.

2	If adding/substituting *the claimant*, the applicant files:
	a) the application notice, *and*
	b) the proposed amended claim form and particulars of claim, *and*
	c) the signed, written consent of the new claimant to be added/substituted, *and*
	    Note: if this consent is not filed, the order and the addition/substitution of the new party as claimant, will not take effect until the signed, written consent of the new claimant is filed.
	d) evidence setting out the proposed new party's interest in or connection with the claim (PD19A:1.3).
	    ♦ Substitution only: evidence must also show the stage the proceedings have reached and what change has occurred to cause the transfer of interest or liability (PD19A: 5.2).

3a	**Addition only:** the application notice is filed under *r 23.3* and served under *r 23.4* (PD19A: 1.4) (see pp 415-416).
3b	**Substitution only:** the application notice is filed under *r 23.3* (PD19A: 1.4) (see p 415).
4*	The hearing is held (if appropriate).
5*	An order giving permission to amend will, unless the court orders otherwise, be drawn up (PD19A: 1.5).
6*	The order must be served on: a) all parties to the proceedings, *and* b) any other person affected by the order. It will be served by the court unless the parties wish to serve it or the court orders them to do so (PD19A: 1.5)
7*	The court may give consequential directions about: a) filing and serving the claim form on any new defendant, *and/or* b) serving relevant documents on the new party, *and/or* c) the management of the proceedings.
8a	If adding/substituting *a claimant*, the court may direct (PD19A: 3): a) a copy of the order to be served on every party and any other person affected by the order, *and/or* b) copies of the statements of case + any documents referred to in those to be served on the new party, *and/or* c) the applicant must file, within 14 days an amended claim form and particulars of claim.
8b	If adding/substituting *a defendant*, the court may direct (PD19A: 3): a) the claimant to file with the court, within 14 days (or as ordered), an amended claim form and particulars of claim for the court file, *and/or* b) a copy of the order to be served on all parties to the proceedings and any other person affected by it, *and/or* c) the amended claim form + particulars of claim, forms for admitting, defending, acknowledging the claim + statements of case + any other documents referred to in those, must be served on the new defendant, *and/or* d) unless the court orders otherwise, the amended claim form + particulars of claim must be served on defendants. **Note:** A new defendant does not become a party until the amended claim form has been served on him.

(Side labels: laimant, claimant, efendant)

Removing a party (after service)

The Court may (r 19.2):

- Delete a party if: it is not desirable for that person to be a party

Procedure: the steps in the table above with a '*' apply here, with the following amendments (PD19A: 4):

Steps	
2	Replace steps 2 and 3 above with: the claimant must file with the court an amended claim form and particulars of claim.
8	Replace step 8 above with: a copy of the order must be served on every party and on any other person affected by the order.

V   Statements of truth (*Part 22*)

➤   **In the following documents:** The following documents must be verified by a statement of truth:

- ◆ all statements of case (claim form, particulars of claim, defence, counterclaim reply etc.), *and*
    - • if a statement of case is amended, the amendments must be verified by a statement of truth.
- ◆ a response providing further information, *and*
- ◆ witness statements (including expert's reports), *and*
- ◆ application notices if an applicant wishes to rely on matters set out in it as evidence, *and*
- ◆ certificates of service, *and*
- ◆ application notices for a third party debt order (*r 72.3*), a hardship payment order (*r 72.7*) or a charging order (*r 73.3*) (see pp 475-476).

Note: A statement of truth not contained in the document it verifies, must clearly identify that document.

➤   **What it is:** a statement that the party putting forward the document (or in a witness statement, the maker of the witness statement) (or in a certificate of service, the signor of the certificate) believes that the facts stated in the document are true.

- ◆ **Litigation friends:** If a party is conducting proceedings with a litigation friend, the statement of truth is a statement that the litigation friend believes the facts stated in the document being verified are true.

➤   **Who signs it:** (see p 384 for electronic document filing rules). The statement of truth must be signed by:

- ◆ in the case of a statement of case, a response or an application, the party or litigation friend, *or* the solicitor on behalf of the party or litigation friend, *or*
- ◆ in the case of a witness statement, the maker of the statement.

Note 1: Signature by a registered company - signature must be by a person holding a senior position (defined on p 395) in the company/corporation, who must state the office/position held.

Note 2: Signature by partnership - signature must be by any of the partners, or a person having the control or management of the partnership business.

Note 3: Signature by solicitor - if a party has a solicitor, the solicitor may sign but the statement refers to the *client's belief*, not his own. The solicitor must sign his own name, *not* that of his firm. He must state the capacity in which he signs and the name of his firm where appropriate. The court takes it to mean:

- ◆ that the client on whose behalf he has signed had authorised him to do so, *and*
- ◆ that before signing he explained to the client that in signing the statement of truth he would be confirming the client's belief that the facts stated in the document were true, *and*
- ◆ that before signing he informed the client of the possible consequences if it should subsequently appear that the client did not have an honest belief in the truth of those facts (see below).

➤   **No statement of truth:** a statement of case is effective unless struck out, *but* a party cannot rely on it as evidence of any matters in it (and for a witness statement, the court may direct that it is not admissible).

➤   **Penalty for false statement:** contempt of court proceedings may be brought against the signor (*r 32.14*).

Form of the Statement of Truth (*PD22*)

➤   **For a statement of case**, a response, an application notice or a notice of objections:
'[I believe][the (claimant etc.) believes] that the facts stated in this [name document being verified] are true.'
➤   **For a witness statement:** 'I believe that the facts stated in this witness statement are true.'
➤   If the statement of truth is contained in a separate document, that document must be headed with the title of the proceedings and claim number. The document being verified should be identified as follows:

- ◆ claim form: 'the claim form issued on [date]'
- ◆ particulars of claim: 'the particulars of claim issued on [date]'
- ◆ statement of case: 'the [defence or as may be] served on the [name of party] on [date]'
- ◆ application notice: 'the application notice issued on [date] for [set out the remedy sought]'
- ◆ witness statement: 'the witness statement filed on [date] or served on [party] on [date]'

VI   Service of documents (in the jurisdiction only. Service out of the jurisdiction is outside the scope of this book)

A   Service of a claim form

1   Methods of service of the claim form

> In exceptional circumstances, the court may dispense with service of a claim form (r 6.16(1)).

A claim form may be served by any of the following methods (r 6.3):		
NB: The rules below apply unless the CPR, any other enactment, a PD or a court order, say so(r 6.1)		
Method of service (r 6.3)	**Date of deemed service if served in the UK** (r 6.14, r 7.5)	**Rules about the method of service**

Personal service (r 6.5)
 	
Notes for whole box:
1. The white text in black boxes is the 'relevant step' for the purpose of time of service of a claim form (see pp 377 and 407).
2. See the provisions about time on p 382
 	
'European Lawyer' has the meaning set out in EC(SL)O 1978 Art 2
 	
Service of the claim form out of the jurisdiction is subject to rr 6.30 -6.47 (not dealt with in this book)
	Second business day after completing the relevant step listed in the 'Served by:' column in the table on the right	➤ Personal service may be used (and must be used if the *CPR*, any other enactment, a *PD* or a court order, say so) (r 6.5(1)-(2)).
		
		Party to be served — **Served by** (r 6.5(3)):
		◆ Individual — ◆ **leaving it with that individual**
		◆ Company or other corporation — ◆ **leaving it with a person holding a senior position within the company or corporation**
		   • A person holding a senior position means (*PD6A: 6.2*):
		     ■ For a registered company or corporation: a director, the treasurer, the secretary of the company or corporation, the chief executive, a manager or other officer of the company or corporation, *and*
		     ■ For a corporation which is not a registered company: in addition to the list in the previous bullet, the mayor, the chairman, the president, a town clerk or similar officer of the corporation.
		◆ Partnership (where partners are being sued in the name of their firm) — ◆ **leaving it with:**
		   • **a partner, or**
		   • **a person who, at the time of service, has the control or management of the partnership business at its principal place of business.**
		
		➤ **Solicitor (which includes anyone authorised to conduct litigation under *LSA 2007* (r 6.2(d))) within the jurisdiction or an EEA state (or a European Lawyer in an EEA state):** A claim form must be served at the relevant solicitor's/European Lawyer's business address (ie: personal service cannot be used - unless the *CPR*, any other enactment, a *PD* or a court order, say otherwise) (r 6.5(2)), where ...
		  ◆ ... the defendant has given, in writing, the business address within the jurisdiction, Scotland or Northern Ireland (or within an EEA state) of a solicitor (or a European Lawyer within any other EEA state) as an address at which the defendant may be served with the claim form (r 6.7(1)(a), r 6.7(2)(a)-(b) and r 6.7(3)(a)), or
		  ◆ ... a solicitor (or a European Lawyer) acting for the defendant has notified the claimant, in writing, that the solicitor (or a European Lawyer) is instructed by the defendant to accept service of the claim form on behalf of the defendant at a business address within the jurisdiction (or within an EEA state) (r 6.7(1)(b), r 6.7(2)(c) and r 6.7(3)(b)).
		➤ **Crown:** For proceedings against the Crown (eg: judicial review), the claim form must be served as follows (r 6.10):
		  • service on the Attorney General must be on the Treasury Solicitor.
		  • service on a government department must be on the solicitor acting for that department.

A claim form may be served by any of the following methods (*r 6.3*) (continued):		
NB: The rules below apply unless the CPR, any other enactment, a PD or a court order, say so(*r 6.1*)		
Method of service (*r 6.3*)	**Date of deemed service if served in the UK** (*r 6.14, r 7.5*)	**Rules about the method of service**
First class post *or* Document exchange (ie: DX) *or* Other service which provides for delivery on the next business day	Second business day after **posting, leaving with, delivering to or collection by the relevant service provider**	➤ Service is effected by (*PD6A 3.1*): ◆ placing the document in a post box, *or* ◆ leaving the document with, or delivering the document to, the relevant service provider, *or* ◆ having the document collected by the relevant service provider. ➤ Service by document exchange (DX) may take place only where the party or the solicitor acting for that party has not indicated in writing that they are unwilling to accept service by DX (*PD6A 2.1*) and: ◆ the address at which the party is to be served includes a numbered box at a DX, *or* ◆ the writing paper of the party who is to be served or of the solicitor acting for that party sets out a DX box number.
Leaving it at a place specified in: ◆ *r 6.8* (see p 391), *or* ◆ *r 6.9* (see p 391), *or* ◆ *r 6.10* (see 'Crown' p 389)	Second business day after **delivering to or leaving the document at the relevant place**	
Fax *or* Other means of electronic communication	**Fax:** Second business day after **completing transmission of the fax** **Other electronic method:** Second business day after **sending the email or other electronic transmission**	➤ (Subject to the provisions of *r 6.23(5)-(6)* - see p 397...) where a document is to be served by fax or other electronic means (*PD6A 4.1*): ◆ the party who is to be served or the solicitor acting for that party must previously have indicated in writing to the party serving: • that the party to be served or the solicitor is willing to accept service by fax or other electronic means, *and* • the fax number, e-mail address or other electronic identification to which it must be sent, *and* ◆ the following are to be taken as such indications: • a fax number set out on the writing paper of the solicitor acting for the party to be served, *or* • an e-mail address set out on the writing paper of the solicitor acting for the party to be served but only where it is stated that the e-mail address may be used for service, *or* • a fax number, e-mail address or electronic identification set out on a statement of case or a response to a claim filed with the court. ➤ Where a party intends to serve a document by electronic means (other than by fax) that party must first ask the party who is to be served whether there are any limitations to the recipient's agreement to accept service by such means (eg: the format in which documents are to be sent and the maximum size of attachments that may be received) (*PD6A: 4.2*). ➤ Where a document is served by electronic means, the party serving the document need not in addition send or deliver a hard copy (*PD6A: 4.3*).
By any method authorised by the court under *r 6.15* (ie: alternative service, see p 392)		
By any method specified in a contract if there is a claim solely in respect of that contract (*r 6.11*).		
➤ A company may also be served by any of the methods of service permitted under *CA 2006* (eg: sending to the registered office) (*r 6.3(2)*). ➤ An LLP may also be served by any of the methods of service permitted under *CA 2006* as varied by regulations under *LLPA 2000* (eg: sending to the registered office) (*r 6.3(3)*).		
Notes for whole box: 1. The white text in black boxes is the 'relevant step' for the purpose of time of service of a claim form (see pp 377 and 407). 2. See the provisions about time on p 382		

2   Place of service of the claim form

> **NOTE:**
> Rules about service on Solicitors or European Lawyers (see p 389)
> and rules about service out of the jurisdiction (rr 6.30-6.47, not dealt
> with in this book) take precedence over the rules on this page

➤ **Address given (before service) by defendant for service:** Where a defendant has given an address at which he may be served, then (r 6.8):

◆ the defendant may be served with the claim form at an address at which the defendant resides or carries on business within the UK (or any other EEA state) and which the defendant has given for the purpose of being served with the proceedings, *or*

◆ in any claim by a tenant against a landlord, the claim form may be served at an address given by the landlord under *LTA 1987 s 48*.

➤ **Address not given by defendant for service:** Where a defendant has not given an address where he may be served **and the claimant does not wish to effect personal service**, then the following applies (r 6.9):

Address for service if address not given and no solicitor	
Nature of defendant to be served	Place of service
Individual	◆ usual or last known residence
Individual being sued in the name of a business	◆ usual or last known residence of the individual, *or* ◆ principal or last known place of business
Individual being sued in the business name of a partnership	◆ usual or last known residence of the individual, *or* ◆ principal or last known place of business of the partnership
Limited liability partnership	◆ principal office of the partnership, *or* ◆ any place of business of the partnership within the jurisdiction which has a real connection with the claim.
Corporation (other than a company) incorporated in England and Wales	◆ principal office of the corporation, *or* ◆ any place within the jurisdiction where the corporation carries on its activities and which has a real connection with the claim.
Company registered in England and Wales	◆ principal office of the company, *or* ◆ any place of business of the company within the jurisdiction which has a real connection with the claim.
Any other company or corporation	◆ any place within the jurisdiction where the corporation carries on its activities, *or* ◆ any place of business of the company within the jurisdiction.

➤ Where a claimant has reason to believe that the address of the defendant in any of these 3 entries is an address at which the defendant no longer resides or carries on business, the claimant must take reasonable steps to ascertain the address of the defendant's current residence or place of business ('current address') (r 16.9(3)).

◆ Where, having taken these reasonable steps, the claimant:

• ascertains the defendant's current address, the claim form must be served at that address, *or*

• is unable to ascertain the defendant's current address, the claimant must consider whether there is:

■ an alternative place where service may be effected, *or*

■ an alternative method by which service may be effected.

NOTE: If there is such a place where, or a method by which, service may be effected, the claimant must make an application to serve at the alternative place or by the alternative method (see p 392).

➤ Where the claimant cannot ascertain the defendant's current residence or place of business *and* cannot ascertain an alternative place or an alternative method, then the claimant may serve on the defendant's usual or last known address in accordance with the table above (r 16.9(4)).

'Alternative' service (*r 6.15, PD6A: 9*)

➤ Where it appears to the court that there is a good reason to authorise service by a method, or at a place, not otherwise permitted, the court order service by an alternative method or at an alternative place (*r 6.15(1)*).

- ◆ On an application under this rule, the court may order that steps already taken to bring the claim form to the attention of the defendant by an alternative method or at an alternative place is good service (*r 6.15(2)*).

➤ Any application for an order for 'alternative' service:

- ◆ may be made without notice (*r 6.15(3)(b)*), *but*

- ◆ must always be supported by evidence (*r 6.15(3)(a)*). Evidence must state:

  - ● If the application is made before the document is served, the application must be supported by evidence stating (*PD6A: 9.1*):
    - ▪ the reason why an order is sought, *and*
    - ▪ what alternative method or place is proposed, *and*
    - ▪ why the applicant believes that the document is likely to reach the person to be served by the method or at the place proposed.

  - ● If the application is made after the applicant has taken steps to bring the document to the attention of the person to be served by an alternative method or at an alternative place, the application must be supported by evidence stating (*PD6A: 9.2*):
    - ▪ the reason why the order is sought, *and*
    - ▪ what alternative method or alternative place was used, *and*
    - ▪ when the alternative method or place was used, *and*
    - ▪ why the applicant believes that the document is likely to have reached the person to be served by the alternative method or at the alternative place.

  - ● Examples (*PD6A: 9.3*):
    - ▪ **1:** An application to serve by sending a SMS text message (or leaving a voicemail message) at a particular telephone number saying where the document is must be accompanied by evidence that the person serving the document has taken, or will take, appropriate steps to ensure that the party being served is using that telephone number and is likely to receive the message.
    - ▪ **2:** An application to serve by e-mail to a company (where paragraph 4.1 does not apply) must be supported by evidence that the e-mail address to which the document will be sent is one which is likely to come to the attention of a person holding a senior position in that company - and senior position is defined on p 395.

➤ Any order for 'alternative' service must specify (*r 6.15(4)*):

- ◆ the method or place of service, *and*

- ◆ the date on which the claim form is deemed served, *and*

- ◆ the period for filing an acknowledgment of service, filing an admission or filing a defence.

➤ Under *r 6.15*, the court has power retrospectively to sanction service which has otherwise been bad.

- ◆ However, this will only be done in an exceptional case (*Kuenyehia and Others v International Hospital Group Ltd* [2006] EWCA Civ 21).

3   Special situations

Service (relating to a contract) on an agent of a principal who is out of the jurisdiction (r 6.12)

➤   The court may, on application, permit a claim form relating to a contract, to be served on the defendant's agent where:

◆   the defendant is out of the jurisdiction, *and*

◆   the contract to which the claim relates was entered into within the jurisdiction with or through the defendant's agent, *and*

◆   at the time of the application either the agent's authority has not been terminated or the agent is still in business relations with the defendant.

➤   Such an application may be made without notice but must always be supported by evidence setting out:

◆   details of the contract and that it was entered into within the jurisdiction or through an agent who is within the jurisdiction, *and*

◆   that the principal for whom the agent is acting was, at the time the contract was entered into and is at the time of the application, out of the jurisdiction, *and*

◆   why service out of the jurisdiction cannot be effected.

➤   An order must state the period within which the defendant must respond to the particulars of claim.

➤   Where the court makes an order under this rule:

◆   a copy of the application notice and the order must be served with the claim form on the agent, *and*

◆   unless the court orders otherwise, the claimant must send to the defendant a copy of the application notice, the order and the claim form.

➤   The court may nevertheless still order alternative service (see p 392).

Service of the claim form on children and protected parties (r 6.13)

➤   **Not a protected party:** Where the defendant is a child who is not also a protected party (see p 399) the claim form must be served on:

◆   one of the child's parents or guardians, *or*

◆   if there is no parent or guardian, an adult with whom the child resides or in whose care the child is.

➤   **A protected party:** Where the defendant is a protected party (see p 399), the claim form must be served:

◆   on one of the following with authority in relation to the protected party as:

●   the attorney under a registered enduring power of attorney, *or*

●   the donee of a lasting power of attorney, *or*

●   the deputy appointed by the Court of Protection, *or*

◆   if there is no such person, on an adult with whom the protected party resides or in whose care the protected party is.

➤   The court may make an order permitting a claim form to be served on a child or protected party (or on a person mentioned above in this box). Such an application may be made without notice.

➤   The court may order that, although a claim form has been sent/given to someone other than a child/protected party (or to a person mentioned above in this box), it is to be treated as if it had been properly served.

➤   The rules in this box do not apply where the court has made an order allowing a child to conduct proceedings without a litigation friend (see p 400).

4   Mechanics of service of the claim form

➤ The court serves the claim form (*r 6.4(1)*).

◆ **Exception 1:** where a rule or practice direction provides that the claimant must serve it.

◆ **Exception 2:** the claimant notifies the court that the claimant wishes to serve it.

◆ **Exception 3:** the court orders or directs otherwise.

➤ **Service by the Court:**

◆ Where the court serves the claim form:

● the court decides which method of service is used (*r 6.4(2)*), although first class post is normally used (*PD6A: 8.1*), *and*

● the claimant must, in addition to filing a copy for the court, provide a copy for each defendant to be served (*r 6.4(3)*), *and*

● the court sends to the claimant a notice which includes the date on which the claim form is deemed served under *r 6.14* (*r 6.17(1)*), see pp 389-390, *and*

● the court also serves or delivers a copy of any notice of funding that has been filed, if it was filed at the same time as the claim form and copies of it were provided for service (*PD6A: 8.2*).

◆ The claim form will be deemed to be served unless the address for the defendant on the claim form is not the relevant address for the purpose of *rr 6.7, 6.8, 6.9* or *6.10* (*r 6.18(2)*).

➤ **Service by the Court (problems):**

◆ Where the court serves the claim form by post and the claim form is returned to the court, the court sends notification to the claimant that the claim form has been returned (*r 6.18(1)*). The court will not try to serve the claim form again (*r (6.4(4)*).

◆ Where the court bailiff is to serve a claim form and the bailiff is unable to serve it on the defendant, the court sends notification to the claimant (*r 6.19*). The court will not try to serve the claim form again (*r (6.4(4)*).

➤ **Service by the Claimant:** Where the claimant serves the claim form, the claimant (*r 6.17(2)*):

◆ must file a certificate of service within 21 days of service of the particulars of claim (unless all the defendants to the proceedings have filed acknowledgments of service within that time), *and*

● The claimant is not required to and should not file with the certificate of service (if already filed with the court) a further copy of (*PD6A: 7.1*) the claim form or the particulars of claim (if not in the claim form) or any document attached to the particulars of claim.

NB: *r 7.4* requires the claimant to file a copy of the particulars of claim (where served separately from the claim form) within 7 days of service on the defendant.

◆ may not obtain default judgment (see p 421) unless a certificate of service has been filed.

Certificate of service for a claim form (*r 6.17*)

➤ **A certificate of service:** must state (if service was under *rr 6.7, 6.8, 6.9* or *6.10*), the category of address at which the claimant believes the claim form has been served and:

◆ for personal service: the date of personal service, *or*

◆ for first class post, DX or other next business day delivery service: the date of posting or leaving with, delivering to or collection by a service provider, *or*

◆ for delivery of a claim form at a permitted place: the date delivered to or left at a permitted place, *or*

◆ for fax: the date of completion of transmission, *or*

◆ for email: the date of sending of electronic transmission/email, *or*

◆ for alternative service: as required by the court.

B Service of documents other than a claim form

1   Methods of service of documents (but not a claim form) (in the jurisdiction only)

> The court may dispense with service of any document which is to be served in the proceedings (*r 6.28(1)*).
> An application for such an order must be supported by evidence and may be made without notice (*r 6.28(2)*).

A document may be served by any of the following methods (*r 6.20*):

NB: The rules below apply unless the CPR, any other enactment, a PD or a court order, say so(*r 6.1*)

Method of service (*r 6.20*)	Date of deemed service if served in the UK (*r 6.26*)	Rules about the method of service
Personal service (*r 6.22*) *Note for whole box: See the provisions about time on p 382*	If the document is served personally before 4.30pm on a business day, on that day *or* in any other case, on the next business day after that day.	➤ Personal service may be used (and must be used if the *CPR*, any other enactment, a *PD* or a court order, say so) (*r 6.22(1)-(2)*). **Party to be served** / **Served by** (*rr 6.5(3), 6.22(3)*): ◆ Individual — ◆ leaving it with that individual ◆ Company or other corporation — ◆ leaving it with a person holding a senior position within the company or corporation • A person holding a senior position means (*PD6A: 6.2*): ▪ For a registered company or corporation: a director, the treasurer, the secretary of the company or corporation, the chief executive, a manager or other officer of the company or corporation, *and* ▪ For a corporation which is not a registered company: in addition to the list in the previous bullet, the mayor, the chairman, the president, a town clerk or similar officer of the corporation. ◆ Partnership (where partners are being sued in the name of their firm) — ◆ leaving it with: • a partner, *or* • a person who, at the time of service, has the control or management of the partnership business at its principal place of business. ➤ Personal service cannot be used (unless the *CPR*, any other enactment, a *PD* or a court order, say so) (*r 6.22(2)*), where ... ◆ **Solicitor or European Lawyer:** ... the party to be served has given the business address of a solicitor/European Lawyer acting for him (*r 6.23*), *or* ◆ **Crown:** ... proceedings are against the Crown (eg: judicial review). Service is at the same address as for a claim form, see p 389 (*r 6.23(7)*).
First class post *or* Document exchange (ie: DX) *or* Other service which provides for delivery on the next business day	Second day after it was posted (for post only), left with, delivered to or collected by the relevant service provider provided that day is a business day *or* if not, the next business day after that day.	➤ Service is effected by (*PD6A 3.1*): ◆ placing the document in a post box, *or* ◆ leaving the document with, or delivering the document to, the relevant service provider, *or* ◆ having the document collected by the relevant service provider. ➤ Service by document exchange (DX) may take place only where the party or the solicitor acting for that party has not indicated in writing that they are unwilling to accept service by DX (*PD6A 2.1*) and: ◆ the address at which the party is to be served includes a numbered box at a DX, *or* ◆ the writing paper of the party who is to be served or of the solicitor acting for that party sets out a DX box number.
Leaving it at a place specified in *r 6.23* (see p 397)	If it is delivered to or left at the permitted address on a business day before 4.30pm, on that day, *or* in any other case, on the next business day after that day.	

A document may be served by any of the following methods (r 6.20) (continued):

NB: The rules below apply unless the CPR, any other enactment, a PD or a court order, say so(r 6.1)

Method of service (r 6.20)	Date of deemed service if served in the UK (r 6.26)	Rules about the method of service
Fax or Other means of electronic communication **Note for whole box:** See the provisions about time on p 382	**Fax:** If the transmission is completed on a business day before 4.30pm, on that day *or* in any other case, on the next business day after the day on which it was transmitted. **Other electronic method:** If the email/communication is sent on a business day before 4.30pm, on that day *or* in any other case, on the next business day after the day on which it was sent.	➤ (Subject to the provisions of r 6.23(5)-(6) - see p 397...) where a document is to be served by fax or other electronic means (PD6A 4.1): ◆ the party who is to be served or the solicitor acting for that party must previously have indicated in writing to the party serving: • that the party to be served or the solicitor is willing to accept service by fax or other electronic means, *and* • the fax number, e-mail address or other electronic identification to which it must be sent, *and* ◆ the following are to be taken as such indications: • a fax number set out on the writing paper of the solicitor acting for the party to be served, *or* • an e-mail address set out on the writing paper of the solicitor acting for the party to be served but only where it is stated that the e-mail address may be used for service, *or* • a fax number, e-mail address or electronic identification set out on a statement of case or a response to a claim filed with the court. ➤ Where a party intends to serve a document by electronic means (other than by fax) that party must first ask the party who is to be served whether there are any limitations to the recipient's agreement to accept service by such means (eg: the format in which documents are to be sent and the maximum size of attachments that may be received) (PD6A: 4.2). ➤ Where a document is served by electronic means, the party serving the document need not in addition send or deliver a hard copy (PD6A: 4.3).

By any method authorised by the court under *r 6.27* (ie: alternative service, see pp 392 and 397)

➤ A company may also be served by any of the methods of service permitted under *CA 2006* (eg: sending to the registered office) (r 6.20(2)).

➤ An LLP may also be served by any of the methods of service permitted under *CA 2006* as varied by regulations under *LLPA 2000* (eg: sending to the registered office) (r 6.20(3)).

> Service of documents out of the jurisdiction is subject to additional rules, *rr 6.30 -6.47* (which are not dealt with in this book)

Examples of deemed service of a document (PD6A: 10)

➤ 1: Where the document is posted (by first class post) on a Monday (a business day), the day of deemed service is the following Wednesday (a business day).

➤ 2: Where the document is left in a numbered box at the DX on a Friday (a business day), the day of deemed service is the following Monday (a business day).

➤ 3: Where the document is sent by fax on a Saturday and the transmission of that fax is completed by 4.30pm on that day, the day of deemed service is the following Monday (a business day).

➤ 4: Where the document is served personally before 4.30pm on a Sunday, the day of deemed service is the next day (Monday, a business day).

➤ 5: Where the document is delivered to a permitted address after 4.30pm on the Thursday (a business day) before Good Friday, the day of deemed service is the following Tuesday (a business day) as the Monday is a bank holiday.

➤ 6: Where the document is posted (by first class post) on a bank holiday Monday, the day of deemed service is the following Wednesday (a business day).

2 Place of service of a document which is not a claim form

If the court orders alternative service, these rules do not apply (r 6.23(8)).

➤ A party to proceedings (after proceedings have started) must give an address (including, unless the court orders otherwise, a full postcode - or EEA equivalent, if applicable) at which that party may be served with documents relating to those proceedings (*r 6.23(1)*).

➤ Except where any other rule or practice direction makes different provision, a party's address for service (where any document must be sent or transmitted to, or left - unless it is served personally or unless the court orders otherwise) must be (*rr 6.23(2), 6.23(3), 6.23(4)*):

- the business address within the UK (or any other EEA state) of a solicitor acting for the party to be served, *or*

- the business address in any EEA state of a European Lawyer nominated to accept service of documents, *or*

- where there is no solicitor acting for the party to be served or no European Lawyer nominated to accept service of documents, an address within the UK (or within any other EEA state) at which the party resides or carries on business, *or*

- where none of the above apply, the party must give an address for service within the UK.

➤ If a party indicates or is deemed to have indicated that they will accept service by:

- fax, the fax number given by that party must be at the address for service (*r 6.23(5)*), *or*

- electronic means other than fax, the email address or electronic identification given by that party will be deemed to be at the address for service (*r 6.23(6)*).

> Service of documents out of the jurisdiction is subject to additional rules, *rr 6.30 -6.47* (which are not dealt with in this book)

> 'European Lawyer' has the meaning set out in *EC(SL)O 1978 Art 2*

'Alternative' service (*r 6.15, r 6.27, PD6A: 9*)

➤ The rules are identical to those in the section on serving a claim form (see p 392), save that:

- references to a claim form are read as references to a document, *and*

- references to a defendant are read a references to a party.

Change of address for service (*r 6.24*)

➤ Where the address for service of a party changes, that party must give notice in writing of the change as soon as it has taken place to the court and every other party.

3   Special situations

Service of a document which is not the claim form on children and protected parties (r 6.25)

➤ Any document (apart from an application for an order appointing a litigation friend) which would otherwise be served on a child or a protected party must be served on the litigation friend conducting the proceedings on behalf of the child or protected party.

  ◆ An application for an order appointing a litigation friend where a child or protected party has no litigation friend must be served in accordance with *r 21.8* (see pp 399 and 400).

➤ The court may make an order:

  ◆ permitting a document to be served on the child or protected party or on some person other than the person specified as above.

    ● An application for such an order may be made without notice.

  ◆ that, although a document has been sent or given to someone other than the person specified above, the document is to be treated as if it had been properly served.

➤ This rule does not apply where the court has made an order allowing a child to conduct proceedings without a litigation friend.

---

4   Mechanics of service of a document which is not the claim form (but subject to rules about service out of the jurisdiction (*rr 6.30-6.47*, not dealt with in this book) and to rules relating to service out of the jurisdiction on solicitors, European Lawyers and parties (see p 397))

➤ A party to proceedings will serve a document which that party has prepared (*r 6.21(1)*).
  ◆ **Exception 1:** where a rule or practice direction provides that the court must serve it.
  ◆ **Exception 2:** the court orders or directs otherwise.

➤ The court will serve a document which it has prepared (*r 6.21(2)*).
  ◆ **Exception 1:** where a rule or practice direction provides that a party must serve it.
  ◆ **Exception 2:** the court orders or directs otherwise.
  ◆ **Exception 3:** the party on whose behalf the document is to be served notifies the court that the party wishes to serve it.

➤ **Service by the Court:** Where the court serves a document:

  ◆ the court decides which method of service is used (*r 6.21(3)*), although first class post is normally used (*PD6A: 8.1*), *and*

  ◆ if the document has been prepared by a party, that party must provide a copy for the court and for each party to be served(*r 6.4(4)*), *and*

  ◆ which is delivery of a defence or which notifies a claimant that the defendant has filed an acknowledgment of service, the court also serves or delivers a copy of any notice of funding that has been filed, if it was filed at the same time as the defence or acknowledgment of service and copies of it were provided for service (*PD6A: 8.2*).

Certificate of service for a document that is not claim form (r 6.29)

➤ A certificate of service: where this is required, it must state:
  ◆ for personal service: the date and time of personal service, *or*
  ◆ for first class post, DX or other next business day delivery service: the date of posting or leaving with, delivering to or collection by a service provider, *or*
  ◆ for delivery of a document at a permitted place: the date delivered to or left at a permitted place, *or*
  ◆ for fax: the date and time of completion of transmission, *or*
  ◆ for email: the date and time of sending of electronic transmission/email, *or*
  ◆ for alternative service: as required by the court.

C   Starting proceedings

I	Identifying the parties (and some extra procedural points that result)	IV	Initial documents needed to file with the claim form
II	Selecting the court	V	The claim form
III	Hearings	VI	Particulars of claim

I   Identifying the parties (and some extra procedural points that result)

1   Joint claimants (*r 19.3*)

➤ Where a claimant claims a remedy to which someone else is jointly entitled, all persons jointly entitled must be parties unless the court orders otherwise.

◆ A person not agreeing to be a claimant must be made a defendant, unless a court orders otherwise.

2   Joining possible claims

➤ A claimant may use a single claim form to start all claims which can be conveniently disposed of in the same proceedings (*r 7.3*). A claimant does not need leave of the court for this.

3   If claimant/defendant is trading under another name

4   If claimant/defendant is suing/being sued in a representative capacity

5   If claimant/defendant is a firm

6   If claimant/defendant is a partnership: see also p 391

➤ Where a partnership has a name, unless inappropriate, claims must be brought against the name which that partnership had at the time the cause of action accrued (*PD21: 5A.3*).

◆ Enforcing judgment against the individual partners' own assets is governed by *PD70: 6A*.

◆ Sometimes partnership membership statements are required (*PD21: 5B*).

see p 405

7   If claimant/defendant is a company registered in England & Wales: see pp 391 and 405

8   Claimant or defendant is a protected party (ie: someone who lacks capacity to conduct proceedings) within *MCA 2005* (*Part 21 and PD21*)

➤ A protected party must bring or defend proceedings by a litigation friend (*r 21.2(1)*) (see p 400).

➤ A protected party is referred to in the title as 'A.B. (a protected party by C.D his litigation friend)' (*PD21: 1.1*).

➤ If the protected party has no litigation friend (*r 21.3(2)*):

◆ prior to service of claim form, no applications are allowed without the court's permission, *and*

◆ during proceedings, no steps are allowed without the court's permission *except*: issuing and serving the claim form and applying for appointment of a litigation friend.

➤ If a party becomes a protected party during proceedings, no party may take any step in the proceedings without the permission of the court until the protected party has a litigation friend (*r 21.3(3)*).

➤ When a party ceases to be a protected party, the litigation friend's appointment continues until it is ended by a court order (*r 21.9*).

9   Insurers

➤ In a road traffic accident case, if insurers are involved, the claimant must send a *RTA 1988 s 151/152* notice to the defendant's insurers within 7 days of issuing proceedings. This enables the defendant's insurers to defend the claim, and for the claimant to claim against them if he wins.

10 **Claimant or defendant is a child (ie: under 18 - a minor)** *(Part 21 and PD21)*

➤ A child must bring or defend proceedings by a litigation friend *unless* the court has made an order permitting the child to do so on his own behalf *(r 21.2(2)-(3))*.

➤ Where the child *(PD21: 1.2)*:

♦ has a litigation friend, the child is referred to in the title as 'A.B (a child by C.D his litigation friend)', *or*

♦ conducts proceedings on his own behalf, the child is referred to in the title as 'A.B. (a child)'.

➤ If the child has no litigation friend, and the court has not ordered an exemption *(r 21.3(2))*:

♦ prior to service of the claim form, no applications are allowed without the court's permission, *and*

♦ during proceedings, no steps are allowed without the court's permission except: issuing and serving the claim form and applying for appointment of a litigation friend.

➤ The litigation friend is personally liable for costs, but is usually indemnified for these by the child.

➤ When a child (who is not a protected party) reaches 18, a litigation friend's appointment ceases *(r 21.9)*. The child may adopt or repudiate proceedings on coming of age during the proceedings.

➤ No settlement, compromise or payment and no acceptance of money paid into court is valid, without the approval of the court. Any money won by the child will be dealt with by direction of the court but will usually be paid into court and invested until the child is 18 (although sums may be drawn and paid earlier to the child for his immediate needs) *(r 21.10-21.11)*.

A litigation friend *(Part 21, PD: 21)*

➤ **Duties:** a litigation friend must *(r 21.4)*:
♦ fairly and competently conduct proceedings on behalf of the child or protected party, *and*
♦ have no interest adverse to that of the child or protected party, *and*
♦ where the child or protected party is a claimant, undertake to pay any costs which the child or protected party may be ordered to pay in relation to the proceedings (subject to any right he may have to be repaid from the assets of the child or protected party).

➤ A claimant must apply to the court for an order appointing a litigation friend for the child or protected party if:
♦ a person makes a claim against a child or protected party, *and*
♦ the child or protected party has no litigation friend, *and*
♦ the court has not made an order that a child can conduct proceedings without a litigation friend, *and*
♦ either someone who is not entitled to be a litigation friend files a defence or the claimant wishes to take some step in the proceedings.

➤ To become a litigation friend *by court order (r 21.6, r 21.8, PD21: 3.3)*:
♦ An application for an order appointing a litigation friend may be made by a person who wishes to be the litigation friend or a party.
  ● The application must be supported by evidence which shows that the proposed litigation friend consents to act and can comply with the 'Duties' above.
  ● The application must be served on every person on whom the claim form must be served and, if it is in respect of a protected party, also on the protected party - unless the court orders otherwise.

➤ To become a litigation friend *without a court order (r 21.5)*:
♦ If the potential litigation friend is a deputy appointed by the Court of Protection under *MCA 2005* with power to conduct proceedings on the protected party's behalf, he must file an official copy of the order of the Court of Protection which confers his power to act either:
  ● where the deputy is to act as a litigation friend for a claimant, at the time the claim is made, *or*
  ● where the deputy is to act as a litigation friend for a defendant, at the time when he first takes a step in the proceedings on behalf of the defendant.
♦ If the potential litigation friend is anyone else, that person must file a certificate of suitability stating that he consents to act, that he satisfies the conditions specified in the 'Duties' point above and that he knows or believes that the [claimant] [defendant] [is a child] [lacks capacity to conduct the proceedings]. This must be filed either:
  ● where the person is to act as a litigation friend for a claimant, at the time when the claim is made, *or*
  ● where the person is to act as a litigation friend for a defendant, at the time when he first takes a step in the proceedings on behalf of the defendant.
♦ The litigation friend must:
  ● serve the certificate of suitability on every person on whom the claim form should be served, *and*
  ● file a certificate of service when filing the certificate of suitability.

II   Selecting the court

A   Courts generally

High Court	County Courts
There is 1 High Court divided into: **Chancery Division** (includes: ◆ Patent Court ◆ Companies Court) **Family Division** Used for: landlord and tenant disputes, trusts, contentious probate, partnership actions, intellectual property actions and actions requesting equitable remedies **Queens Bench Division** (includes: ◆ Commercial Court ◆ Admiralty Court) Used for: claiming damages in contract actions and tort actions	There are *many* county courts ◆ The Central London County Court Business List is sometimes used for certain high value business/commercial transactions ◆ The Central London Civil Trial Centre is at the Central London County Court. More complex County Court cases are heard here, especially those expected to last for more than 1 day. Cases may be referred here by any London County Court

B   Where to *start* a claim *(PD7A: 2)*

➤ In general *(and subject to the rest of the rules in this section)*, any action which both the High Court and the county courts have jurisdiction to deal with may be started in either the High Court or a county court.

   ◆ Note: in calculating the *value* of a claim in this section see the large grey box on p 406.

   ◆ The jurisdiction of the High Court and the county courts is as follows:

The jurisdiction of the courts at commencement of a claim *(CCA 1984, HCCCJO 1991)*	
Jurisdiction of the High Court	**Jurisdiction of the county courts**
Tort claims over £25,000 (Note overlap with county courts)	Tort claims up to £50,000 *(CCA 1984 s 15)*
Contract claims over £25,000 (Note overlap with county courts)	Contract claims up to £50,000 *(CCA 1984 s 15)*
Personal injury claims worth £50,000 or more	Personal injury claims worth under £50,000 *(SI 1991/724)*
Libel (unless the parties agree otherwise)	Equitable interests and land charges disputes where the property has a value of £30,000 or less *(CCA 1984 s 23)*
Slander (unless the parties agree otherwise)	**Note:** A claim may be started using Money Claim Online if the only remedy claimed is a specified amount of money less than £100,000 (excluding any interest or costs claimed) and the claimant is not a child or protected party (ie: someone who lacks capacity to conduct proceedings) or funded by legal aid. The claim must be against 1 defendant or 2 defendants if the claim is for a single amount against each of them *(PD7E: 4)*.
Search orders (authorises a party to search for documents or property at their opponent's premises)	
Freezing injunctions (to freeze assets)	
Judicial review	

➤ **Claims of damages or a specified sum: the £25,000 rule**

   ◆ worth more than £25,000 *may* be commenced in the High Court or the county courts (up to £50,000).

   ◆ worth £25,000 or less *must* be commenced in the county courts.

➤ **Personal injury action: the £50,000 rule**

   ◆ worth £50,000 or more - *must* be commenced in the High Court

   ◆ worth less than £50,000 - *must* be commenced in the county courts.

➤ **Claimant's belief:** the High Court (and not a county court) should hear a case if (subject to the above) a claimant believes the following factors are of a sufficiently high level:

Claimant's factors
1 **Financial value of the claim and the amount in dispute**
2 **Complexity:**   of facts, legal issues, remedies or procedures involved
3 **Importance of the outcome:**   to the public in general

C Transfer of a claim after the claim has been started *(Part 30)*

➤ A claim will usually proceed in the court in which it was commenced.

➤ However, in certain cases the claim can be transferred to a different court. This happens if a court does not have jurisdiction (see the table on p 401) or if the following rules apply:

1   County Court transfer to another County Court *(r 30.2(1)-(3))*

➤ A county court may order proceedings before that court, or any part of them (eg: a counterclaim) to be transferred to another county court if it is satisfied that:

a) an order should be made having regard to the 'transfer criteria' (see box on p 403), *or*

b) the following proceedings could be more conveniently or fairly taken in that other county court:

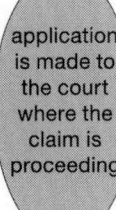

◆ the detailed assessment of costs, *or*

◆ the enforcement of a judgment or order, *or*

application is made to the court where the claim is proceeding

c) proceedings have been started in the wrong county court in which case the Court may order they:

◆ be transferred to the county court in which they ought to have been started, *or*

◆ continue in the county court in which they have been started, *or*

◆ be struck out.

d) the rules for 'Automatic Transfers' apply (claim is for a specified amount, was commenced in a court which is not the defendant's home court, has not otherwise been transferred to another defendant's home court under an application to set aside or vary default judgment and the defendant is an individual), see p 434 for detail.

2   High Court transfer within itself *(r 30.2(4)-(6))*

➤ The High Court may, having regard to the 'transfer criteria' (see box on p 403), order proceedings in the Royal Courts of Justice (RCJ) or a district registry (DR) , or any part of such proceedings (eg: a counterclaim) to be transferred:

◆ from the RCJ to a DR, *or*

◆ from a DR to the RCJ, *or*

◆ from a DR to another DR.

An application for an order must, if the claim is proceeding in a DR, be made to that DR

➤ A DR may order proceedings before it for detailed assessment of costs to be transferred to another DR if it is satisfied that the proceedings could be more conveniently or fairly taken in that other DR.

3   High Court transfer to a County Court

➤ **Discretionary transfer:** the High Court can transfer whatever it wants to a county court *(CCA 1984 s 40)*.

◆ This might occur in the following types of cases:

a) cases that *could* only be started in the High Court, eg: slander, libel.

b) cases that *should* never have started in the High Court *must* be moved to a county court *(CCA 1984 s 40)*, eg: a personal injury action worth less than £50,000.

c) cases that can be heard in either court.

➤ **Automatic transfer:** there will be automatic transfer to a county court unless a 'statement of value' showing the action is worth at least £15,000 (or a statement saying why the action ought to be heard in the High Court) is delivered at the appropriate time.

4   **General power of High Court to transfer to a county court and a county court to High Court**

> ➤ Generally, the High Court has power to transfer cases to a county court and a county court has power to transfer cases to the High Court (*CCA 1984 ss 40-42*). It must take account of the 'transfer criteria' (*r 30.3*).

Transfer criteria (*r 30.3*)

➤ The following are matters which the court must have regard to when considering whether to make a transfer order:

- ◆ the financial value of the claim and the amount in dispute, if different, *and*

- ◆ whether it would be more convenient or fair for hearings (including the trial) to be held in some other court, *and*

- ◆ the availability of a judge specialising in the type of claim in question, *and*

- ◆ whether the facts, legal issues, remedies or procedures involved are simple or complex, *and*

- ◆ the importance of the outcome of the claim to the public in general, *and*

- ◆ the facilities available to the court at which the claim is being dealt with, particularly in relation to:

  - • any disabilities of a party or potential witness, *or*

  - • any special measures needed for potential witnesses, *or*

  - • security, *and*

- ◆ whether the making of a declaration of incompatibility under *HRA 1998 s 4* has arisen or may arise, *and*

- ◆ High Court Factors - ie: factors that might include a court more to having a case heard in the High Court (*PD29: 2.6*):

  - • professional negligence claims.

  - • Fatal Accident Act claims.

  - • fraud or undue influence claims.

  - • defamation claims.

  - • claims for malicious prosecution or false imprisonment.

  - • claims against the police.

  - • contentious probate claims.

Transfer procedure (*r 30.4*)

➤ Where the Court orders proceedings to be transferred, the court from which they are to be transferred must give notice of the transfer to all the parties.

Application to set aside a transfer order (*PD30: 6*)

➤ Where a party may apply to set aside an order for transfer the application should be made to the Court which made the order.

➤ Such application should be made in accordance with *Part 23*, see p 415.

Competition law claims (*r 30.8*)

➤ Where there is a competition claim under *CA 1998 Part I* or *TFEU Articles 101/102*, a special transfer procedure applies.

III Hearings

Hearings - miscellaneous provisions *(Part 39)*	
In public *(r 39.1)* Note: see also telephone hearings p 417	➤ A hearing is in public, *unless* ◆ publicity would defeat the object of the hearing, *or* ◆ the hearing involves matters relating to national security, *or* ◆ confidential information is involved and publicity would damage that confidentiality, *or* ◆ privacy is necessary to protect the interests of a child or a protected party, *or* ◆ it is the hearing of an application made without notice and a public hearing would be unjust to the respondent, *or* ◆ the hearing involves uncontentious matters arising in the administration of trusts or a deceased person's estate, *or* ◆ the court considers a private hearing necessary in the interests of justice. ➤ The court may order the identity of a party or witness not be disclosed if this is necessary to protect the interests of that party or witness.

Failure to attend trial
(r 39.3)
	➤ The court may proceed in a party's absence, *but*
	◆ if no party attends, the court may strike out the whole of the proceedings.
	◆ if the claimant does not attend, the court may strike out the claim and any defence to a counterclaim.
	◆ if the defendant does not attend, it may strike out the defence and/or counterclaim *(r 39.3(1))*.
	➤ If a court strikes out proceedings (or any part of proceedings) under *r 39.3* it may subsequently them *(r 39.3(2))*.
	➤ A party who does not attend and has a order or judgment made against it under *r 39.3* may apply for that order or judgement to be set aside *(r 39.3(3))*.
	◆ An application for proceedings to be restored or an order/judgment to be set aside must be supported by evidence *(r 39.3(4))*
	◆ The court may only grant an application to restore proceedings or set aside an order/judgment if the applicant:
	  a) acted promptly when he found out that the claim had been struck out or the order/judgment set aside, *and*
	  b) had a good reason for not attending the trial, *and*
	  c) has a reasonable prospect of success at trial *(r 39.3(5))*.

Timetable for trial *(r 39.4)*	➤ When the court sets a timetable for a trial under: ◆ *r 28.6* (Fast track) (see p 439), *or* ◆ *r 29* (Multi track) (see p 441) ... ... it will do so in consultation with the parties.
Trial bundles *(r 39.5)*	➤ A claimant must file a trial bundle containing documents required by any relevant practice direction and any court order, unless the court orders otherwise. ➤ The trial bundle must be filed not more than 7 days and not less than 3 days before the start of the trial (see p 455).
Representation at trial of companies/ corporations *(r 39.6)*	➤ An employee may represent a company or corporation at trial if that employee has been authorised by the company or corporation to appear at trial on its behalf and the court gives permission.

IV Initial documents needed to file with the claim form

➤ Documents to file with the claim form include:
◆ the particulars of claim (if not on the claim form or if not being served after the claim form), *and*
◆ for a legally assisted claimant, a notice of funding + any amendments (*Costs PD: 19*), *and*
◆ the relevant defence / admission / acknowledgment of service forms, *and*
◆ the fee, *and*
◆ any relevant litigation friend documents (see p 400).

V   The claim form (*Part 7*)

A   General

➤ Proceedings are started when the court issues a claim form at the request of the claimant (*r 7.2(1)*).

   ◆ A claim form is issued on the date entered on the form by the court (*r 7.2(2)*).

➤ Drafting the claim form must be done on *Form N1* (*PD7A: 3.1*).

➤ There are 2 other ways of starting claims. These are where there is:

   ◆ no substantial dispute of fact or certain special types of applications. *Part 8* procedures apply and *Form N208* (*PD7A: 3.1*) is used as the claims form. *Part 8* proceedings are not dealt with in this book.

   ◆ a specialist jurisdiction (known as a 'list') (eg: the Commercial Court) (not dealt with in this book).

B   Procedure for the claimant's solicitors to issue the claim form

Steps	
1	Prepare at least 3 copies of the claim form and all documents accompanying it (see steps 4 and 5 below); one for the claimant, one for each defendant and one for the court.
2	Sign the copies.
3	Prepare the 'Response Pack' consisting of: 1) the correct admissions form; 2) the correct defence form; *and* 3) the acknowledgement of service form.
4	If the claimant is legally funded, prepare the notification of legal funding and copies (*Costs PD: 19*).
5	If the claimant is a child or protected party, prepare the litigation friend documents (see p 400).
6	Prepare the court fee - cheques are payable to 'HM Paymaster General'.
7	Take, or send (include the SAE if so), the claim form and response pack and any of the above documents to the court, together with the court fee.
8	The court will issue a claim number, seal the documents and issue the claim form.
9	Once issued the claim form can be served within 4 months (within the jurisdiction) (see p 377).

Filling in the parties on the claim form	
Party	**Wording on claim form**
Individual	➤ Insert all known forenames and surname, whether Mr, Mrs, Miss, Ms or Other (eg: Dr) and residential address (**including** postcode and telephone number) ➤ Where the defendant is a proprietor of a business, a partner in a firm or an individual sued in the name of a club or other unincorporated association, the address for service should be the usual or last known place of residence **or** principal place of business of the company, firm or club or other unincorporated association
Child (ie: under 18) *or* protected party under *MCA 2005*	➤ See pp 399-400 for correct form in title and procedure
Trading under another name	➤ Insert the words: 'trading as' and the trading name, eg: 'Mr X trading as X's dairies'
Suing or being sued in a representative capacity	➤ State the capacity, eg: 'Mr X as the representative of Ms Y (deceased)'
A firm	➤ Insert the firm name followed by 'a firm', eg: 'X - a firm' ➤ Insert an address for service which is either a partner's residential address or the principal or last known place of business
A partnership	➤ Insert the partnership name followed by 'a firm', eg: 'X - a firm' ➤ Other details are as per 'A firm' above
A company registered in England and Wales	➤ Insert the company name and an address which is either the company's registered office or any place of business that has a real, or the most, connection with the claim eg: the shop where goods were brought ➤ Verify the company's details with a company search

Drafting the claim form (PD7A: 3, PD7A: 4, r 16.2, r 16.3, PD16: 2)

Front page of the claim form

'Defendant' Insert: all defendants' names *and* addresses

'Claimant' Insert: all claimants' names *and* addresses

'Claim No.' The Court will insert this

Court will insert the issue date

'In the' Insert:
a) '[name] County Court', *or*
b) 'High Court of Justice [name] Division [name] District Registry', *or*
c) 'High Court of Justice [name] Division, Royal Courts of Justice'

'Defendant's name and address' Insert name and address of the particular defendant who will get this copy

'Brief details of claim' Insert (r 16.2):
◆ concise statement of nature of claim, *and*
◆ remedy being sought

Court seal will go here together with stamped date of issue

'Amount claimed'

If a fixed amount insert any amount here from 'Value' plus interest (r 16.2(1)(cc))	If not a fixed amount insert 'Unspecified'

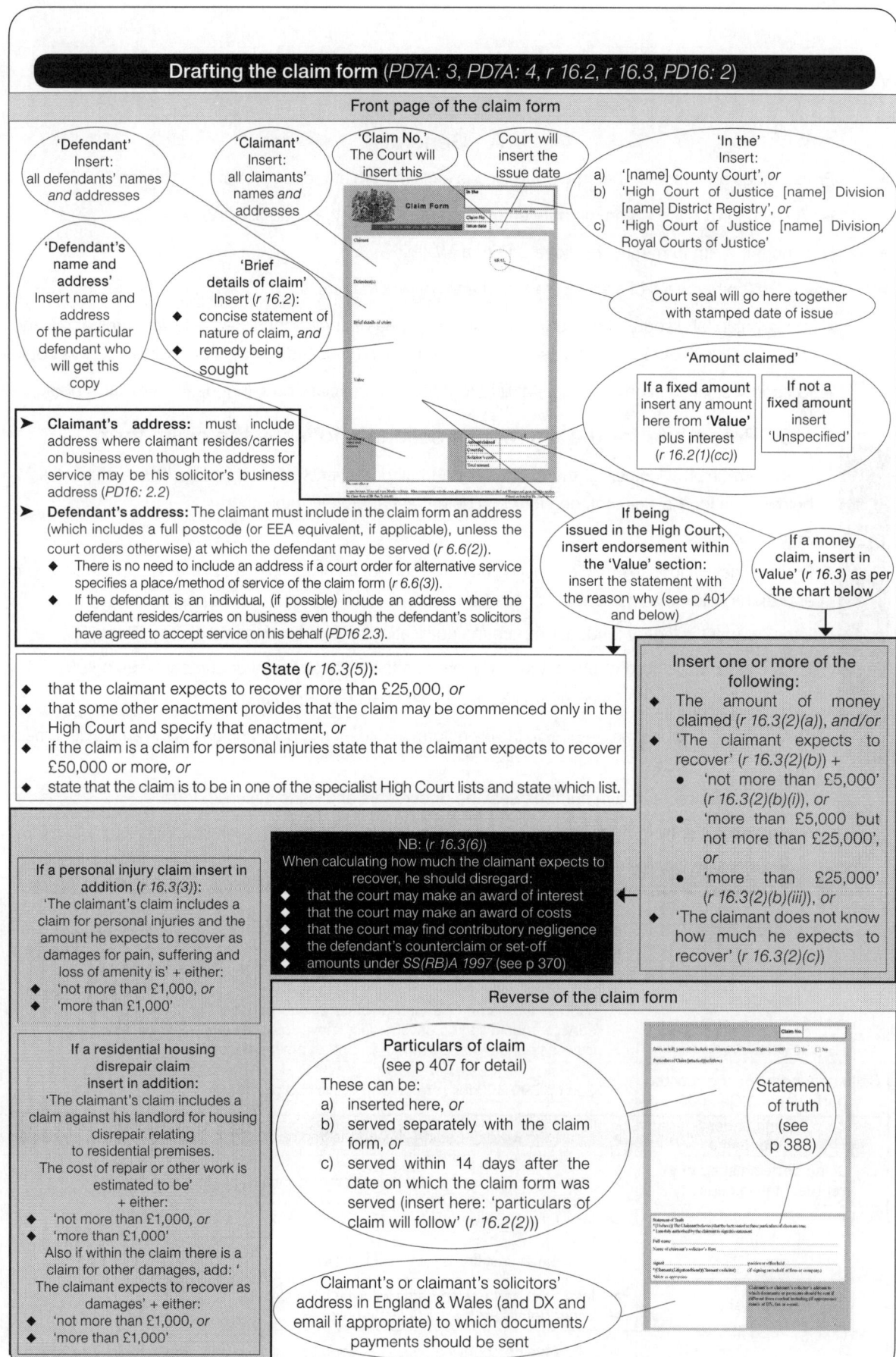

➤ **Claimant's address:** must include address where claimant resides/carries on business even though the address for service may be his solicitor's business address (PD16: 2.2)

➤ **Defendant's address:** The claimant must include in the claim form an address (which includes a full postcode (or EEA equivalent, if applicable), unless the court orders otherwise) at which the defendant may be served (r 6.6(2)).
  ◆ There is no need to include an address if a court order for alternative service specifies a place/method of service of the claim form (r 6.6(3)).
  ◆ If the defendant is an individual, (if possible) include an address where the defendant resides/carries on business even though the defendant's solicitors have agreed to accept service on his behalf (PD16 2.3).

If being issued in the High Court, insert endorsement within the 'Value' section: insert the statement with the reason why (see p 401 and below)

If a money claim, insert in 'Value' (r 16.3) as per the chart below

State (r 16.3(5)):
◆ that the claimant expects to recover more than £25,000, *or*
◆ that some other enactment provides that the claim may be commenced only in the High Court and specify that enactment, *or*
◆ if the claim is a claim for personal injuries state that the claimant expects to recover £50,000 or more, *or*
◆ state that the claim is to be in one of the specialist High Court lists and state which list.

Insert one or more of the following:
◆ The amount of money claimed (r 16.3(2)(a)), *and/or*
◆ 'The claimant expects to recover' (r 16.3(2)(b)) +
  ● 'not more than £5,000' (r 16.3(2)(b)(i)), *or*
  ● 'more than £5,000 but not more than £25,000', *or*
  ● 'more than £25,000' (r 16.3(2)(b)(iii)), *or*
◆ 'The claimant does not know how much he expects to recover' (r 16.3(2)(c))

If a personal injury claim insert in addition (r 16.3(3)):
'The claimant's claim includes a claim for personal injuries and the amount he expects to recover as damages for pain, suffering and loss of amenity is' + either:
◆ 'not more than £1,000, *or*
◆ 'more than £1,000'

NB: (r 16.3(6))
When calculating how much the claimant expects to recover, he should disregard:
◆ that the court may make an award of interest
◆ that the court may make an award of costs
◆ that the court may find contributory negligence
◆ the defendant's counterclaim or set-off
◆ amounts under SS(RB)A 1997 (see p 370)

If a residential housing disrepair claim insert in addition:
'The claimant's claim includes a claim against his landlord for housing disrepair relating to residential premises. The cost of repair or other work is estimated to be' + either:
◆ 'not more than £1,000, *or*
◆ 'more than £1,000'
Also if within the claim there is a claim for other damages, add: ' The claimant expects to recover as damages' + either:
◆ 'not more than £1,000, *or*
◆ 'more than £1,000'

Reverse of the claim form

Particulars of claim (see p 407 for detail)
These can be:
a) inserted here, *or*
b) served separately with the claim form, *or*
c) served within 14 days after the date on which the claim form was served (insert here: 'particulars of claim will follow' (r 16.2(2)))

Statement of truth (see p 388)

Claimant's or claimant's solicitors' address in England & Wales (and DX and email if appropriate) to which documents/payments should be sent

VI   Particulars of claim

➤   Particulars of claim form the main statement of case that sets out the claimant's case.

➤   Particulars of claim must (*r 7.4*):

a)   be contained in the claim form, *or*

b)   be served with, but separate to, the claim form, *or*

c)   be served on the defendant within 14 days after service of the claim form (provided the relevant step to do with service of the claim form (see white text in black boxes on pp 389 - 390) is taken before 12 midnight on the calendar day 4 months after issue of the claim form - see p 377).

   • If the particulars of claim are not included in or have not been served with the claim form, the claim form must also contain a statement that particulars of claim will follow (*PD7A: 6.1, PD16: 3.3*).

   ◆ If practicable, the particulars of claim should be set out in the claim form (*PD16: 3.1*).

➤   Where the claimant serves particulars of claim at a different time to the claim form, he must, within 7 days of service on the defendant, file a copy of the particulars with the court (see p 377) (except in certain exceptional circumstances to do with: (i) the Production Centre, or (ii) Money Claim Online; neither of which are covered in this book) (*r 7.4(3)*).

➤   When particulars of claim are served on a defendant, whether they are contained in the claim form, served with it or served subsequently, they must be accompanied by (*r 7.8(1)*):

a)   a form for defending the claim, *and*

b)   a form for admitting the claim, *and*

c)   a form for acknowledging service.

Compulsory matters (*PD16: 8.1, 8.2*)

➤ The claimant must set out specifically the following matters where he wishes to rely on them in support of his claim

   ◆ any allegation of fraud
   ◆ the fact of any illegality
   ◆ details of any misrepresentation
   ◆ details of all breaches of trust
   ◆ notice or knowledge of a fact
   ◆ details of unsoundness of mind or undue influence
   ◆ details of wilful default
   ◆ any facts relating to mitigation of loss or damage
   ◆ **Conviction:** a claimant who wants to rely on evidence under *s 11 CEA 1968* of a conviction must include:
      • a statement that he wants to rely on a conviction under *s 11 CEA 1968* , *and*
      • the type of conviction, finding or adjudication and its date, *and*
      • the court which made the conviction, finding or adjudication, *and*
      • the issue in the claim to which it relates.

   ◆ **Certain special types of damages:** a claimant seeking aggravated damages, exemplary damages or provisional damages must include a statement to that effect and the grounds for claiming them

---

Interest (*r 16.4(2)*)

➤ A claimant seeking interest must state the following:

a)   a statement to that he is seeking interest, *and*

b)   a statement that:

   i)   that he is seeking interest under the terms of a contract, *or*

   ii)   that he is seeking interest under an enactment (state which), ★ *or*

   iii) that he is seeking interest on some other basis (state which) (eg: see p 370), *and*

c)   (if the claim is for a specified amount of money), he must state:

   i)   the percentage rate at which interest is claimed, ★ *and*

   ii)   the date from which it is claimed, *and*

   iii) the date to which it is calculated (must not be later than the date the claim form is issued), *and*

   iv)   the total amount of interest claimed to the date of calculation, *and*

   v)   the daily rate at which interest accrues after that date

> High Court interest is sought under *SCA 1981 s 35A*

> County Court interest is sought under *CCA 1984 s 69*

> For debt actions, interest may have been set by an agreement - if not then the rate is set by statutory instrument (now 8%) (see p 470)

Drafting the particulars of claim (r 7.4, PD7A: 6, r 16.4, PD16: 3-9)

Particulars of claim which are served separately from the claim form must contain (PD16: 3.8):
- the name of the court in which the claim is proceeding, *and*
- the claim number, *and*
- the title of the proceedings, *and*
- the claimant's address for service.

Give a concise statement of the facts on which the claimant relies (r 16.4)
- It is good practice to set this out as numbered paragraphs
- Examples of typical facts (in addition to the compulsory matters) to include are set out below:

Breach of contract	Problem with goods	Personal injury
• whether contract is oral or written	• price of the goods	• date and place of the accident
• date of + parties to the contract	• date the goods were sold	• names of those involved
• purpose of the agreement	• particulars of goods	• allegation of negligence
• consideration (unless under seal)	• date delivery was due	• (with 'particulars of negligence')
• the term breached		

Compulsory matters which must specifically be stated if relied on (PD16: 8.1):

Breach of contract claims (PD16: 7)	Personal injury claims (PD16: 4)

Written agreement:
• attach or serve a copy of the contract/documents constituting the agreement (**Note:** the original(s) should be available at the hearing)
• attach any general conditions of sale incorporated in the contract
(but where any of the above are bulky, attach or serve only the relevant parts of the contract/documents).
Oral agreement:
• set out the contractual words used and state by whom, to whom, when and where they were spoken
Agreement by conduct:
• specify the conduct relied on and state by whom, when and where the acts constituting the conduct were done
	• state the claimant's date of birth
	• state brief details of the claimant's personal injuries
	• attach a schedule of details of any past and future expenses and losses which he claims
	• (if relying on evidence of a medical practitioner) attach or serve a report from a medical practitioner about the personal injuries which he alleges in his claim
	• (if a provisional damages claim), add a statement:
	  1) that he is seeking an award of provisional damages under either SCA 1981 s 32A or CCA 1984 s 51, *and*
	  2) that there is a chance that at some future time the claimant will develop some serious disease or suffer some serious deterioration in his physical or mental condition, *and*
	  3) specifying the disease or type of deterioration in respect of which an application may be made at a future date.
	(see p 428 (*Part 41*) for more details)

Fatal accident claims (PD16: 5)	Others claims (PD16: 6, r 19.5A)
• state that the claim is brought under the *FAA 1976* • state the dependants on whose behalf the claim is made • state the date of birth of each dependant • state details of the nature of the dependency claim **Note:** A fatal accident claim may include a claim for damages for bereavement. The claimant may also bring a claim under the *LR(MP)A 1934* on behalf of the estate of the deceased	For: • Hire purchase claims • Wrongful interference with goods certain details must be included (not listed here)

A claimant who wishes to rely on certain matters must specifically state them (see 'Compulsory matters' box on p 407)	Particulars of claim must include (r 16.4(1)): • if the claimant is seeking aggravated damages or exemplary damages, a statement to that effect and his grounds for claiming them, *and* • if the claimant is seeking provisional damages, a statement to that effect and his grounds for claiming them.	**Drafting tip** • A typical claim is structured using the formulation: **DUTY** ↓ **BREACH** ↓ **LOSS**
A claimant who seeks interest must state he is seeking interest and add certain details (r 16.4) (see 'Interest' box on p 407)		
Add the prayer for relief headed 'AND THE CLAIMANT CLAIMS:' Specify exactly what the claimant wants the court to order		
Add a statement of truth (see p 388) (PD16: 3.4) '[I][the claimant] believe[s] that the facts stated in these particulars of claim are true.'		

D Defendant's options

1	Draft a full or partial defence and/or counterclaim (*Part 20*)	p 410
2	Make an admission of all or part of the claim	p 411
3	Acknowledge service (delaying the time for service of a defence)	p 413
4	Dispute the court's jurisdiction	p 413
5	Strike out a statement of case (may also be made with 8 below)	p 380
6	Transfer the claim to a different court	p 402 / p 413
7	Join a third party to the claim or make an additional claim (*Part 20*)	p 418-419
8	Seek summary judgment	p 420
9	Set aside a default judgment	p 421
10	Find out further information about the claim	p 422
11	Seek security for costs	p 428
12	Seek a consent order	p 424
13	Seek an interim remedy of the type listed on p 425	p 425

> Including:
>
> ♦ an interim injunction
>
> ♦ an interim declaration
>
> ♦ an order for the detention, custody or preservation of property or inspection or taking of a sample or carrying out of an experiment on or with property, *and* authorising a person to enter land in the possession of a party to carry out that order.
>
> ♦ a 'freezing injunction
>
> ♦ a 'search order'.
>
> ♦ an order for disclosure of documents or inspection of property
>
> ♦ an order for an interim payment made under *r 25.6* (see p 427).

14	Make (or accept on a counterclaim) a *Part 36* offer or payment or other type of settlement	pp 429-433
15	Require the claimant to admit facts or part of the case	p 450
16	Require the claimant to prove the authenticity of a document	p 450

Claiming additional liability if legally funded (*Costs PD: 19*)

Note: A party who will claim an additional liability under a funding arrangement must give other parties information about this (eg: in the defence, acknowledgement etc.), but there is no need to specify the amount of additional liability separately nor to state how it is calculated until it is assessed.

I Defence and counterclaim

A The defence

Times for filing/serving are set out on p 377

➤ A defence is the statement of case setting out the defence to the claimant's particulars of claim.

➤ **Dealing with the claimant's allegations:** In his defence, the defendant must state (*r 16.5(1)-(5)*):

♦ which allegations he admits, *and*

♦ which allegations he is unable to admit or deny, but which he requires the claimant to prove, *and*

♦ which of the allegations in the particulars of claim he denies.

• He must state his reasons for denying any allegation, *and*

• if he is putting forward a different version of events, he must state his own version.

➤ **Failing to deal with an allegation:** If the defendant is silent as to an allegation (*r 16.5(1)-(5)*):

a) if the claim includes a money claim, it is deemed that he requires any allegation relating to the amount of money claimed be proved by the claimant *unless* the defendant expressly admits the allegation.

b) if he has set out in his defence *the nature of his case in relation to the issue to which that allegation is relevant*, it is counted as if he requires that allegation to be proved.

See p 380 Ground 1 for consequences of a bare denial

c) if a and b above do not apply, it is counted *as if admits that allegation*.

➤ **Disputing the statement of value in the statement of claim:** the defendant must state why he disputes it *and* (if he can), give his own statement of the value of the claim (*r 16.5(6)*).

➤ **Representative capacity** (*r 16.5(7)*): if a defendant acts in a representative capacity, he must state what it is.

➤ **Address for service** (*r 16.5(8)*): the defendant must give an address for service *unless* he has filed an acknowledgment of service under *Part 10* (see p 413).

➤ **Statement of truth:** the defence must be verified by a statement of truth (see p 388) (*PD16: 11, Part 22*).

♦ The wording is: '[I believe][the defendant believes] that the facts stated in the defence are true.'

➤ **A defence of set-off** (*r 16.6*): where a defendant contends he is entitled to money from the claimant *and* relies on this as a defence to the whole or part of the claim, the contention may be included in the defence and set off against the claim, whether or not it is also an additional claim under *Part 20* (see pp 418-419).

Compulsory matters to insert in the defence (*PD16: 12, 13.1*)

The defendant must set out specifically the following matters where he wishes to rely on them in support of his claim:

♦ Limitation defence: the defendant must give details of the expiry of any relevant limitation period he has relied on

♦ Personal injuries claim:
• where claimant attached a medical report about his alleged injuries, defendant should:
  a) state in the defence whether, concerning the matters in the medical report, he:
    ▪ agrees with those matters, *or*
    ▪ disputes those matters (giving his reasons), *or*
    ▪ neither agrees nor disputes but has no knowledge of those matters, *and*
  b) if he has obtained his own medical report on which he intends to rely, attach his own medical report to his defence.
• where claimant included a schedule of past and future expenses and losses, defendant should include in, or attach to, his defence a counter-schedule stating which items he:
  ▪ agrees, *or*
  ▪ disputes (supplying alternative figures where appropriate), *or*
  ▪ neither agrees nor disputes but has no knowledge of

B The counterclaim

➤ Where a defendant serves a counterclaim (ie: an additional claim - see pp 418-419), the defence and counterclaim should normally form one document with counterclaim following on from the defence.

II   Admissions

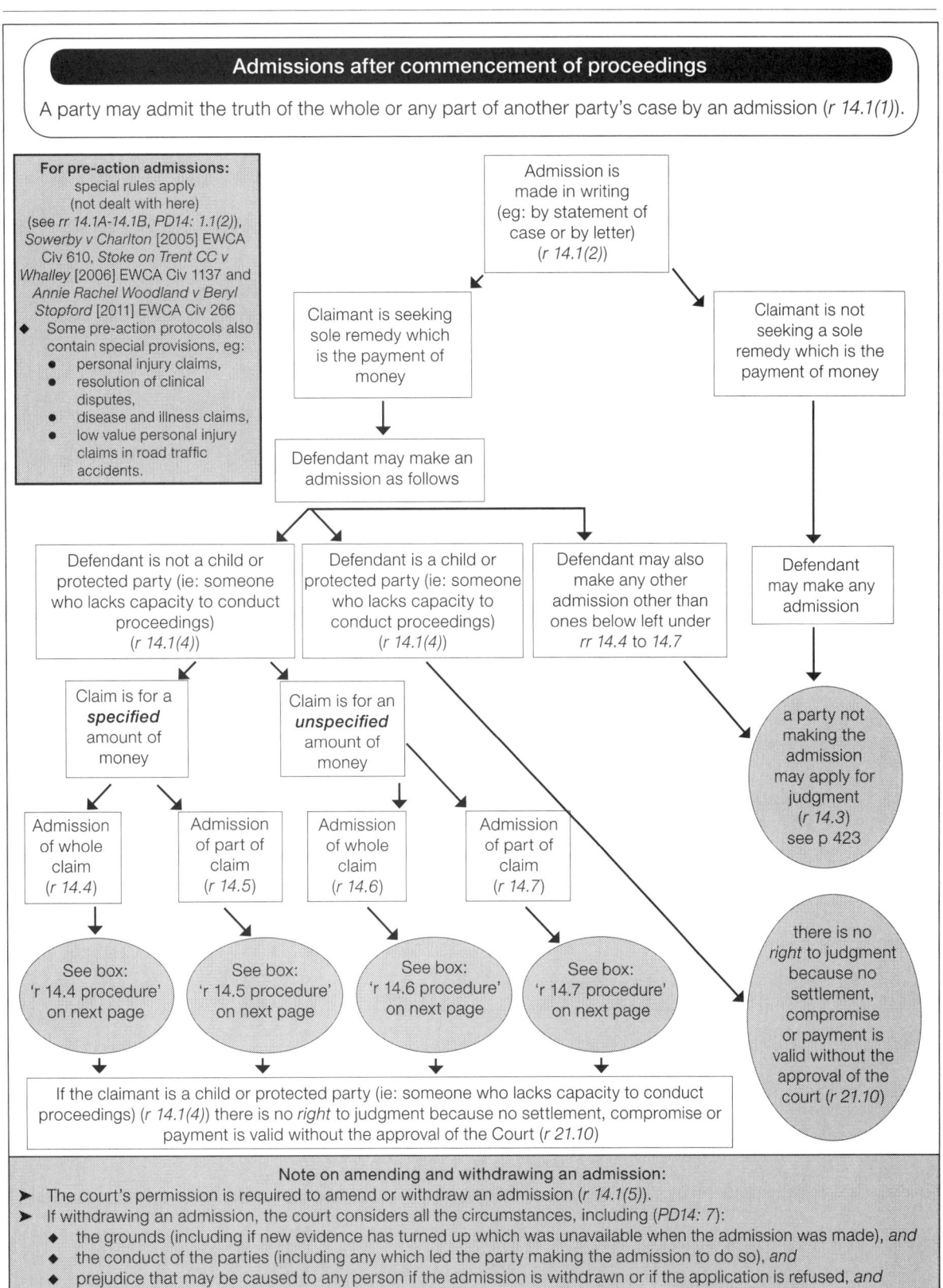

Admissions after commencement of proceedings

A party may admit the truth of the whole or any part of another party's case by an admission (r 14.1(1)).

For pre-action admissions: special rules apply (not dealt with here) (see rr 14.1A-14.1B, PD14: 1.1(2)), *Sowerby v Charlton* [2005] EWCA Civ 610, *Stoke on Trent CC v Whalley* [2006] EWCA Civ 1137 and *Annie Rachel Woodland v Beryl Stopford* [2011] EWCA Civ 266
- ◆ Some pre-action protocols also contain special provisions, eg:
  - ● personal injury claims,
  - ● resolution of clinical disputes,
  - ● disease and illness claims,
  - ● low value personal injury claims in road traffic accidents.

Admission is made in writing (eg: by statement of case or by letter) (r 14.1(2))

Claimant is seeking sole remedy which is the payment of money

Claimant is not seeking a sole remedy which is the payment of money

Defendant may make an admission as follows

Defendant is not a child or protected party (ie: someone who lacks capacity to conduct proceedings) (r 14.1(4))

Defendant is a child or protected party (ie: someone who lacks capacity to conduct proceedings) (r 14.1(4))

Defendant may also make any other admission other than ones below left under rr 14.4 to 14.7

Defendant may make any admission

Claim is for a **specified** amount of money

Claim is for an **unspecified** amount of money

Admission of whole claim (r 14.4)

Admission of part of claim (r 14.5)

Admission of whole claim (r 14.6)

Admission of part of claim (r 14.7)

a party not making the admission may apply for judgment (r 14.3) see p 423

See box: 'r 14.4 procedure' on next page

See box: 'r 14.5 procedure' on next page

See box: 'r 14.6 procedure' on next page

See box: 'r 14.7 procedure' on next page

there is no *right* to judgment because no settlement, compromise or payment is valid without the approval of the court (r 21.10)

If the claimant is a child or protected party (ie: someone who lacks capacity to conduct proceedings) (r 14.1(4)) there is no *right* to judgment because no settlement, compromise or payment is valid without the approval of the Court (r 21.10)

Note on amending and withdrawing an admission:
- ➤ The court's permission is required to amend or withdraw an admission (r 14.1(5)).
- ➤ If withdrawing an admission, the court considers all the circumstances, including (PD14: 7):
  - ◆ the grounds (including if new evidence has turned up which was unavailable when the admission was made), *and*
  - ◆ the conduct of the parties (including any which led the party making the admission to do so), *and*
  - ◆ prejudice that may be caused to any person if the admission is withdrawn or if the application is refused, *and*
  - ◆ when the application to withdraw is made, in particular relating to the date/period fixed for trial, *and*
  - ◆ prospects of success (if the admission is withdrawn) of the claim in relation to which the offer was made, *and*
  - ◆ the interests of the administration of justice.

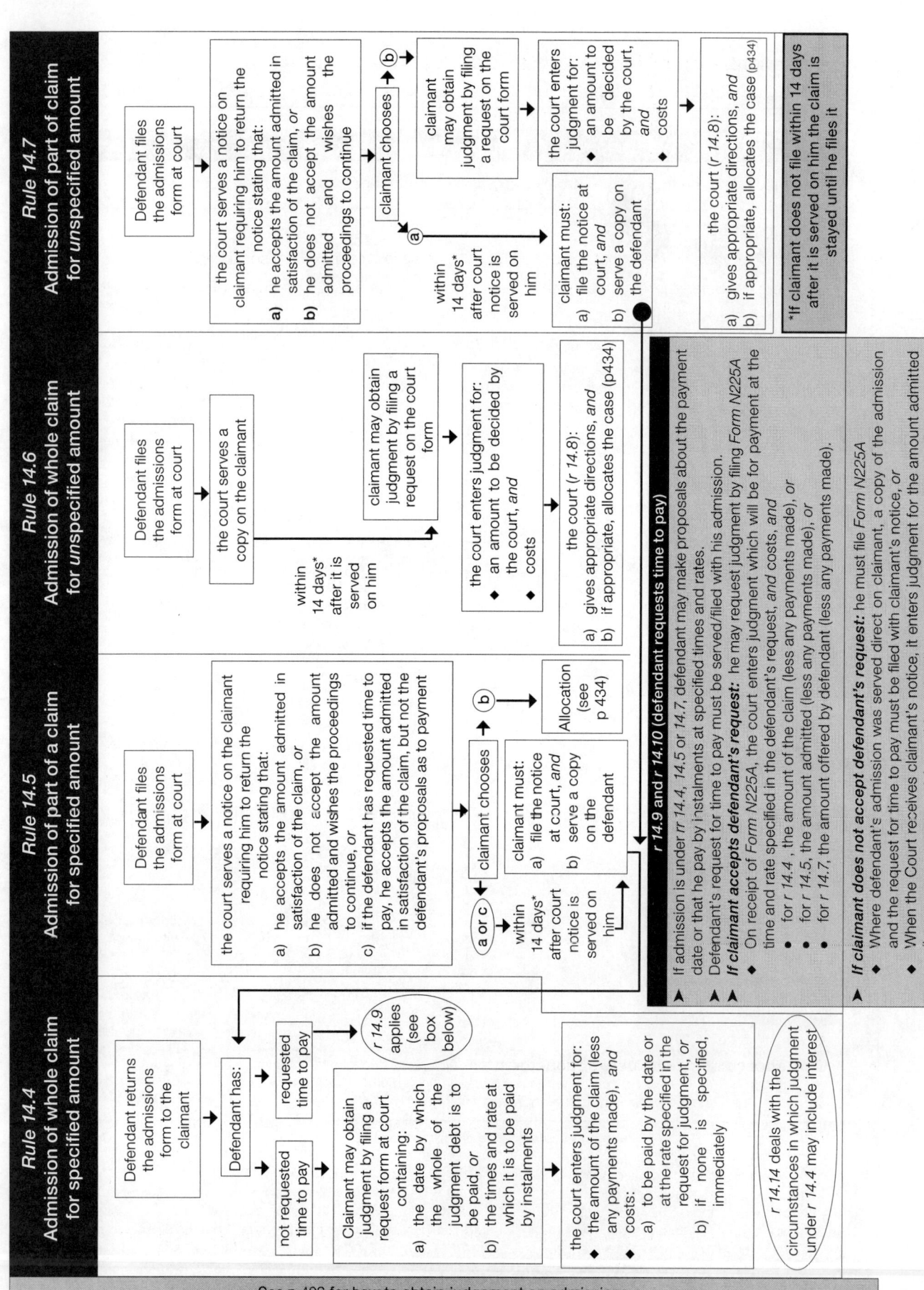

III   Acknowledgement of service (*Part 10, PD:10*)

➤ A defendant must file an acknowledgment of service (*Form N9*) if:

◆ he is unable to file a defence within the period specified (see p 377 and below), *or*

◆ he wishes to dispute the court's jurisdiction (see below).

    Note: A defendant who files an acknowledgment of service does not, by doing so, lose any right that he may have to dispute the court's jurisdiction (see below) (*r 11(3)*).

➤ **Period:** The general rule is that the period for filing an acknowledgment of service is:

◆ where the defendant is served with a claim form which states that particulars of claim are to follow, 14 days after service of the particulars of claim, *and*

◆ in any other case, 14 days after service of the claim form.

➤ The claimant may obtain default judgment (see p 421) if:

◆ a defendant fails to file an acknowledgment of service within the period specified above, *and*

◆ does not within that period file a defence (see p 410) or serve or file an admission (see pp 411-412).

➤ On receipt of an acknowledgment of service, the court must notify the claimant in writing.

➤ An acknowledgment of service must be signed by the defendant or his solicitor and include the defendant's address for service, or if represented by a solicitor, his solicitor's address.

IV   Disputing the court's jurisdiction (*Part 11*)

➤ A defendant may apply to the court for an order declaring that the court has no such jurisdiction or should not exercise any jurisdiction which it may have, if he:

◆ disputes the court's jurisdiction to try the claim, *or*

◆ argues that the court should not exercise its jurisdiction.

➤ A defendant making such an application *must* first file an acknowledgment of service (see above).

➤ **Period:** An application must be made within 14 days after filing an acknowledgment of service (and must be supported by evidence).

◆ The defendant accepts that the court has jurisdiction to try the claim if he:

    ● files an acknowledgment of service, *and*

    ● does not make such an application within 14 days after filing an acknowledgment of service.

➤ **Court makes a declaration:** that it has no jurisdiction/will not exercise its jurisdiction and may also:

◆ set aside the claim form, *and/or*

◆ set aside service of the claim form, *and/or*

◆ discharge any order made before the claim was commenced or served, *and/or*

◆ stay the proceedings.

➤ **Court does not make a declaration, then:**

◆ the acknowledgment of service ceases to have effect, *and*

◆ the defendant may file a further acknowledgment of service within 14 days or such other period as the court may direct, *and*

    ● If the defendant does file a further acknowledgment of service, he is treated as having accepted that the court has jurisdiction to try the claim.

◆ the court must give directions for filing and service of the defence in a *Part 7* claim (or filing of evidence in a *Part 8* claim) if a further acknowledgment of service is filed.

Note: Where a defendant disputes the court's jurisdiction he must file written evidence but he need not in a *Part 7* claim file a defence before the application hearing (or in a *Part 8* claim file any other written evidence).

E   Claimant's options

1	Obtain judgment after the defendant admits all or part of the claim	p 423
2	Reply to a counterclaim made by the defendant	p 414
3	Strike out a statement of case (may also be made with 6 below)	p 380
4	Transfer the claim to a different court	p 402
5	Join a third party to the claim or make an additional claim (*Part 20*)	p 418-p 419
6	Seek summary judgment	p 420
7	Seek a default judgment	p 421
8	Find out further information about a defendant's case	p 422
9	Seek a consent order	p 424
10	Seek an interim remedy of the type listed on pp 425-428	p 425

> Including:
> - an interim injunction
> - an interim declaration
> - an order for the detention, custody or preservation of property or inspection or taking of a sample or carrying out of an experiment on or with property, *and* authorising a person to enter land in a party's possession to carry out the order.
> - a 'freezing injunction'
> - a 'search order'
> - an order for disclosure of documents or inspection of property
> - an order for an interim payment made under *r 25.6* (see p 427).

11	Accept (or make on a counterclaim) a *Part 36* offer/payment/other settlement	pp 429-433
12	Seek a discontinuance of the action	p 423
13	Require the defendant to admit facts or part of the case	p 450
14	Require the defendant to prove the authenticity of a document	p 450

Claiming additional liability if legally funded (*Costs PD: 19*)

Note: A party who will claim an additional liability under a funding arrangement must give other parties information about this (eg: in the claim form etc.), but there is no need to specify the amount of additional liability separately nor to state how it is calculated until it is assessed.

Reply and defence to counterclaim (*r 15.8, r 16.7, PD15: 3.2A*)

➤ If a claimant files a reply to the defence, he must (*r 15.8*):

- file his reply when he files his allocation questionnaire, *and*
- serve his reply on the other parties at the same time as he files it.

➤ A statement of truth is required (see p 388).

➤ A claimant filing a reply to a defence who fails to deal with a matter raised in the defence, is taken to require that matter to be proved (*r 16.7*).

> If the allocation questionnaire filing date is later than the defence to counterclaim filing date, the court normally orders the defence to counterclaim to be filed by the same date as the reply. If the court does not order this, the reply and defence to counterclaim may form separate documents

➤ A claimant who does not file a reply to the defence is not taken to admit matters raised in it (*r 16.7*).

F   Applications for court orders (*Part 23*)

I	Generally	IV	Consent orders
II	Making an application	V	Declaratory judgments
III	The applications		

I   Generally

> ➤   An 'application notice' is a document in which an applicant states his intention to seek a court order (*r 23.1*).
>
> ➤   An applicant must file an application notice *unless*:
>
> a)   a rule or *PD* permit otherwise, *or*
>
> b)   the court dispenses with the requirement for an application notice (*r 23.3*).

➤   An application should be made as soon as it is apparent that it is necessary or desirable (*PD23A: 2.7*).

➤   Whenever possible, an application should be made so that it can be considered at any other hearing (eg: case management conference, allocation or listing hearing) for which a date has already been fixed or is about to be fixed (*PD23A: 2.8*).

    ◆   If a date for a hearing has been fixed and a party does not have sufficient time to serve an application notice, he must inform the other parties and the court (in writing) as soon as possible of the nature of the application and the reason for it (*PD23A: 2.10*) (unless circumstances require secrecy (*PD23A: 4.2*)).

       ●   The party wishing to make the application should make the application orally at the hearing.

    ◆   At the hearing, the court may wish to review the conduct of the case and give any necessary case management directions (*PD23A: 2.9*).

       ●   The parties must be ready to assist the court and answer questions the court asks for this purpose.

II   Making an application

A   Which court?

Which court?

➤   An application must be made to the court in which the claim was started (*r 23.2*) unless:

◆ a claim has not been started ⟶	... the court in which the claim is most likely to be started (except when there is good reason otherwise)
◆ the claim has been transferred to another court ⟶	... the court to which the claim has been transferred
◆ the parties have been notified of a fixed date for trial ⟶	... the court where the trial is to take place
◆ proceedings to enforce judgement have begun ⟶	... any court which is dealing with the enforcement of the judgement (unless a practice direction provides otherwise)

B The application notice: contents, form and procedure

	Application notice: contents, form and procedure
Contents and Form	➤ An application notice must state the order an applicant seeks and (briefly) why the applicant seeks the order (*r 23.6*). ➤ An application notice must be signed and include (*PD23A: 2.1*): ◆ the title of the claim, *and* ◆ the reference number of the claim, *and* ◆ the full name of the applicant, *and* ◆ where the applicant is not already a party, the address for service, *and* ◆ a request for a hearing or a request that the application be dealt with without a hearing. ➤ An application notice must be verified by a statement of truth (*Part 22*) if the applicant wishes to rely on matters set out in the application as evidence.
Procedure	**Steps** **1** The applicant files the application notice at court. **2** A copy of the application notice must be served on each respondent (unless a rule, *PD* or court order provide otherwise) (*r 23.4*). A copy an application notice must be served as soon as practicable after the notice is filed and (unless a rule or *PD* specify otherwise) must be served at least 3 days before the court is to deal with the application (*r 23.7(1)*). ◆ If an application notice is served and the period of notice is shorter, the court may direct that sufficient notice has been given (*r 23.7(4)*). ◆ The application notice must be served as soon as practicable after it has been issued and, if there is to be a hearing, at least 3 days before the hearing date - unless the court otherwise directs or unless the application is to be made without notice or unless there is to be a telephone hearing, (*PD23A: 4.1*). ◆ Where there is to be a telephone hearing the application notice must be served as soon as practicable after issue and in any event at least 5 days before the hearing date (*PD23A: 4.1A*). ◆ Where an application notice should be served but there is not sufficient time to do so, informal notification of the application should be given unless the circumstances of the application require secrecy (*PD23A: 4.2*). **3a** **Hearing requested:** on receipt of the application notice the court notifies the applicant of the time and the date for the hearing (*PD23A: 2.1*). **3b** **Request for no-hearing:** as the Master or District Judge determines, the court *either:* ◆ if the application **is suitable** for consideration without a hearing, informs the applicant and the respondent and gives directions for the filing of evidence, *or* ◆ if the application **is not suitable** for consideration without a hearing, notifies the applicant and the respondent of the time and date for the hearing and may give directions as to the filing of evidence (*PD23A: 2.3-2.5*). > ● The court may deal with the application without a hearing if *either* (*r 23.8*): > ■ the parties agree to the terms of the order sought, *or* > ■ the parties agree that the court dispose of the application without a hearing, *or* > NB:the parties should inform the court in writing and each party should confirm that all evidence and other material on which that party relies has been disclosed to the other parties to the application (*PD23A: 11.1*). > ■ the court does not consider that a hearing would be appropriate. ➤ If the court is to serve a copy of the application notice, the applicant must file a copy of any written evidence in support when he files the notice itself (*r 23.2(7)*). ➤ An application notice must be served with: ◆ a copy of any written evidence in support (unless that evidence has already been filed or served on the respondent) (*r 23.7(5)*), *and* ◆ a copy of any draft order which the applicant has attached to the application, *and* ◆ a statement of costs as soon as possible and, in any event, at least 24 hours before any interim hearing (*Costs PD: 13.5(4)*). ➤ Costs of interim hearings are routinely assessed at the conclusion of the hearing by summary assessment, see p 465.

Applications totally without merit (*r 23.12, r 3.11, PD3C*)

➤ If the court dismisses an application and it considers that the application is totally without merit, the court order must record that and the court must consider whether it is appropriate to make a civil restraint order (see p 381).

C Applications made without service of an application notice

➤ A court may dispose of an application without notice only (*PD23A: 3*):

- ◆ where there is exceptional urgency, *or*

- ◆ where the overriding objective is best furthered by doing so, *or*

- ◆ by consent of all the parties, *or*

- ◆ with the court's permission, *or*

- ◆ where a hearing date has been fixed and there is not sufficient time to serve a notice (*PD23A: 2.10*), *or*

- ◆ where a court order, rule, or *PD* permits.

➤ If the court makes an order (granting or dismissing the application) a copy of the application notice and any evidence in support must be served ...

...on any party or person against whom the order was made and against whom the order was sought ...

...*unless* the court orders otherwise (*r 23.9(2)*).

➤ An order granted with respect to an application made without notice must contain a statement of the right to have the order set aside or varied (*r 23.9(3)*).

➤ A person who was not served with a copy of an application notice may apply to have the order set aside or varied (*r 23.10(1)*).

- ◆ This application to set aside or vary must be made within 7 days after the date on which the order was served on the person who wishes to make that application for set aside/variation (*r 23.10(2)*).

Telephone hearings (*PD23A: 6.1, 6.1A, 6.2-6.5*)

➤ At a telephone conference-enabled county court or district registry of the High Court, allocation hearings, listing hearings, interim applications, case management conferences, pre-trial reviews with a time estimate of no more than 1 hour, all must be conducted by telephone unless the court orders otherwise.
- ◆ This not apply where:
  - • the hearing is of an application made without notice to the other party, *or*
  - • all the parties are unrepresented, *or*
  - • more than 4 parties wish to make representations at the hearing (for this purpose where 2 or more parties are represented by the same person, they are to be treated as 1 party), *or*.
  - • there is a request for a direction that a hearing should not be conducted by telephone (which must be made: i) at least 7 days before the hearing or a shorter time the court permits, *or* ii) by letter).
    - ■ The applicant should indicate on his application notice if he seeks such a court order. Where he has not but nevertheless wishes to seek an order, the request should be made as early as possible.
➤ No party or representative of a party may attend the judge in person without the other party's agreement.
➤ If a telephone application is sought, the application notice should indicate this. If it does not indicate this, a request for a telephone hearing should be made as early as possible.
➤ The following directions will apply to telephone hearings, subject to any direction to the contrary:
- ◆ The applicant's legal representative must arrange the telephone conference for the precise time fixed by the court (giving the operator the telephone numbers of all those participating and the sequence in which they are to be called). The telecom provider must be on an approved court list.
- ◆ The sequence in which the participant's are to be called is:
  a) the applicant's legal representative and (if on a different number) his counsel, *then*
  b) the legal representative (and counsel) of all the other parties, *then*
  c) the judge.
- ◆ Each speaker must remain on the line after being called by the operator. The call must be connected at least 10 minutes before the time fixed for the hearing.
- ◆ When the judge has been connected the designated legal representative (or his counsel) (usually the applicant's legal representative) introduces the parties in the usual way.
- ◆ The judge may require a party to stop using a speakerphone if it causes anyone to have difficulty in hearing.
- ◆ The telephone charges of the party initiating the call are treated as part of the costs of the application.
➤ The designated legal representative must file and serve a case summary and draft order no later than 4pm on the last working day before the hearing on the multi-track (and in any other case, if the court so directs).
➤ Where a party seeks to rely on any other document at the hearing, he must file and serve the document no later than 4 pm on the last working day before the hearing.

III   The applications

A   Making an additional claim (including a counterclaim) (*Part 20*)

Purpose: Additional claims are made under *Part 20*. It applies to (*r 20.2*):

◆ a **counterclaim** by a defendant against the claimant or against the claimant and some other person, *and/or*

◆ an **additional claim** by a defendant against any person (whether or not already a party) for contribution or indemnity or some other remedy, *and/or*

◆ where an additional claim has been made against a person who is not already a party, any additional claim made by that person against any other person (whether or not already a party).

	Counterclaims		Contribution/Indemnity against a party (*r 20.6*)	Other (*r 20.7*)
	Against claimant (*r 20.4*)	Other (*r 20.5*)		
Procedure for making an additional claim	Defendant files particulars of the counterclaim. If the counterclaim is filed with the defence, court's permission is not needed. If the counterclaim is not filed with defence, the court's permission is needed	Defendant applies to court for an order that the person be added as an additional party. The application is without notice (unless the court orders otherwise). When making the order, the court will give case management directions	A defendant who has filed an acknowledgement of service or defence, files a notice containing a statement of the nature and grounds of his additional claim for contribution/ indemnity and serves it on the party. The court's permission is needed unless he files and serves it with his defence or, if his claim is against a party added to the claim later, within 28 days after that party files his defence.	A defendant does not need the court's permission to make an additional claim if that claim is issued before or at the same time as he files his defence (otherwise the court's permission is needed). An additional claim is made when the court issues the appropriate claim form. Particulars of an additional claim must be contained in or served with the claim form
Application for the court's permission to issue a counterclaim or other additional claim	➤ An application must be supported by evidence stating (*PD20: 2*): ◆ the stage which the action has reached (including, where possible, a timetable of the action to date; if delay is a factor in the application, an explanation should be given), *and* ◆ the nature of the additional claim or details of the question/issue which needs to be decided, *and* ◆ a summary of the facts on which the additional claim is based, *and* ◆ the name and address of any proposed additional party.			
	Counterclaims against an existing party only (*r 20.8(1)(a)*)	Contribution/Indemnity (*r 20.8(2)*)		Other (*r 20.8(1)(b)*)
	On every other party when a copy of the defence is served	Not applicable		On the person against whom it is made within 14 days after the date on which the additional claim is issued by the court
Service of an additional claim (*r 20.8*)	➤ If the additional claim form is served on a non-party it must be accompanied by (*r 20.12(1)*): ◆ a form for defending the claim, *and* ◆ a form for admitting the claim, *and* ◆ a form for acknowledging service, *and* ◆ a copy of every statement of case which has been served in the proceedings and such other documents as the court may direct. ➤ A person who is not already a party to the proceedings on whom an additional claim is served becomes a party on service of the additional claim (*r 20.10(1)*). ➤ A copy of the additional claim form must be served on every existing party (*r 20.12(2)*).			

(A continued...) Making an additional claim (including a counterclaim (*Part 20*)

Should an additional claim be a separate claim?	➤ When considering whether to permit an additional claim to be made, to dismiss an additional claim or to require an additional claim to be dealt with separately, the court may have regard to (*r 20.9(1)-(2)*): ◆ the connections between the additional claim and the claim made by the claimant against the defendant, *and* ◆ whether the additional claimant seeks substantially the same remedy as some other party seeks from him, *and* ◆ whether the additional claimant wants the court to decide any question connected with the subject matter of proceedings: i) between existing parties, but also between existing parties and a person not already a party, *or* ii) against an existing party in a different capacity to that in which that existing party is already a party to the proceedings.
General application of *CPRs*	➤ The *CPRs* generally apply to additional claims as to any other claim, *except* that (*r 20.3*):

All claims	For counterclaims
◆ the general rules applicable to time limits for serving a claim form (see p 377) do not apply (see p 418 for the rules which do apply)(*r 20.3(2)*). ◆ the claim need not include a statement of value (which would otherwise be needed under *r 16.3(5)*) to commence a claim in the High Court, see p 406) (*r 20.3(2)*). ◆ The preliminary stage of case management, at allocation (see p 434), does not apply (*r 20.3(2)*).	◆ *Part 14* (Admissions) applies (see pp 411-412) (*r 20.3(4)*). ◆ *Part 12* (Default judgment) applies (see p 421) (*r 20.3(3)*).
	Additional claims other than counterclaims
	◆ *rr 14.3-14.14* (Admissions - see pp 411-412) do not apply (*r 20.3(4)*). ◆ *Part 12* (Default judgment - see p 421) does not apply (*r 20.3(3)*).

> ➤ If the additional claim is not a counterclaim or claim for contribution/indemnity, and the party against whom the additional claim is made fails to file an acknowledgment of service or defence in respect of the additional claim then (*r 20.11*):
>
> a) the party against whom the additional claim is made is deemed to admit the additional claim and is bound by any judgment in the main proceedings so far as that judgment is relevant to any matter arising in the additional claim, *and*
>
> b) if default judgment is given against the additional claimant, the additional claimant may obtain judgment in respect of the additional claim by filing a request in the relevant practice form.
>
> NB: The court's permission is needed to enter judgment under 'b' if the additional claimant has not satisfied the default judgment against him *or* wishes to obtain judgment for any remedy other than a contribution or indemnity (*r 20.11(3)*).
>
> ◆ An application for the court's permission may be made without notice, unless the court directs otherwise (*r 20.11(4)*).
>
> ◆ A court may at any time set aside or vary a judgment under 'b'.

Case management (*r 20.13, PD20: 5*)	➤ Where a defence to an additional claim is filed, the court considers the conduct of the case and gives appropriate directions (*r 20.13(1)*). ◆ Where the defendant to an additional claim files a defence (other than to a counterclaim), the court arranges a hearing to consider case management of the additional claim. This will normally be at the same time as a case management hearing for the original claim and any other additional claims. The court arranges a hearing and gives notice of the hearing to each party likely to be affected by any order made at the hearing (*PD20: 5.1-5.2*). ➤ At the hearing, the court may (*PD20: 5.3*): ◆ treat the hearing as a summary judgment hearing. ◆ order the dismissal of the additional claim. ◆ give directions as to how a claim or issue set out in or arising from the additional claim should be dealt with. ◆ give directions as to the extent to which the additional defendant will take part in the trial of the claim and will be bound by any judgment or decision in the action. ◆ When giving directions, the court must ensure as far as practicable the claims are managed together (*r 20.13(2)*).

B Summary judgment (Part 24)

Purpose: the claimant or defendant seeks judgment quickly and cheaply without the expense and delay of a trial

Grounds (r 24.2)	A **claimant** has no real prospect of succeeding on the claim or an issue A **defendant** has no real prospect of successfully defending the claim or issue	+	There is no other compelling reason why the cause or issue should be disposed of at trial

Procedure (r 24.4)

➤ A claimant may not apply until the defendant has filed an acknowledgement of service or a defence *unless* the court gives permission or a *PD* provides otherwise (eg: the claimant seeks an order for specific performance (PD24: 7.1(b))).

➤ An application must (*PD24:2(3)*):

a) identify concisely any point of law or provision in a document on which the applicant relies, *and/or* b) state that it is made because the applicant believes that on the evidence the respondent has no real prospect of succeeding on the claim or issues, or of successfully defending the claim or issue	+	The applicant knows of no other reason why the disposal of the claim or issue should await trial

  • If the application relies on written evidence but does not contain that written evidence, the application should identify that evidence (PD24: 2(4)).

  • The application should draw the respondent's attention to r.24.5(1) governing evidence (PD24: 2(4)).

➤ If a claimant applies before a defence has been filed, the defendant need not file a defence before the hearing.

➤ The parties will have at least 14 days notice of the date fixed for the hearing and the issues which it is proposed that the court will decide.

> Where the claimant has failed to comply with *Practice Direction (Pre-Action Conduct)* (see p 373) or any relevant pre-action protocol, an action for summary judgment will not normally be entertained before the defence has been filed or, alternatively, the time for doing so has expired (*PD24:2(6)*).

Evidence (r 24.5)

Hearing fixed as a result of an application by a party		Hearing fixed by the court of its own volition	
Respondent (r 24.5(1))	Applicant (r 24.5(2))	Any party (r 24.5(3)(a))	Any party in reply (r 24.5(3)(b))
At least 7* days before the hearing file written evidence and serve copies on the other parties to the application ...	At least 3 days before the hearing file written evidence and serve copies on the respondent ...	At least 7* days (unless the court orders otherwise) before the hearing file written evidence and serve copies on the other parties to the application ...	At least 3 days (unless the court orders otherwise) before the hearing file written evidence and serve copies on the respondent ...

... unless evidence has already been filed or served on the appropriate party (r 24.5(4))

* 4 days before the hearing if an order for specific performance is sought (PD24: 7.3).

Possible orders (r 24.6)

➤ The orders which the court (usually a Master or a District Judge) may make include (PD24: 3(1), 5.1):

a) judgment on the claim.

b) striking out or dismissal of the claim.

c) dismissal of the application.

d) a conditional order.

  • Eg: an order requiring a party to pay money into court or take a specified step *and* providing for that party's claim to be dismissed or statement of claim struck out if he does not comply (PD 24: 5.2).

  • Made if it appears possible but improbable that a claim/defence will succeed (PD 24: 4).

➤ If the application is not dismissed or an order is not made disposing of the claim, the court will give case management directions (PD24: 10).

Summary judgment is **not** available against a defendant in proceedings (r 24.3):
   ◆ for possession of residential premises against a tenant, or mortgagor or a person holding over after the tenancy ends, *or*
   ◆ for an admiralty claim *in rem*.

C Default judgment (Parts 12 and 13)

Purpose:	The claimant wants to obtain judgment when the defendant (*rr 12.1-12.2*):

a) has failed to file an acknowledgement of service, *or*

b) has failed to file a defence ...

but not for a claim under *CCA 1974*, under the *Part 8* procedure, *or* where a rule or *PD* provides that a claimant may not obtain default judgment (eg: *PD12: 1.2-1.3*) *or* for non-counterclaim additional claims (*r 20.3(3)*).

Grounds	➤ The claim has been properly served and (*r 12.3(1)-(2)*): a) the defendant has not filed an acknowledgment of service or a defence and the time limit has expired, *or* ◆ A certificate of service on the court file is sufficient evidence that particulars of claim have been served on the defendant (*PD12: 4.1*) b) an acknowledgment of service has been filed but a defence has not been filed and the time limit has expired, *or* c) in a counterclaim made under *r 20.4* (see p 418) a defence has not been filed and the time limit has expired... *... provided that* it is not the case that (*r 12.3(3)*): ◆ the defendant has applied for summary judgment and that application has not been disposed of, *or* ◆ the defendant has applied to have the claimant's statement of claim struck out under *r 3.4* (see p 380), and that application has not been disposed of, *or* ◆ the defendant has satisfied the whole claim (including costs), *or* ◆ it is a money claim and the defendant has filed or served on the claimant an admission of liability to pay all the money claimed with a request for time to pay.	Where the claimant has served the claim form, the claimant may not obtain default judgment unless a certificate of service has been filed (see p 394) (*r 6.17(2)*).

Procedure	➤ The claimant **files a request** on the relevant practice form if the claim is for (*r 12.4(1)*): a) a specified amount of money, *and/or* b) an amount of money to be decided by the court, *and/or* *The **request** may specify the date by which the debt is to be paid, or the time/rate for instalments (r 12.5(1)) and interest (r 12.6(1))* c) delivery of goods (if the claim form gives the defendant the alternative of paying their value). ➤ The claimant **makes an application** under *Part 23* (see p 415) if the claim (*r 12.4(2)*): ◆ includes a claim for any remedy other than those set out in a) to c) above, *or* ◆ the claimant seeks a judgment for costs (which are not fixed costs - see p 464) only (*r 12.9*), *or* ◆ is against a child, a protected party (ie: someone who lacks capacity to conduct proceedings), a claim in tort by one spouse/civil partner against the other (*r 12.10(a)*), *or* ◆ is against a defendant who has not filed an acknowledgment of service *and* is a State, diplomat, immune under the *IOA 1968* or *IOA 1981*, or has been served out of the jurisdiction (where permission of the court is not required), *or* is domiciled in Scotland, Northern Ireland or a territory to which the Brussels or Lugano Conventions apply *or* is a Member State of the EU (except Denmark) (*r 12.10(b)*). NB: If the defendant is an individual, the claimant must provide the defendant's date of birth (if known) in Part C of the application notice (*r 12.4(2)*).

Judgment (on a request)	➤ If a claim is for a specified sum of money, the judgment is for the amount of the claim (less any payments made) and costs (*r 12.5(2)*): a) to be paid by the date or at the rate specified in the request, *or* b) if no date/rate are specified, immediately. ➤ If a claim is for an unspecified amount of money, judgment is for an amount to be decided by the court and costs (*r 12.5(3)*). ➤ If a claim is for the delivery of goods the judgment requires the defendant to deliver the goods (or if he does not) to pay the amount decided by the court and costs (*r 12.5(4)*). ◆ If judgment is for an amount decided by the court, it gives directions and may allocate the case (*r 12.7*).

Setting aside a judgment in default

Grounds	➤ The court **must** set aside judgment if (*r 13.2*): a) any of the conditions for obtaining that judgment were not satisfied, *or* b) the whole of the claim was satisfied before judgment was entered. ➤ The court **may** set aside judgment if (*r 13.3*): a) the defendant has a real prospect of successfully defending the claim, *or* b) there is some other good reason why the judgment should be set aside or varied or the defendant should be allowed to defend the claim.

D   Further information *(Part 18)*

Purpose: to clarify any matter which is in dispute in proceedings or provide additional information with regard to such a matter - even if the matter is not contained in or referred to in the statement of case

Format of request	➤ A written request specifying the clarification or information sought, stating the time by which a response must be served (the time for response must be 'reasonable' *(PD18: 1.1)*). ➤ The request: ◆ must be concise and strictly confined to matters 'reasonably necessary and proportionate' *(PD18: 1.2)*, *and* ◆ should take the form of a single comprehensive document, not be piecemeal *(PD18: 1.3)*, *and* ◆ should be a separate document *unless* it is brief *and* the reply is likely to be brief, in which case it may in the form of a letter *(PD 18:1.4)*, *and* ◆ should *(PD 18:1.6(a))*: • be headed with name of the court, the title and number of the claim, *and* • in the heading state it is a request under *Part 18*, identify both parties, use separate numbered paragraphs for each request, *and* • identify each document and the paragraph/words to which a request relates. ➤ If convenient, numbered paragraphs should appear on the left of the page so that a response may appear on the right (if the request is in this form any extra copy should be served for use by the respondent) *(PD18: 1.6(2))*. **Service of the Request** *(PD 18: 1.7)* ➤ Subject to the provisions as to use of email and fax (see p 396 and p 397), a Request should be served by email if reasonably practicable.
Format of reply	➤ In writing, dated, signed by the respondent or his legal representative *(PD18: 2.1)*. ➤ A point by point reply to the request. ➤ For each point, repeat the request verbatim and provide a reply (unless the format suggested in *PD18: 1.6(2)* is used (see above)). ➤ A response must be verified by a statement of truth *(PD18: 3)* (see p 388). ➤ The person making a reply must file it at court and serve it on the other parties. ➤ If a party objects to complying with a request or is unable to do so within the time stated in that request, that party must *(PD18: 4)*: ◆ promptly inform the party making the request, *and* ◆ give reasons (eg: disproportionate expense), *and* ◆ give a date by which he expects to be able to comply.
Court application	➤ An application under *Part 23* (see p 415), with *(PD18: 5)*: ◆ the text of the order sought, *and* ◆ a description of the response, if any ... *plus* ... ◆ costs if sought *(PD18: 5.8)*. ➤ If a party has not responded to a request served on him and at least 14 days have passed since the request was served and the time stated in it for a response has expired *(PD18: 5.5)*: ◆ the applicant need not serve a copy of the application notice on the party to whom the request was made, *and* ◆ the court may deal with the application without a hearing ... *otherwise* ... ... the application notice and any order made must be served on all other parties to the claim *(PD18: 5.6-5.7)*

	E Judgment on admissions
Purpose:	to reduce/avoid the expense of a trial by resolving agreed issues beforehand
Time	➤ If a claim form states that particulars of claim will follow, 14 days after the service of those particulars *otherwise* 14 days after service of the claim form (*r 14.2*) (see p 377).
Procedure	➤ A party gives written notice that it admits the whole or part of another party's case (*r 14.1(1)-(2)*). ➤ The claimant may enter judgment (*r 14.1(4)*) (see p 411-412). If the claim relates to a specified amount of money, or an unspecified amount of money (*rr 14.4-14.7*): **Steps** **1** The defendant files the relevant *Practice Form* with the court. **2** The court serves a notice on the claimant, requiring him to return the notice. **3** Within 14 days the claimant must file the notice and serve a copy on the defendant (otherwise proceedings are stayed until the notice is filed). ➤ A defendant may request time to pay (*rr 14.9-14.13, PD 14: 5-6*). ◆ A claimant will not accept a defendant's proposals for payment must file a notice in set form. ◆ The court determines the time and rate of payment. • If the amount outstanding is less than £50,000 a court officer may make this determination (there is no hearing). • A judge may make this determination at a hearing. If a judge holds a hearing: ▪ the court gives each party at least 7 days' notice of the hearing, *and* ▪ where the claim was not started at the defendant's home court or subsequently transferred there, it will transferred there if: a) the claim is for a specified amount of money, *and* b) the defendant is an individual, *and* c) the claim was not started in a specialist list. • If a court officer makes the determination, or a judge does so without a hearing, either party may apply for a redetermination within 14 days of service of the determination on the applicant.

	F Discontinuance (*Part 38*)
	Purpose: Discontinuance halts the action.
	The defendant is entitled to costs (other than in respect of claims allocated to the small claims track) to the date notice of discontinuance is served on the defendant for the part of the proceedings that are discontinued (*r 38.6*) ◄───
Claimant's right to discontinue	➤ The claimant may discontinue without seeking leave. *But* if the court has granted an interim injunction or any party has given an undertaking to the court the claimant must obtain the court's permission (*r 38.2(2)(a)*). ➤ If the claimant has received an interim payment *either* the defendant must consent in writing *or* the court gives permission (*r 38.2(2)(b)*). ➤ If there is more than one claimant, *either* every other claimant must consent in writing *or* the court gives permission (*r 38.2(2)(c)*).
Claimant	a) File a notice of discontinuance (*r 38.3(1)(a)*): ◆ stating that a copy has been served on every other party (*r 38.3(2)*). ◆ (if the consent of another party is needed), attaching a copy of that consent (*r 38.3(3)*). ◆ (if there is more than 1 defendant), stating against which defendant the claim is discontinued (*r 38.3(4)*). b) Serve a copy of the notice on every party to the proceedings (*r 38.3(1)(b)*).
Defendant	➤ May apply to have a notice of discontinuance set aside (*r 38.4(1)*). ➤ An application may not be made more than 28 days after the date on which the notice was served on that defendant (*r 38.4(2)*).
Consequences	1) The permission of the court is need for the claimant to subsequently make a claim against the same defendant if (*r 38.7*): a) the claimant discontinued the claim after the defendant filed a defence, *and* b) the new claim arises out of facts which are the same, or substantially the same, as those out of which the original claim arose. 2) If proceedings are only partly discontinued *and* the claimant fails to pay costs under *r 38.6* (or to make a payment under *LSA 2007 s 194(3)* (payment to a prescribed charity in respect of pro bono representation) within 14 days of the date on which: i) the parties agreed the sum payable by the claimant, *or* ii) the court ordered the costs to be paid or the payment to be made, then the court may stay the rest of the proceedings until the costs are paid or payment made (*r 38.8*).

IV   Consent orders

Consent orders (and judgments) (r 40.6)

Purpose: To obtain a court order without a hearing, thus saving time and costs.

➤ A consent order (or judgment) is drawn up in the terms agreed, expressed as being 'By Consent', and signed by the legal representative acting for each of the parties to whom the order relates, or by a litigant in person (*r 40.6(7)*).

➤ A consent order (or judgment) may be drawn up and sealed by a court officer if (*r 40.6(2)*):

a)   none of the parties is a litigant in person, *and*

b)   the court's approval is not required by the *CPR*, a *PD* or any enactment, *and*

c)   *either (r 40.6(3))*:

   i)   the order (or judgment) is for:

- payment of an amount of money (including damages or the value of goods to be decided by the court).
- delivery up of goods with or without the option of paying the value of the goods or the agreed value.

   ii)   the order is for:

- dismissal of any proceedings (wholly or in part).
- stay of proceedings (the terms agreed may be recorded in a schedule to the order, or elsewhere).
- stay of enforcement (unconditionally, or on condition that money due is paid by instalments specified in the consent order).
- setting aside of a default judgment (*Part 13*) which has not been satisfied.
- payment out of money which has been paid into court.
- discharge from liability of any party.
- payment, assessment or waiver of costs, or such other provision for costs as may be agreed.

   NB: see p 468 for the drawing up and filing of judgments and orders - those rules apply to judgments and orders entered and sealed by a court officer (*r 40.6(4)*).

➤ If a court officer may not draw up and seal a consent order (or judgment), any party may apply for an order (or judgment) in the terms agreed (*r 40.6(5)*).

   ◆ The court may deal with the application without a hearing (*r 40.6(6)*).

Form of consent order (PD40B: 3.4)

➤ A consent judgment or order must:

   ◆ be drawn up in the terms agreed, *and*

   ◆ bear on it the words 'By Consent', *and*

   ◆ be signed by:
- solicitors or counsel acting for each of the parties to the order, *or*
- where a party is a litigant in person, the litigant.

A special type of consent order (known as a Tomlin order)

➤ Purpose: To stay the action by consent of both parties on terms set out in a schedule to a court order.

➤ Procedure: Both parties submit a consent order. The agreement terms are set out in a schedule to the order.

   ◆ If enforcement is necessary, an application can be made to court for specific performance or an injunction.

➤ Any payment to be made under an order is *not* treated as being paid under a judgment, so statutory interest is not available as it is on judgments under *JA 1838 s 17*.

V   Declaratory judgments

➤ The court may make binding declarations whether or not any other remedy is claimed (*r 40.20*).

G Interim remedies (*Parts 25 and 41*)

> I   *Part 25* interim remedies generally
>
> II   Making an application for a *Part 25* interim remedy
>
> III   An application for further damages under *Part 41*

I   *Part 25* interim remedies generally

➤   An order may be made at any time (including before proceedings are started and after judgment) (*r 25.2(1)*).

     ◆   Before a claim is made, a court will only grant an interim remedy if the matter is urgent *or* it is desirable to do so in the interests of justice (*r 25.2(2)(b)*).

➤   If a court grants an interim remedy before a claim commences, it should give directions that a claim be commenced (unless it is an order for disclosure or inspection before start of a claim) (*r 25.2(3)-(4)*).

➤   A defendant may not apply for an interim order before he has filed an acknowledgment of service or a defence (*r 25.2(2)(c)*), unless he has the court's permission.

Types of *Part 25* interim remedies (*r 25.1*)

a)   an interim injunction (prohibiting a person from doing, or requiring a person to do, something).

b)   an interim declaration.

c)   an order for the:
    i)   detention, custody or preservation of property, *and/or*
    ii)   inspection of property, *and/or*
    iii)   taking of a sample of property, *and/or*
    iv)   carrying out of an experiment on or with property, *and/or*
    v)   sale of property which is perishable or which it is desirable to sell quickly, *and/or*
    vi)   payment of income from property until the claim is decided, *and*

d)   an order authorising a person to enter land to carry out an order under (c)(i) to (vi) above.

e)   an order to deliver up goods (under *Torts (Interference with Goods) Act 1977*).

f)   an order (known as a 'freezing injunction'), restraining a party from:

g)   removing from the jurisdiction assets located here, *or*

h)   dealing with any assets (irrespective of whether the assets are located in the jurisdiction ...

i)   directing a party to provide information about assets which are, or may be, the subject of an injunction under (f) above.

j)   an order requiring a party to admit another party to premises to preserve evidence etc. made under *CPA 1997 s 7* (known as a 'search order').

i)   an order for disclosure of documents or inspection of property before a claim has been made under *SCA 1981 s 33* or *CCA 1984 s 52*.

j)   an order for disclosure of documents or inspection of property against a non-party made under *SCA 1981 s 34* or *CCA 1984 s 53*.

k)   an order for an interim payment made under *r 25.6* (see p 427).

l)   an order for a specified fund to be paid into court or secured, in cases of dispute over rights to it.

m)   an order permitting a party seeking to recover personal property, to pay money into court pending the outcome of proceedings and directing that, if he does, the property shall be given to him.

n)   an order directing a party to prepare and file accounts relating to a dispute.

o)   an order directing any account to be taken or inquiry to be made by the court.

p)   an order under *Art 9* of Directive 2004/48 on the enforcement of intellectual property rights (ie: an order in intellectual property proceedings making the continuation of an alleged infringement subject to the lodging of guarantees).

II Making an application for a *Part 25* interim remedy

➤ A court may grant an interim remedy on an application made without notice, if it appears that there are good reasons for not giving notice (*r 25.3(1)*).

➤ An application must be supported by evidence, unless the court orders otherwise (*r 25.3(2)*).

  ◆ If notice has not been given, evidence in support of the application must state reasons why notice has not been given.

➤ The general rules relating to applications in *Part 23* apply (see p 415 et seq).

A Injunctions

1 Jurisdiction

➤ The judge with jurisdiction to conduct the trial has the power to grant an injunction (*PD25A: 1.3*).

  ◆ However, in the High Court, Masters and District Judges may grant injunctions (*PD25A: 1.2*):

  a) by consent (a Master or District Judge may, with consent, vary or discharge an order granted by any judge (*PD25A: 1.4*)), *and*

  b) in connection with a charging order and the appointment of a receiver, *and*

  c) in aid of execution of judgments.

➤ A High Court judge, or any other judge duly authorised, may grant 'search orders' and 'freezing injunctions' (*PD25A: 1.1*).

2 Making an application

➤ The application notice must state the order sought *and* the date, time and place of hearing (*PD25A: 2.1*).

  ◆ For court service, the applicant must file sufficient copies for the court and each respondent (*PD25A: 2.3*).

  ◆ A draft order should be filed, plus a disk containing the draft in a format specified in the *PD* (*PD25A: 2.4*).

➤ The application notice and evidence must be served as soon as practicable after issue (*PD25A: 2.2*) and in any event not later than 3 days before the hearing.

3 Evidence

➤ Evidence must generally be set out (*PD25A: 3.2*):

  a) in a witness statement, *or*

  b) a statement of case (if it is verified by a statement of truth), *or*

  c) the application itself (if it is verified by a statement of truth).

➤ However, an application for a 'freezing injunction'/'search order' must be supported by affidavit.

➤ In either case, all material facts of which the court should be aware should be set out (including, if appropriate, why notice is not given) (*PD25A: 3.3-3.4*).

4 Urgent applications and applications without notice

➤ These are usually dealt with at a hearing, but in cases of 'extreme urgency' may (if and only if the applicant is acting by counsel or solicitors) be by telephone (*PD25A: 4*).

	B Interim payments
	Purpose: The claimant wants an advance from the defendant against a debt or damages.
Note: a)	Before applying to court, it is wise to negotiate with an insurance company for a voluntary payment.
b)	If resolving the case takes longer than expected, the claimant can make additional applications.

Conditions	➤ The court is satisfied that *either* (*r 25.7(1)*):
	a) the defendant has admitted liability to pay damages or a sum of money to the claimant, *or*
	b) the claimant has obtained judgment for damages or a sum of money (not costs) to be assessed, *or*
	c) the claimant would obtain judgment for a substantial amount of money (not costs) at trial (whether or not the defendant is the only defendant or one of a number of defendants to the claim), *or*
	d) the claimant is seeking an order for possession of land *and* the court is satisfied that, if the case went to trial, the defendant would be liable (even if the claim for possession fails) to pay the claimant a sum for the use and occupation of the land while the claim is pending, *or*
	e) in a claim with 2 or more defendants and the order is sought against any one or more, that:
	  ◆ if the claim went to trial, the claimant would obtain judgment for a substantial amount of money (not costs) against at least one defendant (but the court cannot determine which), *and*
	  ◆ all the defendants are either:
	    ● a defendant that is insured in respect of the claim, *or*
	    ● a defendant whose liability will be met by an insurer under *RTA 1988 s 151* or an insurer acting under the MIB Agreement (or the MIB where it is acting itself), *or*
	    ● a defendant that is a public body.

Amount	➤ A 'reasonable proportion of the damages' which 'the court considers just' taking account of (*r 25.7(4)-(5)*): a) the sum likely to be recovered by the claimant, *and* b) any contributory negligence, *and* c) any counterclaim or set-off on which the defendant is likely to rely.
Legal help	➤ Interim payments are paid directly to the claimant ie: are *not* subject to a statutory charge (see pp 443 et seq)
Time	➤ The time for acknowledging service has expired (ie: 14 days after service of claim) (*r 25.6(1)*)
Applicant	➤ A copy of the application notice must be served at least 14 days before a hearing and be supported by evidence (*r 25.6(3)*) which deals with (*PD25B: 2.1*): a) the sum of money sought by way of interim payment, *and* b) the items or matters in respect of which interim payment is sought, *and* c) the sum of money for which final judgment is likely to be given, *and* d) the reasons for believing the conditions set out in *r 25.7* (see above) are satisfied, *and if appropriate* e) any other relevant matters (eg: why the plaintiff needs the money), *and* f) states, in a personal injury action, details of special damages and past and future loss, *and* g) in a claim under the *FAA 1976*, details of the persons on whose behalf the claim is made. ➤ A medical report or statement of special damages should be exhibited (*PD25B: 2.2*).

Respondent/ Applicant	➤ The respondent may serve written evidence in reply.
	  ◆ The respondent must file the evidence and serve copies on every other party to the application at least 7 days before the hearing (*r 25.6(4)*).
	  ◆ If the order is not by consent and the defendant is liable to pay recoverable amounts to the Secretary of State under the *SS(RB)A 1997*, the defendant should obtain a certificate (and this certificate should be filed at the hearing of the application) (*PD25B: 4*).
	➤ An applicant wishing to rely on written evidence in reply must file written evidence and serve a copy on the respondent at least 3 days before the hearing (*r 25.6(5)*).

Consequences	1) The secrecy rule applies after this order - ie: the trial judge is not told about it until liability and quantum are resolved, unless the defendant agrees (*r 25.9*). 2) A preamble to a final judgment should set out the amounts and dates of any interim payment(s). Any final judgment is reduced by the amount of any interim payment(s) (*PD25B: 5*). 3) The court may order the claimant to repay the defendant (with interest) any surplus if the final award exceeds the interim payment (*r 25.8*).

C Security for costs (rr 25.12 - 25.15)

Purpose: to order the claimant (or another person) to give security (in any form the court may direct) for the costs incurred by the defendant in the action or in other proceedings

Procedure	Application supported by written evidence.
Grounds	◆ The court is satisfied that, having regard to all the circumstances of the case, it is just to make an order, *and* ◆ a) The claimant is resident outside the jurisdiction but not resident in a Brussels contracting state (ie: under the Brussels Convention, a Lugano contracting state (ie: under the Lugano Convention) or a state under *EU Regulation 44/2001* on jurisdiction, *or* b) the claimant is a company or other body and there is reason to believe that it will be unable to pay the defendant's costs if ordered to do so, *or* c) the claimant has changed his address since the claim was commenced with a view to evading the consequences of litigation, *or* d) the claimant failed to give his address in the claim form, or gave an incorrect address in that form, *or* e) the claimant is acting as a nominal claimant and there is reason to believe that he will be unable to pay the defendant's costs if ordered to do so, *or* f) the claimant has taken steps in relation to his assets that would make it difficult to enforce an order for costs against him.

A legally aided claimant
Where a legally aided client who has Cost Protection (see p 467) is required to give security for costs, the amount of that security shall not exceed the amount (if any) which is a reasonable one having regard for all the circumstance's (including the client's financial resources and his conduct).
(CLS(C)R 2000 r 6)

III   An application for further damages under *Part 41*

Provisional damages in personal injury claims (r 41.1-41.3)

Purpose: In a personal injury claim, a claimant may want provisional damages assuming his health will not deteriorate

Grounds	a) The particulars of claim include a claim for provisional damages, *and* b) the court is satisfied that the injured person will not develop disease or suffer deterioration *and* the injured person is entitled to apply for further damages at a future date if he develops the disease or suffers the deterioration.
Order (r 41.2)	◆ The order for provisional damages must specify (each) disease or (each) type of deterioration for which an application may be made at a future date and the period within which each application may be made (a claimant may subsequently make more than 1 application to extend this time).
Claimant applying for further damages (r 41.3)	◆ Only 1 more application is allowed for each disease/deterioration set out in the special damages award. ◆ The claimant must give at least 28 days notice to the defendant of his intent to apply for further damages. ● If the claimant knows that the defendant is insured and the identity of the insurers, the claimant must also give 28 days written notice to the insurers. ◆ Within 21 days after the end of the 28 day period, the claimant must apply for directions.

H Offers to settle (*Part 36*)

I	*Part 36* - and other - offers to settle	V	Form and content of offer
II	Timings	VI	Clarification, withdrawal,
III	Special rules: offer by a defendant		acceptance
IV	Interest	VII	Consequences of acceptance

I   *Part 36* - and other - offers to settle

➤ A party can make an offer to settle in any way he chooses but (*r 36.1(2), r 44.3*):

   ◆ if made in accordance with *Part 36,* it has the consequences in Section VII (p 432).

   ◆ if not made in accordance with *Part 36,* it does not have the consequences in Section VII (p 432) but the court will still take the offer into account when deciding costs.

➤ A *Part 36* offer is treated as 'without prejudice except as to costs' (*r 36.13(1)*).

➤ The fact that a *Part 36* offer has been made must not be told to the trial judge or any judge allocated in advance to conduct the trial, until the case has been decided (*r 36.13(2)*).

   ◆ Exceptions (*r 36.13(3)*).

      ● if the defence of tender before claim has been raised, *or*

      ● if the proceedings have been stayed following acceptance of a *Part 36* offer, *or*

      ● if the offeror and the offeree agree in writing that it should not apply.

> *Part 36* has special rules (not dealt with in this book) about offers to settle where the parties have followed the pre-action protocol for Low Value Personal Injury Claims in Road Traffic Accidents and have started proceedings under *Part 8* in accordance with *PD8B* (*rr 36.16-36.22*).

II   Timings

➤ A *Part 36* offer may be made at any time (including before commencement of proceedings) (*r 36.3(2)*).

➤ A *Part 36* offer is made when it is served on the offeree (*r 36.7(1)*), NOT when it is received by the offeree.

➤ A change in a *Part 36* offer is effective when notice of the change is served on the offeree (*r 36.7(2)*).

III   Special rules: offer by a defendant

➤ An offer by a defendant to pay a sum of money in settlement must be an offer to pay a *single sum of money* if it is to be counted as a *Part 36* offer (*r 36.4(1)*).

   ◆ This does not apply in cases of offers for periodical payments and provisional damages.

➤ An offer that includes an offer to pay all or part of the sum, if accepted, at a date later than 14 days after the date of acceptance will not be treated as a *Part 36* offer unless the offeree accepts the offer (*r 36.4(2)*).

IV   Interest

➤ A *Part 36* offer offering to pay/accept a sum of money is treated as inclusive of all interest until (*r 36.3(3)*):

   ◆ the end of THE SPECIFIED PERIOD (see p 430) in the written offer (if the offer is made 21 or more days before the trial starts), *or*

   ◆ 21 days after the date the offer was made (if the offer is made less than 21 days before trial starts).

V   Form and content of offer

Form and content of a *Part 36* Offer (*r 36.2*)

➤ A *Part 36* offer **must**:
  ◆ be in writing, *and*
  ◆ (if the offer is made 21 or more days before the start of the trial) specify a period of not less than 21 days within which the defendant will be liable for the claimant's costs in accordance with *Rule 36.10* if the offer is accepted, (known as "**THE SPECIFIED PERIOD**"), *and*
  ◆ state:
    • that it is intended to have the consequences of *Part 36*, *and*
    • whether it relates to:
      ▪ the whole of the claim, *or*
      ▪ part of the claim (and if so, which part), *or*
      ▪ an issue that arises in the claim (and if so, which issue), *and*
      ▪ whether it takes into account any counterclaim.
➤ A *Part 36* offer may relate only to liability.

➤ A *Part 36* offer **must not** include an offer in relation to costs.
  ◆ Eg: Saying "This offer is inclusive of interest and costs" or saying "The claimant will accept £6,000 towards legal costs", means it is not a *Part 36* offer.
➤ A *Part 36* offer must not be time limited (*C v D* [2011] EWCA Civ 646).
  ◆ Eg: Saying "This offer is open for 21 days", means it is not a *Part 36* offer.

Extra requirements for *Part 36* offers for personal injury claims for future pecuniary loss (*r 36.5*)

➤ A *Part 36* offer may contain an offer to pay/accept:
  ◆ the whole or part of the damages for future pecuniary loss in the form of:
    • a lump sum, *or*
    • periodical payments, *or*
    • both a lump sum and periodical payments, *or*
      ▪ NB: If *Part 36* offer offers to pay/accept damages as both a lump sum and periodical payments, the offeree may only give notice of acceptance of the offer as a whole.
    • the whole or part of any other damages in the form of a lump sum.
➤ A *Part 36* offer:
  ◆ must state the amount of any offer to pay the whole or part of any damages in the form of a lump sum, *and*
  ◆ may state:
    • what part of the lump sum, if any, relates to damages for future pecuniary loss, *and*
    • what part relates to other damages to be accepted in the form of a lump sum, *and*
  ◆ must state what part of the offer relates to damages for future pecuniary loss to be paid or accepted in the form of periodical payments and must specify:
    • the amount and duration of the periodical payments, *and*
    • the amount of any payments for substantial capital purchases and when they are to be made, *and*
    • that each amount is to vary by reference to the retail prices index (or to some other named index, or that it is not to vary by reference to any index), *and*
  ◆ must state either that any damages which take the form of periodical payments will be funded in a way which ensures that the continuity of payment is reasonably secure in accordance with *DA 1996 s 2(4)* or how such damages are to be paid and how the continuity of their payment is to be secured.
➤ If the offeree accepts a *Part 36* offer which includes payment of any part of the damages as periodical payments, the claimant must, within 7 days of acceptance, apply to court for a suitable order.

Extra requirements for *Part 36* offers to settle a claim for provisional damages (*r 36.6*)

➤ The *Part 36* offer must specify whether or not the offeror is proposing that the settlement shall include an award of provisional damages.
➤ If the *Part 36* offer agrees to an award of provisional damages, the offer must state:
  ◆ that the sum offered is in satisfaction of the claim for damages on the assumption that the injured person will not develop the disease or suffer the type of deterioration specified in the offer, *and*
  ◆ that the offer is subject to claimant making any claim for further damages within a limited period, *and*
  ◆ what that limited period is.
➤ If the offeree accepts the *Part 36* offer to settle a claim for provisional damages, the claimant must, within 7 days of acceptance, apply to the court for an order for a suitable order.

Extra requirements for *Part 36* offers where some money would be a compensation payment under *SS(RB)A 1997* (*r 36.15*)

➤ The *Part 36* offer should state either:
  ◆ that the offer is made without regard to any liability for recoverable amounts (being a recoverable benefit under *SS(RB)A 1997* or a recoverable lump sum payment under *SS(RB)(LSP)R 2008*), *or*
  ◆ that it is intended to include any deductible amounts (under *SS(RB)A 1997* or *SS(RB)(LSP)R 2008*).
    • Where this applies:
      ▪ before making the offer, the offeror must apply for a certificate, *and*
      ▪ the offer must state the amount of gross compensation, the name and amount of any deductible benefit by which that gross amount is reduced and the net amount of compensation.
        - Special rules apply if the offeror has applied for, but not received, a certificate.

VI Clarification, withdrawal, acceptance

A Clarification

➤ Within 7 days of a *Part 36* offer being made, the offeree may request clarification of the offer (*r 36.8(1)*).

➤ If the offeror does not give the clarification within 7 days of receiving the request for clarification, the offeree may apply for an order that he does so (*r 36.8(2)*).

  ◆ This does not apply if the trial has started (*r 36.8(2)*).

  ◆ If a court order is made, the court must specify the date when the Part 36 offer is to be treated as having been made (*r 36.8(3)*).

B Withdrawal

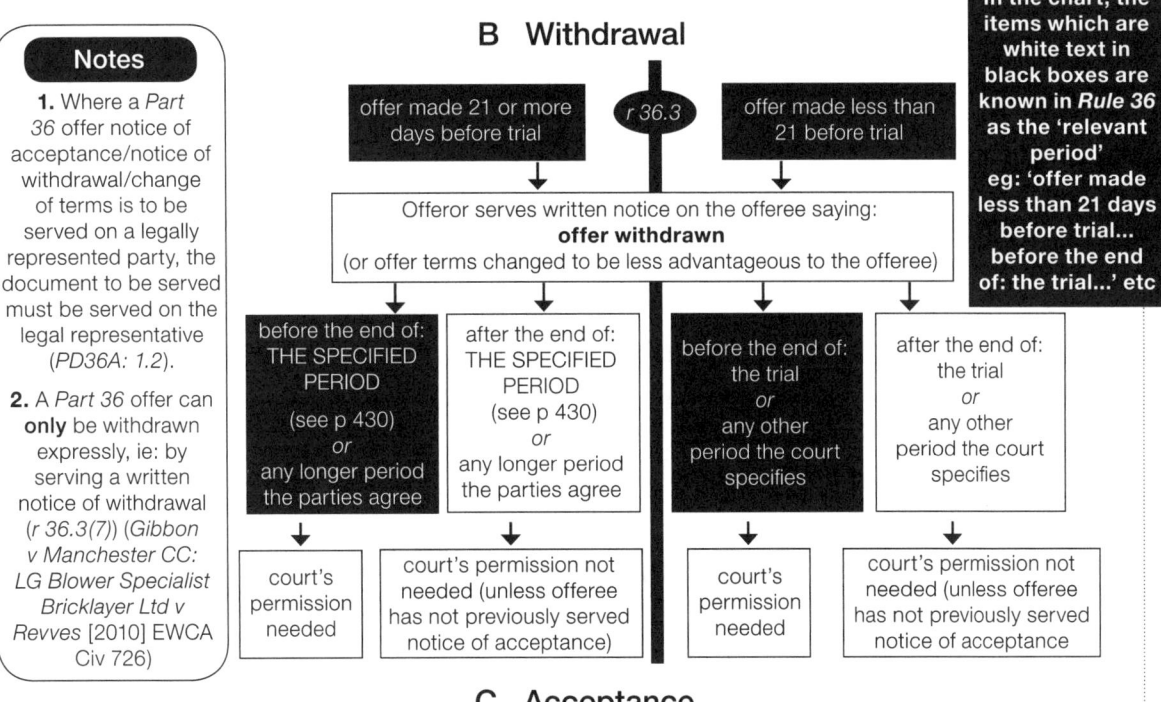

Notes

1. Where a *Part 36* offer notice of acceptance/notice of withdrawal/change of terms is to be served on a legally represented party, the document to be served must be served on the legal representative (*PD36A: 1.2*).

2. A *Part 36* offer can **only** be withdrawn expressly, ie: by serving a written notice of withdrawal (*r 36.3(7)*) (*Gibbon v Manchester CC: LG Blower Specialist Bricklayer Ltd v Revves* [2010] EWCA Civ 726)

In the chart, the items which are white text in black boxes are known in *Rule 36* as the 'relevant period' eg: 'offer made less than 21 days before trial... before the end of: the trial...' etc

C Acceptance

➤ A *Part 36* offer is accepted by serving written notice of the acceptance on the offeror (*r 36.9(1)*) and filing the offer with the court where the case is proceeding (*PD36A: 3.1*).

➤ A *Part 36* offer may be accepted at any time (whether or not the offeree has subsequently made a different offer) unless the offeror serves notice of withdrawal on the offeree (*r 36.9(2)*).

➤ The court's permission to accept is *not* needed - except in the following circumstances (*r 36.9(3)*):

  ◆ acceptance is on behalf of a child or protected party (ie: someone who lacks capacity to conduct proceedings) (*r 21.10*), *or*

  ◆ certain cases where a claimant wants to accept an offer by one (or more) of several defendants (*r 36.12(4)*) (see p 433), *or*

  ◆ if the offer contains deductible amounts (see p 430) *and* the relevant period has expired *and* further deductible amounts have been paid to the claimant since the date of the offer, *or*

  ◆ the trial has started.

  NB: If the court has given permission, unless all the parties have agreed costs, the court makes an order dealing with costs (and may order that the usual *Part 36* costs consequences apply).

➤ A *Part 36* offer may not be accepted after the end of the trial but before judgment is handed down (unless the parties agree otherwise) (*r 36.9(5)*).

VII Consequences of acceptance

A Prior to judgment

➤ Where a *Part 36* offer is accepted within the 'relevant period' (see p 431), the claimant is entitled to the costs of the proceedings up to the date on which notice of acceptance was served on the offeror (*r 36.10(1)*).

- ◆ Costs are on the standard basis if the amount of costs is not agreed (*r 36.10(3)* and see *r 44.4(2)*).

  - The claimant's costs include any costs incurred in dealing with the defendant's counterclaim if the *Part 36* offer states that it takes into account the counterclaim (*r 36.10(6)*).

- ◆ However, this is subject to the court ordering otherwise, where (*r 36.10(2)*):

  - a defendant's *Part 36* offer relates to part only of the claim, *and*

  - at the time of serving notice of acceptance within the relevant period the claimant abandons the balance of the claim.

- ◆ However, if the parties do not agree the liability for costs, the court will make an order as to costs where *r 36.10(5)*:

  - a *Part 36* offer was made less than 21 days before the start of trial is accepted, *or*

  - a *Part 36* offer is accepted after expiry of the 'relevant period' (see p 431).

    - ▪ Where this happens, unless the court orders otherwise *r 36.10(5)*:

      a) the claimant is entitled to the costs of the proceedings up to the date on which the 'relevant period' expired, *and*

      b) the offeree will be liable for the offeror's costs for the period from the date of expiry of the 'relevant period' to the date of acceptance.

The effect of acceptance of a Part 36 offer (*r 36.11*)

➤ If a *Part 36* offer is accepted, the claim will be stayed (*r 36.11(1)*).

- ◆ For a *Part 36* offer relating to the whole claim the stay is upon the terms of the offer (*r 36.11(2)*).

- ◆ For a *Part 36* offer relating to a part of the claim the claim is stayed as to that part only upon the terms of the offer (*r 36.11(3)*).

➤ If court approval is needed before a settlement is binding, the stay applies only after approval (*r 36.11(4)*).

- ◆ Any stay will not affect the power of the court to enforce the terms of a *Part 36* offer or to deal with any question of costs (including interest on costs) relating to the proceedings (*r 36.11(5)*).

➤ Unless the parties agree otherwise in writing, if a *Part 36* offer by a defendant is (or includes) paying a single sum of money, that sum must be paid to the offeree within 14 days of the date of (*r 36.11(6)*):

- ◆ acceptance, *or*

- ◆ (if applicable) an order for an award of provisional damages or order for an award of periodical payments, unless (in either case) the court orders otherwise.

➤ If the accepted sum is not paid within 14 days or such other period as has been agreed, the offeree may enter judgment for the unpaid sum (*r 36.11(7)*).

➤ If a *Part 36* offer is not for a single sum of money (or is for a single sum of money where a party alleges that the other party has not honoured the offer terms) that party may apply to enforce the terms of the offer without the need for a new claim (*r 36.11(8)*).

Acceptance of a *Part 36* offer made by one or more, but not all, defendants (*r 36.12*)

➤ If defendants are sued jointly/in the alternative, the claimant may accept the offer if (*r 36.12(2)*):

◆ he discontinues his claim against those defendants who have not made the offer, *and*

◆ those defendants give written consent to the acceptance of the offer.

➤ If defendants are sued severally, the claimant may (*r 36.12(3)*):

◆ accept the offer, *and*

◆ continue with his claims against the other defendants if he is entitled to do so.

➤ Otherwise the claimant must apply to the court for an order to accept the *Part 36* offer (*r 36.12(4)*).

B After judgment

What a claimant gets	What a defendant gets
➤ If a judgment against the defendant is at least as advantageous to the claimant as the proposals contained in a claimant's *Part 36* offer, the court will order that the claimant is entitled to (*r 36.14(3)*): ◆ interest on the whole or part of any sum of money (excluding interest) awarded at a rate not exceeding 10% above base rate for some or all of the period starting with the date on which the 'relevant period' (see p 431) expired, *and* ◆ his costs on the indemnity basis from the date on which the 'relevant period' expired (see p 431), *and* ◆ interest on those costs at a rate not exceeding 10% above base rate.	➤ If a claimant fails to obtain a judgment more advantageous than a defendant's *Part 36* offer, the court will order that the defendant is entitled to (*r 36.14(2)*): ◆ his costs from the date on which the relevant period expired, *and* ◆ interest on those costs.

> Where the court awards interest and also awards interest on the same sum and for the same period under any other power, the total rate of interest may not exceed 10% above base rate (*r 36.14(5)*).

➤ The boxes above:

◆ are subject to the court considering that it would be unjust to make those orders.

● The court will take into account all the circumstances of the case including (*r 36.14(4)*):

■ the terms of any *Part 36* offer, *and*

■ the stage in the proceedings when any *Part 36* offer was made, including in particular how long before the trial started the offer was made, *and*

■ information available to the parties at the time when the *Part 36* offer was made, *and*

■ the conduct of the parties with regard to the giving or refusing to give information for the purposes of enabling the offer to be made or evaluated.

◆ do not apply if the *Part 36* offer was (*r 36.14(6)*):

● withdrawn, *or*

● changed so that its terms are less advantageous to the offeree, and the offeree has beaten the less advantageous offer, *or*

● made less than 21 days before trial (unless a court abridged the 'relevant period' (see p 431).

I   Allocation (and automatic transfer) (*Part 26*)

On the sooner of (*r 26.3(2)*):
all defendants have filed their defences
or
the period for filing the last defence has expired (see p 377)

↓

the court serves the allocation questionnaire on each party (*r 26.3(1)*) *unless*:
a)   there is admission of part of a specified sum (*r 14.5*) (see pp 411-412), *or*
b)   the defence is 'the debt has already been paid' (*r 15.10*), *or*
c)   the court has said there is no need for an allocation questionnaire

Note:
The date for filing the allocation questionnaire cannot be varied by agreement between the parties (*r 26.3(6A)*)

Where the claim:
(*rr 26.2(1), 26.2(3), 26.3(3)*)
a)   is for a specified amount, *and*
b)   was commenced in a court which is not the defendant's home court, *and*
c)   has not otherwise been transferred to another defendant's home court under an application to set aside or vary default judgment, *and*
d)   the defendant is an individual

the date for filing is specified in the allocation questionnaire (*r 26.3(1)*)
(NB: this must be at least 14 days after the date it is deemed to be served by the court) (*r 26.3(6)*)

file:
♦   allocation questionnaire
♦   the fee, see p 381
♦   estimate of costs in set form* (*Costs PD: 6*)
♦   if the claimant has a reply, file the reply (*r 15.8*)

*do not need to include additional liability arrangements (see p 467)

Failure to file
(*PD26: 2.5*)
a)   no party files within time:
♦   file is referred to a judge for directions,
♦   the judge usually orders that, unless an allocation questionnaire is filed within 3 days from service of that order, the claim and any counterclaim will be struck out.
b)   not all parties (but at least 1 does) file:
♦   court may allocate the claim to a track if it has enough information to do so, *or*
♦   court may order that an allocation hearing is listed and that all/any parties must attend

Possible (Pre-) Allocation Hearing (see box on p 435)

... then the claim is transferred to the home court of the first defendant to file a defence

Note: Where a claimant notifies the court under *r 15.10* or *r 14.5* (see above) that he wishes the proceedings to continue, the court transfers the proceedings to the defendant's home court when it receives that notification. If proceedings are *not* automatically transferred the court serves an allocation questionnaire on each party at this time (*rr 26.2(4), 26.3(4)*)

When (*r 26.5*):
♦   every defendant has filed an allocation questionnaire, *or*
♦   the period for filing the allocation questionnaires has expired, *or*
♦   any stay has expired (see 'stay' box on p 435)

Court allocates the case to a track
(see 'Allocation Factors' box on p 435)
(and it may also hold an 'allocation hearing' see box on p 435) (*r 26.5(4)*):
Note: parties may all consent to a different track

Multi track
(*r 26.6(6)*)
The normal track for any claim for which the small claims track or the fast track is not the normal track

---

Small claims track (*r 26.6(1)-(3)*)

for any claim which has a value of not more than £5,000 *BUT* if the claim is for personal injuries or residential premises, this is only the normal track for:
a)   personal injuries, if:
♦   the value of the claim is not more than £5,000, *and*
♦   the value of any claim for damages for personal injuries is not more than £1,000
b)   a claim which includes a claim by a tenant of residential premises against a landlord where:
♦   the tenant is seeking an order requiring the landlord to carry out repairs or other work to the premises (whether or not the tenant is also seeking some other remedy), *and*
♦   the cost of the repairs or other work to the premises is estimated to be not more than £1,000, *and*
♦   the value of any other claim for damages is not more than £1,000

Fast track (*r 26.6(4)-(5)*)
for any claim:
a)   where small claims track is not the normal track, *and*
b)   the value is not more than £25,000, *and*
c)   the court considers that the trial is likely to last for no longer than 1 day, *and*
d)   oral expert evidence at trial will be limited to:
♦   1 expert per party in relation to any expert field, *and*
♦   expert evidence in 2 expert fields
Note: The court, in particular, takes account of limits on disclosure, the extent of expert evidence and whether the trial is likely to last more than 1 day

The court serves on each party (*r 26.9*):
♦   notice of allocation on every party
♦   a copy of the allocation questionnaires filed by the other parties
♦   a copy of any further information provided by another party about his case (whether by order or not)

Allocation Factors (*rr 26.7-26.8*)

- ➤ When deciding the track for a claim, the court must have regard to:
  - ◆ the financial value, if any, of the claim.
    - ● The court may direct the claimant to justify the amount.
    - ● The amount should disregard:
      - ▪ any amount not in dispute, *and*
        - ❶ Note: an amount for which the defendant does not admit liability is in dispute.
        - ❷ Note: a part amount for which judgment has been entered (eg: summary judgment) is not in dispute.
        - ❸ Note: a part amount claimed as a distinct item which the defendant admits he is liable for is not in dispute.
        - ❹ Note: a sum offered and accepted in satisfaction of any item which is part of the claim is not in dispute.
        Note: Therefore, if there is a claim above £5,000 and the defendant makes, before allocation, an admission that reduces the amount in dispute to a figure below £5,000, the small claims track is the normal track. As to recovery of pre-allocation costs, the claimant can, before allocation, apply for judgment with costs on the amount of the claim that has been admitted.
      - ▪ any claim for interest, *and*
      - ▪ costs, *and*
      - ▪ any contributory negligence.
    - ● Where 2 or more claimants have started a claim (using 1 claim form) against the same defendant and each claimant's claim is separate from the other claimants, the court considers the financial value of each separately.
  - ◆ the nature of the remedy sought.
  - ◆ the likely complexity of the facts, law or evidence.
  - ◆ the number of parties or likely parties.
  - ◆ the value of any counterclaim or other additional claim (see p 418) and the complexity of any matters relating to it.
    - ● If there is more than 1 money claim (eg: where there is an additional *Part 20* claim) the court will not generally aggregate the claims but generally regards the largest of them as determining the financial value of the claims.
  - ◆ the amount of oral evidence which may be required.
  - ◆ the importance of the claim to persons who are not parties to the proceedings.
  - ◆ the views expressed by the parties (including any other information the parties may provide).
  - ◆ the circumstances of the parties.

Stay (*r 26.4, PD26: 3*)

- ➤ When filling in the allocation questionnaire, a party may request the proceedings be stayed while all try to settle.
- ➤ The court stays proceedings (in whole or in part) for 1 month (or other specified period it considers appropriate) if:
  - ◆ all parties request a stay, *or*
  - ◆ the court, on its own, considers that such a stay would be appropriate.
- ➤ The parties may apply to extend any stay. (This may be by letter to the court.)
  - ◆ The extension is generally for no more than 4 weeks unless clear reasons are given to justify a longer time.
- ➤ After a stay, the claimant must tell the court if a settlement has been reached.
- ➤ **No settlement:** If the claimant does not tell the court by the end of the period of the stay that a settlement has been reached, the court gives such directions as it considers appropriate.
- ➤ **Settlement:** Where the whole proceedings are settled during a stay, any of the following are treated as an application for the stay to be lifted:
  - a) an application for a consent order (in any form) to give effect to the settlement, *or*
  - b) an application for the approval of a settlement where a party is a person under a disability, *or*
  - c) giving notice of acceptance of money paid into court in satisfaction of the claim or applying for money in court to be paid out.

Allocation Hearings or Pre-Allocation Hearings (*PD26: 2.4, 5, 6*)

- ➤ When there is *any* type of hearing or a special allocation hearing, the court may at any time before allocation:
  - ◆ dispense with the need for allocation questionnaires, hold an allocation hearing, make an order for allocation and give directions for case management, *or*
  - ◆ fix a date for allocation questionnaires to be filed and give other directions.
- ➤ Where the court orders a *special* allocation hearing, it gives the parties at least 7 days notice and brief reasons.
- ➤ A legal representative at an allocation hearing should be the person responsible for the case and *must* be familiar with the case and able to provide the court with information it is likely to need to take decisions about allocation and case management. He must also have sufficient authority to deal with any issues that arise.
- ➤ The court may also deal with summary disposal of issues at any pre-allocation hearing (eg: summary judgment).

The duty of consultation (*PD26: 2.3*)

- ➤ The parties should consult each other and co-operate in completing the allocation questionnaires.
- ➤ They should try to agree the case management directions which they will invite the court to make.
  - ◆ The process of consultation must not delay the filing of the allocation questionnaires.

J Small claims track (*Part 27*)

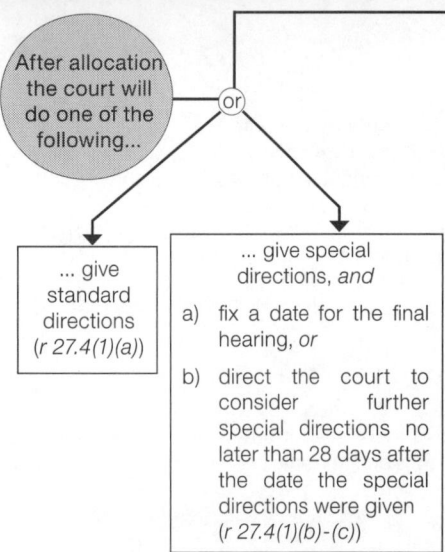

After allocation the court will do one of the following...

or

... give standard directions
(r 27.4(1)(a))

... give special directions, *and*

a) fix a date for the final hearing, *or*

b) direct the court to consider further special directions no later than 28 days after the date the special directions were given
(r 27.4(1)(b)-(c))

... fix a date for a preliminary hearing:

a) ◆ if the court considers special directions are needed to ensure a fair hearing, *and*

   ◆ it appears necessary for a party to attend court to ensure he understands what he must do to comply with special directions, *or*

b) to enable the court to dispose of the claim as a party has no real prospect of success at a final hearing, *or*

c) to enable the court to strike out a statement of case, or part of a statement of case, as that struck out wording discloses no reasonable grounds for bringing or defending the claim
(rr 27.4(1)(d), 27.6(1))

... give notice that the court proposes to deal with the claim without a hearing and invite the parties to notify the court by a specified date if they agree
(r 27.4(1)(e))

The court gives the parties at least 21 days' notice of the date fixed for the final hearing (unless the parties agree to accept less notice), and informs them of the time allowed for the final hearing *(r 27.4(2))*

Standard Directions *(PD27: App. B)*
(where the District Judge gives no other directions)

1   Each party must deliver to every other party and to the court office copies of all documents on which he intends to rely at the hearing no later than [   ] [14 days before the hearing]. (These should include the letter making the claim and the reply.)

2   The original documents must be brought to the hearing.

3   [Notice of hearing date and time allowed.]

4   The parties are encouraged to contact each other with a view to trying to settle the case or narrow the issues. However the court must be informed immediately if the case is settled by agreement before the hearing date.

5   No party may rely at the hearing on any report from an expert unless express permission has been granted by the court beforehand. Anyone wishing to rely on an expert must write to the court immediately on receipt of this Order and seek permission, giving an explanation why the assistance of an expert is necessary.

Sample Special Directions *(PD27: App. C)*

◆ The [ ] must clarify his case. He must do this by delivering to the court office and to the [ ] no later than [ ] [a list of [ ]] [details of [ ]]

◆ The [ ] must allow the [ ] to inspect by appointment within [ ] days of receiving a request to do so.

◆ The hearing will not take place at the court but at [ ].

◆ The [ ] must bring to court at the hearing the [ ].

◆ Signed statements setting out the evidence of all witnesses on whom each party intends to rely must be prepared and copies included in the documents mentioned in paragraph 1. This includes the evidence of the parties themselves and of any other witness, whether or not he is going to come to court to give evidence.

◆ The court may decide not to take into account a document [or video] or the evidence of a witness if these directions have not been complied with.

◆ If he does not [do so] [ ] his [Claim][Defence] [and Counterclaim] will be struck out and (specify consequence).

◆ It appears to the court that expert evidence is necessary on the issue of [ ] and that that evidence should be given by a single expert to be instructed by the parties jointly. If the parties cannot agree about who to choose and what arrangements to make about paying his fee, either party MUST apply to the court for further directions. The evidence is to be given in the form of a written report. Either party may ask the expert questions and must then send copies of the questions and replies to the other party and to the court. Oral expert evidence may be allowed in exceptional circumstances but only after a further order of the court. Attention is drawn to the limit of £200 on expert's fees that may be recovered.

◆ If either party intends to show a video as evidence he must:

a) contact the court at once to make arrangements for him to do so, because the court may not have the necessary equipment, and

b) provide the other party with a copy of the video or the opportunity to see it at least [ ] days before the hearing.

1   **Conduct of a hearing**

➤ The court may, if all the parties agree, deal with the claim without a hearing (*r 27.10*).

➤ The court may adopt any method of proceeding at a hearing that it considers fair (*r 27.8(1)*).

♦ Hearings are informal (*r 27.8(2)*).

➤ Strict rules of evidence do not apply (*r 27.8(3)*).

♦ The court need not take evidence on oath (*r 27.8(4)*).

♦ The court may limit cross-examination (*r 27.8(5)*).

● Eg: a judge may (*PD27: 4.3*):

▪ ask questions of any witness before allowing another person to do so, *or*

▪ refuse to allow cross-examination of any witness until all the witnesses have given evidence-in-chief, *or*

▪ limit cross-examination of a witness to a fixed time/subject/issue.

➤ The court must give reasons for its decision (*r 27.8(6), see also PD27: 5.1-5.5* and box below).

➤ The hearing will generally be conducted in public (*PD27: 4.1(1)*).

Recording of the hearing and reasons for the judgment (*PD27: 5.1-5.5*)

➤ A hearing that takes place at the court will be tape recorded by the court.

➤ A party may obtain a transcript of such a recording on payment of the proper transcriber's charges.

➤ The judge may give reasons for his judgment as briefly and simply as the nature of the case allows. He will normally do so orally at the hearing, but he may give them later at a hearing either orally or in writing.

➤ Where the judge decides the case without a hearing (or a party who has given appropriate notice does not attend the hearing) the judge will prepare a note of his reasons and the court will send a copy to each party.

---

2   **Representation**

➤ A case may be presented by a party, a lawyer or a lay representative (*PD27: 3.2(1)*).

♦ A 'lay representative' is a person other than a barrister, a solicitor or a legal executive employed by a solicitor (*PD27: 3.1(2)*)

➤ A lay representative may not exercise his right of audience (*LR(RA)O 1999, PD27: 3.2(2)*):

a) if his client does not attend the hearing, *or*

b) at any stage after judgment, *or*

c) on an appeal brought against any decision made by the district judge in the proceedings.

● The court has a general discretion to hear anybody, even in circumstances excluded by the *LR(RA)O 1999 (PD 27:3.3(3)*).

➤ A corporate party may be represented by any of its officers or employees (*PD27: 3.2(4)*).

3   **Experts**

➤ An expert may not give evidence at a hearing without the court's permission (*r 27.5*).

4   Non-attendance

Party does not attend *and*: i) gives the court and the other party written notice (an '**Excuse Notice**'), at least 7 days before the hearing that he will not attend, *and* ii) has served on the other party at least 7 days before the hearing date any other documents which he has filed with the court, *and* iii) in the Excuse Notice requests the court to decide the claim in his absence	**Claimant** does not attend the hearing *and* no Excuse Notice is given	**Defendant** does not attend the hearing *or* give an Excuse Notice *and* the claimant attends or gives an Excuse Notice
↓	↓	↓
The court will take into account that party's statement of case and any other documents that party has filed with the court and served (*r 27.9(1)*)	The court may strike out the claim (*r 27.9(2)*)	The court may decide the claim on the basis of the claimant's evidence alone (*r 27.9(3)*)

If neither party attends, or gives notice, the court may strike out the claim and any defence or counterclaim (*r 27.9(4)*)

The court has a general power to adjourn a hearing, eg: a party wishes to attend but cannot do so for a good reason (*PD27: 6.2*)

Setting aside judgment and rehearing under *Part 27*

➤ A party may apply for an order setting aside judgment and for the claim to be reheard if (*r 27.11(1)*):

a) he was not present or represented at the hearing of the claim, *and*

b) did not give an Excuse Notice.

Procedure	➤ Party applies not more than 14 days after the day on which notice of the judgment was served on him (*r 27.11(2)*).
Grounds	➤ The court may grant the application only if the applicant (*r 27.11(3)*): a) had a good reason for not: i) attending, *or* ii) being represented, *or* iii) giving an Excuse Notice, *and* b) has reasonable prospect of success at the hearing.
Order	➤ The court fixes a new hearing for the claim. ➤ The new hearing may take place immediately after the hearing of the application and may be dealt with by the same judge.

Appeals under the small claims track

• An appeal from a decision of a small claims track court is made under *Part 52* as for other appeals (see p 478).

➤ However, for a small claims track appeal, unlike for other appeals:

◆ the appellant only needs to file the following documents (and no other documents are required) (*PD52: 5.8*):

• a sealed copy of the order being appealed, *and*

• the order giving or refusing permission to appeal (and the reasons), *and*

• a record of the reasons of the judgement of the lower court but only:

▪ to enable the court to decide if permission should be granted to appeal, *or*

▪ if permission has been granted, to enable it to decide the appeal.

◆ the respondent may provide a skeleton argument, but is not required to do so (*PD52: 7.7A*).

K Fast Track

```
Allocation to the fast track
```
↓
```
Case management 1
The court gives directions including (rr 28.2(2), 28.3(1)-(2)):
◆  a)  fixing the trial date, or
    b)  fixing a period (not exceeding 3 weeks) within which the trial
        is to take place, and/or
◆  a)  disclosure of documents, and/or
    b)  service of witness statements, and/or
    c)  expert evidence.
◆  disclosure (standard - see pp 443-445, non-standard or none).
```
↓
```
Notice of allocation
The court sends this to the parties and it includes:
◆  the trial date or trial period (r 28.2(3)), and
◆  date for filing the pre-trial checklist.
```
↓
```
Pre-trial checklist
(r 28.5(1))
No later than 2 weeks before the date specified in the
notice of allocation for the return of the completed
checklist (or in any later direction of the court) the
court sends the parties a pre-trial checklist (listing
questionnaire) (unless it considers one is not needed)
```
↓
```
DATE (given in allocation notice (see above)
for parties to file:
◆  the pre-trial checklist (and usually the fee, see
   p 381).
◆  costs estimate (PD28: 6.1).
```
↓
```
Exchange
The parties are encouraged to exchange copies
of the pre-trial checklists before they are filed
to avoid the court being given conflicting or
incomplete information (PD28: 6.1).
```
↓
```
Case management 2
The court:
As soon as practicable after the date specified for filing
a completed pre-trial checklist the court will:
◆  gives appropriate directions and further steps to be
   taken for the trial, including a trial timetable,
◆  fix the date for the trial (or, confirms it if one has been
   given).
```
↓
```
Notice of Trial
The court gives the parties
notice of trial.
```
↓
```
Trial
(see p 459)
```

standard period between giving of directions and trial is not more than 30 weeks (r 28.2(4))

Minimum
2 weeks

date specified for filing a pre-trial checklist is not more than 8 weeks before the trial date or the beginning of the trial period (r 28.5(2))

Minimum
3 weeks
(r 28.6(2))

**Fast Track case management
(ie: Directions hearings
at allocation/listing hearings)
(r 28.5(3)-(4), PD28: 2, 6)**

➤ Case management is generally given
  at 2 stages in the case:
  ◆ at allocation to the fast track, and
  ◆ on filing a pre-trial checklist.
➤ It is usual not to hold a hearing for
  directions as the parties are expected
  to cooperate in directions.
➤ **The Court will hold a hearing to give
  directions when it is 'necessary or
  desirable'.**
➤ If this is because of the default of a
  party (or his legal representative) it
  usually involves a sanction (see
  p 381).
➤ **The Court may give directions at any
  hearing on the application of a party
  or on its own initiative.**
➤ When any hearing has been fixed it
  is the duty of the parties to consider
  what directions the court should
  be asked to give and to make any
  application that may be appropriate
  to be dealt with at that hearing.
➤ When the Court fixes a hearing to
  give directions it will give the parties
  at least 3 days notice of the hearing.

Note Items in bold also apply to multi-track

Problems with the pre-trial checklist

➤ The court may give directions
  (including fixing a hearing) if:
  a) a party files a completed pre-trial
     checklist but another party does
     not, or
  b) a party has failed to give all the
     information requested by the pre-
     trial checklist, or
  c) the court considers it is necessary
     to enable it to decide what directions
     to give to complete preparation of
     the case for trial.
➤ Where the court holds a hearing the
  date must be as early as possible and
  the parties are given at least 3 days'
  notice of the date.
➤ No party files: if no party files a
  completed pre-trial checklist by
  the specified date, the court orders
  that unless it is filed within 7 days
  from service of that order, the claim/
  defence/ counterclaim will be struck
  out without further court order.
➤ A party files: where a party files a pre-
  trial checklist but another party does
  not do so, the court normally gives
  listing directions, fixing/confirming
  the trial date and provide for steps to
  be taken to prepare the case for trial.

439

Directions on allocation (*PD28: 3-4*)

➤ The court's first concern is to ensure that issues between parties are identified and necessary evidence is prepared + disclosed. If in doubt about directions, the court holds a hearing (listed as promptly as possible).

➤ The court may have regard to any document filed with an allocation questionnaire containing further information *provided* that the document states either that its contents have been agreed with every other party or that it has been served on every other party and when it was served.

Agreed directions	No agreed directions
The court may approve these if:	The court's general approach is:
◆ the parties have filed these, *and*	◆ to give directions for the filing and service of any further information required to clarify either party's case,
◆ the court considers that they are suitable, *and*	
◆ they set out a timetable (referring to calendar dates) for steps to prepare the case, *and*	◆ to direct standard disclosure (see pp 443-445) between the parties,
◆ they include a date or a trial period (which must not be longer than 3 weeks) when it is proposed that the trial will take place (where the latest proposed date for the trial or the end of the trial period is not later than 30 weeks from the date of the directions order), *and*	◆ to direct the simultaneous exchange of witness statements,
	◆ to give directions for a single joint expert unless there is good reason not to do so,
◆ they include provisions about disclosure of documents, *and*	◆ if no directions for a single expert are given:
• these may limit disclosure to standard disclosure between all parties or to less than that, *and/or*	• to direct simultaneous exchange of experts' reports
• these may direct that disclosure take place by supply of copy documents without a list (but it must in that case either direct that the parties must serve a disclosure statement with the copies or record that they have agreed to disclose in that way without such a statement)	• (if experts' reports are not agreed) to direct a discussion between experts and preparation of a report.
	Note: If the court does not approve agreed directions but gives directions itself without a hearing, it takes the parties' proposed directions into account in deciding on directions
◆ they include provision about both factual and expert evidence (eg: none is required), *and*	
◆ they contain other appropriate provisions.	

➤ **Typical timetable:** (periods from notice of allocation)

◆ Disclosure	4 weeks
◆ Exchange of witness statements	10 weeks
◆ Exchange of experts' reports	14 weeks
◆ Sending of pre-trial checklists by the Court	20 weeks
◆ Filing of completed pre-trial checklists	22 weeks
◆ Hearing	30 weeks

If the court thinks that some/ all steps in the timetable are unnecessary it may omit them - eg: if Practice Direction (Pre-Action Conduct) or any pre-action protocols have been complied with or other steps have already been taken

➤ **Varying the Court's directions** - the procedure is outside this book but is set out in *r 28.4* and *PD28: 4*.

Directions on listing (*PD28: 7*)

➤ The court must confirm or fix the trial date, specify the place of trial and give a time estimate.
   ◆ The trial date must be fixed and the case listed on the footing that the hearing will end on the same calendar day as that on which it commenced.

➤ The parties should seek to agree directions (see practice box above) and may file the proposed order. (The court may make an order in those terms or it may make a different order.)
   ◆ Agreed directions should include provisions about evidence (including expert evidence, see p 458), a trial timetable and time estimate, preparation of a trial bundle, other matters needed to prepare the case for trial.

➤ **Varying the Court's directions** - the procedure is outside this book but is set out in *r 28.4* and *PD28: 4*.

Fast track standard directions (*PD28: Appendix*)

➤ Standard Directions are listed in the Appendix to *PD28* but include provisions on:

- ◆ FURTHER STATEMENTS OF CASE
- ◆ REQUESTS FOR FURTHER INFORMATION
- ◆ DISCLOSURE OF DOCUMENTS
- ◆ WITNESSES OF FACT
- ◆ QUESTIONS TO EXPERTS
- ◆ REQUESTS FOR INFORMATION ETC.
- ◆ DOCUMENTS TO BE FILED WITH PRE-TRIAL CHECKLIST
- ◆ DATES FOR FILING PRE-TRIAL CHECKLIST AND THE TRIAL
- ◆ DIRECTIONS FOLLOWING FILING OF PRE-TRIAL CHECKLIST

L Multi-Track

```
┌─────────────────────────────────┐
│   Allocation to the multi-track │
└─────────────────────────────────┘
              ↓
```

Case management 1
The court (r 29.2(1)-(2)):
◆ a) gives directions for the management of the case and sets a timetable for the steps to be taken between the giving of directions and the trial, or
b) fixes:
   i) a case management conference, and/or
   ii) a pre-trial review.
◆ gives any other directions relating to case management.
◆ fixes the trial date or period in which the trial is to take place.

Notice of allocation
The court sends this to the parties and it includes (r 29.2(2)-(3)):
◆ the trial date or trial period, and
◆ date for filing the pre-trial checklist.

Pre-trial checklist
(r 29.6(1) and (4))
No later than 14 days before the date specified in the notice of allocation for the return of the completed checklist (or in any later direction of the court) the court sends the parties a pre-trial checklist (listing questionnaire) (unless it considers one is not needed)

Minimum 14 days

DATE (given in allocation notice (see above) for parties to file:
◆ the pre-trial checklist (and usually the fee, see p 381).
◆ costs estimate (PD29: 8.1).

Exchange
The parties are encouraged to exchange copies of the pre-trial checklists before they are filed to avoid the court being given conflicting or incomplete information (PD29: 8.1(5))

Pre-trial review
The Court *may* (but does not have to) decide to:
◆ hold a pre-trial review, or
◆ cancel a previously fixed pre-trial review.
If so, it serves a notice of its decision at least 7 days before the date fixed for the hearing/cancelled hearing

date specified for filing a pre-trial checklist is not more than 8 weeks before the trial date or the beginning of the trial period (PD29: 8.1(3))

Case management 2
The court (r 29.8, PD29: 8.1(6)):
As soon as practicable after:
a) each party has filed a completed pre-trial checklist, or
b) the court has held a listing hearing, or
c) the court has held a pre-trial review,
   the court will:
◆ set a trial timetable (*unless* one has already been fixed, or the court considers that it would be inappropriate to do so),
◆ fix or confirm the date for the trial or the week within which the trial is to begin.

Notice of Trial
The Court gives the parties notice of the trial timetable and the date or trial period

Trial
(see p 459)

Multi-Track case management (ie: Directions hearings)
(r 29.3, 29.6, PD29: 3, 5, 8)

➤ Any time after the claim has been allocated the court may fix:
   ◆ a case management conference, or
   ◆ a pre-trial review.
   Note: at such hearings, if a party is legally represented, that representative must be familiar with the case and have authority to deal with any issues that are likely to arise.

➤ A party must apply to court if he wishes to vary any dates fixed for:
   ◆ a case management conference
   ◆ a pre-trial review
   ◆ return of a pre-trial checklist
   ◆ the trial
   ◆ the trial period.
   Note: Any date set by the court or the *CPR* for doing any act may not be varied by the parties if it makes it necessary to vary any of these dates.

➤ The court may give directions without a hearing.

➤ Whether or not the court has fixed a trial date or period, it may either:
   ◆ give directions for certain steps to be taken and fix a date for a case management conference or a pre-trial review to take place after they have been taken, or
   ◆ fix a date for a case management conference.

➤ Items in bold in the case management box for 'Fast Track' apply here.

➤ If the court fixes a hearing to give directions it gives the parties at least 3 days' notice of the hearing unless a pre-trial review (see chart left).

➤ Where a party applies for a direction not included in a set case management timetable he must do so as soon as possible so as to minimise the need to change the timetable.

Problems with the pre-trial checklist

➤ Items in bold in this section under 'Fast Track' apply here too.

➤ Where the court holds a hearing the date must be as early as possible and the parties are given at least 3 days' notice of the date (unless a pre-trial review - see left).

➤ **A party files:** where a party files a pre-trial checklist but another party does not do so, the court will fix a hearing. Whether or not the defaulting party attends the hearing, the court will normally fix or confirm the trial date and make other orders about the steps to be taken to prepare the case for trial.

Directions on allocation (PD29: 4)

➤ The court tailors directions to the needs of the case and the steps which the parties have already taken to prepare the case of which it is aware. In particular it will have regard to the extent to which *Practice Direction (Pre-Action Conduct)* or any pre-action protocol has or (as the case may be) has not been complied with.

➤ The court's first concern is to ensure that issues between parties are identified and necessary evidence is prepared + disclosed. If in doubt about directions, the court holds a hearing (listed as promptly as possible).

➤ The court may have regard to any document filed with an allocation questionnaire containing further information *provided* that the document states either that its contents have been agreed with every other party or that it has been served on every other party and when it was served.

Agreed directions	No agreed directions

The court may approve these if:
 ◆ the parties have filed these, *and*
 ◆ the court considers they are suitable, *and*
 ◆ they set out a timetable (referring to calendar dates) for steps to prepare the case, *and*
 ◆ they include a date/trial period (which must not be later than reasonably necessary), *and*
 ◆ they include provisions about disclosure of documents, *and*
   ● these may limit disclosure to standard disclosure between all parties or to less than that, *and/or*
   ● these may direct that disclosure take place by supply of copy documents without a list (but it must in that case either direct that the parties must serve a disclosure statement with the copies or record that they have agreed to disclose in that way without such a statement)
 ◆ they include provision about both factual and expert evidence (eg: none is required), *and*
 ◆ they contain other appropriate provisions.
	The court's general approach is:
	 ◆ to give directions for the filing and service of any further information required to clarify either party's case,
	 ◆ to direct standard disclosure (see pp 443-445),
	 ◆ to direct the simultaneous exchange of witness statements,
	 ◆ to give directions for a single joint expert unless there is good reason not to do so,
	 ◆ if no directions for a single expert are given:
	   ● to direct simultaneous exchange of experts' reports
	   ● (if experts' reports are not agreed) to direct a discussion between experts and preparation of a report
	   NB: if expert evidence is required on issues of liability and amount of damages, the court may direct that the exchange of reports that relate to liability are exchanged simultaneously and those relating to amount of damages are exchanged sequentially.
	 ◆ to list a case management conference after the date for compliance with directions,
	 ◆ to specify a trial period.
	 Note: If the court does not approve agreed directions but gives directions itself without a case management conference, it takes any proposed directions into account in deciding on directions.

➤ **Varying the Court's directions** - the procedure is outside this book but is set out in *PD29: 6*.

Directions on listing (PD29: 9)

➤ The court must fix the trial date or week, give a time estimate and fix the place of trial.

➤ The parties should seek to agree directions and may file the proposed order. (The court may make an order in those terms or it may make a different order.)
  ◆ Agreed directions should include provisions about evidence (especially expert evidence - see p 458), a trial timetable and time estimate, preparation of a trial bundle, other matters for preparation for trial.

➤ **Varying the Court's directions** - the procedure is outside the scope of this book but is set out in *PD29: 6*.

What happens at a case management conference? (PD29: 5)

➤ A review of the steps taken in the preparation of the case (especially compliance with any directions).

➤ The court gives directions about steps to progress of the claim in accordance with the overriding objective.

➤ The court records agreements reached between parties about issues + conduct of the claim.

➤ Topics usually considered include:
  ◆ whether the claimant has made his claim clearly (especially any amount he is claiming),
  ◆ whether any amendments are required to the claim, a statement of case or any other document,
  ◆ what disclosure of documents (if any) and factual evidence is necessary,
  ◆ what expert evidence is reasonably required and how and when it should be obtained and disclosed,
  ◆ what arrangements should be made to clarify, obtain further information or put questions to experts,
  ◆ whether it is just and saves costs to order a split trial or the trial of one or more preliminary issues.

➤ The court will not at this stage give permission to use expert evidence unless it can identify each expert by name or field in its order and say whether his evidence is to be given orally or by the use of his report.
  ◆ A party who obtains expert evidence before obtaining a direction about it does so at his own risk as to costs, *except* where he obtained the evidence in compliance with a pre-action protocol.

➤ The parties and their legal advisers should:
  ◆ ensure that all documents that the court is likely to ask to see are brought to the hearing,
  ◆ consider whether the parties should attend,
  ◆ consider whether a case summary will be useful (containing a brief chronology of the claim, the issues of fact which are agreed or in dispute and the evidence needed to decide them, maximum 500 words and prepared by the claimant and agreed with the other parties if possible) , *and*
  ◆ consider what orders each wishes to be made and give notice of them to the other parties.

M Disclosure and Inspection (*Part 31*)

I	Generally
II	Disclosure
III	Inspection

I Generally

➤ 'Disclosure' is a statement by a party that a document exists or has existed (*r 31.2*).

➤ The duty to disclose is limited to a document which is or has been in a party's control (*r 31.8*), ie:

    a) it is or was in his physical possession, *or*

    b) he has or has had a right to possession of it, *or*

    c) he has or has had a right to inspect or take copies of it.

Documents and copies

➤ A 'document' is anything in which information of any description is recorded (*r 31.4*).

    ◆ A 'copy' is anything onto which information recorded in a document has been copied (by whatever means, whether directly or indirectly) (*r 31.4*).

        • A copy which contains a modification, obliteration or other marking or feature on which a party intends to rely or which adversely affects his case or another party's case or supports another party's case is a separate document (*r 31.9*).

        • A party need not disclose more than one copy of a document (*r 31.9*).

➤ Any duty of disclosure continues until the proceedings are concluded (*r 31.11(1)*).

    ◆ If a document comes to a party's notice during proceedings, he must immediately notify every other party (*r 31.11(2)*).

    ◆ Disclosure and/or inspection may take place in stages if the parties agree or the court so directs (*r 31.13*).

➤ A party may not rely on any document which he fails to disclose or to which he does not permit inspection, unless the court gives permission for him to rely on it (*r 31.21*).

Claim to withhold disclosure or inspection (*r 31.19*)

➤ A person may apply, without notice (and supported by evidence), for an order permitting him to withhold disclosure of a document on the ground that disclosure would damage the public interest.

Order for specific disclosure or inspection (r 31.12)

➤ A court may make an order for specific disclosure or inspection (r 31.12(1)).

Discovery	Inspection
➤ An order that a party must (r 31.12(2)): ◆ disclose documents or classes of documents specified in the order, *and/or* ◆ carry out a search to the extent specified in the order, *and/or* ◆ disclose any documents located as a result of that search.	➤ An order that a party must permit inspection of a document (or class of documents) which that party disclosed, being a document which: ◆ adversely affects his own case, *or* ◆ adversely affects another party's case, *or* ◆ supports another party's case ... ... but is a document which that party considered would be disproportionate to the issues in the case to permit inspection (r 31.12(3)).

II   Disclosure

Before proceedings / By a person not party to proceedings

	Before proceedings	By a non party
Application (supported by evidence)	Under *SCA 1981 s 33* or *CCA 1984 s 52* (Sch 2 r 16)	Under *SCA 1981 s 34* or *CCA 1984 s 53* (Sch 2 r 17)
Grounds	a) the respondent is likely to be party to subsequent proceedings, *and* b) the applicant is likely to be a party to those proceedings, *and* c) if proceedings had started the respondent's duty of standard disclosure would extend to the documents, *and* d) disclosure before the start of proceedings is desirable to: i) dispose fairly of the anticipated proceedings, *or* ii) assist in resolving the dispute without proceedings, *or* iii) save costs.	a) the documents are likely to support the case of the applicant or adversely affect the case of another party, *and* b) disclosure is necessary to *either*: i) dispose fairly of the proceedings, *or* ii) save costs.
Order	◆ Must ... • specify the documents or classes of documents for disclosure, *and* • require the respondent to specify those document which are no longer in his control or in respect of which he claims a right or duty to withhold inspection. ◆ May ... • require the respondent to indicate what has happened to documents which he no longer controls, *and* • specify the time and place for disclosure and inspection.	

➤ 'Standard disclosure' requires a party to disclose only the documents (*r 31.6*):

  ◆ on which he relies, *and*

  ◆ which adversely affect his own case or another party's case or support another party's case, *and*

  ◆ which he is required to disclose by a *PD*.

➤ Standard disclosure is normal (*PD31A: 1.1*) and is ordered unless the court directs otherwise (*r 31.5(1)*).

  ◆ The court may dispense with or limit standard disclosure (*r 31.5(2)*).

  ◆ The parties may agree in writing to dispense with or limit standard disclosure (in which case the agreement should be lodged with the court (*PD31A: 1.4*))(*r 31.5(3)*).

Duty of search (*r 31.7*)

➤ For standard disclosure a party has a duty to make a reasonable search for documents which (*r 31.7(1)*):

  ◆ adversely affect his own case or another party's case or support another party's case, *or*

  ◆ he is required to disclose by a *PD*.

➤ 'Reasonableness' in ascertained by reference to a number of factors, include (*r 31.7(2)*):

  ◆ the number of the documents,

  ◆ the nature and complexity of the proceedings,

  ◆ the ease and expense of retrieval of any particular document,

  ◆ the significance of any document which is likely to be located as a result of the search.

Procedure for standard disclosure (*r 31.10*)

Parties	➤ Each party must make and serve on every other party a list in practice *Form N265* (*r 31.2, PD31A: 3.1*). ◆ The parties may agree in writing to disclose documents without making a list and to disclose without making a disclosing statement (*r 31.8*).

List	➤ The list must:
	
	◆ identify the documents in a convenient order and manner as concisely as possible (*r.31.10(3)*).
	
	• Usually this means: listed in date order, numbered consecutively, and concisely described. A large number of documents in a particular category may be listed as such (*PD31A: 3.2*)
	
	◆ indicate documents for which a right or duty to withhold inspection is claimed *and* those documents which are no longer in that party's control (*plus* what has happened to those documents) (*r 31.10(4)*).
	
	◆ include a disclosure statement which (*r 31.10(4)-(5)*):
	
	• sets out the extent of the search, *and*
	
	  ▪ The statement should state that the belief of the disclosing party that the extent of the search is reasonable in all the circumstances.
	
	  ▪ Attention should be drawn to limitations adopted for proportionality reasons and reasons should be given (eg: expense, difficulty, marginal relevance) (*r 31.7(3)*), *PD31A: 4.2*)
	
	• certifies that the party making the disclosure understands the duty to disclose, *and*
	
	• certifies that the best of that party's knowledge he has carried out the duty to disclose.
	
	◆ if the person making the statement is a company, firm, association or other organisation (*r 31.10(7)*):
	
	• identify the person making the statement (name, address, position or the basis on which he makes the statement (*PD31A: 4.3*)), *and*
	
	• explain why that person is considered the appropriate person to the make the statement.

Electronic Documents (PD31B)

An 'Electronic Document' (or 'ED') means any document held in electronic form (including email and other electronic communications (eg: text messages, voicemail, word-processed documents and databases), documents stored on portable devices (eg: memory sticks and mobile phones). It includes documents stored on servers and back-up systems, documents that have been 'deleted' and data about data (ie: metadata) and other embedded data which is not typically visible on screen or a print out (*PD31B: 5(3)*).

Scope of PD31B

➤ *PD31B* is to encourage and assist the parties to reach agreement in relation to ED disclosure in a proportionate and cost-effective manner (*PD31B: 2*).

◆ Unless the court orders otherwise, *PD31B* only applies to proceedings that are (or are likely to be) allocated to the multi-track (*PD31B: 3*).

General principles

➤ When considering ED disclosure, the parties and their legal representatives should bear in mind the following general principles (*PD31B: 6*):

◆ EDs should be managed efficiently in order to minimise the cost incurred, *and*

◆ technology should be used in order to ensure that document management activities are undertaken efficiently and effectively, *and*

◆ disclosure should be given in a manner which gives effect to the overriding objective, *and*

◆ EDs should generally be made available for inspection in a form allowing the receiving party the same ability to access, search, review and display the documents as the disclosing party, *and*

◆ disclosure of EDs which are of no relevance to the proceedings may place an excessive burden in time and cost on the party to whom disclosure is given.

As soon as litigation is contemplated

➤ As soon as litigation is contemplated, the parties' legal representatives must notify their clients of the need to preserve disclosable documents (*PD31B: 7*).

◆ The documents to be preserved include EDs which would otherwise be deleted in accordance with a document retention policy or otherwise deleted in the ordinary course of business.

Before the first Case Management Conference

➤ Before the first Case Management Conference, the parties and their legal representatives must discuss:

◆ the use of technology in the management of EDs and the conduct of proceedings, in particular for the purpose of (*PD31B: 8*):

● creating lists of documents to be disclosed, *and*

● giving disclosure by providing documents and information about documents in electronic format, *and*

● presenting documents and other material to the court at the trial, *and*

◆ the disclosure of EDs (*PD31B: 9*).

● In some cases (eg: heavy and complex cases) it may be appropriate to begin discussions before proceedings are commenced (*PD31B: 9*).

● The discussions should include (where appropriate) (*PD31B: 9*):

■ categories of EDs within the parties' control, the computer systems, electronic devices and media on which any relevant documents may be held, storage systems and document retention policies, *and*

■ the scope of the reasonable search for EDs required by *r 31.7* (see p 445), *and*

■ the tools and techniques (if any) which should be considered to reduce the burden and cost of disclosure of EDs, including:

a) limiting disclosure of documents or certain categories of documents to particular date ranges, to particular custodians of documents, or to particular types of documents, *and*

b) the use of agreed Keyword Searches, *and*

c) the use of agreed software tools, *and*

d) the methods to be used to identify duplicate documents, *and*

e) the use of data sampling, *and*

f) the methods to be used to identify privileged documents and other non-disclosable documents, to redact documents (if appropriate), and for dealing with privileged or other documents which have been inadvertently disclosed, *and*

g) the use of a staged approach to the disclosure of EDs, *and*

■ the preservation of EDs (to prevent loss of such documents before the trial), *and*

■ the exchange of data about EDs in an agreed electronic format using agreed fields, *and*

■ the formats in which EDs are to be provided on inspection and the methods to be used, *and*

■ the basis of charging for or sharing the cost of the provision of EDs, and whether any arrangements for charging or sharing of costs are final or are subject to re-allocation in accordance with any order for costs subsequently made, *and*

■ whether it would be appropriate to use the services of a neutral electronic repository for ED storage.

➤ Documents submitted to the court before the first Case Management Conference should include a summary of matters on which the parties agree about ED disclosure and of matters on which they disagree (*PD31B: 14*).

Electronic Documents (continued) (*PD31B*)

ED Questionnaire

➤ Sometimes, the parties should use an EDQuestionnaire (the form is set out in *PD31B: Schedule*) to provide information to each other about the scope, extent and most suitable format for ED disclosure (*PD31B: 10*).

   ◆ Answers to the EDQuestionnaire must be verified by a statement of truth (*PD31B: 11*).

   ◆ The person signing the EDQuestionnaire should attend the first Case Management Conference, and any subsequent hearing at which disclosure is likely to be considered (*PD31B: 16*).

No appropriate agreement about ED disclosure

➤ If the parties indicate that they cannot reach agreement about ED disclosure (and that no agreement is likely), the court will give written directions about disclosure or order a separate hearing about disclosure. If the court considers that any agreement about ED disclosure is inappropriate or insufficient, the court will give directions about disclosure. In either case, the court will consider making an order that the parties must complete and exchange all or any part of an EDQuestionnaire within 14 days (or such other period the court directs) (*PD31B: 15, 18*).

➤ If at any time it becomes apparent that the parties cannot reach agreement about ED disclosure, the parties should seek directions from the court at the earliest practical date (*PD31B: 17*).

➤ If a party gives ED disclosure without first discussing with other parties how to plan and manage it, the court may require that party to carry out further document searches or repeat other steps already carried out (*PD31B: 19*).

'reasonable search'

➤ The 'reasonable search' (under *r 31.7* - see p 445) for standard disclosure is affected by EDs (*PD31B: 20*).

   ◆ The extent of the search which must be made will depend on the circumstances of the case including, in particular, the factors referred to in *r 31.7(2)* (see p 445).

   ◆ The parties should remember that the overriding objective includes dealing with the case in proportionate ways.

➤ Possible factors in deciding the reasonableness of a search for EDs include (but are not limited to) (*PD31B: 21*):

   ◆ the number of documents involved, *and*

   ◆ the nature and complexity of the proceedings, *and*

   ◆ the ease and expense of retrieval of any particular document, including the:

      • accessibility of EDs including e-mail communications on computer systems, servers, back-up systems and other electronic devices or media that may contain such documents taking into account alterations or developments in hardware or software systems used by the disclosing party and/or available to enable access to such documents, *and*

      • location of relevant EDs, data, computer systems, servers, back-up systems and other electronic devices or media that may contain such documents, *and*

      • likelihood of locating relevant data, *and*

      • cost of recovering any EDs and cost of disclosing and providing inspection of any relevant EDs, *and*

      • likelihood that EDs will be materially altered in the course of recovery, disclosure or inspection, *and*

   ◆ the availability of documents or contents of documents from other sources, *and*

   ◆ the significance of any document which is likely to be located during the search.

➤ Depending on the circumstances, it may be reasonable to search all of the parties' electronic storage systems, or to search only some part of those systems (*PD31B: 22*).

   ◆ Eg: it may be reasonable to decide not to search for documents coming into existence before a particular date, or to limit the search to documents in particular places, or to documents falling into particular categories.

➤ Sometimes a staged approach is appropriate, with disclosure initially of limited categories of documents only. Such categories may subsequently be extended/ limited depending on the results initially obtained (*PD31B: 23*).

➤ The primary source of disclosure of EDs is normally reasonably accessible data. A party requesting under *r 31.12* (see p 444) specific disclosure of EDs which are not reasonably accessible must demonstrate that the relevance and materiality justify the cost and burden of retrieving and producing them (*PD31B: 24*).

Keywords, Metadata

➤ It may be reasonable to search for EDs by Keyword Searches or other automated methods of searching if a full review of each document would be unreasonable (*PD31B: 25*). However, it will often be insufficient to use simple Keyword Searches or other automated methods of searching alone (*PD31B: 26*). The parties should consider supplementing such searches with additional techniques (eg: individually reviewing certain documents or categories of documents (eg: important documents generated by key personnel) and taking such other steps as may be required in order to justify the selection to the court) (*PD31B: 27*).

➤ A party requesting disclosure of additional Metadata or forensic image copies of disclosed documents (for example in relation to a dispute concerning authenticity) must demonstrate that the relevance and materiality of the requested Metadata justify the cost and burden of producing that Metadata (*PD31B: 28*).

Disclosure, Inspection

➤ If a party is giving disclosure of EDs, *PD31A: 3* (see p 445) is amended in various ways (*PD31B: 30*) and there is a mandated specific form in which the list of documents must be given (*PD31B: 31*).

➤ The parties should co-operate at an early stage about the format in which EDs are to be provided on inspection. In case of difficulty or disagreement, the matter should be referred to the court for directions at the earliest practical date, if possible at the first Case Management Conference (*PD31B: 32*).

➤ Save where otherwise agreed/ordered, electronic copies of disclosed documents should be provided in their Native Format, so as to preserve Metadata relating to the date of creation of each document (*PD31B: 33*).

➤ A party should provide any available searchable OCR versions of EDs with the original. A party may however choose not to provide OCR versions of redacted documents. If OCR versions are provided, they are provided on an 'as is' basis, with no assurance to the other party that the OCR versions are complete or accurate (*PD31B: 34*).

III   Inspection

➤ When a document has been disclosed to a party, that party has the right to inspect that document *unless* (*r 31.3*):

a) the document is no longer in the possession of the party who disclosed it, *or*

b) the party disclosing the document has a right or duty to withhold inspection, *or*

c) the party disclosing the document ...

... (which adversely affects his own case or another party's case or supports another party's case) ...

... considers that it would be disproportionate to issues to permit inspection and he stated in his disclosure statement that inspection of the document would not be permitted as to do so would be disproportionate, *or*

d) certain rules (in *r 78.26* - not dealt with in this book) apply about disclosure and inspection of evidence arising out of mediation of certain cross-border disputes.

➤ A party may inspect a document mentioned in (*r 31.14*):

◆ a statement of case, a witness statement or a witness summary, *or*

◆ an affidavit, *or*

◆ an expert's report (although material instructions on the basis of which the report was prepared need only be available for inspection if the court so orders having reasonable grounds for believing that the statement of instructions is inaccurate or incomplete) if the expert's report has not been previously disclosed in proceedings and provided that that party gets a court order first.

Inspection of witness statements ... or not
➤ A witness statement which stands as evidence in chief is open to inspection during the course of the trial unless the court otherwise directs (*r 32.13(1)*).
➤ However, a party may apply for a direction that a witness statement should not be open for inspection (*r 32.13(2)*).

| Grounds for the court's refusing inspection | ➤ The court is satisfied that the statement (or words or passages in the statement) should not be open to inspection due to (*r 32.13(3)-(4)*):
a) the interests of justice, *or*
b) the public interest, *or*
c) the nature of any expert medical advice in the statement, *or*
d) the nature of any confidential information in the statement, *or*
e) the need to protect the interests of any child or protected party |

> ie: someone who lacks capacity to conduct proceedings

➤ A party must give written notice of a wish to inspect a document. The party who disclosed the document must permit inspection not more than 7 days after receipt of this notice (*r 31.15*).

◆ A party may request a copy and if that party also undertakes to pay reasonable copying costs, the party who made the disclosure must supply a copy not more than 7 days after receiving the request.

➤ If a party accidentally allows inspection of a privileged document, the party who inspected it may use it, or its contents, only with the permission of the court (*r 31.20*).

Privilege

➤ Some documents are recognised by law as 'privileged', they must be disclosed *but* do not have to be available for inspection. The following categories of documents are privileged:

legal professional privilege

1 **Solicitor-client correspondence**, for the purpose of legal advice.

2 **Solicitor-third party correspondence**, if created after litigation is commenced, *or* if created with a view to starting litigation or to obtain evidence or advice.

3 **Client-third party correspondence**, if the primary purpose at the time of creation was to see if legal advice should be obtained for existing or contemplated litigation.

4 **'Without prejudice' evidence of negotiations** (unless as evidence of a settlement which was reached where the dispute is whether any settlement was reached at all!).

5 **Public policy material**, eg: defence, NSPCC, social work and probation records.

6 **Material incriminating a party to the proceedings** (in UK criminal or penal proceedings).

➤ Secondary evidence of a privileged document is admissible, unless prevented by an injunction (but see 'Professional ethics' in the 'Conduct' section).

➤ Privilege belongs to the client, so the solicitor may not waive it without the client's authority.

Privilege: restrictions on categories 1 to 3 above

➤ The Court of Appeal in *Three Rivers District Council v Bank of England (Disclosure) (No 3)* [2003] EWCA Civ 474 restricts the scope of legal professional privilege:

◆ Legal advice privilege will only apply to advice given in relation to a client's legal rights and obligations. However, what amounts to legal rights and obligations is less clear.

◆ Legal advice privilege can no longer be assumed despite the existence of a solicitor's retainer. Not all correspondence between client and solicitor will automatically qualify for the protection of legal advice privilege.

N   Evidence

I   Generally

➤ The court has a general power to control evidence by giving directions as to (*r 32.1*):

- the issues which require evidence, *and*

- the nature of the evidence which the court requires to decide those issues, *and*

- the way in which evidence is to be placed before the court ...

  ... even if this involves excluding evidence which would be otherwise admissible (*r 32.2*).

  - Any fact which needs to be proved by the evidence of a witness is usually proved *either* at trial (by the witnesses' oral evidence given in public) *or* at any other hearing by evidence in writing (*r 32.3*).

    - At a **hearing other than trial,** a party may rely on his statement of case or his application notice provided that the statement or application notice are verified by a statement of truth (*r 32.6*).

  - The court may allow a witness to give evidence through a video link or by other means (*r 32.3*).

➤ Contempt of court proceedings may be brought (by the Attorney General, or with the court's permission) against a person who makes, or causes to be made, a false statement in a document verified by a statement of truth without an honest belief in the statement's truth (*r 32.14*).

Notice to admit or produce documents (*r 32.19*)
◆ A party is deemed to admit the authenticity of a document disclosed to him under *Part 31* (see pp 443 et seq) unless he serves notice that the wishes the document to be proved at trial.
◆ A notice must be served by the latest date for serving witness statements or within 7 days of disclosure of the document - whichever is later.

Notice to admit facts (*r 32.18*)	
◆ A party may serve notice on another party requiring him to admit facts, or part of the case, specified in the notice	
Service	◆ No later than 21 days before the trial.
Admission	◆ The admission may be used against the party making it only in the proceedings in which the notice to admit is served and only by the party who served the notice.
	◆ The court may allow a party to amend or withdraw an admission on such terms as it thinks fit.

II   Witnesses (Statements, summaries)

➤   A witness statement is a written statement signed by a person; it contains the evidence which that person would be allowed to give orally (*r 32.4(1)*).

◆   The court (*r 32.4(2)-(3)*):

• **will order** a party to serve on the other parties any witness statement on which that party intends to rely on in relation to any issues of fact to be decided at trial, *and*

▪ At trial where a witness is called to give oral evidence, a witness statement will stand as a witnesses' evidence in chief unless the court orders otherwise (*r 32.5(2)*).

▪ If a witness statement (or summary) is not served within the time limit specified by the court, the witness may not be called to give oral evidence unless the court gives permission (*r 32.10*).

▪ If a party who has served a witness statement does not call the witness to give evidence at trial or put the witness statement in as hearsay evidence, any other party may put the witness statement in as hearsay evidence (*r 32.5(5)*).

• **may direct** the sequence in which statements are served and whether statements are to be filed.

◆   A witness statement must comply with the relevant *PD* (*r 32.8*).

• If a statement does not comply with *Part 32* or *PD32,* the court may refuse to admit it as evidence and may refuse to allow costs arising from its preparation) (*PD32: 25.1*).

Witness statements

➤   A witness statement must (*PD32: 17-20*):

◆   be headed with the name and number of the proceedings and the Court or Division.

◆   state at the top right hand corner of the first page:

• the party on whose behalf it is made, *and*

• the initials and surname of the witness, *and*

• the number of the statement in relation to that witness, *and*

• the identifying initials and number of each exhibit referred to, *and*

• the date the statement was made.

◆   if practicable, be in the witnesses' own words.

◆   be expressed in the first person.

◆   state the full name of the witness, the witnesses' place of residence (or if he is making the statement in a professional or business capacity - the address at which he works, his position and the name of his firm/employer).

◆   the witness' occupation (or if the witness has none, his description).

◆   whether the witness is a party to the proceedings or is the employee of such a party.

◆   indicate which statements are from the witnesses' own knowledge and which are from his information and belief (and any source for such information and belief).

◆   be verified by a statement of truth: 'I believe that the facts stated in this witness statement are true' (see p 388).

➤   Any exhibit should be verified and identified by the witness.

➤ If a party is required to serve a witness statement for use at trial but cannot obtain a witness statement, that party may apply to court for permission to serve a witness summary instead of the statement (*r 32.9(1)*).

◆ The application is an application without notice.

◆ A 'witness summary' is a summary of the evidence (if known) which would be included in a witness statement or (if the evidence is not known) matters about which the party serving the summary wishes to question the witness (*r 32.9(2)*).

Plans, photographs, models, etc (*r 33.5*)

➤ Where evidence (eg: a plan, a photograph, business records which may be given in evidence under *CEA 1995 s 9*, or a model) is **not**:

a) contained in a witness statement, affidavit or an expert's report, *or*

b) to be given orally at trial, *or*

c) evidence in respect of which a hearsay notice must be given under *r 32.2*, ...

... that evidence may only be receivable if the party intending to rely on the evidence gives notice to the other parties (unless the court orders otherwise).

◆ Where evidence is to be given as evidence of a fact, notice must be given not later than the last day for serving witness statements, *unless either*

● the evidence forms part of expert evidence, in which case notice is given when the expert's report is served on the other party, *or*

● there is not to be a witness statement *or* the evidence is solely to disprove an allegation made in a witness statement, in which case notice is at least 21 days before the hearing the evidence is to be put.

◆ If evidence is produced for a reason other than as evidence of fact or expert evidence, the party intending to rely on it must give at notice at least 21 days before the hearing.

➤ A party must give other parties every opportunity to inspect the evidence and agree its admission without further proof.

III   Opinion

➤ A witness may only testify as to matters observed by him and may not give his *opinion* about those matters.

➤ Opinion 'evidence' is inadmissible unless it is:

1   **expert opinion** (*CEA 1972 s 3(1)*).

◆ This is opinion on any relevant matter on which the expert is qualified to give expert evidence.

2   **perception** (*CEA 1972 s 3(2)*).

◆ The witness conveys relevant facts personally perceived by him. The reason for this relaxation is that it is not always possible to separate facts from inferences.

IV   Expert evidence

➤ See p 458.

V   Hearsay

Hearsay: a statutory meaning

➤   Hearsay is 'a statement made by someone *other* than the person *now* giving evidence, intended to prove the truth of the matter stated' whether first hand hearsay (ie: reported directly from a source) or multiple hearsay (coming from a source *via* intermediaries).

Hearsay: a plain English meaning (!)

➤   Hearsay is an assertion, other than one made by a person while giving oral evidence in the proceedings, if the assertion is used to prove the truth of what it asserts.

Hearsay procedure (*CEA 1995*)

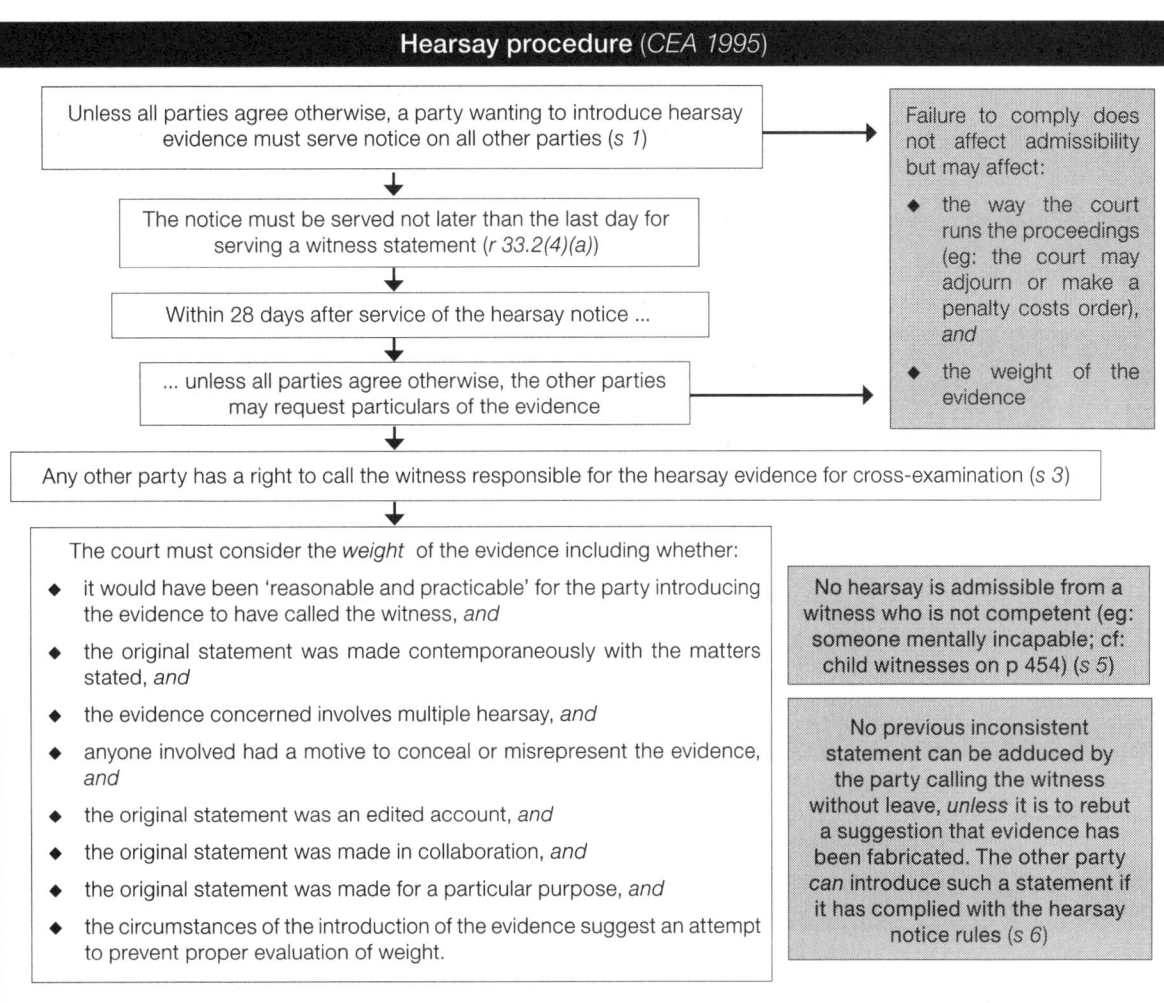

Unless all parties agree otherwise, a party wanting to introduce hearsay evidence must serve notice on all other parties (*s 1*)

↓

The notice must be served not later than the last day for serving a witness statement (*r 33.2(4)(a)*)

↓

Within 28 days after service of the hearsay notice ...

↓

... unless all parties agree otherwise, the other parties may request particulars of the evidence

Failure to comply does not affect admissibility but may affect:

◆   the way the court runs the proceedings (eg: the court may adjourn or make a penalty costs order), *and*

◆   the weight of the evidence

Any other party has a right to call the witness responsible for the hearsay evidence for cross-examination (*s 3*)

↓

The court must consider the *weight* of the evidence including whether:

◆   it would have been 'reasonable and practicable' for the party introducing the evidence to have called the witness, *and*

◆   the original statement was made contemporaneously with the matters stated, *and*

◆   the evidence concerned involves multiple hearsay, *and*

◆   anyone involved had a motive to conceal or misrepresent the evidence, *and*

◆   the original statement was an edited account, *and*

◆   the original statement was made in collaboration, *and*

◆   the original statement was made for a particular purpose, *and*

◆   the circumstances of the introduction of the evidence suggest an attempt to prevent proper evaluation of weight.

No hearsay is admissible from a witness who is not competent (eg: someone mentally incapable; cf: child witnesses on p 454) (*s 5*)

No previous inconsistent statement can be adduced by the party calling the witness without leave, *unless* it is to rebut a suggestion that evidence has been fabricated. The other party *can* introduce such a statement if it has complied with the hearsay notice rules (*s 6*)

Published works

➤   Published works and records are admissible as evidence of the facts contained (*CEA 1995 s 7*).

Contents of a hearsay notice

➤ A hearsay notice must state:

a) identify the hearsay evidence (*r 33.2(3)(a)*), *and*

b) state that the party serving the notice will rely on the hearsay evidence at trial (*r 33.2(3)(b)*), *and*

c) if the witness is not being called to give evidence, gives the reason why the witness will not be called (*r 33.2(3)(c)*).

- If the witness is not being called to give evidence, the party intending to rely on the hearsay evidence must, when he serves the witness statement inform the other parties that the witness is not being called to give evidence and give the reason why the witness is not being called (*r 33.2(3)(c)*).

- If the hearsay is in a document, the party proposing to rely on the hearsay evidence must supply a copy to any party who requests a copy (*r 32.2(4)(b)*).

Cross-examination	Credibility
➤ Any other party may apply to the court for permission to call the maker of statement to be cross-examined on the contents of the statement (*r 33.4(1)*).	➤ If any other party wishes to call evidence to attach the credibility of the person who made the statement, that party must give notice of this intention to the party who proposes to give hearsay evidence (*r 33.5(1)*).
◆ An application must be made not more than 14 days after the day on which the notice is served on the applicant (*r 33.4(2)*).	◆ Notice must be given not more than 14 days after the day on which the hearsay notice was served on the party who wishes to dispute credibility (*r 33.5(2)*).

➤ 1 notice may deal with more than 1 witness.

➤ The duty to give a notice of intention to rely on hearsay evidence does not apply (*r 33.3*):

a) to evidence at hearings other than trials, *or*

b) an affidavit or a witness statement which is to be used at trial but which does not contain hearsay evidence, *or*

c) to a statement which a party to a probate action wishes to put in evidence and which is alleged to have been made by the person whose estate is the subject of the proceedings, *or*

d) where a *PD* excludes the requirement to give such a notice.

Business records

➤ Although hearsay, business records are admissible in evidence (*CEA 1995 s 9(1)*).

- ◆ To be accepted as a business record, a document must be certified by an officer of the business (*CEA 1995 s 9(2)*).

- ◆ Computerised statements are also *prima facie* admissible as hearsay (*CEA 1995 ss 1-2*).

VI   Notarial acts and instruments

➤ A notarial act or instrument may be received in evidence without further proof as duly authenticated unless the contrary is proved (*r 32.20*).

O Trial preparations

I   Making up the trial bundle
II   Should counsel be instructed?
III   Ensuring attendance of witnesses or taking depositions
IV   Expert evidence

I   Making up the trial bundle (r 39.5, PD39A: 3)

Steps

1   Check through the court's case management directions to see where the trial will be.

2   Check whether any relevant hearings are needed to 'flesh out' existing directions (eg: listing hearings, case management conferences, pre-trial review).

3   The court will consult the parties when it sets a timetable for a trial under (r 39.4):

♦   r 28.6 (fast track - fixing/confirming the trial date and giving directions), or

♦   r 29.8 (multi-track - setting a trial timetable and fixing/confirming the trial date or week).

4   The contents of the trial bundle should be agreed where possible.

5   **Not more than 7 days and not less than 3 days before the start of the trial,** the claimant's solicitor files the trial bundle containing copies of (NB: originals should be available at trial):

♦   the claim form and all statements of case,

♦   a case summary and/or chronology where appropriate,

♦   requests for further information and responses to the requests,

♦   any notices of intention to rely on evidence (eg: photographs) (see p 452) which are *not*:

  • contained in a witness statement, affidavit or experts report, *or*

  • being given orally at trial, *or*

  • hearsay evidence,

♦   all witness statements being relied on as evidence,

♦   any witness summaries,

♦   any medical reports and responses to them,

♦   any experts' reports and responses to them,

♦   any order giving directions as to the conduct of the trial,

♦   any notices of intention to use hearsay evidence (see p 454),

♦   any other necessary documents.

> **Trial bundles** should be paginated and indexed with a description of each document. If the total number of pages is more than 100, place numbered dividers between groups of documents. The bundle should be contained in a ring binder or lever arch file. Where there is more than 1 bundle, each should be distinguishable (eg: by different colours or letters). If there are numerous bundles, a core bundle should be prepared containing the core documents essential to the proceedings, with references to supplementary documents in the other bundles

6   The parties should also agree where possible that:

♦   documents contained in the bundle are authentic even if not disclosed, *and*

♦   documents in the bundle may be treated as evidence of facts stated within even if a hearsay notice has not been served (see p 454).

7   Where it is not possible to agree the contents of the bundle, a summary of the points on which the parties are unable to agree should be included.

8   The party filing the trial bundle should supply identical bundles to all the parties to the proceedings and for the use of the witnesses.

NB: a reading list together with an estimated length of reading time and an estimated length of the hearing signed by all advocates is also required to be lodged.

II   Should counsel be instructed?

Steps	
1	**A brief: usually needed if a barrister is instructed**
2	**A conference may be necessary**
3	**The barrister's fee**

1   A brief: usually needed if a barrister is instructed

➤ A brief is the traditional presentation of the case to the barrister who will appear at the hearing.

➤ The brief should include:

- ◆ the heading of the action, *and*

- ◆ a list of enclosures being forwarded to counsel (eg: client's statement, witness statements, pleadings, any legal aid certificate, experts' reports, *relevant* correspondence, pleadings, setting down bundle, trial bundle, counsel's earlier advice, etc).

➤ It should then:

- ◆ identify the client.

- ◆ set out *both* sides of the case.

- ◆ indicate the solicitor's view, and draw attention to where advice is specifically needed.

- ◆ formally request counsel to carry out the task required.

➤ The back sheet should be endorsed with:

- ◆ the title of the action.

- ◆ a definition of what the instructions are.

- ◆ counsel's name and that of his chambers.

- ◆ the solicitor's firm's name, address and reference.

- ◆ if relevant, the legal aid reference number.

Note: the third person is traditionally used in writing to counsel.

2   A conference may be necessary

➤ This is useful if the facts are complex, or if counsel wishes to assess a client as a witness, or to fully comprehend and assess his injuries.

- ◆ The solicitor should arrange this with the counsel's clerk if it is thought necessary.

➤ A written opinion may be specifically requested.

- ◆ Costs will not be allowed unless the court decides the need for the conference was reasonable.

3   The barrister's fee

➤ If legal aid funding covers it, the fee will be paid from legal aid.

➤ A solicitor negotiates the fee on behalf of a private client. The solicitor is liable to counsel for the fee, so a solicitor should ensure that he has been put in funds by a client before the barrister is instructed.

- ◆ The appearance fee is payable once the brief is delivered, but it is usually waived or reduced if the action settles before the hearing.

- ◆ The fee covers 1 day, unless otherwise agreed. A 'refresher' is due on subsequent days.

III   Ensuring attendance of witnesses or taking depositions (*Part 34*)

➤ The solicitor must check the availability of witnesses.

➤ Sometimes witnesses may not attend court voluntarily and it is necessary to compel them to do so by a witness summons.

♦ **Expert witnesses:** may prefer to be summonsed as the obligation helps break appointments.

♦ **Police officers**: *must* be summonsed, as they will not otherwise give evidence in a civil matter.

Witness summons (*rr 34.2-34.7, PD34A: 1, 3*)	
Purpose:	A witness summons is a document issued by the court requiring a witness to: ♦ attend court to give evidence, *and/or* ♦ produce documents to the court
Time	➤ General rule: must be served **at least 7 days** before the date on which the witness is required to attend. ♦ A court may change this time limit.
Procedure for issue	**Steps** 1 A witness summons must be in the specified form. 2 There must be a separate witness summons for each witness. 3 Obtain the court's permission to issue the summons if summons is to be issued: a) less than 7 days before the date of the trial, *or* b) for a witness to attend court to give evidence or to produce documents on any date except the date fixed for the trial, *or* c) for a witness to attend court to give evidence or to produce documents at any hearing except the trial. 4 Issue the summons - 2 copies of the witness summons should be filed with the court for sealing. ♦ 1 copy will be kept on the court file. **Note:** A witness summons is issued on the date entered on the summons by the court.
Procedure for service	**Steps** 1 A witness summons will be served by the court *unless* the issuing party indicates in writing, at the time of issue, that he will serve it himself. 2 Prepare the 'witness sum' to pay the witness for travelling expenses and loss of time as follows: ♦ the witness's expenses for travelling to court and returning to his home or place of work, *and* ♦ a sum for time during which earnings or benefit are lost (or a lesser sum it may be proved the witness will lose by attending court. 3 Decide who is to serve the witness summons (see below). 4a **Self-service:** 1 Notify the court in writing that self-service will be the method of service 2 Serve the witness summons and offer the witness the 'witness sum' at the time. 4b **Service by the court:** 1 Deposit, in the court office, the 'witness sum' 2 The court will serve the witness summons

Depositions (*rr 34.8-34.11*)

➤ At times, a party may wish to apply for a witness to be examined *before* a hearing or trial.

♦ Such a witness is called a 'deponent' and his evidence is called a 'deposition'.

• The examination is usually conducted as if the witness were giving evidence at a trial.

➤ A deposition may be given in evidence at a hearing or trial *unless* the court orders otherwise.

♦ However, the court *may* require a deponent to attend the hearing and give evidence orally.

➤ If deposition evidence is to be used, notice must be served at least 21 days before the hearing/trial.

➤ If a deposition is used at trial, it is treated as a witness statement for the purposes of prior inspection.

IV   Expert evidence (*Part 35*)

➤   **Needed?** Expert evidence is restricted to what is reasonably required to resolve the proceedings (*r 35.1*).

➤   **Duty:** It is the duty of experts to help the court on the matters within their expertise. This overrides any obligation to the person from whom experts have received instructions or by whom they are paid (*r 35.3*).

➤   **Permission:** No party may call an expert or use an expert's report without the court's permission (*r 35.4(1)*).

◆   When parties apply for permission they must identify the field in which the expert evidence is required and, where practicable, name of the proposed expert (*r 35.4(2)*).

◆   The court may limit a party's expert's fees/expenses that may be recovered from any other party (*r 35.4(4)*).

➤   **The report:** Expert evidence must be given in a written report unless the court directs otherwise (*r 35.5(1)*).

➤   **Questions:** A party may put to an expert (proportionate) written questions about his report (*r 35.6(1)*).

◆   The answers become part of the report (*r 35.6(3)*).

◆   Unless the court orders otherwise, or the parties agree, questions (*r 35.6(2)*):

●   may be put once only, *and*

●   must be put within 28 days of service of the expert's report, *and*

●   must be for the purpose only of clarification of the report.

◆   Not answering means the evidence may be disregarded and there may be costs penalties (*r 35.6(4)*).

◆   The party instructing the expert must pay the fees for answering the questions (*PD35: 6.2*).

➤   **Joint experts:** Where 2 or more parties wish to submit expert evidence on a particular issue, the court may direct that the evidence on that issue is given by 1 joint expert (*r 35.7(1)*).

◆   Where the parties cannot agree on that expert, the court can select the expert from a list prepared by the parties or direct that the expert is selected in some other manner entirely (*r 35.7(2)*).

◆   A party instructing an expert must, at the same time, send a copy to other relevant parties (*r 35.8(2)*).

◆   The court has a wide discretion to make orders as to the expert's role and his fees(*r 35.8(3)-(4)*).

◆   The instructing parties are usually jointly and severally liable for the expert's fees and expenses (*r 35.8(5)*).

➤   **Court's discretion:** The court has a wide discretion with regard to experts (*r 35.12*). It may eg: direct that the experts discuss certain matters between themselves, prepare a statement of agreed and non-agreed issues, give the expert directions (particularly if the expert requests them), etc.

➤   **Instructions to an expert:** are not privileged against disclosure but the court will not order disclosure of a specific document or allow cross-examination of the expert in court, *unless* it thinks there are reasonable grounds to consider the instructions were inaccurate or incomplete. If the court thinks so, it will allow the cross-examination where it appears to be in the interests of justice to do so (*r 35.10(4), PD35: 5*).

➤   **Non-multi-track:** On the small claims/fast track, if permission for expert evidence is given, the court will:

◆   not direct an expert to attend a hearing unless it is necessary to do so in the interests of justice (*r 35.5(2)*), *and*

◆   normally only allow evidence from 1 expert on a particular issue (*r 35.4(3A)*).

Content of the expert's report (*r 35.10, PD35: 3*)

➤   The experts report should be addressed to the court and must:
◆   give details of the expert's qualifications,
◆   give details of any literature or other material which has been relied on in making the report,
◆   contain a statement setting out the substance of all facts and instructions which are material to the opinions expressed in the report or upon which those opinions are based,
◆   make clear which of the facts stated in the report are within the expert's own knowledge,
◆   say who carried out any examination/measurement/test/experiment used for the report, give the qualifications of that person, and say whether or not the test or experiment has been carried out under the expert's supervision,
◆   if there is a range of opinion on matters in the report, summarise the range and give reasons for the expert's own opinion,
◆   contain a summary of the conclusions reached,
◆   if the expert is not able to give an opinion without qualification, state the qualification,
◆   contain a statement that the expert understands their duty to the court, and has complied with that duty and is aware of the requirements of *Part 35, PD35* and the Protocol for Instruction of Experts to give Evidence in Civil Claims,
◆   contain a statement of truth (see p 388): '"I confirm that I have made clear which facts and matters referred to in this report are within my own knowledge and which are not. Those that are within my own knowledge I confirm to be true. The opinions I have expressed represent my true and complete professional opinions on the matters to which they refer.'

P The trial

Steps

1

The claimant's side makes the opening speech

➤ This involves taking the judge through the statements of case and introducing agreed exhibits.

➤ The judge may dispense with this (particularly in fast track cases - *PD28: 8.2*).

2

The claimant gives evidence

➤ This is done by oral examination, but examination-in-chief is conducted by using the witness statement exchanged previously, unless the court decides otherwise.

➤ The sequence of questioning is:

  ◆ examination-in-chief by the claimant's side,

  ◆ cross-examination by the defendant's side,

  ◆ re-examination (on points arising from the cross-examination) by the claimant's side.

➤ The defendant's case must be put to the claimant during cross-examination.

➤ Each side should check the admissibility rules (see p 450 et seq).

3

The claimant's side presents evidence

➤ This is done by oral examination of the witnesses.

➤ The sequence of questioning is:

  ◆ examination-in-chief by the claimant's side. (This is conducted by using the witness statements exchanged previously, unless the court decides otherwise.)

  ◆ cross-examination by the defendant's side,

  ◆ re-examination (on points arising from the cross-examination) by the claimant's side.

➤ The defendant's case must be put to the witness.

➤ Each side should check the admissibility rules (see p 450 et seq).

➤ If a witness gives consistently unfavourable or adverse answers to the surprise of the claimant, the claimant's side should ask the judge to declare the witness hostile.

  ◆ If the judge does so, previously inconsistent statements can be put to the witness (see *CEA 1995 s 6* and the law on hearsay p 453).

4

The defendant's side makes its opening speech

➤ The defendant's side may make an opening speech.

➤ The judge may dispense with this (particularly in fast track cases - *PD28: 8.2*).

cont.
5

The defendant gives evidence

➤ This is done by oral examination, but examination-in-chief is conducted by using the witness statement exchanged previously, unless the court decides otherwise.

➤ The sequence of questioning is:

 ◆ examination-in-chief by the defendant's side,

 ◆ cross-examination by the claimant's side,

 ◆ re-examination (on points arising from the cross-examination) by the defendant's side.

➤ The claimant's case should be put to the defendant.

➤ Each side should check the admissibility rules (see p 450 et seq).

6

The defendant's side presents the evidence

➤ This is done by oral examination of the witnesses.

➤ The sequence of questioning is:

 ◆ examination-in-chief by the defendant's side. (This is conducted by using the witness statements exchanged previously, unless the court decides otherwise.)

 ◆ cross-examination by the claimant's side,

 ◆ re-examination (on points arising from the cross-examination) by the defendant's side.

➤ The claimant's case must be put to the witness.

➤ Each side should check the admissibility rules (see p 450 et seq).

➤ If a witness gives consistently unfavourable or adverse answers to the surprise of the defendant, the defendant's side should ask the judge to declare the witness hostile.

 ◆ If the judge does so, previously inconsistent statements can be put to the witness (*CFA 1995 s 6* and see the law on hearsay p 453).

7

The defendant's side's closing speech

➤ The defendant may make a closing speech.

8

The claimant's side's closing speech

➤ The claimant may make a closing speech.

9

Judgment is given and any necessary orders are made

Are leading questions allowed?		
Examination-in-chief	✘	(except to obtain a denial of the other party's case)
Cross examination	✔	
Re-examination	✘	(except to obtain a denial of the other party's case)

Q Costs

I   Basis on which costs are awarded

➤ Costs awarded are a *reasonable* amount in respect of all costs *reasonably* incurred (*r 44.4(1)*).

➤ There are 2 bases on which a Court may assess and award costs (the choice is up to the judge)(*r 44.4(2)*):

   1 **Standard basis (most usual)** (*r 44.4(2)*)

      ◆ The costs must also be proportionate to the matters in issue.

      ◆ Doubts over what is 'reasonable' or 'proportionate' are resolved in favour of the paying party.

   2 **Indemnity basis (rare)** (*r 44.4(3)*) - see also *Noorani v Calver* [2009] EWHC 592

      ◆ Doubts over what is 'reasonable' are resolved in favour of the receiving party.

II   Duty to notify client of costs orders

➤ Where a party has a solicitor and the party is not present when the order is made, the party's solicitor must notify his client in writing of the costs order *and* why the order was made (*r 44.2*).

   ◆ This notification must be no later than 7 days after the solicitor receives notice of the order (*r 44.2*).

III Costs orders and the court's discretion

➤ The court may make an order about costs at any stage in a case (*Costs PD: 8.3(1)*).

➤ The court has discretion as to (*r 44.3(1)*):

   ◆ whether costs are payable by one party to another, *and*

   ◆ the amount of those costs, *and*

   ◆ when costs are to be paid.

> Costs may also be agreed between the parties

> The court may at any stage in a case order any party to file an estimate of costs and to serve copies on all other parties

➤ If the court makes a costs order (*except* an order for fixed costs) it may either (*r 44.7*):

   ◆ make a summary assessment of the costs (see p 465), *or*

   ◆ order detailed assessment of the costs by a costs officer (see p 466).

➤ **General rule:** the unsuccessful party is ordered to pay the costs of the successful party (*r 44.3(2)*).

➤ **Not using the general rule:** in deciding what order (if any) to make about costs, a court has regard to all the circumstances, including (*r 44.3(4) - 44.3(5)*):

   ◆ **the conduct of all the parties before (especially the extent of any compliance with the Practice Direction (Pre-Action Conduct) or any pre-action protocol) and during the proceedings,** *and*

   ◆ whether it was reasonable for a party to raise, pursue or contest a particular allegation or issue, *and*

   ◆ whether a claimant who has wholly or partly succeeded in his claim, exaggerated his claim, *and*

   ◆ the manner in which a party has pursued or defended his case or a particular allegation or issue, *and*

   ◆ whether a party has succeeded on part of his case, even if he has not been wholly successful, *and*

   ◆ any payment into court (or admissible offer to settle) made by a party which is drawn to the court's attention (which is not made in accordance with *Part 36* (see also p 429 et seq)).

If the court decides (or does not) to make an order about costs ... (r 44.3, Costs PD: 8.5)

➤ **General rule:** the unsuccessful party is ordered to pay the costs of the successful party.
 ◆ If the factors on the previous page apply, the court may use its discretion to make one of several possible orders, including the following:

Order	Effect	Usual reasoning of court
costs *or* costs in any event	The 'winner' in the costs order is entitled to costs for the relevant part of the proceedings, whatever other costs orders are made in the proceedings	The loser's conduct is unreasonable *or* costs relate to a collateral issue
costs in the case *or* costs in the application	The 'winner' in the costs order, at the end of the proceedings, is entitled to costs for the relevant part of the proceedings	Costs are preliminary to trial and conduct of both parties is reasonable
costs reserved	The decision about costs is deferred to a later occasion. If no later order is made the costs will be costs in the case	It is not yet possible to make a decision on the reasonableness of either party's conduct
Claimant's/ Defendant's costs in the case/ application	◆ If the 'winner' in the costs order is awarded costs at the end of the proceedings, he is entitled to his costs for the relevant part of the proceedings ◆ If any other party is awarded costs at the end of the proceedings, the party in whose favour the final costs order is made is not liable to pay the costs of any other party for the relevant part of the proceedings	Named party's conduct is only considered reasonable if he succeeds later at trial. The loser's conduct is unreasonable
costs thrown away	Where, eg: a judgment or order is set aside, the 'winner' in the costs order is entitled to the costs which have been incurred as a consequence. This includes the costs of: ◆ preparing for + attending any hearing where the judgment/order which has been set aside was made, ◆ preparing for + attending any hearing to set aside the judgment or order in question, ◆ preparing for + attending any hearing at which the court orders an adjournment, ◆ any steps taken to enforce a judgment or order which was later set aside.	The loser's conduct is unreasonable *or* costs relate to a collateral issue
costs of and caused by	Where, eg: a costs order is made on an application to amend a statement of case, the 'winner' in the costs order is entitled to costs of preparing for + attending the hearing and costs of any consequential amendments to his documents	The loser's conduct (which may be reasonable) causes the other party to incur consequential costs
costs here and below	The 'winner' in the costs order is entitled to his costs in respect of the proceedings in the court making the order and also (generally) to costs of the proceedings in any lower court	The 'winner' was correct in having the hearing in a higher court during the proceedings
no order as to costs (r 44.13) *or* each party pays its own costs	Each party is to bear his own costs of the relevant part of the proceedings, whatever costs order the court makes at the end of the proceedings	Merits (or lack of merits) of both sides are equal
Costs forthwith	The 'winner' in the costs order, is entitled to costs and to have these assessed immediately.	Costs are unusually heavy or loser's conduct is unreasonable and the court wishes to express disapproval

Where the court makes an order or direction on an application without notice and its order does not mention costs, it will be deemed to include an order for applicant's costs in the case (r 44.13(1A))

Possible costs orders (r 44.3(6)-(8))

 ◆ pay a proportion of another party's costs
 ◆ pay a stated amount in respect of another party's costs
 ◆ pay costs from or until a certain date only
 ◆ pay costs incurred before proceedings have begun
 ◆ pay costs relating to particular steps taken in the proceedings
 ◆ pay costs relating only to a distinct part of the proceedings
 ◆ pay interest on costs from or until a certain date, including a date before judgment

Where the court has ordered a party to pay costs, it may order an amount to be paid on account before the costs are assessed

Factors the court takes into account in deciding the amount of costs (*r 44.5*)

- ◆ the conduct of all the parties, including in particular:

  - • conduct before and proceedings, *and*

  - • the efforts made, if any, before and during the proceedings in order to try to resolve the dispute.

- ◆ the amount or value of any money or property involved.

- ◆ the importance of the matter to all the parties.

- ◆ the complexity of the matter or the difficulty/novelty of questions raised.

- ◆ the skill, effort, specialised knowledge and responsibility involved.

- ◆ the time spent on the case.

- ◆ the place and circumstances of the work.

IV   Costs at trial

A   Which type of costs rules apply for costs at trial?

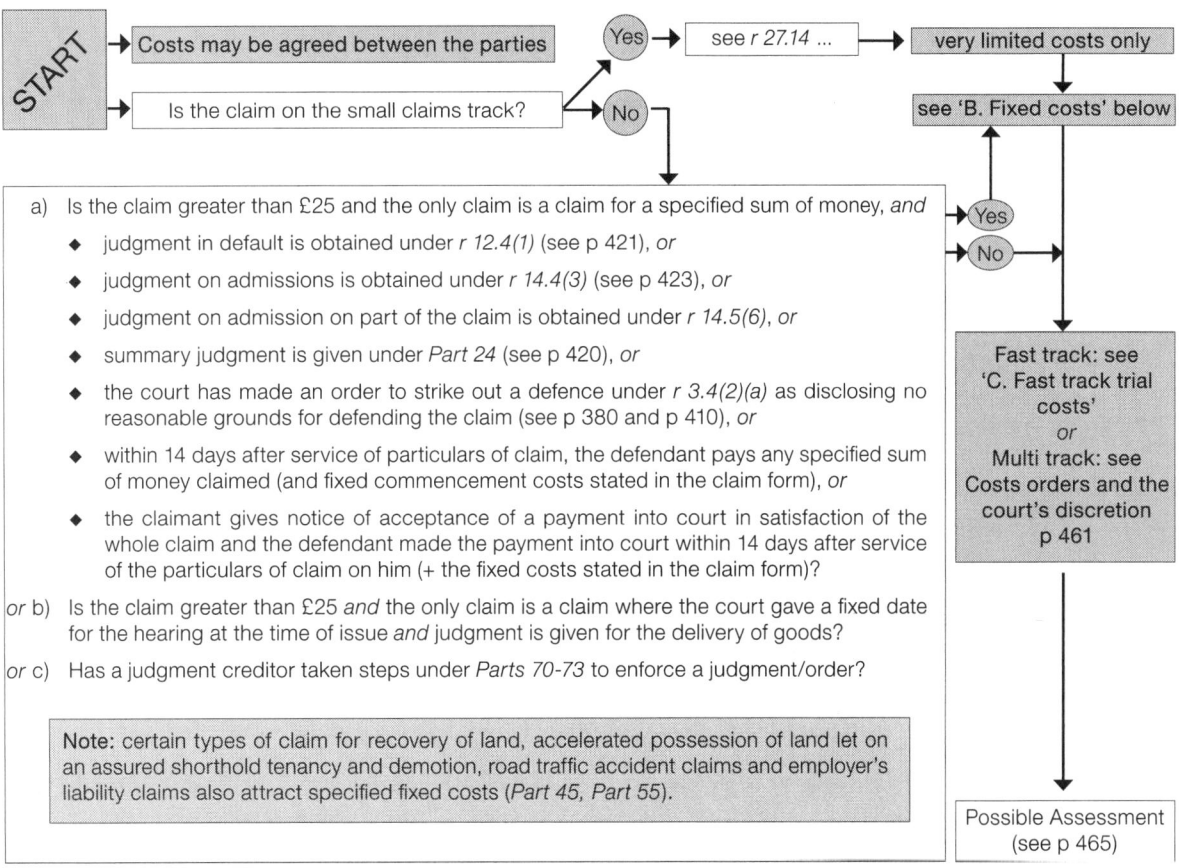

Note: certain types of claim for recovery of land, accelerated possession of land let on an assured shorthold tenancy and demotion, road traffic accident claims and employer's liability claims also attract specified fixed costs (*Part 45, Part 55*).

B Fixed costs (*Part 45*)

➤ The amount of fixed costs (solicitors charges) claimable are (*Part 45, Section I*):

- ◆ fixed commencement costs by reference to Table 1 in *Part 45* (NB: the amount claimed in the claim form - or the value of goods claimed if specified - is used to determine the band in Table 1 that applies to the claim). The bands in Table 1 are:

  - ● i) >£25 to £500, ii) >£500 to £1,000, iii) >£1,000 to £5,000 or the only claim is for delivery of goods and no value is specified on the claim form, *or* iv) the value of the claim is >£5,000, *and*

- ◆ certain additional costs for certain types of service of documents, *and*

- ◆ fixed costs on judgment entry *but* only if the claimant has claimed fixed commencement costs on the claim form *and* if he is given judgment for certain types of claim (set out in Table 3 in *Part 45*), *and*

- ◆ certain miscellaneous fixed costs (set out in Table 4 in *Part 45*).

➤ *Part 45, Section II* sets out costs for costs-only proceedings, or proceedings for approval of a settlement/ compromise for or against a child or protected party (ie: someone who lacks capacity to conduct proceedings), where: i) the dispute arises from a road traffic accident, *or* ii) the agreed damages include personal injury and/or property damages, *or* iii) the total value of the agreed damages does not exceed £10,000, *or* iv) if a claim had been issued for the amount of agreed damages, the small claims track would not have been the normal track.

> *Part 45, Sections III, and IV* set out the percentage increase allowed under a CFA which provides for a success fee where the dispute: i) arises from a road traffic accident or ii) is between an employee and his employer arising from a bodily injury sustained by the employee. *Section V* provides for fixed recovery success fees in employer liability disease claims. *Section VI* provides for fixed costs in certain low value personal injury claims from road traffic accidents. *Section VII* provides the scale of costs for claims in a patents county court. *Section VIII* provides for fixed costs for successful monetary recovery in a county court by HMRC

C Fast track trial costs (*Part 46*)

➤ General rule: this applies *only* where, *at the date of the trial*, the claim is allocated to the fast track. Costs are awarded for an advocate who prepares for/appears at the trial, based on value of the claim as follows:

'Value of claim'	£3000 or less	£3,000+ to £10,000	£10,000+ to £15,000	More than to £15,000
Costs	£485	£690	£1,035	£1,650
NB: Sometimes the court may vary the amounts payable under the general rule				

➤ The court may also apportion costs to reflect the respective degrees of success on the issues at trial.

1 **Claim is only for the payment of money and claimant gets costs:** 'value of claim' = total amount of the judgment excluding interest, costs and any reduction made for contributory negligence.

2 **Claim is only for the payment of money and defendant gets costs:** 'value of claim' = the amount specified in the claim form (excluding interest and costs), *or*, if no amount is specified, the maximum amount the claimant reasonably expected to recover (see the statement of value in the claim form), *or* more than £15,000, if the claim form states that the claimant cannot reasonably say how much is likely to be recovered.

3 **Claim is only for a remedy other than the payment of money:** 'value of claim' = more than £3,000 but not more than £10,000, unless the court orders otherwise.

4 **Claim includes a claim for payment of money and for a remedy other than the payment of money:** 'value of claim' = the highest of the values under 1, 2 and 3 above.

Note on counterclaims: If a defendant counterclaim has a higher value than the claim and the claimant succeeds at trial on both the claim *and* counterclaim, 'value of claim' = the value of the defendant's counterclaim.

➤ There are certain special rules where an advocate acts for more than 1 claimant/defendant.

Note on 'additional liability': the court may also make an award in respect of 'additional liability' (*r 46.3(2A)*).

V   Costs in special cases

➤   For solicitor and own client costs, see pp 6 and 33 et seq.

➤   For costs pursuant to a contract, costs payable to non-parties, trustees/PRs, children, protected parties or litigants in person or costs due to pre-claim disclosure, there are special rules not listed here (*Part 48*).

Orders in respect of pro bono representation (*r 44.3C*)

➤   Where the court makes an order under *LSA 2007 s 194(3)*:

◆   the court may order the payment to the prescribed charity of a sum no greater than the costs specified in *Part 45* to which the party with pro bono representation would have been entitled under *Part 45* and in respect of that representation had it not been provided free of charge, *or*

◆   where *Part 45* does not apply, the court may determine the amount of the payment (other than a sum equivalent to fixed costs) to be made by the paying party to the prescribed charity by:

●   making a summary assessment... *or*

●   making an order for detailed assessment ...

...   of a sum equivalent to all or part of the costs the paying party would have been ordered to pay to the party with pro bono representation for that representation, had it not been provided free.

➤   Where the court makes an order under *LSA 2007 s 194(3)*, the order must specify that the payment by the paying party must be made to the prescribed charity.

VI   Assessment: general

➤   Where the court does not order fixed costs (or no fixed costs are provided for) the amount of costs payable will be assessed by the court. This will be by summary or detailed assessment (*r 44.7*).

◆   A costs order is decided by a detailed assessment unless the order says otherwise (*Costs PD: 12.2*).

➤   **General rule:** detailed assessment of costs of any proceedings (or any part) should not take place until the conclusion of the proceedings, but the court *may* order them to be assessed immediately (*r 47.1*).

➤   **The 2 types of assessment are summary assessment and detailed assessment:**

1   **Summary assessment**

➤   **General rule:** Whenever a court makes an order about costs which does not provide for fixed costs to be paid the court should consider whether to make a summary assessment of costs (*Costs PD: 13.1*). Usually, the court makes a summary assessment (unless there is good reason not to (*Costs PD: 13.2*)):

a)   at the end of a fast track trial, when the order will deal with the costs of the whole claim, *or*

b)   at the end of any other hearing which has lasted not more than 1 day, when the order will deal with the costs of the application or matter to which the hearing related.

NB: the general rule is that there is no summary assessment if the court has ordered 'costs in the case'.

➤   **Written statement** (*Costs PD: 13.5(2)-(3)*): Each party claiming costs drafts a written costs statement (excluding any additional liability) showing in a schedule: hours claimed, hourly rates, fee earner grade, amount + nature of disbursements (except counsel's fee for appearing at the hearing), solicitor's costs for attending/appearing at the hearing, counsel's fees for the hearing, and VAT - all signed by the party/his solicitor.

➤   **Serving the statement** (*Costs PD: 13.5(4)*): As soon as possible (and in any event not less than 24 hours before the hearing) the statement must be filed and copies served on any party who might pay those costs.

➤   **The hearing:** The court specifies the amount payable separately as base costs and as additional liability (for solicitor's charges, disbursements and allowable VAT) and amounts awarded as Fast Track Trial Costs.

2   Detailed assessment

Steps

1   <u>Drafting the bill</u> - **Receiving party drafts a bill of costs - include** (*Costs PD: 4.1-4.4, 4.9, 4.13*):

- title page containing the full title of the proceedings and the name of the party whose bill it is,
- a description of the document giving the right to assessment and certain background information,
- items of costs claimed under the certain headings,
- summary showing the total costs claimed on each page of the bill,
- schedules of time spent on non-routine attendances,
- certain certificates (eg: legal aid certificate and any other relevant certificates).

Note 1:   Each item claimed in the bill of costs must be consecutively numbered.

Note 2:   The bill of costs must not contain claims for costs or court fees relating solely to the detailed assessment proceedings other than costs claimed for preparing and checking the bill.

2   <u>Serving the bill</u> - **Receiving party serves the bill of costs, notice of commencement and various other documents** (*rr 47.6-47.8, Costs PD: 32*)

- This must be done within 3 months of the date of judgment, direction, order, award, right to costs arose (for *Part 36*) etc., otherwise the party may be penalised for the delay.

3   <u>Disputing the bill?</u> - (*rr 47.9, 47.13, 47.14, Costs PD: 40*)

- Paying party (and any other party) may dispute the bill - this must be done by serving points of dispute within 21 days after the date of service of the notice of commencement, on the receiving party and every other party. The parties may agree to vary this period (*Costs PD: 35.1*).
- Within 21 days after service of the points of dispute, the receiving party may serve a reply.
- Within 3 months of the expiry of the period for starting detailed assessment proceedings, the receiving party must file a request for a detailed hearing. This must be accompanied by a copy/copies of:
  - the notice of commencement; the bill of costs; the document giving the right to detailed assessment; the points of dispute (annotated to show agreed/disputed items and their value); replies served; costs orders made by the court; fee notes + other written evidence served on the paying party; if there is a dispute about the receiving party's liability to pay costs to his solicitors, any written information/letter provided by the solicitor explaining calculation of charges; a statement signed by the receiving party/his solicitor giving contact details of the receiving + paying party and other persons who have served points of dispute and giving a time estimate for the hearing.
- Not less than 7 days before the hearing and not more than 14 days before (*Costs PD: 40.11-12*), the receiving party must file with the court papers supporting the bill: ie: instructions + briefs to counsel (in chronological order); all advices, opinions, drafts in response; reports + opinions of medical and other experts; correspondence files and attendance notes; papers relevant to additional liability.
- The detailed assessment hearing is held.

4   <u>Default costs certificate</u> - **an order to pay the costs to which it relates** (*rr 47.11-47.12*)

- The receiving party may file a request for a default costs certificate if he has not been served with any points of dispute or if the 21 days in '3' above has expired.

5   <u>Interim costs certificate</u> (*r 47.15*)

- The court may at any time after the receiving party has filed a request for a detailed assessment hearing, issue an interim costs certificate for such sum as it considers appropriate.

6   <u>Final costs certificate</u> (*r 47.16*)

- When a completed bill is filed (which must be within 14 days after the end of the detailed assessment hearing) the court will issue a final costs certificate and serve it on the parties. It will include an order to pay the costs to which it relates, unless the court orders otherwise.

7   <u>Appeal</u> - **there are limited rights to appeal** (*rr 47.20-47.23*) (see p 478).

VII Assessment: legally aided client (*r 47.17, Costs PD: 21,22*)

➤ **Summary Assessment:**

◆ The court must not make a summary assessment of the costs of a receiving party who is an LSC funded client (*Costs PD: 13.9*).

◆ The court may make a summary assessment of costs payable by an LSC funded client (*Costs PD:13.10*).

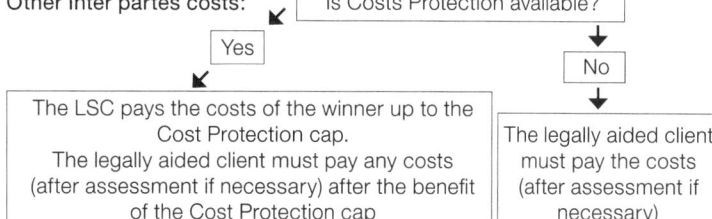

The LSC funded client is the... (*r 47.17, Costs PD: 21, CLS(CP)R 2000*)	
...winner	**...loser**

The costs of the winner's solicitor:

◆ there may be a detailed assessment hearing for the winner's 'solicitor and own client costs'

Other Inter partes costs:

◆ there may be an order for other inter partes costs to be decided by assessment if not agreed:

  • If there is a detailed assessment, a bill of costs may be at 2 rates:
    i) at the prescribed rate (payable by the LSC), *and*
    ii) at a 'private individual's rate' (paid by the other side)

Usually, money recoverable through recovery of inter partes costs will pay for the costs of the winner's solicitor. However the LSC may keep:

◆ any *inter partes* costs awarded in favour of the winner, *and*

◆ any contributions made by the legally helped party, *and*

◆ **the statutory charge** (ie: the LSC has the first call on any damages won).

The costs of the loser's solicitor:

◆ the loser's solicitor can claim these costs by filing a legal aid schedule for the prescribed rates (and following the **'Summary Assessment'** procedure above if appropriate)

Other Inter partes costs:

Is Costs Protection available?

Yes → The LSC pays the costs of the winner up to the Cost Protection cap. The legally aided client must pay any costs (after assessment if necessary) after the benefit of the Cost Protection cap

No → The legally aided client must pay the costs (after assessment if necessary)

Before the LSC can be ordered to pay the whole or any part of the costs incurred by a non-legally aided party:

◆ proceedings must be finally decided in favour of the non-funded party, *and*

◆ unless there is good reason for a delay, the non-funded party must provide written notice of intention to seek an order against the LSC within 3 months of the costs order, *and*

◆ the court must be satisfied that it is 'just and equitable' in the circumstances that costs should be made out of public funds, *and*

◆ (in a court of first instance), the proceedings must have been instituted by the LSC funded client and the non-funded party is an individual and will suffer financial hardship unless the order is made

The LSC keeps any contribution paid by the losing LSC funded client

---

➤ Generally, 'Costs Protection' is available to an LSC funded client but not in respect of **Help at Court** or **Legal Help**

◆ In the case of Legal Help, if he later receives Legal Representation/Family Help/Family Mediation for the same dispute (but not any of these three in family proceedings), then costs protection does apply.

➤ Costs Protection is given by *AJA 1999 s 11*: '[that] costs cannot exceed the amount it is reasonable for [an LSC funded client] to pay having regard to all the circumstances including the financial resources of all the parties to the proceedings and their conduct in connection with the dispute to which the proceedings relate.'

Additional Liability (*r 44.3A*) (see also pp 31 et seq)

➤ Additional liability is (*r 43.2(o)*):
  ◆ a percentage increase in solicitor's charges, *or*
  ◆ the litigation insurance premium.
➤ Additional liability is assessed (either by summary assessment or detailed assessment) at the end of proceedings (or part of proceedings) to which the funding arrangement relates.

VIII Costs capping orders (*rr 44.18-44.20, Costs PD: 23A*)

➤ In exceptional circumstances, a court can make an order limiting the amount of future costs (including disbursements) which a party may recover under a costs order subsequently made – a 'costs capping order'.

◆ 'Future costs' means costs for work after the date of the order but excluding any additional liability.

R   Enforcing judgments

I	Judgment and orders	IV	Interest on judgment debts
II	Reciprocal enforcement	V	Methods of enforcement (extracting
III	Investigating the debtor's means		a judgment debt from a debtor)

I   Judgment and orders (*Part 40*)

1   Form

➤ Every judgment/order must bear: the date on which it is given/made and the court seal (*r 40.2(2)*).

2   Drawing-up and filing

> **Exception:** Judgments/orders in the QBD at the RCJ are drawn up by the parties (unless it is an order by the court on its own initiative or unless the court otherwise orders) (*r 40.3(4)*).

➤ By the court unless *either*:

   a) the court orders or permits a party to draw it up *or* dispenses with the need to draw it up, *or*

   b) the order is a consent order (*r 40.3(1)*).

   ◆ If a party draws up an order, that party must file it no later than 7 days after the date on which the order is ordered or permitted to be drawn up so that the court can seal it. *If he does not do so in this period,* any other party may draw it up and file it (*r 40.3(3)*).

3   Service and effect

➤ If a party draws up a judgment/order and the court is to serve it, that party must file a copy to be retained by the court *plus* sufficient copies for service on himself and on the other parties.   When the court has sealed the judgment/order it serves (see p 395 et seq) a copy on each party (*r 40.4(1)*).

➤ An order which is not made at trial must (unless the court orders otherwise) be served on the applicant, the respondent any other person who the court orders to be served (eg: where a party is acting by a solicitor the party in addition to the solicitor) (*r 40.4(2), 40.5*).

➤ A judgment/order takes effect from the day it is given/made, or any date the court specifies (*r 40.7*).

4   Set aside and correction

➤ Any person (even if not a party) directly affected may apply for set aside or variation (*r 40.9*).

➤ The court may correct accidental errors; a party may apply for correction without notice (*r 40.12*).

5   Compliance

➤ A party must comply with a judgment/order for the payment of amount of money (including costs) within 14 days of the date of the judgment/order *unless* a) the judgment/order specifies otherwise, b) the *CPR* specify otherwise (eg: *Part 12* (default judgment) and *Part 14* (judgment on admissions)), or c) the court has stayed the proceedings or judgment (*r 40.11*)).

II   Reciprocal enforcement (*Part 74*)

➤ **Enforcing a foreign judgment in England and Wales:** Judgments from EU states (*EC Reg 44/2001* and see also *Part 74*) and certain other countries (*AJA 1920, FJ(ER)A 1933*) may be registered in English courts and enforced (*CJJO 2001 and CJJ(AICS)O 2001*).

➤ **Enforcing an English judgment outside the jurisdiction:** English judgments may be registered and enforced elsewhere in the UK (eg: Jersey), in EU member states and in certain other European countries (*CJJA 1982*). There is also provision for reciprocal enforcement of some other foreign judgments (*AJA 1920, FJ(ER)A 1933*). *EU Reg 44/2001* is also relevant (see above).

   ◆ If a country is not covered, fresh proceedings should be started there. There may also be other alternatives, such as arbitration.

III   Investigating the debtor's means

Investigating and tracing a debtor

Steps

1 **Use an enquiry agent**
- ◆ This is to investigate and trace a debtor (set a cost ceiling to limit the expense).
- ✓ This is relatively fast and may unearth more than an oral examination will.
- ✗ It is more expensive than an oral examination.

2 **Seek an order to obtain information from judgment debtors** (*Part 71*)
- ◆ This is an examination of the means of a debtor while he is under oath.

Procedure for oral examinations

Part 71 contains rules which provide for a judgment debtor to be required to attend court to provide information, for the purpose of enabling a judgment creditor to enforce a judgment or order against him.

Preparing to apply for the Order
➤ A judgment creditor may apply for an order requiring:
- ◆ a judgment debtor, or if a company, an officer of that company, to provide information about:
  - ● the judgment debtor's means, *or*
  - ● any other matter about which information is needed to enforce a judgment or order.
➤ An application must be issued in the court which made the judgment or order but if the proceedings have since been transferred to a different court, it must be issued in that court.

↓

Application
➤ The applicant (judgment creditor) prepares an application (which may be without notice) which must state:
- ◆ the name and address of the debtor,
- ◆ which judgment or order the judgment creditor is seeking to enforce,
- ◆ the amount presently owed (if the application is to enforce a judgment or order for money),
- ◆ if the debtor is a company, the name, address and position of the officer to be ordered to attend court,
- ◆ whether the applicant wishes the questioning to be conducted before a judge (and giving reasons),
- ◆ which documents are to be produced, *and*
- ◆ which matters the applicant wishes the judgment debtor (or officer of the judgment debtor) to be questioned about (if the application is to enforce a judgment or order which is not for money).

↓

Consideration of the application
➤ A court officer considers the application without a hearing, *but*:
- ◆ may, when appropriate, refer it to a judge, *and*
- ◆ will refer it to a judge, if the applicant requests questioning before a judge.

→

Service of the order
➤ Not less than 14 days before the hearing, the applicant (or someone on his behalf) must serve the order personally on the person ordered to attend unless:
- ◆ the court orders otherwise, *or*
- ◆ these are county court proceedings and the applicant is an individual litigant in person, when the order will be served by the court bailiff.
➤ If the order is to be served by the applicant, he must inform the court not less than 7 days before the date of the hearing if he has been unable to serve it.

←

The hearing
The court officer examines the debtor who is on oath. If the hearing is before a judge, the creditor examines the debtor. The evidence is tape recorded.
The creditor may request a costs order.

Note: The debtor may offer to pay by instalments and the creditor can decide whether to accept or not.

Note: Failure to attend or answer, results in an order by a High Court/circuit judge for committal to prison ('suspended' when issued for the first time).

Issue of the order
➤ The court issues an order specifying:
- ◆ compulsory attendance, usually at the county court for the district where the debtor resides, at a specified time,
- ◆ when attending, the obligation to produce at court documents described in the order,
- ◆ the obligation to answer on oath such questions as the court may require, *and*
- ◆ a notice warning of imprisonment for contempt of court in the event of non-compliance.

←

Travelling expenses
A person ordered to attend may, within 7 days of being served with the order, ask the applicant to pay him a sum reasonably sufficient to cover his travelling expenses to and from court.

↓

Filing the affidavit
➤ The applicant must file an affidavit by the person who served the order (unless it was served by the court) giving details of how and when it was served, stating:
- ◆ that the person ordered to attend court has not requested payment of his travelling expenses, *or*
- ◆ that the applicant has paid a sum in accordance with such a request, *and*
- ◆ in any event, stating how much of the judgment debt remains unpaid.
➤ The applicant must either file the affidavit not less than 2 days before the hearing or produce it at the hearing.

IV Interest on judgment debts (*Judgment Act 1838 s 17*)

➤ Interest (under *JA 1838 s.17* or *CCA 1984 s 74*) runs from the date a judgment is given *unless* the *CPR* or a *PD* provide differently or the court orders otherwise (*r 40.8*).

High Court: Interest on judgment debts

➤ **High Court:** all judgment debts currently carry interest at 8% (see p 370) from the date the judgment is entered until final payment, regardless of whether the sum represents damages or costs.

➤ Where a county court judgment is being enforced in the High Court, the judgment is treated as one of the High Court for enforcement purposes.

County Courts: Interest on judgment debts

➤ **County Court:** (*County Court (Interest on Judgment Debts) Order 1991*) (as amended)

A Judgments over £5,000

a) all judgments over £5,000 carry interest at 8% from the date judgment is entered until final payment.

b) when enforcement proceedings begin, interest ceases to run *unless* the proceedings produce no payment.

  ◆ If anything at all is recovered, then the balance of the debt becomes interest-free.

c) An application to enforce interest must be made. This must be done with a certificate setting out:

  ◆ the amount of interest claimed, *and*

  ◆ the sum on which the interest is claimed, *and*

  ◆ the dates to and from which interest has accrued, *and*

  ◆ the rate of interest.

NB: If a judgment before trial leaves quantum to be assessed, interest runs from the date of final judgment (*Thomas v Bunn* [1991] 1 AC 362).

NB: Interest does *not* accrue on instalments (or judgment for deferred sums), until the instalment falls due.

B Judgments £5,000 and under

a) If a debt is a qualifying debt under the *LPCD(I) 1998,* it will attract interest under *LPCD(I) 1998* at the specified rate (see pp 360 and 370).

V Methods of enforcement (*Part 70*)

A Procedural matters

➤ A judgment creditor may, except where an enactment, rule or PD provides otherwise (*r 70.2*):

♦ use any method of enforcement which is available, *and*

♦ use more than one method of enforcement, either at the same time or one after another.

➤ A judgment creditor wishing to enforce a High Court judgment or order in a county court must apply to the High Court for an order transferring the proceedings to that county court (*r 70.3*).

♦ The judgment creditor must file the following documents in the county court with his application notice or request for enforcement: (*PD70: 3.1*):

• a copy of the judgment or order, *and*

• a certificate verifying the amount due under the judgment or order, *and*

• if a writ of execution has previously been issued in the High Court to enforce the judgment or order, a copy of the relevant enforcement officer's return to the writ, *and*

• a copy of the order transferring the proceedings to the county court.

➤ If a judgment or order is given or made in favour of or against a person who is not a party to proceedings, it may be enforced by or against that person by the same methods as if he were a party (*r 70.4*).

➤ If a judgment or order is set aside, any enforcement of the judgment or order ceases to have effect unless the court otherwise orders (*r 70.6*).

➤ If a judgment creditor is claiming interest on a judgment debt, he must include in his application or request to issue enforcement proceedings details of (*PD70: 6*):

♦ the amount of interest claimed and the sum on which it is claimed, *and*

♦ the dates from and to which interest has accrued, *and*

♦ the rate or rates of interest applied and (if more than one rate, the relevant dates and rates).

B Methods of enforcement

Information requests and orders

➤ Currently, creditors can only obtain information to assist them in determining how to enforce a civil judgment debt is by way of an Order to Obtain Information.

♦ This requires the debtor to attend court, which is problematic if the debtor is not co-operating.

➤ *TCE 2007 ss 95-105 [not yet in force] allows courts to request information from HMRC, certain government departments and certain third parties (including banks and credit reference agencies) on a judgment debtor who has failed to respond to the judgment or to comply with court-based methods of enforcement to assist with the enforcement of a judgment debt.*

♦ *Such information will include name, address, date of birth, National Insurance number and the name and address of the debtor's employer.*

Enforcement Methods (PD70: 1)	Assets which can be enforced against	Pros (✓) and cons (✗)
1 Writ of fieri facias or warrant of execution	Most forms of personal property owned by the judgment debtor, capable of seizure and sale	✓ Often the quickest way of getting payment of a judgment debt ✓ Simple procedure ✓ Most popular method of enforcement ✓ Works for individual and corporate debtors ✗ Will only work if debtor has enough goods which can be sold at auction to meet the judgment and enforcement officer's charges or enough money to pay the judgment debt ✗ Permission required to issue it once 6 years has passed since date of the judgment or order. (If permission is granted, recovery of interest on the judgment debt is limited to 6 years) ✗ Judgment debtor can refuse bailiff entry to a private residence
2 Third party debt order	Money debts owed by a third party to a judgment debtor	✓ Takes effect relatively quickly ✓ Ensures that a debt is paid in cash ✗ One of the least used methods of enforcement ✗ Evidence to support an application (ie: that the debtor is owed money by a third party/has a bank account and details) can be hard to find ✗ No application for a third party debt order against a joint bank account can be made unless the judgment debt is a joint debt of all the account holders ✗ Third party debt orders cannot attach future debts ✗ A third party debt order cannot be used to enforce against foreign debts (*Societe Eram Shipping Company Limited v Cie Internationale de Navigation* [2004] 1 AC 260, *Kuwait Oil Tanker Company SAK v UBS AG* [2003] UKHL 31).
3 Charging order and order for sale, stop notice or stop order	◆ Land ◆ Securities ◆ Funds in court ◆ Dividends and interest ◆ Interest in a trust	✓ Judgment creditor can wait before enforcing by seeking an order for sale. (If property prices are dropping, one should wait for them to rise again) ✓ Interest continues to run on sum secured from date of judgment to receipt of final monies - though delay in seeking charging order of over 6 years may result in interest being limited to 6 years (*Lowsley v Forbes* [1999] AC 329). ✓ No limitation problems in seeking charging orders and orders for sale because these are not viewed as fresh action on a judgment and therefore are not subject to the 6 year limitation period under *LA 1980 s 24(1)*. ✗ A slow method of enforcement in 3 stages: (i) application for interim charging order, (ii) application for final charging order and (iii) order for sale ✗ Not likely to be effective if there is not substantial equity in a property or if the property is jointly owned or occupied by others than judgment debtor
4 Attachment of earnings order (AEO)	Cash (part of debtor's wages will be paid into court and released to judgment creditor)	✓ Inexpensive and fairly easy method of enforcement ✓ Automatic deduction from wages so does not rely on debtor making payment ✗ Often not very satisfactory. Low payments often ordered ✗ Debtor needs to be in paid employment ✗ Interest does not accrue to the debt. It can take many years to recover in full. ✗ Use of attachment of earnings order may preclude use of other methods of enforcement (leave of the court to levy execution is needed whilst an attachment of earnings order is in force)
5 Appointment of receiver by way of equitable execution under CPR 69	Property of the judgment debtor which is not suitable for other methods of enforcement (e.g. future debts).	✓ Court can appoint receiver by way of equitable execution over foreign and future debts (*Masri v Consolidated Contractors International UK Ltd and others (No 2)* [2008] EWCA Civ 303) ✗ It is rarely used and only available where other methods of legal enforcement are not available (*Morgan v Hart* [1914] 2 KB 183)
	◆ Despite reference to "equitable execution", the debtor's interest can be legal or equitable. ◆ Interest must be assignable ie: NOT some pensions, salaries of public officers and property the subject of contractual restriction on assignment	
6 Bankruptcy or winding up	Assets of the judgment debtor that get divided amongst his creditors by the trustee in bankruptcy following an order for bankruptcy / Assets of the company judgment debtor that get divided amongst its creditors by the liquidator following a winding up order	
Note: See p 463 for costs of enforcing judgments		

Changes to the law by TCE 2007 [not yet in force]

Changes to writs of fieri facias and warrants of execution

➤ *TCE 2007 ss 62-90 [not yet in force] changes the law with respect to the table on p 472.*

➤ *The main changes to be brought into force are as follows:*

 ◆ *Writs of fieri facias are to be renamed writs of control.*

 ◆ *Warrants of execution and warrants of distress are to be renamed warrants of control.*

 ◆ *There is to be a unified enforcement procedure (set out in TCE 2007 Schedule 12) for writs of control and warrants of control.*

 ◆ *There is provision for regulations to specify fees, charges and expenses that can be charged by a person in connection with taking control of goods (eg: fees charged by an enforcement agent for taking control of goods).*

 ● *Such regulations will specify when and how such fees, charges and expenses will be recoverable from the debtor (including when such amounts can be deducted from the proceeds of sale of any goods).*

 ● *Such regulations may also specify that any disputed amount of such fees, costs and expenses is to be assessed in accordance with rules of court.*

 ◆ *Rules are set out for remedial action and the level of damages available to a debtor against an enforcement agent who breaches the procedure.*

 ● *There is no provision for the debtor's right to bring a claim against an enforcement agent whose actions were not authorised at the outset because this is already covered by the existing law of tort.*

 ● *Circumstances are also specified when a creditor can bring a claim against the debtor and new offences are created of intentionally obstructing an enforcement agent in the lawful exercise of his power and interfering with goods seized.*

➤ *TCE 2007 s 67 transfers the district judge's responsibility for the execution of warrants of control issued by a county court to any person authorised by or on behalf of the Lord Chancellor. In practice, the warrants will be executed by county court bailiffs.*

➤ *TCE 2007 s 70 gives the High Court the power to stay execution of a writ of control in line with the county court's power to stay execution.*

 ◆ *The power may only be exercised where the court is satisfied that the debtor is unable to pay any sum or instalment of any sum recovered against him.*

Changes to charging orders

➤ *At present, a court cannot make a charging order when payments due under an instalment order to secure a sum are not in arrears. Sometimes, this can prejudice the creditor eg: a debtor with large debts, who meets his instalments, can benefit from a property sale without paying off the debt.*

➤ *TCE 2007 removes this restriction and enables access to charging orders when a debtor is not yet in arrears with an instalment order. As a safeguard, Lord Chancellor will be able to set financial thresholds beneath which a court cannot make a charging order or order for sale (so as to ensure that charging orders are not used to secure payment of disproportionately small judgment debts).*

Changes to attachment of earnings orders

➤ *Earnings information provided by debtors is often unreliable. TCE 2007 therefore makes provision for a new method of calculation of deductions from earnings based on fixed rates.*

➤ *If a debtor changes job and does not tell the court his new employer's details, any AEO lapses. TCE 2007 allows courts/fines officers to obtain the new employer's details from HMRC.*

1 Writ of fieri facias or warrant of execution *(HCCJO 1991 Art 8, HCCJ(A)O 1996, Sch 1 r 46, r 47, Sch 2 r 26)*		
	High Court	**County Court**
Purpose	➤ A writ of fieri facias requires a sheriff or enforcement officer to seize and sell a debtor's goods for the purpose of recovering a sum due under a High Court judgment or order.	➤ A warrant of execution empowers a district judge to seize and sell a debtor's goods for the purpose of recovering money payable under a county court judgment or order. ◆ The warrant requires the sum to be recovered by seizure and sale of the debtor's goods. ◆ A warrant of distress may be issued by a magistrates' court for the purpose of recovering a sum adjudged to be paid by a conviction or order of the court.
What judgments are enforceable and where?	High Court judgments County Court judgments if £600 or over	County Court judgments under £5,000 (unless proceedings are under *CCA 1984*)
	◆ If a debt is payable by instalments, the claim form can be issued for an instalment or the whole amount	
Procedure	➤ The creditor completes: ◆ 2 copies of the writ of *fieri facias*, *and* ◆ a *praecipe* for a writ of *fieri facias* ➤ He sends these to the court office together with the judgment and assessment notice (if costs are involved) ➤ NB: If enforcing a county court judgment, the creditor completes a combined certificate of judgment and request for writ of *fieri facias* too	➤ The creditor completes a form of request for a warrant of execution. ➤ He files it at the court with a fee
Execution	➤ The court seals the claim form, returns one copy to the creditor who forwards it to the under-sheriff for the county where the debtor resides or carries on his business. ➤ The under-sheriff sends it to an officer for execution	➤ The enforcement agent for the district where the debtor resides or carries on business executes the warrant
	It may not be executed on Sunday, Good Friday or Xmas Day.	
	The creditor should tell the officer about all seizable items of which he knows eg: the type and registration number of a car. The relevant court officer seizes the goods and auctions them off to pay the debt and expenses	

Items exempt from seizure *(Law of Distress (Amendment) Act 1888 s 4, AJA 1956 s 37)*

- ◆ Goods on hire or hire-purchase
- ◆ Tools, books, vehicles and items necessary for the debtor's personal use in his job or business. A vehicle will be seized unless the debtor satisfies the officer that no reasonable alternative transport is possible and that mobility is essential
- ◆ Clothing, bedding, furniture, provisions and household equipment for the basic domestic needs of the debtor and his family.
  - • Microwaves (when a conventional oven is present), stereos, TVs and videos are *not* regarded as being vital for domestic survival!

Methods of seizure

- ◆ The following are forbidden for the court officer: a) forcible entry to premises, *or* b) taking goods from the debtor's person.
- ◆ 'Walking possession' is a method by which the sheriff/other enforcement officer or bailiff agrees not to remove items if the debtor agrees not to dispose of them or permit them to be moved. (This gives the debtor an extra chance to meet the claim, or oppose seizure.)
- ◆ The debtor may apply for suspension of execution. If he succeeds, the writ of *fieri facias* is suspended conditionally on payment by specified instalments.

2 Third party debt orders (*Part 72*)

Purpose and Conditions	➤ *Part 21* contains rules which provide for a judgment creditor to obtain an order for the payment to him of money which a third party who is within the jurisdiction owes to the judgment debtor. ➤ The debt *must* belong to the judgment debtor solely and beneficially. ➤ The third party must be within the jurisdiction of UK courts.
Procedure outline	➤ The creditor makes an application for an interim third party debt order. ➤ If granted, the creditor needs to ask the court for a final third party debt order. ➤ Each application for a third party debt order: ◆ may be made without notice, *and* ◆ must be issued in the court which made the judgment/order being enforced but if the proceedings have since been transferred to a different court, it must be issued in that court.
Application for a third party debt order	➤ The application notice must contain the following information: ◆ the name and address of the judgment debtor, ◆ details of the judgment or order sought to be enforced, ◆ the amount of money remaining due under the judgment or order, ◆ if the debt is payable by instalments, the amounts which are due and remain unpaid, ◆ the name and address of the third party, ◆ if the third party is a bank or building society: • its name and branch address where the debtor's account is believed to be held, *and* • the account number or, if not known, the fact it is not known, ◆ confirmation that to the best of the judgment creditor's knowledge or belief the third party: • is within the jurisdiction, *and* • owes money to or holds money to the credit of the judgment debtor, ◆ if the judgment creditor knows or believes that any person other than the judgment debtor has any claim to the money owed by the third party: • his name and (if known) his address, *and* • such information as is known to the judgment creditor about his claim, ◆ details of other applications for third party debt orders by the creditor for the same debt, ◆ the sources/grounds of the creditor's knowledge/belief for the 3 preceding ◆ points, *and* ◆ **verification by a statement of truth.** ➤ The application will initially be dealt with by a judge without a hearing.
Consideration of the application for interim third party debt order	➤ The judge may make an interim third party debt order: ◆ fixing a hearing to consider whether to make a final third party debt order, *and* ◆ directing that until that hearing the third party must not make any payment which reduces the amount he owes the judgment debtor to less than the amount specified in the order. ➤ An interim third party debt order will specify the amount which the third party must retain. ➤ An interim third party debt order becomes binding on a third party when it is served on him. ➤ The hearing date must not be less than 28 days after the interim third party debt order is made.
Service of interim third party debt order	➤ Copies of the interim order, the application notice and supporting documents must be served: ◆ on the third party, not less than 21 days before the date fixed for the hearing, *and* ◆ on the judgment debtor not less than: • 7 days after a copy has been served on the third party, *and* • 7 days before the date fixed for the hearing. ➤ If the judgment creditor serves the order, he must either file a certificate of service not less than 2 days before the hearing, *or* produce a certificate of service at the hearing.
Obligations of third parties served with interim order	➤ A bank/building society must search to identify all accounts held with it by the judgment debtor and must disclose relevant details to the court and the creditor within 7 days of being served. ➤ A non-bank/building society must notify the court and the creditor in writing within 7 days of being served, if he claims not to owe any money or to owe less than amounts specified.
The hearing for the final order	➤ The court may: ◆ make a final third party debt order, ◆ discharge the interim third party debt order and dismiss the application, ◆ decide any issues in dispute, *or* ◆ direct a trial of any such issues, and if necessary give directions. ➤ The court may, on an application by a debtor opposing the application, transfer it to the court for the district where the judgment debtor resides/carries on business, or to another court. ➤ There is provision for an individual debtor to ask for a hardship payment order if the debtor or his family are suffering hardship in meeting ordinary living expenses. ➤ There is provision for the debtor or the third party to object to the issue of a final third party debt order by filing written evidence of the grounds of objection at least 3 days before the hearing. ➤ A final third party debt order is enforceable as an order to pay money. ➤ If the creditor is awarded costs he shall, unless the court otherwise directs, retain those costs out of the money recovered and the costs are deemed to be paid first out of the money he recovers.

3	Charging orders over land or securities (*Charging Orders Act 1979, Part 73*)			
Charging orders against a judgment debtor's interest in assets				
Practical matters	➤ If seeking charges against land: do an index map search to discover if the land is registered. ➤ Search for prior encumbrances and give written notice of the order to prior chargees.			
Which judgments are enforceable?	**In the High Court:**	High Court judgments for over £5,000 County Court judgments for over £5,000	**In a County Court:**	All High Court judgments All County Court judgments
Procedure outline	➤ The creditor makes an application for a charging order. ➤ The application: ◆ may be made without notice, *and* ◆ must be issued in the court which made the judgment/order being enforced but if the proceedings have since been transferred to a different court, it must be issued in that court. But: • If the application is made under a council tax regulations, it must be issued in the county court for the district in which the relevant dwelling is situated. • If the application is for a charging order over an interest in a fund in court, it must be issued in the court in which the claim relating to that fund is or was proceeding. • The enforceability limits above will always override.			
Application for a charging order	➤ The application notice must contain the following information: ◆ the name and address of the judgment debtor, ◆ details of the judgment or order sought to be enforced, ◆ the amount of money remaining due under the judgment or order, ◆ if the debt is payable by instalments, the amounts which are due and remain unpaid, ◆ if the creditor knows of any other creditors of the debtor, their names and (if known) addresses, ◆ identification of the asset or assets which it is intended to charge, ◆ details of the judgment debtor's interest in the asset ◆ the names and addresses of people who must be served (see below), *and* ◆ **verification by a statement of truth.** ➤ The application will initially be dealt with by a judge without a hearing.			
Consideration of the application	➤ The judge may make an interim charging order: ◆ imposing a charge over the debtor's interest in the asset to which the application relates, *and* ◆ fixing a hearing to consider whether to make a final charging order.			
Service of the interim charging order	➤ Copies of the interim order, the application notice and supporting documents must be served not less than 21 days before the date fixed for the hearing on: ◆ the judgment debtor; ◆ such other creditors as the court directs; ◆ if the order relates to an interest under a trust, on such of the trustees as the court directs; ◆ if the interest charged is in securities other than securities held in court, then generally, the keeper of the register, ◆ if the interest charged is in funds in court, the Accountant General at the Court Funds Office. ➤ If the judgment creditor serves the order, he must either file a certificate of service not less than 2 days before the hearing, *or* produce a certificate of service at the hearing.			
The hearing for the final order	➤ The court may: ◆ make a final charging order confirming that the charge imposed by the interim charging order shall continue, with or without modification, ◆ discharge the interim charging order and dismiss the application, ◆ decide any issues in dispute, *or* ◆ direct a trial of any such issues, and if necessary give directions. ➤ There is provision for the debtor or the third party to object to the issue of a final charging order by filing written evidence of the grounds of objection at least 7 days before the hearing. ➤ If the court makes a final charging order which charges securities other than securities held in court, the order will include a stop notice unless the court otherwise orders. ➤ Any order must be served on everyone on whom the interim charging order was served. ➤ The court may, on an application by a debtor opposing the application, transfer it to the court for the district where the judgment debtor resides/carries on business, or to another court.			
Getting the money	➤ By sale of the property. This is achieved by applying to a court with jurisdiction with a *Part 8* claim form, a copy of the charging order and written evidence. ➤ Where property is owned by more than one person, sale cannot be ordered. However, the creditor may instead be entitled to apply for an order for sale under *TLATA 1996 s 14*.			
Stops orders and stop notices against a judgement debtor's interest in assets				
➤ A 'stop order' is an order of the High Court not to take, in relation to funds in court or securities specified in the order, certain steps listed in *Charging Orders Act 1979 s 5(5)*. A 'stop notice' is similar but the steps cannot be taken without first giving notice to the person who obtained the notice.				

Left margin: **What is it?** A way to secure payment of money ordered to be paid under a judgment or order of the High Court or a county court by placing a charge onto the debtor's property (usually a house or land or securities such as shares). Once an order is in place, a creditor can apply to court for sale of the charged property. It can be made absolute or subject to conditions.

	4 **Attachment of earnings order** (*Attachment of Earnings Act 1971, Sch 2 r 27*)
	County Court only - High Court proceedings are transferred to the County Court

<table>
<tr><td rowspan="20" style="writing-mode:vertical">**What is it?** A way to secure payment of certain debts by requiring an employer to make deductions direct from an employed debtor's earnings. Currently, the rate of deductions under an AEO made to secure payment of a judgment debt is calculated by a county court using information provided by the debtor.</td></tr>
<tr><td>Conditions</td><td>The debtor is employed (not self-employed or unemployed).
The sum due exceeds £50</td></tr>
<tr><td>Application</td><td>File an application form
↓
The court informs the debtor of the application and asks him to:
◆ pay the sum due, *or*
◆ file a statement of means form</td></tr>
<tr><td rowspan="10">*If* the debtor replies</td><td>**Steps**
1 The court makes a diary entry when the form is returned.</td></tr>
<tr><td>2 The court then fixes repayment according to the following 2 guidelines:
   a) 'normal deduction rate' (this is the amount of money to be deducted), *and*
   b) 'protected earnings rate' (this is an amount the debtor must be left with - a 'safety net' for the debtor).</td></tr>
<tr><td>3 The order is served on the debtor and the employer and a copy sent to the creditor.</td></tr>
<tr><td style="text-align:center">The service is as per the rules on p 395 et seq.
↓

Where an order is sent by the court and it is returned undelivered the court sends notice of non-service to the judgment creditor together with a notice saying he may request bailiff service. A bailiff serves by:
◆ inserting the order, enclosed in an envelope addressed to the debtor through the debtor's letter box, *or*
◆ delivering the order to some person (apparently not less than 16 years old) at the debtor's address, *or*
◆ delivering the order to the debtor personally</td></tr>
<tr><td>4 The employer must forward to the court:
   a) the deduction, *and*
   b) up to £1 for himself for administrative expenses on each deduction under the order (*AtEA 1971 s 7*).</td></tr>
<tr><td>5 If either party object or court staff consider that the statement has insufficient information, a judge hears the matter, but meanwhile the employer complies with the order unless varied.</td></tr>
<tr><td>6 If the debtor tells the court he un/self-employed, the application is dismissed.</td></tr>
<tr><td rowspan="4">*If* the debtor *does not* reply</td><td>**Steps**
1 The court automatically issues an order to produce a statement of means.
2 The bailiff serves this personally on the debtor.
   (If the creditor provides the employer's name and address, the court may ask the employer for a statement of earnings).</td></tr>
<tr><td>3 If the debtor does not respond at all, the court automatically issues a 'notice to show cause' which the bailiff serves.</td></tr>
<tr><td>4 Failure to attend a subsequent hearing before a district judge will ultimately lead to committal to prison.</td></tr>
</table>

5 **Appointment of a receiver** (*CPR r 69*) (not dealt with here)

6 **Bankruptcy (individual) or winding up (company)**

Steps
1 If no execution has so far been levied, issue a statutory demand.
2 If execution has been levied but is unsatisfied, see the procedures for bankruptcy/winding up on p 333 et seq.

S   Appeals

A very simplified table of possible Appeal Courts (AJA(DA)O 2000, Part 52, PD52)

Type of claim	Appeal from	Appeal to	Permission needed?	Powers on Appeal
An interim decision on any *Part 7* claim OR A final decision on a *Part 7* claim, other than a claim allocated to the multi-track OR Any decision on a *Part 8* claim	**County Court** a District Judge	Circuit Judge in the county court	Yes unless the appeal is against: ♦ a committal order, *or* ♦ a refusal to grant habeas corpus, *or* ♦ certain actions under *Children Act 1989* (*r 52.3*) To obtain leave, an application must be made to: a) the lower court at the hearing at which the decision was made, *or* b) the appeal court **Permission may be granted if:** ♦ the court considers the appeal would have a real prospect of success, *or* ♦ there is some other compelling reason	The appeal court has all the powers of the lower court (*r 52.10*) eg: to affirm, set aside, vary an order or judgment eg: to refer any claim or issue for determination by the lower court eg: to order a new trial/ hearing eg: to make an order for interest payment eg: to make a costs order *BUT* the appeal is limited to a review of the decision of the lower court unless it is in the interests of justice to hold a rehearing (*r 52.11*)
	County Court a Circuit Judge	Single Judge of the High Court		
	High Court a Master or a District Judge of the High Court			
A final decision on a *Part 7* claim allocated to the multi-track	**County Court** a District Judge or a Circuit Judge	Court of Appeal (*SCA 1981 ss 15-18*)		
	High Court a Master or a District Judge of the High Court			
Any decision of a High Court Judge	**High Court** a High Court Judge			Note: for extra provisions on small claims track appeals, see p 438
Any decision of the Court of Appeal	**Court of Appeal**	Supreme Court	Yes apply to the Court of Appeal but if refused, apply to the Supreme Court	
Costs an authorised costs officer on a detailed assessment (but not if LSC funded) (*rr 47.20-47.23*)	Costs a costs judge or a District Judge of the High Court		No	Costs power to re-hear proceedings and make any order/ directions appropriate

➤   An appeal is allowed if:

♦   a decision of a lower court was:

•   wrong, *or*

•   unjust because of a serious procedural or other irregularity in the proceedings of the lower court.

Note: Judicial review as an 'appeal' against decisions is not dealt with in this table. It is covered by *Part 54*	Note: References to the ECJ or the European Court of Human Rights are not dealt with in this table	Note: Certain specialised jurisdictions (eg: insolvency) and any appeals from tribunals are not dealt with in this table

This chapter examines:

Note: The law as set out in this section of the *Legal Practice Companion:*
◆ applies to adults only unless the text specifically indicates otherwise, *and*
◆ does not cover the special rules on terrorism, sexual offences, fraud and drugs, unless the text specifically indicates otherwise, *and*
◆ ignores most transitional rules.

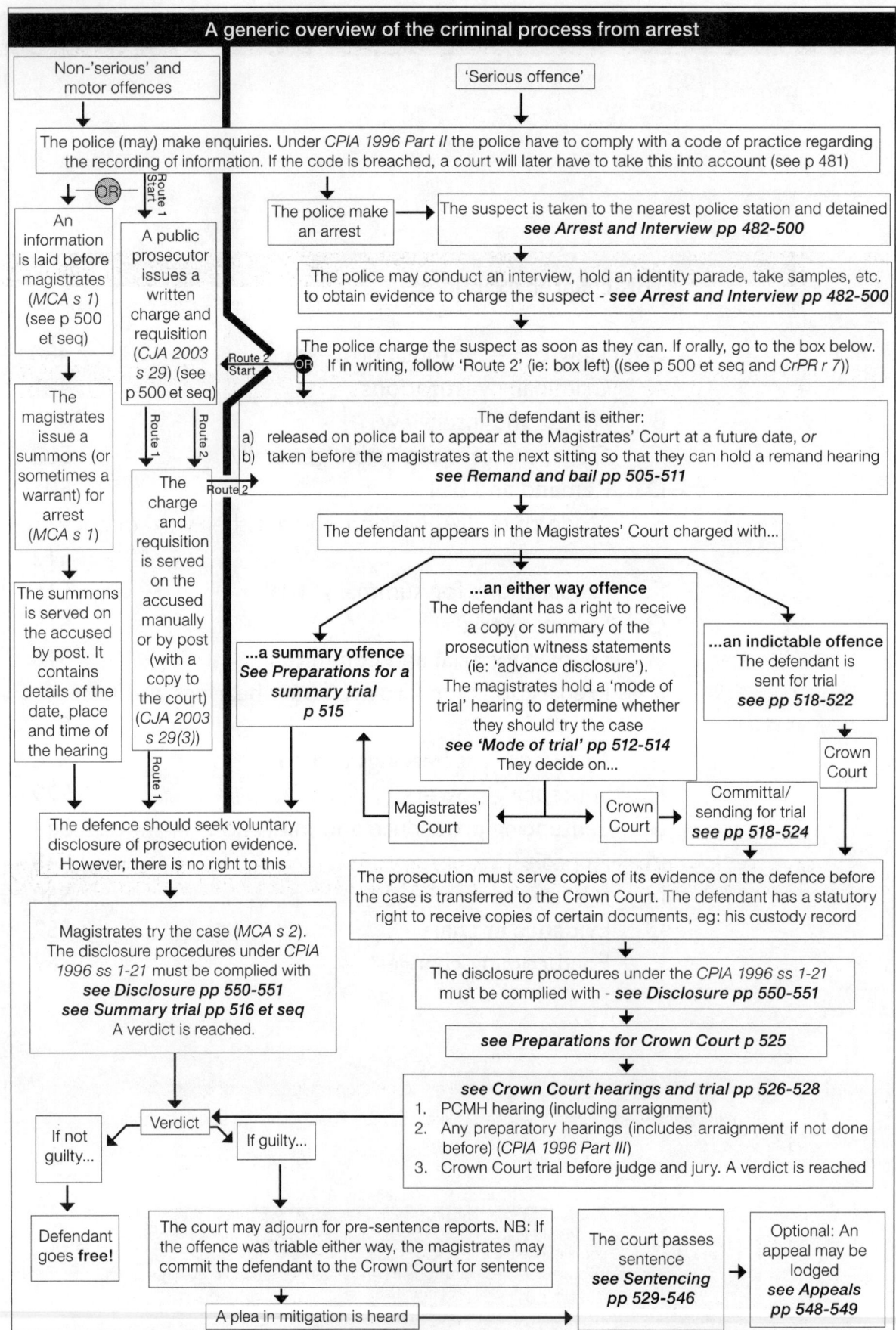

A generic overview of the criminal process from arrest

| Non-'serious' and motor offences | | 'Serious offence' |

The police (may) make enquiries. Under *CPIA 1996 Part II* the police have to comply with a code of practice regarding the recording of information. If the code is breached, a court will later have to take this into account (see p 481)

Route 1 Start — OR

An information is laid before magistrates (*MCA s 1*) (see p 500 et seq)

A public prosecutor issues a written charge and requisition (*CJA 2003 s 29*) (see p 500 et seq)

Route 2 Start — OR

The police make an arrest → The suspect is taken to the nearest police station and detained *see Arrest and Interview pp 482-500*

The police may conduct an interview, hold an identity parade, take samples, etc. to obtain evidence to charge the suspect - *see Arrest and Interview pp 482-500*

The police charge the suspect as soon as they can. If orally, go to the box below. If in writing, follow 'Route 2' (ie: box left) ((see p 500 et seq and *CrPR r 7*))

The magistrates issue a summons (or sometimes a warrant) for arrest (*MCA s 1*)

Route 1 / **Route 2**

The charge and requisition is served on the accused manually or by post (with a copy to the court) (*CJA 2003 s 29(3)*)

Route 2

The defendant is either:
a) released on police bail to appear at the Magistrates' Court at a future date, *or*
b) taken before the magistrates at the next sitting so that they can hold a remand hearing *see Remand and bail pp 505-511*

The defendant appears in the Magistrates' Court charged with...

The summons is served on the accused by post. It contains details of the date, place and time of the hearing

Route 1

...a summary offence *See Preparations for a summary trial p 515*

...an either way offence The defendant has a right to receive a copy or summary of the prosecution witness statements (ie: 'advance disclosure'). The magistrates hold a 'mode of trial' hearing to determine whether they should try the case *see 'Mode of trial' pp 512-514* They decide on...

...an indictable offence The defendant is sent for trial *see pp 518-522*

Crown Court

Magistrates' Court ↔ Crown Court → Committal/ sending for trial *see pp 518-524*

The defence should seek voluntary disclosure of prosecution evidence. However, there is no right to this

The prosecution must serve copies of its evidence on the defence before the case is transferred to the Crown Court. The defendant has a statutory right to receive copies of certain documents, eg: his custody record

Magistrates try the case (*MCA s 2*). The disclosure procedures under *CPIA 1996 ss 1-21* must be complied with *see Disclosure pp 550-551* *see Summary trial pp 516 et seq* A verdict is reached.

The disclosure procedures under the *CPIA 1996 ss 1-21* must be complied with - *see Disclosure pp 550-551*

see Preparations for Crown Court p 525

see Crown Court hearings and trial pp 526-528
1. PCMH hearing (including arraignment)
2. Any preparatory hearings (includes arraignment if not done before) (*CPIA 1996 Part III*)
3. Crown Court trial before judge and jury. A verdict is reached

Verdict → If not guilty... / If guilty...

Defendant goes **free!**

The court may adjourn for pre-sentence reports. NB: If the offence was triable either way, the magistrates may commit the defendant to the Crown Court for sentence

The court passes sentence *see Sentencing pp 529-546*

Optional: An appeal may be lodged *see Appeals pp 548-549*

A plea in mitigation is heard

A Criminal investigations

➤ A code of practice applies for criminal investigations conducted by police officers (*CPIA 1996 s 23(1)*).

➤ The code provides that there are different functions to be performed by (*para 3.1*):

  ◆ the investigator,

  ◆ the officer in charge of an investigation,

  ◆ the disclosure officer.

Duty to retain material

➤ The investigator has a duty to retain material obtained in a criminal investigation which may be relevant to the investigation (*para 5.1*).

Time to retain material

➤ All material which may be relevant to an investigation must be retained until a decision is taken whether to institute proceedings against a person for an offence (*para 5.7*).

➤ If a criminal investigation results in proceedings being instituted, all material which may be relevant must be retained at least until (*paras 5.8-5.10*):

  ◆ the prosecutor decides not to proceed with the case, *or*

  ◆ the accused is acquitted, *or*

  ◆ the accused is convicted.

    • If the accused is convicted the material must be retained until the later of:

      ▪ the convicted person is released from custody, *or*

      ▪ 6 months from the date of conviction, *or*

      ▪ if an appeal is in progress, the time that the appeal is determined, *or*

      ▪ if the Criminal Cases Review Commission (see p 549) is considering an application:
        - the time it decides not to refer the case to the Court of Appeal,
        - the time that the appeal is determined.

Preparation of schedules (*para 6.6 and 7.1*)

➤ The following schedules must be prepared and given to the prosecutor if:

  ◆ the accused is charged, *and*

    a) the offence is triable only on indictment, *or*

    b) the offence is triable summarily *and* the accused is considered likely to plead not guilty, *or*

    c) the offence is triable either way *and*

      i) it is considered that the offence is likely to be tried on indictment, *or*

      ii) it is considered that the accused is likely to plead not guilty at a summary trial.

    NB: If, in (b) or (c)(ii), it is considered that the accused will plead guilty, and contrary to this, he pleads not guilty, then a schedule must be prepared as soon as practicable (*para 6.8*).

➤ Material which may be relevant to an investigation, which the disclosure officer believes will *not* form part of the prosecution case must be listed on a schedule (*para 6.2*).

Non-sensitive material (*para 6.3*)	Sensitive material (*para 6.4*)
Material which the disclosure officer does not believe is sensitive must be listed on a schedule of non-sensitive material	Material which is believed to be sensitive must be: ◆ listed on a schedule of sensitive material, *or* ◆ (in exceptional circumstances) revealed to the prosecution.

B   Arrest and interview

References in this section are to PACE, unless otherwise stated.

References such as 'C: 2.1' are to the relevant paragraph of the PACE Codes of Practice (which do not have statutory force, but with which the police must comply). Eg: 'C: 2.1' refers to paragraph 2.1 of Code C.

I	Dealing with crime without arrest ... or with a special type of arrest
II	Powers of arrest
III	Voluntary attendance
IV	Detention before charge
V	Interview
VI	Inferences from silence
VII	Identification
VIII	Taking samples
IX	Charge
X	Other rights at a police station
XI	Detention after charge: 1 of 3 alternatives
XII	What happens next

The 8 *PACE* codes of practice

➤ **Code A:**

  ◆ For the exercise by police officers of statutory powers of stop and search, *and*

  ◆ For the requirement of police officers and police staff to record public encounters

➤ **Code B:**

  ◆ For searches of premises by police officers and the seizure of property found by police officers on persons or premises.

➤ **Code C:**

  ◆ **for detention, treatment and questioning of persons by police officers**

➤ **Code D:**

  ◆ **for identification of persons by police officers**

➤ **Code E:**

  ◆ **on audio recording interviews with suspects**

➤ **Code F:**

  ◆ **on visual recording with sound of interviews with suspects**

➤ **Code G:**

  ◆ for the statutory power of arrest by police officers

➤ **Code H:**

  ◆ on the treatment of persons in connection with *Terrorism Act 2000 s 41* and *Sch 8*

(Codes in **bold** are dealt with in this book)

I   Dealing with crime without arrest ... or with a special type of arrest

Penalty notices (CJPA 2001 s 2 as amended by ABA 2003 s 87)

➤ Police may issue penalty notices on the spot/at a police station to offenders over 10 for certain disorder offences. However, if a police officer believes the courts are more appropriate, all usual powers (eg: arrest) are available. A penalty notice is notice of the opportunity to discharge any liability to conviction by paying a fixed penalty. There is no criminal conviction or admission of guilt associated with payment of the penalty, but the alleged offender may opt for trial by a court - risking conviction. Failure to pay the penalty/opt for trial can lead to a fine of 1.5 times the penalty amount.

Conditional cautions (CJA 2003 ss 22-27, PJA 2006 s 17 (in pilot areas only) and s 18)

➤ A 'conditional caution' for an offence is half way between a simple caution and a full charge.

➤ It is a caution which has conditions attached to it with which the offender must comply.

➤ It can be given if 5 requirements are satisfied:

   a) there is evidence against the offender, *and*

   b) that a 'relevant prosecutor' (defined in *s 27*) considers that the evidence would be sufficient to charge him and that a conditional caution should be given, *and*

   c) the offender admits the offence, *and*

   d) the offender has been made aware of what the caution (and failure to comply) would mean, *and*

   e) that he signs a document containing details of the offence, the admission, the offender's consent to the caution, and the conditions imposed.

➤ Conditions can be attached only to facilitate the rehabilitation of the offender or to ensure the offender makes reparation for the offence. *PJA 2006 s 17* provides that (currently in pilot areas only), in addition, a conditional caution may contain conditions which have the object of punishing the offender - these are presently only financial penalties (which are subject to a maximum) (*PJA(11)O 2009*).

➤ **Arrest for failing to comply with conditional caution** (*PJA 2006 s 18* inserting *CJA 2003 s 24A*):

   ◆ A constable has a power of arrest without warrant where an offender is suspected of having breached the conditions of a conditional caution without reasonable excuse.

   ◆ Where a person is arrested in this way, a prosecutor must determine whether he has failed to comply with the conditions attached to his caution and, if so, whether there was a reasonable excuse.

     ● If there is no reasonable excuse, the offender can be charged with the original offence in respect of which the conditional caution was given.

       ■ Where further investigations are necessary to establish the circumstances of the suspected non-compliance with conditions, the offender may be released without charge and on bail.

     ● Alternatively, the offender can be released without charge and without bail and with or without any variations in the conditions attached to the caution. (This may happen if the prosecutor determined that there was a reasonable excuse or that there had been no actual non-compliance.)

   ◆ The offender may be kept in police detention to be dealt with (eg: a person might be detained until a relevant prosecutor is available to make a charging decision).

➤ If the offender fails without reasonable excuse to satisfy the conditions attached to the conditional caution, he may be prosecuted for the original offence.

II Powers of arrest

A Powers to arrest

1 Arrest powers for a constable for ANY OFFENCE

➤ *PACE s 24* and *Code G* deal with statutory powers of police to arrest persons suspected of involvement in a criminal offence (*G: 1.1*).

➤ The right to liberty is a key principle of *HRA 1998*. Arrest is an obvious and significant interference with that right (*G: 1.2*).

➤ Arrest must be fully justified and officers exercising the power should consider if the necessary objectives can be met by other, less intrusive means (*G: 1.3*).

➤ Arrest must never be used simply because it can be used. Absence of justification for exercising the powers of arrest may lead to challenges should the case proceed to court. When the power of arrest is exercised it is essential that it is exercised in a nondiscriminatory and proportionate manner (*G: 1.3*).

➤ If *PACE s 24* and *Code G* are not observed, both the arrest and the conduct of any subsequent investigation may be open to question (*G: 1.4*).

➤ A lawful arrest requires 2 elements (*G: 2.1*):

Element 1: A person's involvement or suspected involvement or attempted involvement in the commission of a criminal offence, *and*

Element 2: reasonable grounds for believing that the person's arrest is necessary.

➤ Arresting officers must inform a person arrested that they have been arrested, even if this fact is obvious, and of the relevant circumstances of the arrest in relation to both elements and to inform the custody officer of these on arrival at the police station (*G: 2.2*).

Element 1: Involvement in the commission of an offence

➤ **Involvement in the commission of an offence:** A constable may arrest without warrant in relation to any offence (*s 24(1)-(6)* and *G: 2.3*) (except for one exception, not dealt with here). A constable may arrest anyone:

◆ who is about to commit an offence or is in the act of committing an offence (*s 24(1)*), *or*

◆ whom the officer has reasonable grounds for suspecting is about to commit an offence or to be committing an offence (*s 24(1)*), *or*

◆ whom the officer has reasonable grounds to suspect of being guilty of an offence which he has reasonable grounds for suspecting has been committed (*s 24(2)*), *or*

◆ anyone who is guilty of an offence which has been committed or anyone whom the officer has reasonable grounds for suspecting to be guilty of that offence (*s 24(3)*).

➤ In considering the individual circumstances, the constable must take into account the situation of the victim, the nature of the offence, the circumstances of the suspect and the needs of the investigative process (*G: 2.8*).

Element 2: Necessity

➤ The power of arrest is only exercisable if the constable has reasonable grounds for believing that it is *necessary* to arrest the person (G: 2.4) based on the following exhaustive criteria ((s 24(4)-(6)) and G: 2.9).

a) to enable the name of the person in question to be ascertained (in the case where the constable does not know, and cannot readily ascertain, the person's name, or has reasonable grounds for doubting whether a name given by the person as his name is his real name), *or*

b) correspondingly as regards the person's address, *or*

- An address is a satisfactory address for service of summons if the person will be at it for a sufficiently long period for it to be possible to serve him or her with a summons; or, that some other person at that address specified by the person will accept service of the summons on their behalf (G: 2.9).

c) to prevent the person in question:

i) causing physical injury to himself or any other person, *or*

ii) suffering physical injury, *or*

iii) causing loss or damage to property, *or*

iv) committing an offence against public decency (only applies where members of the public going about their normal business cannot reasonably be expected to avoid the person in question), *or*

v) causing an unlawful obstruction of the highway, *or*

d) to protect a child or other vulnerable person from the person in question, *or*

e) to allow the prompt and effective investigation of the offence or of the conduct of the person in question, *or*

- Eg (G: 2.9): Where there are reasonable grounds to believe that the person:
  - has made false statements, *or*
  - has made statements which cannot be readily verified, *or*
  - has presented false evidence, *or*
  - may steal or destroy evidence, *or*
  - may make contact with co-suspects or conspirators, *or*
  - may intimidate or threaten or make contact with witnesses, *or*
  - where it is necessary to obtain evidence by questioning.

- Eg (G: 2.9): When considering arrest in connection with an indictable offence, there is a need to:
  - enter and search any premises occupied or controlled by a person, *or*
  - search the person, *or*
  - prevent contact with others, *or*
  - take fingerprints, footwear impressions, samples or photographs of the suspect

- Eg (G: 2.9): ensuring compliance with statutory drug testing requirements.

f) to prevent any prosecution for the offence from being hindered by the disappearance of the person in question.

2   Arrest powers for non-constables for ANY OFFENCE

➤ The powers of summary arrest below are exercisable only if:

♦ the person making the arrest has reasonable grounds for believing that for any of the reasons in the box below it is necessary to arrest the person in question, *and*

♦ it appears to the person making the arrest that it is not reasonably practicable for a constable to make it instead.

Reasons for arrest *(s 24A(4))*
➤ To prevent the person in question: ♦ causing physical injury to himself or any other person, *or*   ♦ suffering physical injury, *or*   ♦ causing loss of or damage to property, *or*   ♦ making off before a constable can assume responsibility for him.

NB: This does not apply to the offences of racial hatred or hatred against persons on religious grounds or grounds of sexual orientation under *POA 1986 ss 17-29N* (ie: *Parts 3* and *3A*) (*s 24A(5)*).

➤ Subject to the first arrow bullet above, a person other than a constable may arrest without a warrant (*s 24A*):

♦ anyone who is in the act of committing an indictable offence, *or*

♦ anyone whom he has reasonable grounds for suspecting to be committing an indictable offence.

➤ Subject to the first arrow bullet above, where an indictable offence has been committed, a person other than a constable may arrest without a warrant:

♦ anyone who is guilty of the offence;

♦ anyone whom he has reasonable grounds for suspecting to be guilty of it.

B   Rules immediately following arrest

Records of arrest *(Code G: 4)*
➤ The arresting officer is required to record in his pocket book or by other methods used for recording information (*G: 4.1*):   ♦ the nature and circumstances of the offence leading to the arrest, *and*   ♦ the reason or reasons why arrest was necessary, *and*   ♦ the giving of the caution, *and*   ♦ anything said by the person at the time of arrest.   ➤ The record must be made at the time of the arrest unless impracticable to do (*G: 4.2*).   ♦ If not made at that time, the record should then be completed as soon as possible thereafter.   ➤ On arrival at a police station, the custody officer must open the custody record. The information given by the arresting officer on the circumstances and reason or reasons for arrest must be recorded as part of the custody record. Alternatively, a copy of the record made by the officer (under *G: 4.1* must be attached as part of the custody record (*G: 4.3*)).

1 **Arrest away from a police station**

➤ There are 3 options:

   a) take the arrested person to the police station, *or*

   b) release the arrested person without bail, *or*

   c) release the arrested person on bail (see box below).

➤ If a person is arrested at a place other than at a police station, that person should be taken to the police station as soon as practicable (*s 30(1A)*).

   ◆ A person arrested by a constable at any place other than a police station *must* be released without bail if before that person reaches a police station, a constable is satisfied that there are no grounds for keeping him under arrest or releasing him on bail under *s 30A* (*s 30(7)-(7A)*).

   ◆ A constable who releases a person in this way must record the fact that he has done so as soon as practicable after the release (*s 30(8)-(9)*).

➤ However, nothing written above prevents a constable delaying taking a person to a police station or releasing him on bail if the presence of the person at a place (other than a police station) is necessary in order to carry out such investigations as it is reasonable to carry out immediately (*s 30(10)-(10A)*).

   ◆ Where there is any such delay, the reasons must be recorded when the person first arrives at the police station or (as the case may be) is released on bail (*s 30(11)*).

Arrest away from a police station: street bail (*ss 30A, 30B, 30C, 30D* and *PJA 2006 s 10*)

➤ If a person is arrested other than at a police station, a constable may release that person on bail at any time before he arrives at a police station ('street bail').

➤ A person released on street bail must be required to attend a police station.

➤ A constable granting bail may attach conditions relevant and proportionate to the suspect/the offence.

   ◆ The conditions that can be imposed must be necessary to secure that the person surrenders to custody, that the person does not commit an offence while on bail, or that the person does not interfere with witnesses or otherwise obstruct the course of justice. (Where the person is under the age of 17 conditions may also be applied for their welfare, or in their own interest.)

   ◆ No recognizance, security or surety may be taken and no requirement to reside in a bail hostel may be imposed.

➤ The constable must give that person a notice in writing before he is released stating:

   ◆ the offence for which he was arrested, *and*

   ◆ the ground on which he was arrested, *and*

   ◆ that he is required to attend a police station (it *may* also specify the police station which he is required to attend and the time when he is required to attend).

      • If the notice does not include this last item, the person must subsequently be given a further notice in writing which contains that information.

➤ Nothing prevents the re-arrest without a warrant of a person released on bail in this way if new evidence justifying a further arrest has come to light since his release.

➤ Failure to attend a police station at a specified time means a constable may arrest that person without a warrant.

---

2 **Arrest at a police station (or away from a police station and person then taken there)**

➤ The custody officer (at least a sergeant) must decide to (see also Section IX p 499):

   Note: A suspect is treated as arrested if he returns to a police station to answer to bail.

   a) charge the suspect immediately (*s 37(7)(d)*), *or*

   b) release the suspect (whether on bail or not) without charge (*s 37(7)(b)-(c)*), *or*

   c) detain the suspect before charge (see Section IV p 489), *or*

   d) i) release the suspect on bail (with/without conditions as in the box above) and without charge, *or*

      ii) keep the suspect in police detention...

      ... in either case to allow the CPS to decide whether to charge the suspect with an offence or not or whether to give a caution or not (*s 37(7)(a)* and *s 37A-37D*).

Cautions: wording

➤ Wording: 'You do not have to say anything. But it may harm your defence if you do not mention when questioned something which you later rely on in court. Anything you do say may be given in evidence.' (C:10.5, see pp 491-492).

➤ When a requirement to caution arises at a time when the restriction on drawing adverse inferences from silence applies, the wording is: 'You do not have to say anything, but anything you do say may be given in evidence.' (C: Annex C: 2, see pp 491-492)

➤ A caution *must* be given:

   a) on, or just before, arrest (C:10.4), *and*

   b) on a custody officer authorising detention (it must be given in a written form) (C:3.2), *and*

   c) before an interview (C:10.1), *and*

   d) following a break in questioning (C:10.8), *and*

   e) when charging a detained person (C:16.2).

Table of various offences

Offence	Type	Magistrates' maximum penalty	Crown court maximum penalty
		cf: Mandatory and racially aggravated sentences p 530	
Theft (TA 1968 s 7)	Either way	6 months [to be 12 months when CJA 2003 s 282 is in force] £5,000 fine (MCA 1980 s 32, CJA 1982 s 37) This is the General Magistrates' Sentencing Power ('GMSP')	7 years Unlimited fine (CJA 2003 s 163)
Burglary (TA 1968 s 9)	Either way		10 years (14 on indictment if a dwelling) Unlimited fine (CJA 2003 s 163)
	Indictment		
Fear/provocation of violence (POA 1986 s 4)	Summary		Not applicable
Actual bodily harm (OAPA 1861 s 47)	Either way		5 years Unlimited fine (CJA 2003 s 163)
Robbery (TA 1968 s 8)	Indictment	Not applicable	Life Unlimited fine (CJA 2003 s 163)
Careless driving (RTA 1988 s 3) (RTOA 1988 Sch 2)	Summary	£5,000 fine Endorsement of licence: obligatory Disqualification: discretionary, else endorse 3-9 points Disqualification until a re-test is discretionary	Not applicable
Dangerous driving (RTA 1988 s 2) (RTOA 1988 Sch 2)	Either way	GMSP	2 years, unlimited fine
		Disqualification: obligatory Endorsement of offence on licence: obligatory with 3-11 points A re-test before requalifying is obligatory	
Taking a conveyance (TA 1968 s 12) (RTOA 1988 Sch 2)	Summary	GMSP Disqualification: discretionary	Not applicable
Aggravated vehicle taking (TA 1968 s 12A) (RTOA 1988 Sch 2)	Either way	GMSP	2 years (14 years if death results) Unlimited fine (CJA 2003 s 163)
	Summary if aggravating feature is that damage is worth £5,000 or less	*and* Endorsement on licence is obligatory: endorse 3-11 points Disqualification: obligatory	

III   Voluntary attendance

➤ An individual attending voluntarily at a police station may leave at will (s 29).

➤ If prevented from leaving, he must be informed that he is under arrest (s 29).

IV Detention before charge

➤ A person at a police station to answer to bail is treated as under arrest for the relevant offence (s 34(7)).

➤ **Following arrest**

 ◆ Detention is permitted if the custody officer has reasonable grounds to believe *either* (s 37(2)):

 a) that there is insufficient evidence to charge the suspect and detention is necessary to obtain that evidence by questioning, *or*

 b) it is necessary to secure or preserve evidence, or to obtain it by questioning.

➤ The police should interview the suspect as soon as possible and decide immediately after an interview whether a charge will be brought - if no charge is brought, release should be immediate (s 34(2), s 41(7)).

Detention timetable (before charge)		➤ Any time during which the suspect was on bail pauses the detention 'clock' and is not included in the time elapsed (s 34(7) and s 47(6) by P(DB)A 2011).		c = custody officer i = at least an inspector s = at least a superintendent m = magistrate	
Monday 1.00 pm		Arrival at the police station. Detention clock begins to run (s 41(2)(a)(i))		b) it is an indictable offence, *and* c) the investigation is being conducted diligently and expeditiously NB:This new authorisation is only possible if it is: i) before 24 hours from when the detention clock began to run (s 42(4)), *and* ii) after the second review	s
Monday 1.10 pm		Detention is 'authorised' (when no warrant) by the custody officer under the grounds in s 37(2)	c	Tuesday 1.00 pm cont. — 24 hour offset cont.	
Monday 7.10 pm	+6 hours offset	Latest time for first review of detention. Detention may continue if the original grounds are still valid (s 40(3)) NB: The suspect or his solicitor may make representations	i	Wednesday 1.00 am — 36 hour offset	The superintendent's authority expires. Charge or release *unless* a magistrate grants warrant of further detention (s 43) (NB only for an indictable offence)	m
Tuesday 4.10 am	+9 hour offset	Latest time for second review; thereafter reviews at 9 hourly intervals (s 40(3))	i	Thursday 1.00 pm — 72 hour offset	The magistrate's warrant expires. Charge or release *unless* a magistrate grants extension of warrant of further detention (s 44)	m
Tuesday 1.00 pm	24 hour offset	Charge, or release (on bail or not) (s 41(7)) *unless* a superintendent has reasonable grounds to believe: a) grounds in s 37(2) still exist, *and*	s	Friday 1.00 pm — 96 hour offset	Charge or release (s 44 (3)(b)) **MAXIMUM LIMIT**	

Black background offsets are based from time detention was authorised and are cumulative offsets
White background offsets are based from time of arrival at police station and are absolute offsets

Safeguards on interview at a police station

 ◆ **Rest:** for a continuous period of 8 hours in 24 hours, preferably at night (C:12.2).
 ◆ **Drink or drugs:** no questioning if the suspect is unable to grasp the significance of questions due to drink or drugs, *unless* the superintendent or an officer of higher rank authorises it for the protection of people or property (C:11.18).
 ◆ **Interview room:** heated, lighted, ventilated; chair for the defendant to sit on (C:12.4, 12.6).

 ◆ **Breaks:** at recognised meal times, refreshments every 2 hours (C:12.8).
 ◆ **Identification:** a policeman must identify himself and anyone else present before interview (C:12.7).
 ◆ **Juveniles (under 17):** accompanied by an 'appropriate' adult (a parent/guardian or social worker) for certain situations (C:1.7, 11.15).
 ◆ **Mentally disordered:** accompanied by an 'appropriate' adult (a relative/other responsible person or a special social worker) for certain situations (C:1.7, 11.15).

A solicitor's role at the police station

➤ A solicitor should go prepared and take *PACE, PACE Codes*, copies of relevant LSC funding application forms, a letter (on headed paper) for the suspect explaining the solicitor's offer to advise the suspect if he requests it and a standard pro forma for taking instructions, pen and paper.
➤ A solicitor should keep account of passing time with reference to the time limits for detention.
➤ A solicitor should attend any interview at which the client is questioned.
➤ A solicitor should ask for the investigating officer; seek details of why a client is detained and evidence against him.
➤ A solicitor should ask, as soon as he arrives at the police station, to see the custody record (the police must agree under C:2.4) and ask to speak to the custody officer.
➤ A solicitor should take a contemporaneous note of all that occurs. The solicitor may later be a witness!

V   Interview

➤ An interview is the questioning of a person regarding their involvement or suspected involvement in a criminal offence or offences (for which a caution would need to be given under *C:10.1*) (*C:11.1A*).

➤ After arrest, an interview should not be held until the suspect reaches the police station *unless* delay would endanger persons or evidence, alert others, or cause serious loss or damage to property (*C:11.1*).

➤ Prior to the commencement or recommencement of an interview, the suspect must be reminded that he has a right to free legal advice and that the interview can be delayed for this (*C:11.2*), see p 499.

➤ At the start of an interview at a police station, any significant statement/silence made before a suspect's arrival must be put to him. He must be asked if he would like to confirm, deny, or add anything (*C:11.4*).

➤ No oppression may be used by police during questioning (*C:11.5*).

➤ Any interview before charge (or for which a suspect has not been informed he may be prosecuted) must cease when the officer in charge of the investigation (*C:11.6*):

   ◆ is satisfied all relevant questions about the offence have been put to the suspect, *and*

   ◆ has taken account of any other available evidence, *and*

   ◆ (or for a detained suspect the custody officer) reasonably believes there is sufficient evidence to provide a realistic prospect of conviction for that offence if the person was prosecuted for it.

➤ A record must be made during an interview (or as soon as practicable after it) (*C:11.7-11.14*).

➤ Interviewing is forbidden after the suspect has been charged, *unless* it is necessary to (*C:16.5*):

   ◆ minimise harm to a person or the public, *or*

   ◆ clarify ambiguity in an answer or statement, *or*

   ◆ enable the defendant to comment on new information unearthed since he was charged.

➤ See interviews and other legal rights (p 499) and advice on the qualified right to silence (p 491 et seq).

Recording an interview	
Audio recording of interview (*Code E*)	**Non-taped interview**

➤ Compulsory *unless* offence is a purely summary offence (*F:3.1(a)*).
 ◆ A master recording and a working copy are made (*E:2.2*).
 ◆ The master recording is sealed, and signed by the suspect and the interviewing officer (*E:2*).
 ◆ The defence may access the working copy.
 ◆ A written summary is sent to the defence who may agree that it is admissible as evidence.
    • If the defence objects, a full transcript is made and the seal on the master recording is broken in court.
 ➤ *E:7* allows audio recording to a secure digital network, instead.
 ◆ Interview record files are stored in read only format, firstly on secure non-removable storage devices to ensure integrity. They are then transferred to a remote network device (*E:17.6*).
	➤ Summary offences only
	 ◆ An accurate written record must be made (*C:11.7*).
	 ◆ The record must be made during the interview or as soon as practicable after it (*C:11.7-11.8*).
	 ◆ An interviewee must read and sign the record (*C:11.11*). Refusals to do so must be recorded. Note: *C:11E* says that if the suspect agrees, the words are 'I agree that this is a correct record of what was said' and he signs his signature.
	 ◆ The interview record will be served on the defence.
	    • If the defence agrees, the record is admissible.
	    • If the defence objects, oral evidence is admissible and the officer may refresh his memory from contemporaneous notes.

Visual recording of interview (*Code F*)	
➤ PACE s 60A allows visual recording of interviews but there is no statutory requirement to visually record interviews. ◆ The rules are broadly the same as for audio interviews. ◆ Each party must be present if the seal on the master recording is broken (*F:6.4*). ◆ Again, *F:7* allows recordings to be made to a secure digital network, instead.	**Outside the context of an interview** ➤ Comments made by the suspect should be (*C:11.13*): ◆ recorded in writing and signed by the officer concerned, ◆ shown to the suspect, who must have an opportunity to read, time and sign them. A refusal to sign should be recorded.
Written statement under caution	
This is a prepared statement by the suspect setting out his version of events. It may also be a confession. The rules and the form are set out in *Annex D to Code C*	

VI   Inferences from silence

➤   The *CJPO 1994* cuts down on a suspect's/accused's right to remain silent. The rules are:

	s 34		s 36	s 37
Situation	a) Before being charged, *and* b) while being questioned under caution by a constable, *and* c) the constable is trying to discover whether, or by whom, an offence has been committed	On a suspect being charged or officially informed he may be prosecuted for an offence	a) On being arrested, *and* b) with an object, substance or mark: 　i) on his person, *or* 　ii) in or on his clothing or footwear, *or* 　iii) in his possession, *or* 　iv) in any place in which he is, at the time of his arrest, *and* c) the constable reasonably believes that the object, substance or mark has something to do with the suspect participating in a specified offence, *and* d) the constable informs the suspect of his suspicions and asks him to account for the object, substance or mark	a) On being arrested, *and* b) the suspect is at a place where a constable reasonably believes that the person's presence may be to do with participation in an offence, *and* c) the constable reasonably believes that the suspect's presence has something to do with the suspect participating in a specified offence, *and* d) the constable informs the suspect of his suspicions and asks him to account for his presence

ss 34, 36 and 37 will most often apply only to interviews in police stations (because of the general rule prohibiting interviews outside police stations). The usual interview safeguards for police station interviews will, of course, still apply

Consequ-ences apply if:	a) Suspect fails to mention a fact he might reasonably be expected to mention, *and* b) he later relies on that fact in his defence		Suspect fails or refuses to provide an explanation	Suspect fails or refuses to provide an explanation
Consequ-ences	The court or magistrates can 'draw such inferences as appear proper' from the silence as applied to: 1 a submission of 'no case to answer' in a trial (see p 517 and p 526) 2 determining the guilt or innocence of a defendant at trial NB: Such inferences do not decide the matter alone, there must be other factors too (*CJPO 1994 s 38*)			

Practical advice on silence in light of case law

➤ If advising a suspect to stay silent, one should record the reason to avoid 'adverse inferences' at trial (see p 566).
➤ It is wrong to advise clients to answer only some questions but not others, as the *whole* interview will be admissible and the silences will be hard to explain.
➤ The idea that 'an inference can never strengthen the prosecution case but only weaken a defence case once it has been found there is a case to answer' has been eroded by case law:
  ◆ If the defence makes a submission of no case to answer, the prosecution may still respond that the defence has relied on facts not mentioned on an earlier occasion (*R v Hart* & *R v McLean* [1998] CLY 1056). This is significant in:
    • cases where a client has had a 'no comment' interview and then answered questions in a second interview or had several no comment interviews but later hands in a prepared statement when charged. If a solicitor believes there is no case to answer, he should advise the client to stay silent throughout. (Although it might be sensible to make a prepared statement, this should be kept in the solicitor's papers for use only if the judge dismisses the defence submission that there is no case to answer).
    • identification cases where there is going to be a case to answer at any stage because it is critical to raise any alibi at the first possible opportunity and at a time when the police can still check the alibi without the suspect being able to brief the alibi witness (see *R v Taylor* 1999 Crim LR 77).
  ◆ Solicitors and clients should not give reasons for a client staying silent unless they are content for the prosecution to inspect the solicitor's notes of the private consultation which preceded that interview, because the giving of reasons waives legal privilege (*R v Condron* [1997] 1 WLR 827 and *R v Bowden* [1999] 2 Cr App R 176). This is significant since *CPIA 1996 s 66* has been in force because a witness summons may now be made against defence solicitors requiring their attendance with their notes at the trial.

Principles from *R v Cowan; Gayle; Ricciardi* [1995] 3 WLR 818 CA

➤ In normal circumstances, the burden of proof of proving the silence and inferences from it, is on the prosecution.

➤ The defendant's entitlement to remain silent is his right and choice.

➤ An inference from a failure to answer questions cannot on its own prove guilt (*CJPO 1994 s 38(3)*)

➤ A tribunal of fact (eg: the trial court) must first have established a case to answer before drawing a *s 34* inference.

➤ A tribunal of fact (eg: the trial court) might draw an adverse inference, if despite:

◆ any evidence relied on to explain the silence, *or*

◆ the absence of any evidence to explain the silence ...

... the tribunal concluded that silence could only sensibly be attributed to:

◆ the defendant having no answer, *or*

◆ the defendant has no answer that would stand up to interrogation.

Advising on silence at police stations

Effect of keeping silent	Risk of damage to client's case (see factors below)	Best advice to a client	
Adverse inferences will be drawn	**Low risk** There is no risk or a minimal risk in terms of possible damage to the client from the interview	Advise the client to answer the questions	There are strong arguments that it will not be appropriate for a jury to draw inferences from silence if a solicitor has advised silence. However, the reasoning of the lawyer for this advice must constitute a good objective reason for the silence (*R v Argent* [1997] 2 Crim App R 27, *R v Betts and R v Hall* [2001] 2 Cr App R 16)
Adverse inferences may or may not be drawn	**Medium risk** The risk from the interview is that the client might not perform well or might come across badly	Advise the client to give a written statement	
No adverse inferences will be drawn	**High risk** The risk from the interview is that the client will say something damning, possibly because he is frightened, confused or does not understand what is happening	Advise the client not to answer any questions but to remain totally silent or respond 'no comment' to everything that is asked	see *R v Knight* [2004] 1 WLR 340

Factors to consider in evaluating risk

◆ whether an early explanation will avoid the suspect being charged at all
◆ the evidence the police already have - if this is overwhelming, a confession may be advisable to help later in mitigation
◆ the capacity of a suspect to handle the stresses of an interview (eg: maturity, age and psychological ability to handle the interview)
◆ the gravity of the offence
◆ whether the suspect has any prior experience of either questioning or custody

VII Identification

➤ There are identification issues if there is disputed identification evidence (see Disputed identification (Turnbull guidelines) and the warning at trial, p 557).

➤ There are 6 methods of identification (methods B to D are listed in *D:3.4 to 3.10*):

A Court identification.	**D** Group identification (*Annex C to Code D*).
B Video identification (*Annex A to Code D*).	**E** Showing of photographs (*Annex E to Code D*).
C Identification parade (*Annex B to Code D*).	**F** Confrontation (*Annex D to Code D*).

1 Suspect is not known by police

➤ A witness may be taken to a particular place to try to identify a person they have seen on a previous occasion. Although the variables (eg: number, age, sex, race of people) and manner of identification cannot be controlled, the safeguards applicable to methods B to D should be followed as far as practicable (*D:3.2*).

➤ A witness must not be shown photographs, computerised or artist's composite likenesses or 'E-fit' images if the identity of the suspect is known to the police and the suspect is available to take part in a video id, an id parade or a group id. If the suspect's identity is not known, the showing of such images to a witness must be done in accordance with *Annex E* rules (not dealt with here) (*D:3.3*).

2 Suspect is known (ie: enough information to justify arrest), available and consents to B to D

➤ All id procedures must performed by an inspector or above unconnected with the investigation (*D:3.11*).

➤ The suspect is initially offered either a video identification or an identification parade (*D:3.14*) or if the officer in charge of the investigation considers more satisfactory than those choices and the identification officer considers it practicable to arrange, he is offered a group identification (*D:3.16*) .

3 Suspect is known but is not available or does not consent to B to D

➤ The identification officer may make arrangements for a video identification (using still images if necessary). Any moving/still images may be used and may be obtained covertly. Alternatively, the identification officer may make arrangements for a group identification. (These rules also be applied to juveniles where the parent/guardian consent is refused) (*D: 3.21*).

➤ If methods B to E are not practicable, the identification officer may arrange a confrontation (*D: 3.23*).

➤ Any refusal of consent by the suspect is noted and **this may be used in evidence against him at trial.**

Matters to be explained to the suspect before methods B, C & D above (*D: 3.17*)

- ◆ the purposes of the video identification or identification parade or group identification,
- ◆ the suspect's entitlement to free legal advice,
- ◆ the procedures for holding it (including the suspect's right to have a solicitor or friend present),
- ◆ that the suspect does not have to take part in a video identification, id parade or group identification,
- ◆ that **if the suspect does not consent** to, and take part in, a video identification, identification parade or group identification, **the refusal may be given in evidence** in a subsequent trial and police may proceed covertly without his consent or make other arrangements to test whether a witness can identify the suspect,
- ◆ whether, for the purposes of the video identification, images of the suspect have previously been obtained and if so, that he may co-operate in providing further images for use in place of those previously taken,
- ◆ where appropriate, the special arrangements for juveniles or mentally vulnerable people,
- ◆ that if the suspect should significantly alter his appearance between being offered an identification procedure and any attempt to hold an identification procedure, this may be given in evidence if the case comes to trial, and the identification officer may then consider other forms of identification,
- ◆ that a video or photograph may be taken of the suspect when they attend for any identification procedure,
- ◆ whether the witness has been shown photographs, a computerised or artist's composite likeness or similar likeness or picture by the police during the investigation before the identity of the suspect became known,
- ◆ that if the suspect changes his appearance before a identification parade it may not be practicable to arrange one on the day in question or subsequently and because of the change of appearance, the identification officer may then consider alternative methods of identification,
- ◆ that the suspect or his solicitor will be provided with details of the description of the suspect as first given by any witnesses who are to attend the video identification, id parade, group identification or confrontation.

A   Court identification

> **Used as a last resort (its evidential value is limited as the witness is 'identifying' a man in the dock).**
> The witness is asked whether he recognises the prisoner in the dock.
> Consent is *not* required.

B   Video identification (*Code D: Annex A*)

> A witness is shown moving images of a known suspect, together with similar images of others who resemble the suspect.
> The set of images must include at least 8 others *in addition* to the suspect who so far as possible resemble the suspect in age, general appearance and position in life (*D:2 Annex A*).
> If the suspect has an unusual physical feature (eg: facial scar, tattoo, etc.) hairstyle or hair colour which does not appear on the images of the other people that are available to be used, steps may be taken to conceal the location of the feature on the images of the suspect and the other people *or* to replicate that feature on the images of the other people (*D:2A Annex A*).
> All subjects are filmed in the same position, doing similar things, under identical conditions unless: (i) the identification officer reasonably believes it is not practicable due to a suspect's refusal to cooperate *and* (ii) the different conditions would not point a witness to an individual image (*D:3 Annex A*).
> Each person is identified by number (*D:5 Annex A*).
> The suspect or his lawyer are shown the sequence first to see if they object (*D:7 Annex A*).
> The witness must *not* be told if another witness has made an identification or communicate with any other witness (*D:10 Annex A*).
> Only 1 witness views the set of images at any one time and is told the person they saw earlier may or may not be in the sequence of images to follow (*D:11 Annex A*).
> Once the witness has seen the sequence and has indicated he does not want to view it again, he is asked to identify by number anyone he saw on a previous occasion (*D:12 Annex A*).

C   Identification parade (*Code D: Annex B*)

> A suspect must be given a reasonable opportunity to have a solicitor or friend present (*D:1 Annex B*).
> An id parade may happen in a normal room or a room with a screen permitting witnesses to see the id parade without being seen. The procedures for the composition and conduct of the id parade are the same in both cases, but an id parade with a screen may take place only when the suspect's solicitor, friend or appropriate adult is present or the id parade is recorded on video (*D:2 Annex B*).
> Before the id parade takes place the suspect or his solicitor must be provided with details of the first description of the suspect by any witnesses who are to attend the id parade. Where a broadcast or publication is made, the suspect or their solicitor should also be allowed to view any material released to the media by the police to recognise or trace the suspect, provided it is practicable to do so and would not unreasonably delay the investigation (*D:3 Annex B*).
> 8 persons *in addition* to the suspect take part who so far as possible resemble the suspect in age, height, general appearance and position in life (*D:9 Annex B*).
> Where the suspect has an unusual physical feature, eg: a facial scar or tattoo which cannot be replicated on other members of the id parade, steps may be taken to conceal the location of that feature on the suspect and the other members of the identification parade if the suspect and their solicitor or appropriate adult agree, eg: by use of a plaster or a hat (*D:10 Annex B*).
> When the suspect is brought to the place where the id parade is to be held, the suspect or his lawyer are asked whether they have any objection to the arrangements for the id parade or to any of the other participants in it and to state the reasons for the objection (*D:12 Annex B*).
> The suspect may select his own position in the line, but may not otherwise interfere with the order of the people forming the line. Where there is more than one witness the suspect must be told, after each witness has left the room, that they can if they wish change position in the line. Each position in the line must be clearly numbered, whether by means of a numeral laid on the floor in front of each identification parade member or by other means (*D:13 Annex B*).
> The witness must *not* be told if another witness has made an identification or communicate with any other witness (*D:14 to 16 Annex B*).
> When the identification officer or civilian support staff is satisfied that the witness has properly looked at each member of the id parade, they ask the witness whether the person they saw on an earlier relevant occasion is on the identification parade and, if so, to indicate the number of the person concerned (*D:17 Annex B*).
> If the witness wishes to hear any identification parade member speak, adopt any specified posture or see an identification parade member move, the witness must first be asked whether he can identify any person(s) on the identification parade on the basis of appearance only. When the request is to hear members of the identification parade speak, the witness must be reminded that the participants in the identification parade have been chosen on the basis of physical appearance only. Members of the identification parade may then be asked to comply with the witness's request to hear them speak, to see them move or to adopt any specified posture (*D:18 Annex B*).
> A video recording must normally be taken of the identification parade. Where that is impracticable a colour photograph must be taken. A copy of the video recording or photograph shall be supplied on request to the suspect or his solicitor within a reasonable time (*D:23 Annex B*).

D Group identification (*Code D: Annex C*)

➤ Group identifications may take place either with the suspect's consent or covertly without his consent (*D:2 Annex C*).

➤ The location of the group identification is a matter for the identification officer, although he may take into account any representations made by the suspect, appropriate adult, his solicitor or friend (*D:3 Annex C*).

➤ The place where the group identification is held should be one where other people are either passing by or waiting around informally, in groups such that the suspect is able to join them and be capable of being seen by the witness at the same time as others in the group. Eg: people leaving an escalator, pedestrians walking through a shopping centre, passengers on railway and bus stations, waiting in queues or groups (*D:4 Annex C*).

➤ If the group identification is to be held covertly, the choice of locations are limited by the places where the suspect can be found and the number of other people present at that time. In these cases suitable locations might be along regular routes travelled by the suspect, including buses or trains or public places frequented by the suspect (*D:5 Annex C*).

➤ Although the number, age, sex, race and general description and style of clothing of other people present at the location cannot be controlled by the identification officer, in selecting the location the officer must consider the general appearance and numbers of people likely to be present (*D:6 Annex C*).

➤ Immediately after a group identification procedure has taken place a colour photograph or a video should be taken of the general scene, where this is practicable, so as to give a general impression of the scene and the number of people present. Alternatively, if it is practicable, the group identification may be video recorded (*D:8 Annex C*).

➤ An identification carried out remains a group identification notwithstanding that at the time of being seen by the witness the suspect was on his or her own rather than in a group (*D:10 Annex C*).

➤ A suspect must be given a reasonable opportunity to have a solicitor or friend present (*D:13 Annex C*).

➤ The witness must *not* be told if another witness has made an identification or communicate with any other witness (*D:14 to 17 Annex C*).

➤ Witnesses must be brought to the place where they are to observe the group one at a time. Immediately before the witness is asked to look at the group the person conducting the procedure must tell the witness that the person they saw may or may not be in the group and that if they cannot make a positive identification they should say so. The witness must then be asked to observe the group in which the suspect is to appear (*D:18 Annex C*).

➤ There are special rules for moving groups (*D:19-24 Annex C*) and stationery groups (*D:25-29 Annex C*).

➤ If the suspect unreasonably delays joining the group, or having joined the group, deliberately conceals himself from the sight of the witness, this may be treated as a refusal to co-operate in a group identification (*D:30 Annex C*).

➤ If the witness identifies a person other than the suspect that person should be informed what has happened and asked if they are prepared to give their name and address (*D:31 Annex C*).

➤ When finished, the suspect must be asked if he wants to comment on the conduct of the procedure (*D:32 Annex C*).

➤ If identification is carried out covertly, a suspect has no right to have a solicitor, appropriate adult or friend present. Also any number of suspects may be identified at the same time (*D:35-36 Annex C*).

E Showing of photographs (*Code D: Annex E*)

➤ An officer of the rank of sergeant or above is responsible for supervising and directing the showing of not less than twelve photographs at a time, which shall, as far as possible, all be of a similar type . The actual showing may be done by a constable or civilian support staff (*D:1 and 4 Annex E*).

➤ The supervising officer confirms that the first description of the suspect given by the witness has been recorded before the witness is shown the photographs (*D:2 Annex E*).

F Confrontation (*Code D: Annex D*)

➤ A witness is confronted with the suspect and asked if it is the correct person.

➤ Before the confrontation takes place the witness must be told that the person they saw may or may not be the person they are to confront and that if he or she is not that person then the witness should say so (*D:1 Annex D*).

➤ Before the confrontation takes place the suspect or their solicitor must be provided with details of the first description of the suspect given by any witness who is to attend the confrontation. Where a broadcast or publication is made, the suspect or his solicitor must be allowed to view any material released by police to the media (to recognise or trace the suspect) provided that it is practicable to do so and would not unreasonably delay the investigation (*D:2 Annex D*).

➤ Force may not be used to make the face of the suspect visible to the witness (*D:3 Annex D*).

➤ Confrontation must take place in the presence of the suspect's solicitor, interpreter or friend unless this would cause unreasonable delay (*D:4 Annex D*).

➤ The suspect is confronted independently by each witness, who is asked "Is this the person?". If a witness identifies the person but cannot confirm it, he is asked how sure he is that the person is the same as earlier (*D:5 Annex D*).

➤ The confrontation normally takes place in the police station, either in a normal room or in one equipped with a screen permitting a witness to see the suspect without being seen. A room equipped with a screen may be used only when the suspect's solicitor, friend or appropriate adult is present or the confrontation is recorded on video (*D:6 Annex D*).

➤ After the procedure each witness shall be asked whether they have seen any broadcast or published films or photographs or any descriptions of suspects relating to the offence and their reply is recorded (*D:7 Annex D*).

VIII Taking samples

Concept of a recordable offence
➤ In practice, all offences which are punishable with imprisonment are recordable offences, as are around 60 other more minor offences. Details are in *NPR(RO)R 2000*.

A Fingerprinting

➤ **Consent:** Except as set out below, no person's fingerprints may be taken without consent (*s 61(1)*).

  ◆ Consent must be in writing if it is given at a time when at a police station (*s 61(2)*).

When consent is not needed

➤ No consent is needed if:

The police may require attendance at a police station in certain circumstances to take fingerprints (s 63A(4) and Schedule 2A)

s 61(3)	◆ ... the person is detained after arrest for a recordable offence, *and* ◆ he has not had his fingerprints taken in the course of the investigation of the offence by the police
s 61(4)	◆ ... the person has been charged with (or informed that he will be reported for) a recordable offence, *and* ◆ he has not had his fingerprints taken in the course of the investigation of the offence by the police

s 61(4A-4B)	◆ ... the person has answered to bail at a court or police station, *and*
	◆ the court or an officer (being at least an inspector) authorises them to be taken, if:
	  ● the person who answered to bail has answered to bail for a person whose fingerprints were taken previously and there are reasonable grounds for believing that he is not the same person, *or*
	  ● the person who answered to bail claims to be a different person from a person whose fingerprints were taken on a previous occasion

s 61(5A) inserted by CSA 2010 s 2(1)	◆ ... the person has been arrested for a recordable offence and released *and*:
	  ● for a person on bail, he has not had his fingerprints taken in the course of the investigation of the offence by the police, *or*
	  ● in any case, he has had his fingerprints taken in the course of that investigation but *s 61(3A)* (above) applies

s 61(5B) inserted by SA 2010 s 2(2)	◆ ... the person was not detained at a police station and he has been charged with (or informed that he will be reported for) a recordable offence *and*:
	  ● he has not had fingerprints taken in the course of the investigation of the offence by the police, *or*
	  ● he has had fingerprints taken in the course of that investigation but *s 61(3A)* (above) applies

s 61 (6)(a)	◆ ... the person has been convicted of a recordable offence, *and* (i) or (ii) apply:
s 61 (6)(b)	◆ ... the person has been given a caution in respect of a recordable offence which, at the time of the caution, he has admitted, *and* (i) or (ii) apply:
s 61 (6)(c)	◆ ... the person has been warned/reprimanded under *CDA 1998 s 65* for a recordable offence, *and* (i) or (ii) apply:

s 61(6A-6B)	◆ ... a constable takes a person's fingerprints reasonably suspecting that the person is committing or attempting to commit an offence, or has committed or attempted to commit an offence, *and*:
	  ● the name of the person is unknown to, and cannot be readily ascertained by, the constable, *or*
	  ● the constable has reasonable grounds for doubting whether a name given by the person is his real name

s 61(6D-6E)	◆ ... under the law in force in a country/territory outside England & Wales the person has been convicted of an offence under that law (whether or not he has been punished for it), *and* ◆ the act constituting the offence would constitute a qualifying offence if done in England & Wales (whether or not it constituted such an offence when the person was convicted), *and* ◆ the person has not had his fingerprints taken on a previous occasion under this power or he has had his fingerprints taken on a previous occasion under that power but *s 61(3A)* (above) applies.

> For ss *61(3)-(4)*, where a person has already had fingerprints taken, that is disregarded if the fingerprints previously taken are not a complete set or any fingerprints taken previously are not of sufficient quality to allow satisfactory analysis, comparison or matching (*s 61(3A)*)

> **Authorisation:** An officer may give an authorisation under *s 61(4A)* orally or in writing but, if he gives it orally, he must confirm it in writing as soon as is practicable (*s 61(5)*).

> (i) the person must not have had fingerprints taken since being convicted, cautioned or warned or reprimanded, *or*
(ii) he had his fingerprints taken since but the *s 61(3A)* box above applies (*s 61(6ZA)* (inserted by *CSA 2010 s 2(3)*))

> The taking of fingerprints under *s 61(6A)* does not count under *PACE* as taking them in the course of the investigation of an offence by the police (*s 61(6C)*)

496

➤ **Who may take fingerprints:** The power to take the fingerprints of a person without consent is exercisable by any constable (*s 61(8B)*), except that powers under *s 61(6)* or *ss 61(6D-6E)* can only be exercised with the authorisation of an officer of at least the rank of inspector and then only if that officer is satisfied that taking the fingerprints is necessary to assist in the prevention or detection of crime (*s 61(6ZB)-61(6ZC) and s 61(6F)-61(6G)*).

Safeguards for fingerprints

➤ Where a person's fingerprints are taken without consent, before his fingerprints are taken he must be told (and it must be recorded as soon as practicable after the fingerprints are taken) (*s 61(7)*):
  ◆ the reason for taking the fingerprints, *and*
  ◆ the power pursuant to which they are being taken, *and*
  ◆ where the authorisation of the court or an officer is required for the exercise of the power, the fact that the authorisation has been given.

➤ If a person's fingerprints are taken at a police station (or under *s 61(4A)/(6A)* at a place other than at a police station), whether with or without consent (*s 61(7A)*):
  ◆ before the fingerprints are taken, an officer must inform him that they may be the subject of a speculative search, *and*
  ◆ the fact that the person has been informed of this possibility shall be recorded as soon as is practicable after the fingerprints have been taken.

➤ If a person is detained at a police station when the fingerprints are taken, the reason for taking them (and, in the case falling within *s 61(7A)* above, the fact referred to in the second diamond bullet) must be recorded on his custody record (*s 61(8)*).

B   Intimate samples

➤ **Intimate samples are** (*s 65*): Blood, semen or any other tissue fluid, urine, pubic hair, dental impressions or a swab taken from any part of a person's genitals or from a person's body orifice other than the mouth.

➤ **In police detention:** an intimate sample may be taken from a person only if (*s 62(1)*):
  ◆ a police officer of at least the rank of inspector authorises it to be taken, *and*
  ◆ consent is given.

➤ **Not in police detention:** an intimate sample may be taken from a person from whom, in the course of the investigation of an offence, two or more non-intimate samples suitable for the same means of analysis have been taken which have proved insufficient, if (*s 62(1A)*):
  ◆ a police officer of at least the rank of inspector authorises it to be taken, *and*
  ◆ the appropriate consent is given.

➤ **Grounds for authorisation:** An officer may only give authorisation if he has reasonable grounds (*s 62(2)*):
  ◆ for suspecting involvement in a recordable offence of the person who will be sampled, *and*
  ◆ for believing that the sample will tend to confirm or disprove his involvement.

➤ **Authorisation:** may be given orally (confirmed in writing as soon as practicable) or in writing (*s 62(3)*).

➤ **Consent:** must be given in writing (*s 62(4)*).

➤ **Who may take the sample** (*s 62(9)-(9A)*):
  ◆ Urine may be taken by anyone.
  ◆ A dental impression may be taken only by a registered dentist.
  ◆ For any other form of intimate sample, it may be taken only by a registered medical practitioner or a registered health care professional.

➤ **Refusal of consent:** without good reason means a jury may draw such inference as they like (*s 62(10)*).

Safeguards for samples

➤ Before a sample is taken, an officer must inform the person of (*ss 62(5)-(6)*):
  ◆ the reason for taking it (including the nature of the offence in which it is suspected he has been involved) (the '**Reason**'), *and*
  ◆ the fact that authorisation has been given and the *PACE* section under which it has been given (the '**Facts**'), *and*
  ◆ if the sample was taken at a police station, the fact that the sample may be the subject of a speculative search (the '**Search Fact**').

➤ After a sample is taken, these must be recorded as soon as practicable (and if taken from a person detained at a police station, recorded in the custody record) (*ss 62(7)-(8)*):
  ◆ the Reason and the Facts, and if the sample was taken at a police station, the Search Fact, *and*
  ◆ the fact that the appropriate consent was given.

The police may require attendance at a police station in certain circumstances to take intimate samples (s 63A(4) and Schedule 2A)

C Non-intimate samples

➤ **Non-intimate samples are** (s 65): Non-pubic hair, nail (or under a nail), a swab taken from any part of a person's body other than a part from which a swab taken would be an intimate sample, saliva, skin impression.

➤ An non-intimate sample may be taken from a person only with consent (ss 63(1)) unless...:

	When consent is not needed

➤ No consent is needed if the person...

s 63(2A) s 63(2B) s 63(2C)	◆ ... is in police detention because of his arrest for a recordable offence, *and* ◆ ... has not had a non-intimate sample of the same type and from the same part of the body taken in the course of the investigation of the offence by the police, or he has had such a sample taken but it proved insufficient
s 63(3)	◆ ... is being held in custody by the police on the authority of a court, *and* ◆ an officer of at least the rank of inspector authorises it to be taken without the appropriate consent (and only when 'Grounds for authorisation' are the same as for intimate samples, see p 497 (s 63(4)))

s 63(ZA)	◆ ... has been arrested for a recordable offence and released (s 63(3ZA), *and*
	  ● for a person on bail, he has not had a non-intimate sample of the same type and from the same part of the body taken from him in the course of the investigation of the offence by the police, *or*
	  ● in any case, he has had a non-intimate sample taken from him in the course of that investigation but it was not suitable for the same means of analysis or it proved insufficient

s 63(3A)	◆ ... (whether or not in police detention or held in custody by the police on the authority of the court) has been charged with (or informed that he will be reported for) a recordable offence and the person (s 63(3A)):
	  ● has not had a non-intimate sample taken from him in the course of the investigation of the offence by the police, *or*
	  ● has had a non-intimate sample taken from him in the course of that investigation but it was not suitable for the same means of analysis or it proved insufficient, *or*
	  ● has had a non-intimate sample taken from him in the course of that investigation and the sample was destroyed by statutory rule and it is disputed, in relation to any proceedings relating to the offence, whether a DNA profile relevant to the proceedings is derived from the sample

s 63(3B, 3BA, 3BB, 3BC)	◆ ... has been convicted of a recordable offence (s 63(3B)), *or* ◆ ... has been given a caution in respect of a recordable offence which, at the time of the caution, he has admitted, *or* ◆ ... has been warned or reprimanded under *CDA 1998 s 65* for a recordable offence, **AND**, for any of the 3 diamond points above, *either*: a) a non-intimate sample has not been taken from the person since he was convicted, cautioned or warned or reprimanded, *or* b) such a sample has been taken from him since then but it was not suitable for the same means of analysis, or it proved insufficient **AND** only an officer of at least inspector rank can authorise this and only then if taking the sample is necessary to assist in the prevention or detection of crime
s 63(3E, 3F, 3G, 3H)	◆ ... has been convicted (under the law in force in a country or territory outside England & Wales) of an offence under that law (whether or not he has been punished for it), *and* ◆ the act constituting the offence would constitute a qualifying offence if done in England & Wales, *and* ◆ either the person has not had a non-intimate sample taken from him on a previous occasion under this exception or he has had such a sample taken from him on a previous occasion under that subsection but the sample was not suitable for the same means of analysis or it proved insufficient, *and* ◆ at least an inspector authorises this and the officer is satisfied that taking the sample is necessary to assist in the prevention or detection of crime

The police may require attendance at a police station in certain circumstances to take non-intimate samples (s 63A(4) and Schedule 2A)

➤ **Grounds for authorisation:** An officer may only give authorisation if he has reasonable grounds (s 63(4)):
  ◆ for suspecting involvement in a recordable offence of the person who will be sampled, *and*
  ◆ for believing that the sample will tend to confirm or disprove his involvement.

➤ **Authorisation:** may be given orally (confirmed in writing as soon as practicable) or in writing (s 63(5)).

➤ **Consent:** must be given in writing (s 63(2)).

➤ **Who may take the sample without consent** (s 63(9ZA): any constable.

➤ The 'Safeguards for samples' box (see p 497) also applies to non-intimate samples.

D Other powers (ss 54A, 64A, 60AA, 61A)

➤ There are powers to take photographs, remove disguises and to take impressions of footwear.

IX   Charge

➤   When the officer in charge of the investigation reasonably believes there is sufficient evidence to provide a realistic prospect of conviction he must without delay inform the custody officer who is responsible for considering (or referring to the CPS to decide) whether the detainee should be charged (*C:16.1 - 16.1B*).

X   Other rights at a police station

Right to legal advice

➤   All detainees must be informed that they may at any time consult and communicate privately with a solicitor, whether in person, in writing or by telephone, and that free independent legal advice is available (*C: 6.1*).

On arrest (*PACE s 58*)

➤   This is a right which a suspect has on arrival at the police station, and subsequently whenever he requests it.

➤   Legal advice from a *particular* solicitor can be delayed for up to 36 hours from the time detention was originally authorised if:

a)   the investigation concerns an indictable offence, *and*

b)   a superintendent, or a higher officer, authorises the delay, *and*

c)   there are reasonable grounds for believing that this will prevent interference with evidence or people *or* alert others still at large *or* hinder the recovery of property.

➤   If legal advice from a particular solicitor is delayed on the basis of the reasons above, access to another solicitor must be offered (*Code C, Annex B, Paragraph 3*).

➤   The defendant must be told of an attempt by a solicitor (on the solicitor's arrival) to contact him (*Code C:6.15*).

At interview

➤   A person who has requested legal advice may not be interviewed (or continue to be interviewed) unless he has received that legal advice, unless *either* (*C:6.6*):

a)   legal advice is barred under *PACE s 58* (see above) *or:*

b)   a superintendent, or a higher officer has reasonable grounds for believing that *either:*

    i)   delay will lead to interference with or harm to evidence, harm to persons or property, alert others or hinder the recovery of property, *or*

    ii)   the solicitor has been contacted and agreed to attend but waiting for his arrival will cause unreasonable delay to the investigation (*C:6.6*), *or*

c)   an inspector authorises an interview *and* the nominated solicitor cannot be contacted or will not attend, *and* the defendant refuses the duty solicitor (*C:6.6*), *or*

d)   an inspector authorises an interview *and* the defendant changes his mind about wanting legal advice and agrees in writing or on the record of the interview (eg: video, tape, etc.) (*C:6.6*).

➤   The solicitor may intervene during the interview (*C:6D*):

◆   to clarify or challenge improper questions or the manner in which they are put.

◆   to advise the client not to reply.

◆   to give further legal advice.

➤   The interviewer may not exclude a solicitor from the interview unless his conduct is such that an interviewer is unable properly to put questions to the suspect and an officer of at least superintendent rank is first consulted and he first speaks to the solicitor (unless a superintendent is unavailable, in which case an inspector not connected to the investigations must do this) (*C:6.10*).

Reminders of the right to legal advice

➤   There is a right to be reminded of the right to legal advice (*C: 6.5, Annex B*):

◆   when first brought to the police station (or if attending voluntarily)

◆   before the start or recommencement of an interview at a police station.

◆   before a review of detention.

◆   after a charge if:

    ●   a police officer wants to draw a suspect's attention to the written or oral statement of another person, *or*

    ●   if further questions are to be put to a suspect about the offence.

◆   before an identification parade or a request for an intimate body sample.

Right to have someone informed of arrival at the police station

➤   The right can be delayed for up to 36 hours if (*C: 6.5, Annex B*):

a)   the investigation concerns an indictable offence, *and*

b)   an inspector, or higher officer, authorises it, *and*

c)   there are reasonable grounds for believing that this will prevent interference with evidence or people, alert others still at large, or hinder the recovery of property.

XI   Detention after charge: 1 of 3 alternatives

1   **The custody officer *must* release the accused unconditionally (which is unusual) or on police bail (*s 38*).**

➤ Police bail might be conditional upon the accused attending court on a particular date, etc. (*PACE 1984 s 47*) (This is the most usual and likely occurrence out of the options on this page.)

➤ Conditions may be set if necessary (*BA 1976 s 3A*):

i)   to ensure that the accused surrenders to custody, *and/or*

ii)   to ensure that the accused does not commit an offence while on bail, *and/or*

iii)   to ensure that the accused does not interfere with a witness or obstruct justice, *and/or*

iv)   for the accused's own protection or, if he is a child/young person, for his own welfare/interests.

➤ NB: The police have a power of arrest if a suspect fails to answer to police bail (*s 46A*).

or **2**   **The custody officer *must* keep the accused in police detention if** (*CJPO 1994 s 25*)**:**

➤ ... (unless the custody officer finds that there are 'exceptional circumstances') the suspect is charged with murder, attempted murder, manslaughter, rape or attempted rape and (*CJPO 1994 s 25*):

◆ has a previous conviction for any one of these (or for culpable homicide) from a court in any part of the UK (or the equivalent to any one of these or to culpable homicide in another EEA State), *and*

◆ in the case of a previous conviction in the UK for manslaughter or culpable homicide, if 18 or over, he was then sentenced to imprisonment (or, if under 18 - ie: a child or young person - to long-term detention) (or in the case of a previous conviction in another EEA State for manslaughter or culpable homicide, if 18 or over, he was then sentenced to detention (or, if under 18 to detention for more than 2 years).

➤ Note: He must then be brought before a magistrate as soon as possible (*s 46(1)*).

or **3**   **The custody officer *may* keep the accused in police detention if** (*s 38(1)*)**:**

a)   he is charged with murder (but subject to the rules above when he *must* be kept in), or

b)   his name or address is unascertainable or doubtful, *or*

c)   detention is necessary because he has reasonable grounds to believe the suspect will fail to appear at court to answer to bail, *or*

d)   (if arrested for an imprisonable offence), detention is necessary to prevent commission of an offence, *or*

e)   (if arrested for a non-imprisonable offence), detention is necessary to protect anyone else from physical injury or damage to property, *or*

f)   detention is necessary to prevent interference with the administration of justice or investigations, *or*

g)   detention is necessary for the suspect's own protection, *or*

h)   in a case where a sample may be taken under *s 63B*, he has reasonable grounds for believing detention is necessary to enable the taking of a Class A drugs sample.

➤ Note: He must then be brought before a magistrate as soon as possible (*s 46(1)*).

XII   What happens next

A What happens post charge: dangerous/careless driving

➤ Dangerous or careless driving (*RTOA 1988 s 1*): If there is no accident as a result of these offences, there can be no conviction for these offences, unless as a preliminary:

a)   the defendant is warned at the time of the offence that a prosecution is possible, *or*

b)   a summons is served on the defendant within 14 days, *or*

c)   within 14 days, a notice of intended prosecution is served on the person who was the registered vehicle keeper at the time of the offence.

B   What happens post charge: summary offences

➤ **If the defendant has been charged in writing:** within 6 months of the commission of the offence (usually), a public prosecutor issues a written charge (alleging that he has committed an offence) and requisition (requiring him to attend the Magistrates' Court and setting out where and when) (on pilot only at present) (*CJA 2003 s 29* and *s 30(5)*).

➤ **If the defendant has been charged orally**: within 6 months of the commission of the offence (usually), a prosecutor must 'lay an information' at a Magistrates' Court (*MCA 1980 ss 18, 127*).

◆ *MCA 1980 s 1* says that on receiving a formal statement (ie: an 'information') alleging that someone has committed an offence, the court may issue a summons requiring that person to attend court (or, if an offence which must or may be tried in the Crown Court or punishable with imprisonment, a warrant for that person's arrest - but warrants are not dealt with in this book).

➤ A prosecutor who wants the court to issue a summons must (*CrPR r 7.2(1)*):

◆ serve an information in writing on the court officer, *or*

◆ unless other legislation prohibits this, present an information orally to the court, with a written record of the allegation that it contains.

➤ A public prosecutor issuing a written charge must notify the court officer immediately (*CrPR r 7.2(3)*).

➤ A single document may contain more than 1 information or more than 1 written charge (*CrPR r 7.2(4)*).

➤ Where an offence can be tried only in a Magistrates' Court, then (unless other legislation otherwise provides) not more than 6 months after the offence alleged (*CrPR r 7.2(5)*):

◆ a prosecutor must serve an information (ie: lay an information) on the court officer or present it to the court, *or*

◆ a public prosecutor must issue a written charge.

➤ For a summary offence linked with an indictable or 'either way' offence: see 'Mode of trial'/Allocation, p 512.

C   What happens post charge: indictable and 'either-way' offences

➤ As 'B' above save that where an offence can be tried in the Crown Court, then within any time limit that applies to that offence (*CrPR r 7.2(6)*):

◆ a prosecutor must serve an information (ie: lay an information) on the court officer or present it to the court, *or*

◆ a public prosecutor must issue a written charge.

➤ Time limits for when an indictment must be drawn up are on p 526.

Information/charge (*CrPR r 7.3*)

➤ An allegation of an offence in an information or charge must contain:

◆ a statement of the offence that describes the offence in ordinary language and identifies any legislation that creates it, *and*

◆ such particulars of the conduct constituting the commission of the offence as to make clear what the prosecutor alleges against the defendant.

➤ More than 1 incident of the commission of the offence may be included if those incidents taken together amount to a course of conduct having regard to the time, place or purpose of commission.

The summons, warrant or requisition (*CrPR r 7.4*)

➤ The court may issue or withdraw a summons or warrant:

◆ without giving the parties an opportunity to make representations, *and/or*

◆ without a hearing, or at a hearing in public or in private.

➤ A summons/warrant/requisition may be issued in respect of more than 1 offence.

➤ A summons or requisition must, in respect of the defendant:

◆ contain notice of when and where he is required to attend court, *and*

◆ specify each offence in respect of which it is issued, *and*

◆ for a requisition, identify the person under whose authority it is issued, *and*

◆ for a summons, identify the court that issued it (unless that is otherwise recorded by the court officer) and the court office for the court that issued it.

➤ A summons may be contained in the same document as an information.

➤ A requisition may be contained in the same document as a written charge.

➤ Where the court issues a summons:

◆ the prosecutor must serve it on the defendant and notify the court officer, *or*

◆ the court officer must serve it on the defendant and notify the prosecutor.

➤ Where a public prosecutor issues a requisition that prosecutor must:

◆ serve on the defendant the requisition and the written charge, *and*

◆ serve a copy of each on the court officer.

C   Court matters applicable generally

    I   The overriding objective
    II   Criminal case management
    III   Variations to orders and time
    IV   Hearings

I   The overriding objective

Rules of the court

➤ Rules of court practice and procedure are governed by the **Criminal Procedure Rules** (*CrPR*).

    ◆ Definitions of terms in the *CrPR* are listed in *r 2.2* and also in a glossary at the back.

    ◆ Each *Part* contains rules - notation is as follows: eg: *r 7.2(2)* refers to rule 7.2(2) in *Part 7*.

➤ The *CrPR* are a step towards the creation of a new, consolidated criminal procedural code.

➤ There is a Consolidated Criminal Practice Direction which can be found at: http://www.justice.gov.uk/ guidance/courts-and-tribunals/courts/procedure-rules/criminal/practice-direction/pd_consolidated. htm .

The court's overriding objective in applying the *CrPR* (*r 1*)

➤ The *CrPR* are a code with the overriding objective that criminal cases be dealt with justly, ie:

    a) acquitting the innocent and convicting the guilty, *and*

    b) dealing with the prosecution and the defence fairly, *and*

    c) recognising the rights of a defendant, particularly those under *ECHR Art 6*, *and*

    d) respecting interests of witnesses, victims and jurors and keeping all informed of progress, *and*

    e) dealing with the case efficiently and expeditiously, *and*

    f) ensuring that appropriate information is available when bail and sentence are considered, *and*

    g) dealing with the case in ways that take into account the gravity of the offence alleged, the complexity of what is in issue, the severity of the consequences for the defendant and others affected and the needs of other cases.

➤ The court must further the overriding objective in particular when:

    ◆ exercising any power given to it by legislation (including these *CrPR*), *and*

    ◆ applying any practice direction, *and*

    ◆ interpreting any rule or practice direction.

➤ Each participant, in the conduct of each case, must:

    ◆ prepare and conduct the case in accordance with the overriding objective, *and*

    ◆ comply with the *CrPR*, practice directions and directions made by the court, *and*

    ◆ at once inform the court and all parties of any significant failure by anyone to take any procedural step required by the *CrPR*, any practice direction or any direction of the court.

II   Criminal case management

The court's general powers of case management (rr 3.2, 3.3, 3.5)

➤ The court must further the overriding objective by actively managing the case (and giving any appropriate direction as soon as possible), including:

- early identification of the real issues and the needs of witnesses, *and*
- achieving certainty as to what must be done, by whom, and when, in particular by the early setting of a timetable for the progress of the case, *and*
- monitoring the progress of the case and compliance with directions, *and*
- ensuring that evidence, disputed or not, is presented in the shortest and clearest way, *and*
- discouraging delay, dealing with as many aspects of the case as possible on the same occasion, and avoiding unnecessary hearings, *and*
- encouraging the participants to co-operate in the progression of the case, *and*
- making use of technology.

➤ Each party must actively assist the court in fulfilling its duty to actively manage a case (and applying for a direction if needed to further the overriding objective).

➤ The court may give any direction and take any step actively to manage a case unless that direction or step would be inconsistent with legislation. In particular, the court may:

- nominate a judge, magistrate or justices' legal adviser to manage the case, *and*
- give a direction on its own initiative or on application by a party, *and*
- ask or allow a party to propose a direction, *and*
- for the purpose of giving directions, receive applications/representations by letter, telephone and any other means of electronic communication (and conduct a hearing by such means), *and*
- give a direction: (i) at hearing (in public or in private) *or* (ii) without a hearing, *and*
- fix, postpone, bring forward, extend, cancel or adjourn a hearing, *and*
- shorten or extend (even after it has expired) a time limit fixed by a direction, *and*
- require that issues in the case be determined separately, and decide in what order, *and*
- specify the consequences of failing to comply with a direction.

➤ If a party fails to comply with a rule or a direction, the court may:

- fix, postpone, bring forward, extend, cancel or adjourn a hearing, *and/or*
- exercise its powers to make a costs order, *and/or*
- impose such other sanction as may be appropriate.

Case progression officers (r 3.4)

➤ At the start of the case (unless the court directs otherwise) each party must nominate an individual responsible for progressing that case and tell other parties and the court who he is and how to contact him.

➤ In managing the case, the court must (if appropriate) nominate a court officer (a 'case progression officer') to be responsible to progress the case and ensure the parties know who he is and how to contact him.

➤ The case progression officer must:

- monitor compliance with directions, *and*
- ensure that the court is kept informed of events that may affect the progress of that case, *and*
- ensure that he can be contacted promptly about the case during ordinary business hours, *and*
- act promptly and reasonably in response to communications about the case, *and*
- if he will be unavailable, appoint a substitute to fulfil his duties.

III   Variations to orders and time

Varying a court direction (r 3.6)

➤   A party may apply to vary a direction if:
- the court gave it without a hearing, *or*
- the court gave it at a hearing in his absence, *or*
- circumstances have changed.

➤   A party who applies to vary a direction must:
- apply as soon as practicable after he becomes aware of the grounds for doing so, *and*
- give as much notice to the other parties as the nature and urgency of his application permits.

Varying a time limit (r 3.7)

➤   The parties may agree to vary a time limit fixed by a direction, but only if:

a) the variation will not affect the date of any hearing that has been fixed or significantly affect the progress of the case in any other way, *and*

b) the court has not prohibited variation by agreement, *and*

c) the court's case progression officer is promptly informed.

➤   The court's case progression officer must refer the agreement to the court if he doubts anything in (a) above is satisfied.

IV   Hearings

Rules as to hearings (r 3.8)

➤   At every hearing, if a case cannot be concluded there and then the court must give directions so that it can be concluded at the next hearing or as soon as possible after that.

➤   At every hearing the court must, where relevant:
- if the defendant is absent, decide whether to proceed nonetheless, *and*
- take the defendant's plea (unless already done) or if no plea can be taken then find out whether the defendant is likely to plead guilty or not guilty, *and*
- set, follow or revise a timetable for the progress of the case, which may include a timetable for any hearing - including the trial or (in the Crown Court) the appeal, *and*
- in giving directions, ensure continuity in relation to the court and to the parties' representatives where that is appropriate and practicable, *and*
- where a direction has not been complied with, find out why, identify who was responsible, and take appropriate action.

➤   In order to prepare for a trial in the Crown Court, the court must conduct a plea and case management hearing unless the circumstances make that unnecessary.

➤   In order to prepare for the trial, the court must take every reasonable step to encourage and to facilitate the attendance of witnesses when they are needed.

D   Remand and bail

I   Remand generally: in custody or on bail ?
II   Bail

I   Remand generally: in custody or on bail ?

➤   Remand is considered at every adjournment. It is to ensure the defendant will appear at the next hearing.

➤   The defendant has a right to bail. It is for the prosecution to show why this should not be granted.

Remand in custody	Remand on bail
Remand before conviction or sending for trial/committal for trial (*MCA 1980 s 128*)	

➤ Remand for a maximum of 8 days at a time.
  ◆ This can be extended for another 8 days at a time if another hearing approves it.
➤ However, custody can be extended for 8 days at a time *without the defendant being present*, if:
  ◆ the defendant consents, *and*
  ◆ a solicitor is acting, *and*
  ◆ there have not been more than 3 consecutive remand hearings in the defendant's absence.
➤ A court can remand a defendant in custody for up to 28 days (*MCA 1980 s 128A*) if:
  ◆ it has previously remanded him in custody for the same offence, *and*
  ◆ he is in court, *and*
  ◆ it can set a date for the next stage of proceedings to occur, so he can be remanded until then.
➤ For a summary offence, the maximum time limit for an adult to be in custody from his first appearance until the start of the summary trial is 56 days (*PO(CTL)R 1987 r 4A*).
➤ For an either way/indictable offence, the maximum time limits for an adult for cumulative detention are (*PO(CTL)R 1987 r 5, POA 1985 ss 22, 22B*):
  ◆ for up to 56 days in a Magistrates' Court before a summary trial.
  ◆ for up to 70 days before committal proceedings.
  ◆ for up to 112 days in the Crown Court between committal for trial and the start of the trial.
  ◆ for up to 182 days in the Crown Court between sending for trial and the start of the trial (less any period in custody).
    • Solicitors should mark the Crown Court file with the period so as to make an application for bail when the period has expired. Bail must then be given.
    • If the time limits expire, the proceedings are stayed. Certain types of proceedings can be reinstituted afresh within 3 months.
NB: The defence should *not* warn the prosecution when the time limits are about to expire.
NB: A court may extend a limit if the prosecution has acted with all due diligence and expedition *and* there is good and sufficient cause.
	➤ The maximum time limit is unlimited (!) with the defendant's consent.

Remand after committal (*MCA 1980 s 6(3)*)	
➤ Remand until the case is heard (this can take months), subject to the limits above. *This will be replaced by similar provisions regarding sending for trial when CJA 2003, s 41 and Schedule 3 are brought into force abolishing committal.*	➤ Remand on conditions set by the court until the case is heard.
Remand after conviction, until the next hearing (most probably sentencing) (*MCA 1980 s 10(3)*)	
➤ Magistrates' Courts may remand in custody for up to 3 weeks. ➤ The Crown Court may remand until the next hearing, whenever that is.	➤ Magistrates' Courts can remand for up to 4 weeks. ➤ The Crown Court may remand until the next hearing.

Protocol for the Effective Handling of Custody Time Limit Cases in the Courts

➤   Since 1 April 2009, a 'Protocol for the Effective Handling of Custody Time Limit Cases in the Magistrates' and Crown Courts' has applied. See http://www.lawsociety.org.uk/documents/downloads/dynamic/ctlprotocolmay09.pdf

II   Bail

A   Right to bail (*BA 1976 s 4*)

The 'general right' to bail

➤ There is a 'general right' to bail for:

| Note: The 'general right' is subject to the rules on refusing bail - see "C. Refusing Bail" on p 507 |

   a) an accused before conviction when he (*BA 1976 s 4(1)-(2)*):

◆ appears or is brought before a Magistrates' Court or the Crown Court in the course of or in connection with proceedings for an offence, *or*

◆ applies to a court for bail (or for a variation of bail conditions) in connection with the proceedings,

   b) an offender after conviction during an adjournment for reports (*BA 1976 s 4(4)*),

   c) an offender who, after being convicted of an offence, appears or is brought before a Magistrates' Court or the Crown Court for breach (*BA 1976 s 4(3)*):

◆ of a requirement of a community order (*CJA 2003 Schedule 8* and see p 537), *or*.

◆ of a reparation order (*PCC(S)A 2000 Schedule 8* and see p 542), *or*

◆ or revocation/amendment of a youth rehabilitation order (*CJA 2008 Schedule 2* and see p 543).

➤ NOTE: there is *no* right to bail:

   a) for someone before the Crown Court awaiting sentence, *or*

   b) for someone before the Crown Court awaiting appeal against conviction or sentence, *or*

   c) unless the Court or constable (as applicable) finds there to be 'exceptional circumstances' in a case where someone who is charged with murder, attempted murder, manslaughter, rape or attempted rape and (*BA 1976 s 4(8), CJPO 1994 s 25*):

● has a previous conviction for any one of these (or for culpable homicide) from a court in any part of the UK (or the equivalent to any one of these or to culpable homicide in another EEA State), *and*

● in the case of a previous conviction in the UK for manslaughter or culpable homicide, if 18 or over, he was then sentenced to imprisonment (or, if under 18 - ie: a child or young person - to long-term detention) (or in the case of a previous conviction in another EEA State for manslaughter or culpable homicide, if 18 or over, he was then sentenced to detention (or, if under 18 to detention for more than 2 years)).

B   Procedure for bail hearings

Steps	
1	The prosecution objects to bail.
2	The defence applies for bail.
3	Evidence is called (rules of evidence do not apply - *Re Moles* [1981] Crim LR 170).
4	The court decides on remand in custody or on bail.
5	The court must give a note stating whether or not bail will be granted, together with reasons why and a list of any conditions it imposes and reasons for those conditions (*BA 1976 s 5(3)*).

Duty to hear further applications (*MCA 1980 ss 10, 18* and *SCA 1981 s 81*)

Magistrates' Court	Crown Court
➤ There is a duty on the court to hear further applications for bail if a defendant is still in custody and the right to bail still applies	➤ There is a duty on the court to hear further applications for bail if a defendant is still in custody and the right to bail still applies ➤ There is a duty to hear further applications from those in custody: ◆ prior to trial, sentence and appeals *and* ◆ when a Magistrates' Court has refused bail after adjournment *and* a certificate of full argument is presented to court.

Hearing before a High Court judge in chambers (a last resort) (*CJA 1967 s 22*)

| ✘ As a civil matter, no CDS legal funding is available | ✘ In practice, no court will later grant bail if a High Court judge refuses it |

Bail and murder

➤ A person charged with murder (including one charged with murder and other offences) may not be granted bail except by a judge of the Crown Court (*CJA 2009 s 115*).

◆ The power of magistrates to consider bail in murder cases has been removed.

C Refusing bail

Sometimes, the court *may* refuse bail and sometimes the court *must* refuse bail.

➤ **RULES:** The rules are different as to whether the offence in question is:
1 non-imprisonable (as to which see Section 1 below), *or*
2 imprisonable, when it depends on whether the offence (or one of the offences) of which he is accused/convicted is:
   a) imprisonable and IS a summary offence OR IS one of certain offences listed in *MCA 1980 Schedule 2* (involving criminal damage), where the value involved is less than the relevant sum (currently £5000) (as to which see Section 2a below), *or*
   b) imprisonable and IS NOT a summary offence AND IS NOT one of certain offences listed in *MCA 1980 Schedule 2* (involving criminal damage), where the value involved is less than the relevant sum (currently £5000) (as to which see Section 2b below).

1 Non-imprisonable offences

➤ The court <u>may</u> refuse bail if any of the following grounds apply (*BA 1976 Schedule 1 Part 2*):

◆ It appears to the court that, having been previously granted bail, the defendant failed to surrender to custody and the court believes, in view of that failure, that the defendant, if released on bail (whether subject to conditions or not) would fail to surrender to custody (*para 2*).

◆ The court is satisfied that the defendant should be kept in custody for his own protection or, if he is a child or young person, for his own welfare (*para 3*).

◆ The defendant is in custody pursuant to a court sentence (*para 4*).

◆ The defendant, having been released on bail, has been arrested for absconding and the court is satisfied that there are substantial grounds for believing that if released on bail (whether subject to conditions or not) he would fail to surrender to custody, commit an offence on bail or interfere with witnesses or otherwise obstruct justice (*para 5*).

2a Imprisonable offence(s) which: IS a summary offence OR IS one of certain offences listed in *MCA 1980 Schedule 2* (involving criminal damage), where the value involved is less than the relevant sum

➤ The court <u>may</u> refuse bail if any of the following apply (*BA 1976 Schedule 1 Part 1A*):

◆ It appears to the court that, having been previously granted bail, he has failed to surrender to custody and the court believes, in view of that failure, that the defendant, if released on bail (whether subject to conditions or not) would fail to surrender to custody (*para 2*).

◆ It appears to the court that the defendant was on bail in criminal proceedings on the date of the offence and the court is satisfied that there are substantial grounds for believing that the defendant, if released on bail (whether subject to conditions or not) would commit an offence while on bail (*para 3*).

◆ The court is satisfied that there are substantial grounds for believing that the defendant, if released on bail (whether subject to conditions or not), would commit an offence while on bail by engaging in conduct that would, or would be likely to, cause physical or mental injury, or fear of such injury (*para 4*).

◆ The court is satisfied that the defendant should be kept in custody for his own protection or, if he is a child or young person, for his own welfare (*para 5*).

◆ Having been released on bail in or in connection with the proceedings for the offence, was arrested under *BA 1976 s 7* (liability to arrest for absconding or breaking conditions of bail) (see p 511) and the court is satisfied that there are substantial grounds for believing, if released he would (*para 7*):
  ● fail to surrender to custody, *or*
  ● commit an offence while on bail, *or*
  ● interfere with witnesses, *or*
  ● otherwise obstruct the course of justice (whether in relation to himself or any other person).

◆ The court is satisfied that it has not been practicable to obtain sufficient information for the purpose of taking a bail decision due to lack of time since proceedings started (*para 8*).

2b **Imprisonable offence(s) which: IS NOT a summary offence AND IS NOT certain offences listed in *MCA 1980 Schedule 2* (involving criminal damage), where the value involved is less than the relevant sum**

➤ The court <u>may</u> refuse bail if any of the following apply (*BA 1976 Schedule 1 Part 1*):

♦ The court is satisfied that substantial grounds exist to believe that a defendant would (*para 2*):

- fail to surrender to custody, *and/or*

- commit another offence (see also the 'Factors' box on p 509), *and/or*

- interfere with witnesses or obstruct the course of justice.

♦ The court is satisfied that the defendant should be kept in custody for his own protection or, if he is a child or young person, for his own welfare (*para 3*).

♦ The defendant is in custody pursuant to a court sentence (*para 4*).

♦ The court is satisfied that it has not been practicable to obtain sufficient information for the purpose of taking a bail decision due to lack of time since proceedings started (*para 5*).

♦ There is adjournment for enquiries/reports for which the defendant needs to be in custody (*para 7*).

➤ The court <u>must</u> refuse bail if either of the following apply:

Scenarios when the court MUST refuse bail	
BA 1976 Schedule 1 Part 1 CJA 2003 ss 14-15, CJA(14)O 2006	*BA 1976 Schedule 1 Part 1, CJA 2009 s 114*

♦ The defendant is over 18 (*para 2A, para 6*), <u>and</u>
♦ the defendant is liable on conviction to life imprisonment, detention at Her Majesty's pleasure or custody for life (*CJA(14)O 2006*), <u>and</u>
♦ <u>either</u>:
  • it appears to the court that he was on bail in criminal proceedings on the date of the offence (*para 2A*), *or*
  • it appears to the court that having been released on bail in or in connection with the offence, he failed to surrender to custody (*para 6*) ...
♦ ... <u>unless:</u>
  • (under *para 2A*) the court is satisfied that there is no significant risk of the defendant committing an offence while on bail (whether subject to conditions or not), *or*
  • (under *para 6*) the court is satisfied that there is no significant risk that, if released on bail (whether subject to conditions or not), he would fail to surrender to custody.
	♦ A defendant is charged with murder must not be granted bail unless the court is of the opinion that there is no significant risk that, if released on bail, he or she would commit an offence that would be likely to cause physical or mental injury to another person (*para 6ZA*).

Factors in considering the above sets of grounds

➤ Strictly speaking, the court only has to consider the factors below in relation to the grounds under *BA 1976 Schedule 1 Part 1, paras 2* and *6* (ie: 2 of the grounds listed for refusing an imprisonable offence) or the opinion under *para 6ZA* (see the previous page).

   ◆ However, in practice these factors apply to all the grounds.

➤ Factors (*BA 1976 Schedule 1 Part 1, para 9*):

   ◆ the nature and seriousness of the offence or default (and the probable method of dealing with the defendant for it),

   ◆ the character, antecedents, associations and community ties of the defendant,

   ◆ the defendant's record as respects the fulfilment of his obligations under previous grants of bail in criminal proceedings,

   ◆ (except in the case of a defendant whose case is adjourned for inquiries or a report), the strength of the evidence of his having committed the offence or having defaulted,

   ◆ if the court is satisfied that there are substantial grounds for believing that the defendant, if released on bail (whether subject to conditions or not), would commit an offence while on bail, the risk that the defendant may do so by engaging in conduct that would, or would be likely to, cause physical or mental injury to any person other than the defendant,

   ◆ any other relevant factors.

➤ When a court decides whether it is satisfied that there are substantial grounds for believing that the defendant, if released on bail (subject to conditions or not), would commit an offence while on bail (part of the first ground for refusing bail for an imprisonable offence), the court must give particular weight to the fact that the defendant was on bail in criminal proceedings on the date of the offence, *provided that* the defendant is under 18 and it appears to the court that he was on bail in criminal proceedings on the date of the offence (*BA 1976 Schedule 1 Part 1, para 9AA*).

Refusal of bail and Class A drugs (*CJA 2003 s 19, BA 1976 s 3(6C)-(6F)*)

➤ Unless the court is satisfied that there is no significant risk of a defendant committing an offence while on bail, bail *must* be refused if the defendant is an adult *and*:

   ◆ the defendant has been charged with an imprisonable offence, *and*:

   ◆ there is drug test evidence that the person has a specified Class A drug in his body, *and*

   ◆ either the offence is a drugs offence associated with a specified Class A drug or the court is satisfied that there are substantial grounds for believing that the misuse of a specified Class A drug caused or contributed to that offence or provided its motivation, *and*

   ◆ the person does not agree to undergo an assessment as to his dependency upon or propensity to misuse specified Class A drugs or, has undergone such an assessment but does not agree to participate in any relevant follow-up offered.

Drugs (*BA 1976 s 4(9)*)

➤ In deciding under *BA 1976 Sch 1, Parts 1 or 2*, the court must consider any misuse of controlled drugs.

Prosecution appeals about the grant of bail

➤ If new evidence comes up after bail is granted by a Magistrates' Court for an either way or indictable offence, the prosecution can ask the court to reconsider the decision to grant bail (*BA 1976 s 5B*).

➤ If a Magistrates' Court grants bail to a person charged with/convicted of an imprisonable offence, the prosecution may appeal the granting of bail to the Crown Court (*B(A)A 1993 s 1(1), CJA 2003 s 18*).

D Bail conditions (*BA 1976 s 3*)

➤ A person granted bail in criminal proceedings shall be under a duty to surrender to custody (*BA 1976 s 3(1)*).

➤ He may be required to comply, before release on bail or later, with court requirements (*BA 1976 s 3(6)*):

♦ to secure that he surrenders to custody, *and/or*

♦ to secure that he does not commit an offence while on bail, *and/or*

♦ to secure that he does not interfere with a witness, or obstruct the course of justice in relation to himself or another, *and/or*

♦ for his own protection or, if he is a child/young person, for his own welfare/interests, *and/or*

♦ to secure that he makes himself available for enquiries to be made to assist the court in dealing with him for the offence, *and/or*

♦ to secure that he (before the time for him to surrender to custody ie: his next appearance in Court) attends an interview with an authorised legal advisor.

Conditions which a court *may* set	
Condition	**Rules**
surety	➤ The sum depends on a surety's wealth, character, previous convictions, or proximity to the defendant. ➤ The surety pays the money to the court if the defendant defaults on his bail conditions - no money is paid to the court on bail being granted.
security	➤ The defendant surrenders his money, chattels, passport, etc.
reporting	➤ Reporting to the police station at specified intervals.
curfew	➤ Compulsory attendance between certain times at a certain place.
residence	➤ Residence, for example, in a bail hostel. ➤ (If so, the defendant may also be required to comply with bail hostel rules (*BA 1976 s 3(6ZA)*).)
non-communication with a prosecution witness	➤ This may involve alternative accommodation for the defendant (possibly in a bail hostel) if a prosecution witness is a relative living in the same house.
electronic monitoring	➤ **For children and young persons** (*BA 1976 s 3AA, CJA 2008 s 51 and Schedule 11*), only if: ♦ the child or young person is at least 12 years old, *and* ♦ the child or young person: • is charged with or has been convicted of a violent or sexual offence (or an offence punishable in the case of an adult with imprisonment for a term of 14 years or more), *or* • is charged with or has been convicted of one or more imprisonable offences which, together with any other imprisonable offences of which he has been convicted in any proceedings amount (or would, if he were convicted of the offences with which he is charged, amount) to a recent history of repeatedly committing imprisonable offences while remanded on bail or to local authority accommodation, *and* ♦ the court is satisfied that the necessary provision for dealing with the person concerned can be made under arrangements for the electronic monitoring of persons released on bail that are currently available in each local justice area which is a relevant area, *and* ♦ a youth offending team has informed the court that in its opinion the imposition of electronic monitoring requirements will be suitable in the case of the child or young person. ➤ **For persons 17 years old and above** (*BA 1976 s 3AB, CJA 2008 s 51 and Schedule 11*), only if: ♦ the court is satisfied that without the electronic monitoring requirements the person would not be granted bail, *and* ♦ the court is satisfied that the necessary provision for dealing with the person concerned can be made under arrangements for the electronic monitoring of persons released on bail that are currently available in each local justice area which is a relevant area, *and* ♦ if aged 17, a youth offending team has informed the court that in its opinion the imposition of electronic monitoring requirements will be suitable in his case.
Conditions which a court *must* set	
➤ If the defendant is accused of murder, the court must set as a condition that he be medically examined (unless previous reports of his medical condition are satisfactory) (*BA 1976 s 6A*).	

Appeal against certain bail conditions (*CJA 2003 s 16*)

➤ A right of appeal to the Crown Court exists against imposition by magistrates of certain bail conditions relating to residence, provision of a surety or a security, curfew, electronic monitoring or contact.

➤ Breach of a bail condition entitles the police to arrest the defendant - the breach is not an offence, but it may provide a ground on which bail can be withdrawn (*BA 1976 s 7*).

◆ The defendant must be produced before a properly constituted court within 24 hours of arrest (excluding Sundays, Good Friday and Xmas Day - *R v Glen Parva Young Offender Institution ex p G* [1998] QB 877).

E Surrender and absconding

1 Surrender

➤ A defendant granted bail must surrender at the time and place appointed (*BA 1976 s 6*).

➤ Failure to surrender is an offence unless there is a 'reasonable' cause.

◆ The defendant has the burden of proof in showing a 'reasonable' cause (*BA 1976 ss 6(2), 6(3)*).

• Failure to give to a person granted bail a copy of the record of the decision shall not constitute a reasonable cause for that person's failure to surrender to custody (*BA 1976 s 6(4)*).

◆ The court may issue a warrant for the defendant's arrest (*BA 1976 s 7(1)-(2)*).

2 Absconding

➤ An offence of failing to surrender (ie: absconding) is punishable either on summary conviction or as if it were a criminal contempt of court (*BA 1976 s 6(5)*).

➤ Where a magistrates' court convicts a person of an offence of absconding, the court may send him in custody or on bail to the Crown Court for sentence (*BA 1976 s 6(6)*):

◆ if it thinks that the circumstances of the offence are such that greater punishment should be inflicted for that offence than the court has power to inflict, *or*

◆ in a case where it sends that person for trial to the Crown Court for another offence, that it would be appropriate for him to be dealt with for the absconding offence by the court before which he is tried for the other offence.

➤ Penalties (*BA 1976 s 6(7)*):

◆ **Magistrates** may impose a fine of up to £5,000 and a sentence of up to 3 months.

◆ The Crown Court may impose an unlimited fine and a sentence of up to 1 year.

➤ Time limits (*BA 1976 s 6(10)-(12)*):

◆ Where a person has been released on bail granted by a constable, a magistrates' court cannot try that person for absconding unless:

• an information is laid for the absconding offence within 6 months from the time of its commission, *or*

• an information is laid for the absconding offence no later than 3 months from the time of the occurrence of the first of the following events below to occur after the commission of the relevant offence:

■ the person surrenders to custody at the appointed place, *or*

■ the person is arrested, or attends at a police station, in connection with the absconding offence or the offence for which he was granted bail, *or*

■ the person appears or is brought before a court in connection with the absconding offence or the offence for which he was granted bail.

E   Mode of trial/Allocation on an 'either way' offence

➤ This page shows the law as it stands before *CJA 2003 s 41* and *Schedule 3* is brought into force.

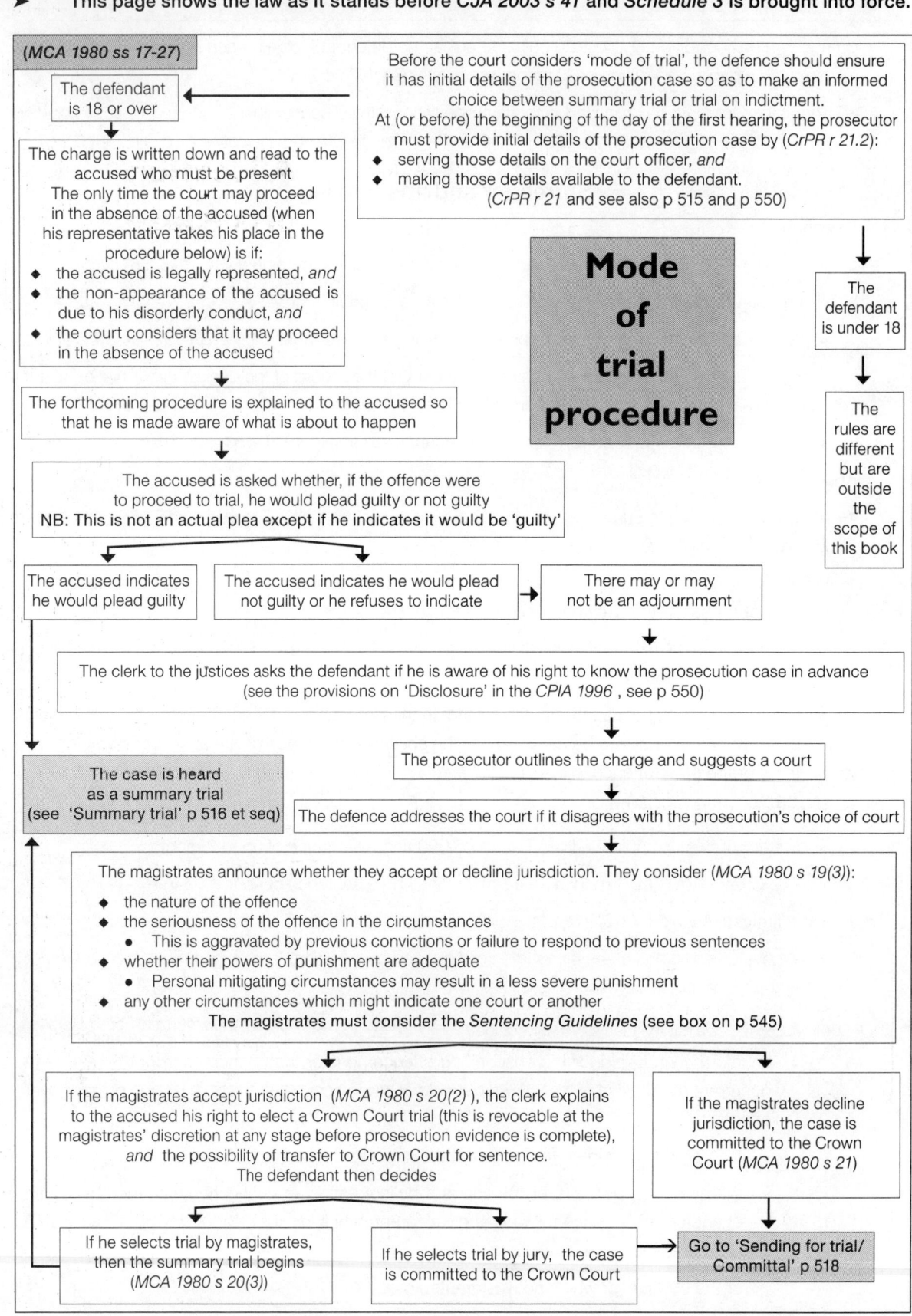

(*MCA 1980 ss 17-27*)

The defendant is 18 or over

The charge is written down and read to the accused who must be present
The only time the court may proceed in the absence of the accused (when his representative takes his place in the procedure below) is if:
◆ the accused is legally represented, *and*
◆ the non-appearance of the accused is due to his disorderly conduct, *and*
◆ the court considers that it may proceed in the absence of the accused

Before the court considers 'mode of trial', the defence should ensure it has initial details of the prosecution case so as to make an informed choice between summary trial or trial on indictment.
At (or before) the beginning of the day of the first hearing, the prosecutor must provide initial details of the prosecution case by (*CrPR r 21.2*):
◆ serving those details on the court officer, *and*
◆ making those details available to the defendant.
(*CrPR r 21* and see also p 515 and p 550)

Mode of trial procedure

The defendant is under 18

The rules are different but are outside the scope of this book

The forthcoming procedure is explained to the accused so that he is made aware of what is about to happen

The accused is asked whether, if the offence were to proceed to trial, he would plead guilty or not guilty
NB: This is not an actual plea except if he indicates it would be 'guilty'

The accused indicates he would plead guilty

The accused indicates he would plead not guilty or he refuses to indicate

There may or may not be an adjournment

The clerk to the justices asks the defendant if he is aware of his right to know the prosecution case in advance (see the provisions on 'Disclosure' in the *CPIA 1996* , see p 550)

The prosecutor outlines the charge and suggests a court

The case is heard as a summary trial (see 'Summary trial' p 516 et seq)

The defence addresses the court if it disagrees with the prosecution's choice of court

The magistrates announce whether they accept or decline jurisdiction. They consider (*MCA 1980 s 19(3)*):
◆ the nature of the offence
◆ the seriousness of the offence in the circumstances
  • This is aggravated by previous convictions or failure to respond to previous sentences
◆ whether their powers of punishment are adequate
  • Personal mitigating circumstances may result in a less severe punishment
◆ any other circumstances which might indicate one court or another
The magistrates must consider the *Sentencing Guidelines* (see box on p 545)

If the magistrates accept jurisdiction (*MCA 1980 s 20(2)*), the clerk explains to the accused his right to elect a Crown Court trial (this is revocable at the magistrates' discretion at any stage before prosecution evidence is complete), *and* the possibility of transfer to Crown Court for sentence.
The defendant then decides

If the magistrates decline jurisdiction, the case is committed to the Crown Court (*MCA 1980 s 21*)

If he selects trial by magistrates, then the summary trial begins (*MCA 1980 s 20(3)*)

If he selects trial by jury, the case is committed to the Crown Court

Go to 'Sending for trial/ Committal' p 518

➤ *This page shows the law after CJA 2003 s 41 and Schedule 3 are brought into force [not yet in force].*

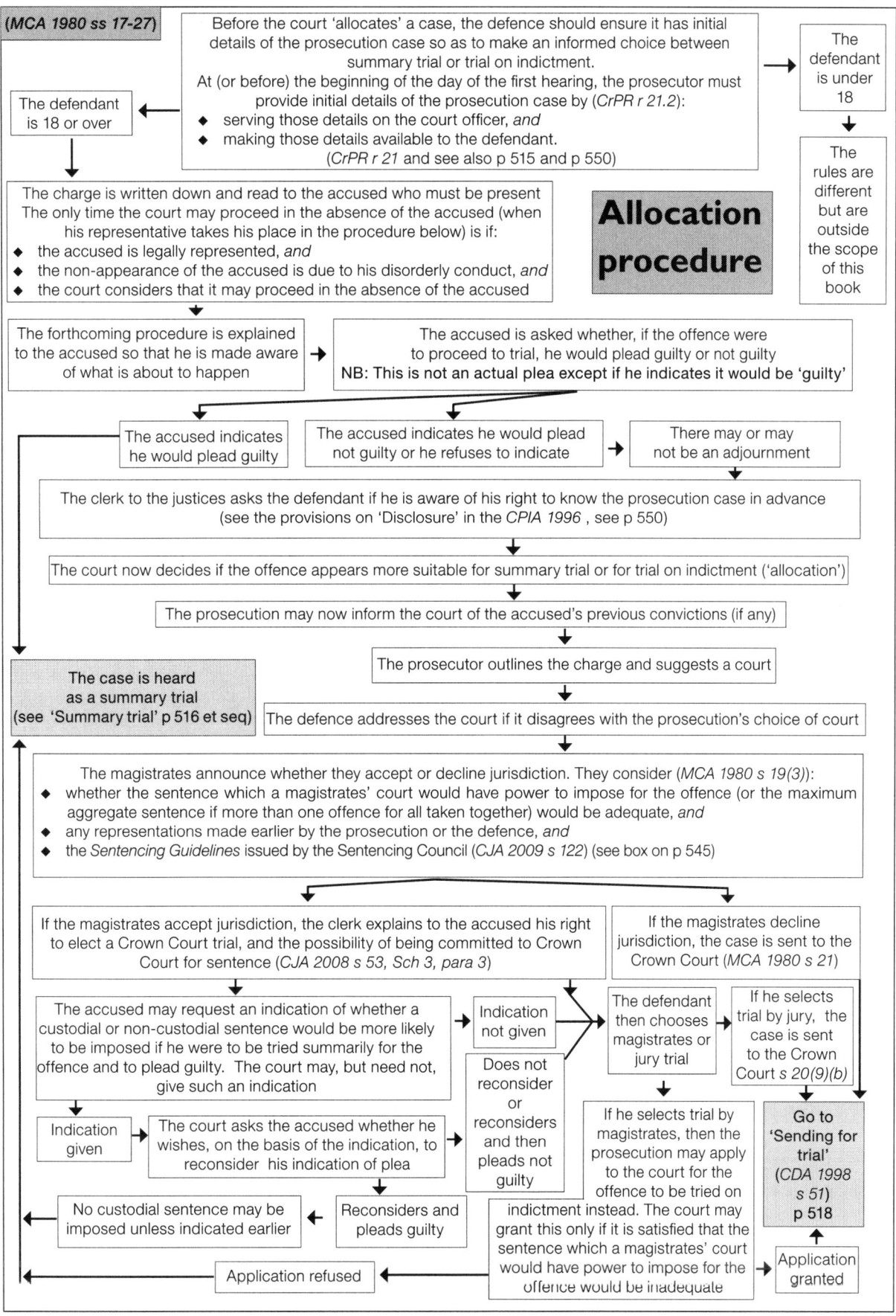

(MCA 1980 ss 17-27)

Before the court 'allocates' a case, the defence should ensure it has initial details of the prosecution case so as to make an informed choice between summary trial or trial on indictment.
At (or before) the beginning of the day of the first hearing, the prosecutor must provide initial details of the prosecution case by (CrPR r 21.2):
♦ serving those details on the court officer, *and*
♦ making those details available to the defendant.
(CrPR r 21 and see also p 515 and p 550)

The defendant is under 18

The defendant is 18 or over

The rules are different but are outside the scope of this book

Allocation procedure

The charge is written down and read to the accused who must be present
The only time the court may proceed in the absence of the accused (when his representative takes his place in the procedure below) is if:
♦ the accused is legally represented, *and*
♦ the non-appearance of the accused is due to his disorderly conduct, *and*
♦ the court considers that it may proceed in the absence of the accused

The forthcoming procedure is explained to the accused so that he is made aware of what is about to happen

The accused is asked whether, if the offence were to proceed to trial, he would plead guilty or not guilty
NB: This is not an actual plea except if he indicates it would be 'guilty'

The accused indicates he would plead guilty

The accused indicates he would plead not guilty or he refuses to indicate

There may or may not be an adjournment

The clerk to the justices asks the defendant if he is aware of his right to know the prosecution case in advance
(see the provisions on 'Disclosure' in the CPIA 1996 , see p 550)

The court now decides if the offence appears more suitable for summary trial or for trial on indictment ('allocation')

The prosecution may now inform the court of the accused's previous convictions (if any)

The prosecutor outlines the charge and suggests a court

The case is heard as a summary trial (see 'Summary trial' p 516 et seq)

The defence addresses the court if it disagrees with the prosecution's choice of court

The magistrates announce whether they accept or decline jurisdiction. They consider (MCA 1980 s 19(3)):
♦ whether the sentence which a magistrates' court would have power to impose for the offence (or the maximum aggregate sentence if more than one offence for all taken together) would be adequate, *and*
♦ any representations made earlier by the prosecution or the defence, *and*
♦ the Sentencing Guidelines issued by the Sentencing Council (CJA 2009 s 122) (see box on p 545)

If the magistrates accept jurisdiction, the clerk explains to the accused his right to elect a Crown Court trial, and the possibility of being committed to Crown Court for sentence (CJA 2008 s 53, Sch 3, para 3)

If the magistrates decline jurisdiction, the case is sent to the Crown Court (MCA 1980 s 21)

The accused may request an indication of whether a custodial or non-custodial sentence would be more likely to be imposed if he were to be tried summarily for the offence and to plead guilty. The court may, but need not, give such an indication

Indication not given

The defendant then chooses magistrates or jury trial

If he selects trial by jury, the case is sent to the Crown Court s 20(9)(b)

Does not reconsider or reconsiders and then pleads not guilty

Indication given

The court asks the accused whether he wishes, on the basis of the indication, to reconsider his indication of plea

If he selects trial by magistrates, then the prosecution may apply to the court for the offence to be tried on indictment instead. The court may grant this only if it is satisfied that the sentence which a magistrates' court would have power to impose for the offence would be inadequate

Go to 'Sending for trial' (CDA 1998 s 51) p 518

No custodial sentence may be imposed unless indicated earlier

Reconsiders and pleads guilty

Application refused

Application granted

Defendant elects summary trial and subsequently changes his mind before all the prosecution evidence has been heard

➤ The magistrates have discretion to refer the case to the Crown Court (*MCA 1980 s 25*).
➤ This will be repealed when *CJA 2003 s 41* and *Schedule 3* is brought into force. It will be replaced with a new prosecution right to challenge as per the chart on the preceding page.

Summary offences linked to indictable offences which may be tried in the Crown Court

CJA 1988 s 40(1): Defendant accused of...	CJA 1988 s 41(1): Defendant accused of an offence which is...
... common assault, taking a conveyance, driving whilst disqualified, certain types of criminal damage, assaulting a prison custody officer or a secure training centre custody officer *and* a) i) the summary offence is based on the same facts or evidence as the indictable offence, *or* ii) the summary offence is of a similar character to the indictable offence with which the defendant is also charged, *and* b) facts/evidence relating to the offence were disclosed "to examining justices in the presence of the person charged" *[to be changed to: "by material served on the person charged" when CJA 2003 s 41 is brought into force [not yet in force].]*	a) punishable with imprisonment or involves obligatory or discretionary disqualification from driving, *and* b) it appears to the court that the summary offence arises out of circumstances which are the same as, or connected with, those giving rise to the offence that is triable 'either way' *CJA 1988 s 41(1) and its consequences will be repealed when CJA 2003 s 41 is brought into force because the existing rules will be subsumed into the new rules for sending for trial [not yet in force]*

Subsequent procedure for trial

The Crown Court must treat the summary offence as an indictable offence, but must deal with the offender as a Magistrates' Court would have done	Evidence for the summary offence is not heard at committal. In the Crown Court the procedure depends on the plea: a) guilty plea: the court sentences for the summary offence with the same powers as a Magistrates' Court b) not-guilty plea: the summary offence is sent to the magistrates for trial

Advice to a client about selecting a court for trial: factors to consider

1 **Previous conviction?**

   ✗ **Magistrates' Court:** magistrates may be seen as case-hardened, and may already be familiar with a police officer or with the defendant.

   ✓ **Crown Court:** conviction is thought by some to be less likely in a Crown Court where juries can be seen as sympathetic.

2 **If there is a question of admissibility of evidence ...**

   ✗ **Magistrates' Court:** magistrates decide matters of fact and law (ie: when giving a verdict, magistrates must attempt to 'forget' evidence which they have heard before holding it to be inadmissible).

   ✓ **Crown Court:** a Crown Court judge rules on the law, the jury decides matters of fact (ie: the jury is sent out while the judge decides evidential matters, so jurors never hear evidence unless it is admissible).

3 **Questions of cost**

   ✓ **Magistrates' Court:** costs will be lower.

   ✗ **Crown Court:** costs will be higher.

4 **Questions of stress**

   ✓ **Magistrates' Court:** less publicity means less stress.

   ✗ **Crown Court:** more publicity means more stress.

5 **Is the defendant in custody?**

   ✓ **Magistrates' Court:** delay before trial is shorter (usually about 1 month).

   ✗ **Crown Court:** delay before trial is longer (about 6 months).

6 **Sentence**

   ✓ **Magistrates' Court:** sentences are less severe than in the Crown Court (but the defendant may be referred to the Crown Court for sentencing for certain crimes).

   ✗ **Crown Court:** sentences are more severe than in the Magistrates' Court.

F   Preparations for summary trial

➤ The solicitor should:

- ◆ Ensure that he has a copy of the custody record (see *Code C:2.4,* p 489).

- ◆ Ensure, where identification is disputed, that he has a copy of the original description from which the identification was made, see p 493 and note points on p 557.

- ◆ Obtain a copy of the charge sheet.

- ◆ Interview the client and take a detailed statement and full instructions as soon as possible.

- ◆ Interview witnesses: take a proof of evidence signed and dated by the witness.
  - ● When interviewing a prosecution witness, it is good practice to have an independent party present, and to write to the prosecution to let them know the interview has taken place; this avoids any suspicion of putting pressure on a witness.
  - ● During an interview, challenge the witness's version of events. (**Note:** 'preparing a witness' for cross-examination is forbidden.)

- ◆ Visit the area of the alleged offence, and prepare plans if appropriate.

- ◆ Seek expert evidence: if the client is LSC funded, obtain the LSC's authorisation for the expenditure.

- ◆ Ensure he has disclosure of the prosecution case (see box below).

- ◆ Put the prosecution case to the defendant, and note any comments he makes on it.

- ◆ Decide whether witnesses should attend.
  - ● **Note:** where a witness will not need to be cross-examined, a statement submitted under *CJA 1967 s 9* will be sufficient, see p 563.

- ◆ If a witness is needed, write to him asking for written confirmation that he will turn up at a specified time.
  - ● If this confirmation is not forthcoming, the solicitor should write to the relevant court officer using the unanswered letter as proof that the witness is unlikely to attend of his own accord.
  - ● If a JP is satisfied that a person is likely to be able to give material evidence (or produce any document or thing likely to be material evidence) at the summary trial **and it is in the interests of justice to issue a summons to secure the attendance of that person to give evidence** (or produce the document or thing), the JP issues a summons directed to that person requiring him to attend before the court at the time and place appointed in the summons (*MCA 1980 s 97, CrPR r 28*). See also the rules on this on p 522.
    - ■ The court may issue an arrest warrant if a witness fails to obey the summons (*MCA 1980 s 97(3)*).

- ◆ Decide if a witness anonymity order is needed and make any relevant applications (*CJA 2009 ss 86-97*).

The solicitor should ensure he has disclosure of the prosecution case

➤ At (or before) the beginning of the day of the first hearing, the prosecutor must provide initial details of the prosecution case by (*CrPR r 21.2*):
- ◆ serving those details on the court officer, *and*
- ◆ making those details available to the defendant.

➤ Initial details of the prosecution case must include (*CrPR r 21.3*):
- ◆ a summary of the evidence on which that case will be based, *or*
- ◆ any statement/document/extract setting out facts or other matters on which that case will be based, *or*
- ◆ any combination of such a summary, statement, document or extract, *and*
- ◆ the defendant's previous convictions. (This should be checked for inaccuracies.)

➤ *CPIA 1996 ss 1-21* and the common law contain the disclosure rules (see p 550). A solicitor should ask for full voluntary disclosure now as the main statutory disclosure will be after plea. He should get:
- ◆ details of any evidence the prosecution possesses which is favourable to the defence.
- ◆ a record of any prosecution interviews with the defendant.
- ◆ the names and addresses of witnesses the prosecution will not call.
- ◆ a list of the witnesses interviewed by the police who the prosecution do *not* intend to call.
- ◆ a statement of the defendant's criminal record, details of the criminal records of prosecution witnesses and co-defendants.

G Summary trial

Pre-trial hearings (*MCA 1980 ss 8A-8D*)

➤ *MCA 1980 ss 8A-8D* are intended ensure more efficient and uniform preparation of cases for trial in the Magistrates' Courts and to bring the powers of lay magistrates and judges in pre-trial hearings heard in the magistrates' courts into line with those of the Crown Court.

➤ The magistrates may hold a 'pre-trial hearing' before a summary trial (ie: where the accused has pleaded not guilty) at any time before it has begun to hear evidence from the prosecution at the trial.

➤ The court can make a ruling on:

◆ any question as to the admissibility of evidence, *and/or*

◆ any other question of law relating to the case.

➤ Before making a ruling:

◆ the court must have given the parties an opportunity to be heard, *and*

◆ it must have appeared to the court that it is in the interests of justice to make the ruling, *and*

◆ if the defendant is not legally represented, the court must have asked the defendant whether he wishes to be granted a right to representation funded by the LSC as part of the CDS, and if he does, decided whether or not to grant him that right.

➤ There are restrictions on reporting matters at the pre-trial hearing.

Joinder

➤ Co-defendants tried on 1 'information' for the same offence are tried together, unless there is a conflict of interest. Conviction of one does not prevent the acquittal of the other (eg: *Barsted v Jones* (1960) 124 JP 400).

➤ Defendants tried on separate 'informations' can be tried together if the defence agrees. But the court always has discretion to consider that as the facts are the same, or that as the offences are similar and related, a joint trial is 'in the interests of justice' (*Chief Constable of Norfolk v Clayton* [1983] 2 AC 473).

Defect in process

➤ If the defence is misled by an error in the 'information', summons or warrant, then it may seek an adjournment to rethink its case. It has no other remedy in these circumstances (*MCA 1980 s 123*).

Costs

➤ **The defendant is acquitted (not LSC funded)** (*POA 1985 s 16(1)*): Costs are met from central funds, *unless* the defendant brought suspicion on himself by his own conduct (*POA 1985 s 16(7)*).

➤ **The defendant is acquitted (he is LSC funded):** Costs are not met by central funds, but by the LSC. Any contribution the defendant has made may be refunded (*POA 1985 s 21(4A)*) unless there are exceptional circumstances.

➤ **The defendant is convicted:** Costs must be met by the defendant where the court is satisfied that he has the means and ability to pay (*POA 1985 s 18(1)*). (Costs must be met by the LSC if the offender is an assisted person, but may be subject to a RDCO, see p 30.) The court makes an order for a specified sum (*POA 1985 s 18(3)*).

Procedure (*MCA 1980 s 9 and CrPR r 37*)

Steps	
1	Unless already done (eg: if a summary trial has started from sending for trial/a mode of trial hearing where the charge has already been read to the defendant: *CPIA 1996*), then the justices' legal adviser or the court must (*CrPR r 37.2(2)*): ◆ read the allegation of the offence to the defendant, *and* ◆ explain, in terms the defendant can understand (with help, if necessary) the allegation and what the procedure at the hearing will be, *and* ◆ ask whether he has been advised about the potential effect on sentence of a guilty plea, *and* ◆ ask whether the defendant pleads guilty or not guilty, *and* ◆ take the defendant's plea of guilty or not guilty.
2	(i) If he pleads 'guilty', the court proceeds to sentence (*CrPR r 37.7 and r 37.10*) - see the procedure on p 546) . (ii) If he pleads 'not guilty' (or does not enter a plea), although he can alter this at any time before sentence, the procedure continues as below.
3	The statutory disclosure procedure applies from this point (see p 550) and the disclosure of expert evidence procedure applies too (see p 565).
4	The prosecutor may summarise the prosecution case, identifying relevant law and facts (*CrPR r 37.3(3)(a)*).
5	The prosecutor must introduce the evidence on which the prosecution case relies (*CrPR r 37.3(3)(b)*).
6	At the end of the prosecution case, if the defendant's asks, or on its own initiative, the court may acquit on the ground that the prosecution evidence is insufficient for any reasonable court properly to convict, *but* must not do so unless the prosecutor has had an opportunity to make representations (*CrPR r 37.3(3)(c)*). This is done by the defence submitting 'no case to answer' (see p 524 for a discussion of this) if *either*: a) there is no evidence to prove an essential element of the offence, *or* b) the prosecution evidence is so discredited under cross-examination *or* so manifestly unreliable that no reasonable tribunal could convict on it. ⟶ ◆ For the effect of 'adverse inferences' on a defendant's decision not to testify, see p 566. ◆ The prosecution may reply to this submission. ◆ If the submission is accepted, the case is dismissed, otherwise step 7 applies.
7	The justices' legal adviser or the court must explain, in terms the defendant can understand (with help, if necessary) the right to give evidence and the potential effect of not doing so at all, or of refusing to answer a question while doing so (*CrPR r 37.3(3)(d)*). ◆ The legal representative of the defence must tell the court at this point that the defendant will give evidence, else the magistrate will give a 'silence warning' (see p 566) (*CJPO 1994 s 35*).
8	The defendant may introduce evidence (*CrPR r 37.3(3)(e)*).
9	A party may introduce further evidence if it is then admissible (eg: because it is in rebuttal of evidence already introduced) (*CrPR r 37.3(3)(f)*).
10	The prosecutor may make final representations in support of the prosecution case, if the defendant is represented by a legal representative or (whether represented or not) the defendant has introduced evidence other than his or her own (*CrPR r 37.3(3)(g)*).
11	The defendant may make final representations about the case (*CrPR r 37.3(3)(h)*).
12	If a party wants to introduce evidence/make representations after that party's opportunity to do so, the court may refuse to receive any such evidence or representations and, in any event, must not receive any such evidence or representations after it has announced its verdict (*CrPR r 37.3(4)*).
13	The magistrates reach a majority verdict and then consider an appropriate sentence and costs. (i) If the court convicts, it must give sufficient reasons to explain its decision and the court proceeds to sentence (*CrPR r 37.3(5), CrPR r 37.10*) - see the procedure on p 546. (ii) If the court acquits, it may give an explanation of its decision and it may exercise any power it has to make a civil behaviour order and a costs order (*CrPR r 37.3(6)*).

It is not acceptable for defence lawyers to base submissions on the absence of prosecution evidence if prior notice of that omission has not been given to the Crown (*R v Penner* [2010] EWCA Crim 1155)

H Sending for trial and committal

>   I   Sending for trial or committal?
>   II   Sending for trial
>   III   Committal

I Sending for trial or committal?

➤ This section governs the next steps in the procedure when an accused is charged with an offence which is an either way offence or triable only on indictment.

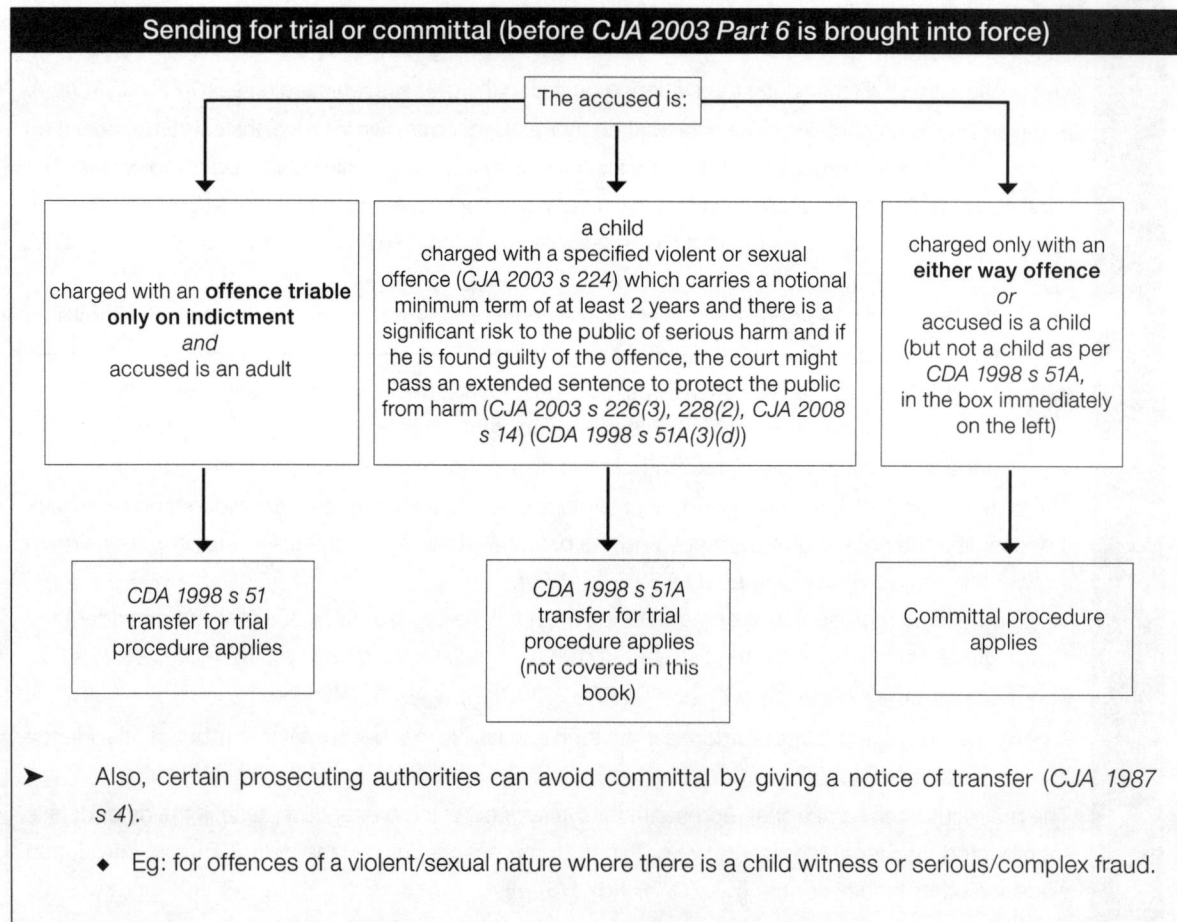

Sending for trial or committal (before *CJA 2003 Part 6* is brought into force)

The accused is:

charged with an **offence triable only on indictment** *and* accused is an adult	a child charged with a specified violent or sexual offence (*CJA 2003 s 224*) which carries a notional minimum term of at least 2 years and there is a significant risk to the public of serious harm and if he is found guilty of the offence, the court might pass an extended sentence to protect the public from harm (*CJA 2003 s 226(3), 228(2), CJA 2008 s 14*) (*CDA 1998 s 51A(3)(d)*)	charged only with an **either way offence** *or* accused is a child (but not a child as per *CDA 1998 s 51A*, in the box immediately on the left)
CDA 1998 s 51 transfer for trial procedure applies	*CDA 1998 s 51A* transfer for trial procedure applies (not covered in this book)	Committal procedure applies

➤ Also, certain prosecuting authorities can avoid committal by giving a notice of transfer (*CJA 1987 s 4*).

♦ Eg: for offences of a violent/sexual nature where there is a child witness or serious/complex fraud.

Sending for trial or committal (after CJA 2003 ss 41-42 are brought into force) [not yet in force]

➤ *After CJA 2003, Part 6 (ss 41-42) is brought into force, committal will be abolished and all cases will be sent for trial [Not yet in force].*

II   Sending for trial

➤   An adult before a Magistrates' Court who is charged with an offence triable only on indictment is immediately sent to the Crown Court for trial (*CDA 1998 s 51(1)*).

- ◆   The accused is sent for trial (*CDA 1998 s 51*):

  - ●   for the indictable-only offence, *and*

  - ●   for any either way or summary offence with which he is charged which:

    - ■   appears to the court to be related to the indictable-only offence, *and*

    - ■   (in the case of a summary offence only), is punishable with imprisonment or involves obligatory or discretionary disqualification from driving.

- ◆   Any other adult who is charged jointly with the accused with an either way offence which is related to the indictable-only offence, is also immediately sent to the Crown Court for trial of the either way offence (*CDA 1998 s 51*).

- ◆   A child jointly charged with the accused for the indictable offence is, if the court considers it necessary in the interests of justice, sent immediately to the Crown Court for trial (*CDA 1998 s 51*).

The above text will be replaced when CJA 2003 s 41 is brought into force [not yet in force]

➤   *An adult before a Magistrates' Court is immediately sent to the Crown Court for trial as per the 'sending for trial' box on p 518 (CDA 1998 s 51(1)).*

➤   *Where the court sends an adult for trial, it also sends him at the same time to the Crown Court for trial for any either-way or summary offence with which he is charged and which (CDA 1998 s 51(3)):*

- ◆   *(if it is an either-way offence) appears to the court to be related to the main offence for which he is sent for trial, or*

- ◆   *(if it is a summary offence) appears to the court to be related to the main offence for which he is sent for trial or to the either-way offence if that either way offence is punishable with imprisonment or involves obligatory or discretionary disqualification from driving (CDA 1998 s 51(11)).*

Note: If the adult has already been sent for a trial and subsequently appears or is brought before a Magistrates' Court charged with an either-way or summary offence, the court can also send him for trial for that offence at this later point, if these conditions above are fulfilled (CDA 1998 s 51(4)).

➤   *Where the court has sent an adult (A) for trial and another adult appears or is brought before the court on the same (or a subsequent) occasion who is charged jointly with A with an either-way offence and that either-way offence appears to the court to be related to an offence for which A was sent for trial, then the court sends the other adult to the Crown Court for trial for the either-way offence (CDA 1998 s 51(4)), together with any other linked offences as per the rules in CDA 1998 s 51(3) (CDA 1998 s 51(5)).*

➤   *Special rules apply if a child/young person is charged jointly with an adult (CDA 1998 s 51(7)-(9)).*

- ◆   *In general, a child jointly charged with the accused for the indictable offence is, if the court considers it necessary in the interests of justice, sent immediately to the Crown Court for trial (CDA 1998 s 51(7)).*

➤   *There are special rules also for cases involving children or serious or complex fraud cases (CDA 1998 s 51A-51D).*

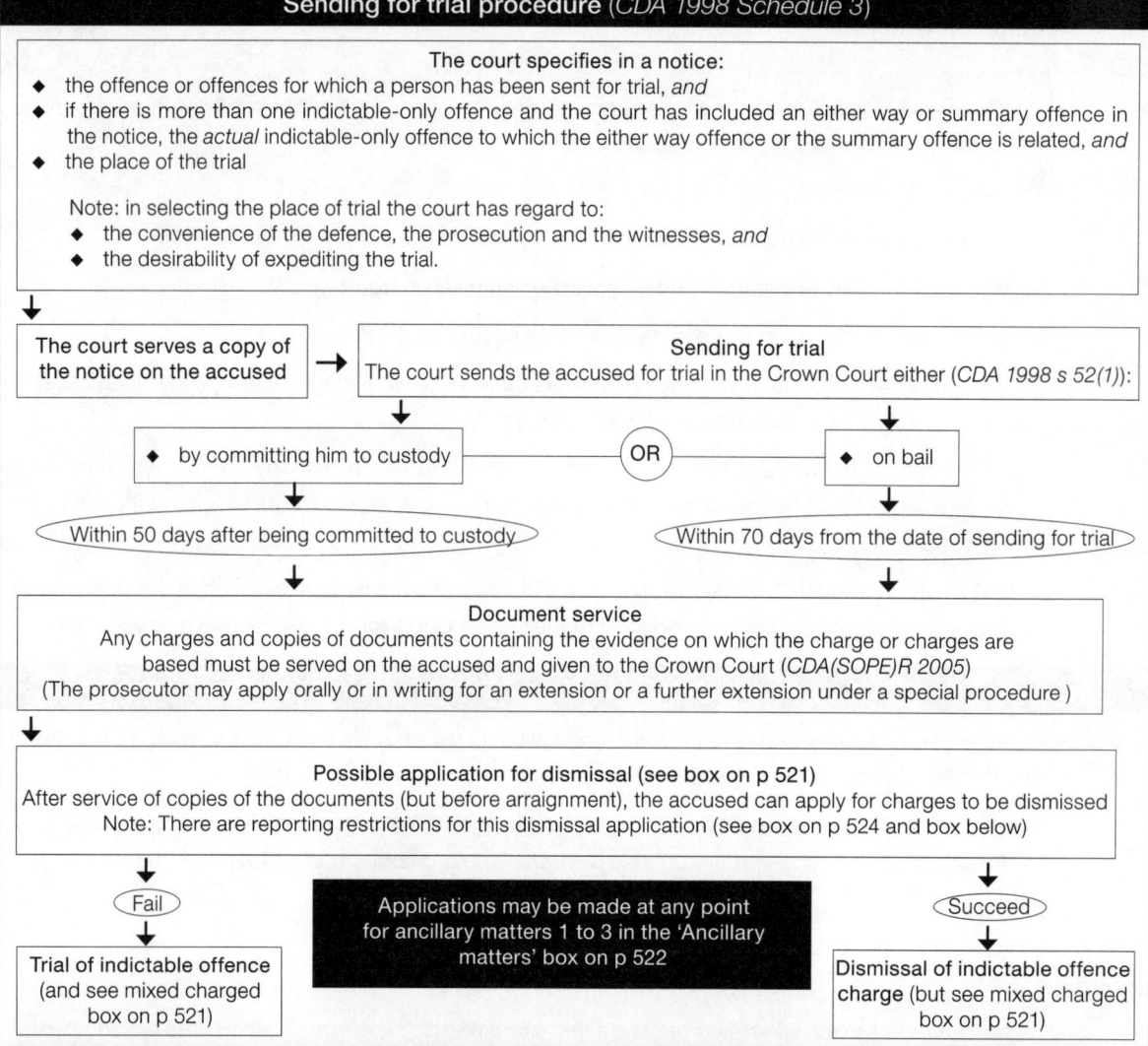

Sending for trial procedure (*CDA 1998 Schedule 3*)

The court specifies in a notice:
- the offence or offences for which a person has been sent for trial, *and*
- if there is more than one indictable-only offence and the court has included an either way or summary offence in the notice, the *actual* indictable-only offence to which the either way offence or the summary offence is related, *and*
- the place of the trial

Note: in selecting the place of trial the court has regard to:
- the convenience of the defence, the prosecution and the witnesses, *and*
- the desirability of expediting the trial.

| The court serves a copy of the notice on the accused | → | **Sending for trial** The court sends the accused for trial in the Crown Court either (*CDA 1998 s 52(1)*): |

- by committing him to custody — OR — on bail

Within 50 days after being committed to custody · Within 70 days from the date of sending for trial

Document service
Any charges and copies of documents containing the evidence on which the charge or charges are based must be served on the accused and given to the Crown Court (*CDA(SOPE)R 2005*)
(The prosecutor may apply orally or in writing for an extension or a further extension under a special procedure)

Possible application for dismissal (see box on p 521)
After service of copies of the documents (but before arraignment), the accused can apply for charges to be dismissed
Note: There are reporting restrictions for this dismissal application (see box on p 524 and box below)

Fail · Succeed

Applications may be made at any point for ancillary matters 1 to 3 in the 'Ancillary matters' box on p 522

Trial of indictable offence (and see mixed charged box on p 521)

Dismissal of indictable offence charge (but see mixed charged box on p 521)

Reporting restrictions (*CDA 1998 Schedule 3*) (*Also CDA 1998 s 52A [not yet in force]*)

➤ It is unlawful to publish in the UK a written report or include for reception in the UK a report of any allocation or sending proceedings, unless a court orders otherwise.

➤ Defendant(s) may object to the lifting of reporting restrictions. If a lifting order is to be made, the court can only lift the restrictions if it is 'in the interests of justice'.

➤ However, the following matters may be reported:

- the identity of the court and the name of the justice or justices
- the name, age, home address and occupation of the accused
- in the case of an accused charged with an offence in respect of which notice has been given to the court under *s 51B*, any relevant business information
- the offence or offences, or a summary of them, with which the accused is or are charged
- the names of counsel and solicitors engaged in the proceedings
- where the proceedings are adjourned, the date and place to which they are adjourned
- the arrangements as to bail
- whether a right to representation funded by the LSC as part of the Criminal Defence Service was granted to the accused or any of the accused.

Application for dismissal of main indictable offence

➤ After service of copies of the documents (but before arraignment), the accused can apply orally or in writing for the main indictable offence for which he was sent for trial to be dismissed (*CDA 1998, Schedule 3 para 2*).

➤ It is possible to obtain the attendance of prosecution witnesses for cross-examination if it is in the interests of justice to do so.

◆ *This will be repealed when CJA 2003 s 41 is brought into force.*

Mixed charges *(CDA 1998 Schedule 3 paras 6-7)*

➤ If the accused is sent to the Crown Court for:

◆ a main indictable offence *and* other either way offences:

• if the accused succeeds in having the main indictable offence for which he was sent for trial dismissed, then the Crown Court holds a plea-before venue hearing to ascertain if the either way offence should be tried in the Crown Court or the Magistrates' Court.

■ If the accused pleads guilty, then the court immediately proceeds to sentence.

■ If the accused pleads not guilty, there is a full mode of trial hearing (see p 512).

• if the accused fails in having the main indictable offence dismissed, then the Crown Court considers that main indictable offence and the either way offence.

◆ an indictable offences *and* other summary offences:

• if the accused is convicted on the indictable offence for which he was sent for trial, the Crown Court considers whether the summary offence is related to any of those indictable offences. If they are related, the court states to the person the substance of the summary offence and asks him whether he pleads guilty or not guilty.

■ If the accused pleads guilty, the Crown Court convicts him of the summary offence, but may deal with him for the summary offence only in a manner in which a Magistrates' Court could have dealt with him.

■ If the accused pleads not plead guilty, the powers of the Crown Court cease in respect of the summary offence and the matter goes for trial to the Magistrates' Court.

Ancillary matters

1 **Witness summons to ensure witnesses attend the Crown Court trial:** *CP(AW)A 1965 s 2* contains the rules for issue of a witness summons by the Crown Court. It applies when a person is likely to be able to give evidence likely to be material evidence (or produce any document or thing likely to be material evidence) for any criminal proceedings before the Crown Court, and it is in the interests of justice to issue a summons to secure the attendance of that person to give evidence or to produce the document or thing (usually to compel any witness with material evidence to attend trial who will not attend voluntarily). *CrPR r 28* governs the procedure which is very strict.

➤ Some of the rules that apply are:

These rules are also applicable in the Magistrates' Court - see p 515

◆ A party who wants the court to issue a witness summons, warrant or order must apply as soon as practicable after becoming aware of the grounds for doing so (*CrPR r 28.3*). The party applying must:

- identify the proposed witness, *and*
- explain what evidence the proposed witness can give or produce, *and*
- explain why it is likely to be material evidence, *and*
- explain why it would be in the interests of justice to issue a summons/order/warrant.

◆ the court may also make a witness summons of its own motion (*CP(AW)A 1965 s 2D, CrPR r 28.1(1)(b)*).

➤ A Crown Court judge punishes disobedience of such a summons as contempt (*CP(AW)A 1965 s 3*).

➤ (Committal only:) A Magistrates' Court which commits a person for trial must immediately remind him of his right to object, within 14 days, to a statement or deposition being read as evidence at the trial without oral evidence being given by the person who made the statement or deposition, and without the opportunity to cross-examine that person (*CrPR r 10.4*).

◆ General rule (if a defendant does not object): all statements of a particular witness forming part of the committal bundle are read at trial instead of the witness being called to give oral evidence (*CPIA 1996 Schedule 2*).

2 **LSC funding:** The defence can apply for an extension of LSC funding to cover a Crown Court trial. It also confirms whether or not the defendant's financial circumstances are altered.

3 **Bail** (For committal the reference is: *MCA 1980 s 6(3)*): Bail is usually extended until trial. If the defendant is in custody, he can make a bail application.

4 **Fix a date for a PCMH:** Magistrates fix a date for a plea and case management hearing (p 527).

III   Committal

Note: It is proposed that committal will be abolished when CJA 2003, s 41 and Schedule 3 is brought into force.

➤ Committal proceedings are the means by which a Magistrates' Court decides if there is sufficient evidence to send an accused to the Crown Court.

➤ There are 2 types of committal hearing, both in *MCA 1980 s 6: s 6(1)* committal and *s 6(2)* committal.

s 6(1) committal	*s 6(2)* committal
Committal **with** consideration of evidence	Committal **without** consideration of evidence

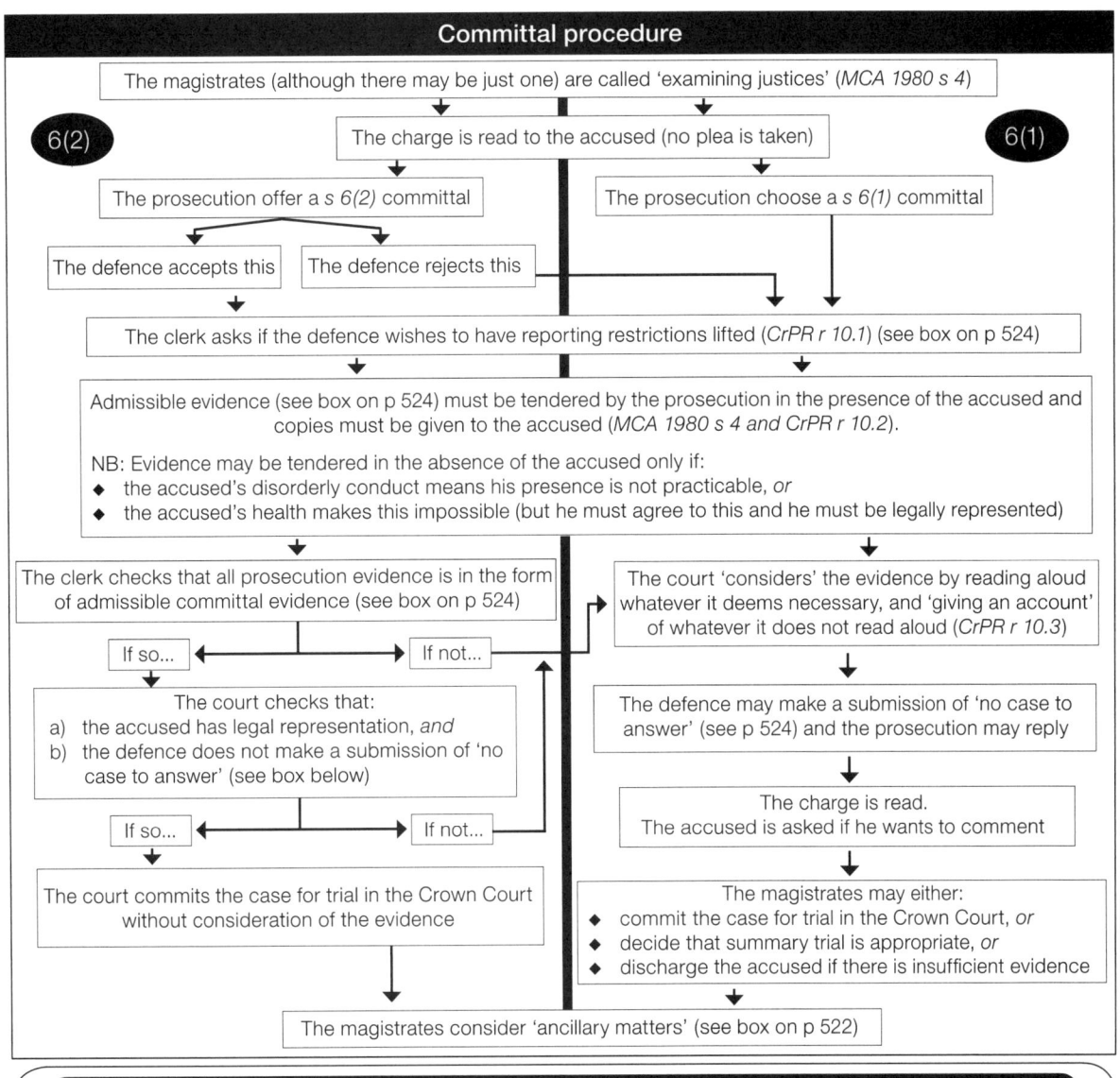

Committal procedure

The magistrates (although there may be just one) are called 'examining justices' (*MCA 1980 s 4*)

6(2) · 6(1)

The charge is read to the accused (no plea is taken)

The prosecution offer a *s 6(2)* committal

The prosecution choose a *s 6(1)* committal

The defence accepts this — The defence rejects this

The clerk asks if the defence wishes to have reporting restrictions lifted (*CrPR r 10.1*) (see box on p 524)

Admissible evidence (see box on p 524) must be tendered by the prosecution in the presence of the accused and copies must be given to the accused (*MCA 1980 s 4 and CrPR r 10.2*).

NB: Evidence may be tendered in the absence of the accused only if:
- the accused's disorderly conduct means his presence is not practicable, *or*
- the accused's health makes this impossible (but he must agree to this and he must be legally represented)

The clerk checks that all prosecution evidence is in the form of admissible committal evidence (see box on p 524)

The court 'considers' the evidence by reading aloud whatever it deems necessary, and 'giving an account' of whatever it does not read aloud (*CrPR r 10.3*)

If so... — If not...

The court checks that:
a) the accused has legal representation, *and*
b) the defence does not make a submission of 'no case to answer' (see box below)

The defence may make a submission of 'no case to answer' (see p 524) and the prosecution may reply

If so... — If not...

The charge is read.
The accused is asked if he wants to comment

The court commits the case for trial in the Crown Court without consideration of the evidence

The magistrates may either:
- commit the case for trial in the Crown Court, *or*
- decide that summary trial is appropriate, *or*
- discharge the accused if there is insufficient evidence

The magistrates consider 'ancillary matters' (see box on p 522)

Which committal should be chosen?

- ➤ A *s 6(2)* committal is quicker and will usually be preferable.
- ➤ A *s 6(2)* committal can only take place if:

6(2) · 6(2)

a) all evidence tendered by the prosecution at committal is (see p 524 for in-depth definitions):
- in the form of written statements, *or*
- in the form of documents or exhibits referred to in the written statements, *or*
- in the form of depositions, *or*
- in the form of documents or exhibits referred to in depositions, *or*
- any particular document allowed by statute, *and*

b) the defendant has a solicitor acting for him, *and*

c) the defence do not claim that the prosecution has insufficient evidence.

Prosecution reasons:	Defence reasons:
identification is at issue - the Attorney General has advised that *s 6(2)* is only suitable if the prosecution, defence and court are satisfied about reliability of identification evidence	◆ to submit no case to answer, *or* ◆ to obtain publicity (it may help trace witnesses), *or* ◆ to persuade a court to commit on a lesser charge.

6(1) · 6(1)

Test for committal to the Crown Court

➤ The test is whether, having heard the case, there is sufficient evidence to put the accused on trial for indictment (ie: if a reasonably minded jury, properly directed, would convict on the evidence provided). If so, then the magistrates will commit the case to the Crown Court for trial.

Test for a submission of 'no case to answer'

➤ *R v Galbraith* [1981] 1 WLR 1039 - taken at its highest, could a jury convict on the evidence?

◆ This 'depends on the view to be taken of a witness's reliability, or other matters ... within the jury's province, and where *one possible view* of the facts is that there is evidence on which the jury could properly convict [and if all these apply, then a submission will fail]'.

Admissible committal evidence (*MCA ss 5A-5D*)

➤ Admissible committal evidence is evidence that is tendered by, or on behalf of, the prosecutor, *and* is:
  ◆ **a written statement**, *or*
    ● this is a statement that:
      ■ purports to be signed by the person making it, *and*
      ■ contains a declaration by that person that:
        - it is true to his best knowledge and belief *and*
        - if tendered in evidence the person would be liable to prosecution if it contained anything he knew to be false or untrue, *and*
      ■ has been given together with any documents or exhibits it refers to (or copies have been given) (these must be inspectable if copies are not available) to each of the other parties before being tendered by the prosecutor, *and*
      ■ contains the defendant's age (but only if he is under 18).

> A document is anything in which any information of any description is recorded (*MCA 1980 s 5A(6)*)

  ◆ **a deposition**, *or*
    ● this is a document that:
      ■ has been sent to the prosecutor after the *MCA 1980 s 97A(9)* procedure, *and*
      (NB: the *MCA 1980 s 97A* procedure is often used when an evidence statement has been taken from someone who may not voluntarily give evidence at committal and is made to do so pursuant to a witness summons, or is arrested to do so, see p 515.)
      ■ has been given together with any documents or exhibits it refers to (or copies have been given) (these must be inspectable if copies are not available) to each of the other parties before the inquiry as 'examining justices' begins.
  ◆ **documents or other exhibits referred to in written statements or depositions**, *or*
  ◆ **a documentary hearsay statement**, *or*
    ● the prosecution must have signed a certificate that there is reasonable cause to believe the evidence may be properly used at trial.
  ◆ **any other document allowed by statute**.

Reporting restrictions (*MCA 1980 s 8*)

➤ The press may report the names of defendants/witnesses, the charge and result of the proceedings.

➤ The press may not report evidence (to prevent a jury being prejudiced).

➤ A single defendant may ask that restrictions be lifted (eg: to obtain publicity to help trace witnesses).

◆ If a co-defendant requests, restrictions are lifted if it is 'in the interests of justice' (*MCA 1980 s 8(2A)*).

Preparations for Crown Court hearings and trial

Between committal and trial

1   **Make all relevant preparations as for summary trial (see p 515)** *and get the committal bundle.*

2   **Apply to the Crown Court or a High Court judge in chambers for bail, if necessary.**

3   **Brief counsel** (see box below for *'Format of a brief to counsel'*).

4   **Ensure that the prosecution has turned over all relevant material (following the disclosure procedure, see p 550).**

5   **Ensure that witnesses can attend as planned.**

> ➤ This is achieved by applying for any necessary witness summons (see p 522).

6   **Exchange any expert witness statements with the prosecution as soon as practicable after committal** (*CrPR r 33*)(see also p 565).

> ➤ A party introducing expert evidence must serve it on the court officer and each other party as soon as practicable and, in any event, with any application relying on that evidence (*CrPR r 33.4(1)*).

> ➤ Another party can require a copy of, or a reasonable opportunity to inspect a record of, any examination, measurement, test or experiment on which the expert's findings and opinion are based, or that were carried out in the course of reaching those findings and opinion, and anything on which any such examination, measurement, test or experiment was carried out (*CrPR r 33.4(1)*).

> ➤ A party may not introduce expert evidence if that party has not complied with the rules above, unless every other party agrees or the court gives permission (*CrPR r 33.4(2)*).

7   **Take instructions on mitigation.**

8   **Obtain disclosure of prosecution materials (see p 515) and materials unused by the prosecution** (a common law right and cf: *R v Ward* [1993] 1 WLR 619).

Format of a brief to counsel

1   **Heading:** case, title, court, relevant LSC funding certificate or fee, case number.

2   **List of enclosures**

> ➤ Eg: LSC representation order, list of previous convictions, bundle of witness statements, comments on witness statements, bail notice, indictment, custody record.

3   **Prosecution allegations**

> ➤ Direct counsel to specific allegations in the witness statements.

> ➤ Define facts which are not in dispute.

4   **Defence allegations**

> ➤ Give a brief statement of the relevant law.

> ➤ Apply the law to the circumstances of the case.

5   **Note any evidential problems** (see pp 552 et seq)

> ➤ Character: Examine whether admission of character evidence will need to be adduced (see pp 554 et seq). (Rules for when convictions are spent are in *ROA 1974*.)

> ➤ Evidence: admissible as an exception to the rule against hearsay (ie: opinion, *res gestae*, etc).

> ➤ Confessions: point out any grounds for exclusion.

> ➤ Corroboration: note where this is needed, and highlight any suitable evidence, see p 557.

> ➤ Discuss briefly the reasons for and against the defendant testifying, see pp 554 et seq. State:
>   a) why any difficulty is likely to arise, *and*
>   b) any consequences which follow.

6   **Mitigation:** give any relevant information.

7   **Request:** 'Would counsel please advise ... and attend court on ... at ...'.

J Crown Court hearings and trial

The indictment and following procedure

The indictment

➤ The prosecution is responsible for seeing that an indictment is drafted.
➤ An indictment is a statement of offences (called 'counts') with which an accused is charged.
  ◆ A 'count' is an individual charge (defined formally below).
➤ The prosecutor must serve a draft indictment on the Crown Court officer not more than 28 days (although the Crown Court can extend this even after it has expired) after (*CrPR r 14.1(1)-(2)*):
  ◆ service on the defendant and on the Crown Court officer of copies of the documents containing the evidence on which the charge or charges are based, in a case where the defendant is sent for trial, *or*
  ◆ a High Court judge gives permission to serve a draft indictment, *or*
  ◆ the Court of Appeal orders a retrial, *or*
  ◆ the committal or transfer of the defendant for trial.
➤ Unless the Crown Court otherwise directs, the court officer must sign and date the draft, which then becomes an indictment and serve a copy of the indictment on all parties (*CrPR r 14.1(3)*).
➤ An indictment is in a specified form and must contain, in a paragraph called a 'count' (*CrPR r 14.2(1)*):
  ◆ a statement of the offence, describing it in ordinary language and identifying any legislation that creates it, *and*
  ◆ particulars of the conduct making clear what the prosecutor alleges against the defendant.
➤ More than 1 incident of the offence may be included in a count if those incidents taken together amount to a course of conduct having regard to the time, place or purpose of commission (*CrPR r 14.2(2)*).
➤ **Joinder:** An indictment may contain more than 1 count if all the offences charged are founded on the same facts or form or are a part of a series of offences of the same or a similar character (*CrPR r 14.2(3)*).
➤ Counts must be numbered consecutively (*CrPR r 14.2(4)*).
➤ An indictment may contain (*CrPR r 14.2(5)*):
  ◆ any count charging substantially the same offence as one specified in the notice of the offence(s) for which the defendant was sent for trial/committed for trial or specified in the notice of transfer given by the prosecutor, *and*
  ◆ any other count based on the prosecution evidence already served which the Crown Court may try.
➤ 2 or more accused may be joined in one indictment.

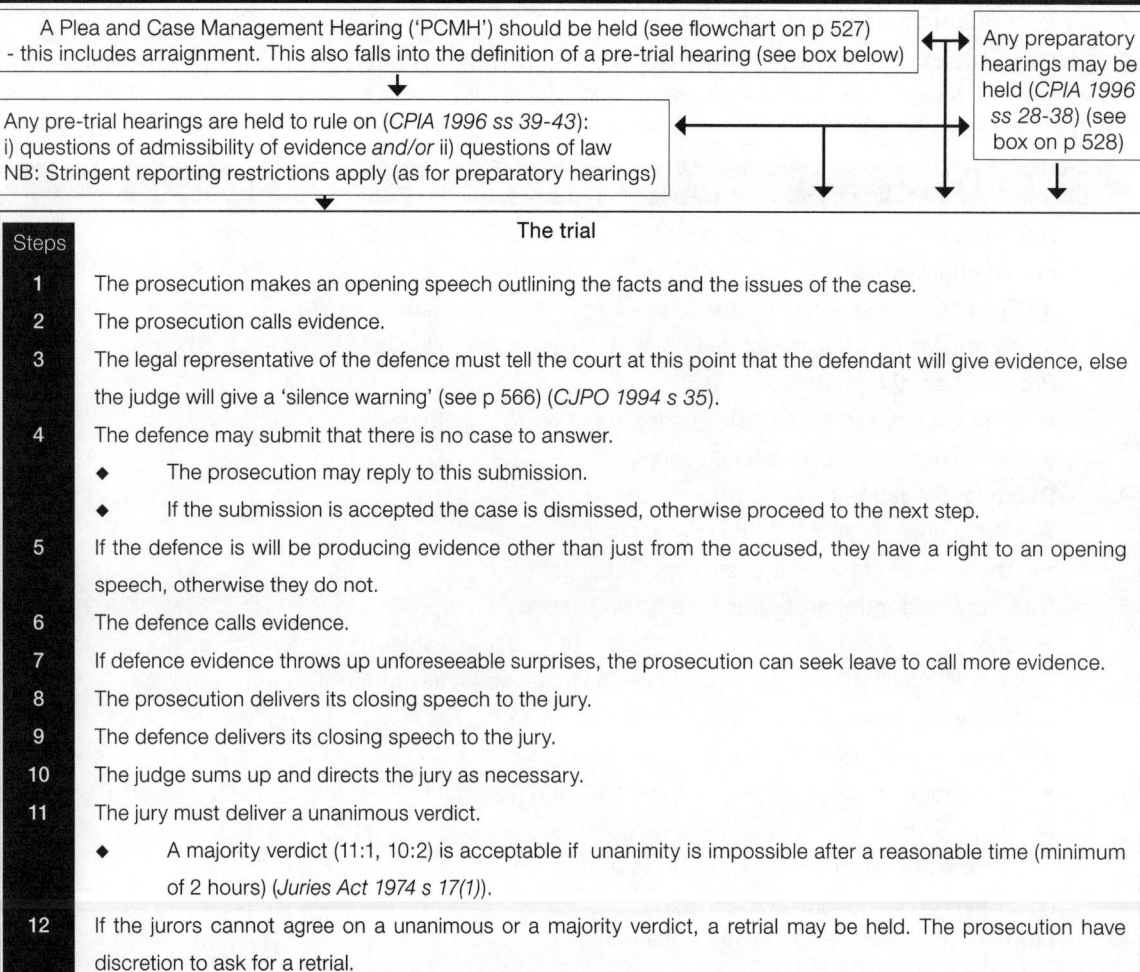

A Plea and Case Management Hearing ('PCMH') should be held (see flowchart on p 527) - this includes arraignment. This also falls into the definition of a pre-trial hearing (see box below)

Any pre-trial hearings are held to rule on (*CPIA 1996 ss 39-43*):
i) questions of admissibility of evidence *and/or* ii) questions of law
NB: Stringent reporting restrictions apply (as for preparatory hearings)

Any preparatory hearings may be held (*CPIA 1996 ss 28-38*) (see box on p 528)

The trial

Steps	
1	The prosecution makes an opening speech outlining the facts and the issues of the case.
2	The prosecution calls evidence.
3	The legal representative of the defence must tell the court at this point that the defendant will give evidence, else the judge will give a 'silence warning' (see p 566) (*CJPO 1994 s 35*).
4	The defence may submit that there is no case to answer.
	◆ The prosecution may reply to this submission.
	◆ If the submission is accepted the case is dismissed, otherwise proceed to the next step.
5	If the defence is will be producing evidence other than just from the accused, they have a right to an opening speech, otherwise they do not.
6	The defence calls evidence.
7	If defence evidence throws up unforeseeable surprises, the prosecution can seek leave to call more evidence.
8	The prosecution delivers its closing speech to the jury.
9	The defence delivers its closing speech to the jury.
10	The judge sums up and directs the jury as necessary.
11	The jury must deliver a unanimous verdict.
	◆ A majority verdict (11:1, 10:2) is acceptable if unanimity is impossible after a reasonable time (minimum of 2 hours) (*Juries Act 1974 s 17(1)*).
12	If the jurors cannot agree on a unanimous or a majority verdict, a retrial may be held. The prosecution have discretion to ask for a retrial.

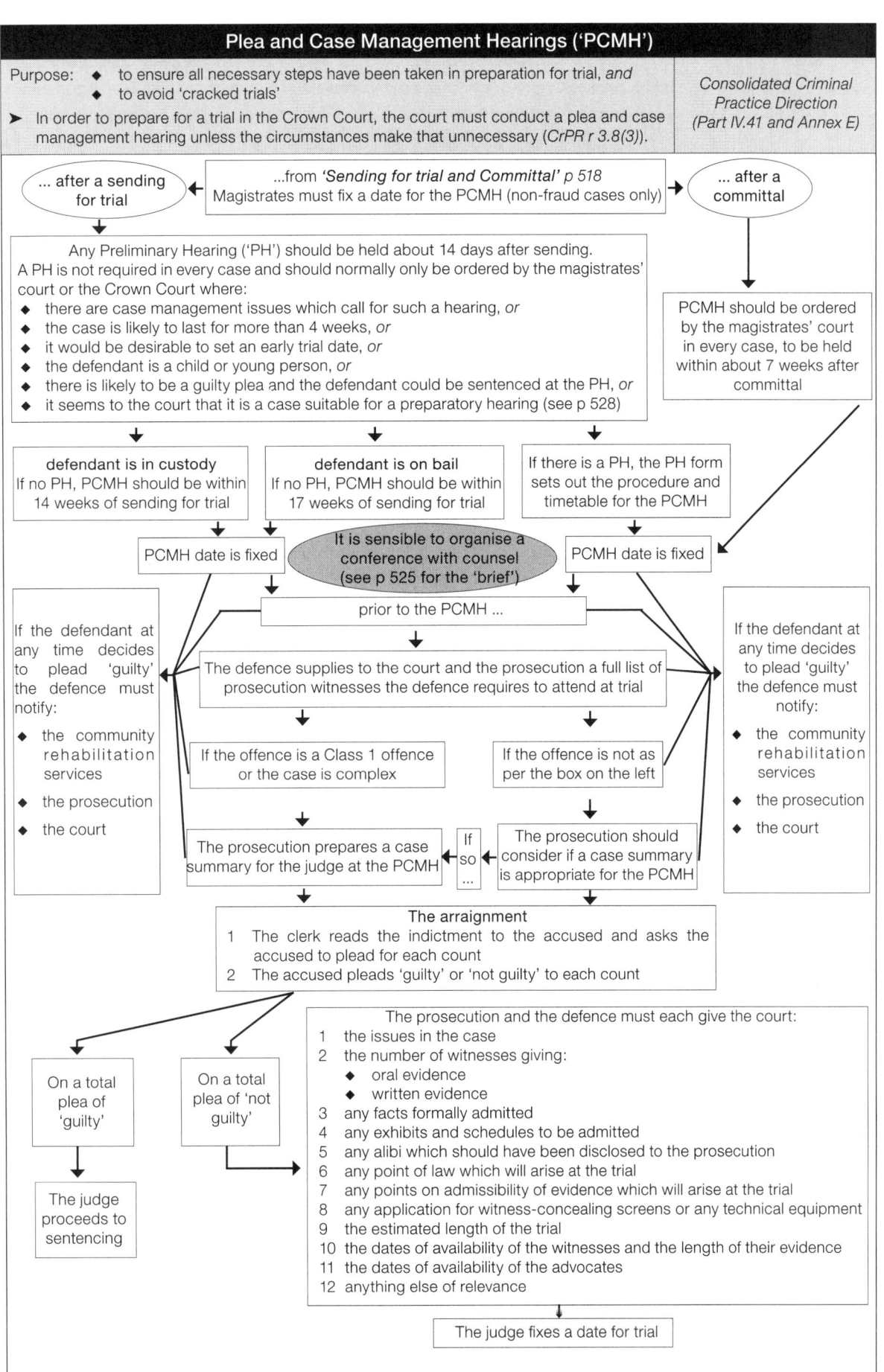

Plea and Case Management Hearings ('PCMH')

Purpose:
- to ensure all necessary steps have been taken in preparation for trial, *and*
- to avoid 'cracked trials'

➤ In order to prepare for a trial in the Crown Court, the court must conduct a plea and case management hearing unless the circumstances make that unnecessary (*CrPR r 3.8(3)*).

Consolidated Criminal Practice Direction (Part IV.41 and Annex E)

... after a sending for trial ◄ ...from *'Sending for trial and Committal'* p 518 — Magistrates must fix a date for the PCMH (non-fraud cases only) ► ... after a committal

Any Preliminary Hearing ('PH') should be held about 14 days after sending. A PH is not required in every case and should normally only be ordered by the magistrates' court or the Crown Court where:
- there are case management issues which call for such a hearing, *or*
- the case is likely to last for more than 4 weeks, *or*
- it would be desirable to set an early trial date, *or*
- the defendant is a child or young person, *or*
- there is likely to be a guilty plea and the defendant could be sentenced at the PH, *or*
- it seems to the court that it is a case suitable for a preparatory hearing (see p 528)

PCMH should be ordered by the magistrates' court in every case, to be held within about 7 weeks after committal

defendant is in custody
If no PH, PCMH should be within 14 weeks of sending for trial

defendant is on bail
If no PH, PCMH should be within 17 weeks of sending for trial

If there is a PH, the PH form sets out the procedure and timetable for the PCMH

PCMH date is fixed

It is sensible to organise a conference with counsel (see p 525 for the 'brief')

PCMH date is fixed

If the defendant at any time decides to plead 'guilty' the defence must notify:
- the community rehabilitation services
- the prosecution
- the court

prior to the PCMH ...

The defence supplies to the court and the prosecution a full list of prosecution witnesses the defence requires to attend at trial

If the defendant at any time decides to plead 'guilty' the defence must notify:
- the community rehabilitation services
- the prosecution
- the court

If the offence is a Class 1 offence or the case is complex

If the offence is not as per the box on the left

The prosecution prepares a case summary for the judge at the PCMH ◄ If so ... ◄ The prosecution should consider if a case summary is appropriate for the PCMH

The arraignment
1. The clerk reads the indictment to the accused and asks the accused to plead for each count
2. The accused pleads 'guilty' or 'not guilty' to each count

On a total plea of 'guilty'

On a total plea of 'not guilty'

The prosecution and the defence must each give the court:
1. the issues in the case
2. the number of witnesses giving:
   - oral evidence
   - written evidence
3. any facts formally admitted
4. any exhibits and schedules to be admitted
5. any alibi which should have been disclosed to the prosecution
6. any point of law which will arise at the trial
7. any points on admissibility of evidence which will arise at the trial
8. any application for witness-concealing screens or any technical equipment
9. the estimated length of the trial
10. the dates of availability of the witnesses and the length of their evidence
11. the dates of availability of the advocates
12. anything else of relevance

The judge proceeds to sentencing

The judge fixes a date for trial

Preparatory hearings (*CPIA 1996 ss 28-38, CrPR r 15*)

➤ Any time after sending for trial/committal but before a jury has been sworn, a Crown Court judge may hold a preparatory hearing, if he decides that a trial will be so complex or so long or so serious that there will be a substantial benefit for one of the following purposes (*s 29*):
  ◆ to identify the issues likely to be material to the verdict of the jury.
  ◆ to assist the jury's comprehension of such issues.
  ◆ to expedite proceedings before the jury.
  ◆ to assist the judge in the management of the trial.
  ◆ considering questions as to the severance or joinder of charges.

➤ The hearing starts with arraignment (see p 527) (unless done before, eg: at the PCMH) (*s 30*).

➤ The powers of the judge at a preparatory hearing are (*s 31*):
  ◆ to rule on the admissibility of evidence. ──────────────────→
  ◆ to rule on a question of law relating to the case. ──────────→
  ◆ to rule on any question as to the severance or joinder of charges. ──→

> There may be an appeal to the Court of Appeal (only with leave) (*s 35*). No jury may be sworn until after the appeal is heard.

  ◆ to order the prosecutor to give to the court and each accused a written statement (ie: a case statement) of:
    a) the principal facts of the prosecution case, *and/or*
    b) witnesses, *and/or*
    c) exhibits, *and/or*
    d) a proposition of law on which the prosecutor will rely, *and/or*
    e) the consequences of the above.
  ◆ to order, *but only following any order to the prosecution to give a case statement* (and the order has been carried out) the defence to give the prosecution and the court written notice of objections to the prosecution case statement.
  ◆ to order the prosecution to prepare the prosecution evidence and any explanatory material in such a form as appears to the judge to be likely to aid comprehension by a jury and to give it in that form to the court and to the accused or, if there is more than one, to each of them.
  ◆ to order the prosecution to give the court and the accused or, if there is more than one, each of them written notice of documents the truth of the contents of which ought in the prosecutor's view to be admitted and of any other matters which in his view ought to be agreed.
  ◆ to order the prosecution to change its case if there are valid objections raised after the written statement ordered above.
  ◆ to order that sample counts only will be heard by a jury and related counts will not (if in the interests of justice) (*DVCVA 2004 ss 17-21*).

➤ The judge must warn the accused of the consequences of later departing from the case outlined in the defence statement above (*s 31(8)*).
  ◆ The consequences are that at trial a jury may draw 'adverse inferences' following:
    • the judge's comment on this, *and/or*
    • other parties' comments on this (with leave).
  NB: The judge must point out that the jury must have regard to the extent of departure from the case and any justifications for such departure (*s 34*).

Reporting restrictions (*CPIA 1996 ss 37-38*)

➤ There is no reporting allowed of the preparatory hearing (or an appeal from it) until after trial unless a judge authorises it. The following details are allowed to be reported however:
  ◆ the identity of the court and the name of the judge.
  ◆ the details of the accused and witnesses.
  ◆ the details of the offence(s).
  ◆ the name of counsel and solicitors.
  ◆ the details of any adjournment.
  ◆ the details of any bail arrangements.
  ◆ the details of whether LSC funded help was granted or not.

K Sentencing powers

NB: *All sentences are subject to the statutory limits laid down for particular offences.*

I The purpose of sentencing

➤ The purposes of adult sentencing are set out in statute by *CJA 2003 s 142*:

- punishment, *and*

- crime reduction, *and*

- the reform and rehabilitation, *and*

- public protection, *and*

- reparation.

> **Exceptions:**
> - where an offender is under 18 (there are separate purposes for the aims of the youth justice system set out in *CDA 1998*)
> - where the sentence is fixed by law (eg: a mandatory life sentence imposed for murder)
> - where offences require certain custodial sentences

II General rules about increasing and decreasing custodial sentences

➤ **Culpability and harm:** In considering the seriousness of any offence, the court must consider the offender's culpability in committing the offence and any harm which the offence caused, was intended to cause or might forseeably have caused (*CJA 2003 s 143(1)*).

➤ **Previous convictions:** In considering the seriousness of any offence, the court must treat each previous conviction as an aggravating factor having regard, in particular, to the nature of the offence to which the conviction relates and its relevance to the current offence, and the time that has elapsed since the conviction (*CJA 2003 s 143(2)*).

➤ **Offence while on bail:** In considering the seriousness of any offence committed while the offender was on bail, the court must treat the fact that it was committed in those circumstances as an aggravating factor (*CJA 2003 s 143(3)*).

➤ **Reduction in sentence for early guilty plea:** A court can reduce a sentence for an early guilty plea, to encourage defendants who are guilty to save court time and save victims and witnesses unnecessary trouble. The court must take into account when the guilty plea was made and the circumstances in which it was given (*CJA 2003 s 144*).

➤ **Racial or religious element:** A racial or religious element is treated as an aggravating factor which increases the seriousness (*CJA 2003 s 145*).

➤ **Disability or sexual orientation element:** A disability or sexual orientation element to any crime is treated as an aggravating factor which increases the seriousness (*CJA 2003 s 146*).

III   Custodial sentences

A   First custodial sentence

➤ The offender cannot be given a custodial sentence for the first time if he is not legally represented during the sentencing process *unless* (*PCC(S)A 2000 s 83*):

◆ he was granted a right to representation funded by the LSC as part of the Criminal Defence Service but the right was withdrawn because of his conduct, *or*

◆ the offender has not applied for such representation despite previous opportunity to do so.

B Rules for prison sentences of less than 12 months ('Custody plus')
(CJA 2003 ss 181-182 [not yet in force])

➤ *See p 532 for details.*

C   Intermittent custody (on pilot only)
(CJA 2003 ss 183-186)

➤ If a sentence of imprisonment of 14 to 26 weeks has been imposed and the court deems it appropriate, if the offender consents, the custodial part of the sentence can be served intermittently by an 'intermittent custody order'.

➤ The custodial periods are served in short blocks of a few days at a time, while the licence period runs between the blocks (and may continue after the last custodial period).

◆ Only an unpaid work requirement, an activity requirement, a programme requirement and a prohibited activity requirement may be imposed.

➤ If an offender fails to comply with the terms of the community part of the sentence he is returned to custody and the Parole Board will decide when he is to be re-released.

D   Racially or religiously aggravated offences
(CDA 1998 ss 28-32)

➤ *CDA 1998 ss 28-32* adds a set of racially or religiously aggravated crimes where the maximum penalty is greater where the 'racial' or 'religious' factor is proved. Where it *is* proved, the maximum penalty goes up.

◆ Eg: Where it is proved, the maximum custodial penalty (we deal here with indictment convictions only):

• for grievous or actual bodily harm (*OAP 1861 s 20 and s 47*) goes from 5 to 7 years.

• for common assault goes from 6 months to 2 years.

• for criminal damage (*CrDA 1971 s 1(1)*) goes from 10 years to 14 years

• for certain public order offences (eg: *POA 1986 s 4*) goes from 6 months to 2 years.

• for certain sections of the *PHA 1997* goes up.

NB: (*CJA 2003 s 145*)(see p 529) does not apply to these crimes.

E Discretionary custodial sentences

➤ A discretionary custodial sentence may not be imposed if (*CJA 2003 s 152(1)*):

◆ a sentence is fixed by law, *or*

◆ a custodial sentence must be imposed for certain firearms offences (per *FA 1968 s 51A(2)*) or certain repeated offences (*PCC(S)A 2000 ss 110-111* and see p 532) cases of using someone to mind a weapon (*VCRA 2006 s 29*) or if a sentence must be imposed under *CJA 2003 s 225(2)* (see p 532).

➤ **The 'seriousness test' must be satisfied:** A custodial sentence must not be imposed unless the court believes that the offence, or the combination of the offence and one or more offences associated with it, was so serious that neither a fine alone nor a community sentence can be justified for the offence (*CJA 2003 s 152(2)*).

◆ Factors that can affect seriousness are:

● information about the circumstances of the offence (*CJA 2003 s 156(1)*), *and*

● other factors listed on p 529, *and*

● if the offence is one for which an extended sentence can be imposed (see below), the nature and circumstances of the offence and any other offences of which the offender has been convicted anywhere in the world, any pattern of behaviour, information about the offender, (*CJA 2003 s 229*).

➤ **Length of sentence:** the shortest term (not exceeding the permitted maximum) that in the opinion of the court is commensurate with the seriousness of the offence, or the combination of the offence and one or more offences associated with it (*CJA 2003 s 153*).

◆ Limits on length of discretionary custodial sentence:

● **Magistrates' Court:** maximum 6 months for any one offence unless an offence presents a lower maximum penalty (*PCC(S)A 2000 s 78*). [*To be replaced by: 'maximum 12 months for any one offence unless an offence presents a lower maximum penalty' (CJA 2003 s 154) [not yet in force]*.]

■ The minimum is 5 days (*MCA 1980 s 132*).

■ There is a maximum of 6 months [*changed to 65 weeks by CJA 2003 s 155 [not yet in force]*] for 2 offences triable either way (*MCA 1980 s 133(2)*).

● **Crown Court:** up to the maximum set by statute for the offence. If none is set then 2 years on indictment (*PCC(S)A 2000 s 77*) [*to be repealed and replaced*].

Extended sentences for certain violent or sexual offences (*CJA 2003 s 227, CJA 2008 s 15*)

➤ If a 'violent' or 'sexual' offence (*specified in CJA 2003 Schedule 15*) has been committed and the court is of the opinion that there is a significant risk to members of the public of serious harm occasioned by the commission by him of further specified offences (but the court is not required to impose a sentence of imprisonment of life - see p 532) (*CJA 2003 s 227, CJA 2008 s 15*), the court <u>may</u> impose an extended sentence if:

◆ at the time the offence was committed, the offender has been convicted of an offence specified in *CJA 2003 Schedule 15A, or*

◆ if the court were to impose an extended sentence of imprisonment, the term that it would specify as the appropriate custodial term would be at least 4 years.

➤ Term of imprisonment:

◆ The greater of (*CJA 2003 s 227*): ● the 'Length of Sentence' (see above), *or* ● 12 months		◆ an 'extension period' which must be added on for which the offender is subject to a licence and which is of such length as the court considers necessary for the purpose of protecting members of the public from serious harm

The extension period must not exceed:
◆ 5 years for a specified v i o l e n t o f f e n c e, *and*
◆ 8 years for a specified s e x u a l offence.
Also, the term of the whole sentence taken together must not exceed the maximum term permitted for the offence.

Time served on remand in custody is counted as time served as part of sentence unless remand was concurrent with an existing term of imprisonment or it is just in all the circumstances not to give effect to this (*CJA 2003 s 240*). (Credit may also be given for certain bail spent under electronic curfew (*CJA 2003 s 240A by CJA 2008 ss 20-22*).)

F Other mandatory rules on sentences

1   Dangerous offenders *(CJA 2003 s 225, CJA 2008 s 13)*

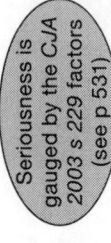

Seriousness is gauged by the CJA 2003 s 229 factors (see p 531)

➤ A court must pass a discretionary life sentence (being a new sentence of imprisonment for public protection) if the seriousness of the offence justifies it, if (*s 225(2)*):

- ◆ the offender is convicted of a specified sexual or violent offence (listed in *CJA 2003 Schedule 15*) carrying a maximum sentence of 10 years or more, *and*

- ◆ the court considers that the offender poses a significant risk of serious harm to the public, *and*

- ◆ the offence carries a maximum sentence of life imprisonment.

➤ A court may impose a sentence of imprisonment for public protection if the seriousness of the offence justifies it, if (*s 225(3)*):

Seriousness is gauged by the CJA 2003 s 229 factors (see p 531)

- ◆ the offender is convicted of a specified sexual or violent offence (listed in *CJA 2003 Schedule 15*) carrying a maximum sentence of 10 years or more, *and*

- ◆ the court considers that the offender poses a significant risk of serious harm to the public,

- ◆ the offender has been convicted certain offences specified in *CJA 2003 Schedule 15A*,

- ◆ the notional minimum term is at least 2 years.

➤ When passing sentence the court must set the relevant part of the sentence that will be served in custody for the purposes of punishment and deterrence.

- ◆ After the offender has served this relevant part then their release will be dependent upon the recommendation of the Parole Board.

➤ This sentence therefore provides for the indeterminate detention of those dangerous offenders who continue to pose a significant risk of harm to the public.

- ◆ Release provisions are set out in more detail in *CJA 2003 s 230* and *Schedule 18*.

2   *Prison sentences of less than 12 months* *(CJA 2003 s 181 [not yet in force], CJA 2008 s 20)*

➤ *In general, all prison sentences of less than 12 months must consist of a short period of custody followed by a longer period on licence, during which the offender has to comply with fixed requirements.*

➤ *The term of the sentence must be expressed in weeks, must be at least 28 weeks, must not be more than 51 weeks in respect of any one offence, and must not exceed the maximum term permitted for the offence.*

➤ *A court may specify the number of days which an offender must serve in prison and the number of days on which he is released on licence (subject to specified licence conditions called a 'custody plus order').*

- ◆ *The licence conditions are the same as the Community Order requirements (see p 537) but the requirements shaded in grey cannot be imposed as licence conditions.*

➤ *The court must specify both the 'custodial period' and the 'licence period'. During the licence period the offender is to be subject to conditions specified in the 'custody plus order'.*

- ◆ *The custodial period must be between 2 and 13 weeks.*

- ◆ *The licence period must be at least 26 weeks.*

➤ *Where a court imposes two or more terms of imprisonment in accordance to be served consecutively:*

- ◆ *the aggregate length of the terms of imprisonment must not be more than 65 weeks, and*

  - • *Take account of all custody periods but only the longest of the licence periods.*

- ◆ *the aggregate length of the custodial periods must not be more than 26 weeks.*

3   Minimum 3 years for burglary *(PCC(S)A 2000 s 111)*

➤ A convicted burglar must be sentenced to minimum 3 years for a third domestic burglary, unless particular circumstances relate to the offence/offender and would make it unjust in all the circumstances.

IV Suspended sentences (CJA 2003 ss 189-194)

A Imposition of a suspended sentence
(CJA 2003 s 189)

➤ A court which passes a sentence of imprisonment (or, for someone aged 18 to under 21, detention in a young offender institution) for at least 14 days but not more than 12 months (or in a Magistrates' Court, for at least 14 days but not more than 6 months) may suspend that sentence for between 6 months and 2 years while ordering the offender to undertake certain requirements in the community.

   ◆ The period during which the offender undertakes requirements is called 'the supervision period' and the entire length of suspension is called 'the operational period'.

➤ The custodial part of the sentence will not take effect unless the offender fails to comply with the imposed requirements or if he commits another offence within the period of suspension.

➤ The length of time the offender undertakes requirements may be less (but not more) than the entire period of suspension, but the supervision period and the operational period must each last 6 months to 2 years.

➤ The supervision period must not exceed the operational period.

➤ A suspended sentence may be combined with a fine/compensation order, but not a community sentence.

B Imposition of requirements
(CJA 2003 s 190)

➤ The requirements that can be attached are the same as in the 'Requirements' box on p 537.

   ◆ Where the court imposes a curfew requirement or an exclusion requirement, it must also impose an electronic monitoring requirement unless electronic monitoring is not available in the local area or someone else whose consent is required (eg: a landlord) withholds that consent.

C Review of a suspended sentence order
(CJA 2003 ss 191-192)

➤ The courts have a discretion to provide that a suspended sentence order be subject to periodic review at a review hearing. A review hearing is conducted by the court responsible for the order.

D Breach and revocation of a suspended sentence order
(CJA 2003 s 193 and Schedule 12)

➤ If the responsible officer thinks that the offender has failed without reasonable excuse to comply with any of the community requirements of a suspended sentence order, the officer must give him a warning.

➤ If the offender fails again to comply without reasonable excuse within 12 months of the warning, the responsible officer must cause an information to be laid and the court may issue a summons, or if the information is in writing and on oath, issue a warrant for his arrest.

➤ If it is proved that the offender has breached the order (of if an offender is convicted of an offence committed during the operational period of a suspended sentence (other than one which has already taken effect)) then the court must consider his case and the court may:

   ◆ order that the suspended sentence takes effect with its original term, or

   ◆ order that the sentence is to take effect with a lesser term, or

   ◆ amend the order by imposing more onerous community requirements, extending the supervision period or extending the operational period.

533

Suspended sentencing powers (CJA 2003 Schedule 12)

Magistrates' Court	Crown Court
➤ Can issue a summons for an offender to appear before a court (or a warrant for his arrest) if the offender has failed to comply with any community requirements of the order in cases where the suspended sentence order was made by a magistrates' court (or which was made by the Crown Court and includes a direction that any failure to comply with the community requirements of the order is to be dealt with by a magistrates court).	➤ The Crown Court can issue a summons or warrant for the offender to appear before it where:
◆ The summons will specify the court reviewing the order if the order contains provision for review.	◆ the order was made by the Crown Court, *and*
➤ If the offender does not appear in response to a summons the court can issue a warrant for his arrest.	◆ does not include a direction that any failure to comply with the community requirements of the order is to be dealt with by a magistrates' court.
➤ If an offender breaches a suspended sentence by failing to comply with a community requirement (or by committing a further offence) there is a presumption that the suspended sentence will be activated, unless the court finds that it would be unjust to do so.	➤ If the offender does not appear in response to a summons, a warrant for his arrest can be issued.
➤ If it activates the suspended sentence, the court can set a shorter term or custodial period for the offender to serve if it wishes.	
◆ If the court finds that it would be unjust to activate the suspended sentence it can keep the sentence suspended but amend the order to make the community requirements more onerous or to extend either the supervision or operational periods.	
◆ The court must state the reasons for choosing this option.	
◆ It must also take into account the extent to which the offender complied with the requirements of the order and the facts of the subsequent offence.	
➤ A magistrates' court can commit the offender to the Crown Court (including orders which were made by the Crown Court and include a direction that any failure to comply with community requirements is to be dealt with by a magistrates' court.)	
◆ If the proceedings occur in the Crown Court the determination of breach is to be made by the court and not a jury.	

➤ When the suspended sentence is activated, the court must make a custody plus order (ie: it has to set the licence conditions that will apply on the offender's release from custody at the end of custodial period of his sentence). The court may decide whether the new sentence is to take effect immediately or after any other sentence that the offender is serving (subject to the rules affecting consecutive sentences).

V   Fines and other sums imposed on conviction (CJA 2003 ss 162-165)

➤   **Crown Court:** Where a person is convicted on indictment of any offence (except an offence where the sentence is fixed by law) the court can generally impose a fine instead of or in addition to any other sentence (subject to any enactment to the contrary) (*CJA 2003 163*).

➤   Before fixing a sum the court must:

- ◆ inquire into the offender's financial circumstances (*CJA 2003 s 164(1)*), *and*

- ◆ ensure the penalty reflects the seriousness of the offence (*CJA 2003 s 164(2)*), *and*

- ◆ consider the case circumstances, including the state of an offender's finances insofar as they are known, or appear to the court (*CJA 2003 s 164(3)*).

➤   If the offender is under 18, the parents must pay the fine (*PCC(S)A 2000 s 137*).

Methods used by the Magistrates' Courts to enforce payment of fines (or other sums)

➤   The Magistrates' Court may use the following methods to enforce immediate payment of the sum. The Court:

a) may order the offender to be searched for money to meet the fine (*MCA 1980 s 80(1)*),

b) if the offence is imprisonable, may order detention at a police station until 8am next day (*MCA 1980 s 136*),

c) on conviction (or after), may make a money payment supervision order specifying terms of payment and placing the offender in someone's care (usually an officer of a local probation board) who should advise and befriend the offender with a view to inducing him to pay and avoid imprisonment. No offender's consent is needed (*MCA 1980 s 88*),

d) may issue a warrant of distress *[soon to be renamed a 'warrant of control' under TCE 2007 s 62: not yet in force]* to seize and sell the offender's goods to meet the sum (*MCA 1980 s 76*),

e) may order the offender's immediate imprisonment.

➤   If the offender fails to pay any sum imposed on conviction (eg: fines, costs or sums to be paid under compensation or confiscation orders) within the time allowed, the Magistrates' Court may issue a summons or warrant requiring the offender to appear or issue a warrant to arrest him and bring him before the court to conduct a means inquiry (*MCA 1980 s 83*). The Magistrates' Court may enforce payment by several methods (not detailed here).

- ◆ By *CA 2003 s 97* and *Schedule 5*, the court may:

    i)   make an attachment of earning order,

    ii) make an order for deductions of benefits,

    iii) make collection orders to be enforced by fines officers (*see also FCR 2006*),

    iv) order vehicles to be clamped and sold to pay fines (*see also FCR 2006*).

- ◆ In default of paying a fine, magistrates may impose an attendance centre requirement (for a person under 25) or unpaid work or a curfew requirement and can also disqualify for driving for up to 12 months (*CJA 2003 ss 300-301, CJA 2008 s 40, PCC(S)A 2000 s 60*).

- ◆ The court may order the discharge of fines by unpaid work (on pilot test in certain areas) (*DELIW(PS)O 2004*) (*CA 2003 s 97 and Schedule 6*).

VI   Community sentences (*CJA 2003 ss 147-151, 177-180*)

A   Definition

➤   A community sentence means a sentence which consists of or includes (*CJA 2003 s 147*):

   ◆   a community order (see p 537), *or*

   ◆   a youth rehabilitation order, which may impose a number of requirements (see p 543) (*CJA 2008 ss 1-8*)..

B   Imposition of a community sentence

➤   A community order is available to the courts as an option only for offences punishable with imprisonment (*CJA 2003 s 150A, CJA 2008 s 11*) [*except for 1 exception below under CJA 2003 s 151: not yet in force*].

➤   A community sentence may not be imposed if a sentence (*CJA 2003 s 150*):

   ◆   is fixed by law, *or*

   ◆   falls to be imposed for certain firearms offences (per *FA 1968 s 51A(2)*) or falls to be imposed for certain repeated offences (*PCC(S)A 2000 ss 110-111* and see p 532) or for an offence of using someone to mind a weapon (*VCRA 2006 s 29*) or under a requirement to impose a sentence of imprisonment for life or detention for life (*CJA 2003 ss 225-226* and see p 532).

➤   A court must not pass a community sentence unless it believes that the offence (or the combination of the offence and one or more offences associated with it) was serious enough to warrant one (*CJA 2003 s 148(1)*).

   ◆   Requirements forming part of the community sentence must be the most suitable ones for the offender and the restrictions on the liberty of the offender (eg: a curfew requirement) must be in line with the seriousness of the offence (*CJA 2003 s 148(2)*).

➤   *A court may pass a community sentence instead of imposing a fine, if it considers that it would be in the interests of justice to do so, even though the offence itself in issue does not warrant a community sentence - but only if the offender was 18 or over when convicted, and the offender has committed 3 or more offences since the age of 16, for each of which, he has received a fine in the past (CJA 2003 s 151 [not yet in force]).*

➤   Just because a community sentence may be passed for an offence or just because particular restrictions on liberty may be imposed by a community order/youth rehabilitation order, does not *require* a court to pass such a sentence or to impose those restrictions because of *s 148* (*CJA 2003 s 148(5)*), *CJA 2008 s 10*).

➤   If an offence is not serious enough for a community sentence, a fine, conditional discharge or absolute discharge might be appropriate.

➤   For certain orders a pre-sentence report is needed (*CJA 2003 s 156*).

C   Breach and revocation of a community sentence
(*CJA 2003 s 179 and Schedule 8*)

➤   Non-compliance penalties (following a warning) are:

   ◆   imposition of more onerous requirements, *or*

   ◆   dealing with the offender for the original offence as if the community order had not been made, *or*

   ◆   if non-compliance is wilful and persistent, custody.

➤   If the defendant re-offends, re-sentencing is possible.

➤   Magistrates can revoke an order which they imposed.

➤   The Crown Court alone may revoke the order if it imposed the original sentence.

D Community Orders

➤ The following community orders (known as 'requirements') may be imposed (*CJA 2003 s 177(1)*).

   ◆ Certain requirements are subject to restrictions (*CJA 2003 s 177(2)*).

   ◆ If the court makes a community order that includes a curfew or exclusion requirement, it must also impose an electronic monitoring requirement unless electronic monitoring is not available in the local area or if someone whose consent is required (eg: a landlord) withholds it (*CJA 2003 s 177(3)*).

➤ The court must consider compatibility of the various requirements it proposes (*CJA 2003 s 177(6)*).

➤ The court should try to avoid any order which clashes with an offender's religious beliefs or with times of education and employment (*CJA 2003 s 217*).

Requirements (*CJA 2003 ss 147-151, 177-180, 199-223*)

➤ The court may impose on the offender one or more of the following requirements:

◆ **Unpaid work requirement:**	unpaid work, eg: clearing canals, removing graffiti etc. (For between 40 and 300 hours.) (*CJA 2003 ss 199-200*).
◆ **Activity requirement:**	certain defined activity at a defined place, time, for a certain number of days, eg: receiving help with employment or group work on social problems, etc. (For maximum 60 days.) (*CJA 2003 s 201*).
◆ **Programme requirement:**	the offender must take part in an accredited programme on a certain number of days, eg: anger management course, sex offending court, substance misuse course, etc (*CJA 2003 s 202*).
◆ **Prohibited activity requirement:**	the offender must not take part in a certain activity, eg: not contacting a certain person (*CJA 2003 s 203*).
◆ **Curfew requirement:**	the offender must remain at a specified place for certain periods of time (From between 2 to 12 hours in any given day.) (*CJA 2003 s 204*).
◆ **Exclusion requirement:**	the offender must not enter a certain place or area during a period specified (Order can last maximum 2 years.) (*CJA 2003 s 205*).
◆ **Residence requirement:**	the offender must stay at a specified place for a set period (*CJA 2003 s 206*).
◆ **Mental health treatment requirement:**	...as part of a community sentence or suspended sentence, the offender undergo mental health treatment for a certain period (*CJA 2003 ss 207-208*).
◆ **Drug rehabilitation requirement:**	...as part of a community sentence or suspended sentence, the offender must undergo drug rehabilitation and testing (*CJA 2003 ss 209-210*).
◆ **Alcohol treatment requirement:**	...as part of a community sentence or suspended sentence, the offender must undergo alcohol treatment (*CJA 2003 s 211*).
◆ **Supervision requirement:**	The offender must attend appointments to promote his rehabilitation (*CJA 2003 s 213*).
◆ **Attendance centre requirement:**	For offenders under 25 only, the offender must attend an attendance centre for a specified number of hours (Maximum once a day for a maximum of 3 hours on each occasion and for an aggregate maximum of 12 to 36 hours.) (*CJA 2003 s 214*).
◆ **Electronic monitoring requirement:**	The offender must be electronically tagged (*CJA 2003 s 215*).

➤ The offender must be at least 18 for these requirements (*CJA 2003 s 177(1), CJA(8)O 2005, CJA(8)(A)O 2007* and *CJA(8)(A)O 2009*); but youth rehabilitation orders apply to under-18s (*CJA 2008 ss 1-8*).

For the meaning of items shaded in grey, see Section 2 on p 532.

VII Discharges *(PCC(S)A 2000 ss 12-15)*

➤ A court can issue a discharge if in the circumstances (the nature of the offence, the defendant's character), punishment is inexpedient.

◆ **An absolute discharge:** if the offender is morally blameless, but technically guilty.

◆ **A conditional discharge:** if the offender has a previously clean record, the offence is trivial, and the publicity and court appearance are sufficient ordeal.

• A conditional discharge is for up to 3 years only.

• If the offender commits an offence during this time, he may be re-sentenced for the original offence.

VIII General disqualification from driving

➤ If a person is convicted of any offence (except those mentioned in the point below), then the Crown Court or a Magistrates' Court may, in addition to, or instead of, dealing with him in any other way, order him to be disqualified from holding or obtaining a driving licence for such period as it thinks fit *(PCC(S)A 2000 s 146(1))*.

◆ The power to disqualify 'instead of' under *s 146(1)* does not apply to cases where a person is convicted of murder or where the sentence is imposed under *(PCC(S)A 2000 Chapter III)* (automatic life sentence for second serious offence) but the power to disqualify 'in addition to' still applies *(PCC(S)A 2000 s 146(2))*.

◆ The power is also subject to *PCC(S)A 2000 s 146(3)* ie: that disqualification under *s 146* may not be imposed unless the court has been told that the power to make such an order is exercisable by that court.

Driving disqualification and custody (CJA 2009 s 137 and Sch 16) *[not yet in force]*

➤ *Where an offender is disqualified from driving under PCC(S)A 2000 s 146 (or RTOA 1988 ss 34 and 35 - see p 539 et seq) and a custodial sentence is also imposed for the same offence, then there is an extension in the length of the period of a driving disqualification imposed (PCC(S)A 2000 s 147A by CJA 2009 s 137 and Sch 16 - and also RTOA 1988 s 35A).*

◆ *The court must determine the appropriate discretionary period of disqualification and then add on the appropriate extension period.*

• *This 'extension period' is defined in PCC(S)A 2000 s 147A(4) (and RTOA 1988 s 35A(4)) and takes account of that part of the sentence which the offender will serve in prison.*

➤ *If an offender is disqualified at the same time as he is imprisoned for another offence (or at a time when they are already in prison for another offence), the court is required to have regard to the diminished effect of disqualification as a distinct punishment and to have regard to that consideration if, and to the extent that, it is appropriate to do so (PCC(S)A 2000 s 147B and RTOA 1988 s 35B).*

IX   Motoring penalties

1   Endorsement (*RTOA 1988 ss 28, 33, 96, 97* and *Schedule 2*)

➤ Endorsement is mandatory for i) dangerous driving, ii) aggravated vehicle taking, iii) careless driving, iv) causing death by careless or inconsiderate driving (*RSA 2006 s 20*, inserting *RTA 1988 s 2B*), v) causing death by driving: unlicensed, disqualified or uninsured drivers (*RSA 2006 s 21*, inserting *RTA 1988 s 3ZB*), vi) furious driving (*RSA 2006 s 28*).

➤ Conviction for 2 (or more) offences on the same occasion leads to an endorsement for the offence with the 'higher' number of points allowed. However, the court may wish to exercise its discretion and award more than just the points for the 'higher' offence (*RTOA 1988 s 28(4)-28(6)*).

➤ When a court makes an order for obligatory disqualification for 1 offence, it may not at the same time endorse penalty points for another offence committed on the same occasion (*Martin v DPP* (2000) 164 JP 405).

2   Disqualification (*RTOA 1988 ss 28, 33, 34, 96, 97* and *Schedule 2*)

a) **Obligatory:**   for i) dangerous driving, ii) aggravated vehicle taking, iii) causing death by careless or inconsiderate driving (*RSA 2006 s 20*, inserting *RTA 1988 s 2B*), iv) causing death by driving: unlicensed, disqualified or uninsured drivers (*RSA 2006 s 21*, inserting *RTA 1988 s 3ZB*).

◆ **Period:** Where a person is convicted of an offence involving obligatory disqualification, the court must order him to be disqualified a period of not less than "12 months" (unless the court for special reasons thinks fit to order him to be disqualified for a shorter period or not to order him to be disqualified) (*RTOA 1988 s 34(1)*).

● The phrase "12 months" in the diamond bullet above, should be read as "3 years" where a person has, within 10 years of the commission of the offence, been convicted of (*RTOA 1988 s 34(3)*): causing death by careless driving when under the influence of drink or drugs (*RTA 1988 s 3A*), or driving or attempting to drive while unfit (*RTA 1988 s 4(1)*) or driving or attempting to drive with excess alcohol (*RTA 1988 s 5(1)(a)*) or failing to provide a specimen where that is an offence involving obligatory disqualification (*RTA 1988 s 7(6)*) or failing to allow a specimen to be subjected to laboratory test where that is an offence involving obligatory disqualification (*RTA 1988 s 7A(6)*).

> **Ignore any 'Extension periods' when calculating the '56 days or more' (see p 538)**

● The phrase "12 months" in the diamond bullet above, should be read as "2 years" where a person has had more than one disqualification for a fixed period of 56 days or more within 3 years immediately preceding the offence and the person has been convicted of manslaughter or causing death by dangerous driving (*RTA 1988 s 1*) or causing death by careless driving while under the influence of drink or drugs (*RTA 1988 s 3A*).

● See also the box on p 538 for details of 'extension periods'.

b) **Discretionary:** i) careless driving, ii) taking a conveyance, iii) theft of a motor vehicle, iv) furious driving (*RSA 2006 s 28*).

◆ **Period:** Where a person is convicted of an offence involving discretionary disqualification, and either there are less than 12 penalty points to be taken into account on that occasion or the offence is not one involving obligatory endorsement, the court may order him to be disqualified for such period as the court thinks fit (*RTOA 1988 s 34(2)*).

c) Under the penalty points system (*RTOA 1988 s 35*)

➤ Penalty points are dealt with first.

◆ If there are 12 or more penalty points from:

• the current conviction (ignoring any order for disqualification for committing the offence) *plus*

• points previously endorsed for offences within 3 years immediately before the commission of the present offence,

THEN disqualification is obligatory.

◆ Points prior to a previous disqualification are ignored.

➤ The court will go on to consider discretionary disqualification if the driver is not automatically disqualified by having 12 points or more but if the offender has 12 or more penalty points, the court must disqualify the offender for a minimum period (*RTOA 1988 s 35(1)*).

• **Minimum period** (*RTOA 1988 s 35(2)*): If the offender:

> Ignore any 'Extension periods' when calculating the 56 days (see p 538)

• has no previous disqualification of at least 56 days (imposed within 3 years of the commission of the offence now being sentenced), the minimum period of disqualification is 6 months.

• has one previous disqualification of at least 56 days (imposed within 3 years of the commission of the offence now being sentenced), the minimum period of disqualification is 1 year.

• has 2 or more previous disqualifications of at least 56 days (imposed within 3 years of the commission of the offence now being sentenced), the minimum period of disqualification is 2 years.

• See also the box on p 538 for details of 'extension periods'.

3 **Avoiding disqualification and endorsement**

a) Avoiding obligatory disqualification or obligatory endorsement

➤ A 'special reason' must be present ie: a mitigating circumstance (eg: a boomerang thrown across the windscreen).

➤ 'Special reasons' are connected with the commission of the offence, but are *not* personal to the offender (*Whittal v Kirby* [1947] KB 194).

➤ A 'special reason' is not anything which could constitute a defence to the charge in law.

b) Avoiding discretionary disqualification

➤ *Any* mitigating factor relevant to the offence should be used to avoid discretionary disqualification.

➤ The factor may be *either* connected with the circumstances *or* personal to the offender. (For example, an obligatory situation or loss of job is relevant here.)

c) Avoiding disqualification under the points system

➤ Disqualification is mandatory unless there are mitigating circumstances.

➤ All circumstances are relevant except ((*RTOA 1988 s 35(4)*):

i) the triviality of the offence, *or*

ii) hardship (unless exceptional), *or*

iii) circumstances taken into account to avoid or reduce disqualification under the points system during the last 3 years.

Note: i) a driver can have 7-12 points and escape disqualification.

ii) disqualification wipes a licence clean of all the old points.

iii) if 2 offences are committed simultaneously, both of which carry a point penalty, the court only adds the 'higher' of the penalties to the licence, unless it sees fit to order otherwise.

X   Example ancillary orders

1   Compensation order *(PCC(S)A 2000 ss 130-134)*

➤ The order is for the offender to pay compensation to a victim.

➤ Generally this order is *not* available for motoring offences (the victim can claim from the offender's insurers) *(PCC(S)A 2000 s 130(6))*.

➤ Magistrates' limit: £5,000 *(PCC(S)A 2000 s 131)*; Crown Court: unlimited.

➤ The court has the power to make an attachment of earnings order to ensure that the compensation is paid *(CPIA 1996 s 53)*. NB: Consent of the offender is required.

> NB: A £15 surcharge is payable by an offender on conviction which contributes to the Victims Fund *(DVCAVA 2004 s 14 inserting CJA 2003 ss 161A-161B)*

2   Forfeiture order *(PCC(S)A 2000 s 143)*

➤ Property in the offender's possession, or control, is forfeit by this order if the property is used for committing or facilitating the offence, *or* intended for use in connection with the offence, *or* held unlawfully.

3   Confiscation orders (seizure of proceeds of crime) *(PCA 2002 ss 6-91)*

➤ An order confiscates the proceeds of crime *(s 6)*.

➤ Interest is payable on unpaid orders *(s 12)*, with custody in default *(s 38)*.

➤ May be made only in the Crown Court after a conviction in the Crown Court or the magistrates' court.

◆ Where the conviction takes place in the magistrates' court, a confiscation order can only be made if the defendant is either committed to the Crown Court for sentence or committed to the Crown Court for sentence and confiscation under *s 70*).

➤ An offender who gives reasonable grounds to believe that he is living off crime must account for his assets and will have them confiscated to the extent that he is unable to account for their lawful origin.

4   Restitution order *(PCC(S)A 2000 ss 148-149)*

➤ The order is to compensate, or restore to a victim, goods stolen from him.

5   Costs order *(POA 1985 s 18)*

➤ On conviction, 'just and reasonable' costs may be awarded to the prosecution (payable by the offender).

➤ On acquittal, if the defendant is not LSC funded, the court can order his costs to be paid from central funds. This is usual unless, eg: the acquittal was on a technicality *or* the defendant brought suspicion on himself by his conduct *(POA 1985 s 16)*.

➤ On acquittal, contributions paid by a legally aided defendant may be repaid (subject to the above).

6   Committal to the Crown Court for sentence *(PCC(S)A 2000 s 3)*

➤ The offender must be aged over 18.

➤ The conviction must be for an either way offence *and* when the offence (or a combination of associated offences) is so serious that the Crown Court should, in the court's opinion, have the power to deal with the offender in any way it could deal with him if he had been convicted on indictment *(PCC(S)A 2000 s 3, CJA 2003 s 41 and Sch 3, CJA 2008 s 53 and Sch 13)*.

7   **Deferment of sentence** *(PCC(S)A 2000 s 1)*

➤ Passing a sentence may be deferred for up to 6 months.

➤ The offender must consent.

➤ The offender must comply with requirements set by the court (eg: see box on p 537) *(CJA 2003 s 278)*.

➤ If the offender is convicted during the interval of another offence, he can be sentenced for both offences. The court will have the same powers as on conviction for the original offence.

➤ The power to defer a sentence is used to assess:

   ◆ the offender's conduct after conviction, *or*

   ◆ any change in the offender's circumstances (marriage, etc).

➤ The court specifies the conduct it expects, and the sentence it will impose if this is not complied with.

XI   Summary of some youth sentences

➤ No sentence of imprisonment may be passed on an offender under 21 *(PCC(S)A 2000 s 89)*.

Some youth sentences										
Age Sentence	Under 21	20-19	18	17	16	15	14	13	12	Under 12
community sentence						see p 536				
detention and training order	half the sentence is a period of training in detention; half is supervision in the community. Imposed where a court could impose imprisonment if the offender was over 21. Orders may be for 4, 6, 8, 10, 12, 18 or 24 months. *(PCC(S)A 2000 s 100)*						only if a persistent offender			only if to protect the public from harm
reparation order				imposed to allow the offender to make reparation for the offence otherwise than by payment of compensation. Maximum work is 24 hours in aggregate. The consent of the offender is needed *(PCC(S)A 2000 s 73)*.						
detention in a young offender institution	if convicted of an offence punishable by imprisonment if he was over 21. Minimum term: 21 days. Maximum term: the maximum term for the offence *(PCC(S)A 2000 s 97)*.			*Note:* *detention in a young offender's institution is due to be abolished when CJCSA 2000 s 61 is brought into force [not yet in force]*						
detention at Her Majesty's Pleasure				if convicted of murder and was under 18 at the time the offence was committed *(PCC(S)A 2000 s 90)*.						
detention under *(PCC(S)A 2000 s 91)*				a) If the offence is punishable with minimum 14 years imprisonment *or* b) indecent assault on a woman or man			As age 14-18 and also: c) death by dangerous driving, *or* d) death by careless driving while affected by alcohol			

Youth rehabilitation orders (CJA 2008 ss 1-8)

➤ *CJA 2008 s 1* and *Schedule 1* provide for youth rehabilitation orders (YROs).

➤ This is a community sentence for offenders aged under 18.

   ◆ It combines several older community sentences into one new generic community sentence.

➤ When imposing a YRO, the court can choose from a menu of different requirements that the offender must comply with. These include:

   ◆ an activity requirement, *and*

   ◆ a supervision requirement, *and*

   ◆ if the offender is aged 16 or 17, an unpaid work requirement, *and*

   ◆ a programme requirement, *and*

   ◆ an attendance centre requirement, *and*

   ◆ a prohibited activity requirement, *and*

   ◆ a curfew requirement, *and*

   ◆ an exclusion requirement, *and*

   ◆ a residence requirement, *and*

   ◆ a local authority residence requirement, *and*

   ◆ a mental health treatment requirement, *and*

   ◆ a drug treatment requirement, *and*

   ◆ a drug testing requirement, *and*

   ◆ an intoxicating substance treatment requirement, *and*

   ◆ an education requirement.

➤ A YRO may also impose an electronic monitoring requirement (*CJA 2008 Schedule 1 para 26*).

   ◆ An electronic monitoring requirement must be imposed where a YRO imposes a curfew or exclusion requirement unless in the particular circumstances of the case, the court is satisfied it would be inappropriate to do so or it is not practicable for the certain reasons set out.

➤ *CJA 2008 s 1(3)-(4)* and *Schedule 1 paras 3-4* provide for a YRO with intensive supervision and surveillance and a YRO with fostering.

   ◆ *CJA 2008 s 1(4)* provides that a court may not impose a YRO with intensive supervision and surveillance or a YRO with fostering unless the offence is punishable with imprisonment and the court is satisfied that the offence (on its own or with others) is so serious that, but for the availability of these orders, a custodial sentence would be appropriate (or where the offender is under 12, would be appropriate if the offender had been 12).

      • For offenders under 15, the court must be satisfied that they are persistent offenders.

➤ *CJA 2008 s 1(6)* applies the restrictions which apply to other community sentences under *CJA 2003 ss 148* and *150* to the YRO, ie:

   ◆ a YRO must not be imposed on an offender unless the court considers the offence or offences serious enough to warrant it, and

   ◆ requirements forming part of the YRO must be the most suitable for the offender, and

   ◆ restrictions on liberty imposed must be commensurate with the seriousness of the offence.

➤ A YRO is not available in a case where the penalty is fixed by law, such as murder, or where there is a mandatory custodial sentence.

L   Sentencing procedure and mitigation

- I   Sentencing Guidelines
- II   Court procedure
- III Preparing a plea in mitigation
- IV   Pre-sentence report and drug test

I   Sentencing Guidelines

Sentencing Council

- ➤ The Sentencing Council prepares Sentencing Guidelines which may be general in nature or specific to an offence or category of offence and which may be about any sentencing matter (*CJA 2009 ss 118-136*).
  - ◆ The Sentencing Council consists of 14 members: 8 judicial members and 6 non-judicial members.
- ➤ Sentencing Guidelines may be general in nature or specific to an offence or category of offence (*CJA 2009 s 120*).
  - ◆ The Council *must* prepare guidelines on the reduction of sentence for a guilty plea and on the application of the totality principle.
  - ◆ The Council *may* prepare sentencing guidelines about any other sentencing matter.
  - ◆ When it draws up guidelines, the Council must have regard to current sentencing practice, the need to promote consistency in sentencing, the impact of sentencing decisions on victims of crime, the need to promote public confidence in the criminal justice system, the cost of different sentences and their effectiveness in reducing re-offending, and the Council's monitoring of the application of its guidelines.
- ➤ For offence specific guidelines, the guidelines should (*CJA 2009 s 121*):
  - ◆ if reasonably practicable, divide the offence into levels of seriousness based on the offender's culpability and/or the harm caused and any other particularly relevant factors, *and*
  - ◆ state the range of sentences appropriate for a court to impose for the offence, *and*
  - ◆ list any relevant aggravating and mitigating factors that are likely to apply to the offence and the relevant mitigating factors personal to an offender, *and*
  - ◆ include criteria and guidance on the weight to be given to an offender's previous convictions and other aggravating and mitigating circumstances where these are significant to the offence or the offender being sentenced.
- ➤ The Council may prepare guidelines for Magistrates' Courts on how to allocate cases either to a Magistrates' Court for summary trial or the Crown Court for trial on indictment (*CJA 2009 s 122*).

➤ Every court must follow any Sentencing Guidelines, unless it is satisfied that it would be contrary to the interests of justice to do so (*CJA 2009 s 125*). (The interests of justice exception qualifies the duties mentioned below.)

- ◆ Where there are offence-specific guidelines relevant to the offender's case a court must sentence within the offence range set out in the guideline. Where those guidelines specify different levels of seriousness of the offence, the court must if possible decide which category most resembles the offender's case in order to identify the sentencing starting point. The court's duty is to sentence within the range of sentences for the offence as a whole (as opposed to the range specified for the particular level).

- ◆ The duty to follow the Sentencing Guidelines is subject to various statutory provisions, eg: restrictions on imposing community sentences and imposing discretionary custodial sentences or the requirement that custodial sentences should be for the shortest term commensurate with the seriousness of an offence and the requirements for minimum sentences in certain cases. If a court imposes a sentence of a different kind or outside the range indicated in a Sentencing Council guideline, it is obliged to state its reasons for doing so (*CJA 2003 s 174(2)(a)*).

➤ The full Sentencing Guildeines are to be found at http://sentencingcouncil.judiciary.gov.uk/guidelines/guidelines-to-download.htm.

Sentencing Guidelines

Steps

1 A court will work out the offence seriousness (culpability and harm):

A. A court should identify the appropriate starting point by:

➤ ... considering which of the examples of offence activity corresponds most closely to the circumstances of the case to identify the appropriate starting point, *and*

➤ ... basing starting points on a first time offender pleading 'not guilty', *and*

➤ ... referring within the guidelines, to the page numbers indicated, where the starting point is, or range includes, a fine, community order or custodial sentence.

B. A court should consider the effect of aggravating and mitigating factors (see below).

➤ They should move up or down from the starting point to reflect aggravating or mitigating factors that affect the seriousness of the offence to reach a provisional sentence.

➤ Non-exhaustive aggravating and mitigating factors are set out; relevant factors are also identified in the individual offence guidelines.

➤ There should be no double-counting any aggravating or mitigating factors in the description of the activity used to reach the starting point.

➤ The range is the bracket into which the provisional sentence will normally fall but the court is not precluded from going outside the range where the facts justify it.

➤ Previous convictions which aggravate the seriousness of the current offence may take the provisional sentence beyond the range, especially if there are significant other aggravating factors present.

2 A court forms a preliminary view of the appropriate sentence, then considers offender mitigation.

➤ Some factors are: genuine remorse, admissions to police in interview and ready cooperation with authorities.

3 A court will consider a reduction for a guilty plea.

➤ The sliding scale reduction for a guilty plea to punitive elements of the sentence should be applied.

➤ The application of the reduction may take the sentence below the range in some cases.

4 A court will consider ancillary orders, including compensation.

5 A court will decide sentence and give reasons by:

➤ reviewing the total sentence to ensure that it is proportionate to the offending behaviour and properly balanced, *and*

➤ giving reasons for the sentence passed, including any ancillary orders, *and*

➤ stating if the sentence has been reduced to reflect a guilty plea; indicating what the sentence would otherwise have been, *and*

➤ explaining if the sentence is of a different kind or outside the range indicated in the guidelines.

Overarching principles: seriousness - list of aggravating factors

Factors indicating higher culpability:

- Offence committed whilst on bail for other offences
- Failure to respond to previous sentences
- Offence was racially or religiously aggravated
- Offence motivated by, or demonstrating, hostility to the victim based on his or her sexual orientation (or presumed sexual orientation)
- Offence motivated by, or demonstrating, hostility based on the victim's disability (or presumed disability)
- Previous conviction(s), particularly where a pattern of repeat offending is disclosed
- Planning of an offence
- An intention to commit more serious harm than actually resulted from the offence
- Offenders operating in groups or gangs
- 'Professional' offending
- Commission of the offence for financial gain (where this is not inherent in the offence itself)

- High level of profit from the offence
- An attempt to conceal or dispose of evidence
- Failure to respond to warnings or concerns expressed by others about the offender's behaviour
- Offence committed whilst on licence
- Offence motivated by hostility towards a minority group, or a member or members of it
- Deliberate targeting of vulnerable victim(s)
- Commission of an offence while under the influence of alcohol or drugs
- Use of a weapon to frighten or injure victim
- Deliberate and gratuitous violence or damage to property, over and above what is needed to carry out the offence
- Abuse of power
- Abuse of a position of trust

Factors indicating a more than usually serious degree of harm:

- Multiple victims
- An especially serious physical or psychological effect on the victim, even if unintended
- A sustained assault or repeated assaults on the same victim
- Victim is particularly vulnerable
- Location of the offence (for example, in an isolated place)
- Offence is committed against those working in the public sector or providing a service to the public

- Presence of others e.g. relatives, especially children or partner of the victim
- Additional degradation of the victim (e.g. taking photographs of a victim as part of a sexual offence)
- In property offences, high value (including sentimental value) of property to the victim, or substantial consequential loss (e.g. where the theft of equipment causes serious disruption to a victim's life or business)

Overarching principles: seriousness - list of mitigating factors

Factors indicating lower culpability:

- A greater degree of provocation than normally expected
- Mental illness or disability

- The fact that the offender played only a minor role in the offence
- Youth or age, where it affects the responsibility of the individual defendant

II   Court procedure

Magistrates' Court

➤ **The court may** (*CrPR 37.10(2)*):
- ◆ exercise its power to require:
  - a statement of the defendant's financial circumstances, *and*
  - a pre-sentence report, *and*
- ◆ (and in some circumstances must) remit the defendant to a youth court for sentence where:
  - the defendant is under 18, *and*
  - the convicting court is not itself a youth court.

➤ **The prosecutor must** (*CrPR 37.10(3)*):
- ◆ summarise the prosecution case, if the sentencing court has not heard evidence, *and*
- ◆ identify any offences to be taken into consideration in sentencing (ie: admitted by the offender), *and*
  - The offender signs a 'taking into consideration' form.
  - The offender may not be subsequently charged with these. A compensation order can be made in respect of these offences.
- ◆ provide information relevant to sentence, *and*
- ◆ where it is likely to assist the court, identify any other matter relevant to sentence, including:
  - aggravating and mitigating factors, *and*
  - the legislation applicable, *and*
  - any Sentencing Guidelines, or guideline cases.

➤ **The defendant must** (*CrPR 37.10(4)*):
- ◆ provide information relevant to sentence, including details of financial circumstances.

➤ Where the defendant pleads guilty but wants to be sentenced on a different basis to that disclosed by the prosecution case (eg: because the prosecution and defence accounts of the facts differ greatly, or to resolve the respective liability of 2 or more defendants) (*CrPR 37.10(5)*):
- ◆ the defendant must set out that basis in writing, identifying what is in dispute, *and*
- ◆ the court may invite the parties to make representations about whether the dispute is material to sentence, *and*
- ◆ if the court decides that it is a material dispute, the court will invite such further representations or evidence as it may require *and* decide the dispute.

NOTE: Any such hearing is known as a 'Newton hearing' (*R v Newton* (1983) 77 Cr App R 13).

➤ Where the court has power to order the endorsement of the defendant's driving licence, or power to order the disqualification of the defendant from holding or obtaining one (*CrPR 37.10(6)*):
- ◆ if other legislation so permits, a defendant who wants the court not to exercise that power must introduce the evidence or information on which the defendant relies, *and*
- ◆ the prosecutor may introduce evidence, *and*
- ◆ the parties may make representations about that evidence or information.

NOTE: On a driving offence when disqualification is an issue, 'special reasons' for avoiding disqualification are given by the defendant on oath.

➤ Before the court passes sentence (*CrPR 37.10(7)*):
- ◆ the court must:
  - give the defendant an opportunity to make representations and introduce evidence relevant to sentence, *and*
  - where the defendant is under 18, give the defendant's parents, guardian or other supporting adult, if present, such an opportunity as well, *and*
- ◆ the justices' legal adviser or the court must elicit any further information relevant to sentence that the court may require.

NOTE: This is known as a plea in mitigation.

➤ If the court requires more information, it may exercise its power to adjourn the hearing for not more than 3 weeks at a time, if the defendant will be in custody - else 4 weeks at a time (*CrPR 37.10(8)*).

➤ When the court has taken into account all the evidence, information and any report available, the general rule is that the court will (*CrPR 37.10(9)*):
- ◆ pass sentence there and then (taking into account the Sentencing Guidelines - see p 545), *and*
- ◆ explain the sentence, the reasons for it and its effect, in terms the defendant can understand (NB: under *CJA 2003 ss 174, 270*, the court MUST state in open court the reasons for its deciding on the sentence), *and*
- ◆ consider exercising any power it has to make a costs or other order.

➤ Despite the general rule (*CrPR 37.10(10)*):
- ◆ the court must adjourn the hearing if:
  - the case started with a summons or requisition, and the defendant is absent, *and*
  - the court considers:
    - ◾ passing a custodial sentence, *or*
    - ◾ imposing a disqualification (unless it has already adjourned the hearing to give the defendant to attend)
- ◆ the court may exercise any power it has to:
  - commit the defendant to the Crown Court for sentence (and in some cases it must do so), *or*
    - ◾ For an offence triable 'either way', the court decides if it is appropriate to commit for sentence to the Crown Court (see p 524) (*PCC(S)A 2000 s 3*).
    - ◾ This also applies if the defendant pleaded guilty before the mode of trial procedure (*PCC(S)A 2000 s 4*).
  - defer sentence for up to 6 months.

III Preparing a plea in mitigation

Preparing a plea in mitigation

Steps

1 Make a realistic assessment of the likely sentence and consult the Sentencing Guidelines.

2 For likely custodial sentences:

- Consider whether the case is so serious that only a custodial sentence will suffice.
- Consider any relevant factors such as:
  - any early admissions, particularly with evidence of real remorse,
  - any practical steps taken to address addiction,
  - any youth and immaturity,
  - any good character, especially positive good character,
  - any family responsibilities and/or physical and mental disability,
  - whether it is a first custodial sentence.

> Judges can give a defendant an advance indication of the likely sentence on a guilty plea (*R v Goodyear* [2005] EWCA Crim 888)

3 **For all types of sentence:** consider any relevant factors (*CJA 2003 s 166*) such as:

- the offender's age and history: youth or old-age may induce sympathy.
- the circumstances of the offence: provocation, stress, drug dependency.
  - **Note:** voluntary ingestion is *not* good mitigation.
- the effect of any increases in 'seriousness' or aggravating factors (see p 529 and p 531).
- subsequent behaviour:
  - **remorse**
  - **guilty plea and the time and circumstances of this plea** (*CJA 2003 s 144*).
    - i) There may be a discount on *custodial* sentences of up to a third (see the Sentencing Guidelines).
    - ii) If the defendant has no choice but to plead guilty, there is still a discount given (*R v Forbes* [2005] EWCA Crim 2069).
  - **assisting police** - eg: naming others, revealing stolen property, confessing, saving police time.
  - **reparation** - voluntary rectification of damage and motive are important.

Note: Character witnesses and letters of reference are admissible in a plea for mitigation.

IV Pre-sentence report and drug test

➤ This is compiled by an officer of a local probation board or social worker.

➤ It *must* be ordered (if the offender is aged over 18) before (*CJA 2003 s 156(3)-(4)*):
- imposing a custodial sentence *unless* the court feels it is unnecessary, *or*
- making a community sentence unless the court considers it unnecessary.

NB: There are slightly altered rules for offenders aged under 18 (*CJA 2003 s 156(5)*).

➤ It *may* be ordered before imposing any other sentence, usually when it is anticipated that the accused will plead guilty and he is aged 30 or less.

➤ *If the court is considering passing a community sentence or a suspended sentence, it may order a pre-sentence drug test to test for Class A drugs (CJA 2003 s 161, CJA 2008 Sch 4 para 78) [not yet in force]."*

➤ The pre-sentence report may be oral or in writing (but must be in writing if the offender is under 18) (*CJA 2003 s 158, CJA 2008 s 12*).

M   Appeals

A   From Magistrates' Court to Crown Court

➤ **From Magistrates' Court to Crown Court** (*MCA 1980 ss 108-110 and CrPR 63*)

♦ The defence only can appeal against conviction or sentence.

♦ **Conviction:**

- if the offender pleaded guilty, there is only a right to appeal against a conviction if the plea was equivocal (ie: a non-genuine plea of guilty) (*MCA 1980 s 108*).

- the Crown Court can remit an equivocal plea to the Magistrates' Court with a direction to enter a plea of 'not guilty'.

♦ **Sentence:** may be heavier or lighter, provided the magistrates would be empowered to impose it.

♦ **Procedure:**

Steps	
1	An appellant must serve an appeal notice on the Magistrates' Court officer and every other party not more than 21 days after (*CrPR r 63*): ♦ sentence or the date sentence is deferred, whichever is earlier, if the appeal is against conviction or against a finding of guilt, *or* ♦ sentence, if the appeal is against sentence, *or* ♦ the order or failure to make an order about which the appellant wants to appeal, in any other case. ♦ The Crown Court can grant leave to appeal after this.
2	The appeal is heard by a Crown Court judge or a recorder sitting with 2 to 4 magistrates. ♦ If the appeal is against conviction, there is a rehearing following exactly the same process as for a summary trial (*SCA 1981 s 79(3)*). ♦ If the appeal is against sentencing, the prosecution merely outlines the case facts, and the defence makes a plea in mitigation.
3	The court can confirm, reverse or vary the magistrates' decision. It can also remit the matter (with its opinion) to the Magistrates' Court, *or* it may make any order it thinks just, exercising any powers the magistrates might have used (eg: concerning costs and compensation) (*SCA 1981 s 48*).

B   From Magistrates' Court to Divisional Court

➤ **From Magistrates' Court to Divisional Court** (the QBD of the High Court) by way of case stated (*CrPR r 64*):

♦ **Grounds:** the magistrates' decision is wrong in law, or exceeds their authority (*MCA 1980 s 111*).

♦ There is a hearing of legal argument (no evidence is called).

♦ The High Court may reverse, affirm, or amend the decision. It can also remit the matter (with its opinion) to the Magistrates' Court or the Crown Court, or it may make any order it thinks fit, exercising any powers the magistrates might have used (eg: concerning costs and compensation) (*SCA 1981 s 28A*). The High Court may also send the case back for amendment.

C From Crown Court to the Court of Appeal

➤ **From Crown Court to the Court of Appeal**

- Against conviction or sentence (*CAA 1968 ss 1, 2, 9, 11, CAA 1995* and *CrPR r 68*).

- On a question of law or fact, leave is required.

- The prosecution cannot appeal against acquittal (except in limited circumstances if new and compelling evidence and in the interests of justice) or sentence.

- The Attorney General may, with leave of the Court of Appeal, refer lenient Crown Court sentences for certain types of case to the Court of Appeal for review. The Court of Appeal passes the appropriate sentence in accordance with the Crown Court's powers (*CJA 1988 ss 33-36* and *CrPR r 70*).

- If the defendant is acquitted in the Crown Court, the prosecution can appeal on a point of law (*CJA 1972 s 36* and *CrPR r 70*). The defendant stays acquitted, but the Court of Appeal rules on the point of law.

A summary table of appeals to higher courts		
Who appeals	**Reason for appeal**	**Court where the appeal is heard**
Appeal from the Magistrates' Court (*MCA 1980 s 108*)		
Defence only	Conviction	Crown Court appeal hearing
	Excessive sentence	
Defence *or* Prosecution	Ultra vires	Queen's Bench Division of the High Court for judicial review
Prosecution only	Lenient sentence	No right of appeal
	Acquittal	
Appeal from the Crown Court (*CAA 1968, CAA 1995*)		
Defence only	Excessive sentence	Court of Appeal
	Conviction unsafe (ie: law or fact)	Court of Appeal, with leave (full court may instruct CCRC (below) to investigate (*CJA 2003 s 313*))
Defence *or* Prosecution	Ultra vires	No provision for judicial review in the High Court
Prosecution only	Lenient sentence	Attorney General can refer the case to the Court of Appeal (Note: in the Magistrates' Court there is no such right) (*CJA 1988 Part IV ss 35-36*)
	Acquittal	Court of Appeal. Limited right of appeal for certain specified offences only under limited circumstances, if new and compelling evidence and it is in the interests of justice to allow the appeal. The DPP must consent to such an appeal
	Question of law following acquittal	Court of Appeal. The defendant *stays* acquitted, but court rules on the point of law anyway

➤ It should also be noted that the Magistrates' Court has power to hear 'appeals' from itself under certain circumstances (*MCA 1980 s 142 (as amended by ss 26-28 CAA 1995)*). However, this topic is not dealt with in this chapter.

➤ The Criminal Cases Review Commission ('CCRC') has powers to refer certain types of cases to appeal (*CAA 1995, Part II*).

N   Disclosure

References are to CPIA 1996.

➤ *CPIA 1996 ss 1-21* contains a procedure for advance disclosure of evidence by both sides.

◆ Common law rules applying to the prosecution are disapplied (see box below).

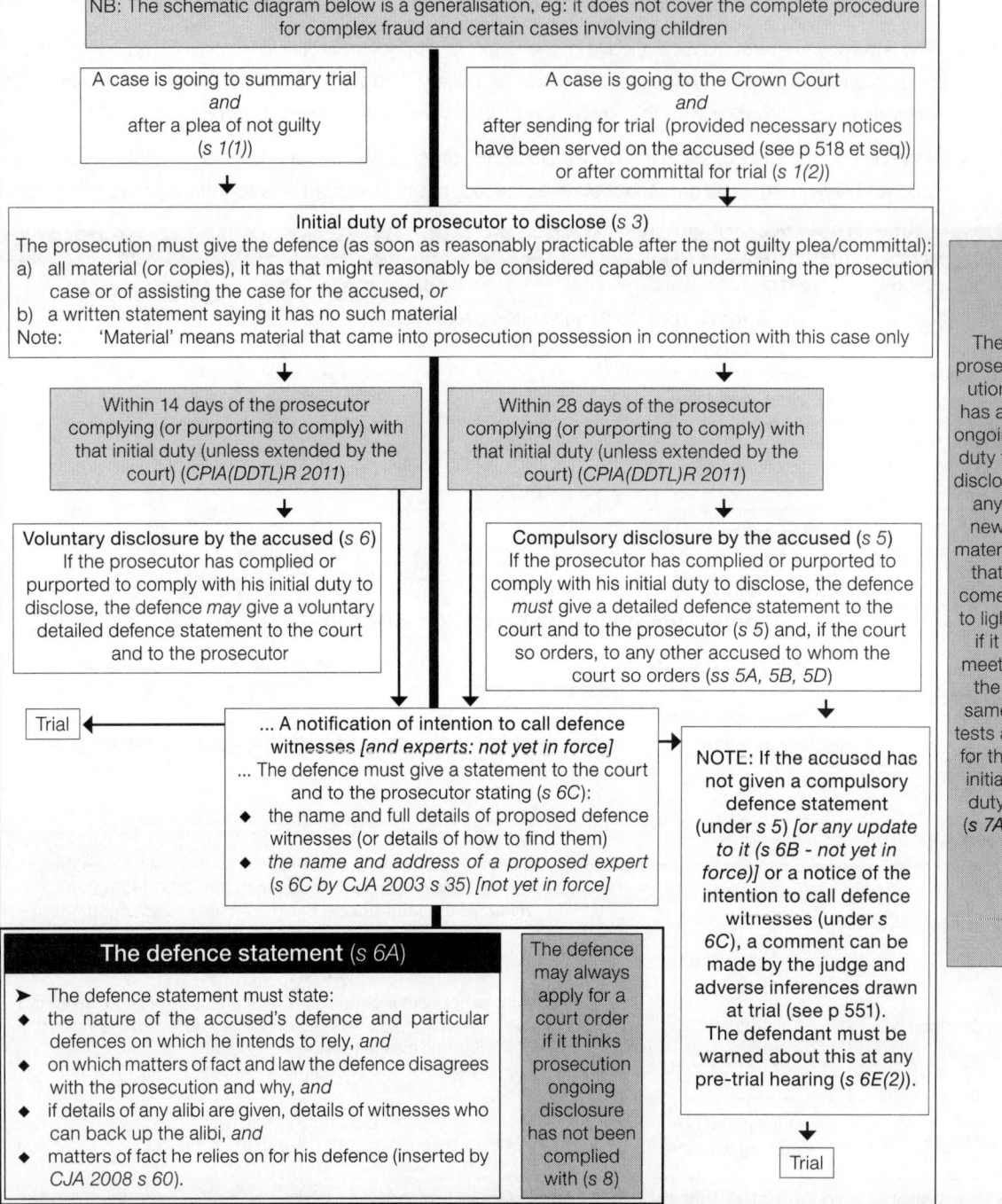

NB: The schematic diagram below is a generalisation, eg: it does not cover the complete procedure for complex fraud and certain cases involving children

A case is going to summary trial
and
after a plea of not guilty
(s 1(1))

A case is going to the Crown Court
and
after sending for trial (provided necessary notices have been served on the accused (see p 518 et seq)) or after committal for trial *(s 1(2))*

Initial duty of prosecutor to disclose *(s 3)*
The prosecution must give the defence (as soon as reasonably practicable after the not guilty plea/committal):
a) all material (or copies), it has that might reasonably be considered capable of undermining the prosecution case or of assisting the case for the accused, *or*
b) a written statement saying it has no such material
Note: 'Material' means material that came into prosecution possession in connection with this case only

Within 14 days of the prosecutor complying (or purporting to comply) with that initial duty (unless extended by the court) *(CPIA(DDTL)R 2011)*

Within 28 days of the prosecutor complying (or purporting to comply) with that initial duty (unless extended by the court) *(CPIA(DDTL)R 2011)*

Voluntary disclosure by the accused *(s 6)*
If the prosecutor has complied or purported to comply with his initial duty to disclose, the defence *may* give a voluntary detailed defence statement to the court and to the prosecutor

Compulsory disclosure by the accused *(s 5)*
If the prosecutor has complied or purported to comply with his initial duty to disclose, the defence *must* give a detailed defence statement to the court and to the prosecutor *(s 5)* and, if the court so orders, to any other accused to whom the court so orders *(ss 5A, 5B, 5D)*

Trial ←

... A notification of intention to call defence witnesses *[and experts: not yet in force]*
... The defence must give a statement to the court and to the prosecutor stating *(s 6C)*:
◆ the name and full details of proposed defence witnesses (or details of how to find them)
◆ *the name and address of a proposed expert (s 6C by CJA 2003 s 35) [not yet in force]*

NOTE: If the accused has not given a compulsory defence statement (under *s 5*) *[or any update to it (s 6B - not yet in force)]* or a notice of the intention to call defence witnesses (under *s 6C*), a comment can be made by the judge and adverse inferences drawn at trial (see p 551). The defendant must be warned about this at any pre-trial hearing *(s 6E(2))*.

Trial

The defence statement *(s 6A)*

➤ The defence statement must state:
◆ the nature of the accused's defence and particular defences on which he intends to rely, *and*
◆ on which matters of fact and law the defence disagrees with the prosecution and why, *and*
◆ if details of any alibi are given, details of witnesses who can back up the alibi, *and*
◆ matters of fact he relies on for his defence (inserted by CJA 2008 s 60).

The defence may always apply for a court order if it thinks prosecution ongoing disclosure has not been complied with *(s 8)*

The prosecution has an ongoing duty to disclose any new material that comes to light if it meets the same tests as for the initial duty *(s 7A)*

Changes to common law rules? *(s 21)*

➤ The common law rules of disclosure continue to apply in the period between accusation (charge or summons) and a plea of not guilty/committal: *R v DPP ex parte Lee* [1999] 2 All ER 737.

Problems with ...

... the defence statement, notice of witnesses and trial

1. If the defence statement (under *s 5* compulsory disclosure) (*s 11(2)*): ◆ is not given (under *s 5* disclosure), *or*	**OR** **2. If the defence statement (under *s 6* voluntary disclosure) (*s 11(3)*):** **OR**	**3. If the defence gives a witness notice out of time or later calls a witness at trial (other than himself) not adequately identified in the witness notice (*s 11(4)*):**

↓

- is out of time (according to the periods laid down by rules made under *s 12*), *or*
- does not give an updated defence statement, if relevant, or gives it out of time, *or*
- contains inconsistent defences, *or*
- is different from a defence later put forward at trial, *or*
- relies on a matter (or any particular of any matter of fact) in breach of *s 6A* (see p 550) he was meant to put into the defence statement ('****')
- does not contain alibi details and details of those who will support that alibi, but such evidence is later used at trial

↓

At trial (*s 11*):
- the court can comment on this
- any other party can comment on this (without leave. However, if *** (above) applies and it is not a point of law or a point of authority, leave is needed. Also, if 3 (above) applies, leave is also needed.)

Note: it must have regard to the degree of any difference between the defence and the defence statement and the justification for any difference

↓

The jury and the court:
may draw adverse inferences as to guilt (but cannot convict solely on this)

... time limits for disclosure

➤ All prosecution and defence disclosure must occur within time limits set down by the Secretary of State (under *s 12*).

- These time limits may be set as the Secretary of State sees fit (eg: the 14/28 day rules for certain disclosure, see previous page).
- There are various transitional provisions that say that if no regulations are made, the various stages of disclosure must occur 'as soon as practicable' after certain events listed (eg: prosecution disclosure is as soon as reasonably practicable after certain events such as a plea of 'not guilty' or committal for trial) (*s 13*).

➤ If the prosecutor does not comply with his time limits (*s 10*), then ...

- ... unless the accused would be denied a fair trial as a result ...
- ... this is not on its own an abuse of process leading to a stay of proceedings.

... confidentiality

➤ *ss 17-18* provide that any material disclosed by the prosecutor is confidential.

- Various new criminal offences are set out for breach of that confidentiality.

Prosecutor will not disclose material 'in the public interest' (*ss 14-16*)

➤ The prosecutor as a general rule must disclose all material.

➤ However, the prosecutor may apply to the court for non-disclosure if it would not be 'in the public interest'. The court may grant such an application.

- **In summary trial**, as long as it is before the verdict, the accused can apply at any time for a review of non-disclosure.
- **In other cases**, as long as it is before the verdict:
  - the court has a duty to keep any non-disclosure under review, *and*
  - notwithstanding the court's duty, the accused can apply at any time for a court review.

➤ If:
- a person claiming to have an interest in the material applies for a review of the non-disclosure, *and*
- he shows that he was involved in bringing the material to the attention of the prosecutor,
... *then* he must be heard before any order for non-disclosure is made.

➤ A third party who has material which has previously been inspected by the prosecution or which is in the possession of the prosecution, may be required to disclose this to the defence.

- This will be subject to a hearing if necessary on:
  - public interest, *or*
  - confidentiality.

O   Evidence at trial

I	Evidential proof	V	Admissibility of evidence (all categories except hearsay)
II	Implications for 'character'		
III	Evidential safeguards	VI	Admissibility of evidence (hearsay)
IV	Witness's competence and compellability	VII	Inferences from silence at trial

I   Evidential proof

A   Burden of proof

➤ **The prosecution** must prove guilt 'beyond reasonable doubt'.

➤ **The defence** has an 'evidential burden' (ie: it must introduce necessary evidence before the court).

◆ Occasionally, it may be necessary to establish a defence on the balance of probabilities, such as:

a) insane automatism (*Bratty v AG for Northern Ireland* [1963] AC 386).

b) insanity *(Sodeman v The King* [1936] 2 All ER 1138).

c) diminished responsibility (*Homicide Act 1957 s 2*).

B   Proof by evidence

➤ **Everything must be proved *except*:**

◆ facts which are formally admitted by the defence and the prosecution (*CJA 1967 s 10*).

◆ where judicial notice is taken of a point of fact (eg: dogs bark, they do not quack).

◆ where judicial notice is taken of a point of law (eg: traffic must stop at a red light).

◆ circumstantial evidence (rebuttable): where there is an *inference* of fact drawn from *proven* facts.

● Examples include:

i) doctrine of recent possession: someone possessing goods illegally came by them illicitly.

ii) doctrine of continuance: a given state of affairs continues (*R v Balloz* (1908) 1 Cr App R 258).

C   Types of evidence

➤ **Oral evidence:** this carries most weight.

➤ **Real evidence:** this consists of objects (eg: weapons).

➤ **Documentary evidence:** this includes recordings and photographs.

◆ A document must be authenticated by demonstrating in what circumstances it was created.

◆ A copy is admissible (*CJA 2003 s 133*).

➤ **Written statements and depositions (see p 524):** any that were used at committal may be used at trial, as long as they have been signed by a magistrate.

➤ **Video recording evidence:** allowed in limited circumstances *[to be widened when CJA 2003 s 137-138 is brought into force [not yet in force]]*.

> A person giving oral evidence may refresh his memory from a document made or verified by him at an earlier time if (*CJA 2003 s 139*):
>
> ◆ he states in his oral evidence that the document records his recollection of the matter at that earlier time, *and*
>
> ◆ his recollection of the matter is likely to have been significantly better at that time than it is at the time of his oral evidence.

D   Finding the facts

Sequence for examination of witnesses

Steps	
1	Examination-in-chief
2	Cross-examination
3	Re-examination

1   Examination-in-chief

➤ This is where a side calls its own witness and asks questions of that witness.

➤ A witness may refresh his memory from a contemporaneous document.

➤ No leading questions are permitted, except to obtain a rebuttal or denial of the opponent's case.

➤ Even if a witness gives unfavourable answers, the side which called the witness cannot contradict or discredit the witness *unless*:

♦ the witness is declared hostile. To achieve this, an application must be made to the judge (*CPA 1865 s 3*)). If this is done:

● the party calling a witness may cross-examine him and ask leading questions, *and*

● the witness can be confronted with statements made previously by him which are inconsistent with his testimony (see p 564).

2   Cross-examination

➤ After a side has called its witness for examination-in-chief, the other side may cross-examine the witness.

➤ The cross-examiner will seek to:

a) put his view of the case to a witness, *and*

b) extract useful information from the witness, *and*

c) challenge a witness's credibility.

♦ The questions must be relevant to the evidence about the offence before the court.

♦ A witness's answer is *final* unless the witness:

i) is biased (*R v Shaw* (1888) 16 Cox 503), *or*

ii) has given evidence which is inconsistent with a previous statement (*CPA 1865 ss 4-5*) (see also p 564), *or*

iii) has a relevant conviction (*CPA 1865 s 6*), *or*

iv) has a reputation for untruthfulness (*Toohey v Metropolitan Police Comm.* [1965] AC 595).

3   Re-examination

➤ There may now be a re-examination by the other side after the cross-examination on matters brought up during the cross-examination.

➤ This may be done in an attempt to undo any damage from the cross-examination.

II Implications for 'character'

References in this section are to CJA 2003

➤ All common law rules governing the admissibility of evidence of bad character in criminal proceedings have been abolished (*s 99*). (This is subject to *s 118* which preserves the common law rule that a person's reputation is admissible to prove his bad character.).

Meaning of 'bad character' (ss 98, 112)

➤ Evidence of a person's 'bad character' means **evidence of, or of a disposition towards, misconduct** on his part, other than evidence which:

a) has to do with the alleged facts of the offence with which the defendant is charged, *or*

b) is evidence of misconduct in connection with the investigation or prosecution of that offence.

◆ 'Misconduct' means the commission of an offence or other reprehensible behaviour.

➤ Evidence of a person's 'bad character' therefore includes evidence of previous convictions (cf. *R v Hanson, R v Gilmore and R v Pickstone* [2005] 1 WLR 3169), evidence on charges being tried concurrently, evidence relating to offences for which a person has been charged (but the charge was not prosecuted or acquitted), evidence that a person is racist etc.

➤ The Crown is able to lead at trial evidence of the defendant's bad character if the defendant has passed through one of the '7 gateways' (and the additional statutory requirements are met (*s 101*)):

a) all parties to the proceedings agree to the evidence being admissible, *or*

b) the evidence is adduced by the defendant himself or is given in answer to a question asked by him in cross-examination and intended to elicit it, *or*

c) it is important explanatory evidence, *or*

d) it is relevant to an important matter in issue between the defendant and the prosecution, *or*

e) it has substantial probative value in relation to an important matter in issue between the defendant a co-defendant, *or*

f) it is evidence to correct a false impression given by the defendant, *or*

g) the defendant has made an attack on another person's character.

> ◆ The court must not admit evidence on these 2 items if, on an application by the defendant to exclude it, it appears to the court that the admission of the evidence would have such an adverse effect on the fairness of the proceedings that the court ought not to admit it.
> ● The court must have regard, in particular, to the length of time between the matters to which that evidence relates and the matters which form the subject of the offence charged.

➤ The court must either direct the jury to acquit (or if it considers that there ought to be a retrial, discharge the jury) if (*s 107*):

◆ evidence of his bad character has been admitted under grounds c to g above, *and*

◆ the court is satisfied at any time after the close of the case for the prosecution that:

● the evidence is contaminated, *and*

● the contamination is such that, considering the importance of the evidence to the case against the defendant, his conviction of the offence would be unsafe.

➤ Offences committed under the age of 14 are only admissible if the offence for which the defendant is now being tried (over the age of 21) and the offence for which the defendant was convicted under the age of 14 are both triable only on indictment and the court is satisfied that the interests of justice require it to be admissible (*s 108*).

Ground	Phrase	Meaning
		Meaning of phrases used in grounds a to g above (*ss 102-106*)
c	Evidence is 'important explanatory evidence' if:	◆ without it, the court or jury would find it impossible or difficult properly to understand other evidence in the case, *and* ◆ its value for understanding the case as a whole is substantial.

d	'Matters in issue between the defendant and the prosecution' include:	◆ the question whether the defendant has a propensity to commit offences of the kind with which he is charged, except where his having such a propensity makes it no more likely that he is guilty of the offence. This includes evidence of previous convictions.
		  ● This can be established by evidence that he has been convicted of an offence of the same description as the one with which he is charged, or an offence of the same category as the one with which he is charged.
		    ■ This does not apply in the case of a particular defendant if the court is satisfied, by reason of the length of time since the conviction or for any other reason, that it would be unjust for it to apply in his case.
		◆ the question whether the defendant has a propensity to be untruthful, except where it is not suggested that the defendant's case is untruthful in any respect.
		NB: Only prosecution evidence is admissible.

e	'Matter in issue between the defendant and a co-defendant'	➤ Evidence which is relevant to the question whether the defendant has a propensity to be untruthful is admissible only if the nature or conduct of his defence is such as to undermine the co-defendant's defence.
		➤ Evidence is only admissible if:
		  ◆ it is to be (or has been) adduced by the co-defendant, *or*
		  ◆ a witness is invited to give (or has given) it in cross-examination by the co-defendant.

f	'Evidence to correct a false impression'	➤ The defendant gives a false impression if he is responsible for the making of an express or implied assertion which is apt to give the court or jury a false or misleading impression about the defendant.
		  ◆ A defendant is treated as being responsible for the making of an assertion if:
		    ● the assertion is made by the defendant in the proceedings (whether or not in evidence given by him), *or*
		    ● evidence of the assertion is given and the assertion was made by the defendant:
		      ■ on being questioned under caution before charge about the offence, *or*
		      ■ on being charged with the offence /informed he might be prosecuted for it, *or*
		    ● the assertion is made by a witness called by the defendant, *or*
		    ● the assertion is made by any witness in cross-examination in response to a question asked by the defendant that is intended to elicit it, or is likely to do so, *or*
		    ● the assertion was made by any person out of court, and the defendant adduces evidence of it in the proceedings.
		  ◆ A defendant who would otherwise be treated as responsible for the making of an assertion is not so treated if, or to the extent that, he withdraws it.
		  ◆ Where it appears to the court that a defendant, by his conduct (including appearance or dress), seeks to give an impression about himself that is false or misleading, the court may if it appears just to do so treat the defendant as being responsible for the making of an assertion which is apt to give that impression.
		NB: Only prosecution evidence is admissible.

g	'Attack on another person's character'	➤ A defendant does this if:
		  ◆ he adduces evidence attacking the other person's character,
		    ● ie: that he has committed an offence (whether a different offence from the one with which the defendant is charged or the same one), or has behaved, or is disposed to behave, in a reprehensible way.
		  ◆ he asks questions in cross-examination that are intended to elicit such evidence, or are likely to do so, *or*
		  ◆ evidence is given of an imputation about the other person made by the defendant:
		    ● on being questioned under caution, before charge, about the offence with which he is charged, *or*
		    ● on being charged with the offence or officially informed that he might be prosecuted for it.
		NB: Only prosecution evidence is admissible.

General rules about use of 'bad character' evidence

➤ A court, when considering the relevance or probative value of bad character evidence, must assume that the evidence is true (*s 109*).

 ◆ BUT when the evidence is so unreliable that no reasonable jury could believe that it was true, the judge does not have to assume the evidence is true.

➤ A court must give reasons for its rulings under these provisions (*s 110*).

 ◆ These must be given in open court and, in the magistrates' courts, entered into the register of proceedings, ensuring that a record is kept.

 ◆ This applies to rulings on whether an item to evidence is evidence of bad character, rulings on questions of admissibility and exclusion and any decision to withdraw a case from the jury.

➤ Bad character evidence that is admissible in relation to one charge in the proceedings is not automatically admissible in relation to another charge in the same proceedings, but must instead meet the provisions of this part of *CJA 2003* to be admissible in respect of that charge (*s 112(2)*).

➤ Nothing here affects the exclusion of evidence by *CPA 1865 s 3* (impeaching the credit of own witness by general evidence of bad character: hostile witness) (*s 112(3)*), see p 553.

Non-defendant's 'bad character' (*s 100*)

➤ Evidence of the bad character of a person other than the defendant is admissible if:

 ◆ it is important explanatory evidence, *or*

  • This means that: a) without it, the court or jury would find it impossible or difficult properly to understand other evidence in the case, and b) its value for understanding the case as a whole is substantial.

 ◆ it has substantial probative value in relation to a matter which is a matter in issue in the proceedings and is of substantial importance in the context of the case as a whole, *or*

  • In assessing the probative value the court must have regard to the following factors (and to any others it considers relevant):

   ▪ the nature and number of the events, or other things, to which the evidence relates,

   ▪ when those events or things are alleged to have happened or existed,

   ▪ the nature and extent of the similarities and the dissimilarities between each of the alleged instances of misconduct where: the evidence is evidence of a person's misconduct, and it is suggested that the evidence has probative value by reason of similarity between that misconduct and other alleged misconduct,

   ▪ the extent to which the evidence shows or tends to show that the same person was responsible each time, where:

    i) the evidence is evidence of a person's misconduct, *and*

    ii) it is suggested that that person is also responsible for the misconduct charged, *and*

    iii) the identity of the person responsible for the misconduct charged is disputed.

 ◆ all parties to the proceedings agree to the evidence being admissible.

➤ **Leave of the court is needed except where all parties agree.**

III   Evidential safeguards

1   Corroboration

➤ At common law, one witness is sufficient in all cases.

➤ By statute, corroboration (ie: independent supporting evidence) is required to convict a defendant of perjury (*Perjury Act 1911 s 13*) and speeding (except if the evidence is from a speed camera). The judge must tell the jury this.

➤ In other cases, where it is felt that further proof might be needed to support certain evidence, it is within the discretion of the judge to give the jury a corroboration warning, ie: the jury should be warned that further proof is desirable.

➤ Contents of a corroboration warning:

- ◆ A judge should point out to the jury why evidence is suspect, or identify corroborative evidence and non-corroborative evidence, as a warning that there is a danger in relying on the evidence.

- ◆ Magistrates warn themselves (!) - the defence can remind them in its closing speech.

When is a warning necessary?		
When corroboration itself is essential	When a corroboration warning is mandatory	When a corroboration warning is desirable
For charges of: ◆ treason ◆ perjury ◆ speeding	There *used to be* a mandatory warning for the following 2 instances, but this has now been abolished by *CJPO 1994 ss 32-33*. However, a court may still give such a warning even though this is undesirable as it is contrary to the intention of the *CJPO 1994* (*R v Makanjuola*; *R v Easton*, [1995] 2 Cr App R 469) ◆ An accomplice gives evidence ◆ A victim of an alleged sexual offence gives evidence	◆ A prosecution witness has an interest in giving false evidence (eg: to preserve his own reputation or he bears a grudge) (*R v Cheema* [1994] 1 WLR 147) ◆ A defendant tries to incriminate a co-defendant ◆ A witness is shown to be unreliable (eg: a mental patient)

2   Disputed identification (Turnbull guidelines) (*R v Turnbull [1977] QB 224*)

➤ In a case where disputed identification of the defendant is the sole or a substantial issue, there is a danger of wrongful conviction unless the following procedure is complied with:

Steps

1 Evidence of identification is admissible if:
- ◆ the evidence is visual *and*
- ◆ on at least 2 occasions, the defendant was purported to be seen (eg: at the crime and at an identification parade).

2 The judge or magistrates must consider the soundness of the evidence by contemplating the following 6 factors:

1	the length of observation	4	conditions
2	whether the defendant was already known to the witness	5	distance
3	how close the witness's description is to the police description	6	lighting

3 If the identifying evidence is poor, then the judge or magistrates must order an acquittal.

4 If the evidence is sound, the judge gives the jury a **Turnbull warning**. He must warn the jury (or magistrates must warn themselves!):
- ◆ of the dangers of relying on identification evidence, *and*
- ◆ to consider factors 1 to 6 above in evaluating the evidence.

IV   Witness's competence and compellability

Competent (meaning)	Compellable (meaning)
A 'competent' witness can lawfully give evidence	A 'compellable' witness can be required to testify

Unsworn evidence

➤ The following witnesses may not give sworn evidence (*YJCEA 1999 s 55*):

♦ someone who has not yet reached 14 years old, *or*

♦ someone who has not a sufficient appreciation of the solemnity of the occasion *and* the responsibility to tell the truth when taking an oath. (NB: 'sufficient appreciation' is assumed unless there is contrary evidence.)

Competent?

➤ Everybody is competent to give evidence except someone who (*YJCEA 1999 s 53*):

♦ cannot understand questions put to him and give answers which can be understood, *or*

♦ (as a prosecution witness) currently stands charged in the criminal proceedings.

Compellable?

Defendant as a prosecution witness	Defendant as a defence witness
➤ *Not* compellable (*CEA 1898 s 1*). (Also *not* competent - see above.)	➤ *Not* compellable (*CEA 1898 s 1*). ➤ His evidence is admissible against a co-defendant that he implicates. ➤ If he testifies, he must be called before any other witnesses for the defence (*PACE s 79*). ➤ If he decides not to testify, this can have adverse consequences, see p 566. ➤ The judge will comment adversely if the defence raises issues, but gives no evidence in support. ➤ The prosecution may comment on his refusal to testify (*CJPO 1994 Schedule 10 para 2*). ➤ A co-accused may comment freely on a defendant's refusal to testify.

Present spouse as a prosecution witness	Present spouse as a defence witness
➤ Compellable only if the defendant is charged with (*PACE s 80(3)*): ♦ an assault on the spouse. ♦ an assault or sexual offence on a victim aged under 16.	➤ Compellable, unless the accused and the spouse are jointly charged) (*PACE ss 80(2), 80(2A), s.80(4), 80(4A)*).

Former spouse
➤ Compellable (*PACE s 80(5)*).

Is a co-defendant compellable?	

➤ Whether a co-defendant is compellable to testify against a fellow defendant and the admissibility of his evidence depends on the co-defendant's plea as follows:

The co-defendant on a plea of...	
'guilty' (and therefore no longer on trial)	**'not guilty'**
Compellable	*Not* compellable
He is like any other witness and any statements made to the police, or a confession, will be inadmissible against the defendant as they will be hearsay	His confession, or statements made to the police, are only admissible against himself. (Evidence not made on oath by the co-defendant is not evidence against the defendant - it is inadmissible and must be disregarded)
A corroboration warning is not necessary (*CJPO 1994 s 32,* see p 557)	Some corroboration warning is desirable, see p 557
Cross-examinable on his record	Cross-examination: a defendant may be asked anything, even if it would incriminate him (subject to *CEA 1898 s 1(2),* see p 560)
Note: A defendant is innocent until he *pleads* guilty	**Note:** A defendant is competent as witness to his own alibi, or to authenticate a document

V   Admissibility of evidence (all categories except hearsay)

Special measures and admissibility

➤ *YJCEA 1999 ss 16-33* introduces court powers to make special measures (eg: evidence by video link or from behind a screen) for vulnerable witnesses (eg: witnesses who are less than 18, or with a mental disorder, or who are in fear or distress). This evidence is admissible as if given normally.

➤ There are 7 primary types of *in*admissible evidence:

1   At common law

➤ The common law discretion of a judge to prevent an unfair trial is preserved by *PACE s 82(3)*.

➤ There is discretion to exclude evidence improperly obtained by the prosecution.

➤ Usually the discretion might be applied if the prejudicial effect on the jury of the evidence outweighs its true probative value.

➤ However, the discretion is very rarely exercised because as a *matter of law* much improperly obtained evidence is admissible. The following examples are admissible:

♦ evidence from the illegal search of a person (*Kuruma, Son of Kariu v The Queen* [1955] AC 197).

♦ evidence obtained by an agent provocateur (*R v Sang* [1980] AC 402).

2   *PACE s 78*

➤ The court has a general discretion to exclude evidence, if an admission of the evidence 'would have such an adverse effect on the fairness of the proceedings that the court ought not to admit it' given all the circumstances, including how the evidence was obtained.

3 Irrelevant evidence

4 Self-made evidence

> ➤ A witness may not support his evidence at trial by introducing a statement he made on a previous occasion.

> ➤ This is inadmissible *unless* it involves:

> a) previous exculpatory statements to the police, *or*

> b) statements that come under *res gestae* - 'circumstances of spontaneity or involvement in the event', so there is no possibility of concoction or distortion (see '*res gestae*' on p 565), *or*

> c) evidence that rebuts the suggestion that the witness has recently fabricated his testimony.

Admissible
self-made
evidence

5 Privileged evidence

> ➤ Privileged material is inadmissible and falls within these categories:

> a) **legal professional privilege:** eg: client-solicitor communications, or those with third parties, in contemplation of proceedings (*Parkins v Hawkshaw* (1817) 2 Stark NP 239).

> b) **against self-incrimination:** an answer which may lead to a criminal charge for a witness (*R v Garbett* (1847) 2 C&K 474, and *Evidence Act 1851 s 3*). However, this does not apply if a defendant elects to testify (*CEA 1898 s 1(2)*).

6 Public interest immunity

> ➤ Evidence that for reasons of public interest is inadmissible.

> ➤ Such reasons include:

> ◆ state interests (*D v NSPCC* [1978] AC 171).

> ◆ details of the prevention, detection and investigation of crime, eg: identity of a police informant, unless this is necessary to prove a defendant's innocence (*R v Turner* [1995] 1 WLR 264).

7 Similar fact evidence

> ➤ This is evidence that the defendant has committed offences before, similar to the ones now before the court.

> ➤ This is inadmissible because:

> a) the prejudice created by such evidence outweighs any probative value it may have (*DPP v Kilbourne* [1973] AC 729), *and*

> b) it is irrelevant, since irrespective of the number of similar crimes which have been committed, these crimes cannot connect a person with the crime in front of the court (*R v Miller* [1952] 2 All ER 667).

> ➤ However, if the prosecution can convince the judge/magistrates that in a particular case a) and b) are untrue *and* that the evidence is relevant, the judge/magistrates may rule that the similar fact evidence is admissible.

> ➤ An accused can *always* introduce similar evidence against a co-accused because the judge has no discretion to exclude it (*R v Miller* [1952] 2 All ER 667).

VI Admissibility of evidence (hearsay)

General principles

➤ *CJA 2003 s 114* removes the common law rule against the admission of hearsay evidence.

➤ *CJA 2003 s 114 (1)-(3)* set out the following circumstances in which a statement which is not made in oral evidence during criminal proceedings can be used as evidence of the facts stated within it:

    a) a statutory provision makes it admissible (and these are primarily listed on p 562), *or*

    b) a common law rule preserved by *CJA 2003 s 118* makes it admissible (see p 565), *or*

    c) all parties to the proceedings agree to it being admissible, *or*

    d) the court is satisfied that it is in the interests of justice for it to be admissible (*s 114(d)*).

➤ To allow the statement under ground (d) above, the court must have regard to the following factors (and to any others it considers relevant):

    ◆ how much probative value the statement has (assuming it is true) in relation to a matter in issue in the proceedings, or how valuable it is for the understanding of other evidence ('first factor'),

    ◆ what other evidence has been/can be given on the matter/evidence mentioned in the first factor,

    ◆ how important the matter/evidence in the first factor is in the context of the whole case,

    ◆ the circumstances in which the statement was made,

    ◆ how reliable the maker of the statement appears to be,

> In deciding whether to admit hearsay, a judge must have regard to all of these listed factors but need not reach a conclusion on each of them (*R v Taylor* (2006) The Times 7 February)

    ◆ how reliable the evidence of the making of the statement appears to be,

    ◆ whether oral evidence of the matter stated can be given and, if not, why it cannot,

    ◆ the amount of difficulty involved in challenging the statement,

    ◆ the extent to which that difficulty would be likely to prejudice the party facing it.

Some definitions used in the first factor (*CJA 2003 s 115*)	
'statement'	'matter'

◆ any representation of fact or opinion made by a person by whatever means; and it includes a representation made in a sketch, photofit or other pictorial form.
NB: This changes the common law position.
	◆ is a relevant matter only if one of the purposes of the person making the statement appears to the court to have been:
	  ● to cause another person to believe the matter, or
	  ● to cause another person to act or a machine to operate on the basis that the matter is as stated.

An extra power to exclude superfluous 'out of court' statements (*CJA 2003 s 126*)

➤ The court has a discretion to exclude superfluous out of court statements if it is satisfied that the value of evidence is substantially outweighed by the undue waste of time which its admission would cause.

    ◆ The common law power for the court to exclude evidence if its prejudicial effect is out of proportion to its probative value and the discretion contained in *PACE s 78* is specifically preserved.

Statements by a machine (*CJA 2003 s 129*)

➤ If a statement generated by a machine is based on information input into the machine by a human, the output of the device is only admissible where it is proved that the information was accurate.

    ◆ The common law presumption that a mechanical device is properly set/calibrated is preserved.

Hearsay notices (CrPR r 34)

➤ A hearsay notice is required to admit statutory hearsay in court (but is no longer required for hearsay based on common law rules (eg: res gestae). A notice is needed if either party wishes to rely on:
- ◆ s 114(d) (interests of justice), or
- ◆ s 116 (unavailable witnesses), or
- ◆ s 121 (multiple hearsay).

➤ There is no need for a hearsay notice for hearsay evidence that is admissible under any of the following sections of CJA 2003:
- ◆ CJA 2003 s 117 (business and other documents) - see below,
- ◆ CJA 2003 s 118 (preservation of certain common law categories of admissibility) - see pp 554, 561 and 565
- ◆ CJA 2003 s 119 (inconsistent statements) - see p 564,
- ◆ CJA 2003 s 120 (other previous statements of witness) - see p 564,
- ◆ CJA 2003 s 127 (expert evidence: preparatory work) - but see CrPR r 33.4 and p 565.

➤ However, a notice of opposition to hearsay is required in **all** cases, whether or not a hearsay notice is given (CrPR r 34.3).

A Statutory hearsay (admissible)

1 Documentary hearsay: admissible

Witness statements (CJA 2003 s 116)	Business documents (CJA 2003 s 117)
First hand hearsay only	**First hand and multiple hearsay**
Oral or documentary	Documentary only
Admissible if:	Admissible if:

◆ The witness's oral evidence would have been admissible itself, *and*
 	
◆ The person who made the statement is identified to the court's satisfaction, *and*
 	
    • This will enable the opposing party to challenge the absent witness's credibility (s 124).
 	
◆ A party (or someone acting on his behalf) has not caused the unavailability of the declarant, and
 	
◆ One of the following 2 conditions is fulfilled:
 	
  1. the witness is unable to attend because:
 	
  a) he is dead, *or*
 	
  b) he is unfit to be a witness because of his bodily or mental condition, *or*
 	
  c) he is outside the UK and it is not reasonably practicable to secure his attendance, *or*
 	
  d) he cannot be found although such steps as it is reasonably practicable to take to find him have been taken
 	
or **2. through fear**, he does not give (or does not continue to give) oral evidence in the proceedings, either at all or in connection with the subject matter of the statement, and the court gives leave for the statement to be given in evidence.
 	
    • 'Fear' is widely construed eg: it includes fear of death/injury of another person or of financial loss
 	
    • Leave may only be given under ground e if the court considers that the statement ought to be admitted in the interests of justice, having regard to:
      ■ the statement's contents,
      ■ any risk that its admission or exclusion will result in unfairness to any party to the proceedings (and in particular to how difficult it will be to challenge the statement if the relevant person does not give oral evidence),
      ■ the fact that a direction under YJCEA 1999 s 19 (special measures for the giving of evidence by fearful witnesses etc) could be made in certain cases,
      ■ any other relevant circumstances.
	◆ The document or the part containing the statement was created or received by a person in the course of a trade, business, profession or other occupation, or as the holder of a paid or unpaid office, *and*
	
	◆ The person who supplied the information had or may reasonably be supposed to have had personal knowledge of the matters dealt with, *and*
	
	◆ Each person (if any) through whom the information was supplied received the information in the course of a trade, business, profession or other occupation, or as the holder of a paid or unpaid office.
	
	NB: A document prepared for pending or contemplated criminal proceedings or for a criminal investigation is only admissible if:
	
	    ◆ either of the '2 conditions' is satisfied, *or*
	
	    ◆ the person who supplied the information contained in the statement cannot reasonably be expected to have any recollection of the matters dealt with in the statement (having regard to the length of time since he supplied the information and all other circumstances).
	
	➤ The court may make a direction that a statement is inadmissible if satisfied that the statement's reliability as evidence for the purpose for which it is tendered is doubtful in view of:
	
	    ◆ its contents, *or*
	
	    ◆ the source of the information contained in it, *or*
	
	    ◆ the way in which or the circumstances in which the information was supplied or received, *or*
	
	    ◆ the way in which or the circumstances in which the document concerned was created or received.

2 Written statements: admissible

➤ A statement defined as follows is admissible in trials (*CJA 1967 s 9(1)*).

a) the statement purports to be made by the signatory, *and*

b) there is a declaration that it is true to the best of the witness's knowledge and belief, and it was made in full knowledge of the danger of a prosecution for falsehood, *and*

c) a copy is served before any hearing on all parties *and* none object within 7 days of service.

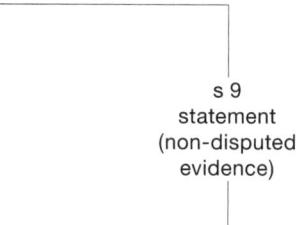

s 9
statement
(non-disputed
evidence)

➤ When a party wants to introduce a written statement in evidence under *CJA 1967 s 9* (*CrPR r 27*), the statement must contain:

◆ at the beginning, the witness' name and, if under 18, the witness' age, *and*

◆ a declaration by the witness that it is true to the best of the witness' knowledge and belief and that the witness knows that if it is introduced in evidence, then it would be an offence wilfully to have stated in it anything that the witness knew to be false or did not believe to be true, *and*

◆ if the witness cannot read the statement, a signed declaration by someone else that that person read it to the witness, *and*

◆ the witness' signature, *and*

◆ if the statement refers to a document or object as an exhibit, a description of that exhibit as to identify it clearly (and the exhibit must be labelled or marked correspondingly, and the label or mark signed by the maker of the statement.

3 Confessions: admissible

i) Confessions generally

➤ A confession is:
'any statement wholly or partly adverse to the person who made it, whether made to a person in authority or not and whether made in words or otherwise' (*PACE s 82(1)*).

➤ A part-confession is admissible in total. If there are periods of silence followed by periods of speaking, the whole is admissible.

➤ A confession from a co-defendant cannot be used by the other defendant if obtained in breach of *PACE ss 76* or *78* (see below) (*PACE s 76A inserted by CJA 2003 s 128*).

◆ However, unlike for the prosecution, the co-accused only needs to satisfy the court on the balance of probabilities that the confession was not obtained in breach of *PACE ss 76* or *78*.

ii) Excluding confessions

➤ The following 3 points show ways to attempt to exclude a confession:

❶ *PACE s 76(2)*

◆ A confession is inadmissible *unless* the prosecution show 'beyond reasonable doubt' that the confession was not obtained in one of the following 2 ways:

• by **oppression** of the person who made it, *or*

• in consequence of anything said or done which was likely, in the circumstances at the time, to render **unreliable** any confession which might be made by him in consequence thereof.

♦ **Oppression:** the Court of Appeal has defined this as the 'exercise of authority or power in a burdensome, harsh or wrongful manner; unjust or cruel treatment of subjects ... the imposition of unjust or unreasonable burdens' (*R v Fulling* [1987] QB 426). ('Oppression' includes 'torture, inhuman and degrading treatment and the use or threat of violence' (*PACE s 76(8)*).)

♦ **Unreliability:** a breach of a *PACE* Code is, in itself, not sufficient. There must be a causal link between the breach and the unreliability. Demonstrative police misconduct is unnecessary.

❷ *PACE s 78* - see p 559.

❸ **At common law** - see p 559.

iii) **The admission of evidence from an excluded confession**

➤ Factual evidence gained from an excluded confession: Facts are admissible (*PACE s 76(4)(a)*).

➤ Expression: A confession is admissible as evidence that the defendant writes, speaks or expresses himself in a certain way, irrespective of whether the confession itself is excluded (*PACE s 76(4)(b)*).

---

4   **Hearsay and previous statements by witnesses**

➤ If a witness admits that he has made a previous inconsistent statement (or it is proved that he made one), it is not only evidence which undermines his <u>credibility</u> (as someone who makes inconsistent statements) but also evidence of the <u>truth</u> of its contents (*CJA 2003 s 119*).

➤ Other previous statements of the witness are also admissible as evidence of the truth of their contents (not only to bolster the credibility of the witness's oral evidence). This applies when (*CJA 2003 s 120* and *CJA 2009 s 112, CJA(4)O 2010*):

♦ A previous statement is admitted as evidence to rebut a suggestion that the witness's oral evidence is untrue, *or*

♦ A witness is 'refreshing his memory' from a previously written document. If he is cross-examined on the document and it is received in evidence, the statement will be evidence of any matter contained within it, *or*

♦ A previous statement is admissible as evidence of the facts within it provided that, while giving evidence, the witness states that, to the best of his belief, he made the statement and, to the best of his belief, it states the truth (*CJA 2003 s 120(4)*) . At least one of the following must also apply:

● The statement describes or identifies a person, place or thing (which includes objects such as a car registration number), *or*

● The statement was made when the incident was fresh in the witness's memory and he cannot reasonably be expected to remember the matters stated (ie: this goes to the weight of the evidence, but should not make it inadmissible), *or*

● The statement is a complaint by a victim of the alleged offence to which the proceedings relate, about conduct which, if proved, would constitute the offence or part of the offence - and the witness gives oral evidence before the statement is adduced. There is a further requirement for such a statement to be admissible which is that the complaint must not have been made as a result of a threat or a promise.

A note on multiple hearsay (*CJA 2003 s 121*)

➤ Multiple hearsay: where information passes through more than one person before it is recorded.
➤ Multiple hearsay is admissible in 2 circumstances only:
  ♦ under the exceptions for business documents (*CJA 2003 s 117*) or previous statements of witnesses (inconsistent or otherwise) (*CJA 2003 s 119-120*), or
  ♦ all parties to the proceedings agree, or
  ♦ the court uses its discretion to admit the statement.
    ● The test for exercise of discretion is whether the court is satisfied that the value of the evidence in question (taking into account how reliable the statement appears to be) is so high that the interests of justice require the later statement to be admissible for that purpose.

B Common law hearsay (admissible) (unchanged by *CJA 2003 s 118*).

1 *Res gestae* (*Ratten v The Queen* [1972] AC 378): **admissible**

➤ *Res gestae* is:

◆ a statement by the doer of an act, which is related to the act and is contemporaneous with it.

◆ a spontaneous statement at the time of an event.

◆ a statement made at the time of an event, and which shows a state of mind, emotion or intention.

◆ an expression of physical sensation felt at the time.

➤ *Res gestae* is admissible if a judge can disregard the possibility that the statement was concocted or distorted (*R v Andrews (Donald)* [1987] AC 281).

➤ A classic example of *res gestae* is a dying declaration (*Mills v The Queen* [1995] 3 All ER 865).

2 **Opinion: admissible**

➤ Opinion is admissible if *either*:

a) a witness recalls his personal perception at the time, *or*

b) the evidence is from an expert witness. The opinion must be pertinent to the expert's expertise.

● If an expert is present, all can see copies of his report.

● If an expert is absent, leave of court is required to admit an expert's report (*CJA 1988 s 30(2)*).

➤ Advance disclosure of an expert witness's evidence is compulsory (*PACE s 81* and *CrPR r 33.4*).

3 **Public information: admissible**

➤ Published works dealing with matters of a public nature (such as histories, scientific works, dictionaries and maps) are admissible as evidence of facts of a public nature stated in them.

➤ Public documents (such as public registers, and returns made under public authority with respect to matters of public interest) are admissible as evidence of facts stated in them.

➤ Records (such as the records of certain courts, treaties, Crown grants, pardons and commissions) are admissible as evidence of facts stated in them.

➤ Evidence relating to a person's age or date or place of birth may be given by a person without personal knowledge of the matter.

4 **Reputation or family tradition: admissible**

➤ Evidence of reputation or family tradition is admissible to prove/disprove the pedigree or existence of a marriage, existence of any public/general right or the identity of any person/thing.

5 **Admissions by agents: admissible**

➤ An admission made by an agent of a defendant is admissible against the defendant as evidence of any matter stated, or a statement made by a person to whom a defendant refers a person for information is admissible against the defendant as evidence of any matter stated.

6 **Common enterprise: admissible**

➤ A statement made by a party to a common enterprise is admissible against another party to the enterprise as evidence of any matter stated.

VII   Inferences from silence at trial

➤ The following sections of the *CJPO 1994* can each adversely affect the defendant at trial.

s 35 CJPO 1994

The defendant
(of any age)
fails to give
evidence at
trial

↓

Sub-procedure for s 35

➤ At the end of the prosecution case, *unless the legal representative of the defendant informs the court that the defendant will give evidence,* the judge will ensure that the defendant knows that inferences may be drawn from his refusal to testify

➤ This procedure is covered by *The Consolidated Criminal Practice Direction Part IV.44.*

s 34 CJPO 1994

Situation 1: questioning before charge

a) The defendant had not yet been charged, *and*
b) was being questioned under caution by a constable, *and*
c) the constable was trying to discover whether, or by whom, an offence had been committed, *and*
d) the defendant failed to mention a fact he might reasonably be expected to mention at the time, *and*
e) the defendant later (at trial) relies on that fact in his defence

Situation 2: questioning at time of charge

a) At the time that the defendant was charged or officially informed he might be prosecuted for an offence, *and*
b) the defendant failed to mention a fact he might reasonably be expected to mention at the time

YJCEA 1999 s 58 says that no inferences from silence are permissible where a defendant had no prior access to legal advice

s 37 CJPO 1994

a) At the time that the defendant was arrested, *and*
b) the defendant was at a place where a constable reasonably believed that the person's presence might be to do with participation in an offence, *and*
c) the constable reasonably believed that the presence of the defendant at that time and place could be attributed to the defendant participating in a specified offence, *and*
d) the constable informed the defendant of his suspicions and asked him to account for his presence, *and*
e) the defendant failed or refused to provide an explanation

s 36 CJPO 1994

a) The defendant was arrested, *and*
b) with an object, substance or mark:
   i) on his person, *or*
   ii) in or on his clothing or footwear, *or*
   iii) in his possession, *or*
   iv) in any place in which he was at the time of his arrest, *and*
c) the constable reasonably believed that the object, substance or mark had something to do with the defendant participating in a specified offence, *and*
d) the constable informed the defendant of his suspicions and asked him to account for the object, substance or mark, *and*
e) the defendant failed or refused to provide an explanation

Consequences of an adverse inference of silence

➤ In the Crown Court, arguments about the admissibility of the defendant's silence when previously being interviewed (ie: any case above apart from *s 35*) take place in the absence of the jury.

◆ The judge decides on admissibility and the jury decides whether inferences may be drawn.

➤ In the Magistrates' Court, the magistrates decide everything.

➤ The magistrates or jury can 'draw such inferences as appear proper' from the silence as applied to:

1 a submission of 'no case to answer' in a trial (see pp 516 et seq and p 526).

2 determining the guilt or innocence of a defendant at trial.

Note: such inferences must not decide the matter alone - there must be other factors too (CJPO 1994 s 38).

➤ The defence needs to introduce evidence in order to put forward a 'good reason' for the defendant's silence, so as to avoid the 'adverse inferences' from the silence (*R v Cowan; Gayle; Ricciardi* [1995] 3 WLR 818 CA).

◆ This case also shows that *s 35* is not only meant to be invoked in exceptional cases.

P   Forthcoming changes

Part 3 of Legal Aid, Sentencing And Punishment Of Offenders Bill: published on 21 June 2011

Part 3, Chapter 1: Sentencing

➤   Chapter 1 changes some general sentencing provisions in *CJA 2003* and other legislation. In particular it:

- ◆   imposes a duty on courts to consider the imposition of compensation orders for certain offences, *and*
- ◆   simplifies the provision setting out the court's duty to give reasons for and to explain the effect of a sentence imposed by the court (see p 544), *and*
- ◆   amends the court's power to suspend a prison sentence by increasing the length of sentences that can be suspended, giving the court discretion not to impose community requirements as part of the sentence and enabling it to impose a fine for breach of a suspended sentence order, *and*
- ◆   makes changes in relation to community orders for adults and offenders who are less than 18.
  - •   These are non-custodial sentences with specific treatment or behaviour requirements attached.
  - •   Chapter 1 clarifies when community orders end and makes amendments to certain requirements (eg: curfew requirements and mental health, drug rehabilitation and alcohol treatment requirements). (It also creates a new power to prohibit foreign travel as part of an order.)

➤   Chapter 1 also amends sentencing provisions *PCC(S)A 2000* that apply to youths (see p 542). These:

- ◆   will enable a court to impose a penalty for breach of a Detention and Training Order even where the Order has finished its term, *and*
- ◆   will amend referral orders to provide more flexibility and discretion for their repeated use.

➤   Chapter 1 also repeals a number of unimplemented provisions in *CJA 2003* including those relating to:

- ◆   Custody Plus (see pp 530 and 532), *and*
- ◆   intermittent custody (enabling splitting a sentence: part in prison and part in the community), *and*
- ◆   an unimplemented increase in magistrates' courts' sentencing powers (see p 488).

Part 3, Chapter 2: Bail

➤   Chapter 2 makes changes to restrict the court's powers to remand adult unconvicted defendants in custody where there is no real prospect that the defendant would receive a custodial sentence if convicted.

- ◆   A court would still be able to remand in custody for the defendant's own protection, or where there was a risk of further offending involving domestic violence.

➤   Chapter 2 amends the definition of 'young person' in *BA 1976* to include 17 year olds. This is made as a consequence of changes to the provisions about remands for youths (which are in Chapter 3).

Part 3, Chapter 6: Out of court disposals

➤   Chapter 6 contains amendments to the legislation under which police constables may issue a penalty notice for disorder and authorised persons may give conditional cautions (see p 483).

- ◆   This includes the introduction of a penalty notice with an education option and provision for conditional cautions to be given without the need to refer the case to the relevant prosecutor.
- ◆   The amendments also allow new types of conditions to be attached to a conditional caution given to a foreign national offender without leave to enter or stay in the UK.

➤   Chapter 6 creates a new kind of youth caution and makes youth conditional cautions more flexible.

Part 3, Chapter 7: Knives and offensive weapons

➤   Chapter 7 creates new offences of threatening with an offensive weapon or an article with a blade or point thereby creating an immediate risk of serious physical harm. There will be a minimum sentence of 6 months imprisonment for over 18s found guilty (unless this would be unjust in all the circumstances).

INDEX

Index   570

Index

Subject	Page	Subject	Page

M